"Gerald Bray is one of our leading evangelical scholars and teachers and he has given us here a magisterial overview of Christian belief and doctrine. A great example of theology in the service of the church."

> TIMOTHY GEORGE, Founding Dean, Beeson Divinity School; General Editor, *Reformation Commentary on Scripture*

"Soaked in the depth and breadth of the Christian tradition, Gerald Bray brings a rich wisdom to his exceedingly accessible Systematic Theology. Freshly organizing his approach around love, Bray does not fall into cheap sentimentality, but instead carefully teases out the drama and story of divine love and how it should inform our understanding of countless areas of theology and life. Students and laity in particular will find this volume immensely helpful, and I heartily recommend it to all!"

> KELLY M. KAPIC, Professor of Theological Studies, Covenant College

"Intimidated by theology books? This is the book for you. Here you'll find a firm place to stand to take in the full panorama of Christian belief—centered around the wonderful and worship-inspiring truth of the love of God, and firmly anchored in the sure and certain word of God. If you've read Lewis's *Mere Christianity* or Stott's *Basic Christianity* and you long to know more, then you're ready to move on to Gerald Bray's *God Is Love*."

> STEPHEN J. NICHOLS, Research Professor of Christianity and Culture, Lancaster Bible College; author, *Welcome to the Story*

"*God Is Love* is a warm, conversational, and contemporary systematic theology written by one of evangelicalism's leading thinkers. But it is much more. It is biblically saturated, historically rooted theological wisdom for the people of God."

> CHRISTOPHER W. MORGAN, Dean, School of Christian Ministries, California Baptist University; editor, *Suffering and the Goodness of God*

"Gerald Bray delivers on his promise—he teaches Christians about the God who is love and about the love that this triune God shows to others. He keeps this promise by pointing insistently to God's gracious speech in the Bible, and by showing consistently how it all hangs together in the story of this God and his gospel. This book is a gripping lesson from a master teacher. For introduction to biblical doctrine—its sources and its implications—Christians will find no better aid than this new treasure."

> MICHAEL ALLEN, Assistant Professor of Systematic Theology, Knox Theological Seminary; author, *Reformed Theology*

GOD

IS

LOVE

A BIBLICAL AND SYSTEMATIC THEOLOGY

GERALD BRAY

CROSSWAY

WHEATON, ILLINOIS

God Is Love: A Biblical and Systematic Theology

Copyright © 2012 by Gerald Bray

Published by Crossway
      1300 Crescent Street
      Wheaton, Illinois 60187

Cover design: Faceout Studio

Cover image: Shutterstock

First printing 2012

Printed in the United States of America

Scripture quotations are from the ESV® Bible (*The Holy Bible, English Standard Version®*), copyright © 2001 by Crossway. Used by permission. All rights reserved.

All emphases in Scripture quotations have been added by the author.

Hardcover ISBN: 978-1-4335-2269-7
ePub ISBN: 978-1-4335-2272-7
PDF ISBN: 978-1-4335-2270-3
Mobipocket ISBN: 978-1-4335-2271-0

Library of Congress Cataloging-in-Publication Data
Bray, Gerald Lewis.
God is love : a biblical and systematic theology / Gerald Bray.
   p. cm.
  Includes bibliographical references and index.
  ISBN 978-1-4335-2269-7 (hc)
   1. Theology, Doctrinal—Popular works. I. Title.
BT77.B755   2012
230—dc23   2011039137

Crossway is a publishing ministry of Good News Publishers.

SH		22	21	20	19	18	17	16	15	14	13	12
15	14	13	12	11	10	9	8	7	6	5	4	3	2	1

CONTENTS

PREFACE

The book you hold in your hands is the fruit of many years of teaching theology to students in different parts of the world. It was a basic premise of the fathers of the early church and of the Protestant Reformers that the church's doctrine should be drawn exclusively from the Bible, as the revealed Word of God. *Sola Scriptura* was their watchword, and the present volume tries to be as faithful to that precept as possible. Subjects not fully covered by the sacred text, like church government for example, are treated only briefly, and the position taken here is that such matters belong to the category of "things indifferent."

The main purpose of this book is to set out what God has revealed to us. That revelation is sufficient for our needs but it is not exhaustive and we must not press things beyond what he has chosen to tell us. At the heart of Christian theology there lies a personal relationship with God. Like all personal relationships, it is based on a degree of knowledge undergirded by trust. What we do not know we leave to God's judgment, because we believe that we can trust him to act in ways consistent with what he has told us. In human relationships we trust people all the time, even though we are fallible creatures and liable to disappoint others and be disappointed ourselves. How much more should we be prepared to trust God, who is infallible and will never let us down?

The Bible is the record of a relationship between God and man. It explains how God loves what he has made and wants us to enjoy the fruits of his creative acts in fellowship with him. But it also tells us how some of the highest creatures rebelled against him and rejected his love, and that the leader of that rebellion seduced the human race into following him. Out of this tragedy has come the message that God has not abandoned us but instead has revealed an even deeper love by sending his only Son to live our life, to die in our place, and to rise again from the dead so that we might dwell with him in eternity.

Centuries of experience and reflection have produced an enormous body of commentary that seeks to probe the meaning of the mystery of God's love, giving rise to many controversies in the course of time. A companion volume to this one will address these things and show how one debate led to another.

For the present, however, our aim is to show how Christian belief is firmly grounded in God's Word, so that we may have a sure and comprehensive foundation for what we preach and proclaim. It is beyond the scope of this book to investigate the claims made for particular books to be included in Holy Scripture or the doubts raised against some of the canonical texts. What the ancients called the *Hebraica veritas* (the Hebrew Bible, or Old Testament) and the *Christiana veritas* (the New Testament) remain the foundation of our theology and have been treated as such here. Passages whose authenticity is open to doubt, such as Mark 16:9–20 or John 7:52–8:11, have not been used to support any doctrine, but this should not be understood as a denial of their canonical status. The attribution of particular books to named authors (such as Isaiah or Peter) is likewise respected, even when (as in the case of Matthew) there is no internal evidence to support it.

No author can predict who will read his book, but the aim of this one is to reach those who would not normally find systematic theology appealing or even comprehensible. Technical terminology has been avoided and the concepts underlying it have been explained as simply and directly as possible. Profound simplicity is the hallmark of classical literature and can be seen at its best in the Gospel according to John. "In the beginning was the Word, and the Word was with God, and the Word was God."[1] Nothing could be more straightforward than that, yet the depths of what it means have never been fully sounded by the human mind. Only when we grasp its simple profundity can we begin to understand the Bible and appreciate why it remains the inexhaustible source and wellspring of our spiritual life.

Many people who write theology today anchor themselves firmly in a branch of the Christian church, whether it is Catholic, Protestant, or (Eastern) Orthodox. These people may be conservative, wanting to support and explain the meaning of their tradition, or they may be liberal, intending to question that tradition's received wisdom and reconstruct it on new and untried foundations. This book does neither of these things. Perceptive readers may notice that its author is an ordained clergyman of the Church of England from what is nowadays called the "Evangelical" wing of that church. Although it is firmly Protestant, classical Anglicanism does not promote devotion to a particular founder or doctrines and practices that distinguish it from other churches. It is best understood in terms of what John Stott called *Basic Christianity* or what C. S. Lewis called *Mere Christianity*, the titles of two influential books that have been read far beyond the bounds of the church that produced them.

Basic or mere Christianity is not a shallow faith but draws deeply on the

---

[1] John 1:1.

revelation of God's Word and seeks to embrace all who submit to its authority in sincerity and truth. It is fully Catholic, fully Orthodox, and fully Protestant because it is firmly grounded on the Bible and on its teaching alone. It is also clearly shaped by the teaching of Jesus Christ, who told us that we must be "born again" if we are to enter the kingdom of God. There is no substitute for that spiritual transformation, and the author of this book is one with members of every church or confession who bear witness to the "one thing needful."

The ancient traditions of Christianity on which we draw were formulated at a time when our faith was largely confined to the Mediterranean and European world. We cannot deny that inheritance and ought to be grateful for it, but we must also recognize that in the past two centuries the church has spread far beyond those historical limits and now reaches the ends of the earth. Today the majority of believers is to be found in the "global south," in places where Christianity has either not been present until quite recently or where it was once strong but has since declined and been revivified in modern times. The needs of Christians there are often different from those of believers in the Western world, and this volume seeks to address them as far as it can. The author's aim is to speak with equal clarity to believers in China, Indonesia, and Africa as to those in Europe, America, or Australasia. Whether it will succeed in this only time will tell. No one can predict the future, but it is safe to say that we can no longer confine ourselves to the cultural and geographical limits of the past as we go forward to meet our Lord on his return.

In pursuit of this aim, this volume recognizes that certain issues have shaped and divided the church, and has tried to see those issues in their scriptural context. It avoids detailed discussions of current theological questions where these reflect trends unlikely to have a major, long-term impact, and it avoids giving particular weight to the views of modern theologians who will be forgotten in the next generation. Those who are looking for a guide to current debates or for the kind of theological ping-pong that sets one man's views against another's will have to look elsewhere. So too will those who are impressed by the number of theologians and books an author quotes to support his statements. Eternal truths have a staying power that transient ideas and arguments generally lack, and it is on those that we have sought to concentrate. Each generation seeks to deepen its spiritual experience and make its own contribution to the deposit of faith that was once delivered to the saints, but that faith remains what has been believed everywhere, at all times, by everyone who calls on the name of Christ in sincerity and truth. It is that truth which this book seeks to explain and anchor ever more profoundly in the hearts and minds of God's people.

It remains for me to thank the many people and institutions that have allowed me to write this book and to whom I owe an immense debt of gratitude. The Latimer Trust has been kind enough to sponsor the project from the beginning, and Crossway has made its publication possible. Tyndale House in Cambridge has provided an agreeable atmosphere in which to work, and the book would not have seen the light of day without the support I have received from Beeson Divinity School, where much of the text was written. I am especially grateful to Jonathan Bailes, Joel Busby, Elizabeth Childs, Christopher Culver, Stephen Greene, Jonathan Hicks, Jonathon Lookadoo, Chase Porter, David Tew, and Dominic Zappia who gave generously of their time and energy to help make this volume more accessible to those for whom it is intended. Their encouragement and fellowship in the gospel have done much toward making the whole effort worthwhile.

Gerald Bray
Cambridge
March 14, 2011

PART ONE

THE LANGUAGE OF LOVE

1

THE CHRISTIAN
EXPERIENCE
OF GOD

KNOWING GOD

God is love.[1] Everything we know about him teaches us that, and every encounter we have with him expresses it. God's love for us is deep and all-embracing, but it is not the warmhearted sentimentality that often goes by the name of love today. The love God has for us is like the love of a shepherd for his sheep, as the Bible often reminds us. Sometimes the shepherd can guide his sheep simply by speaking to them and, ideally, that is all that should be needed. But sheep are often slow to respond, and then the shepherd has to nudge them along with his staff. Sometimes he has to grapple with them forcibly and insist that they follow him when they would rather go their own erratic way. But however hard it is for the shepherd to keep his flocks in order, he never abandons them. As the psalmist put it, "You are with me; your rod and your staff, they comfort me."[2] The rod and the staff are the shepherd's instruments of discipline. The sheep may resent them and try to resist their force, but they know that in the end they must go where their shepherd is leading them. As Jesus said, "The sheep hear his voice, and he calls his own sheep by name and leads them out."[3] He is the Good Shepherd, who loved his sheep so much that he gave his life for them. However many have gone astray, we have his assurance that not one of them will be lost.[4]

We know God because we are the sheep who have responded to our

---

[1] 1 John 4:15.
[2] Ps. 23:4.
[3] John 10:3b.
[4] John 10:11; Matt. 18:12–13; Luke 15:4–7; John 18:9.

Shepherd's voice and have experienced his love at work in us. He has rescued us from our folly and reintegrated us into the world that he made for our enjoyment. People who are not Christians also benefit from God's great love for the human race, but they are not his sheep, and so they do not understand God's love or appreciate it as they should. Even if they have a belief in God, they do not know him as a loving Father who has made them, preserved them, saved them from the consequences of their rebellion against him, and given them a new and eternal life. They may follow a religious tradition out of habit or a sense of duty, or because it is part of their cultural inheritance, but they have never met the God they claim to worship. This phenomenon is very common in most parts of the world, where other religions vie with Christianity as an explanation of life's meaning. But it can also be found in and on the fringes of the church, where there are people who think of themselves as Christians but who lack any clear form of belief that would give that claim some meaning. These are the goats, whom we must distinguish from the sheep, however similar they may appear on the surface.

Among the goats, there are many who attend church at certain times in their lives (for baptisms, weddings, and funerals) or for important festivals (such as Christmas or Easter) but that is as far as it goes. Some of them may pray or read the Bible occasionally, especially when they have a particular need, but they treat these spiritual resources like medicines in the cabinet— something to be used when required but otherwise kept safely tucked away in storage. A few actually become members of a church and may get quite involved in it, even to the point of becoming ordained pastors and teachers. They may be idealistic and well-meaning, and believe that the church is an important vehicle for doing good in the world. Some of them may be quite spiritual in their own way, and use prayer as a means of expanding their horizons or getting in touch with their inner selves. They may accept Christian teaching as a help to them in this, but they do not submit to it as their supreme and unquestioned authority. They often welcome insights from other religions or belief systems, and if there are elements of traditional Christianity that they find inconvenient, they either jettison them or reinterpret them to the point where they are no longer offensive—or even recognizable. These people embrace the traditions of the church but their beliefs and behavior are a simulation of true Christian faith and not the real thing. This becomes clear when they come up against the sheep. When that happens, the goats often react by mocking the sheep and deriding what they see as the sheep's naivete. In extreme cases the goats may even try to drive the sheep out of the church because the presence of people who listen to the voice of the Shepherd and follow his teaching is a standing rebuke to their inadequate and superficial piety.

There are other goats who have no faith at all and seldom give the subject much thought, but when the question comes up, they are reluctant to admit their unbelief. Instead, they claim that it is impossible to know whether any religion is true and so they refuse to commit themselves to a decision one way or the other. This is a popular option nowadays, and is the stance most commonly taken by people in the media and public life of what were once (and sometimes still are) officially "Christian" countries. As they see it, getting along with others is possible only if we put religious convictions to one side, which can be done only if those convictions are not essential to the way we think and live. A few people go further than this and openly deny the existence of God. Some of them even attack Christians for what they see as their ignorance, their bigotry, and their immorality. This may seem like an odd accusation, but to them it is justified because Christians believe in a gospel which teaches that those who do not believe in Jesus Christ are eternally damned. To atheists like these, the notion that a good God could tolerate evil and condemn people to suffer is so outrageous that the existence of suffering and evil in the world is accepted as proof that such a being cannot exist. The strange thing is that, although they have no alternative explanation for suffering and evil, they do not hesitate to attack those who do and sometimes even blame them for causing the problem in the first place.

As Christians, we do not invite this kind of opposition, but when we are dealing with people who think differently from us we cannot put the gospel of Christ to one side. Our faith in God is not just a philosophical belief in a supreme being; it is a life-changing experience of the one who has made us what we are. Everything we think, say, and do bears witness to this, and there is no aspect of our lives that is not affected by it. Other people need to understand the all-embracing depth of our convictions, even if they do not share them. Because we love them as we believe God loves them, we have a duty to tell them that what has happened to us can and ought to happen to them too. The treasure we have received is not for hoarding but for sharing, and it is our duty to go out and find those whom God has called to be his sheep.

Having said that, we cannot force our knowledge of God onto others, however much we want them to share it. No one has ever been argued into faith in Christ. Some people have been scared into a kind of belief, perhaps by unexpectedly escaping death in an accident, but such "conversions" usually turn out to be temporary. On a more intellectual plane, Christian faith cannot be found by scientific exploration or discovered by scholarly inquiry.

There have been philosophers who have tried to demonstrate the existence of a supreme being, but even if they conclude that God's existence is probable and easier to accept than any alternative, such an intellectual deduction is not enough to make them Christians. Humbler men and women have joined the church in the hope of finding God, but that is not enough to make them Christians either. Both types of people are wide of the mark because a true Christian is not a sheep who has gone looking for the Good Shepherd and found a man who seems to fit the bill, but someone who has *been looked for and found* by God.

This is made clear in the earliest records of the Christian church. There was no one in the ancient world more dedicated to the service of God or more eager to do his will than the young Saul of Tarsus.[5] He had gone from his home in what is now Turkey to Jerusalem in order to study the wisdom of his ancestors, and by his own account he swallowed every word of it, hook, line, and sinker.[6] His determination to put it into practice was unparalleled. In all probability he was prepared to die for his beliefs, and he was certainly willing to travel far and wide in order to propagate and defend them. But although he believed in God, he had never met him, and did not know who he really was. There were people who told him the truth about Christ, including Stephen, a deacon in the newly emerging Christian church, but Saul refused to listen.[7] Instead, his zeal for what he already believed was inflamed by such provocation, and he was determined to stamp out the Christian church if he could. It was while he was on his way to Damascus to do just that, that Jesus came to him and revealed himself. Saul fell down like a dead man, blinded by the light that shone from heaven. He had no idea what had hit him until a voice came from that light and told him that he was Jesus, the God whom Saul was persecuting. Saul got up from the ground—the word in the original text is the same as the one that means "resurrection from the dead"—and his life would never be the same again.

What had happened to Saul? He did not know what Jesus had taught his disciples because he had not been with them, and there was no way he could have found out otherwise. Whatever he thought about the man who spoke to him from heaven, Saul did not believe that he was a gifted rabbi or religious teacher who had a new or deeper understanding of Judaism than the one he had learned in Jerusalem. The modern notion of "Jesus the great religious teacher" meant nothing to Saul. In no sense could he be described as a "seeker

---

[5]See Acts 9:1–19 for the full story.
[6]See Phil. 3:4–6.
[7]See Acts 7:58.

after truth" who had finally found what he was looking for; he was fully convinced that he knew the truth already, and he did not want any further enlightenment. Even the force of his vision was not enough to give him the understanding he needed. Saul got up from the ground shaken and confused, and it was only when he was taken to Ananias, a Christian elder in Damascus, who explained what had happened to him, that he understood the meaning of his experience and believed. Saul had not found God; God had found him. Ananias did not persuade Saul to believe, nor did he argue about whether God exists. What he did was to clarify for Saul something that he already knew to be true from his experience but was unable to articulate.

The conversion of Saul of Tarsus remains a model for Christians, because although most of us have not had an experience of God as dramatic as his, we can see in it a pattern of knowing God that is as true for us as it was for him. It does not matter what we were in the past—whether we were looking for truth, indifferent to it, or confident that we knew it already. What matters is that now we have found the truth, not because we have stumbled across it or worked our way into it, but because the Truth has found us and made us over into new men and women. As Saul (also known as Paul) was to say in his letter to the Galatians, "I have been crucified with Christ. It is no longer I who live, but Christ who lives in me. And the life I now live in the flesh I live by faith in the Son of God, *who loved me and gave himself for me.*"[8] The words in italics say it all. The man who told his disciples, "I am the way, and the truth, and the life. No one comes to the Father except through me,"[9] had met Saul on the road to Damascus, because he loved him. Jesus had given himself up to death so that Saul could live a new life in union with him. When he fell to the ground, Saul died to his old self, and when he got up again it was as if he had been raised from the dead. Everything that followed was an explanation of that experience, a working out of what it meant for his life and for the life of the world.

COMMUNICATING THIS KNOWLEDGE TO OTHERS

Dying to self and rising again with Christ is the heart of the Christian faith, and the new life we receive is common to all who believe in him. We work out this new life in different ways, but the heart of the matter remains the same, and when we talk about it, what we say resonates with what Paul wrote to the Christians of Galatia. The words we use may be simple and they are often inadequate to express the true dimensions of the reality we have experienced.

---

[8]Gal. 2:20.
[9]John 14:6.

Our message may be abbreviated, either because we cannot say everything at once or because those listening to our account cannot take it all in, or because we do not fully understand it ourselves. We may not know how to express it properly and trip over ourselves when we try to explain it. How many of us can put into words the feelings we have for those who are closest to us? But if human love is a powerful force that cannot be pinned down like that, how much more will this be true of the love of God? It takes careful reflection in order to speak comprehensively, accurately, and convincingly about an experience of something that goes beyond what is merely rational. To guide us in understanding and expressing such deep things, God has raised up teachers and guides, so that we may learn, as Saul learned from Ananias, how to communicate what we have experienced.

To do this effectively, we have to find the right terms—words that will not be misunderstood by those who hear them. Our minds have to be given the right conceptual framework, so that we will not get confused or talk at cross-purposes. We cannot argue other people into believing in God, but we can always say what he means to us and how he should be understood, so that those who do not believe in him know whom they are rejecting. We must be able to tell the world how we understand the universe, our place in it, and the purpose of our existence. Others may disagree with us and offer alternative proposals, but we must put our case as clearly and as coherently as possible, so that they know what they are disagreeing with. Christians who are vague about these things or who cannot articulate their beliefs in a comprehensible manner will never communicate their faith to anyone. God has called us to give a reason for the hope that is within us and to proclaim the message of salvation to all mankind, whether or not they listen to what we are saying.[10] We may not always get through to unbelievers, but we should at least do our best to make sure that, if our message is rejected, the fault for that will lie with them and not with us.

Christian teachers and guides come in different shapes and sizes. Some are "evangelists" or proclaimers of the gospel, whose primary task is to explain our faith to outsiders and urge them to consider Christ's claim on their lives. Others are preachers whose main role is the building up of God's people, so that they will be more settled in their beliefs and better witnesses to the wider world. Then there are teachers, whose duty it is to develop the deeper implications of our faith and provide resources to preachers and evangelists so that they can fulfill their own callings more effectively. Admittedly, this analysis is an abstraction, and each person who is called to bear witness to

[10] 1 Pet. 3:15; Matt. 28:19–20.

Christ will to some extent be all three of these things. But just as some will be called to devote their lives to itinerant evangelism and others will be called to minister to settled congregations, so there will be those who are set apart for the study of the faith itself. These are the theologians, teachers whose primary responsibility is to examine our experience of God and express it in a coherent way. The result of their labors is the body of knowledge that we call theology.

THE SCOPE AND LIMITATIONS OF THEOLOGY

Some people think of theology in terms of a "system" while others shy away from that word because it seems to reduce the complexities of a living relationship to an abstract formula that can be logically dissected and pieced together in the classroom. The systematizer is often tempted to provide solutions to questions that demand an answer if the system is to be complete, but that are unanswerable in the current state of our knowledge. There is no doubt that attempts to claim more than the evidence warrants have brought the discipline of theology into disrepute. To give only a couple of examples, we do not know what God was doing before he created the world, nor can we say why he chose Israel to be his special people.[11] We do not know when the world will end and cannot say why there are so many people who have not had the message of salvation preached to them, through no fault of their own.

No one knows why God permits evil to exist in spite of his own goodness, or why believers who are destined for happiness in the next life have to suffer in this one. Of course, we can suggest possible reasons for some of these things, and occasionally we can make logical deductions about what must be the case. For example, we can surmise that if only a limited number of people have been saved, those who are not included among them have not been chosen by God, but we do not know why they have been passed over, nor can we identify who they are. What we know is that God has told us enough for us to be assured of our own standing before him, and he gives us the hope that he will use our preaching and witness to bring others into the same experience of salvation that we enjoy. Beyond that, we can only speak in generalities and have to admit that there are gaps in our understanding that will not be filled until we are seated with him in his eternal glory.

Frustrating though it may be to our impatient human minds, God has not revealed everything to us. He has given us what we need for the tasks he has assigned to us, and has assured us that what we do for him will be rewarded, but he has not burdened us with knowledge that is too much for us to bear or

---

[11]See Job 38:3–7; Deut. 7:6–8.

irrelevant to what we are called to do. The good theologian must know how to recognize the boundaries of our understanding, and must remind curious souls not to stray beyond the limits that God has imposed on our learning. Knowing more than we are meant to know, or are capable of absorbing, would unsettle us in much the same way that children are upset when they are told things too hard for them to comprehend. We restrict what we tell our children because we love them and want them to grow in wisdom and understanding without being forced into adulthood before they are ready for it. In the same way, God reveals only a part of his being and plan for us until we are ready to enter into the fullness of eternal life. When that happens, we shall see him face-to-face and be able to understand it all.[12]

THEOLOGICAL DISAGREEMENTS

If theology is the analysis of Christian experience, and Christian experience is essentially the same for everyone, why is it that theologians often disagree with one another? There are several possible reasons for this. One is that we are all finite beings with a limited understanding. No one person can see everything with equal clarity, and we must all have the humility to learn from the perspectives of others. The reality we are studying is the same, but if we approach it from different angles or with different ends in view, we must not be surprised if we come up with different interpretations of it. For example, one person may want to know how Jesus Christ relates to the prophets who lived before his time, while another may be more concerned about whether we still have to obey the ancient Jewish law. The former will naturally give a high value to the Old Testament, while the latter will tend to focus on its inadequacies. There is no necessary contradiction here, but if these different approaches are pushed too far or wrongly applied, perspectives that are equally valid and useful in their own context will eventually come into conflict with each other.

The solution to this problem is not to be found in an "either/or" dichotomy but in a "both/and" combination, with each aspect of the question being given its due weight within the framework of the whole. In the case just mentioned, the underlying question is whether the Old Testament has been abolished or fulfilled in Christ. The answer is that both are true, but in different ways. To put it simply, Christ fulfilled the law in a way that has made some parts of it redundant, and so they have been abolished. Problems arise only when "abolish" and "fulfill" are treated as incompatible opposites, and

---

[12]1 Cor. 13:11–12.

people are asked to choose one or the other. If that happens, legitimate differences become irreconcilable, and theologians end up disagreeing with one another as a result.

Another problem is that not every theologian starts from the same fundamental principles. Some think that Christianity is a kind of philosophy and analyze it like that, with the result that they try to make it fit an alien frame of reference and end up distorting it. Others persuade themselves that they have found the essence of the truth in one particular idea, and then ignore or suppress evidence that goes against their theory. For instance, it is easy (and correct) to say that God is love, but if we then go on to argue that a God of love cannot tolerate the existence of evil, we have allowed our understanding of the principle of God's love to take us beyond the evidence and have come to an unwarranted conclusion. In recent times, some theologians have been so concerned to express their faith in the language and concepts of the secular world that they have lost sight of the uniqueness of Christianity. It is never easy to discern when an idea borrowed from an external source can help our understanding of the gospel and when it can only hinder it, and here theologians are as prone to misjudgment as anyone else.

Taking this tendency one step further, some theologians think that it is legitimate (and even necessary) to base their conclusions on data not drawn from God's revelation of himself in Holy Scripture. They may appeal to what they call "nature" as a way of explaining certain things, or rely on popular traditions that have been handed down through the ages. It is relatively easy to detect such errors when they occur in contexts far removed from our own, but harder to see them when they are familiar to us. The faults of earlier generations have often been revealed with the passage of time, and the mistakes we make will probably be clear to our grandchildren, although we cannot see them now. For instance, it used to be thought that Jerusalem was the center of the universe, that God speaks Hebrew as his native language, and that Genesis lists every human tribe and nation that exists in the world. Today we know that these beliefs were false and have abandoned them, despite the fact that they were sincerely held by many godly people for centuries. Before passing judgment on their ignorance, though, we have to remember that we probably have equally odd ideas about some things but do not recognize what they are because our horizons are too limited. These ideas seem obvious to us, but future generations will see things differently and may criticize us for being blind to matters that will seem perfectly clear to them.

When dealing with matters pertaining to God, humility is essential. If our attempts to discover his ways are dissociated from a spirit of reverent worship, what we are seeking will remain hidden from us and the task to which we have been assigned will be left for others to accomplish. In doing theology, we are talking about someone with whom we live in relationship, with all the complexities that any relationship involves. We cannot objectify God and analyze him any more than we can distance ourselves from our parents, spouse, or children and examine them as if our ties to them were purely intellectual. As with our close human relations, our knowledge of God is embedded in a context that we must recognize and respect. Just as we probably would never have known our parents if we were not related to them, so we would not know God if we were not related to him either. The existence of the relationship does not compromise or obscure our knowledge, which would not exist without it, but it does place certain responsibilities on us as to how we express it. A child cannot talk about his parents in the dispassionate way that a biographer would, but a child knows things about his parents that no outsider can fully understand. It is the same in our relationship with God. The Bible never speculates about whether God exists, because it was written by people who knew him and who would have found such a question absurd. As Jesus said to Nicodemus, "Truly, truly, I say to you, we speak of what we know, and bear witness to what we have seen, but you do not receive our testimony."[13] Those who do not know God will never understand who he is or what he is like—you have to meet him first.

Finally, we must remember that the Christian experience of God can never be fully captured in words. Love cannot be reduced to a formula, and there are many ways of expressing it, none of which is exhaustive. The task of the true theologian is to discern which of these ways best reflect the spiritual reality revealed to us in Jesus, and which must be abandoned because they do not express it adequately. It often happens that some aspects of the truth come across better in one system of thought than they do in another, but that the less satisfactory system is also saying things that need to be taken into account. For instance, we know that God is sovereign over his creation and must therefore be in control of everything that happens, but we also know that some of his creatures have rebelled against him of their own free will. How can these apparently incompatible things be reconciled in a logically coherent way? Some have tried to do this by minimizing the extent of divine sovereignty, while others have reacted by regarding human choice as an illusion, but neither of these apparent solutions to the dilemma does justice to the facts. In the end, we may be forced to accept that there is no fully satisfactory way of reconciling these things in our minds, but what to us is an unresolv-

---

[13]John 3:11.

able paradox is merely another indication that God's thoughts are higher than ours can ever be.

What we call "theology" is a work in progress. It is not a fixed body of knowledge that can never grow or develop; it continues to expand as our relationship with God deepens. At the same time, it does not change, because God does not change. Theologians may have to express themselves in new ways when challenged by fresh discoveries that raise questions our ancestors never dreamed of. We may have to adapt our language to different circumstances and present the age-old message of Christ in ways previously unknown. Many theologians are goats, who relish these opportunities and use them to take the church away from its foundations. This has given theology a bad name in many circles. But these are false teachers who must be exposed and avoided. True theologians are sheep who hear their Shepherd's voice and interpret his words for the benefit of the rest of the flock. In this task, theology will continue until the time comes when it will no longer be needed. When that happens we shall know all things, and be enfolded forever in the unchanging and all-encompassing love of God.[14]

---

[14] 1 Cor. 13:8–13.

2

GOD HAS SPOKEN TO US

THE FINITE AND THE INFINITE

When the great prophet Isaiah spoke to ancient Israel about time and eternity, he exclaimed, "The grass withers, the flower fades, but the word of our God will stand forever."[1] Isaiah understood the transitory nature of human existence and would have agreed with Jesus that those who devote themselves to piling up "treasures on earth" will soon discover how misplaced their efforts have been.[2] His focus was on eternity and his thoughts were concentrated on the word of God. Like the other prophets before him, Isaiah believed that God had spoken, and that this message had been given to particular people, including himself, at specific times in human history. God did not always say exactly the same thing, and often his message was not easy to understand, but whatever he said at any given time, it was his word and would last forever. This is because what God does in time reflects who and what he is in eternity. This gives consistency to God's actions even if, in our finitude, we cannot always perceive what that consistency is.

There have always been people who are unable to accept the claim that the infinite can be accurately expressed in finite terms. Philosophers have said that, if God is infinite and we are not, he cannot communicate with us—because our nature is incompatible with his. In one sense this is quite true, and Christians have never denied it. God cannot reveal to us what he is in himself, and even if he wanted to, our finite minds do not have the capacity to understand his infinitude. How can creatures limited by time and space know what it means to be boundless and eternal? We can look at the works of creation

---

[1] Isa. 40:8.
[2] Matt. 6:19–20.

and guess something about what the God who made heaven and earth must be like, but our understanding of him is rather like the understanding of a man who discovers a watch and then tries to guess who the watchmaker might be. He can see that whoever made the watch must have been able to produce such an object, but that is about as far as it goes. He cannot identify or describe the watchmaker in detail, and would not recognize him if he bumped into him accidentally; there is nothing in the watch that enables him to identify its maker with any precision. Even if the man knows a watchmaker, it would still be impossible for him to prove that he was the one who made the watch. In the same way, we can look at the universe and conclude that whoever made it must have had the ability to do so, but that is not enough for us to identify him or to know him in a personal way.

To what extent is it possible for human beings to acquire a knowledge of God by their own efforts? The Bible tells us that the heavens declare the glory of God,[3] and so anyone capable of admiring the heavens ought to have some knowledge of God. The apostle Paul confirms this and adds that God has revealed his eternal power and divine nature to everyone—a truth that we have suppressed in our rebellion against him. For that reason, says Paul, we are without excuse if we deny God's existence.[4] All people have a law written on their hearts that performs much the same function for them as the law of Moses did for the Jews.[5] The rational order of the universe, innate notions of goodness, beauty, and justice, and the sense of our own smallness in relation to the world we live in all suggest that there is a higher power that holds everything together and makes sense of it. Christians, of course, believe that power to be the God of the Bible and interpret these observations and feelings as evidence of his existence.

From a Christian standpoint, this "natural theology" is essentially applied revelation, which is one reason why it is criticized by unbelievers. If natural observation merely serves to confirm what a Christian already knows by faith, the question must arise as to whether Christians have manipulated the data in order to get the result that suits them. In the Christian version of natural theology, there is no room to disagree with the biblical revelation, which remains the touchstone of our knowledge. Christians do not use natural theology as a basis for their faith, but only as an apologetic device by which to demonstrate that what they believe corresponds to what can be seen and known by observation. The validity of natural theology is therefore

---

[3] Ps. 19:1.
[4] Rom. 1:18–20.
[5] Rom. 2:14–16.

decided not by whether it is objectively true but by whether it is useful for evangelistic purposes. If it is, then Christians will use it, but if it is not, they will abandon it and look for some other way of presenting and defending their beliefs.

From a non-Christian standpoint, natural theology is valid only if it is possible to demonstrate by rational deduction, based on observable phenomena, that there is a higher power which may be called "god" (for want of a better term), but which does not necessarily conform to any known deity, not even to the God of the Bible. This kind of theology was called "deism" in the eighteenth century but nowadays is usually termed "theism." It is much less common among nonreligious people than it used to be, but every once in a while there are reports of atheists, like the late Antony Flew (1923–2010), who "convert" to a theistic worldview while remaining skeptical of or indifferent to Christianity. The existence of such people demonstrates that natural theology is more than just an evangelistic device, though whether classical natural theology "proves" the existence of a supreme being remains an open question. Beyond the world of the intellectuals, there are large numbers of unsophisticated people whose views about God and the divine may reasonably be called "theistic" in this sense. They have not thought about the finer points of their belief, and like the eighteenth-century deists they express their opinions in Christian terms because such terms are the ones most familiar to them, but they resist "organized religion" and are unwilling to commit themselves to anything more than a generic form of monotheism.

Within the Christian tradition, natural theology goes back to the Middle Ages. Beginning in the twelfth century and continuing into modern times, Christian theologians and philosophers have set out the proofs for the existence of God in great detail and have used them in different ways as evidence for the truth claims of Christianity. Some theologians have even tried to prove the doctrine of the Trinity by referring to various natural phenomena, which (to their minds at least) make it plausible and even necessary. The biggest difficulty with such proofs is that what seems logical to a Christian may not appear that way to someone whose starting point is different. For example, Christians will agree that God must be the supreme being, the greatest good, and so on if these are the categories being used. But whether this conclusion comes from a logical analysis of the data, or whether it is the result of a faith which insists that the God in whom we already believe must be these things, is not so easy to determine. A Christian who makes an argument for the existence of a supreme being from natural theology would presumably have to conclude that this being is the God whom he worships on the basis of revelation, since otherwise he would not be professing Christian faith. But if that is the case, the conclusion has been determined in advance and the arguments used will be those that support it. If there is any negative evidence, it will be either discounted or reinterpreted to give the desired result.

A problem for Christians is that philosophically based arguments for the existence of God are somewhat generic and not as specific as the biblical data require. For example, it is one thing to say that there must be a first mover or first cause of the universe and to identify this with the God of the Bible (as Christians must obviously do), but it is quite another thing to say that this first cause has a relationship with human beings and has sent his Son into the world to save us from our sins. Those things are essential to our understanding of the God of the Bible, but they are much too specific to be proved by logical deduction. It is therefore very uncertain whether someone who accepts the logical arguments for God's existence will be persuaded to believe what Christians maintain are the most important things about him. To put it simply, a Christian must be a monotheist, but a monotheist does not have to be a Christian. Monotheism is essential to Christianity, but Christianity does not compel all monotheists to accept it as the only truly rational and consistent exposition of monotheistic belief. On the contrary, there are millions of monotheists in the world who reject Christianity precisely because it is incompatible with their view of what rationally consistent monotheism is or should be.

When we turn to the details, we find that, historically speaking, the main "proofs" for the existence of God have been the following:

1. The world consists of different kinds of beings, some of which are clearly "greater" than others. As Anselm of Canterbury (1033–1109) put it, God is the being than which no greater being can exist or even be conceived. Christians naturally believe this about God, but as a logical argument for the necessity of his existence, it is flawed. For a start, how do we determine what "greater" means? Most of us would think that a human being is "greater" than an elephant, a horse, or a stork, but why? Elephants are bigger and stronger than we are, horses can usually run much faster, and storks can fly. If any (or all) of these criteria count as a measure of "greatness," can we really claim that we are greater than they are? There is also the problem that such measurement is open-ended. For example, there is no highest number, because any number we can think of can always be added to. If God is the greatest being, could we not conceive of something even greater than he is, even if that something does not actually exist?

2. We know that everything in the world has a cause, so there must be

a first or supreme cause that set off the chain of causation that we observe. Once again, Christians believe this as part of the doctrine of creation, but proving it rationally is more difficult. Why should there be only one ultimate cause when there are clearly many different effects and many different causes nowadays? And why should the first cause not have been caused in its turn by something else? Where did it come from and how do we know that "the buck stops" with it, as the popular expression goes?

3. The world is too complex to have come into existence by accident. There must be a design in it somewhere, a purpose which we can discern to some extent in the working out of causes and effects. If there is a design, then there must be a designer who is related to his creation but essentially distinct from it. This is the argument of the watch and the watchmaker. The existence of the watch strongly suggests that someone made it, but although the maker must have the ability to make watches, he is not himself a watch or anything like one. This is one of the strongest arguments for the existence of God, and it is not surprising that it has become the basis of the so-called intelligent design theory of origins in recent years. Once again, Christians accept this argument as a matter of course, but it is difficult to prove. There are things in the world that apparently have no "purpose," such as dandelions. There are also a number of animals and birds that have become extinct without causing any major breach in the natural order. Did the dodo have any reason for existing? Finally, is an effect necessarily purposeful? I know what will happen if I drop something—it will fall to the ground. What for? The effect is predictable but its purpose is not, which must make us wonder whether it has any inbuilt purpose at all.

4. Human beings have a sense of good and evil. This must come from somewhere and must be related to some sort of standard. But to what standard? Christians have a ready answer to this, but for others it is more complex. The nature of "good" is not immediately obvious to everyone and may not be objective at all. How can we say that it is innate in us, when so much of our judgment is due to our upbringing and the ideas that have been communicated to us? Would we think the same way if we had not received that sort of education? We do not know, and cannot go back in time to find out. What is certain is that people from different backgrounds and cultures perceive "good" and "evil" differently, even if there are many elements in common. The whole thing seems to be too subjective to allow for easy definition or categorization, which makes it difficult to use as an argument for the existence of a being as clearly defined as the God of the Bible.

5. Human beings have a notion of beauty and proportion. Where does

our aesthetic sense come from and why does it matter so much to us? Here again, Christians accept the argument without question because we believe in a God who has made everything good, but others will retort that beauty is in the eye of the beholder and has no objective existence at all. As with morality, it is too subjective to be very useful as an argument for the existence of an absolute and unchanging God.

Putting all these things together, we have to conclude that, while Christians accept the proofs for God's existence as true, this is not because they are logically watertight but because we already believe what they set out to prove. We probably have to accept that each of them can be refuted and that no one of them provides incontrovertible evidence for God's existence. At the same time, however, it is also possible to argue that although the individual proofs are not compelling, taken together they make a reasonable case for the probability of what they claim. They cannot be proved, but neither can they be *disproved*, and the weight of the evidence leans toward accepting their claims. In the end, however, natural theology is something that Christians will accept to the degree that it accords with biblical revelation, and others will either reject or misunderstand it. It is not enough to lead anyone to Christ, who can be known only by revelation and not deduced from observation of the world around us.

Does this make natural theology useless or a waste of time? Some theologians have thought so and have more or less discounted it for that reason. Others have said that it is a preparation for the gospel, insufficient by itself but a useful grounding in concepts that find their fulfillment in divine self-disclosure. Still others (and this is where we would range ourselves) think of it primarily as part of the preserving work of God in the world. As the apostle Paul put it,

> What can be known about God is plain to them [unbelievers], because God has shown it to them. For his invisible attributes, namely, his eternal power and divine nature, have been clearly perceived ever since the creation of the world, in the things that have been made.[6]

Or as he told the people of Lystra,

> In past generations God allowed all the nations to walk in their own ways. Yet he did not leave himself without a witness, for he did good by giving you rains from heaven and fruitful seasons, satisfying your hearts with food and gladness.[7]

---

[6]Rom. 1:19–20.
[7]Acts 14:16–17.

The proof of God's existence lay in his bounty to those who did not know him or worship him as God. Unlike other deities, he did not take care of his own people exclusively, or respond only to their requests. His universal presence was not merely a means of helping believers wherever they were; rather, it demonstrated his concern for the entire world. Paul's point was that, at the level of nature, God treats all human beings equally, and when the apostles sought to persuade unbelievers of his existence, it was to their innate sense of gratitude for the blessings that they had received that they appealed. One of the most popular American holidays is Thanksgiving Day, which manages to be religious and secular at the same time. The Pilgrim Fathers who first celebrated it did so for religious reasons, but it was essentially a harvest festival that had no place on the church calendar. Today it is a major celebration when people are expected and encouraged to be grateful, but no one specifies to whom thanks should be given. Christians have no problem with this because they thank the God of Jesus Christ, but what about followers of other religions, not to mention atheists and agnostics? You cannot be thankful in the abstract, and most people admit they have received blessings that they have done nothing to deserve, even if they are not clear as to where those blessings have come from. They are usually quite prepared to be grateful for them, though, and this feeling gives Christians an opportunity to talk about God. Perhaps it is here, more than anywhere else, that "natural theology" comes into its own, because it is at this level, more than in the abstract realms of philosophy, that most people are likely to be touched by the Christian claim that there is indeed a God from whom all blessings flow.

Those blessings are granted without discrimination to believers and unbelievers alike. The sun and the rain affect the righteous and the unrighteous in the same way, and everyone benefits (or suffers) from them.[8] Christians receive no special favors because of their faith, nor do others suffer to an exceptional degree because of their unbelief. This may seem unfair to some believers, who think that they ought to be treated better because of their faith, but actually it is a blessing in disguise. It would be all too easy for people to turn to Jesus if they thought there was some material benefit in doing so, only to reveal later that they were not true followers of his at all.[9] Missionaries are familiar with the phenomenon of so-called "rice Christians," that is to say, people who profess Christianity because they think it will bring them some material gain, but whose faith is vague or nonexistent. In recent years we have also seen the spread of the so-called "prosperity gospel," which preaches that believers

---

[8]Matt. 5:45.
[9]See the story of the ten lepers in Luke 17:11–19, where only one returned to give thanks after being healed.

will receive special blessings from God in this life. Messages of that kind have a special appeal to the poor and underprivileged, but they must be resisted. This is not because we do not want to help the poor but because the promise that becoming a Christian will automatically bring material blessing is false and cruel to those who are taken in by it. One of its worst effects is that, if the promised prosperity does not arrive (as it seldom does), the explanation will almost certainly be that the intended recipients are too sinful to be worthy of it. Nothing could be more perverted than a gospel which depends on human performance, yet that is ultimately where prosperity teaching leads. Jesus did not promise his followers an easy life, but the very opposite, and we must not fall into the trap of suggesting otherwise.[10]

There have been long arguments in the history of the church about whether natural theology has any validity. At one extreme are those who believe that the human mind and the world are designed to fit each other perfectly, making it possible for us to come to a knowledge of the Creator by natural investigation and logic. At the other end of the scale are those who deny that natural theology has any value at all. As they see it, studying nature to find God will most likely lead to worshiping nature as God, which is more like paganism than Christianity.[11] The truth, as so often in such matters, seems to lie somewhere in the middle. Natural theology is not entirely useless, and those who know the God of the Bible can easily see and applaud his works in creation.[12] But although there is plenty of evidence in the universe for the existence of God, it is not enough to give us the understanding of our Creator that we get from the Bible. At most we might come to believe in a supreme being who is an intelligent designer, but this concept has come under fire from those who believe that the apparent imperfections of our world make it hard to believe that such a being exists. Those who reject God have been able to put forward nontheistic explanations of the origins of the universe which they think are perfectly adequate and make it unnecessary to believe in the existence of a Creator God. They may be wrong to think this, but since natural theology starts with the same fundamental beliefs as they do, it is unlikely to persuade them of their error.

Furthermore, the assumption that the supreme being must be personal, which comes naturally to those with a Christian heritage, cannot be justified on the basis of natural theology alone. It was not the belief of the ancient

---

[10]Matt. 8:20; 10:38; 16:24; John 16:33.
[11]"Paganism" is a somewhat ill-defined term to describe the unorganized polytheistic religions of the ancient world that Christianity eventually displaced. In modern times, the same phenomenon is usually called "animism."
[12]Ps. 19:1.

Greeks, who invented the notion of a "supreme being," and modern atheists see no more reason than they did for coming to such a conclusion. Men like Plato and Aristotle believed in *it*, not in *him*. They would have thought that the personification of ultimate reality compromised its supremacy by reducing it to the human level (which is what the Greeks had done with their gods). In the final analysis, we have to agree that if we take this line of argument to its logical limits, the philosophers are right to say that we shall never encounter the Christian God. Our finite minds cannot comprehend his infinite nature, and any attempt to do so will end in failure or idolatry—or both. Natural theology has its importance and is taken seriously in the Bible, but it is a preparation for the gospel and not a substitute for it. It gives people enough knowledge for them to be able to respond to the message of salvation but not enough for them to work it out for themselves.

Christians resolve the problem of incompatible natures by saying that communication between God and man is possible by means of what we call the "person." The Bible tells us that human beings are created in the "image" and "likeness" of God,[13] and although there has been much debate about what that means, certain aspects of it are beyond dispute. Every theologian agrees that human beings are the only material creatures that have this image and that its presence in us makes communication with God possible. In theological terms, God is personal by nature and we are personal because we have been created in his image. This common ground established a link between God and man from the very beginning. Even Adam and Eve were in contact with God, as can be seen from the account of creation in Genesis. There is more to the image of God than the ability to communicate with him, but communication is fundamental to any relationship, and it is our relationship with God that gives our existence its purpose and meaning. It is not for nothing that God created the world by his Word, that he spoke to his people through the ages, and that it was the Word that became flesh and dwelt among us.[14]

Our personhood is finite, but it is not bound by the limitations of material finitude in the way that our bodies are. We are capable of thinking beyond space and time, and would not understand what those concepts are if we could not rise above them. We know that one day our human bodies will die and the material world will come to an end. But the Bible assures us that our personhood will not disappear. In the resurrection it will go on existing in a transformed body that is finite but is no longer bound by the constraints of

---

[13]Gen. 1:26–27.
[14]John 1:14.

time and space.[15] How this will happen remains a mystery, but at least we can say that our personal relationship with God will carry over from this life to the next without any fundamental change. This is why we proclaim that we have the "firstfruits" of eternal life here and now. As the apostle Paul said to the Romans:

> We . . . who have the firstfruits of the Spirit, groan inwardly as we wait eagerly for adoption as sons, the redemption of our bodies.[16]

The witness of Scripture is that our creaturely finitude is not an insuperable barrier to communication between God and us. On the contrary, because we are persons created in his image and likeness, we have an inbuilt relationship with him that every human being enjoys and that constitutes the true definition of what it means to be human.[17]

THE SCANDAL OF PARTICULARITY

There are some who accept that divine-human interaction is possible, but who find it scandalous to claim that God revealed himself to particular individuals in a single nation, especially when those individuals had done nothing to deserve it and the nation to which they belonged counted for so little in human history. What disturbs these objectors is the Christian insistence that universal truth can be expressed in only one way.[18] Even if we allow that the prophets of ancient Israel had a glimpse of eternal truth, what is it about them that makes them unique? How can one small group of people dare to claim that they alone have received a message from God, when, by their own admission, that message is of universal validity?

Those who study the ancient world from a secular point of view will come across many great men from Mesopotamia, but Abraham will not be one of them. They will examine the great civilizations of Assyria and Egypt, of Babylon, Persia, Greece, and Rome, but Israel (if it figures at all) will hardly be more than a blip on their mental horizon. To write the history of antiquity putting Israel at the center is rather like writing the history of Europe from the standpoint of Luxembourg, a country that is geographically central but otherwise insignificant. Yet that is precisely what the Bible does, and the truth of its claim has been borne out by events. It is no exaggeration to say that while the great empires of the past have disappeared into history,

---

[15]1 Cor. 15:35–57.
[16]Rom. 8:23.
[17]See Rom. 1:19–21.
[18]John 14:6.

the tiny nation of Israel still exists and has spread its wings to the far corners of the globe, bequeathing to us not only Judaism but Christianity and Islam as well. All over the world, children are still named David and Rebecca, but not Nebuchadnezzar or Nefertiti. Furthermore, while other nations have collapsed and disappeared relatively quickly when subjected to outside pressure, Israel has undergone centuries of relentless persecution and even attempted genocide, but it has withstood every assault. Today it is as strong and influential as it has ever been. For an "insignificant" nation, Israel has gone a long way, and its story is far from over.

That much is clear and must be acknowledged by everyone, even if they can find secular reasons to explain why the Hittites have vanished but not the Hebrews. Jews and Christians are usually happy to acknowledge the force of the secular argument, but they go further and say that Israel has survived because God spoke to the ancient Israelites and made them his people, promising that they would vanquish their enemies and survive until the end of time:

> But you, Israel, my servant, Jacob, whom I have chosen, the offspring of Abraham, my friend; you whom I took from the ends of the earth, and called from its farthest corners, saying to you, "You are my servant, I have chosen you and not cast you off"; fear not, for I am with you; be not dismayed, for I am your God; I will strengthen you, I will help you, I will uphold you with my righteous right hand.[19]

Isaiah's words were directed to a nation that had lost everything—its king, its religious establishment, its social coherence. But out of that ruin, God told Isaiah that he was going to rebuild his people and give them a new vision of his plan and purpose for them. That is exactly what happened. The nation that Jesus was born into was very different from the kingdom given to David a thousand years before, and even more different from the extended family of Abraham, to whom God had promised the land of Canaan a thousand years before that. But at the most fundamental level it was exactly the same—God's chosen people, who gathered around his word and honored it as the charter that guaranteed their existence and their ongoing survival.

No one today would doubt that the long-term survival of the Jewish people, against all the odds, has been a remarkable phenomenon in human history. Whatever we think about the modern state of Israel and its occupation of Palestine nearly two millennia after the destruction of the last previous Jewish state there, we have to admit that there has never been anything like it.

---

[19]Isa. 41:8–10.

Moreover, there will almost certainly never be anything like it again, if only because there is no other nomadic nation with a similar background. The nearest thing to it is the Roma ("Gypsies"), a wandering people who left India a thousand years ago and migrated to Europe, but they have no identifiable homeland to go back to and no sense that they are in temporary (albeit very long-term) exile. The Jewish story is unique, but why has Israel survived when the other ancient nations have all disappeared? It is certainly not because of their numbers or their cultural achievements, both of which have always been relatively few. Even in its heyday, the temple of Solomon in Jerusalem did not match the great shrines of Egypt or Mesopotamia, and there was nothing else in Israel even remotely comparable to the temple in terms of its cultural significance. The nation was constantly being decimated—by wars, by exile, and by intermarriage with foreigners. In 722 B.C. came the sudden loss of ten out of the twelve original tribes, when the northern kingdom of Samaria was extinguished and its inhabitants were taken off into exile and dispersed.[20] But Israel did not disappear because, in spite of everything, it still had the word of God, which as Isaiah said, would stand forever.

The truth is that apart from that word, which we now possess in the form of the Bible, Israel would never have survived. The Bible is Israel's only legacy to the rest of the human race and the measure of its greatness. Furthermore, it is the Bible that tells us the secret of Israel's staying power:

> You are a people holy to the LORD your God. The LORD your God has chosen you to be a people for his treasured possession, out of all the peoples who are on the face of the earth. It was not because you were more in number than any other people that the LORD set his love on you and chose you, for you were the fewest of all peoples, but it is because the LORD loves you and is keeping the oath that he swore to your fathers . . .[21]

From the very beginning, Israel was a nation that knew it had been chosen, called, and set apart by God. What brought the nation together was not a ruthless superhuman power that crushed all opposition to its rule, nor was there any achievement on Israel's part that attracted God to it. The glue that cemented the relationship between God and Israel, and that has bound them to each other through thick and thin, is *love*—God's love for his people and his determination to keep the oath that he swore to their forefathers, that they would continue to exist and to be his people until the end of time. Even when Jerusalem was a smoldering ruin and the people

---

[20]2 Kings 17:6.
[21]Deut. 7:6–8a.

had been slaughtered and scattered to the ends of the earth, this note sounded out loud and clear:

> The steadfast love of the LORD never ceases,
>   his mercies never come to an end;
> they are new every morning,
>   great is your faithfulness.
> "The LORD is my portion," says my soul,
>   "therefore I will hope in him."[22]

Israel has never lacked enemies who have tried to destroy it, as the tale of Haman's attempted genocide makes clear.[23] That story has been repeated many times since then in different forms. Powerful men have tried to wipe Israel off the face of the earth, and some are still trying to do so, but they have all failed and will continue to fail. Unworthy of its calling though Israel undoubtedly is, it is protected by an unseen hand that is stronger than any force that can be unleashed against it. That hand is nothing less than the protecting power of the love of God.

CHRISTIANS AND ISRAEL

As men and women who have been grafted into the nation of Israel by the coming of Jesus Christ, Christians also lay claim to this love and the promises that go with it. Jesus was the Son of God who came to earth as a Jew in order to fulfill the ancient law of his chosen people and the promises connected with it. Most Jews failed to recognize him because the way in which Jesus became their Savior was not what they were expecting. They believed that when "the anointed one"[24] came, he would reestablish the kingdom of David and Solomon and create an empire in which the Jews would lord it over other nations. Instead of that, Jesus asked them to accept that God had sent his Son to die on a cross for the sins of the whole world. Furthermore, he invited men and women from every nation to join that chosen people and constitute a new Israel that was greater than anything David or Solomon had known.

Jews who followed Jesus realized that the Word of God, which they had received as the Law, the Prophets, and the Writings of their ancestors, was above all else a preparation for the coming of the Savior. This belief was not uncommon among Jews of the time and can still be found among them today, but modern orthodox Jews believe that the Messiah is yet to come,

---

[22]Lam. 3:22–24.
[23]Est. 3:6.
[24]In Hebrew *mashiach* (Messiah) and in Greek *christos* (Christ).

while Christians say that he has already appeared and fulfilled the ancient promises in the life, death, and resurrection of Jesus Christ. Both groups agree that the Hebrew Bible (which Christians call the "Old Testament") is the Word of God and that it stands forever, but they differ as to how it should be interpreted.

The New Testament teaches that Christians have been grafted into the nation of Israel, and that all true Israelites believe (or will come to believe) in the claims of Jesus Christ to be their Messiah and Savior.[25] It also teaches that the external features of the Old Testament law that set Israel apart from other nations have now been internalized. Christians are just as distinct from the rest of the world as Jews are, but the nature of that distinction can be perceived only by spiritual means. Circumcision, for example, was a physical rite that set Jews apart from others, but for Christians, it is the "circumcision of the heart" or the spiritual commitment that circumcision symbolized that makes the real difference.[26] Similarly, the temple that was at the heart of ancient Israel has been replaced by Jesus Christ, whose body is the temple.[27] Thanks to our spiritual union with him, we too are temples of the Holy Spirit, and the laws of purity that applied to the ancient building are now to be interpreted in relation to us.[28]

In this connection, the ancient practice of *herem*, or "holy war," which was meant to rid Israel of ungodly people and practices, has been replaced by the concept of spiritual warfare, in which Christians are permanently engaged.[29] As the apostle Paul pointed out, this warfare is not against flesh and blood but against the spiritual forces that control the world we live in.[30] As with circumcision and the temple, holy war is a personal discipline that can never spill over into physical violence or justify the seizure of secular power by a church or religious authority.[31] To put it briefly, what Israel did externally in the context of a nation state, Christians do internally as a people chosen by God from every state and nation. The principles are the same but the way they are worked out is different, which is why Paul was able to say that the law of Israel had been superseded by the gospel of Jesus Christ.[32]

---

[25]Rom. 11:11–24.
[26]Rom. 3:1–4:25.
[27]John 2:19–21.
[28]2 Cor. 6:16.
[29]See Ex. 23:20–33; Deut. 20:1–20.
[30]Eph. 6:10–20.
[31]Nowadays few people are familiar with *herem*, which is no longer practiced by Jews, but we are increasingly acquainted with the Islamic notion of *jihad*, which is similar to it. Liberal Muslims insist that *jihad* is a purely spiritual warfare, while many more conservative Muslims disagree and are prepared to include physical violence as part of it.
[32]Gal. 3:1–29.

DIVINE REVELATION TO ISRAEL

It is the New Testament writers who tell us that, in Old Testament times, the Holy Spirit inspired the prophets and holy men of God to write the sacred Scriptures.[33] The Holy Spirit did not dwell in the hearts of the Israelites in the way that he dwells in the hearts of Christians, but the Old Testament writers longed for this indwelling presence when they spoke about writing the law of God on their hearts, and even of tasting and eating God's Word.[34]

The special character of the Scriptures is revealed in the way that they are called "holy." Christians reject the idea that holiness can be applied to objects—there is no holy land, no holy oil, and no holy people other than believers in Christ, all of whom are sanctified only because they have been united to him. But there is Holy Scripture because the Word of God is present in it, proclaimed by it, and made efficacious through it.[35] How this can be so has been the subject of much debate and not a little dissension, but its importance for the Christian church is such that there can be no escaping the question. The Bible speaks to the church with the voice of God, and its authority is paramount. Jesus demonstrated this when he replied to Satan's temptations, not with his own words but with quotations from Deuteronomy.[36] "It is written" was all that needed to be said for the text to carry the power of God. What makes the Scriptures holy is not their historical accuracy or even their content, but the presence of God in them. These are his love letters to his people, and those who love him hear and cherish the Scriptures for that reason. How much of them we understand is an important but ultimately secondary issue. There will always be more in God's Word than we have grasped, but this does not affect our attachment to the Bible. We treasure his words whether or not we know what they mean, because we sense his presence in them. We are confident that the hidden things of his Spirit will be made clear when the time comes, as they were made clear to people like Simeon and Anna when they saw the baby Jesus.

God's revelation did not originally come in written form, and although there is evidence that he occasionally dictated to the prophets what they should write, dictation was not the usual way in which he communicated what he wanted to say to his people.[37] There was obviously no writing in the garden of Eden, and although it may have existed in the days of Noah and Abraham, there is no sign that God used it in his dealings with either of them. Writing

---

[33] 2 Pet. 1:21.
[34] Ps. 119:11; Jer. 15:16.
[35] 2 Tim. 3:15–16.
[36] Matt. 4:4, 7, 10, quoting respectively Deut. 8:3; 6:16; and 6:13.
[37] See Isa. 8:1, 30:8; Jer. 30:2; Ezek. 43:11.

was certainly known in both Babylonia and Egypt, and the resemblance of parts of Genesis to the written records of those countries suggests that writing may have been used among the early Hebrews as a means of preserving their traditions. It is even possible that parts of our Old Testament were originally composed for secular purposes and later were integrated into the sacred text under the guidance of the Holy Spirit. That is what happened to the decrees of Cyrus,[38] so we should not rule out the possibility and even the likelihood that something similar occurred in earlier times as well.

Leaving such exceptions aside, it is safe to say that God normally spoke to his people through men (and occasionally women) whom he had called to be their spiritual leaders. Whether this communication was oral is harder to say, since it is possible, and at times virtually certain, that he spoke to them in visions and dreams that were later verbalized but which were not strictly "oral" in themselves.[39] This, however, is a subtle distinction. The important point is that God did not communicate with his people directly in writing. Indeed, at times when there were no spiritual leaders, he did not communicate with them at all, as was the case during the long centuries when they were enslaved in Egypt.

The Bible tells us that writing, as a form of communication from God to his people, began with Moses, and more specifically with the giving of the Ten Commandments at Mount Sinai.[40] The early history of the world and of Israel which the Pentateuch records was ascribed by later Israelites to Moses, who was supposed to have compiled and written down the oral traditions of the people. We now accept that the process by which this occurred was more complex than this suggests, and no one can say for sure what part Moses played in it. At one extreme are those who insist that he wrote every word just as we now have them. At the other extreme are those who claim that the stories were put together, if not actually invented, at a much later date and perhaps even after the exile in 586 B.C. With no hard data or indisputable external criteria to go on, it is impossible to be dogmatic about this one way or the other, but the likelihood is that Moses was a significant contributor to the writings attached to his name. Archetypal lawgivers existed in many other ancient societies, and, while there were certainly additions to the basic legal systems they devised, no one would deny that they played a pivotal role in establishing them. If men like Solon and Lycurgus were real people who constructed the framework within which Athenian and Spartan law later

---

[38]2 Chron. 36:23; Ezra 1:2–4.
[39]See Ezek. 1:1; Dan. 8:1–14.
[40]Ex. 24:4; 34:28.

developed, there is no reason to think that Moses was any less historical or that his achievement was substantially different from theirs.

From a theological standpoint, what matters most is that, from the time of Moses onward, God's revelation to Israel through the prophets and others was recorded for posterity. How far this record corresponds to the original revelation is impossible to say because those to whom it was given are not available for comment. Most likely, what we have is a distillation of what was originally revealed to them, giving us the substance of what God said but not every single word. At the end of John's Gospel we read that if everything Jesus said and did had been written down, there would not be enough books in the world to contain the material, and that seems to be a reasonable guide to the relationship between God's revelation to his chosen messengers and what we know of it now.[41]

The advantages of a written text over oral tradition may not have been apparent at the time, but they are obvious to us now. A written text has a fixity and a permanence which an oral record does not have, even if it was handed down for centuries with little or no variation. A book is also a public document in the way that oral tradition is not. Oral records depend on the reliability of those who transmit them, and if the transmitters alter them there is not much that anyone else can do about it. But a written text cannot be so easily changed, even if copyists make mistakes in transcribing it. Writing offers a relatively fixed reference point that does not depend on the transmitter nearly as much as oral communication does, and it makes the texts accessible to people like us, who have no contact with the original author(s) or transmitter(s). If the Word of God is to be passed on intact from one generation to another, writing is the best way of doing it. Scholars like to emphasize the textual variants that occur in different manuscripts, and many claim that the existence of these variants disproves any theory of divine inspiration, but the truth is that very few of these variants have any importance for theology, and many of them can be disregarded because they do not affect the meaning at all. Uncertainties do remain, to be sure, but they are far fewer than critics like to claim or than would exist if we had to depend on oral transmission alone.

We cannot now reconstruct the history of the composition of the Hebrew Bible with any certainty, but it is generally agreed that the "five books of Moses" (Genesis—Deuteronomy), known in Hebrew as the Torah, are the foundation documents to which the books of the Prophets and the so-called "Writings" were later added. The Torah emphasizes that Moses wrote down

---

[41]John 21:25.

what God said to him because God told him to do so, but it was the message, and not the tablets on which it was written, that was regarded as sacred. When Moses came down from the mountain on which God had revealed his law and found the people worshiping a golden calf that they had built in his absence, he was so enraged that he broke the tablets and had to go back up the mountain to get new ones.[42] Many years later, when the people were about to enter the Promised Land, the law was rewritten to take account of the changed circumstances, as the name "Deuteronomy" indicates.[43]

These facts teach us that the tablets on which the law was written were not sacred objects to be venerated in their own right. It was the message they contained that mattered, although that was no excuse to treat the tablets with disrespect or alter what they said. Second, we learn that the law could be (and was) adapted to meet changing circumstances, but without compromising its original purpose. It was given in time, but not frozen by it, so that it was (and is) legitimate to interpret it in ways that go beyond the original context and make it applicable today. This is an important point, since much of what the text says was geared to the life of a nomadic desert people, and is irrelevant to the conditions in which most of us now live. But the principles that led to the framing of the law are still valid, and it is these that have to be used today when the details of the law are applied to our circumstances. Jewish interpreters have been doing this for more than two thousand years, and Christians also do it, albeit in a different way, because we discern the meaning of the law in and through the person and work of Jesus Christ.

After the Torah come the books of the Prophets. Prophecy is an ancient phenomenon, and its origins remain somewhat obscure. There were prophets in the time of Moses, but because they were not appointed by him they were somewhat suspect, although Moses himself accepted them.[44] After that we hear little more about prophecy until the time of Samuel (eleventh century B.C.), by which time prophecy had virtually faded out.[45] At that point God spoke to Samuel, and from then on things changed. Prophecy enjoyed a revival that continued until the time of Malachi (about 400 B.C.), when it ceased once again. During that time, God spoke to individual prophets, who relayed the message to those for whom it was intended. Sometimes a prophet would be called to speak to only one person, such as a king who had done something wrong, but he might equally well be sent to address the entire nation, and

---

[42]Ex. 32:19.
[43]It means "second law" in Greek. There is no equivalent term in the original Hebrew, which just calls the book by its opening line, "These are the words."
[44]Num. 11:26–29.
[45]See 1 Sam. 3:1.

might even be told to go to foreign lands.[46] The early prophets' messages were delivered orally, and it was only in the time of Hezekiah (around 700 B.C.) that they were written down and preserved as distinct collections. This explains why our knowledge of prophets such as Elijah and Elisha comes from the histories of the kings, whereas the sayings of men like Isaiah and Jeremiah are recorded as such, probably because scribes and disciples who accompanied them wrote them down.[47] We are not sure whether these later prophets wrote anything themselves, but even if some of them did, their messages were almost all delivered orally in the first instance and the written form appeared afterwards. In the case of Jeremiah, we know from the existence of different manuscript traditions that the process of putting the prophet's words into written form took many centuries and was not completed until about 200 B.C. or even later.[48] That was probably true of other prophets as well, though direct evidence of this process no longer exists.

The remainder of the Hebrew Bible consists of a miscellaneous collection of books known as the "Writings," which come from a number of different sources. Some of them were attributed to King David (the Psalms) or to his son Solomon (Proverbs, Ecclesiastes, Song of Songs) though the exact nature of the relationship between the books and their supposed "authors" is more complex than such attributions would suggest to the modern reader. For example, we know for certain that the Psalms do not all go back to David, since some of them come from the time of the Babylonian exile, although in the time of Jesus "David" was commonly used as shorthand to refer to them all.[49] The book of Job is anonymous, and may have been composed as a written text without any prehistory of oral transmission—we do not know. But allowing for such possible exceptions, it is fair to say that, for the most part, the Hebrew Bible is a written record of what was originally an oral message, as the apostle Peter recognized when he wrote, "For no prophecy was ever produced by the will of man, but men spoke from God as they were carried along by the Holy Spirit."[50]

A glance at most non-Hebrew Bibles will quickly reveal that the Jewish distinction between the Prophets and the "Writings" is obscured in them. This is because these Bibles follow the order of the books as they were included in

---

[46]Nathan was sent to King David (2 Sam. 12:1–15) and Micaiah to King Ahab (1 Kings 22:13–28). Most of the other prophets spoke to Israel as a whole, even when their prophecies were about the fate of foreign nations, but Jonah was sent to Nineveh and *not* to Israel, which was unusual.

[47]This was certainly the case with Jeremiah, whose scribe was Baruch.

[48]The Greek translation known as the Septuagint, which was made sometime before 200 B.C., has a shorter version of Jeremiah which is arranged differently from the now-canonical Hebrew text.

[49]For example, Acts 4:25–26, quoting Ps. 2:1–2.

[50]2 Pet. 1:21.

the Greek translation known as the Septuagint, which was made at Alexandria sometime in the third century B.C. The Septuagint split the Hebrew prophetic books into two categories, the first of which we now call "historical" and the second "prophetic." It also rearranged the Writings, including some of them in either the historical or prophetic sections. The historical books are Joshua to 2 Kings, but not including Ruth. In the Hebrew Bible, Ruth, Chronicles, and Ezra to Esther are found among the Writings, not the Prophets, but in our Bibles they are attached to the historical books. The remaining prophetic books are Isaiah to Malachi, but Lamentations and Daniel were placed among the Writings in Hebrew. It is good to be aware of this because books that to us seem very similar (such as Kings and Chronicles) were in different categories in Hebrew—the books of the Kings were prophetic and the Chronicles concluded the "Writings," a fact which is now obscured in most non-Hebrew Bibles.

The different arrangement of the books presents no great difficulty, but there is an important discrepancy between the Hebrew Bible and the Septuagint that continues to cause disagreement today. Protestants generally accept the Hebrew canon, though in the Septuagint order and subdivided into thirty-nine books. The main exception to this is in the Psalms, where Protestant Bibles follow the Hebrew and not the Septuagint divisions. The text is fundamentally the same (although many of the Septuagint translations are quite different from the Hebrew text that has come down to us), but the numbering is different. The Septuagint combines Psalms 9 and 10 into one and divides Psalm 147 into two (vv. 1–11 and 12–20), making the numbering one lower for most of the Psalter than it would otherwise be.[51]

Roman Catholics and the Eastern Orthodox prefer the Septuagint canon, which contains books or parts of books that either no longer exist in Hebrew or were written in Greek in the first place. These extra texts have traditionally been known as the Apocrypha, a Greek word that means "hidden," though of course they are not really hidden at all! Today they are often called "deuterocanonical" as a way of indicating their secondary status. The decision about which canon to accept depends on the degree of authority we grant to the ancient Israelite community to determine what the limits of the Old Testament should be. The more we understand ourselves to be in continuity with them, the more we are likely to prefer their canon. But if we believe that we have gone beyond their limitations, we may feel less bound to follow their decisions about what books belonged to Holy Scripture and be more prepared to accept texts that they have rejected.

---

[51]There is an added complication in that the Hebrew Psalm 115 is part of the Septuagint Psalm 113, and what the Septuagint makes Psalms 114 and 115 is combined as Psalm 116 in the Hebrew. (The division follows v. 9.)

As far as the Septuagint is concerned, there is no doubt that it was widely used by the first generation of Greek-speaking Christians, and it is often quoted in the New Testament. The apostles never expressed any reservations about it, and the Dead Sea Scrolls have revealed that sometimes the Septuagint represents an alternative reading of the Hebrew that Jewish editors of a later time apparently rejected. On the other hand, the New Testament never quotes a Septuagint book that is not found in the Hebrew Bible, so the question of whether those books enjoyed any authority in the early church cannot be answered in that way.

A better guide to the authority of the different texts can be found by examining the commentary material that has survived from ancient times. Christians started writing commentaries on the Bible in order to help preachers and teachers understand its more difficult passages. It therefore follows that they wrote only on those books that were used in the life of the church. The astonishing fact is that there are commentaries on every Old Testament book that is in the Hebrew Bible, but none on those that are not.[52] It therefore seems that the Hebrew canon was the one actually used in the church, even if the extra Septuagint books were readily available and copied along with the others. The Holy Spirit spoke to the early Christians and taught them by using the books found in the Hebrew canon, which was the one Jesus must have used. It would not be until the sixteenth century Reformation that there was a final definition of what the canon contained, but the usage of the church from earliest times is a clear indication of how the Spirit was guiding it to a proper understanding of its faith.

DIVINE REVELATION TO THE CHRISTIAN CHURCH

The New Testament is different from the Old because it was given by the Holy Spirit after the coming of Christ. It is therefore more a book of fulfillment than of promise in the Old Testament sense, and what was half-hidden or concealed in the Old is fully revealed and expounded in the New.[53] On the other hand, when the New Testament writers refer to the Scriptures they mean the Old Testament, which they regarded as a distinct body of sacred literature that enjoyed canonical authority even before the coming of Christ.[54] They did not seek to add to that canon, but created a new one based on the

---

[52]The only exceptions are a commentary on Baruch, written by Theodoret of Cyrrhus (fifth century), and one or two others on the longer versions of Esther and Daniel. It should be noted, however, that the reason for the existence of these commentaries is that the texts in question were thought to be part of books that are found in the Hebrew canon (with Baruch belonging to Jeremiah). Not until the time of Bede (673–735) does a fragmentary commentary on Tobit appear, and only after that do we find anything on the other Apocryphal books.
[53]Heb. 1:1.
[54]2 Tim. 3:16; 2 Pet. 1:21.

teaching of the apostles.[55] This took shape gradually, as the apostolic writings that revealed Christ and taught the church about him were recognized and collected. There were other apostolic writings, including some letters of the apostle Paul, that were not preserved, presumably because they were of no spiritual value to the church as a whole.[56] There were also many pseudepigraphal writings that claimed apostolic authority without possessing it. These had to be identified and weeded out, but although the finishing touches were not put on the New Testament canon until the fourth century, it is remarkable how broad an agreement there was about it long before that.

The four Gospels were already accepted as uniquely authoritative in the early second century, as we know from Tatian's failed attempt to reduce them to one.[57] A lot of scholarly speculation has gone into reconstructing the process by which the Gospels were composed, but hard evidence is sparse and many different interpretations are possible. What can be said with certainly is that there was an oral tradition circulating among the first generation of Christians, which was codified and written down in at least three different ways.[58] Whether the Gospel writers (or compilers) based their work on written material, or whether it was all oral tradition, is unknown. It seems probable that the Fourth Gospel represents an independent source, but if other written material existed from which the Synoptic Gospels were composed, none of it has survived in a recognizable form.

As far as the attributions of the individual Gospels to Matthew, Mark, Luke, and John are concerned, the one most likely to be accurate is Luke, who also wrote the Acts of the Apostles as a sequel to his Gospel account. Next would probably come John, the "beloved disciple," who identifies himself in the closing paragraph,[59] though the authenticity of this has been contested. The second-century Christian writer Papias tells us that Mark is essentially the memoirs of Peter which he dictated to his disciple Mark, and that may well be true. Matthew remains anonymous, having no obvious connection to the disciple of that name. In the early church, however, Matthew's Gospel was regarded as the first and most important of the four, which is why it stands at the beginning of our New Testament. Only in modern times have most scholars posited Mark as the earliest Gospel to be written, mainly because it is shorter and less polished than the others and contains virtually noth-

---

[55] 2 Pet. 3:15–16 is the only evidence we have that books now in the New Testament were regarded as Scripture by the first generation of Christians.
[56] See Col. 4:16, which seems to refer to a letter written by Paul to the church at Laodicea.
[57] This was his *Diatessaron*, or "four-in-one."
[58] See 1 Cor. 11:23–26. The three Gospels directly concerned here are Matthew, Mark, and Luke, the so-called "Synoptics."
[59] John 21:20–24.

ing that cannot be found in Matthew and/or Luke as well. It is a reasonable hypothesis, but as with all such things, it cannot be proved, and we must keep an open mind about the matter.

The Gospels and Acts have the feel of official histories, but the letters of Paul and the other apostles are very different. They were occasional pieces, written for the most part to deal with various difficulties that had arisen in the church. In most cases, we can only guess what the problems were from the answers provided, an exercise which is inevitably speculative. In the end, we have to work with the texts as we have them, and while we must not draw conclusions that are wildly improbable, neither must we be too tied to their supposed "background" as the key to their interpretation. Digging up ancient Corinth or Philippi may be interesting and even important in some ways, but the findings of archaeology have to be used with extreme caution, since there is usually no way of knowing whether particular artifacts, inscriptions, or even local customs had any real impact on the life of the church. There are sure to be some allusions in the letters which escape us now, but their general drift is clear, and the principles they enunciate can usually be understood and applied with little or no knowledge of the original context.

The authorship of the epistles presents a particular difficulty, since many scholars doubt whether they can all be ascribed to the people who are supposed to have written them. Here again, speculation takes over from hard evidence, though the apostolic authorship of virtually all of the letters can be credibly defended. The biggest problem is 2 Peter, whose authenticity was widely doubted in ancient as well as in modern times. Because its style is so different from 1 Peter and its content seems to be too "advanced" for the first generation of Christians, it has frequently been regarded as a pseudepigraphal text from the mid-second century. Yet in spite of this, the letter continues to function in the church as a means of teaching and encouraging believers in their faith in a way that is not true of other early Christian literature such as the *Didache* or the *Shepherd of Hermas*. Despite the difficulties surrounding it, therefore, 2 Peter has proved its worth and earned its place in the canon.

The book of Revelation is in a category all its own and has frequently been misunderstood. One of the real advances in twentieth-century biblical scholarship was its rediscovery of the genre of apocalyptic literature, which has made it easier to interpret the last book of the Bible and to justify its place in the canon. For many centuries, Revelation was either ignored or misunderstood because no one really knew what to do with its rich symbolism. Many made the mistake of treating it as literal prophecy, which led to fantastic predictions of the imminent end of time, and so on. Invariably, readings of that kind would turn out to be wrong, and that discredited the book in the eyes of many serious scholars. Now, however, it is possible to appreciate the text of Revelation for what it is and to realize that it is one of the most profoundly theological books in the entire Bible. It may take some time for awareness of this to percolate down to the average churchgoer, who is still liable to be misled by sensational interpretations, but there is a new scholarly consensus on the subject that promises to enhance, not diminish, the book's reputation and usefulness in the life of the church.

The truly remarkable thing about the New Testament is that all branches of the Christian church recognize it and there is no dispute over extra or "apocryphal" books of the kind that there is in the Old Testament.[60] Although no ancient ecclesiastical council decreed it or even discussed the matter, the New Testament canon came together and has stayed together through all the ups and downs of church history, and is still universally agreed upon today. This consensus is the work of the Holy Spirit, persuading the people of God as they read, hear, and apply the sacred texts that these writings, and these alone, bear authentic witness to the apostolic teaching and to the gospel of Christ.

One major difference between the Testaments is to be found in the time and place of their composition. The Old Testament was written by largely anonymous people over many centuries. It describes the growth and development of God's people as their circumstances changed over time. It records the lives of great men like Abraham, Moses, and David, which serve as both a warning and an encouragement to us today. The New Testament, on the other hand, is the product of a single generation. We know the names of most of those who wrote it, but relatively little about the people mentioned in it. We can piece together the character of men like Peter and Paul, but we do not have enough information to be able to reconstruct a complete biography of either man and are not even told when or where they died.

We do not know why the writing of the Old Testament extended over such a long period, but we can make a reasonable guess as to why the New Testament was completed in a single generation. One reason is that it is the record of the apostolic witness. Apostles were people who had seen the risen Christ, and they naturally died out after the first generation.[61] Another reason is that the New Testament writers were conscious of living in the last days, and did not expect any further revelation from God.[62] Perhaps, too, there was the thought that all Christians share the same apostolic faith, which therefore

---

[60]Only the Ethiopian Orthodox Church adds eight extra books, which are, however, peculiar to Ethiopia and unknown elsewhere.
[61]1 Cor. 15:3–9.
[62]Heb. 1:1.

cannot change or develop. Just as those who saw Jesus in the flesh were not specially privileged over later generations who had to rely on the witness of others, so too later generations did not receive any revelation that the first Christians were deprived of.[63] Those saved at the eleventh hour receive the same reward as those who have labored in the vineyard all day long[64] because in Christ Jesus there is no before or after, but only permanent, eternal life shared by all.

At the end of the day, the divine inspiration of the Scriptures is seen in the power they exert in forming and feeding the people of God. The law of Moses would not have been worth preserving otherwise, since much of it has no application outside the ancient covenant community, and that has now disappeared. The Bible is a book for believers who appreciate its teaching and respond to it because in it they hear the voice of the Lord speaking to them. Centuries of common experience have ensured that the Bible remains at the heart of the church's life today, feeding us spiritually as it has fed hundreds of generations before us. Long after the disappearance of the original contexts in which its various parts were written, God continues to use them to inform and instruct those who seek to follow him today.

HOW THE BIBLE WAS REVEALED

The picture that emerges from this is that God spoke to individuals who then recorded his message or passed it on to others to record for them. God presumably communicated to the writers of the Old Testament in Hebrew, or at least that was how they heard him, but we are less sure about the New Testament writers. They certainly *wrote down* what they heard in Greek, but it is possible that God spoke to them in their native Aramaic (a language closely related to Hebrew), and that they translated the message themselves. That was undoubtedly the case with the words of Jesus, who preached and taught in Aramaic, and there are indications that the apostle Paul may have heard God speaking to him in that language as well.[65] Whatever the truth of the matter may be, we can say for sure that although the word of God was spoken in particular human languages, it was not confined to them. Even before the coming of Christ, the Hebrew Bible had been translated into Greek, and Aramaic versions were also appearing, apparently without any objections being raised. Much of what is recorded in the Gospels comes to us in translation, and the original Aramaic is no longer extant. Christians have never

---

[63]John 20:29.
[64]See Matt. 20:1–16.
[65]See Gal. 4:6; 1 Cor. 16:22.

believed that translating God's Word is impossible, although the medieval church in Western Europe discouraged it for other reasons.[66]

To those who find it strange that God should have communicated his universal message to particular individuals in their own language, which then had to be translated (sometimes by those same individuals) into other tongues, several possible explanations can be given, although none of them is expressly mentioned in the Bible itself. First, God relates to us as individuals. Even though we belong to a community, he speaks to us on a one-to-one basis and uses particular people to proclaim his message to the wider group. Even Jesus, despite the fact that he occasionally addressed large crowds of people, often said important things to only one person.[67] The evangelists who recorded Christ's message for posterity were also individual people who shaped their books in ways that reflect their individuality, however much they depended on other sources in the construction of their narrative. There can be no escaping the fact that God's communication to his people passed through individuals who were called and chosen for that purpose.

Second, far from privatizing the message, proceeding by way of one individual to a group guaranteed that everyone would hear the same message from a common source. This was most clearly seen when Peter and the other disciples stood up in Jerusalem on the day of Pentecost to proclaim the news of the risen Lord Jesus, and we are told that everyone present heard them speaking in their own language.[68] The message was one, but the communication was universal and adapted to the needs of each individual hearer.

This is how God continues to speak today. We have the Hebrew and Greek texts in which his message was first recorded and we base our translations on them. Relatively few Christians learn those languages, and nowadays almost no one (other than native speakers) would think of using them in their prayers to God. No Christian doubts that God speaks to us through translations, and we hear him in our own language without any sense that we need an interpreter to understand what he is saying. If doubts arise or people claim to hear something that is incorrect, the ancient records are there to prevent us from going astray, and scholars study them diligently in order to make sure that the content comes across without distortion. God's Word has always overcome the language barrier, and the common witness of Christians around the world shows that they have understood the same message in their native tongues. But without the common reference point represented by the texts in their original

---

[66]The church canonized the Latin Vulgate—itself a translation, of course—and discouraged vernacular translations because it was afraid that they might be heretical.
[67]Nicodemus, for example (John 3), or the woman at the well (John 4).
[68]Acts 2:6–11.

languages, there would be no way of knowing whether we were all talking about the same thing, and if disputes arose about how to interpret them, there would be no authority to which we could turn for help.[69]

If God had revealed himself to every nation in the many and diverse ways in which he revealed himself to Israel before sending his Son to them, it would be almost impossible to know whether Jesus Christ was the Savior of the world.[70] If there were more than one way to God, it would be unclear whether one of them was better than the others, or which one we should prefer and why. Paradoxical as it may seem, insisting on one revelation given through particular individuals to one specially chosen people is the best way to guarantee equal treatment for all, and that may be why it was the way that God actually chose. Scripture is the language of God's love for his people, and if it does not speak to the soul, then it is not doing what we ought to expect from the Word of God. Ultimately, the Bible points us to an experience of God that lies beyond itself but which it confirms and supports as the standard against which everything else must be judged.[71]

THE DIVINE INSPIRATION OF THE BIBLE

A great deal has been written about the inspiration, infallibility, and inerrancy of Holy Scripture, though only the first of these terms is found in the Bible itself.[72] Infallibility and inerrancy are best viewed as logical deductions from the principle of divine inspiration. The former term became current in the nineteenth century, when Protestants applied it to the Bible and Roman Catholics to the papacy, but "inerrancy" is of more recent origin. The general line of argument is that if the Bible is divinely inspired, it must also be infallible because God would not lead his people astray. To be truly infallible, however, it must not contain any errors, because even the smallest mistake might mislead people and cause them to err or (if they discovered the mistake) to doubt the truth of God's Word. Arguments of this kind make logical sense, but they come up against the obvious objections that we do not possess the original manuscripts and that all the copies we have contain errors of various kinds. This means that no truly "inerrant" text exists, but that does not necessarily imply that the copies we have are misleading and says nothing at all about whether they are inspired by God.

A great deal of controversy surrounds these terms, and it is fair to say that

---

[69]There are no perfect texts in the original languages, but the differences among them are minimal and seldom affect the meaning to any significant degree.
[70]See Heb. 1:1–3.
[71]See Isa. 8:20.
[72]2 Tim. 3:16.

in the modern church, belief in what they represent is the hallmark of conservative, and usually evangelical, believers. But it is also fair to say that traditionally orthodox Christians have always believed that the Bible is divinely inspired, and the unique place occupied by its text in Christian worship bears witness to that fact. In ancient times it was commonly believed that poets were inspired by a muse or other genius, who gave them the superhuman talent they possessed. Inspiration applied primarily to the people who composed literary works, and not to the works themselves. In the New Testament, we find both—holy men were moved by the Spirit of God, but the texts they produced were also breathed out by him.[73] This quality was the mark of their holiness and the guarantee of their supreme authority in the life of the church.

"Infallibility" emerged as a way of saying that the Scriptures do not teach error, and "inerrancy" makes it more precise by insisting that they do not contain it either. Both terms have suffered from the excessive zeal of some of their proponents, who have made extravagant claims that go beyond what can be proved from the texts themselves. For example, some have said that Job must have been a historical person, since he is described in that way in the book that bears his name, but it is just as likely that he is a fictional character whom the anonymous author created in order to make a series of important theological points. To use "inerrancy" as an excuse for insisting on the historicity of Job is going too far, and the term loses its credibility when such claims are made on the basis of it.

The best way to look at these words is to see them as essentially juridical terms. The Bible is the written constitution of the church and must be interpreted as such. Its authority is absolute, and therefore it is both infallible and inerrant as far as the life of the church is concerned. No Christian preacher or teacher has any right to distort or minimize its teaching, and every word in it must be carefully weighed and its meaning considered. We do not have to worry if some parts of it (such as the Old Testament food laws) are no longer immediately applicable today, because that is often true of human laws as well. A state constitution almost certainly contains provisions that are now obsolete, but they retain the authority of the document as a whole, and if the circumstances for which they were designed should recur, they would come back into force. The Bible is very much like that, except that it also contains a spiritual message that can be applied in spiritual ways long after the material circumstances in which it was originally revealed have disappeared. If we view matters in that way, then the Bible will not lead us astray, nor will it teach us anything that is false to the Spirit who inspired it.

---

[73] 2 Pet. 1:21; 2 Tim. 3:16.

We do not need to worry too much about the mistakes scribes made in copying, since many of these can be corrected and few have any real significance as far as the meaning of the original is concerned. Some areas of doubt remain, but as long as we do not put too much weight on words or passages that are unclear, this should not affect our understanding of the overall message of the text. More serious are the allegations that the Bible contains errors of fact or of judgment that are not accidental. For example, archaeologists have raised questions about the Israelite invasion of Palestine under Joshua because evidence for the collapse of the walls at Jericho or the destruction of Ai is either missing or does not support the claims made in Scripture.[74] Historians have found no evidence for the existence of Esther or Daniel, and many scholars believe that they were made up in later times for what were essentially political reasons.

The New Testament is less open to this kind of objection because the time period it covers is much shorter and better known, but there are still many details about the life of Jesus and the career of the apostle Paul which are hard to piece together from the texts. Did Jesus cleanse the temple at the beginning of his ministry or at the end, or did he do it twice, as some scholars have tried to argue? More radical scholars might ask whether the event ever happened at all, and suggest that it was concocted by the disciples to make a theological point.[75] These are hard and perhaps impossible questions to answer, partly because the evidence is insufficient for us to decide either way and partly because the intention of the original author(s) is unclear. Scholars do their best to resolve these difficulties, on the reasonable assumption that the problems were not apparent to those who first wrote or read the texts and so there must be some explanation for them. The explanation may not always be what we would expect, and certain questions remain unanswerable in our present state of knowledge, but it would be most unwise to accuse the text of lying or misrepresenting the facts simply because we do not know what they are. The true researcher, like a good detective, will persevere until he has found a solution and refuse to comment on facile theories which discount the witness of the texts. They, after all, are a major part of the evidence we have, and must be treated with due caution and respect.

From the standpoint of the ordinary believer, arguments about the "historicity" of the biblical text are important because our faith is based on truth, but such arguments are not the heart of the matter. The Bible is not the source

---

[74]Josh. 6:20; 8:20.
[75]Matt. 21:12–17; Mark 11:15–18; Luke 19:45–47; John 2:14–16. The first three Gospels place it later, but John puts it at the beginning of Jesus' ministry.

of our doctrine and spiritual life merely because it contains no errors, since the same might be said of a dictionary or computer manual. Infallibility and inerrancy have their place, but divine inspiration remains the key to interpreting the text because that is what makes it the Word of God. The apostle Paul spoke to us all when he wrote to Timothy,

> The sacred writings . . . are able to make you wise for salvation through faith in Christ Jesus. All Scripture is breathed out by God and profitable for teaching, for reproof, for correction, and for training in righteousness, that the man of God may be complete, equipped for every good work.[76]

In other words, the Bible is our textbook for learning and growing in our faith, so that we may be able to live as we should and bear witness to the truth of the gospel we have received in Christ Jesus.

THE INTERPRETATION OF THE BIBLE

The Holy Spirit has given us the Scriptures and informs our hearts and minds as we read them and seek to know how to apply them today. We have the assurance of Jesus that the Spirit of truth will lead us into all truth if we follow his guidance.[77] The nature and content of this truth can be understood if we start with its fundamental principles and work from there. The first is that the Holy Spirit has given us the revelation of God in written form. The main question we must ask of every biblical text is, what does it tell us about God? What does it say about who he is and about what he does? The second question is, what does this text say about us human beings? What are we meant to be and what has gone wrong? The third and final question is, what has God done about this problem and what does he expect of us in the light of what he has done? Seeking answers to these questions will help us interpret the Spirit's message to Christ's people collectively and to each of us as individuals.

This is true even of those parts of the Bible that, on the surface, appear to be the furthest from giving us any instruction about God. Take, for example, the genealogies of 1 Chronicles. There we have page after page of names, many of which we find unpronounceable and most of which are obscure. For every one we recognize there must be fifty that we have never heard of before and will probably never come across again or have any practical use for. What is the point of these lists of names in Scripture? Can it be that God was wasting his time giving us all this information, or that these details have somehow found their way into a divine message where they do not belong? Many read-

[76] 2 Tim. 3:15–17.
[77] John 16:13.

ers are tempted to conclude just that, and ignore such texts. A few people even make fun of them, as if an endless list of "begats" were somehow comical. The believing Christian, however, is not in a position to do this. Somehow or other, he has to make spiritual sense of passages like these, and the way to do that is to follow the guideline questions enumerated above.

What do the genealogies reveal about God? They tell us that he is a faithful Lord, who keeps his covenant from one generation to another. Whoever we are and however far we may have descended from the source of our human life in Adam, we are still part of God's plan. Over the centuries we have developed differently, we have lost contact with one another, and we have even turned on each other in hostility, but in spite of all that, we are still related and interconnected in ways that go beyond our immediate understanding or experience.

Secondly, what do the genealogies say about us? They say that from the world's point of view, most of us are nobodies. We live and die in a long chain of humanity, but there is not much that anyone will remember about us as individuals. Yet without us, future generations will not be born and the legacy of the past will not be preserved. We are part of a great cloud of witnesses, a long chain of faithful people who have lived for God in the place where he put them. Even if we know little about our ancestors, we owe them a great debt of gratitude for their loyalty and perseverance, when they had little or nothing to gain from it or to show for it.

Finally, what do the genealogies say about God's dealings with us? They tell us that we are called to be obedient and to keep the faith we have inherited, passing it on undiminished to the next generation. They remind us that there is a purpose in our calling that goes beyond ourselves. Even if we are not celebrated by future generations and leave little for posterity to remember us by, we shall nevertheless have made an indispensable contribution to the purposes of God in human history. So the genealogies bring us a message from God, even if they appear on the surface to be barren and unprofitable. All we have to do is ask the right questions, and their meaning will be quickly opened up to us.

Asking the right questions about the text of the Bible is also the best way to avoid unnecessary disputes about it. It is often said that a passage of Scripture has as many meanings as there are interpreters, and that the quest for objective truth is bound to disappoint us. The fact that many equally Bible-believing Christians can come up with different and even mutually incompatible interpretations of Scripture is held up as evidence, if not as proof, that it is full of contradictions and can therefore be quoted in support of any number of radically different propositions. But a closer examination of these disagree-ments will almost always show that such criticism is misplaced.

Differences of opinion over what the Bible says and teaches generally arise because the approach being taken to it is wrong. For example, ques-tions may be asked about the historical accuracy of the Bible's accounts of particular events. As the purpose of recounting these events is to explain the ways of God with men and not to give what we would regard as an "objective" report of what went on, the details will be selected in a way that brings out the main purpose of the story. Things that do not contribute to that may be omitted from the biblical account, and information that might be important for other reasons is not necessarily included. This is particularly obvious in the case of the life of Jesus. A modern biographer would want to know when he was born, what his life was like before he burst onto the public stage, and in what year he died. The Gospels tell us none of these things with anything like the precision that a modern historian would look for, but that is not their purpose. The absence of such details about his life does not detract from the fact that Jesus lived the most important life in human history, a claim that is fully expounded in the texts and a judgment that we are glad to accept even without much factual information about it.

Another tendency that causes confusion is our habit of trying to make the Bible say things it was never intended to say. For example, there is very little in the Bible about church worship and government. That the church should conduct worship services and be governed by elders and pastors in an orderly manner is clearly stated,[78] but the details of how this should be done are left tantalizingly vague. Matters of this kind seem to have been left to the discre-tion of particular congregations or church bodies, unless they affected the basic message of the gospel.

Sometimes people go the other way and try to make the text bear the weight of a theological position that lies beyond its scope. This has been very common in modern debates about women's ministry, to take but one obvious example. That there were women in the New Testament church who exercised ministerial functions is clear,[79] but that does not cancel out the leadership role reserved for men, nor does it override the submission to that principle that is demanded of women.[80] Still less can texts that talk about women in other roles be "adapted" to apply to the ordained ministry today.[81] Special pleading

---

[78]1 Cor. 14:40; 1 Tim. 3:1–13; Titus 1:5–16.
[79]Rom. 16:1–2.
[80]1 Tim. 2:8–15. See also 1 Cor. 11:7–10.
[81]See Rom. 16:7 and Gal. 3:28 for particularly egregious examples of such misuse of the texts. Romans 16:7 mentions a woman called Junia who was "well known to the apostle," but some people claim that the verse

of this kind has been rampant in recent years and has persuaded many, not least those who wanted to hear this message anyway, but it is an abuse of the Scriptures and a falsification of their witness that has been brought about by modern desires, not by any inclination to listen to the text or do what it commands.

Many other examples of the misuse of a text can be cited, but it is remarkable how they usually all boil down to one of two things. Either the hermeneutical method being used is faulty, or the issues being discussed are not in the text to begin with. As a revelation given by the Holy Spirit, the Bible must be read in the light of the work the Holy Spirit does in the world, which is to reveal the Father and the Son. But the Father and the Son reveal themselves in the work they have done over many generations in the context of creation, of the covenant made with their chosen people, and of the evolving pattern built into the so-called dispensations of the covenant. These great principles give us a historical and theological framework for interpreting what the Bible means, and if we depart from these principles, we shall quickly fall into error. In ancient times, many biblical texts seemed to be morally objectionable as they stood, or else to contain precepts that could no longer be applied. But instead of seeing these things in their covenant context, many interpreters preferred to interpret them in a figurative way. Thus was born the device of allegory, which interprets biblical texts, especially hard ones, in a spiritualized way that may intend to do great honor to God at the cost of ignoring or even falsifying the literal sense of the text. The Song of Songs is a classic example of this. Unwilling to treat it as a love poem, most early commentators interpreted it as an allegory of God's love for his people. In reaction to that, some modern commentators have gone to the other extreme and regarded it as erotic poetry, with little or no "spirituality" about it at all. Yet if we ask the hermeneutical questions outlined above, we shall soon see that neither of these views is correct.

The Song of Solomon is indeed a book about God, but not in the allegorical way so often chosen by the fathers of the church. The name of God is never mentioned in the text, not because he is not there but because he is hidden. Human love can be a wonderful and passionate thing, but it is riddled with complexities and contradictions. Alongside great exaltation of spirit there comes the threat of abandonment and death. One minute the beloved are caught up in raptured embrace; in the next they are wandering the streets of the city, lost and looking for something they cannot hope to find. Human

---

implies that she was an apostle herself. Galatians 3:28 says that there is no difference between male and female in Christ, but it is talking about salvation, not about ministry in the church, where other factors come into play.

love blossoms for a season but then moves on as a new generation arises and the cycle of life begins again. God keeps the cycle going but he himself is above and beyond it. His love has some similarities with the love of the bridegroom for his bride, or of the lover for his beloved, but in the final analysis it is a different thing altogether. Where human emotions ebb and flow, God's love remains constant. Where human affections are tainted with corruption and bound to the limitations of this world, God's commitment to his people is permanent and unchanging. What is not possible with us is possible with him, and his covenant will endure long after we have passed away. This is the true message of the Song, which we shall discover if we are attentive to the Spirit's voice and the way in which he reveals God to us.

Knowing how to read the Old Testament in the light of the coming of Jesus Christ is the greatest challenge the church has had to face, and one that recurs in every generation. On the one hand, the historical mission of Israel has been accomplished, and the provisions made for it have therefore ceased to apply, at least in their original form. On the other hand, God is the same yesterday, today, and forever, and his word does not change. To the extent that what he said back then reflects his character and his eternal purpose for the human race, it is still valid for us today, even if it has been fulfilled in the life, death, and resurrection of Jesus. It is deciding which precepts belong in which category that challenges us, and we must not be surprised that there are significant differences of opinion about particular issues.

For example, some believe that the fourth commandment ("Remember the Sabbath day") applies to the Christian Sunday, which ought to be as much of a day of rest as its ancient Israelite equivalent was. Others reject this interpretation, claiming that Sabbath observance is no longer mandatory, although most people agree that Sunday ought to be kept as a day of worship.[82] Who is right? Jesus demonstrated by his own teaching and behavior that the rigid Sabbath-keeping typical of some Jews in his day was actually in breach of the law because it was an excuse for evading the more fundamental obligation of showing charity.[83] There is nothing in the New Testament that explicitly sets aside one day a week for the worship of God, although it is clearly necessary for the church to find a time when its members can gather together for that purpose. The conclusion must be that we are entitled to do that, but that whatever arrangements we make, they must not be exaggerated or interpreted in a way that undermines the basic principle of love, which must remain the primary motivation for all our thoughts and actions.

---

[82]Here Seventh-day Adventists are more literal and (in a sense) more logical than most Christians are.
[83]Matt. 12:1–12.

Despite such difficulties, Christians have to remember that the Old Testament speaks about Jesus Christ.[84] Often it does so only indirectly, and in those cases we must try to discern how particular passages speak about him. We must also remember that the Old Testament is a partial revelation of things that have become fully clear in Christ.[85] This is especially obvious in the sacrificial laws, where the lamb slain for the sins of the people is the prototype of Christ's atoning sacrifice on the cross, but it can be applied in different ways to the entire text. If these guidelines are borne in mind, the chances of reading the Old Testament correctly will be greatly increased, even if there is no guarantee that we shall always get it right.

DIVINE REVELATION OUTSIDE THE BIBLE?

Has God ever spoken to people beyond what is recorded for us in the Bible? He most certainly has! The Bible tells us this when it says, "There are also many other things that Jesus did. Were every one of them to be written, I suppose that the world itself could not contain the books that would be written."[86] No doubt John was indulging in a bit of literary hyperbole, but the point is clear: what we have in the Gospels is only a selection, and a small selection at that, of what God did in and through his Son's earthly life. We do not know for sure, but we can reasonably assume that most of the prophets of the Old Testament also prophesied more than is recorded of them. After all, if men like Nathan or Micaiah had not done so, how would anyone have known that they were prophets in the first place? Nor can we say that God stopped speaking to people when the New Testament was completed. In the history of the church there have been countless individuals who have claimed that God has spoken to them in different ways, and we *expect* to hear him speaking to us too. Our relationship with him is a two-way street, and if he encourages us to talk to him in prayer, we must be prepared to hear him talking back to us.

In the course of human history, far too many people have heard God speaking to them for us to doubt that this can happen, but trying to figure out what it means is another story. For example, if I hear a voice telling me to buy a loaf of bread, and I believe that this is God speaking directly to me, there is no way that my belief can be proved or disproved. That may not matter very much if all I am going to do with the bread is eat it as I would eat anything else. We have no right to tell people who make such claims that they cannot be correct, especially since the Bible tells us that God cares about our welfare

---

[84]John 5:39; Luke 24:27.
[85]Heb. 1:1.
[86]John 21:25.

and guides us through life one step at a time.[87] If my relationship with God works itself out in this way, then I must rejoice and be glad that I can feel so close to him. At the same time, we are warned in the Bible not to believe every spirit, and we must be on our guard against the possibility that we are being deceived.[88]

How can we tell when a voice that we hear is God speaking to us? There is no infallible rule to follow here, but there are certain principles we can rely on for guidance. First, anyone who says things about God that contradict the Scriptures has been misled. God will not tell his people to murder, steal, or commit adultery, nor will he give anyone a new revelation of himself that modifies or adds to what we already know. That kind of revelation ceased at the end of the apostolic period, for the very good reason that we are in fellowship with the saints of every age and so cannot know more about God than the first generation of Christians did. Individuals today who claim to have received a message that the church has never heard before, but must now accept, are certainly wrong, and we must not listen to them. For example, from time to time someone predicts that Christ will return on a certain day, even though the New Testament explicitly says that this cannot be known by anyone.[89] Tragedies have occurred when people have listened to such predictions instead of testing what they say by the Word of God, and we must be careful not to fall into such traps.

Beyond that, it is often impossible to say for sure whether what we think is a word from the Lord is genuine, and believers must allow each other the freedom to determine what the right response to such impulses should be. For example, if I believe that God is telling me to open a bakery and there is nothing to stop me from doing so, then perhaps the only way to test this is to open one and see what happens. If the bakery prospers, I may be able to claim that God's word to me has been fulfilled. If it fails, I may have to admit that I was mistaken, or that God wanted me to fail for reasons of his own—perhaps to make me depend more on him and less on my own efforts. Either way, such divine-human communication is between him and me and cannot be interpreted as his will for the wider church. God does not want everyone to open a bakery, and if I insist that my experience must become a model for others or a yardstick for measuring their spirituality, then I have certainly taken things too far.

The key distinction here is the difference between what is private and

---

[87]See Matt. 6:28–32.
[88]1 John 4:1.
[89]Acts 1:7.

what is public. A private communication from God to an individual believer must be received and acted upon by the person concerned, according to the wisdom given him by the Holy Spirit. It is when such things move from the private into the public sphere that we must exercise the greatest caution. The Bible has been given to us as our common guide to God's will, and it remains the permanent, fixed standard by which all other claims to divine guidance must be judged. Anything beyond that is private speculation and cannot be imposed on the church with the authority of God's revelation. Just as someone in secular life has to consider whether a bright idea he has is legal before he acts on it, so a Christian must ask whether what he thinks is a word from the Lord is biblical before he does anything about it. If he decides that it is, then let him test it and see, as long as we all remember that the written Word is the final arbiter given to us by God and is the only authority to which the church is called to submit without reservation.

nice!

3

THE CHRISTIAN WORLDVIEW

THE COHERENCE OF THE UNIVERSE

At the heart of the Christian worldview is the belief that the universe is a coherent whole. Without that belief, modern science would be impossible. The greatest intellectual battles the early church had to fight focused on the doctrine of creation, which was contrary to the prevailing philosophies of the time but had to be asserted if the Christian revelation was to make any sense. But although the early Christians managed to impose their doctrine of creation on Western civilization, they did not overturn ancient Greek science as a whole. For a long time the church simply ignored it, but when interest in the natural world revived in the thirteenth century, theologians of the time took the view that the Bible and ancient Greek science were mutually compatible. According to them, the former spoke authoritatively about heavenly things and the latter equally authoritatively about earthly things. What the Bible said about the world was interpreted in terms of a non-Christian belief system and so its real teaching was obscured. It was only when the biblical doctrine of creation was understood to be something quite different from anything Aristotle, Ptolemy, or Galen had thought that the intellectual conditions needed for modern scientific development were created. This development occurred in the sixteenth and seventeenth centuries and led to some tension between theological traditionalists and scientific modernists. This in turn left the impression that there was a built-in conflict between the Bible and science which could only end in the defeat of the Bible.

Today it is fashionable to point to the case of Galileo (1564–1642), who was persecuted by the Roman Catholic Church for his scientific beliefs. Few people pause to consider the fact that Galileo was condemned not because he opposed the teaching of the Bible but because he had revealed the inadequacy of the ancient Greek science which the church mistakenly regarded as equally infallible. The real lesson from that and other similar episodes is not that the Bible is wrong but that Christians must not commit themselves to any scientific theory as if it were absolute truth or build a theological system on what might one day turn out to be shifting sand.

In fact, most of those who realized that Galileo was right had a strong belief in the truth of the Bible and were not trying to overturn its authority. Many of the world's great scientists have been believing Christians, and a good number still are. Observation suggests that, on university campuses today, scientific departments have a percentage of believing Christians at least as high as if not higher than those found in other faculties. Atheists may regard this as anomalous or perverse, but they cannot deny that it is a fact, and it remains some of the best evidence we have that Christianity and natural science are not incompatible or hostile to each other.

If natural science has disproved the Bible, how can we explain why so many scientists believe in God? The basic reason for their faith must surely be that the coherence of the universe demands an explanation. The more deeply we probe into our world, the more inclined we are to look for an overarching principle that holds it together. The suggestion that such a complex system could have come into being by chance is so improbable as to be virtually incredible. Knowing as we do that even a slight change in the conditions governing our existence would destroy us, it seems far more plausible to suggest that the world can be maintained only by the guiding hand of a supernatural, intelligent power. To believe, as scientific atheists do, that human beings, who in their eyes are just chance products of evolution, thrown up on a single, medium-sized planet in a virtually infinite cosmos, hold the key to understanding a universe which stretches far beyond them is patently absurd. Take away the image and likeness of God, and there is no reason why one species on a single planet should hold the key to understanding the entire universe.

We must also remember that only a tiny minority of highly educated people who have lived on earth for the past century or two have claimed to be able to explain the workings of the universe on a purely materialistic basis. What about everyone else? Should we entrust our fate to a handful of intellectuals who think they are more intelligent than the rest of the human race? Is no other kind of knowledge—artistic sensitivity, for example, or technical skill—of any significance or value? Do we really believe that Shakespeare or Rembrandt knew less about the human condition than Charles Darwin or Richard Dawkins? These questions and many more like them spring to mind when we reflect on the audacity of the people who make such claims. Would human knowledge of ultimate reality, such as it is, suffer any serious loss if every scientific atheist were suddenly to disappear? The answer to this is clearly no. Quite apart from anything else, the knowledge they possess is shared by others who accept it as factually true but who do not draw the same inferences from it about the existence (or nonexistence) of God.

Belief in the coherence of the universe does not compel us to accept that Christian claims about how it was made (creation) and how it is governed (providence) are true, because those claims go beyond mere coherence, but belief in coherence is a necessary start. Nor does belief in the coherence of the universe remove the difficulties raised by the great questions of suffering and evil, whose existence continues to trouble us even if we can sometimes see a certain logic in it. But Christians believe that it is far easier to deal with such problems within the framework of the Christian revelation than it is to believe in chance evolution, where even good and evil have no objective definition. As the old saying goes, "One man's meat is another man's poison," and if moral awareness is based on nothing more than personal preference, or even on what is imagined to be "the greatest good for the greatest number," it is hardly adequate. If there is a right way to live, then it must be based on something more than expediency, which would almost certainly be different for different people. Deciding what is right and wrong is never easy, but it is far better to base one's judgment on some objective criterion than to be guided by nothing more than individual intuition responding to particular circumstances but unrelated to anything beyond them.

DISORDER IN THE UNIVERSE?

The Christian message proclaims that the power governing the universe is the God who has revealed himself in the Bible and who came into the world in the person of Jesus of Nazareth. Those who dispute this claim are invited to put it to the test—"taste and see that the LORD is good!" as the psalmist says.[1] We are also told that this God is love, and that everything he has made reflects and proclaims that love to us. The world was created and is now kept in being by the power of love, which explains why it coheres so well and is so perfectly adapted to our needs. Yet there are some things in the universe that we do not like, and other things that attack us and make life harder than we think it ought to be. There is a force of evil at work in the world that we must resist as best we can. Where this evil comes from and why it is there we cannot say,

---

[1]Ps. 34:8.

but we sense that its presence in our midst is anomalous and out of keeping with the true nature of our universe.

So strong is this feeling that some people deny the existence of God because they cannot accept that evil is compatible with his nature. But this conclusion ignores the fact that our knowledge of evil depends on the revelation that God has given us in the first place. If he had not told us about evil, we would not know what it is and could hardly feel the outrage we do when we encounter it. Without divine revelation, we might wonder what is wrong with the world, but our concept of evil would be blunted, and we would have no corresponding knowledge of good to compare it with. In other words, we would just have to put up with our circumstances, knowing that there is nothing we could ever do to change them. Yet our minds rebel against such a fatalistic conclusion. The existence of evil does not destroy our belief in the essential goodness of the world we live in. On the contrary, we are strengthened in that belief because we sense that evil is an anomaly, and not an inevitable part of the natural order of things. By condemning it as abnormal, we reject it and are disposed to fight against it as an enemy that inhibits our full enjoyment of the world.

Strange as it may seem, the existence of evil teaches us that God's love is something greater and more fundamental to his being than even his goodness is. Those who reject God because they think that the existence of evil is incompatible with his goodness have made the classic mistake of equating goodness with love, and assuming that the one must necessarily imply the other. Of course, we agree that God is both good and loving, and if everything else were as perfect as he is, there would be no distinction between them. Where the difference appears and the primacy of his love over his goodness is revealed, is when that goodness is rejected or denied. If God were good but not loving, he would condemn and destroy anything that turned away from his goodness. Conversely, if he were loving but not good, he could not turn against anyone who rejected his nonexistent goodness. Nor is there anything remarkable about a good God who loves creatures who are as good as he is; that is just what we would expect. But the Christian gospel says that, in his love, God has reached out to those who have rebelled against him and embraced evil. It is the wonder of God's love that he can transcend his own goodness, reach out to those who have denied it, and reconcile them to himself.[2]

For this reason, Christians believe that the love of God is even greater than his goodness, though we do not forget that he remains good in himself, and we proclaim that it is because of his love that his goodness comes to heal

---

[2] See Hab. 1:13.

and restore us. Even in the face of evil, God is love. He reaches out to people he cannot naturally like and enters into fellowship with them, although they have done nothing to deserve it. To the superficial observer, the existence of evil appears to be a disorder in the universe, but even this evil can be used to demonstrate the saving power of the love of God.

THE SUSTAINING LOVE OF GOD

The Bible tells us that God is one, but in that oneness there are three divine persons bound together in the infinite depth and wonder of eternal love. The love he extends to us as his creatures is therefore a natural outworking of the love he has in himself. It is the link between the visible and the invisible, between what is eternal in God and what has been created by him in time. By being made in his image and being invited to participate in that love, we human beings have been dignified to a degree that must be the envy of the rest of the created order. For we are not merely the beneficiaries of God's providential care in the way that birds and flowers are: we are active members of a fellowship of love that establishes our place as children of God and masters of creation.[3] The love that binds us to God is perfect and fully known in him, but in us it is bound by our limitations as his creatures and by the legacy of our rebellion against him—a legacy from which we can never fully escape in this life.

It is easy for us to become so preoccupied with our own condition that we forget how important the love of God is for sustaining the universe. What we can all too easily regard as a hostile environment was created for our enjoyment and is held together by God because he is delighted with it. Jesus reminded his disciples of this when he told them,

> Look at the birds of the air: they neither sow nor reap nor gather into barns, and yet your heavenly Father feeds them. . . . Consider the lilies of the field, how they grow: they neither toil nor spin, yet I tell you, even Solomon in all his glory was not arrayed like one of these.[4]

The natural world is a complex system of interacting organisms that sustain each other in a balanced environment specially designed for each one of them. To study these organisms is to enter a world of microscopic perfection where everything is finely tuned to a degree that makes it inconceivable that it could all have happened by accident. Today there is a growing number of scientists and philosophers who recognize that this fine tuning is one of the

[3]See Matt. 6:25–34.
[4]Matt. 6:26, 28.

most powerful arguments for the existence of God. Christians would go even further and claim that not only does this fine tuning support the fact that God is the Creator of all things, but it shows us that he is also a God of love. It is true that some animals survive by eating others, and many live on plants as well. Yet somehow each species manages to survive and prosper, with none being made extinct due to the greed of another. The sad exception to this rule is man—we are the ones who destroy our environment and upset the natural balance that it contains.

But even then, the power of nature to recover from our depredations is truly remarkable. Trees and vegetation spring up again after they have been cut down, and even some animals that were once thought to be extinct have turned up again, almost as if they had never gone away. When properly managed, rivers that used to be too polluted to sustain life have been restored, and the fish, otters, and other creatures that once dwelt there have made their way back. Landscapes ruined by mining or deforestation have gradually recovered, and in some cases now look not so very different from what they must have been before the devastation began. Even human bodies have innate regenerative powers, and thanks to the discoveries of modern medicine, they can often be brought back to a degree of health and well-being that seems truly miraculous. None of this would be possible, of course, if the potential for it were not already present in the organisms concerned, and the fact that they so often are is a sure sign of God's unfailing love for what he has made.

4

SPEAKING ABOUT GOD

THE WAY OF NEGATION

We can know God's love by experiencing it, but the depths of our experience can never be adequately defined in words. Something will always be left unarticulated, because there is a dimension to the love of God that cannot be captured in concepts available to our finite minds. To put it a different way, although we receive God's love in its fullness, we can never know it fully because our finitude makes it impossible for us to plumb the depths of the divine being. For this reason, some people argue that any words spoken about God are deceptive, because in attempting to define the infinite they distort its true nature. To their minds, theology must be content with saying what God is not. They call this the *way of denial,* or *negation,* because it rejects human words and concepts as both inadequate and misleading in trying to express the reality of God. According to this view, human language can point us in the right direction and give us a foretaste of the glory we are meant to experience in our relationship with God, but it can never take the place of that reality or be an adequate expression of it. The basic principle of this "negative" or "apophatic" theology, as it is called, is that whatever we say about God, it cannot express what he really is. Our minds are shaped by the finite experiences of human beings, which can never be more than pale approximations or analogies of the "real thing" in heaven.

In making this claim, proponents of the way of negation are reminding us of an important truth: love cannot be reduced to a logical formula, or adequately analyzed by the mental constructs of our human brains. There is always something more to love than this, that cannot be neatly packaged by our minds and which, in some of its manifestations at least, may even appear to contradict our innate certainties. For example, we are not surprised to think that God would love things that are as good, just, and perfect as he is, but why should he care for people who are none of these things? What is it that makes him reach out to the least likely among us and draw them to himself? We do not know the answer to this, but if it were not so, none of us would have any chance of being saved from the consequences of our rebellion against him. On the contrary, we would all have been destroyed long ago by the inexorable logic of God's very goodness, justice, and perfection. To the extent that the traditional way of negation bears witness to this truth, it is a valuable and even essential ingredient of the Christian consciousness. It reminds us that there are some things we shall never know about God, and many things about him that we shall be able to express only in a halting and inadequate way. In the words of the apostle Paul,

> Now we see in a mirror dimly, but then face to face. Now I know in part; then I shall know fully, even as I have been fully known. So now faith, hope and love abide, these three; but the greatest of these is love.[1]

Many people equate the way of negation with mysticism, but although the two are closely linked, they are not identical. The way of negation is a philosophical position, whereas mysticism is a spiritual experience, although both can be expressed in intellectual terms and each has given rise to a respectable body of theological literature. People who are inclined to derive their knowledge from books and to process what they learn along the lines laid down by rational thought need to be reminded that, important as those things are, they are not enough. Our knowledge of the divine must be rooted in a life of prayer and devotion that go beyond the limits of our finite minds and allow us to be caught up into the hidden being of God. Most of the time this does not involve anything extraordinary, although such things cannot be ruled out. When God called Moses to meet him on Mount Sinai, he said that he would come in a thick cloud, which suggests that the meeting between the two would be shrouded in mystery.[2] In the New Testament, the apostle Paul tells us that he knew a man who had been caught up into the third heaven, which has always been understood to refer to mystical experience of a kind not given to the average believer.[3] And of course, almost the entire book of Revelation was written by John to record what he saw when he was taken up to heaven and shown the hidden things of God.[4]

---

[1] 1 Cor. 13:12–13.
[2] Ex. 19:9.
[3] 2 Cor. 12:2.
[4] Rev. 4:1–2.

Mystical experiences of various kinds have been reported throughout the history of the church, and some people have even written guidebooks for those seeking such experiences. It is difficult to know what to say about this, because a mystical experience of God is private by definition and therefore virtually impossible for an outsider to evaluate or imitate. However, certain basic principles relating to mystical experiences can be gleaned from the Scriptures. The first is that they are possible but rare. Paul's statement about the man who had had one tells us how unusual they were. He was obviously prepared to accept such experiences as genuine, but he never told people in his churches that they should expect to have them as a matter of course. Second, there is no reason to believe that mystics are superior to other Christians or that God has given them any special authority to teach in the church. What happens to them is between them and the Lord, and is not meant to be imitated by others.

Third, while mystical experiences may deepen a believer's relationship with God, they cannot add anything to it that is not already indicated in the Bible and readily available, at least in principle, to any Christian. Some mystical traditions have claimed that a mystic does not need to participate in the worship of the church or receive the sacraments, because he has risen to a higher spiritual level and can dispense with such mundane things. There is no ground in Scripture for believing that, and anyone who treats mysticism as a way to escape from the fellowship of other Christians cannot be believed or followed. Lastly, a mystic has no authority to disrupt the church or impose himself on it in defiance of its regularly constituted leadership.[5] If these guidelines are firmly in place and respected by those who claim to have had mystical experiences, there should be no difficulty for the rest of the church in accepting them as and when they occur.

THE WAY OF AFFIRMATION

Recognizing the value of the way of negation is important, but it is not the whole story. Our mystical union with God must be proclaimed to the world in language adequate to communicate it, because God's love reaches out to people everywhere and invites them to come into that union. God did not make the world with the intention of hiding himself from it, but in order to express his glory in and through what he has made. Human beings are created in his image and likeness and have been given the capacity to relate to him. Because we have thoughts that we can express in words, it must be possible

---

[5]See 1 Cor. 14:26–40.

for us to talk about this, the most fundamental aspect of our being, and to do so in ways that can be communicated to other people. The need to go beyond the limitations of the finite does not mean that the finite can be ignored or rejected. The fact that the human mind is inadequate to embrace the divine reality in its fullness does not make its mental processes invalid or unreliable within the sphere for which it was created. As finite creatures we live within certain boundaries, but God is present there just as much as anywhere else, and it is there that we are called to testify about him. In order to help us do this properly, God has accommodated himself to our limitations and made our relationship with him possible. The way of negation must therefore be balanced by the *way of affirmation*, which is the positive proclamation of that love of God which comforts us in our finitude and spurs us on to seek the higher knowledge that only our ultimate transition to eternal life will provide.

The way of affirmation relies heavily on the principle of *analogy*. This means that it takes words and concepts drawn from everyday experience and uses them to express something of the transcendent being and majesty of God. For example, when we say that God is our Father, we are taking a common word from everyday life and using it to express the kind of relationship we have with him. Just as a human father procreates outside himself (unlike a human mother) so God has made us outside his own being. We have not emerged from some kind of divine womb, but have been created out of nothing, along with the rest of the world. Just as a human father has the responsibility to provide for his children, to discipline them, and to prepare them for adult life, so God provides for us, rebukes and chastens us when we go wrong, and shapes us so that one day we shall be able to take our place next to him in his heavenly kingdom.

Of course, our human fathers are not perfect, and this is where the analogy breaks down. Eventually we outgrow our human parents and may have children of our own, but that is never true of our relationship with God. With him, we are always children, and paradoxically, as our relationship with him matures, so our sense of total dependence on him grows deeper. Many people have bad experiences of their human fathers, and some have never known them. Children often view their parents as heroes, but sooner or later reality sets in and they realize that they are just as human as everyone else. But that is never true of God, who is and always remains perfect and divine. We may turn away from him, but he never turns away from us, and is always ready to welcome us back into his family when we see the error of our ways and repent.

Analogies of this kind are meant to make us reflect on who we are in relation to God, but they also teach us what we should be like in relation to each other. The Bible talks about believers as brides of Christ and describes our relationship with him as a marriage, partly to make it easier for us to understand what it is like, but partly also to give us a clearer idea of what matrimony ought to be. In this sense, theological analogies are a two-way street, taking us up to God but also bringing him down into our everyday lives. They are deeply affirming of our relationship with him and are one of the best ways we have of exploring and explaining who God is, what he is like, and what he means to us.

What we call "theology" is an expression of this way of affirmation. Despite its limitations, it is a way that is coherent and devoid of internal contradiction, because it derives from the self-revelation of the one true God. For something to be free of contradiction does not mean that it is necessarily free of paradox, and it is important not to confuse these things. For example, we say that God is good but that he permits the existence of evil. Is this a contradiction? Some say that it must be, and so they do not believe in God. But Christians deny that there is any contradiction. However hard it may be for us to reconcile good and evil in our minds, they hold together in our experience and therefore they must make sense in the mind of God. His mind surpasses our understanding, but that is no reason to reject its existence or the power of its logic. God has told us that his ways are higher than our ways, and that we must not expect to know everything about him and his purposes for us.[6] As Christians, we have learned from experience that we must hold these apparently opposite principles together in tension and that it works, even when we cannot fully explain it. God's love reconciles things that we separate and even regard as contradictory, but when we know him in the fullness of his love, we shall see the whole picture, and the paradoxes now present in our finite minds will be resolved once and for all.[7]

RESPONDING TO REVELATION

The way of negation and the way of affirmation are combined and reconciled in God's self-revelation. That revelation is very old, going back to the first days of creation, but it is also new every morning, because he is alive and at work in the world he has created. It is a message conveyed to us in words we can understand—words put in the hearts and on the lips of men chosen and appointed by God for that purpose—but at the same time it passes all human understanding.[8] This revelation is a sign of God's love for us, and if we love

---

[6] Isa. 55:8–9.
[7] 1 Cor. 13:10–12.
[8] Phil. 4:7.

him as we ought to, we shall love that revelation and respect the authority of those assigned to bring it to us. The love of God can be known only in community, whether that is the fellowship of the Trinity of divine persons or the society known to us as the church, the sum total of all the people of God from the beginning of time to its end.

None of us can know the love of God on our own. Even when there is no one near us with whom to share it, we are surrounded by a host of heavenly witnesses, and the voice that speaks to our heart is the same voice that spoke to and through the messengers of old. We are not free to add to that voice or to depart from it; the love of God demands that we submit to him and obey his commands. There are other voices, but those who are faithful to God's love do not listen to them.[9] Not every word is a revelation of the divine, nor is every spiritual experience an encounter with God. Distinguishing the true from the false and clinging to that which is good is vital for the health of any loving relationship, and it is the special task of the theologian to help us keep our eyes fixed on what is right. God's love for us is constant and unchanging, but our love for him has its ups and downs. We are easily distracted and are seldom able to concentrate for long on the object of our desire. Without the teaching and the correction that comes from God's appointed servants, we shall soon go astray and lose the joy of our relationship with him, even if we do not lose the relationship itself. In the depth of his love, God wants what is best for us. It is to help us toward that end that he has given us enough understanding of himself to enable us to attain the goal that all believers must seek.

Every human being is created in God's image and likeness, and is therefore privileged to have a relationship with him, but the quality of that relationship varies enormously from one individual to another. For most people it is broken and dysfunctional, because we have rebelled against God and are no longer willing or able to enter into the kind of communion he intended us to have with him. But for some people, the brokenness of the past has been put right and fellowship with God has been restored. In the context of the human race as a whole, these people may be few in number, though they are an enormous company drawn from every nation, tribe, and language. They are bound together by nothing more than their shared experience of the love of God at work in their lives, but that love is everything to them—it is no less than a new birth, a new creation in which the old has been transformed and revitalized without being denied or discarded. Most of the branches of human learning are equally accessible to everyone, whether or not they are believers, but knowledge of God is the special possession of those who have entered into

---

[9]John 10:7–9.

mystical union with him. This is why it is so difficult to classify theology as a "science." To the outsider, theology is puzzling or simply meaningless, so it cannot be regarded as a science in the same way that chemistry or biology are. But to the believer theology is both meaningful and perfectly rational, because it is an expression of our common experience of God. Moreover, theology is of vital importance to us, because it is the spur we need in order to deepen our relationship with him. In the end, it is the only form of knowledge that really matters, because it alone will remain in eternity, long after every other kind of science has passed away.

5

THE PRACTICE OF THEOLOGY

THE ROLE OF THEOLOGY

The primary purpose of theology is to teach us what should be common to the faith of every believer. The love of God reaches out to each of us individually, and no one person's experience will be exactly the same as another's. But we all have a great deal in common because we know and love the same God. Theology does not focus on us and our feelings but on God and the way he has revealed himself to us. That revelation remains the same from one generation to another and does not change across different countries and cultures. How we perceive and absorb the revelation may vary to some degree, but never to the point where we cease to recognize that we are talking about the same God. We translate our understanding into different languages and adapt how we express it to accommodate the needs of different people, but the kernel of our experience remains the same and binds us together in a single overarching fellowship, which we call the church.

The second task of theology is to define the ways in which our faith ought to be expressed. Every Christian has a way of speaking about his experience of God, and that must be respected, but naive expressions of belief are often open to misunderstanding. For example, many Christians will say that Jesus is the "Son of God" and assume by that that he is inferior to his Father, who in their minds is "God" in a special and unique way. The mistake is understandable, but if it is allowed to go unchecked, it will lead the church into error, as it did in the fourth century when many people fell into the heresy of Arianism.[1] In this sense, the theologian performs a task like that of a medical doctor.

---

[1] Arianism is the belief of Arius (d. 336), who claimed that the Son of God was a creature, and therefore inferior to the Father.

People go to the doctor with their pain, and the doctor is expected to diagnose its cause and treat it. This requires a specialist's knowledge that often outstrips the patient's understanding, but without it a remedy is unlikely. Folk medicine may accidentally lead to a cure, but it may just as easily kill the patient or make his condition worse. Of course doctors are not infallible, and some things are just as mysterious to them as to anyone else, but at least they have an analytical framework within which they can locate particular problems and hopefully avoid erroneous prescriptions. Similarly, a professional theologian is there to guide believers into understanding their experience in the right way and to warn them against false trails that will lead them astray.

Theology also encourages and strengthens our faith by challenging us to go deeper into it. It is very easy to rely on experience alone and assume that, if there is something we are unaware of, it probably does not matter. That is a great mistake. The Bible teaches us that we must not be content with what we already have but must go on to greater things, and theology is there to point the way to a more mature faith. Like the children we are, we constantly need to be challenged with the next hurdle, which we must overcome in order to grow.[2]

Finally, theology reminds us that our minds are limited, and that even when they are fully submitted to God's will there are some things about him that we shall never know. God calls us into fellowship with him and gives us the knowledge we need to make that fellowship real. At the same time, he is greater than we are, and there are things about him that we shall never fully understand. Theology is therefore a call to intellectual humility. It leaves us with paradoxes that cannot be fully resolved and questions to which there is no clear answer. If we can acknowledge this and come to terms with our own limitations, then all will be well. But if we try to go beyond what we are entitled to know, we shall be rebuffed and may have to face the unpleasant consequences of our overweening pride.

THEOLOGY AND PHILOSOPHY

One of the great temptations we face when trying to teach people the love of God is to put it into categories that are not designed to express it. This happens when we conceive of theology as a kind of philosophy, founded on rational principles and built into a system that does not accommodate anomalies or paradoxes. The temptation to do this is great, not least because the concerns of philosophy often touch on matters that Christians regard as theological. It is hardly surprising that, throughout the history of the church,

---

[2]Heb. 5:11–14.

there have been attempts to interpret the biblical revelation of God in philosophical terms, often as a means of bringing the gospel to bear on the intellectual concerns of the day. Many early Christians used Platonic categories to express their beliefs, and in the Middle Ages what was popularly regarded as "Aristotelianism" played the same role.[3] It was this kind of theology that was overturned in the sixteenth and seventeenth centuries, leaving such a bad taste in the mouths of those who supported Galileo against a church that had accepted it all too readily.

More recently, almost every kind of modern philosophy has been taken as a model by at least some theologians, who have used their chosen system of thought as a means of developing a fresh expression of God and his ways. Their hope has been that their theological model would appeal to people whose minds have been shaped by the same intellectual framework. For example, many theologians have looked to Immanuel Kant (1720–1804) and Georg Wilhelm Friedrich Hegel (1770–1831) to provide models for their analysis of God's Word, though the results have not always been particularly happy. In the twentieth century, logical positivism, linguistic analysis, personalism, and even Marxism all made their contribution to the thought of different theologians, who sought to use the insights these methods provided, either as a means of bringing out some aspect of Christianity that had not been fully explored before or as a template for building a new vision of God. There is no reason to suppose that these attempts will come to an end anytime soon, and it seems likely that many theologians will find the philosophies of the future just as suggestive and provocative as those of the past have been.

How valid is a philosophically based approach to theological questions? God is a coherent being and his revelation makes sense, so on the face of things, philosophy is a good starting point for theological inquiry. By applying logic to our thoughts about God, philosophical theology helps us to understand the coherence of his self-revelation and gives us valuable tools for expressing it correctly. Most importantly, philosophy can help us guard against errors by showing us that some assertions are inherently illogical or contradict other things we may want to say about God. To take but one example, we believe that God is all-powerful, but that does not mean that he can destroy himself, because then he would cease to exist and his omnipotence would have no meaning. Rigorous thinking exposes such nonsense and limits what the word "almighty" can mean, but it does not define it any further than

---

[3]Aristotelianism used an inductive method of scientific inquiry, whereas Platonism was deductive, basing its judgments on the notion of an ideal truth. It should be remembered, however, that the historical Aristotle was Plato's disciple and successor, and not as opposed to his ideas as the later systematization of his thought might appear to be.

that. On the other hand, the philosopher who argues that a God who is unable to self-destruct cannot be omnipotent may be logical within the confines of his own mind, but he has failed to understand the being of God, which is not constrained by such human constructs.

The fundamental difficulty with philosophical approaches to God is that they are based on theories developed in order to make sense of the world. In that context, philosophy is a valid discipline. We have been given minds to examine the created order over which God has placed us, and we have a duty to figure out how it operates—so that we can exercise our dominion in a responsible and constructive manner. It is reasonable for us to suppose that the logic we perceive in creation reflects the mind of the Creator, who must have a reason for ordering the material universe in the way that he has done. But to extrapolate from this to the idea that by studying creation we can know the being and mind of God is to go too far. There is no reason to say that the universe is a mirror image of God, and in fact much about the universe suggests that in many ways it is very unlike him—it is visible, for a start! It is true that human beings are made "in the image and likeness of God," but how much this tells us about his nature is hard to say. To use a secular analogy, the queen's head on coinage is undoubtedly an image of her, but it says nothing about what she is like as a person. The link between them is a real one but it is partial and inadequate. To make assumptions about the queen based on the face we see on a coin is highly risky, to put it mildly. In much the same way, the image of God tells us something about him, but we must be careful not to draw unwarranted conclusions from what is only an approximation to the truth.

The human mind is adapted to the purpose for which God has created us, which is to rule over the material world. We can figure out how that world works and apply our knowledge to the task of governing it and developing its potential. The spiritual realm, however, lies outside the human mind's sphere of competence. Because we are spiritual beings, we can know that this other world exists and is of determining importance for our lives, but we cannot figure it out on our own. The religions and philosophies of this world are impressive monuments to the power of the human imagination, but even when they approximate quite well to objectively observable facts, approximations is all that they are—they are not a revelation of God and have no ability to draw us closer to him. Sometimes one or more of them may get something right, and we are glad when they do, but such occurrences are unsystematic and inadequate for the purpose of creating a viable theology. Ultimately, the knowledge we have of God must come from him. It can be understood by the mind and harmonized with what we know about the material creation, but its source lies outside ourselves. It is at this point that philosophy and theology part company, because the foundations on which their knowledge rests are different. The task of a Christian philosopher is to show how his discipline can and must be understood within the parameters laid down by theology, and to show that philosophical attempts to dispense with the need for a divine self-revelation are doomed to failure. His duty is to defend what God has told us about himself by showing how it coheres with material reality, not to build a theory out of that reality which then purports to be a justification of the existence and activity of God.

THE BIBLE AS THE SOURCE OF THEOLOGY

The Bible is the written form of God's self-revelation. It is not an abstract presentation of God's being and activities such as we would expect from a philosophical textbook, but a history of how he dealt with his people over two thousand years. That history illustrates principles that are normative for us today because they reflect the mind of God, and because the events that confirm the validity of those principles actually happened. The modern world is the product of that history, which continues to give us a foundation for living in the present and the hope of a greater fulfillment in the future. We must respect the way in which the Bible has been given to us—a collection of various documents written by many people over a long period of time with a variety of aims in view—and not try to make something out of it that it is not intended to be.

We believe that what the Bible says is true, but we also believe that this truth was revealed in time and space. It must therefore be understood in the light of the historical context in which it was given. Its truth is dependent on the various authors' original intention, even if it is not fully defined by it. A text may come to mean more than what its author understood when he wrote it, and we should not be surprised by this. The framers of the American constitution, for example, could not have known how their words would be applied centuries after their deaths, but no one suggests that it is wrong to adapt those words to deal with new circumstances as they arise. The only question is whether a particular interpretation is faithful to the intention of the original text. All law is like that to some extent, and since the Bible is the law of God for his people, we should not be surprised to find that it is interpreted in ways designed to meet their needs as they arise. If that were impossible, then the Bible would have nothing to say to a world which has to cope with advanced technology and the threat of nuclear warfare. At the same time, as students of American constitutional history are well aware, it is possible to misinterpret, misapply, or simply ignore the most authoritative texts, and those whose responsibility it is to expound them must always be on their guard against these tendencies.

As far as Christians are concerned, the fundamental question about the Bible is whether the teaching of Jesus and the New Testament is the right interpretation of God's revelation to ancient Israel. Today it often seems that Jews and modern scholars are ranged on one side of the argument while Christian tradition and those committed to upholding it are on the other. It is obviously true that the Old Testament was in existence before the coming of Christ and that it meant something to the Israelites, whether or not they shared the Messianic hope of their people. In purely objective terms, we have no way of knowing what the men who wrote and compiled the Old Testament thought about the Messianic hope, and it is probable that some were more aware of it than others. But everyone in ancient Israel knew that the nation's existence had a purpose, and that one day God would fulfill that purpose. The Christian claim is that that day arrived when the Son of God became a man as Jesus of Nazareth. Because of that belief, it is not possible for Christians to read the Hebrew Bible in a purely "neutral" or "objective" fashion. We do not have to resort to allegories or forced interpretations to bring out a Messianic message in every verse, but we do have to accept that the texts were preparing Israel for the Messiah's coming, whether or not the individual Old Testament authors realized it. In that sense, the Old Testament has come to mean more to us than most Jews would regard as legitimate, because we believe that its promises and prophecies have been fulfilled in Christ. Christians must regard as inadequate any interpretation of the Old Testament which does not take that into account.

We must also remember that it is possible to attribute authority to documents that have been forged, falsified, or tampered with. This is why we must do all we can to establish what the text of Scripture is, even though we are dependent on copies of now lost originals. In a few cases, like that of the so-called "longer" ending of Mark,[4] there are genuine grounds for caution, and we should be careful not to base anything we teach on such texts alone. More serious is the problem of falsification known as pseudepigraphy, which many modern scholars claim is common in the New Testament. One of the questions they ask is how many of the letters attributed to the apostle Paul he actually wrote. They are virtually unanimous in rejecting the Pauline author-

---

[4]Mark 16:9–20.

ship of Hebrews, but as the text does not claim to come from him, that is not an insuperable problem for those who believe that it has divine authority. The Pastoral Epistles (1 and 2 Timothy and Titus), however, are a different matter altogether. Not only do they purport to come from Paul himself, but they contain a wealth of personal details which would be lies if that were not the case. Where they are concerned, authorship and authority are closely linked, and to deny one is effectively to renounce the other.

This matters, not only for the integrity of the letters themselves, but also for their authority in the church. Are we happy to submit to the teaching of books that are forgeries, even if the forger says nothing that the supposed author would not have said? Our faith is that of the apostles, so if they did not write some of the epistles that now circulate under their names, why should we bother with them? This has serious practical consequences, not least for the Pastorals, which contain important and detailed instructions for the life of the Christian community. It is no accident that, in modern times, those who in whole or in part have rejected the teachings of the Pastorals have done so by claiming that they are not truly apostolic writings and therefore have no binding authority on us today.

Christians cannot accept this. The New Testament was put together by men who believed that they were compiling authentically apostolic writings, and they did not include books that they knew to be pseudepigraphal. They were familiar with many of the objections that have resurfaced in modern times, and they debated those objections—sometimes for many years. But in the end they overcame whatever doubts they had, and the wisdom of their judgment has been confirmed by subsequent generations, which have continued to honor their decisions as they have seen the fruit of the teaching of those books. The burden of proof must therefore lie with those who dispute the claim to apostolic authorship that the New Testament books make for themselves. Unless the doubters can make their case stick, their claims must be politely but firmly disregarded.

We know that the Bible was written by men inspired by God and that this quality of inspiration carries over to the words of the text, but the exact nature of the relationship between what God said to them and what they wrote eludes our grasp.[5] The written texts were not (or at least were not often) dictated by God directly, but neither were they just meditations about him composed by the prophets and apostles in their more reflective moments. What we have in the Bible is the message that God gave to his chosen messengers. It is what he intended us to have, and its truth is revealed to those

---

[5]See 2 Pet. 1:21.

who approach it in humble reverence and in a spirit of obedience. When we do that, we discover that the Bible is infallible and inerrant in the way that it works in our lives. The physical texts of the Bible have suffered in the course of time, as the many manuscript variations readily demonstrate, but their spiritual message remains unimpaired and is clear enough for even an uneducated reader to understand.

The theology of the Christian church is essentially no more than the teaching of Holy Scripture set out in a coherent way, not to satisfy the logic of human minds but to do justice to the oneness of God and the inner logic and beauty of his plan for the world. Some things in the Bible, such as the Old Testament food laws, have little direct bearing on us today—though they remind us that biblical holiness extends to every aspect of life. Other parts of Scripture, such as the command to kill the children of Babylon,[6] may offend our sense of justice or fairness, but they remind us that we are engaged in spiritual warfare and can give no quarter or comfort to our enemies in that struggle.

As Christians, we receive God's Word as he has given it to us, interpret it as it stands, and submit to it whether or not we like what it says. There are those who claim that human "dignity" allows or even compels us to challenge God and to question him by objecting to his revelation, but this is not the proper attitude of the Christian. Our dignity as human beings lies in our special relationship to God, which manifests itself most clearly in rational and voluntary obedience to his will. It is one thing to be assailed by doubts about God and his purposes for us—all Christians go through periods of doubt—but quite another to set ourselves up as arbiters of what his purposes and actions ought to be. Whatever else we do, we must not let our sense of human dignity become a cloak to disguise our pride, as it often does. When brought face-to-face with the Word of God, the proper response of the Christian is to do what it says, knowing that it has been given to equip us for our task.[7]

When searching the Scriptures to discover God's will for our lives, we must also accept the fact that he has not revealed everything about himself. We have been given what we need to know in order to trust and serve him, but on a number of occasions we are specifically told there are things that have been hidden from our eyes.[8] It is the constant temptation of some theologians to fill in the gaps in our knowledge, to create a system of thought that provides an answer to every question, and to explain the purposes of God in great and comprehensive detail. This is not possible, and we must accept that there is

---

[6]Ps. 137:9.
[7]2 Tim. 3:16–17.
[8]Matt. 20:21–23; 25:13; Acts 1:7.

much that we shall never know. We can always say that God created the world for his glory, but why should a perfect and self-sufficient God have wanted to glorify himself? How was it possible for good creatures to rebel against his will and become evil? When will God wind everything up and restore his creation to the perfection which he originally intended for it? We do not know the answers to such questions. To pretend that we do is to manipulate and misinterpret God's word. A theology rooted in the Bible is therefore bound to be incomplete in some ways, and we must resist the temptation to fill in the gaps with speculations of our own, even when such speculations appear to be helpful.

This does not mean that what is revealed does not sometimes oblige us to draw certain conclusions from what we have been told. An obvious example is the doctrine of the Trinity, which some people have regarded as "unbiblical" because it is not stated in the Bible in so many words. Yet it is clear from the New Testament that the Father is God, the Son is God, and the Holy Spirit is God, although there is only one God. The three persons are associated in the act of baptism, which is the recognized way into the body of the church.[9] The word "Trinity" is just a convenient term to describe the divine persons that spares us the need to write a paragraph every time we want to talk about them. The term itself is not sacred, but it does not contradict anything found in Scripture and is functionally useful to describe what is present in God. For that reason it can be used with a good conscience by believers everywhere. Furthermore, experience has shown that those who object to such words on the ground that they are not found in the New Testament are usually objecting to the doctrine they convey, but concealing that behind an apparently sincere opposition to the use of nonbiblical terms. That tendency was already perceived in the early church and has been frequently denounced since then by perceptive people who have seen through the superficial piety of those who behave in that way. If we meet this kind of objection today, we must not hesitate to expose it for what it is and insist that what we are saying is consistent with the teaching of Scripture.

THINGS UNKNOWN AND THINGS INDIFFERENT

When we come to questions relating to things that have not yet occurred and remain somewhat obscure, such as the end of the world, we have been specifically warned not to speculate beyond what is written.[10] Unfortunately, thousands have done so and have been disappointed by their own self-

---

[9]Matt. 28:19.
[10]Acts 1:7.

deception. Nothing is better documented than the failure of millenarian prophecies to materialize, but they keep reappearing and seducing the minds of people who crave certainty in such matters and cannot let God's Word on the subject stand as it is.

On a less exalted plane, much the same can be said for matters relating to church government. We know that the early church had leaders appointed by the apostles, and we know that they were chosen and appointed for specific tasks. We also know that no church today can function in precisely the way that a New Testament congregation did, if only because there are now no apostles to rule over them. We do not know whether the New Testament churches all had the same form of government, nor is there any biblical answer to such questions as who has the right to preside at the Lord's Supper. These issues and others like them exercise our minds because we have to decide what to do in the church today, but we cannot dogmatize about them on the basis of Scripture because the evidence needed to do so is lacking. We are told that everything ought to be done "decently and in order,"[11] a command which we do our best to fulfill in the way we organize our common life, but however much we may be persuaded that a particular form of church government is the best one, none of us can claim exclusive divine sanction for our practices, and those who do so only succeed in dividing the church. We are free to adopt and to adapt different patterns of ministry and to worship according to necessity or convenience, as long as we respect the New Testament principles of decency and order. Of course, if we are to work together with other churches, the more we can share with them a common pattern of government, the better. But just as no one form is imposed on us in Scripture, so we should not try to impose a single form on others—and the realities of history have ensured that there will always be at least some variation in this area.

One of the most important theological concepts for the life of the wider church is that of *economy*, which allows for flexibility in the way we apply fundamental principles to differing circumstances. To this must be added the subsidiary principle of the so-called *adiaphora*, or things indifferent. The *adiaphora* are those matters on which a local church is free to make its own arrangements and insist on them as part of its internal discipline, without claiming that they have a divine sanction so specific that no other pattern is possible. Both *economy* and the *adiaphora* make us highlight those things that are essential and encourage us to concentrate on them rather than on secondary matters. Such an approach respects the freedom of particular churches to be flexible, without sacrificing the core truths than give us our common iden-

---

[11] 1 Cor. 14:40.

tity as Christians. Like members of a family, we have important resemblances but we are not identical. As in any family, the secret of harmony is to make this diversity work for us by respecting the individuality of each member, without losing sight of the common purpose we all share. In the end, we are all part of a single body, of which Christ is the head, binding us to himself in love. If we can learn that, and grow to appreciate each of the members for who and what they are, loving them as part of our very selves, however much they may differ from us in many ways, then—and only then—is there a real hope that we may grow in the knowledge of God which is our theology, and may use that knowledge both to glorify him and to bear witness to him in the world.

6

THEOLOGY AND FAITH

THE NEED FOR GOOD THEOLOGY

In the modern world there are many who lament the divisions of the Christian church and long for those who profess the name of Christ to be visibly united. That may well be a desirable goal, but solid progress toward it can be made only on the basis of an agreed theology, which we call "orthodoxy" or right belief.[1] It is unfashionable to say this today. There are many, especially in the mainline Protestant denominations, who argue that doctrine is divisive and that a clearly articulated theology is inappropriate to the nature of a Christian fellowship. Following the line taken by Adolf von Harnack (1851–1930) and others of his school, some even think that "dogma," as they like to call it, represents an unwelcome Hellenization of early Christianity that ought to be dispensed with for the health of the church as a whole.[2] To them there is no such thing as orthodoxy—as far as they are concerned, the term represents no more than the beliefs of the party in power who persecuted their enemies and drove them out, labeling them as "heretics" in the process. Unsurprisingly perhaps, those who think this way tend to side with the "heretics" as marginalized victims, and regard their own attempts to rehabilitate them as delayed reparation for the sins of the past. Others may be more orthodox in their basic beliefs but have nevertheless been influenced by a form of spirituality that has persuaded them that intellectualism of any kind is the enemy of the truth and ought to be avoided. To their minds, there is no such thing as "good" theology—it is all bad by definition and potentially harmful to true Christian faith.

---

[1]Strictly speaking, "orthodoxy" means "right worship," but for Christians, to believe in God is to worship him, so the two concepts have come together in practice.
[2]Hellenization was the process by which an idea or doctrine was assimilated to the mindset of the ancient Greek world.

These two groups are polar opposites in many ways, but when it comes to speaking about God they converge to a surprising degree. Sadly, in their different ways, both are enemies of Christ, because it is he who fulfills and validates the word of God revealed to us in Holy Scripture. In his great love for us, God has told us certain things about himself which we must believe and proclaim to the world, whether or not we like what he has told us. Before they fell from grace, Adam and Eve did not know what evil was, even though it already existed and God wanted to protect them from it. That is why he told them not to eat the fruit of the tree of the knowledge of good and evil, for that knowledge was sure to bring them death.[3] But once they did so, in spite of God's command to the contrary, there could be no turning back. For us, to know God is to know the difference between right and wrong and to opt for the former in our dealings with him. If we do not do this, then we are failing to love him as we should, because to love God is to obey his commandments.[4] The sin of Adam and Eve was fundamentally a rejection of God's love for them, and it is only by overcoming that rejection that the relationship we are meant to have with God can be restored. Orthodoxy and heresy are part of the reality in which we live. They are the intellectual manifestations of the spiritual struggle we are called to wage between good and evil. There can be no return to the garden of Eden and no profession of innocence in the great battles we are called to fight as servants of God and soldiers of Christ. Theology is a weapon in that struggle—not the only one, to be sure, but one that we cannot do without.

Christians are called to speak the truth in love, and there is no truth greater than the truth about God.[5] The fall of the human race began with a lie—cleverly disguised and containing more than a grain of truth, to be sure, but a lie nevertheless. Adam and Eve were deceived by it, and in different ways that deception continues to haunt us to this day. God has told us that he is the only God to be worshiped, and that Jesus Christ is the only way by which we can come to know him.[6] Yet today it is fashionable among well-meaning people, including church leaders, to say that there are many paths to God, and that it does not much matter which one we choose. Such people claim to honor Jesus Christ, perhaps because they think he is the clearest or best way to God, and probably because it is the way they have chosen for themselves, but what at first sight appears to be an honor accorded to Jesus is in fact the very opposite. To put him on a pedestal alongside other religious leaders is not

[3]Gen. 2:17.
[4]John 14:15, 21; 1 John 5:3.
[5]Eph. 4:15.
[6]Ex. 20:3; John 14:6.

to honor but to reject the one who said, "No one comes to the Father except through me."[7]

The modern world cannot accept the exclusive nature of Christ's claims, even though they are freely offered to every human being as the way, the truth, and the life. The fact that this offer of salvation treats everyone equally—and ensures that those who receive it get exactly the same thing, regardless of their sex, social status, or ethnic background—is overlooked by people who find it scandalous to think that spiritual truth can be defined in such a narrow way. Yet there is nothing intrinsically incredible in the assertion that Jesus is unique. If there is only one God, it is not unreasonable to say that he has revealed himself in only one way. Indeed, it should be reassuring to be told that this way is the universal standard applicable to everyone. As the apostle Paul put it, the way of Christ is the way of human equality: "as in Adam all die, so also in Christ shall all be made alive."[8] There is no discrimination against anyone.

Christians obey the command of God to follow the one way of salvation made known to the human race, but this is no reason for them to be proud of their faith or of their standing before God. Toward the end of his life, the apostle Paul described himself as "the very least of all the saints."[9] That note of humility is the hallmark of the true believer. How can it be otherwise, when we are saved by grace, not by our own merits, and when we know that the mercy of God shines brightest in those who have been the greatest sinners? To be great in the kingdom of heaven is not a call to use our natural gifts but to understand that the highest place in heaven belongs to those who have been forgiven much and who know just how undeserving they are.[10] A proper sense of humility in the presence of God is essential but it must not be confused with the sort of false modesty shown by those who deny the exclusive nature of Christ's claims and refuse to press them on those of other religions or none.

To fail to proclaim Christ as the only way, truth, and life is not only to deny him to our own hurt but also to deprive others of the opportunity to hear the Word of God—it is an abdication of our responsibility as believers. We cannot force people into the kingdom of God; we cannot even argue them into it by superior logic. The work of convicting hearts and minds is done by the Holy Spirit, without whom our efforts can only be pointless and unfruitful. We preach Jesus Christ, not because we believe that we are superior to others but because we want them to benefit from the same spiritual blessing that we

---

[7]John 14:6.
[8]1 Cor. 15:22.
[9]Eph. 3:8.
[10]Luke 7:47.

have found in him—and only in him. The love of God is not a vague, well-meaning or wishy-washy experience that we can share or not as we choose, but a life-changing message that we must proclaim out of our love for him and out of his love for the world he has made.

THE BASIS OF OUR FAITH

Those who know the love of God in their lives and who are ready to share it with others are united in a common faith that finds its roots and its meaning in him. The portrait we draw of his being and his works from the Scriptures is one that we recognize and share with each other, even if we are not always sure of how best to express some of the details. For instance, we agree that God is invisible and that his Spirit dwells in our hearts by faith, but it is harder to formulate the relationship between his sovereignty and our free will. We know that we make choices by using the rational capacities of our human will, but when we look back on what we have done, we see the hand of God at work in it. We know that God was not standing over us, dictating our decisions before we made them, but we also know that he is in control of our lives, working out what is best for us whether or not we appreciate it at the time. No one disputes either of these things, but relating them to one another involves us in a mystery beyond our understanding.

We cannot escape God's will for our lives, however hard we try, but neither does God force us to be his children against our will—he draws us by his love and frees us to receive him into our hearts. If he does not act, we can do nothing to get closer to him, but when he gets to work in our lives, we feel a great sense of deliverance from the burden of sin and we submit to him willingly, with all our heart, mind, soul, and strength. We give ourselves to him as servants, and by doing that we are set free to become his children, for such is the nature of love.

Why this happens to some people and not to others is a mystery, but that too is the nature of love. In human life we often see people falling in love with each other, but it is by no means always clear why they do so. At the same time, there are people who look for love and fail to find it, and that is another mystery. How is it possible for me to love someone and not be loved back? Why is it that some people's good will, dedication, and willingness to make sacrifices end up producing nothing in return, while other people mistreat those close to them in the most flagrant and abominable ways, but retain the love of those whom they abuse?

We do not know the answers to these questions, even though we observe such things going on around us all the time. But if we cannot explain what we experience at the human level, which we understand and to some extent think we can control, how can we expect to fathom the love of God for his people? Why do we disobey him when he has sacrificed everything for us? Why does he continue to love us, even when we do everything in our power to hurt and deny him? We cannot explain this, but every Christian knows from experience that it is so, and we are grateful to God that in his love he will never abandon us, no matter how far we stray from him.[11]

When we realize this, we can appreciate that theology is God's way of teaching and disciplining his church. Today, the word "discipline" is readily associated with punishment, even if it is self-inflicted for a good purpose, such as athletic achievement or weight loss. But discipline is essentially learning, which in this context means absorbing the commands of God and putting them into practice. Teaching us what we should do and why is the task of theology, but putting it into practice is left to the heart and mind of the individual believer, who is told to go and sin no more.[12] Good theology cannot make people behave like children of God, but unless they have good theology, God's children will not know how they are supposed to act and are much less likely to conform to his will. Letting a child do whatever he wants is not a sign of love, but the very opposite. Children need to be disciplined, since otherwise they will never become the adults they are meant to be. Similarly, God's children also need to be taught how to think and behave, or else they too will never come to the maturity they are meant to have in spiritual things.

Church discipline is too often understood in terms of who should and should not be allowed to belong to the fellowship of believers. People want to know what others believe and what commitment they can expect from them *before* admitting them to membership, which is perfectly understandable. However, the real task of church discipline begins *after* people have joined the fellowship—it is designed to help church members grow, not to chase away those who our human minds think are undesirable. It is hard not to think that the church could avoid a great deal of trouble by realizing that it is a home for sinners, not a company of the righteous who have no need of repentance.[13] It can begin to do this by structuring its sense of discipline to focus not on punishment and exclusion but on forming a Christian mind and heart in those who have come under the teaching of the gospel. If our theology can help us

---

[11]Rom. 8:38–39.
[12]John 8:11.
[13]Luke 5:32.

achieve that, then it has fulfilled its purpose and made its own humble but significant contribution to building the kingdom of God in eternity.

KNOWING THE LOVE OF GOD

The key to the Christian life is knowing the love of God at work in our hearts. Mastering academic theology is no substitute for this, but then neither is preaching the gospel. These things are good and right in their place, but if they are not subjected to a higher spiritual discipline, they are as likely to lead us astray as they are to build others up in their faith. The apostle Paul made this point when he compared himself to an athlete:

> Every athlete exercises self-control in all things. They do it to receive a perishable wreath, but we an imperishable. So I do not run aimlessly; I do not box as one beating the air. But I discipline my body and keep it under control, lest after preaching to others I myself should be disqualified.[14]

Paul lived in a world where things moved at a slow pace and distractions were limited. When he was forced to winter in some port or other, he had months of leisure time on his hands and could reflect deeply on the things of God. Today, we live in a different world. Even when we go away for a few days, we are seldom far from a telephone or a computer. People expect us to stay in touch and to be ready to respond to their requests more or less instantly. Preachers and teachers are under particular pressure, because they are constantly expected to be giving out and do not always have the time they need to refresh themselves. Forced to give an answer to every question, they can easily fall into the trap of giving a standard answer, when they have had no time to reflect on it or to put it into practice in their own lives. Getting ahead of oneself in this way is an occupational hazard of Christian ministry, and those engaged in it have a special duty to protect themselves by making an extra effort to put God first in their lives.

In some churches, a newly ordained minister is expected to commit himself to reading the Bible and praying twice a day—every day. The purpose of this discipline is to preserve him from getting stale by keeping him close to God. In practice, of course, it does not always work out that way. For some, the duty becomes a burden and fulfilling it is no more than a kind of vain repetition, not unlike what Jesus condemned in the pagans of his time.[15] For others, such obligations are meaningless and they ignore them, because they think that spiritual people ought not to be tied down by what they see as legal-

---

[14]1 Cor. 9:25–27.
[15]Matt. 6:7.

ism. But rightly understood, the daily discipline of Bible reading and prayer is essential for growing in the Christian life. Those who abuse or ignore it suffer the consequences, and their ministry is adversely affected as a result. It does not take long for a discerning hearer to distinguish preachers who know what they are talking about from those who do not, and intellectual attainment is seldom the deciding factor in their judgment. What people hear from preachers is what comes from their heart, and if that heart is not right with the Lord, they will hear nothing. The weakness of preaching in so many churches today has more than one cause, no doubt, but this must be one of the main factors involved. "Practice what you preach" is not simply a well-known proverb; it is the essential preparation for any truly successful gospel ministry.

Here we must be humble in our approach to the things of Almighty God, and at the same time forthright in warning ourselves and others of the dangers we face if we are not. The history of the church is littered with the residue of battles between believers who could not keep things in perspective. Fired up by their own understanding of the truth, they showed little respect for others and virtually no understanding of their point of view. Today, when we read the writings of the great Reformers and Puritans of the sixteenth and seventeenth centuries, we are often shocked by their readiness to attack their opponents in the most scurrilous terms, a readiness which (it must be acknowledged) was fully reciprocated by those on the other side. Of course, it was an age of theological controversy and also one of literary hyperbole, and some allowance has to be made for that. The *odium theologicum* ("theologically motivated hatred") so painfully obvious in some of their writings was not invented by them, nor did it fade out with their passing. The sad truth is that some of the greatest men of the church have been among the worst offenders, and even today it is by no means uncommon to hear Christians speak uncharitably about those with whom they disagree. In the final analysis, however, there is no excuse for the behavior of earlier generations in this respect, and it cannot be used as an excuse for us to follow in their footsteps.

Of course, we must never deny or compromise the truth, and at times that means saying hard things to people who do so, especially if they are in responsible positions in the church and ought to know better. But at the same time, we must speak the truth in love, seeking to persuade our opponents of the errors of their ways and not to crush them by superior force or by mere argument. Disarming an opponent by love does not always succeed, but it is the way that Christians should follow, as Jesus taught his disciples to do.[16] If the gospel of Christ comes under attack, we ought to be able to say that this

---

[16]Matt. 5:39.

is the fault of its enemies, and not the result of the behavior of those meant to be its defenders and advocates.

As Christians we are told that we must hold every thought captive to Christ, and that includes what we think both about ourselves and about other people.[17] We are all sinners saved by grace, debtors to the unfathomable riches of God's mercy.[18] Whatever gifts we may have been given and however privileged we may be in terms of our background and education, what really matters is the presence of Christ in our lives. The apostle Paul summed this up well when he wrote,

> Whatever gain I had, I counted as loss for the sake of Christ. Indeed, I count everything as loss because of the surpassing worth of knowing Christ Jesus my Lord. For his sake I have suffered the loss of all things and count them as rubbish, in order that I may gain Christ and be found in him . . .[19]

We live in a media world where much is made of pastors who have built mega-churches, of preachers who have become international stars, and of writers who have sold more than a million copies of their books. All too often, those aspiring to serve in ministry are encouraged to look to them as models and to wonder what they can do to achieve comparable success. In academic life, universities are inundated by students wanting a doctorate because they think it is a necessary qualification for Christian service, and even some churches expect their ministers to have such qualifications.

There is nothing wrong with any of these things in themselves, but if they become idols they will replace God in our lives and do great damage, both to us and to the wider church. There can be no substitute for a humble and contrite heart, as even the great King David had to learn.[20] Sadly, there are many who started off as shining lights for Christ but have since fallen by the wayside, lured away from the truth by the attractions of academia. Having sought to gain the whole world by their brilliance, they have ended up losing their own soul, and the whole church is poorer as a result.[21]

Those who embark on theological study must be warned that they are treading on holy ground, and that they are marked men in the eyes of the world, the flesh, and the Devil.[22] Those who will be found worthy of the task that lies before them are those whose hearts are nourished by love and

---

[17]See 2 Cor. 10:5.
[18]See Eph. 3:7–8.
[19]Phil. 3:7–9a.
[20]Ps. 51:17.
[21]See Mark 8:36.
[22]Eph. 6:10–12.

whose minds are enriched by faith and faithfulness to God and his word. The language of theology is the language of love, because it is in love that God sent his Son to save us.[23] It is in that spirit that we are called to go forward, and in that spirit alone that we shall one day stand in his presence, when all things will be revealed and we shall know even as we have been fully known.[24]

---

[23]John 3:16.
[24]1 Cor. 13:12.

PART TWO

GOD'S LOVE
IN
HIMSELF

7

THE MYSTERY OF
THE TRINITY

THREE PERSONS IN FELLOWSHIP WITH ONE ANOTHER

What does it mean to say that God is love? What does God have to be like for that to be possible? We could perhaps imagine that the world was run by a machine, but its functional regularity would not be enough to make it God. We might even think of the world as being governed by a supreme mind, as many ancient Greek thinkers did, but its intellectual prowess would not be enough to make it God either. Christians believe that God is in control of his universe and that he is the ultimate cause of all things. We are happy to accept that he is the "supreme being," but this is a natural consequence of who he is and not an abstract ideal to which he ought to conform. To put it a different way, we have not concluded that there must be a first cause behind the universe and then called it God, turning it into a personal being in order to make it easier for us to understand. On the contrary, it is because we have met the God who has revealed himself to us in the Bible that we understand that, if we are looking for a first principle behind the universe, it must be him.

Many modern scientists do not believe that there is such a first principle, but that makes no difference to Christians because God does not depend on scientific theories for his existence. However scientists think the universe is constituted, God is still the one who made it. In that sense he is the "first cause," but he is not part of the chain of causality that exists within the universe. If he were, he would not be God because he would not transcend the system he created. The scientific understanding of matter and its origins changes and develops as new discoveries are made, but God remains the same because his being is not dependent or contingent on any particular theory of how the world came into being.

Our knowledge of God is not rooted in mental constructs, even if they are correct, but in personal experience. That experience is not the result of intellectual deduction from the nature of reality, but is the fruit of an encounter expressed in the Bible as a relationship of *faith*.[1] This faith is more than simple belief because it involves commitment of a kind that is possible only between persons. I can believe that the ground beneath my feet is solid enough to build a house on and then construct one on the basis of that belief, but although I might say that I have "faith" in the ground, there is no relationship between us. For example, it would be unreasonable for me to pray to the ground in the hope that it might protect me from earthquakes. The ground does not have a mind or a will that would justify such behavior on my part, and no reciprocal relationship with it is possible. Faith in God, however, involves two-way communication, which means that there is something present both in us and in God that makes such dialogue meaningful. That something is what we call "personhood," and so it is with the personhood of God that our analysis of how we know and experience him must begin.

Many theologians, however, have not begun with this. Works of theology tend to start with a discussion of God's being and its attributes, of which his personhood may be regarded as one. They then go on to talk about that personhood, which in Christian terms means describing him as a Trinity of three equal persons. To put it simply, theologians often begin by saying *what* God is and only after they have explained that do they go on to talk about *who* he is. This approach has the advantage that it starts with the principle that there is only one God, which is fundamental to the Christian faith. In the Old Testament, God revealed himself to his people as a single being, and although the New Testament writers spoke of the Father, Son, and Holy Spirit as fully and equally God, they never lost sight of his fundamental oneness. Christians reject all forms of polytheism and believe in the one God of Israel every bit as much as Jews do. Yet our experience of God goes beyond what is revealed about him in the Old Testament. Much as we insist that he is one, we know that we have come into a relationship with him that involves three distinct persons. Moreover, we cannot say that only one of these persons is fully or truly God in a way that the others are not, because our experience of them tells us that all three are equally divine. The apostle Paul expressed this well when he wrote, "Because you are sons, God has sent the Spirit of his Son into our hearts, crying 'Abba! Father!'"[2] Our knowledge of God comes through the Holy Spirit of the Son, who integrates us into his own relationship with

---

[1] See Heb. 11:1–40 for the clearest and fullest explanation of this.
[2] Gal. 4:6.

the Father, something that would not be possible or meaningful unless each of them was fully divine.

It is only in and through that experience that we come to know that the underlying being of God is one, and begin to understand what that really means. If the fundamental principle of our theology is that God is love, then we must start with the divine persons and not with the unity of God's being. The concept of love implies that there must be someone or something to be loved. Of course it is possible to argue that, even if God were a single person, he would still be self-aware and could love himself, but the biblical idea of love is something more than self-esteem. The love which the Bible speaks about is not a self-centered kind of preening in the mirror, but a concern for others. We are expected to treat others with the same consideration that we would want them to show us. As Jesus put it, we are to love others as we love ourselves.[3] The great Augustine of Hippo (354–430) solved the problem of how the one God could be a God of love by saying that his self-awareness had an identity of its own, which he called the Son, playing on the fact that "conception" can be both physical and intellectual. God conceives of himself as he truly is, and loves that self-awareness as he loves himself. In this way, Augustine identified the primordial God as the Father, his self-awareness as the Son, and the love that the Father has for that self-awareness as the Holy Spirit, who binds the Father and Son together.

But although this is a clever idea, does it make sense to say that God's self-awareness came to earth and died for the human race as the supreme way of manifesting his divine self-love? The analogy breaks down here, because for the incarnate Son of God to give his life for sinful human beings, he must be more than just an idea in the mind of God. This is important, because it was not in God's self-awareness, but in and through the incarnate Son's sacrifice to his Father, that the depths of his love for us were revealed. We can hardly say that an image of the divine mind sacrificed itself on the cross in order to do what the mind wanted, if only because the story of the incarnation, crucifixion, and resurrection of the Son reveals the action of someone who has his own identity and who is more than just an echo or reflection of the mind of God. The love of the Father for the Son and the corresponding love of the Son for his Father are best understood, not as a conceptual act inside the mind of God but as the kind of self-sacrifice that characterizes the relationship of one person to another.

The relationship between the Father and the Son encourages us to think of them as being two persons, however hard it may be to reconcile that idea

---

[3]Matt. 7:12; 19:19.

with the belief that there is only one God. But as Augustine's theory reminds us, Christians go further than this and insist that there are not two persons in God but three. Why this should be so is difficult to explain in purely logical terms. We can readily understand that there must be at least two persons, if one is to suffer and die for the sake of the other, but where a third person fits into this scenario is less obvious. Perhaps the answer lies in the words of Jesus to his disciples shortly before his death, when he told them that it would be better for them if he were to go away, because if he did not do so, the Holy Spirit would not be able to come. The significance of this is that when the Spirit came, he would dwell in the disciples' hearts (which the incarnate Christ did not) and would do greater things in and through them than Jesus was doing when he spoke those words.[4] We can fill in this picture by referring to other parts of the New Testament, where it is made clear that the death of Jesus Christ for our sins did not become effective until he returned to his Father in heaven and offered him the sacrifice that he had made.[5] He is now sitting at the Father's right hand, pleading for us on the basis of that sacrifice, and so a third person becomes necessary in order to apply that work in our hearts. That person is the Holy Spirit, who represents both the Father and the Son and makes them present and active in our lives.[6]

In what sense do the three persons of the Godhead share a common being? This question is not a new one. It lies at the heart of traditional apophatic theology, and has come up again in recent years because of the claim that the terminology traditionally used to describe God was drawn from ancient Greek philosophical concepts that are no longer regarded as valid. Here we are dealing with a half-truth. Ancient Greek philosophers certainly used terms that were later found in Christian theology, but to say that the Christians borrowed those terms from philosophy is misleading. Ancient Greek thought was not systematized to the point where it had a technical vocabulary that was easily recognized as such. Common words like *ousia* ("being") and *hypostasis* ("substance") were employed by different thinkers who gave them meanings of their own, which can sometimes be understood only by reference to the specific context in which they were used. There was great variety and little precision in the way such words were used, so that even if Christians "borrowed" the words, it says little or nothing about what they did with them. In fact, the overall effect of Christian theology was to *create* a technical theological vocabulary out of what had previously been a vague

---

[4]John 16:7.
[5]Eph. 4:8–10; Acts 2:33.
[6]John 14:18–23.

and diffuse philosophical terminology. Many of the controversies that shook the early church can best be understood as attempts to achieve this kind of precision and to make it stick. The reason why it was important for Christians to do this is that, unlike the philosophers, they were not dealing with abstract concepts but with a concrete reality. God had appeared in human flesh, in the man Jesus of Nazareth, and some means had to be found to describe this occurrence accurately and to make sense of it.

Most significantly, the choice of words employed by Christian theologians was not determined by their allegiance to any particular school of ancient Greek philosophy, to all of which they were opposed in principle, but to the witness of their own Scriptures, which gave them the terms that they subsequently developed for theological use. Some of these terms can also be found in philosophical writing, though it is not always clear who borrowed what from whom. It is at least possible, for example, that the later Platonic philosophers, whom we now call Neoplatonists, got some of their ideas from Christianity, and not the other way around, using terms that had been subtly "Christianized" by their opponents.[7] If that is true, it would explain how the Neoplatonists managed to transform what had been an essentially secular way of thinking into a religious worldview that Plato himself would probably have rejected. It is also the case that the most important theological term of them all, the word "person," did not exist in ancient Greek philosophy and was never accepted by its advocates. Even those philosophers who believed in the existence of a supreme being were not prepared to agree that it was a "person," and therefore they rejected out of hand the most basic aspect of both Jewish and Christian belief.

From its earliest days, the Christian church used the word "being" (*ousia*) in order to define God. The exact form of this word is not found in the Bible but the underlying concept certainly is. The God of Israel was always known as Yahweh ("he who is"), and the verb "to be" frequently occurs in the New Testament in connection with God, not least on the lips of Jesus, who was capable of shocking his Jewish hearers by saying such things as, "Before Abraham was, I am."[8] The verb also occurs in a specifically Christian context in the first chapter of Revelation, where God declares that he is "the Alpha and the Omega [the first and the last], . . . *who is and who was and who is to come*, the Almighty."[9] The opening chapters of the

---

[7]The process can be seen in Origen's *Contra Celsum*, a work that aimed to refute the anti-Christian diatribes of the second-century Platonic philosopher Celsus. What comes across though is that Celsus presented Platonism as a philosophy that was able to match everything that Christianity claimed to offer. Without realizing it, Celsus had turned his philosophical beliefs into a religion modeled on Christianity.

[8]John 8:58.

[9]Rev. 1:8.

book of Revelation are especially interesting, because it is not entirely clear who spoke these words. The text ascribes them to "the Lord God," but the context strongly suggests that this was not the Father but the Son. As John explains, "Then I turned to see the voice that was speaking to me, and on turning I saw seven golden lampstands, and in the midst of the lampstands one like a son of man . . ."[10] The man whom he saw was the risen Christ, who then gave him messages for each of the seven churches of Asia. But note that each message concludes with the same statement: "He who has an ear, let him hear what *the Spirit* says to the churches."[11] The Word of God is incarnate in Jesus Christ, who gives it to the churches in and by his Holy Spirit, and all this in the context of the Alpha and Omega, the one who is, who was, and who is to come, the Almighty!

From identifying God the Holy Trinity as "he who is," it was but a short step to referring to him as the ultimate or supreme being. The early Christians did not hesitate to do so, believing that they had good biblical warrant for this assertion, regardless of what any philosopher might think. In modern times, this transition from a verb to a noun has been criticized as an unwarranted "Hellenization" of biblical faith, the first stage on the road from believing in an active, dynamic deity to objectifying him as an immutable first principle. This charge, however, is unfair. The biggest problem the early Christians faced was explaining that if God was to be described as a "being," then his being was radically different from anything that actually exists in creation. Unlike many of the philosophical schools, they did not think of the visible world as a corruption of ultimate being caused by separation from the primordial essence, but as something quite different from it. For a Christian to describe any created thing as a "being" was to invent a new category of existence in time and space, which was incompatible with God's being in eternity. This is why so much early Christian theology was preoccupied with saying what God is *not*, in sharp contrast to the philosophers. The latter generally believed that it was not the supreme being, but those things that had separated themselves and fallen away from it, that had lost something of what truly is, and who could therefore be described as having declined into various forms of "nonbeing." Far from being a poor copy of a philosophical model, Christian theological reflection on the nature of being challenged the reigning philosophical theories of the time and put forward a belief that in many ways was the exact opposite of them. It is to how they did this that we must now turn.

---

[10]Rev. 1:12–13.
[11]Rev. 2:7.

THE TRINITY IS ETERNAL

It is a great mistake to believe that because God revealed his love for us in time and space, the Trinity of divine persons who manifest that love has no existence beyond that temporal and spatial framework. But wrong though it is to think that way, the idea was widely entertained in the earliest centuries of Christianity, and it is easy to understand why. Christians had inherited the monotheism of the Old Testament, and in the polytheistic environment to which they were called to bear witness, any suggestion that there might be more than one God had to be strenuously resisted. Under no circumstances could they afford to define the eternal, absolute being of God within the limits imposed by the temporal and contingent world in which they lived. It seemed natural to them that when God worked in the world he did so through inter-mediaries like angels, who shared enough divine characteristics to be in com-munication with him but who were also capable of adapting themselves to the finite circumstances of the created order to which they essentially belonged. These Christians understood that Jesus and the Holy Spirit were closer to God than angels were, but they did not know how to identify them with the infinite being of God, which to their minds was not capable of adjusting itself to the limitations of time and space. This difficulty led them to think of ways to explain how God could be present in the world by his Son and his Spirit without compromising his transcendent divinity.

The eternal, unchanging reality of the one divine being seemed to the early Christians to be obvious and indisputable. It was the coexistence of three persons of the Godhead within that being that caused them difficulty, which is why that is the main theme of ancient Christian theology. Were these persons to be understood as particular expressions of the one divine being that appeared at different times or in different circumstances (or both)? Were they parts of the divine being that could be distinguished from it, even to the point of separation, as may have happened when the Word of God became flesh?[12] Or was only one of the divine persons truly God, the other two being offshoots of him, sharing some of his characteristics but not all of them? All these views were held by different people in the early church, but none of the views was able to establish itself as the correct one, because in their different ways each of them had been formulated within the conceptual framework of ancient philosophical thought. That is the basic reason why so many were tempted to say that God was one in eternity but three in time and space, a solution that was compatible with different types of Greek philosophy but

---

[12] John 1:14.

which does not accord with the witness of the Bible. Only when the limitations of ancient Greek thought were transcended and replaced by the biblical
worldview could Christian theology find adequate expression, as it eventually
did in the classical creeds of the ancient church.[13]

Two solutions to the apparent dilemma the early Christians faced were
proposed not long after the end of the New Testament period, and for a century or more they made a great impression on the church. The first attempt
to solve the problem was to say that when God decided to create the world,
he brought forth the Son and the Holy Spirit as his two hands, which he then
used to make the universe. As the hands of God, the Son and the Spirit shared
his divine nature but remained distinct from the divine being itself. They came
into existence for a purpose and would presumably disappear back into their
original divinity once that purpose had been accomplished.[14] Unfortunately
for the proponents of this view, the notion that the Son (as God's Word or
reason) and the Holy Spirit (as God's Spirit) are parts of the divine substance
which separated from him to become distinct beings in their own right, is
exploded by the absurdity of the result. God did not lose his mind when the
Son became incarnate, nor did he cease to be spiritual when the Holy Spirit
descended at Pentecost! It is therefore hardly surprising that ideas of that kind
never really got off the ground. More subtle and intellectually more satisfactory was the belief that the second and third persons of the Trinity were inferior to the Father, who alone was fully God, but that too had to be rejected,
because it is not possible to be only partially God. The early Christians canvassed the different options available to them, but in the end they were forced
to work out how it is that three persons can coexist without losing their own
identity or compromising the essential oneness of God's being.

The most popular way of doing this was by a device that has come to be
known as "modalism." It was not uncommon for early Christian thinkers to
suggest that God had revealed himself to his people in different guises, known
as "modes," at different times in history, and this so-called modalism was
popular for a time. It allowed people to argue that in the Old Testament God
had appeared as the Father; in the incarnation of Christ he had come into
the world as the Son; since Pentecost he has dwelt in our hearts as the Holy

---

[13]There were three of these, of which the so-called "Nicene" Creed is the most universal and representative.
It was probably promulgated at or shortly after the first council of Constantinople in 381. The "Apostles'"
Creed can be traced back to the second century, but did not reach its present form until much later and
was never approved by a church council. Finally, the so-called "Athanasian" Creed, the most detailed of the
three, was written by an unknown monk in southern Gaul, sometime around the year 500, and attributed to
Athanasius of Alexandria (296–373), probably because, like Athanasius himself, it was held to be the yardstick
of Christian orthodoxy.
[14]See 1 Cor. 15:28, which might be interpreted in such a way.

Spirit. His three names were held to correspond to the different functions he performed in each of these manifestations. Before the coming of Christ, it was argued, God was worshiped and understood primarily as the Creator. The Old Testament was seen as the book of creation, and the religion of the people was worked out in relation to that, as the Mosaic food laws illustrate. The essential message was that between the Creator and his creatures there is a great gulf fixed, that no one can cross—in either direction. Man cannot become divine any more than God can become human. At first sight this sounds good, and there is undoubtedly a lot in the Hebrew Scriptures to back up this point of view, but it is not the whole story. The Old Testament also portrays God as the Redeemer of his people,[15] and there are many instances where prophets and psalmists were filled with the Spirit of the Lord, suggesting an intimate relationship with the Creator that was somehow able to overcome the great gulf that was supposed to be fixed between him and his creatures. In other words, to see the Old Testament God only in the role of Creator is to diminish the revelation of him that the Scriptures give us, and therefore it must be rejected as inadequate.

Much the same applies to the second part of the formula, which asserts that in Christ God appears primarily as the Redeemer. Once again, there is a certain truth in the statement, but the New Testament is at pains to remind us that Jesus was also the Creator,[16] and to see him exclusively in his Redeemer role is to reduce him to something less than what he really is. The same must be said about the notion that God now appears as the Sanctifier, to whom the name "Holy Spirit" is given. No one questions that sanctification is a vital activity of the Holy Spirit, but if there were no more to God than that, it is hard to see what the point of it would be. As it is, the New Testament makes it clear that the Holy Spirit sanctifies us for obedience to Jesus Christ, according to the foreknowledge of God the Father.[17] In other words, there is a context in which the Spirit's sanctifying work finds its purpose, and that context is the common will and life of the three persons of the Trinity. Seen in this light, modalism hardly does justice to the New Testament witness, where Jesus is regularly portrayed as speaking to his Father, who is clearly someone else—he is not talking to himself.[18] Jesus also speaks about the Holy Spirit as another Comforter or Helper, not as himself reappearing in a different mode.[19]

Modalism may have encouraged some Christians to use the word "person"

---

[15] Job 19:25; Isa. 43:1–3.
[16] John 1:3; Col. 1:16.
[17] 1 Pet. 1:2.
[18] See John 17:1–5 for a very clear example of this.
[19] John 16:7–15.

to describe the three modes of God's activity, and it was certainly a factor that contributed to the unwillingness of many to accept it as a valid way of expressing the divine threeness. "Person" had originally been the word used for "mask" in the ancient Greek theater, where the character being portrayed was identifiable by the mask the actor wore. A change of role meant a change of mask (or person), a device that allowed a single actor to play many different parts. Once the drama was over, the masks would be discarded and the actor's identity would become plain, which is what the modalists thought would happen with God. They believed that at the end of time, when the work of salvation was finally accomplished and creation had been transformed into something eternal and different from what it is now, God would no longer have to play the parts of creator, redeemer, and sanctifier, and so the Trinity of persons by which we know him would give way to the knowledge of the one true God.[20]

The temptation to interpret the persons entirely within the confines of time and space was further encouraged by appealing to the language the Bible uses to describe the Son and the Holy Spirit in relation to the Father. For example, the Son is called the Father's only begotten Son and also "the firstborn of all creation."[21] Taken in isolation, it is not hard to see how verses like these could be used to support the belief that the Son was the first of God's creatures, the only one of his kind to be sure, and enjoying primacy over everything else that exists, but a creature nevertheless. The problems with this kind of interpretation, however, are two. First, these verses must be understood in the context of others which explicitly state that the Son was with the Father from the beginning, and that everything the Father made was made together with him.[22] There is also the quote in the first chapter of Hebrews, taken from Psalm 2:7, where God says, "You are my Son, today I have begotten you."[23] Even if we allow that in the original context this expression referred to King Solomon, whom God had adopted in this way, it is clear that the word "begotten" did not imply any kind of birth within the Godhead. At most, it may have meant that on a particular day, God declared to the king that he was adopting him as his son, thereby establishing a relationship with him equivalent to the one which would normally come into being by physical generation.

But the writer to the Hebrews transposes the meaning of the psalm from time and space to eternity, where the use of the word "today" excludes any possibility of birth or adoption. Moreover, the same writer insists that the

---

[20]See 1 Cor. 15:28 for a verse that was interpreted in that sense.
[21]John 1:14; Col. 1:15.
[22]John 1:1–3.
[23]Heb. 1:5.

psalm refers to a being who is higher than the angels, which rules out any of the ancient kings of Israel. The angels share in everything that belongs to the divine nature, apart from those attributes of divinity that are not compatible with their creaturely status. To be higher than an angel therefore means being higher than the highest of the creatures, and the only being who fits that description is God himself. The use of the word "begotten" is the same as in the original psalm; it does not refer to a physical birth but to a legal relationship. Transposed from time to eternity, the addition of the word "today" underlines the eternal presence of God, for whom there is no yesterday or tomorrow, no past or future—only "now."

In the case of the Holy Spirit, the Bible does not say that he is "begotten" of the Father, because that would make him a second Son, thereby contradicting John 1:14. Instead, we are told that the Holy Spirit "proceeds" from the Father, a present-tense verb which suggests that there was never a time when that was not so.[24] The procession of the Spirit is revealed as an ongoing, permanent reality, not as something that began and was then completed at a particular moment in the past. It is therefore right to say that the Bible teaches us that the Son and the Holy Spirit are present in the Godhead in eternity, and that the love that flows between them and binds them to one another is equally eternal and unchanging.

THE TRINITY IS RELATIONAL

If the love of God is eternal, then the persons who manifest that love must also be eternal, and any theory which suggests that one of them brought the other two into being must be rejected. This is easier said than done, however, because the language of generation and procession used in the Bible clearly suggests that there is a derivation of some kind from the Father, even if this cannot be equated with an event that can be pinpointed in time. The early Christians found nothing more difficult than surmounting the notion of causality among the persons of the Godhead. As a result, we find them using terms such as "eternally begotten" as the best way of reconciling the words of the Bible with their assumption that God's being is eternal, even though the expression itself is a logical contradiction. In making this affirmation they were moving in the right direction and transcending the limitations of time and space that the term "begotten" implies. Nevertheless, it took many centuries for theologians to realize that it was fundamentally wrong to understand the generation of the Son and the procession of the Holy Spirit in terms of

---

[24]John 15:26.

cause and effect, and even today the legacy of a false model of "causation" is capable of producing misinterpretations that can (and do) divide the church.

The first step in overcoming this error was the recovery of the true meaning of the original Hebrew words for "begotten" and "firstborn." It is not always realized today, but for more than a thousand years most Christians had little knowledge of Hebrew and no real understanding of the Old Testament background. Most Christians did not know that the language of sonship used of the second person of the Trinity is derived from a legal context. As the "only begotten" and "firstborn," the Son was the *heir* to all things, and as the heir, he shared the Father's authority over them.[25] In human terms, an heir is normally the son or daughter of the owner, but not necessarily so, since there are many different patterns of inheritance and it is often possible for a person to nominate his heir(s), especially when there is no physical descendant. In the case of God, a natural heir would have to share his divine being and would therefore be just as eternal as he is. On the assumption that the Son is the Father's natural heir, his entitlement to the inheritance must be based on his own divine being, and so by definition he is coeternal with the Father. As for the Holy Spirit, there is no indication that there was ever a time when he did *not* proceed from the Father, so the same may be said of him as well.

The language of generation and procession used in the New Testament must be understood in relational terms, not causal ones. This means that in some mysterious way unknown to us, the three persons of the Godhead must have decided to relate *to each other* in the ways just described. The sonship of the second person is not an accident of birth but the result of a voluntary act—not his alone, but that of all three persons, since they have a single will that is common to them all. Similarly, the identity of the third person is the result of a free choice, made not only by him but by the three persons acting together. Finally, the fatherhood of the first person, though not described in such terms, must also be the result of a free act on the part of all three, a reminder to us of their common mind and purpose. How this can be is a mystery that goes beyond our ability to understand, because it speaks of things that subsist in the eternal being of God, which is incomprehensible to us. When we speak of a "voluntary decision" taken by the three persons acting together, we are using a human concept to explain a divine reality that is worked out in eternity. As far as we are concerned, it has always been like that and always will be—there never was a time when things were or will be otherwise, because there is no time in God.

The mutual relationships of the three persons of the Trinity are perfect

---

[25]See, for example, Matt. 21:33–41. It also underlies 1 Cor. 15:20–28.

and all-embracing. The Father loves the Son and the Holy Spirit fully and absolutely, but in a way that is peculiarly appropriate to his identity as the Father.
The Son also loves the Father and the Holy Spirit to the same degree, but in a
way that is especially indicative of his identity as the Son. The Holy Spirit loves
the Father and the Son likewise, but again in a way that brings out the particular nature of his relationship to each of them. This theme is deeply embedded
in the Scriptures, but it has never been fully elucidated by theologians, probably
because so many of them have been tied to the causation model of Trinitarian
relations which makes a balanced presentation of the subject more difficult.
As a result, a great deal has been written about the ways in which the Son
relates to his Father, but much less about the other way around. There is also a
considerable body of literature dealing with the relationship between the Holy
Spirit and the Son, but much less about the Spirit's relationship to the Father
and almost nothing about the Father's relationship to him.

On the causation model it is easy to see why this should be so, because the
attention paid to the Son-Father relationship, as also to the Holy Spirit–Son
one, reflects the sense that the Son is dependent on the Father and that the
Holy Spirit is likewise dependent on him (as well as on the Son). It is far easier
to find books that explain how the Son fulfilled the will of his Father in his
earthly ministry than it is to find something that discusses the ways in which
the Father guided, sustained, and ultimately vindicated his Son during that
time, or how those events fit into his eternal plan. It is not that these things are
denied—merely that they have not been elaborated to the degree one might
expect. What this shows us is that things that appear to be normal and natural
when one model of the Trinity is followed, look lopsided when another one is
adopted instead. A Trinity of relations must give each of the persons his due
and equal weight, unlike the causation model, in which some relations seem
to be more important than others.

In the relational Trinity, there are some things that all three persons share in
equally, such as the work of creation. It is customary to attribute that primarily
to the Father, but the evidence of Scripture points to the involvement of the Son
and sometimes to the Spirit as well, though that is more open to dispute.[26] This
common action indicates a very high level of mutual interpenetration which is
surely a sign of the love that the persons have for one another, but it is when we
see how they relate to each other that we perceive the divine love most clearly.
The Father shows his love for the Son by supporting him throughout his earthly

---

[26]John 1:3; Col. 1:16; Gen. 1:2. Whether the Bible explicitly states that the Holy Spirit was involved in creation
depends on how the second verse of Genesis is interpreted. Does it refer to the third person of the Trinity or
simply to the spiritual nature of God? Either interpretation is possible, though for obvious reasons, Christians
have often preferred the first option and Jews have rejected it.

ministry of reconciliation, even to the point of raising him from the dead, and finally by exalting him so high that the Son becomes his co-ruler and co-judge.[27] The Father's love for the Holy Spirit is not openly stated, but it becomes clear when we realize that he shared his intentions with the Spirit, who was then sent to reveal them to the apostles and prophets.[28] The love of the Son for the Father is most fully revealed in his act of self-sacrifice on the cross, when he took our place by becoming sin for us, bore our punishment, and reconciled us to God by paying the price demanded by the Father's justice. But at every point in his earthly ministry, the Son made it clear that he had come to do the will of the Father who had sent him, and in his obedience to that will he demonstrated what the demands of love could mean.[29]

The Son's love for the Holy Spirit is not often mentioned in Scripture, but it can be seen in the so-called farewell discourses of Jesus, recorded in John 14–16, where he tells his disciples that he must go away so that the Comforter may come. Jesus adds that when that happens, his followers will do even greater things than he himself has done.[30] For the Son to speak so highly of his successor, even to the point of calling him another Comforter, is surely an act of love, as well as one of humility.[31] The Holy Spirit would come to glorify the Son, but the way was prepared by the Son himself, who commended the Spirit to his disciples before they knew who he was.

The Holy Spirit's love for the Father is closely connected to his love for the Son, and it is doubtful whether they can really be distinguished from one another. It is as the Spirit of the Son that he comes into our hearts, allowing us to pray to the Father in the Son's own words.[32] At the same time, it is as the Spirit sent from the Father that he comes into the world to bear witness to the Son.[33] The two things go together, and remind us that it is in and through the work of the Holy Spirit that the Father and the Son come to dwell in our hearts, making it possible for us not only to experience the love of God at work in our lives but to participate in it as well.[34]

WHAT IS A PERSON?

We may find the controversies about the Trinity that plagued the early church confusing, but one of the main reasons why they occurred was because the

---

[27] 1 Cor. 15:27–8; Phil. 2:9–11.
[28] 2 Pet. 1:21; 1 Tim. 3:16.
[29] John 4:34, 5:30, 6:39–40; Luke 22:42.
[30] John 14:12; 16:12–15.
[31] John 14:16.
[32] Gal. 4:6; Rom. 8:15.
[33] John 15:26.
[34] John 14:23.

Greco-Roman world had no single concept for what we now call "person-hood." Because of that, the early Christians were not sure how to describe the God of the Bible, who reveals himself in what we call "personal" terms. Of course, there were plenty of human beings around back then whom we would not hesitate to describe as "persons," but this analogy would not have been helpful to the fathers of the early church. They were only too well aware that the pagan gods were portrayed as glorified men and women, and they were determined that the Christian God should not be confused with them. In modern usage, "person" is often taken to be synonymous with "individual," but that definition is not very useful either. The word "individual" describes someone who is different from others and separate from them, whereas the word "person" emphasizes the relational aspect of the individual and what links him to others. To put it a different way, there is more to being a person than simply being an individual, whether human or divine, because personhood implies relational identity in a way that individuality does not. In Christian theology, the word "person" is used to describe three different kinds of relations: those within the Godhead, those between human beings, and those between God and the human race. These are all interconnected because of the shared quality of personhood that makes such relations possible.

Given that God is not a human being and that his divine nature is completely different from our human one, finding a way to express this relationship was more difficult for Christians than it would have been for pagans, who thought of the gods in their own image, even if the gods could do things that ordinary humans could not do. Christians had to find a way of explaining how God can relate to human beings, even to the point of becoming one himself, without ceasing to be eternally transcendent. The need to do this was imposed on them by the fact that the Son of God became a man in Jesus Christ, and they had no ready-made vocabulary to describe what had happened. Early Christian theology was not a speculative exercise that tried to figure out how the divine and the human could interact, but an attempt to make sense of an event that changed the way they thought of themselves and the world in which they lived. They did this in Greek, because that was the international language of their time, and they chose words that already existed, since otherwise they would not have been able to preach their message without inventing a jargon of their own that would have been more of a hindrance than a help to communication. But in the process of doing this, they selected their terminology and defined it much more carefully than the ancient Greeks had ever done. This took time and caused misunderstandings, especially when attempts were made to translate Greek terms into Latin. Latin was not as developed a language then as it later became and was therefore less able to accommodate technical theological terms, but as it is from Latin that our own terminology is largely derived, we have to understand how the early church handled its translation difficulties.

Latin appears only once in the New Testament, as one of the three languages in which Pontius Pilate wrote his inscription on the cross of Jesus.[35] It was little used in the first two hundred years of the church's existence, because even in places like Rome and Lyon, where it was the most widely spoken language, the Christian community continued to employ Greek for internal purposes. Translation seems to have occurred first in North Africa, where Tertullian of Carthage (fl. c. 196–212) is credited with having devised a Latin theological vocabulary, most of which is still in common use, as table 7.1 illustrates.[36]

Greek	Latin	English
ousia, ho ōn, to on, to einai	*substantia (essentia, esse)*	substance, essence, being
hypostasis	*persona (subsistentia)*	person, subsistence
physis	*natura*	nature
(prosōpon)	*persona*	person

TABLE 7.1

Latin has a smaller vocabulary than Greek and is less flexible in the way that it can be used, a fact that caused considerable misunderstanding for a long time. In the verb "to be," for example, Greek has three grammatical genders in the present participle, so that a subtle distinction can be (and was) made between the masculine *ho ōn* ("he who is") and the neuter *to on* ("that which is"). The noun "being" (*ousia*) was created from the feminine form *hē ousa*. By contrast, Latin has only one participial form (*ens*) for all three genders. In medieval times that form was also used as a noun meaning "being," but in the ancient world the only way Latin could express "being" was by using the infinitive *esse* ("to be").[37] Apparently in the first century B.C. someone had tried to create *essentia* ("essence") as a translation for *ousia*, but although it sounds perfectly normal to us, the Romans thought it sounded outlandish and did not use it until the controversies of the fourth century forced them to align their theological vocabulary more closely with the Greek.

In Tertullian's day, that had not yet happened, so instead he used the word *substantia*, the term which was then generally accepted as a translation of both *ousia* and *hypostasis*—a good example of what the Greeks meant when

---

[35]Luke 23:38; John 19:20.
[36]The words in parentheses were not used in Tertullian's day but appeared later on, when serious attempts were made to establish formal equivalents for the main theological terms in both languages.
[37]This was also possible in Greek (*to einai*). Note that English is even poorer than Latin in this respect, with only the one word "being" available to translate the many different forms of the Greek verb.

they said that Latin was crude and unsuited to subtle theological discourse! This of course left him with no obvious word for *hypostasis* when it had to be distinguished from *ousia*, as it did in the case of the Trinity. Faced with that challenge, Tertullian came up with the word *persona*, which seems to have come into Latin by way of Etruscan (*phersu*). The Etruscans, however, had taken the word from the Greek *prosōpon*, which originally meant "mask," and so all the problems associated with the Greek word were liable to resurface, as they eventually did.

In creating a Christian theological vocabulary, the Hebrew Bible was not as much help as we might think. In biblical language, human persons are invariably described in some other way, either by a proper name (if a particular individual is being referred to) or by using terms such as "man" or "son of man," which establish relationship on the basis of a shared nature. That was good enough as long as it was just a matter of describing the connections between members of the same species. Just as human beings were linked to one another by their common descent from Adam and Eve, the persons of the Godhead were described in the New Testament in terms of their relationship to the Father.[38] The problem with this way of thinking was that it did not allow for a corresponding relationship between God and man, who are of different species. Old Testament Judaism did not need to worry too much about this; its belief that Adam and Eve were created in the image and likeness of God made it possible for human beings to relate to him without compromising the essential difference between the Creator and his creatures.[39] But Christians could not be content to leave things there because, once the Son of God became a man, a way had to be found to describe that occurrence both adequately and accurately. Jesus Christ was not just a man made in the image of God; he was God himself. It was the incarnation—with its implications for both God and man—that compelled the church to develop the concept of "person" in the way that we understand it today.

Appropriately enough, it was the writer to the Hebrews who described the being and identity of the Son in words that the ESV translates as follows:

> He is the radiance of the glory of God and the exact imprint of his nature,
> and he upholds the universe by the word of his power.[40]

Other modern translations are similar to this one, but they do not do justice to what the writer was trying to say. The difficulty lies in the phrase "exact

---

[38] John 1:14; 15:26.
[39] Gen. 1:26–27.
[40] Heb. 1:3.

imprint of his nature," which is meant to translate the Greek words *charaktēr tēs hypostaseōs autou*. In its literal sense, *charaktēr* does mean an imprint of the kind that is made by a stamp or die, so this can perhaps be accepted as a fair translation of what is meant. The Son is an identical reproduction of the Father, but what does this mean? For the writer to the Hebrews there is no problem—the Son is the express image of *hē hypostasis autou*,[41] a term which is here translated as "his nature." But the Greek language has another word for "nature" (*physis*), which was not synonymous with *hypostasis*. Generally speaking, *hypostasis* was used to identify what an object was, whereas *physis* described what it was like or what it consisted of. Of course the two things are connected because a nature (*physis*) cannot exist without an identity (*hypostasis*) in and through which it is perceived, but they are conceptually distinct and it is not always possible to use them interchangeably. A *hypostasis* can behave unnaturally (i.e., against the innate properties of its *physis*), which happens when an object that cannot normally fly is blown about by the wind, and so a distinction between the terms must be preserved.

The matter is further complicated by the fact that, in ancient times, someone trying to define what a *hypostasis* was would not have thought to describe it as a *physis* but would have said that it was more like an *ousia* ("being"), because it possessed objective existence in a way that a *physis* did not. A *hypostasis* and an *ousia* were both potentially visible, which a *physis* was not; it had to be discerned in one of the other two. If there was a difference between *hypostasis* and *ousia*, it was that one *hypostasis* can have the same nature (*physis*) as other *hypostaseis* and so form what we would call a species, all the members of which share a common *ousia*. For example, when we use the term "human being," we are thinking primarily in terms of a particular individual (a *hypostasis*, in other words). But at the same time, we recognize that the individual in question is human because he shares a common humanity, or "being" (*ousia*), with the rest of us. If we accept this distinction between *hypostasis* and *ousia*, it is obvious that human nature (*physis*) belongs to the *ousia* of our common humanity and not to the *hypostasis* of our individual identity, and so to translate *hypostasis* as "nature" is incorrect.

In the case of God, however, the distinctions between identity, being, and nature, which are so clear when we are talking about human beings, are harder to maintain because God is one. The perfection of God's being (*ousia*) ensures that everything belonging to his nature must be coterminous with it, and that he cannot act in an unnatural way. Thus, if it is the nature of God's being to

---

[41]Note that *hē hypostasis* is in the nominative whereas *tēs hypostaseōs* is in the genitive case; hence the difference in form.

be good and invisible, he is always fully good and completely invisible. If he were not, he would be imperfect and so not God at all. It is this coincidence between God's being and his nature that makes it possible to use one of his characteristics to describe him in his totality, as the Bible does when it calls him the Almighty or the Eternal. To the Jewish mind, the effective oneness of God's being and his nature was essential to the way in which he reveals himself to us. As far as they were concerned, God's *hypostasis* or identity must also be one with his being and nature, since otherwise it would not be a true manifestation of him.

It is here that the writer to the Hebrews introduces something new to the Jewish way of thinking about God. He could not have used the word *ousia* to describe the Son as the "exact replica of his divine being," because it was a fundamental tenet of Jewish monotheism that there is only one divine being, who revealed himself to his people as Yahweh ("he who is"). As we have just explained, what was true of God's being (*ousia*) would also have been true of his nature (*physis*), because monotheism ensured that the two were effectively one and the same, so he could not have used the word *physis* either. For that reason, the translation "exact imprint of his nature" must be rejected as inappropriate and misleading.

But by saying that the Son was the *charaktēr tēs hypostaseōs autou*, the writer to the Hebrews assumed that God the Father was a distinct *hypostasis*, thus allowing for the possibility that the Son was another *hypostasis*, identical to the Father in his divine being and its divine nature but also distinct from him. A way then had to be found to say that there could be more than one *hypostasis* in God, sharing the same singular and indivisible *ousia* and its *physis*.

It was this challenge that led the church to develop the formula which says that in God there are three equally divine *hypostaseis* in one divine *ousia*, and this is now accepted as the standard interpretation. The term *hypostasis* was popular because it occurs in the New Testament, which *ousia* does not—a point that was of some significance to theologians who were determined to stick as closely to the Bible as they could. *Hypostasis* had the further advantage that it could also be used to describe the objective identity of individual human beings, and therefore serve as a conceptual link between God and man.

But as a technical term, *hypostasis* labored under certain disadvantages that became more apparent as Christian theology developed. For one thing, it could be used to describe the identity of any object—a table was a *hypostasis* just as much as a human being was. For another, it was often understood as a copy or reproduction of a common being, making the concrete object it denoted logically subordinate to an underlying concept. In the human context, it gave the impression that individuals were like cookies made from dough—cut-outs from a common generic substance called "humanity," with their different shapes and sizes being attributed to the different kinds of cut-out that they were. As we might say today, people were regarded as "chips off the old block," differing from each other in all sorts of secondary ways but essentially dependent on the block for their common nature.

As these examples illustrate, the difficulty with the term *hypostasis* was that it did not necessarily include either the aspect of agency or the dimension of relationship, both of which are of crucial importance for Christian theology. Three tables in a room are three *hypostaseis* but they cannot act on their own or establish relationships with one another. It was possible to include these aspects in the term when dealing with God and man, but only if it could be assumed that their respective beings (*ousiai*) are intrinsically active and relational, which is by no means obvious. God can exist without having to do anything to maintain himself in being, and if action is intrinsic to his nature, it might be argued by some that his creation must be just as eternal as he is. That view was common among ancient pagans, who could not conceive of a creator who was independent of the material universe, but it is specifically denied by the Bible, not just by its assertion that creation took six days but even more by the statement that, once it was complete, God *rested* on the seventh day.[42] A God who was eternally active by nature would not have been able to do that.

Furthermore, if God were fully defined by his being (*ousia*), it would be inconceivable for him to have relationships since there would be no one and nothing for that *ousia* to relate to. If someone were to reply that the divine *ousia* was *potentially* relational because once God created something else, he would automatically relate to it, that would cause another problem by implying that God is not eternally perfect and self-sufficient in himself. If God had undeveloped potential that could not be realized without bringing something else into being, not only would that make him less than perfect, it would also mean that he would be changing all the time. Whenever something new appeared, he would have to adapt in order to accommodate it and there would be no way of knowing whether his potential was (or could be) fully realized. Something like this has actually been said by the proponents of "process theology," a theory which makes God's being eternal energy and sees the world

---
[42]Gen. 2:3.

as a kind of spin-off from that. The fundamental difficulty with this is that it obliterates the absolute difference between the Creator and his creation, turning Christianity into something more like the ideas of the ancient Greeks than the teaching of the Bible.

To say (as some have done) that God created the world in order to have something to love is to say that his love is not perfect and that he needed the world in order for it to be complete. That cannot be the case, and so it gradually became apparent to the early Christians that the word *hypostasis*, understood as a manifestation of an underlying *ousia* that gave the latter an identity without itself being an agent capable of relationships, was less than ideal for describing the divine threeness. But what term was there that could retain its positive aspects without falling victim to its inherent drawbacks?

This question was eventually answered by making a decisive break with the Greek philosophical tradition and adopting the word *persona* as the preferred term for the threeness in God. By the time that happened, *persona* and its Greek antecedent *prosōpon* had developed a long way from their original meaning of "mask." As far back as the fourth century B.C., a detailed codification of the different theatrical masks (*prosōpa*) had been drawn up by Theophrastus (371?–287? B.C.) in a handy manual for actors, playwrights, and other interested parties, which he not unnaturally called *Characters*. Once that happened, it was a short step toward applying the term *prosōpon* to the natural human face, whose distinctive traits were thought to be indicators of the bearer's character and were interpreted as such by people who were trained to "read" them. The extension of meaning from "mask" to "face" was very rapid, because when the Old Testament was translated into Greek only a couple of generations after Theophrastus, *prosōpon* was already being used as the standard translation of the Hebrew word *panim* ("face"). The interesting thing is that by then it had developed so far away from its original meaning of "mask" that it could be used to describe the exact opposite. Thus we find that the Old Testament term "face to face," which is regularly used to refer to a direct and unmediated meeting with God, is always translated as *prosōpon pros prosōpon* in Greek.[43] The apostle Paul was familiar with this usage and even used *prosōpon* to make the contrast between what is revealed and what is hidden when he told the Corinthians that "now we see in a mirror dimly, but then *face to face*."[44]

---

[43]Gen. 32:30; Ex. 33:11; Num. 14:14; Deut. 5:4; 34:10; Judg. 6:22. Note, however, that in 3 John 14 what must have been the same underlying phrase is rendered in Greek as *stoma pros stoma* ("mouth to mouth").
[44]1 Cor. 13:12.

While this development was taking place in the Greek world, the Romans went a step further and turned *persona* into a legal term. In Roman juridical usage, a *persona* was (and is) someone or something that could sue or be sued in a court of law. This particular usage meant that there were people such as women, children, and slaves, who were not legal "persons" whereas there were institutions (such as businesses) that were. Although this seems anomalous to nonspecialists, this legal use of *persona* has always preserved the essential characteristics of agency and relationality.

Tertullian understood this and felt that the term could be employed for the three *hypostaseis* in God. He took it over and used it with great success, defining the Trinity as three persons in one substance, a formula still in common use today. Unfortunately, when this expression was translated back into Greek, it could be made to sound as though the Romans were saying that there were "three masks in one being." It was therefore not surprising that some Greeks accused the Romans of modalism (which they called Sabellianism after its supposed inventor, an otherwise unknown Sabellius). In return, some Romans suspected the Greeks of believing in tritheism ("three substances in one being"). These were misunderstandings and were eventually recognized as such, but the fact that they could occur shows how difficult it was for the church to come to a common form of expressing this central belief.

It was not until the fourth century that the Greek-speaking Basil of Caesarea (d. 379) recognized that the Romans used *persona* in the sense of *hypostasis*. This seems to have opened the door to the use of *prosōpon*, at least by the school of Antioch. If the Antiochenes had used *prosōpon* to refer to the three members of the Trinity, there might not have been much difficulty in regarding it as synonymous with *hypostasis*. But the Antiochenes used *prosōpon* only in their Christology, where it was clearly distinguished from *hypostasis*. This caused considerable confusion and delayed the acceptance of the word as the equivalent of *hypostasis* for two generations.

Antiochene Christology was developed in reaction to the teaching of Arius (256–336), who argued that the Son of God could not be fully divine because a divine being could not suffer and die. The Son was only the highest of the creatures, closer to God than any other, but still not divine in the absolute sense. Arius's position was soon condemned, but the Antiochenes thought that it revealed an inherent tendency that was typical of the Alexandrian approach to theology. The Alexandrians believed that, in the womb of the Virgin Mary, the Word (*Logos*) of God had taken on human flesh by adding it to his divine nature (*physis*). The Word could therefore suffer and die for our sins, but only to the extent that the human element in his nature was able to suffer and die. The divine element, which was immortal and impassible, did not (and could not) change. The Alexandrians had difficulty in distinguishing the human from the divine in the incarnate Christ because they insisted that he could have only one nature, even after his incarnation. How the human and the divine coalesced in this one nature was never entirely clear, but it seems that the Alexandrians envisaged some kind of merger between them, which naturally favored the divine over the human.

In practical terms, this meant that although the incarnate Son of God had both a human and a divine will, the divine will was naturally stronger and therefore took over the human will, fortifying it and making it incapable of sinning. This led people to ask whether the temptations of Jesus were real; if he could not have sinned, what sense did it make to say that he was tempted? Debates of this kind were common at Alexandria, and in extreme cases its theologians denied that Jesus had a human soul (Apollinarius) or that he was a genuine human being like us (Eutyches). Those extremes were duly condemned, but the fact that they could be proposed at all shows the general tendency of Alexandrian theology. According to the Alexandrians, every nature (*physis*) manifests itself in a corresponding *hypostasis*. Because there was only one *hypostasis* in the Son, which was that of the divine Word, the human nature assumed by that Word in the womb of the Virgin Mary had to be integrated into his divine *hypostasis*; otherwise the unity of the incarnate Christ would not be preserved.

To this, the Antiochenes reacted by saying that the divine Word could not be touched by any human failing and therefore it could not suffer or die. Any suggestion that it could, even by the device of assuming a human nature and using it in order to suffer and die, seemed to them to be a step on the road to denying its absolute divinity, which in their opinion would inevitably lead to Arianism. As they understood it, what happened in the womb of Mary was that the Word joined himself to a human embryo that would have been born as a man even if the Word had deserted it, because it had its own human *hypostasis* ("identity"). That did not happen, of course. Instead, the baby Jesus who came out of Mary's womb was a conjunction of two natures, each of which had its own *hypostasis* and retained its capacity to exist independently of the other.

What the world saw, however, was the conjunction of the two *hypostaseis*, according to which they acted together by mutual agreement. It was this conjunction that the Antiochenes called the *prosōpon* of the incarnate Son. By virtue of the common *prosōpon*, Jesus Christ could suffer and die as a man without his divinity being affected at all. An extreme form of this

Christology even said that when Jesus cried, "My God, my God, why have you forsaken me?"[45] what he meant was that the eternal Word had abandoned the man and left him to die on the cross as nothing more than an ordinary human being. That was going too far, and most Antiochenes held to the view that the conjunction of the two *hypostaseis* remained unimpaired, allowing them to say that the Word accompanied the man in his suffering and death without actually experiencing them. To sum up, Antiochene Christology said that the divine and human natures in the incarnate Son maintained their own identity (*hypostasis*) and their own natural properties. But it also said that because the two natures were permanently conjoined in the one *prosōpon* of Jesus Christ, it was possible to say that the Son of God had suffered and died for our salvation.

The problem, of course, is that we can only say this by transferring the title "Son of God," which properly belongs to the *hypostasis* of the divine nature, to the *prosōpon* in which that *hypostasis* was joined to the human *hypostasis* of Jesus of Nazareth. But if the human *hypostasis* died (according to its nature) and the divine *hypostasis* did not (also according to its nature), what happened to the conjunction? Was the *prosōpon* human, divine, or some combination of the two? If it was a combination, why did it not break apart when one *hypostasis* died and the other did not? In the end, what the Antiochenes rejected as an extreme form of their Christology was no more than its logical conclusion, which left the church without a coherent understanding of whether its Savior was God or a man.

It was the Council of Chalcedon in 451 that broke this logjam by saying that the principles of unity in the incarnate Son, the Alexandrian *hypostasis* and the Antiochene *prosōpon*, were really one and the same. This meant that the council accepted the basic outline of Alexandrian Christology, but in Antiochene dress. The fathers of Chalcedon rejected the Antiochene contention that the *prosōpon* of Christ was no more than the conjunction of his human and divine *hypostaseis*, on the ground that there could be only one *hypostasis* in Christ, as the Alexandrians claimed. At the same time, however, they also rejected the Alexandrian view that the two natures somehow merged into one, agreeing with the Antiochenes that the natures remained distinct. They were able to reach this conclusion because they adopted the position of the Western church, which had always regarded *persona* (*prosōpon*) as equivalent to *hypostasis*. Chalcedonian Christology was immediately embraced by the West, which has never wavered from it. In the East, however, it produced

---

[45] Matt. 27:46.

divisions that still exist, despite many attempts to overcome them.[46] Oddly enough, Chalcedon did not make a specific connection between the divine person of the incarnate Son and the second person of the Trinity, though that was clearly implied in what it said. The omission was put right at the second council of Constantinople in 553, which set the seal on what the Western (Catholic and Protestant) and the main Eastern (Orthodox) churches now regard as the right way to express our theology.

The most important long-term achievement of the Council of Chalcedon was that it transcended the limitations of the thought-world of ancient Greek philosophy, in which both Alexandria and Antioch had been imprisoned, and restructured Christian theology on a new and different basis. It did this by decreeing that a "person" is not to be understood as a manifestation of an underlying substance (*ousia*) that determined what it could and could not do in line with that substance's nature (*physis*). Instead, "person" is to be treated as a theological principle in its own right, logically prior to both the substance and its nature and therefore superior to them. This revolution in theological thinking occurred when the council said that the divine person of the Son of God took on a second nature by becoming man, making his divine *hypostasis* the *hypostasis* of his humanity as well.[47] Subsequent debates established that this second nature was a substance (*ousia*) in its own right, fully equipped with a soul, a mind, and a will that were neither subordinate to the Son's divine nature nor dominated by it. In other words, by saying that the union of the two natures in Christ was hypostatic (i.e., personal), the fathers of Chalcedon made the natures dependent on the one person/*hypostasis* and not the other way around. In the incarnate Christ, the divine *hypostasis* controlled each of its two natures (*physeis*), giving the person of the incarnate Son the freedom to employ them as he chose without being constrained by either of them.

The lasting effect of the Chalcedonian definition of the person and natures of Christ was to bring Christian theology closer to the teaching of the Bible than it had been since New Testament times. The ancient Israelites would not have denied that Yahweh was the "supreme being" but they did not speak in such abstract terms. Their God was never a concept to be understood according to a hierarchy of ideas of which he stood at the top end. To

---

[46]The Alexandrians clung to their earlier position and evolved into what we now know as the "monophysite" church. Some Antiochenes also stuck with their previous views, which they attributed to Nestorius, and so their descendants are now referred to as "Nestorians." Though they were long regarded as heretical by the other churches, modern ecumenical study has generally concluded that their intentions are orthodox even if their terminology appears unsatisfactory from the Chalcedonian point of view. As a result, they are now accepted by such bodies as the World Council of Churches, and are usually known as the "non-Chalcedonian churches of the East."

[47]It was this that was brought out in the years between 451 and 553, and which was finally canonized at the second council of Constantinople.

them he was always what we would call a "person," and we can even say that "being" (Yahweh, "he who is") was his proper name. Jews who spread across the Greco-Roman world absorbed the mindset of Greek philosophy and could interpret their faith in its terms when they had to, but it never came naturally to them. The incarnation of Christ, however, challenged the purely transcendent monotheism of Judaism and forced Christians to tie their doctrine of God to their understanding of humanity. The result was a Savior who was fully divine and fully human, but who remained a single person whose ultimate identity was anchored in the fellowship of the Trinitarian God.

MODERN DIFFICULTIES WITH THE TERM "PERSON"

The use of the word "person" to describe both the members of the Holy Trinity and the principle of unity in the incarnate Christ is now so firmly established in Christian theology that it is almost impossible to dislodge it. Even so, it has been criticized by a number of modern theologians who have claimed that the meaning of the word has changed so much that to go on using it of God is misleading or even wrong. As they see it, the difficulty is that many people nowadays think of a "person" as a "center of consciousness." In Chalcedonian terms, this "center of consciousness" is not a *hypostasis* but part of the substance (*ousia*) or nature (*physis*), which makes it hard to see how there can be more than one of them in God, but only one in the incarnate Christ. They prefer to call Jesus a "person" (in the human sense) and sometimes use the same term for God in his oneness. They are thus forced to look for something else to describe the divine threeness, and often resort to the phrase "modes of being," with its unfortunate echo of ancient modalism.

This line of reasoning sounds plausible at first sight, and it has convinced many, but further reflection will show that it is inadequate. For example, if a person is defined as a "center of consciousness," does a human being who loses consciousness cease to be a person? The question may seem strange, but it is not uncommon for people to claim that someone in a long-term, irreversible coma is no longer a person, which makes it easier to justify terminating what remains of the body's "life." There may be good reasons to doubt whether it is right to prolong bodily existence indefinitely by entirely artificial means rather than let nature take its course, but that is not the same thing as denying the personhood of someone who is in that state. Such an approach suggests that it is possible to deprive human beings of their fundamental dignity as persons merely by making them unconscious, which is grotesque.

Another problem we face today is that the word "personality" has taken on a meaning which is much closer to *physis* than to *hypostasis*. At one time, "personality" meant what we now call "personhood," so that in older works of theology it is possible to find discussions of the "personality" of the Holy Spirit, meaning no more than that he is a person in the same sense that the Father and the Son are persons. But in popular modern usage, "personality" refers to the characteristics that make up and distinguish particular individuals, so that we can speak of someone as having a pleasant "personality," for example. We also accept that, under certain conditions, that kind of personality can change. Traumatic experience or hypnosis can affect the way an individual expresses himself and relates to other people, and then we say that his "personality" has changed. Here it is clear that we are dealing with something that belongs to the nature of a being and not to what classical theology would call its "person." To put it simply, a man whose psychological personality has changed remains objectively (and legally) the same person as he was before.

To suggest otherwise could easily lead to a situation in which a change of personality would be sufficient ground for restructuring a man's social responsibilities in ways that are potentially harmful. Would it ever be right, for example, to legitimize divorce on the grounds that a man's or woman's personality was no longer what it was at the time of the marriage? This is already happening in cases where a man divorces his wife because he has discovered that he is homosexual and therefore unsuited to the heterosexual relationship to which he is officially committed. But if this line of reasoning is accepted as valid, where will it end? The ease with which personality changes can be made and the potential for abuse are such that without a concept of "person" distinct from psychology, the modern preference for noncommittal relationships will almost certainly become the norm, to the detriment of long-term social stability. If a marrying couple can promise that they will be faithful to each other only until their personalities change or until they discover "who they really are," what hope is there for creating a lasting bond between them?

God does not have a "personality" in the modern sense of the word, because he cannot change, but it would be hard to deny that he is somehow personal. Even those who define "person" as "center of consciousness" are usually prepared to accept this, despite the problems it creates for the Trinity and for our understanding of the incarnation of Christ. If the Father, Son, and Holy Spirit are not three "centers of consciousness," what are they? To speak about them as "modes of being," as Karl Barth and others have done, is problematic because that kind of language is liable to land us back in the very modalism that the early church tried so hard to escape from. If we accepted it, how could we say that God became a man in only one of the modes of his being? What would Jesus' "center of consciousness" have been if that were the case? Jesus Christ was obviously a man, but what is it that makes him God as well? Even if his human "center of consciousness" were perfectly in tune with God's, that would still not make him divine. In the final analysis we have to say that the word "person" expresses something about God and about the incarnate Son that cannot be captured by "center of consciousness" or "mode of being." We therefore have to conclude that to abandon "person" in favor of some other concept can only diminish our understanding of who Jesus is, of how he relates to the other members of the Godhead, and of how we relate to him.

The traditional Christian meaning of the word "person" can be maintained and reclaimed for contemporary use if we remember that the closest secular parallels for it are not psychological but judicial. In both law and theology, a person is a responsible agent who possesses an inalienable identity, whether or not he is able to function in the normal human way. When a body dies, we do not throw it out as if it had no further significance, but treat it with the care and respect due to the person to whom it belonged. We do this even though we believe that the person in question no longer inhabits the body. The way we treat the corpse bears witness to our belief that the person who once dwelt in it is still alive. By our attitude toward the body, we demonstrate that we are still related to that person and that we take responsibility for his or her legacy.[48]

The human person is that part of us which cannot be altered. Therefore anything in human nature that is susceptible to change and decay, such as the mind, the consciousness, and the will, cannot be our "person." Fundamentally, the human person is God's image and likeness in us, which makes it possible for us to connect with the divine.[49] Though we dwell in time and space, as human persons we reflect the persons in God to whom we are eternally related. That relationship may be a good one, in which case we are united in fellowship with the persons of the Trinity, or it may be a bad one, in which case we stand condemned in his presence for having rejected the communion that God intended for us to enjoy with him. Either way, we have a relationship with God that can be rightly understood only when expressed in personal terms.

In the end, the best way to think of personhood is to say that being a person means having the capacity to give and receive love. The persons of the Godhead love each other fully and completely. Their mutual love constitutes their being and determines their actions, which are not constrained by the limitations inherent in their divine nature but are governed by the relation-

---

[48]This is one reason why a last will and testament cannot be easily overturned after the death of the person who made it.

[49]Ps. 82:6; John 10:34–35.

ship that each of them has with the others. The incarnation of the Son would have been impossible if the persons of the Trinity were circumscribed by their divine nature. But when the Son demonstrated the depth of his love for his Father by taking on the role of a servant, he assumed a human body and the incarnation became a reality. As human beings, we are persons because we have been made for love—love of God in the first instance, but also love of one another and of ourselves. Our love may be imperfect, it may grow cold, and it may be diverted to things that do not deserve it. But even when we abuse it, it is love which expresses the meaning of our life and which we display in everything we do. We may love the things of this world and show no appreciation for the love of God, but God nevertheless continues to love us as persons, and it is as persons that he calls those whom he has chosen to enter into eternal fellowship with him.[50]

Personal relationship with God is the only way that we can communicate with him because personhood is something that we both share. In his love for us, God has not cut us off from himself because of the mutual incompatibility of our natures. Instead, he has given us a way to connect with him so that we can have fellowship with one another. The ancient Israelites were aware of this, and it amazed them to think that such a miracle was possible:

> Behold, the LORD our God has shown us his glory and greatness, and we have heard his voice out of the midst of the fire. This day we have seen God speak with man and man still live. Now therefore why should we die? For this great fire will consume us. If we hear the voice of the LORD our God any more, we shall die. For who is there of all flesh, that has heard the voice of the living God speaking out of the midst of fire as we have, and has still lived? Go near and hear all that the LORD our God will say, and speak to us all that the LORD our God will speak to you, and we will hear and do it.[51]

As this passage reminds us, our personal relationship with God is properly worked out only if we obey his commands. That way, we shall live and not die by being consumed by the fire of his presence.[52] "If you love me," said Jesus, "you will keep my commandments."[53] This was no more than a reiteration of what God had said to the Israelites in the desert, and it is a reminder that at the heart of our knowledge of God is the life-giving power of love, which is the true measure of our participation in the divine being.[54]

---

[50]Rom. 9:22–25; 2 Tim. 2:20.
[51]Deut. 5:24–27.
[52]Prov. 7:2; Ezek. 18:23, 32; 33:11; Heb. 12:9.
[53]John 14:15.
[54]Ex. 20:6; Deut. 5:10; John 15:10.

8

THE BEING OF GOD

DIVINE SUBSTANCE AND DIVINE NATURE

In our experience of the Trinity, the Son and the Holy Spirit reach out to us in their different ways, but the Father remains hidden from our eyes. It is his particular function to uphold a sense of the transcendence of God's being, which remains fundamentally unlike ours, however close he comes to us in other ways. This task is vitally important because it is a common temptation for us to want to bring God down to our level, and even to reproach him for failing to understand us if he remains above and beyond what we are. Faced with a world that demands an exclusively human Jesus, and which is always trying to interpret human feelings as the work of the Holy Spirit, it is the Father who reminds us that God's ways are not our ways and that, compared with him, we are impotent and unable to create even the simplest natural phenomena.[1] The Father is not the personification of the divine being, but the person of the Godhead who reminds us of what God really is and to whom the work of the Son and the Spirit in our lives is directed.

Is it right to think of God as the supreme being? Christians have always believed that he is, but the concept is more problematic than it may appear at first sight. Can we say that God is a single "substance" without compromising the primacy of the three persons of the Trinity? Many Christians have said that we can, but there has always been a danger that the idea of an abstract "supreme being" will take over and obscure the true nature of the God who reveals himself to us in personal terms. Some theologians have even been tempted to suggest that the divine being constitutes a *fourth* reality in the Godhead. Not only was this in addition to the three persons, but ultimately,

---

[1] Isa. 55:8–9; Job 38:4–39:30.

it was more important than they were because it was common to all of them equally.

This way of thinking was never officially adopted by the church, but it came to full expression in the late seventeenth century and was one of the factors that contributed to the rise of unitarianism. The cult of the "supreme being" or deity began in Britain and reached its apogee in the French revolution. It can be seen in many of the writings of the founders of the United States as well as in innumerable works of nineteenth-century progressive thinkers and twentieth-century liberal clerics. For two hundred years now it has been a mainstay of popular civic religion in many Western democracies and has frequently been assimilated to orthodox Christianity, even though it is a caricature of what the Bible teaches. The confusion has arisen because someone who worships the biblical God will have to agree with the deists that he is the supreme being. The snag is that someone who thinks primarily in terms of a "supreme being" is not worshiping the Christian God but an intellectual idol that he does not know in a personal way, even if he thinks about the deity in personal terms.[2] Deists are not committed to accepting the biblical portrait of God, and they have a marked tendency to modify the biblical view in ways that make him more congenial to them. A particular favorite of theirs is to deny that there is any wrath in God, despite the fact that the Bible often speaks about it.

The early Christians understood the scope for misunderstanding on this point and were uncomfortable about identifying God too closely with the supreme being of the philosophers. A small (but telling) difference shows us what the root of their problem was and how they reacted to it. The philosophers spoke of their supreme being as *to on* (the thing that is) but Christians changed the neuter participle to the masculine *ho ōn*, which to them was the equivalent of Yahweh ("he who is").[3] By doing this, they made it clear that the supreme being is a person who relates to us in personal ways, not an abstract deity—a vital difference that distinguished and still distinguishes Christianity from any kind of philosophy.

The Bible is not hostile to the idea that Yahweh is the supreme being, but the priority in ancient Israel was to impress upon people that there is only one God, to whom they were personally related by the covenant he had established with Israel. This seems obvious to us today, but at that time it was a unique claim, because all the surrounding nations were polytheistic. In their view, the

---

[2]This is common in the Western world because of its Judeo-Christian heritage, but there is no logical reason why the supreme being has to be personal.
[3]Rev. 1:8.

spiritual realm was populated by a number of different beings, of which some could be described as glorified humans but others were monstrous. For these nations, there was no clear divide between the spiritual and the material and no concept of a creation distinct from the divine world. It seemed natural to them that the gods could become human beings, or at least appear in human form and act pretty much in the same way that any of us would. Sexual intercourse with a deity was not only possible but was sought after because it would guarantee increased fertility and bring superhuman creatures into being. All of this was totally foreign to Israel. According to the biblical revelation, the one God is above and beyond any human concept, because he dwells outside the created order altogether. He cannot be compared or assimilated to any creature, spiritual or material. Copulation with him is impossible. Even the greatest human being is in no sense divine, and the same must be said of angels, despite the fact that they are spiritual beings like God himself.

Given this picture of God, it might be asked whether he can properly be described as a "being" at all. If a being can be defined in objective terms, then there is good reason to say that God does not fit into this category because he is infinite. Since any definition of God would be a limitation, and any limitation would be a diminution of his true self, the result would be a mental idol adapted to the capacity of the human brain and for that very reason a travesty of the true God. If a being is something definable in human terms, then God is not and cannot be one! The usual answer to this is that the Bible speaks of God as a being, indeed as *the* Being. His name Yahweh ("he who is") indicates this, as does the description of him as the one "who is and who was and who is to come."[4] At the same time, however, we cannot define him in terms limited to the time and space universe he created, but must do so in the context of the transcendent reality in which he dwells.

Some Christians, however, have gone further than this. In the apophatic tradition, God is infinite and therefore indefinable, even in his transcendent reality. He can be described only as *to mē on* (that which is not), a term which is sometimes misleadingly translated into English as "nonbeing," though "beyond being" would be a better term for it. It is all too easy to develop a mental construct of the divine being and attach properties to it that sound good in the abstract but can cause embarrassment if their logical implications are pressed too far. For example, theologians have long asked how an eternal being can exist in time, as the Son of God did when he was incarnate as Jesus of Nazareth. Those who think of his divinity as a substance have a problem with this because a divine substance cannot exist in time and space without

---

[4]Rev. 1:8.

ceasing to be itself. There is also the difficulty that this substance would have to be shared with the Father and the Holy Spirit, both of whom would therefore be implicated in the incarnation of the Son if he had managed to bring his divine substance with him into the created order. Convolutions of this kind have puzzled many, and the apophatic tradition is a useful antidote to them, because it insists that, whatever the divine being is, it cannot be understood in those terms.

To say that God is a "being" is not to define what that being is but to emphasize that he is objectively there. He is not a figment of our imagination, nor is he some elusive idea that cannot be identified in any very precise way. He communicates with us in personal terms, but his voice is not a sound in a void; there is substance behind it. What kind of substance he is, is another question. Theologians have veered from saying that the divine substance (or being) is an intellectual abstraction that expresses what the three persons of the Godhead have in common, to saying that God's being is an objective reality in its own right which each of the Trinitarian persons encapsulates in his own way.

The being of God is inexpressible in human terms, which means that it cannot be scientifically detected or investigated. If by some chance we were ever to come into contact with his being, we would be destroyed because we would not be able to handle the encounter.[5] The image the Bible uses to make this point is usually that of fire.[6] Fire is real and is vitally important for human life, but we cannot touch it without suffering the consequences. So it is with God. His being and ours cannot coexist in direct contact with each other, but at the same time we cannot exist without him. The persons of the Godhead reveal this incomprehensible divine being to us, making it possible for us to have some connection with it in spite of our radical incompatibility with its nature, but they are not merely expressions of the divine being, nor are they bound by it. If that were the case, the second person of the Trinity could not have become a man, since his divine nature would have prevented such a thing. Only a person in control of his nature can do something that is incompatible with it, and this tells us what the true relationship between the persons of the Trinity and the divine being is.

The Father, Son, and Holy Spirit share the same being, but they are in control of it, not the other way around. The persons can and do communicate with us, and, by the indwelling presence of the Holy Spirit in our hearts we are privileged to share in their divine being by being allowed to participate in some of its characteristics, or attributes. Thus, for example, we can receive the

---

[5]Ex. 33:20.
[6]See Ex. 3:2–6; Heb. 12:29.

gift of eternal life, which properly belongs to God alone. But we can receive it only by transcending the nature we have been given in creation and being transformed by the power of God into spiritual beings capable of standing in his presence.[7] This is possible because, like God, we too are persons who are not bound by our natures any more than the persons of the Trinity are bound by theirs.

The apophatic impulse to go beyond classical notions of "being" has had a particular appeal in the Eastern churches, but it has received an airing in the West as well, particularly now that modern theories of physics appear to have made the classical notion of "substance" untenable. Do we really need to speak about God in this way? At one level, the answer to this must be "no," and if we think of "substance" in the way that Aristotelian physics did, then the terminology must certainly be abandoned, as apophatic theology has always insisted. There is no abstract thing in, under, or behind God that we can define as his "substance" and examine without reference to the persons of the Trinity. We have no access to his divine nature apart from his revelation of himself, and that revelation is personal. We know that in other ways God is utterly unlike us, and that he rebuked people who thought otherwise, but beyond that we cannot go.[8] Having said that, we must also affirm that the three persons of the Trinity share common characteristics, and it is helpful to have a word to describe these, even if that word does not correspond to any identifiable thing.

In the past, when theologians talked about the "substance" of God (what he is), what they were really talking about was his "nature" (what he is like), which is revealed to us in these common characteristics. Thus, for example, to say that God is good, invisible, or omnipotent means that he is completely good, invisible, and omnipotent. All three persons of the Trinity share these attributes, each of which is absolute and thus logically coterminous with his "being." In other words, God is the Supreme Good both because his goodness is absolute and not simply defined in relation to something else, and because there is nothing in him that does not share in this goodness. We cannot say that God is good only when he wants to be, but that he also has a nasty side that comes out from time to time as well. Even when he appears to be turning against us, God is still supremely good, and his punishment of our disobedience reflects that.[9] In a similar way, God is the ultimate Invisible, the only Omnipotent, and so on. Taken together,

---

[7] 1 Cor. 15:50–54.
[8] See, for example, Ps. 50:7–15; Isa. 66:1.
[9] See Jer. 10:24.

these characteristics of his nature add up to his "substance," and that is what we mean when we use the term.

If God's "substance" and his "nature" coincide, can we not just drop the problematic term "substance" and simply speak of his "nature"? There is no great difficulty in doing this where God is concerned, but the concepts do not coincide in his creatures, and when we are comparing God with them it is often useful to maintain the distinction. To understand this, we need only consider that human nature is not the same thing as human being. Human being is what a man or woman is; human nature is what people in general are like. That the two do not coincide can be seen from the fact that it is possible for a human being to go against his nature and do things that are unnatural to him, even if acts of that kind create controversy and may have to be treated as disorders. The important thing is that, while it is possible for human beings to act in this way because our natures can be distinguished from our being, it is not possible for God to do so, because his nature and being are effectively one and the same.

God can never act in a way that is unnatural to him, and if he does something that we do not expect and/or do not like, we cannot explain it by saying that there is something wrong with him. He never acts out of character and never does anything that he might regret when he "comes to his senses," as we might say of human beings. This is particularly important when we consider the nature of God's love. There are always people who think that, if God is love, he can never get angry or punish anyone—because to their minds such behavior is incompatible with love. The biblical evidence that God does punish people is dismissed as an expression of primitive human ideas that are unworthy of him, and those who try to uphold such concepts as the "wrath of God" are ridiculed as crude fundamentalists who have no understanding of what God is really like.[10] But however hard it may be to understand or accept, everything that God does he does in his love and in his goodness. Even his wrath and punishment must be understood in that context.

For God to be angry is not out of character for him but an expression of his nature in relation to particular circumstances. The God who loves us as his creatures also hates us as sinners who have rebelled against him, because he cannot tolerate us in that condition. The paradox is that he hates us because he loves us; if he did not care one way or the other, he might easily be indifferent to us and either do nothing or (more probably) destroy us without giving

---

[10]As a matter of interest, the expression "wrath of God" occurs only once in the Old Testament (Ps. 78:31, KJV) but nine times in the New, of which five are in the book of Revelation (14:10, 19; 15:1, 7; 16:1). The others are in John 3:36; Rom. 1:18; Eph. 5:6; and Col. 3:6.

the matter a second thought. It is God's love that has led him to redeem us, but he has done so because that same love has led him to hate us as we are—in him, the two apparent opposites are reconciled into one. Those who find this difficult to understand need only reflect on the way that parents treat their children when the latter get into trouble or cause embarrassment. There are things that we may be prepared to tolerate in other people's children, and even find amusing at times, things that bring out our anger when we see them in our own offspring. This is not a double standard but a reminder that, when we are dealing with those whom we love and have a special responsibility for, we are less tolerant than we might otherwise be. In the same way, God disciplines those whom he loves, however hard it may be to accept it at the time, and if we are the recipients of such discipline then we ought to be grateful and thank him for taking such good care of us.[11]

To sum up, the characteristics (attributes) of God are qualities that apply to all the persons of the Trinity and may be regarded as inherent in their divinity. They can be subdivided into distinct categories, but what marks them out is the fact that they are quite different from, and frequently the exact opposite of, what we find in God's creatures. So much is this the case that often the only way we can describe them is by negation—God is invisible, immortal, infinite, and so on. Even when God is described in terms that can be applied to human beings and/or other creatures, the scale of application is so different that we have to say that the words are not being used in the same sense. For example, we say that God is good and that his creation is good also, but God's goodness includes moral perfection, which created goodness does not include. Similarly, we believe that God is rational and that human beings are too, but the divine rationality is so superior to the human that it is incomprehensible to us. As the Lord declared through the prophet Isaiah,

> For my thoughts are not your thoughts,
>   neither are your ways my ways, declares the LORD.
> For as the heavens are higher than the earth,
>   so are my ways higher than your ways
>   and my thoughts than your thoughts.[12]

The meaning of these attributes is determined by the nature of the being or substance we are describing, and God's infinitude (as opposed to our creaturely finitude) ensures that it will be quite different in his case from what it is in ours.

---

[11]Prov. 3:11–12; Heb. 12:5–6.
[12]Isa. 55:8–9.

GOD IS ALL-POWERFUL

What is the most fundamental attribute of God? This is a difficult question to answer because so much depends on how we approach the question. If we are thinking in moral terms, then perhaps God's righteousness, his goodness, or his love will be the first thing that springs to our minds. If we are thinking about his greatness, we might consider his infinitude, his immutability, or his impassibility as most deserving of this honor. As even this short list shows, however, each of God's attributes implies the others, which makes it virtually impossible to rank them in order of importance. Take any one of them away and God would cease to be himself. On the other hand, it is clear from the witness of the Bible that there is one divine attribute that stands out above the others, at least as far as we and the rest of his creation are concerned. This is his omnipotence, an attribute which underlies his exercise of absolute sovereignty over everything he has made and provides the context in which we experience and come to understand the true meaning of his other attributes.

Logically speaking, it is difficult to say that "sovereignty" is a divine attribute because it has no meaning apart from creation; it is a relational term that is more meaningful to us than it is to God as he is in himself. This can be seen quite clearly from the names he uses to reveal himself to us. The most common of these is "Lord," though here we have to be careful because very often this word is a substitute for the Hebrew "Yahweh," a name regarded by the Jews as too sacred to pronounce.[13] Instead of attempting to say it, they had a number of substitute words that they used when reading the Bible aloud, of which the most common seems to have been "Adonai" ("my Lord"). By putting the vowels of Adonai together with the consonants YHWH, they could produce "Yahowah," a hybrid name which has come down to us as Jehovah.[14] Nowadays this name has become associated with the Jehovah's Witnesses and so is less used by Christians than it used to be, but it is still familiar enough to remind us that the relational term "Lord" was from very ancient times closely associated with the very being of God.

Lordship is meaningful only when there is something to be lord of, and in that sense the name is external to God himself—it is we who call him Lord because of our subordinate status in relationship to him. It is important because it is a constant reminder of who is in control of our lives and because

---

[13]Hebrew does not normally write the vowels, so the word appears as YHWH in the Old Testament. The vowels have been supplied by scholarly guesswork.

[14]This form occurs seven times in the Authorized (King James) Version of the English Bible (1611), four times on its own (Ex. 6:3; Ps. 83:18; Isa. 12:2; 26:4). Otherwise it appears as part of a place name—Jehovah-jireh (Gen. 22:14); Jehovah-nissi (Ex. 17:15), and Jehovah-shalom (Judg. 6:24). Interestingly, modern versions like the ESV tend to use "Lord" in all these cases (capitalized as LORD to indicate the underlying YHWH).

it can be applied equally to all three persons of the Trinity. The fact that Jesus is regularly called Lord is a sign that he too is God because his lordship means that he is just as sovereign over us as the Father is.[15] It is also a reminder that, although we have been taught to call God our Father, we must never forget that he is also our ruler. We have no right to presume on the intimacy that he has granted us as his children and assume that we can draw near to him as a matter of right. It is an indication of the greatness of his love for us that he has allowed us to become his children by adoption, but the choice is his, not ours.

Even more significant as a sign of God's sovereignty is the fact that he is frequently called the Almighty.[16] This title clearly bears witness to his omnipotence, but we must study its origin and application to appreciate why it is revealed in Scripture as a proper name of God and not simply listed as one of his attributes. The name "Almighty" is the translation of the Hebrew *El-Shaddai* and the Greek *Pantokratōr*, both of which refer more to God's lordship than to his inherent power, though of course the one depends on the other. It is not simply that God is capable of doing whatever he wants to and cannot be hindered in this by any other power in the universe, but that he controls everything and rules his world directly. This is extremely important because it rules out any idea that God might have backed off from certain things or abandoned parts of his creation to hostile powers who have taken control of it and use it to assault us in ways beyond his ability to help.

In the ancient world, there were many spiritual beings to whom the word "god" was applied, just as there were many who were worshiped as "lords." If the God of Israel had been just one god among many, there would have been no reason to regard him as the supreme ruler of the universe, even if he was more powerful than the gods and lords of Israel's neighbors. It was the title "Almighty" which made it clear that the God of the Bible was not to be compared with any other so-called deity, and which ensured that his power would not be thought of as limited to one nation or territory. When the Israelites were sent into exile, God revealed himself to them as the Lord of Babylon and Persia just as much as he was the ruler of Israel, and he told them that he was powerful enough to bring them back to their homeland in due course.[17] With the coming of Christ, God showed his people that he was not confined to the rituals and practices of the Mosaic covenant, nor was his promise of salvation limited only to Jews. The power of the Almighty was, and still is,

---

[15]1 Cor. 15:27–28. The Holy Spirit is also called Lord, though less frequently. See 2 Cor. 3:17.

[16]Among many other instances, see Gen. 17:1; Ex. 6:3; Job 5:17; Ps. 91:1; Ezek. 1:24; 2 Cor. 6:18; Rev. 4:8. The book of Job uses the word no fewer than thirty-one times!

[17]See Isa. 43:1–3, for example.

strong to save men and women, whoever they are and however far they may have strayed from his ways.

What does it mean to say that God is all-powerful? We should dismiss frivolous debates about whether God can commit suicide or do something else that would contradict his nature. Such discussions are meaningless because even if God could commit what we would think of as suicide, it would only mean that he was transforming one kind of life into another, since to him "death" would be no more than another form of life. Questions of this kind fail to understand that the attributes of God are not explanations of who or what he is in himself, since that lies beyond our comprehension; rather, they explain who and what he is in relation to us, his creatures. We perceive him as all-powerful because he has made us, has established and maintains the conditions under which we live, and can remove or destroy those conditions without being restrained or hindered by any external force. If we do not like what God intends to do with us, there is nowhere else for us to turn, no higher court of appeal that might overrule his judgment. It might be possible for us to plead with him in the hope that he may change his mind, but that is a completely different matter. God has told us to bring our requests to him precisely because he has the power to answer them, which he would not be free to do if he were not the Almighty. But at the same time, whatever he decides to do with our prayers, his decision is final. Even the apostle Paul had to accept that God's will for his life was different from what he would have preferred, and Jesus likewise submitted his human will to the divine will that he shared with his Father.[18] None of us is greater than they were, and we must follow their example in this as in all things, believing as they did that "for those who love God all things work together for good, for those who are called according to his purpose."[19]

But what about those who do not love God? What power does he exercise over them? If it is true that he can destroy whatever he has made, why does God permit the continued existence of people and angels who have rebelled against him? In particular, why does he allow them not only to survive but often to thrive and dominate the world in contempt of him and in disregard for his will? The words of the psalmist echo the thoughts of many, then and since:

> As for me, my feet had almost stumbled,
>   my steps had nearly slipped.

---

[18]Matt. 26:42; 2 Cor. 12:8–9; Phil. 1:23–24.
[19]Rom. 8:28.

For I was envious of the arrogant
  when I saw the prosperity of the wicked. . . .

these are the wicked;
  always at ease, they increase in riches.
All in vain have I kept my heart clean
  and washed my hands in innocence.[20]

It is undoubtedly hard to understand how an all-powerful and loving God can permit the continued existence of evil in the world, when presumably he could snuff it out whenever he wanted to, but although this difficulty has haunted Christian theologians from the beginning, it is easier to live with its problems than with those that would be created if his absolute sovereignty were to be denied. A world controlled by God is a world in which he can always act to save us, even if there are forces in it that are prepared to attack and enslave us. If he were not ultimately in control of those forces, we could have no assurance that he is able to help us and could easily find ourselves in the depths of despair. In the end, it is easier to live with the problem of why God allows evil to exist than it would be to live with the problem of why evil forces should be able to thwart his will.

The obvious case of an evil that God continues to permit is the ongoing existence of Satan and his demons. They have rebelled against God, and he has cast them out of his presence with no hope of reconciliation, and yet they have not been eliminated. Why not? Why does God permit them to exist and to go on exercising their power in the world when it seems clear that he does not want them?[21] Are we to say that God does not destroy them because he is somehow prevented from doing so? Surely not! The assertion of the divine omnipotence forces us to conclude that whatever the reason for the continuing existence and activity of these evil powers may be, it is not because God cannot dispose of them if he so chooses. Indeed, we are reminded in the Scriptures that Satan is subject to the sovereignty of God and can act only within the limits God allows.[22] Clearly the Devil and his angels can place no limit on God's power, but although that is good to know and is a great reassurance that our own salvation cannot be diminished or taken away,[23] it does not explain why God is so tolerant of their existence.

The ultimate reason for this is a mystery that is not revealed to us. We know from the opening chapters of Genesis that evil spiritual powers were

[20]Ps. 73:2–3, 12–13.
[21]Hab. 1:13.
[22]Job 1:12.
[23]Rom. 8:38–39.

already at work when God created the world, so there has never been a time when human beings have not had to contend with them.[24] We can suggest that these evil powers have been allowed to continue their activities because God hates nothing that he has made and will not willingly destroy any of his creatures, however much they may rebel against him. We might want to argue that evil forces exist in order to test the faith of the righteous, who would otherwise have nothing to test themselves against. But whatever conclusions we may come to, they are all speculative. All we can say for sure is that God is good, that he hates evil and will one day put an end to it, but that for the time being it continues to exist and exert its influence in the world. We are commanded to put on the whole armor of God and to stand firm against evil, but we are not promised that our resistance will lead to its elimination, something that must await the final judgment at the end of time.[25]

Another question raised by God's omnipotence concerns the freedom of his creatures. Does the almighty power of God mean that I am unable to make my own decisions, even when I think that that is what I am doing? Do I have the freedom to choose between good and evil, or has he already made that choice for me? Can I resist the will of God, or do I inevitably do it, even when I am rebelling against him? The underlying issue here is one of responsibility. If a human being has no power of his own, how can he be held responsible for his actions? This may not matter so much if the actions are good, but why should we go to hell for doing things we cannot avoid? If God did not want us to fall into sin, why did he not intervene to prevent Adam and Eve from giving in to temptation? Surely, we think, an all-powerful God could have done that without any trouble, and saved his creatures all the misery that sin and evil have brought into the world! Quite apart from all the bother that he would have spared us, the Father would have made it unnecessary for his Son to sacrifice himself for our sins. If it was in his power to do that, why did he not do so?

These questions, and others like them, have constantly resurfaced in the history of Christian theology, and it must be admitted that no fully comprehensive and compelling answers to them have ever been found. (If they had been, presumably the questions would have been resolved and we would no longer be asking them.) Nevertheless, there are certain principles revealed to us in Scripture that enable us to focus our minds and at least narrow the range of explanations available to us. First, we can say that God is in control of everything that happens, even if we do not understand why he permits things to exist that appear to oppose his revealed will for us. Second, in this

---

[24]Gen. 3:1–7.
[25]Eph. 6:13; Rev. 20:7–10.

life we are bound by the limitations of our created nature and are not free to go against it without suffering the consequences. There are some things that are simply impossible for us to do—for example, we cannot suddenly decide to live in another century, have different parents, or acquire a new body. Modern medical science has made it possible for us to change sex, but only superficially—a man cannot really become a woman, or vice versa, and people who have undergone such operations often find themselves in an in-between zone where they are not fully accepted by other members of the sex they have chosen to adopt. We cannot grow taller or younger, however much we may wish to do so, nor can we alter our racial or ethnic origins. To some extent we can adopt a different language and culture, but unless we do this at a very young age (when the choice is probably not ours), we are unlikely to succeed completely, and the degree to which our adopted nation will accept us will depend on how open and receptive its social structures are. In all these respects, we are rather like fish in an aquarium—free to swim around, but only within the limits that have been determined for us by our Creator.

As for moral choices, we are not as free to make them as we might think. Adam and Eve could not make such choices because they lacked moral awareness. They disobeyed God because they were tempted by the promise that, if they did so, they would become like him. Until that happened, however, they did not know what good and evil were and so could not make moral choices in the way that we understand the term. That does not excuse their disobedience, of course, but it puts their freedom into its proper context. Initially, God had shielded them from having to make moral decisions by withholding the knowledge of good and evil from them, but that knowledge was present in the garden and available to them if they chose to acquire it. They did so, thinking it would make them free, but instead they discovered that they lost whatever freedom they had had and were subsequently prevented from regaining it.

This is the condition we are in—we did not choose to be sinners, but are born that way whether we like it or not. As a result, we sometimes choose evil even when we think that it is good. We resist God's will even when we are convinced that we are obeying it. It is only when we are set free in Christ that we become aware of this, and the result is the spiritual warfare that is the daily experience of every Christian, because now our liberated minds are at war with the law of sin and death that we have inherited from Adam.[26] My freedom means that I must accept responsibility for this situation, even though I can do nothing about it, because acceptance of that responsibility is the first

---

[26]Rom. 7:21–25.

step on the way toward true deliverance. Even if God could intervene and save me without first convicting me of sin, the result would not necessarily be what I would want, nor would it guarantee that such a salvation was irreversible. To take a human analogy, it is perfectly possible to protect an alcoholic by locking him up and denying him access to the thing he craves. In such circumstances, he could dry out and lead a useful life, but it would be at the expense of his personal freedom. What he might do when released is anyone's guess. Perhaps he would see the error of his former ways and renounce strong drink forever, but it is just as likely that he would go back to alcohol as soon as he could get his hands on it again.

This is not the kind of heaven that God is preparing for us. If we are to be truly free we must be delivered from our sinfulness. That is possible only if we accept responsibility for it, recognize our inability to change ourselves, and turn to him for his saving power to get to work in our lives. In the meantime, God tolerates our sinfulness, not because he likes it but because he loves us and knows that this is the way we must go if we are ever to turn from our sin and enjoy eternal life in fellowship with him. At bottom, the mystery of human freedom is the mystery of divine love—the one cannot exist without the other. God sets us free in the power of his love, and it is by that love that our freedom is preserved. We cannot escape from it, but neither are we limited by it, since God's love, like God himself, is infinite and eternal.

When we realize the implications of this, we can begin to understand that most of the other divine attributes are functions of God's omnipotence and can be properly appreciated only in relation to it. For example, God's invisibility is necessary because otherwise he could not be and act everywhere at the same time, which is a function of his almighty power. If he could be seen, he would be circumscribed by the limitations that visibility imposes, and so would not have the freedom to act in the way that his omnipotence dictates. This point is highlighted for us by Jesus when he tells his disciples that he must go away in order for the Holy Spirit to come, and that when he does, they will do greater things than he could do when he was still with them in the flesh.[27] This cannot mean that the divinity of Jesus was diminished by his incarnation, so it must mean that his humanity imposed real constraints on his power when he was still in the flesh. As a human being, he could not be everywhere at once, nor could he dwell in the hearts of his disciples in the way that his Holy Spirit would do after the day of Pentecost. But now that he has returned to his heavenly glory he is no longer constrained in this way, and in the power

---

[27]John 14:12.

of his divine nature we find that he is always and everywhere present, just as the Father and the Holy Spirit are.[28]

CAN GOD CHANGE OR SUFFER?

Another attribute that is logically dependent on God's omnipotence is his immutability, which in turn is closely linked to his impassibility. These characteristics of God have come under a lot of fire in modern times because many leading theologians have been persuaded that a God who interacts with his creatures (and especially with his human creatures) must change and develop if his relationship with them is to be genuine. To their minds, an immutable God would be unfeeling and therefore uncaring, and if that were so he could not be a God of love. They point out that, in the Old Testament, God occasionally "repented" of something he was planning to do as a result of the prayers of his people,[29] and they hold that up as evidence that he does in fact change in response to human actions. According to this view, when we suffer, God suffers with us; when we repent, he changes his mind and spares us the punishment that was coming to us.

In evaluating the validity of these objections to the traditional view of God's immutability, it is necessary to point out that what we are dealing with is evidence that God's stated purpose is not always fulfilled because circumstances intervene that cause him to change it. This was the case with the punishment he had decreed against Nineveh, as recorded in the book of Jonah. But God's decision to destroy Nineveh was never absolute, as Jonah's career demonstrates. The prophet went (very much against his own will!) to proclaim their upcoming destruction to the Ninevites, but much to Jonah's annoyance, they listened to what he had to say and repented. When that happened, God stayed his judgment because the situation which had initially occasioned it no longer applied. Does this mean that God changed his mind in a way that would deny his inherent immutability?

To this the answer must be no. It is God's eternal and universal intention to punish sin and eliminate evil—that does not change. After Jonah's departure, Nineveh went back to its old ways and in the end it was destroyed, along with all the other great civilizations of antiquity that denied God's power. It is also God's eternal plan and purpose to save those who repent and believe in him. In the case of the Ninevites they repented and their destruction was delayed, but they did not believe and so in the end they were not saved.[30]

---

[28]See John 14:23.

[29]1 Chron. 21:15; Amos 7:6; Jonah 3:10.

[30]In Old Testament times, saving belief would have entailed joining the nation of Israel, which the Ninevites clearly did not do.

God's dealings with them were entirely consistent. As the story of Jonah makes plain, the temporary repentance of the Ninevites was part of God's plan, not just for them but also for Jonah, who had to understand that God's grace and mercy was not restricted to Israel. The one thing perfectly clear from the story is that it was not Jonah who changed God's behavior; if Jonah had had his way, Nineveh would have been destroyed long before he ever got there. What the story of Jonah teaches us is that, although God's outward actions may vary according to circumstances, his inner purpose remains the same because his essential character does not change. Everything God does is consistent with who and what he is. This is what we mean when we talk about divine immutability, and we must be grateful for it. It is our trust in his power to accomplish what he has promised to do that gives us assurance of eternal salvation.

Against this modern perception that God is capable of inner change there stands the ancient and all but universal tradition of theology which says that God is "without body, parts, or passions."[31] In other words, God is not merely invisible, but he has no internal variations and is not susceptible to any outside influences either. Whatever his nature is, it is above and beyond anything that can engage directly with the created order. To imagine God's being as capable of suffering is to diminish his sovereignty. How can anything or anyone he has made be able to harm him? Critics of this position refer to it as "classical theism," and believe that it presents us with a "static" God, as opposed to the "dynamic" deity that they are proposing. To their minds, a "static" God is not merely immutable but is incapable of entering into a relationship with anything outside of himself. Presumably a truly "static" God would have to be totally inert and incapable of doing anything at all, though critics of classical theism seldom go that far.

They do, however, claim that this is the kind of God that most modern atheists have rejected, and argue that this is another reason for abandoning the model, because Christians do not believe in a "static" divine being any more than atheists do. On the contrary, the Bible teaches that God is intimately involved with his creation, and particularly with human beings, to whom he relates in a living, "dynamic" way. This interaction does not diminish his power in the abstract sense, but it commits him to using that power in specific ways which are tied to, and explained by, the nature of the covenant(s) he has made with us. Far from being distant, remote, and incomprehensible, God comes close to us, dwells in our hearts, and responds to all our pain, suffer-

---

[31]The expression comes from the first article of the Thirty-nine Articles of Religion of the Anglican/Episcopal tradition.

ing, and sense of alienation. When we turn against him he feels it deeply—so deeply, in fact, that he sent his Son into the world to reconcile us to him once and for all. This is the experience of the Christian and the essence of the gospel, which must define everything we say and claim to know about God.

At one level, much of this debate is pointless because it is an attempt to harmonize two essentially different things. The so-called classical theists are mainly concerned to protect God's omnipotence and to establish the reliability of his promises. As they see it, a God who is capable of change is one who may decide to abandon his plan to save the human race and do something else instead. After all, they argue, once you admit the possibility of change in God, where will it stop? It is not enough to insist that God will change only in ways that will lead to positive results for us, since there is no way of guaranteeing that. Quite apart from anything else, it may be the case that something we regard as a positive change will disadvantage someone else whose needs and aspirations are different from ours. It often happens in human life that attempts to avoid discrimination against one person or group end up by discriminating against others, as various "affirmative action" programs have discovered.

If God decides to alter his plans in order to benefit one person or group of people, who can say whether another person or group will not suffer because of it? It is even possible to point to a biblical example of how this might happen. The apostle Paul tells us that the Jews have been blinded against receiving Christ until the full number of Gentile believers has been saved.[32] Are we to say that God suddenly decided to apply affirmative action principles to the Gentiles by denying entry into heaven to his own chosen people until the numbers were properly balanced? Has God reneged on his covenant promises to the Jews, and if he has done that, can he not do the same to us as well? Did not Paul himself warn the Gentiles of this, when he said, "Do not become proud, but fear. For if God did not spare the natural branches, neither will he spare you"?[33] Of course Paul did not think that God would change his mind in an arbitrary fashion. As far as he was concerned, God had planned the whole thing from the beginning and was in full control of events. Nor had he changed in the slightest, as Paul makes perfectly clear:

> As regards the gospel, they [the Jews] are enemies for your sake. But as regards election, they are beloved for the sake of their forefathers. For the gifts and the calling of God are irrevocable. For just as you were at one time disobedient to God but now have received mercy because of their disobe-

[32]Rom. 11:25.
[33]Rom. 11:20–21.

dience, so they too have now been disobedient in order that by the mercy shown to you they also may now receive mercy. For God has consigned all to disobedience, that he may have mercy on all.[34]

God's gifts and calling are irrevocable, and even the disobedient receive mercy, whether they are Jews or Gentiles. People and circumstances change, but God does not, and the promises he has made and fulfilled in the work of Jesus Christ are the same yesterday, today, and forever.[35] If that were not so, no one would be able to believe a word God said, and what passes for "salvation" would vary from one individual to the next. The implications of such a doctrine are devastating, and those who think of our relationship to God primarily in terms of emotional involvement have not stopped long enough to consider those implications properly.

At the same time, classical theists do not deny that there is a genuine two-way relationship between God and his people, and they insist just as much as their critics do that this relationship is a living thing. It is not static, but it is not really "dynamic" either. We would do better to say that it is "energetic." The distinction here is based on the difference between *dynamis* and *energeia*, two Greek words that both mean "power" but that are used in different ways. Properly speaking, *dynamis* is what we would call "potential," whereas *energeia* (from which we get the word "energy") is "realized potential." It is wrong to say that God is "dynamic" because he has no unrealized potential in him. There is no part of him that is un- or under-developed. He is not growing into something more perfect than what he already is, and the creation of the universe does not contribute to his own sense of self-fulfillment.

If we were to say that God is continually growing, we would be saying that God is an imperfect being who must grow and expand in order to perfect himself. We would also be saying that he needs his creation in order to do this and is therefore dependent on it to some degree. In reality, though, God's power is not latent or dormant but fully active. This is why it is best to describe him as "energetic," which means that he uses his power to fulfill his purposes in the universe which he has made and continues to uphold. An energetic God is fully interactive with his creation without being subject to or dependent on it, and therefore he does not change because of his contact with it. An energetic God can and does meet us in our particular circumstances and engages with us in appropriate ways without losing his own transcendence in the process. Indeed, it is because he is energetic in this way that we can know that his power is

---

[34]Rom. 11:28–32.
[35]Heb. 13:8.

always available to assist us. It will not fail us when we need him. An energetic God is flexible without being unpredictable or unreliable, and this is what we are after. This is the saving Lord who reveals himself to us in the Bible, and it is in this way that we should understand his relationship to us.

Furthermore, God's energetic being does not work in the world in and of itself as an abstract thing. It is not some kind of heat that penetrates a body, nor is it like the light that illuminates a room. God's energetic being is known to us in and through his three persons, each of whom acts in the fullness of his power. We can therefore say that in the work of the Son and in the work of the Holy Spirit the fullness of God's being is engaged. There is no reason for us to think that God has revealed only part of his power to us, which would imply that there is something beyond what we have experienced in Christ. The gospel message that we have received is not merely a stage on the way to a higher revelation or a preparation for something greater still to come, as was the case of the Mosaic law. In Christ, we have met God in his fullness and experienced his saving power in a complete and definitive way.[36] There is no higher stage still to come and no spiritual truth still waiting to be revealed. Even at the end of time, when the present world will be brought to its conclusion and we shall be taken up into the eternal life of God, it will be in and through Christ, and Christ alone, that this heavenly reality will be opened up to us. He is the Alpha and the Omega, the beginning and the end, the Almighty.[37]

WHAT GOD IS NOT

Another group of divine attributes that belong together includes God's invisibility, incomprehensibility, and infinity. These things can be distinguished in our minds but in the end they amount to much the same thing. All of them are conceptual negatives—they tell us what God is *not* rather than what he is. This does not mean that they are beyond our understanding, but that we cannot measure or define God in ways that are familiar to us. Today, we have little problem accepting that God is invisible, but when the Bible was written this was a major issue. The gods of the other nations were highly visible, at least in the sense that pictures and statues of them could be seen everywhere, but Israel's God was resolutely different from them. The very first commandment after the one that proclaims God's uniqueness forbids the making of any idol to represent him, and this has always been one of his most obvious distinguishing characteristics.[38]

---

[36]Col. 3:9.
[37]Rev. 1:8.
[38]Ex. 20:4.

The reason for this is revealed to us in the Old Testament. For God to be transcendent he *must* be invisible, since otherwise he could not be everywhere at the same time. Those who argue that invisibility compromises the reality of God's existence are simply foolish—the wind is invisible, but no one doubts that it is there! Only an invisible God can say that heaven is his throne and earth is his footstool.[39] Only he can tell his people that they cannot contain him in a house or temple built by human hands.[40] God cannot be pinned down or controlled by us, even when we are doing what he has told us to do in order to please him.[41] He told the Israelites that he would dwell among them and put his name in Jerusalem,[42] but this did not prevent him from being with them when they were sent into exile in Babylon. His presence in one place did not imply that he was absent everywhere else. The pagan peoples prayed to local deities, and either abandoned them or sought new names for them if they moved elsewhere, but that was never the case with Israel. Yahweh was everywhere, unseen but never unknown by his people.

The incomprehensibility of God is an idea that causes difficulties today because the meaning of the word is narrower than it was in ancient times, when "comprehend" had both a physical and an intellectual meaning. That is still true of a word like "grasp," which we can do with our minds as well as with our hands, and so it would perhaps be better to speak about God's "ungraspability," even if there is no such word in the dictionary. God's incomprehensibility means that he cannot be measured or contained either physically or mentally. Whatever impression we have of him can only be partial, and even if it is accurate as far as it goes, it can never be definitive. Remembering that God is greater than we are is extremely important, particularly when it comes to dealing with questions that arise when things go wrong or our lives take an unexpected turn. We tend to want God to be a certain something or to act in a particular way, and find it hard to cope when he does not conform to our expectations. Sometimes he does things that are meant to make us change our way of thinking and develop a deeper understanding of him, but there are other times when we cannot fathom his purposes and have to admit that there are hidden depths in him that we shall never see. If we understood everything about him, his sovereignty would be compromised because we would find ourselves on a level that was capable of knowing everything. Knowledge is power, and if we fully understood God, we would be able to act like him and even displace him in our lives.

---

[39]Isa. 66:1; Acts 7:49.
[40]2 Sam. 7:5–7; 1 Kings 8:19; 2 Chron. 2:6.
[41]Ps. 50:12–13.
[42]1 Kings 11:36; 14:21; 2 Chron. 6:6; 33:4; Ezra 6:12; Isa. 18:7; Jer. 3:17; Rev. 3:12.

Rebellious human beings try to do just this, which is why the first step on the road to salvation is to remember that there is someone above and beyond us who is immeasurably greater than we are or can ever be.

God is not only much greater than we are, but infinitely greater. Infinity is known in mathematics as the endless extension of a principle. A line can stretch to infinity. There is an infinite number of fractions between one and two. And so on. But from a theological point of view, this kind of infinity is just ongoing finitude; it is something contained within the created universe rather than something that exists beyond it, and so it cannot be equated with infinity in the sense that this term applies to God. Divine infinity means that there are no conceivable limitations that can be placed on God. No matter where we go or what we do, we shall never run out of God or leave him behind. However much we develop in ourselves, we shall never outgrow him.

This point needs to be made today because of a widespread belief that "man has come of age" and can now do without God in the world. One of the positive effects of centuries of Christianity is that it has relegated many traditional religious beliefs to the level of superstition. We no longer live in a mental universe that sees evil powers at work behind natural phenomena or that regards every unusual event as a miracle. There may still be unexplained occurrences but there are no longer "acts of God" in the traditional sense. Scientists may not know how to account for everything that happens, but they believe that there is an explanation that does not need to resort to the concept of a God.

In many ways, this development is positive and beneficial to us as human beings, because it enables us to see the world as the coherent universe that it is, and to rule over it as God intended us to do. But if this knowledge persuades us that God is now superfluous and can be dispensed with, then we are greatly mistaken. He has never been part of this world, and is certainly not confined to those aspects of it that we cannot figure out for ourselves. The Bible tells us that the heavens and the earth are "the work of [God's] fingers,"[43] the implication being that it makes no more sense to look for him in the stars or in the natural world than it would to look for the architect in the bricks and mortar of the house he has built. God dwells in another dimension of reality altogether, which we describe as "infinite" because we have no other word for it and can never hope to define it. All we can say for sure is that whatever we think God is like, he is much more, so that even our highest expectations of him will be exceeded many times over as we grow in our knowledge of him.

---

[43]Ps. 8:3.

THE GOODNESS OF GOD

An important subcategory of divine attributes is the one we generally classify as God's moral qualities. Here it is his essential goodness that springs to mind as the most basic concept, and everything associated with that—his truthfulness, faithfulness, and purity—depends ultimately on that goodness. It is because God is good that he is truthful, because he is good that he is reliable, and because he is good that he is consistent. As the apostle James expressed it, "Every good gift and every perfect gift is from above, coming down from the Father of lights with whom there is no variation or shadow due to change."[44] These things are clear to Christians because we have experienced God in this way, but we need to think about them more deeply if we are to understand their meaning properly. What exactly does it mean to say that God is good? When we go back to the Genesis account of creation, we see that this word can be used in two somewhat different senses. On the one hand, there is what we might call structural goodness, which is what the creation story is primarily talking about. When God made the world, he saw that it was very good, meaning that it perfectly realized what he intended. That kind of goodness is inherent in all created things, and we may suppose that it reflects something in the character of God, because he is the perfect being.

But important as this is, it is not the kind of goodness that we immediately think of, even in this context. Adam and Eve were good in that way and remained so, even after they fell. But when we think of them, we think primarily of their moral goodness, which they were unaware of as long as they possessed it and came to recognize only after they had lost it by their disobedience. Human moral goodness is defined in the Bible as obedience to the commands of God, but we can hardly define God's goodness in that way, since he is not required to be obedient to anyone.[45] Goodness in God must therefore be something different from what it is in us, even if the way it manifests itself bears some resemblance to what we would recognize as good.

What do we mean when we say that God is "good"? We may be tempted to reply that his character must correspond to the commandments he has given us, because if it does not, the nature of our fellowship with him would be called into question. We might argue that if God saw nothing wrong with murder, theft, or adultery, it would be hard to see why he would want to prevent us from indulging in them. Presumably he has told us that they are wrong because they go against what he is like in himself. This seems obvi-

---

[44]James 1:17.
[45]See, for example, 1 Sam. 13:8–14.

ous, but a little thought will show that things are more subtle than that. It is all very well for us to say that God does not kill, commit adultery, steal, or bear false witness against his neighbor, but what do such things mean in his case? Who would God steal from, since everything already belongs to him? What neighbors does he have? How could he commit adultery? If he chooses to kill, that is his right, since whatever he destroys is something he has made.[46] The simple truth is that the categories by which we measure goodness do not apply to God, either because they are meaningless in his case or because his sovereign power is not subject to any law. For that reason, a checklist of moral precepts, however valid it may be when applied to us, cannot be the standard by which we measure God's goodness. To do that, we have to go beyond particular examples of goodness as we experience it in our lives, and look for the underlying principle that gives those examples their meaning.

Jesus summarized the moral law in two commandments: first, that we should love God with all our heart, soul, mind, and strength, and second, that we should love our neighbors as ourselves.[47] The first of these obviously cannot apply to God, except perhaps in the sense that the three persons of the Trinity love each other in this totally committed way. The second one, however, does have a relevance to God, because by creating us in his image and likeness, he has established a relationship with us that is not unlike that between human neighbors. In telling us that we must love our fellow men as we love ourselves, God is also telling us that he loves us as he loves himself. There is an interconnectedness in divine and human relationships that is brought out by the love God has for us and that he expects us to have both for him and for one another. It is in this complex structure of relationships that we can see most clearly what the goodness of God means for us.

To love others means we must respect them and avoid doing things that would harm or diminish them. This is as true of God as it is of human beings. We are called to respect God, not just because he is our Creator but also because we are called to love him, and love entails respect. God is not obliged to respect us as his creatures, but because he loves us he also respects us as a sign and outworking of that love. God does not invade our lives or take advantage of his position as our Creator in order to diminish us or to deprive us of what he has given us in our creation. On the contrary, his rule over us is benevolent and helps us to survive and flourish in the world he has made for us to enjoy. As Jeremiah put it,

---

[46]See the argument to this effect in Rom. 9:19–23.
[47]Mark 12:30–31.

> The steadfast love of the LORD never ceases,
>   his mercies never come to an end;
> they are new every morning,
>   great is your faithfulness.[48]

Or as the psalmist sang,

> You prepare a table before me
>   in the presence of my enemies;
> you anoint my head with oil;
>   my cup overflows.
> Surely goodness and mercy shall follow me
>   all the days of my life,
> and I shall dwell in the house of the LORD
>   forever.[49]

Wherever we are and whatever our circumstances may be, the hand of God is upon us, shielding us from harm, bestowing all kinds of blessings on us, and leading us to eternal life in heaven. Everything else proceeds from that, and it is in this daily provision and protection that we come to understand what it means for us to say that God is "good."

There is, however, another way in which God's goodness is known to us, and that is by considering its opposite. Just as Adam and Eve found out what goodness was when they were exposed to evil, so we can measure the goodness of God by contrasting it with the evil that we experience. Everything that comes into our lives from Satan is the opposite of what God wants for us and may be considered "evil." By learning to recognize that and reject it, we come to understand what goodness really is. Fundamental to this is the notion of truthfulness. Like goodness, the question of truthfulness did not arise until evil appeared, since there was nothing to be untruthful about. We see this clearly in the story of the garden of Eden, because after Adam and Eve had disobeyed God, they felt the need to clothe themselves and to hide from him in a way that they had not done before. It was only when they realized that they were naked that the truth of their helplessness dawned on them and they reacted against it. It had always been there, but as long as they were obedient to God it did not matter, because they trusted in him and in his faithfulness to them and it never occurred to them to do anything else.[50] Only when that

---

[48]Lam. 3:22–23.
[49]Ps. 23:5–6.
[50]Gen. 3:7–11.

relationship of trust was broken did the problem arise and the truth become something hard to face.

As human beings, we still spend our lives hiding from the truth one way or another. We cannot face the fact that we are miserable sinners, condemned by our own actions to a life of misery in separation from the God who made us. We may accept that we are less than perfect, but we still want to believe that with some effort on our part, we can put matters right and stand a reasonable chance of keeping God happy, or at least happy enough to let us into heaven. What we cannot accept is that we are so bad that there is no way we could ever earn our way into God's presence, and that he rejects our pitiful efforts to do so precisely because they are so inadequate. Look around at the religions and philosophies on offer in the spiritual marketplace and there is one thing common to them all: they all say that, deep down inside, we are fundamentally good, and with a little help and training we can make ourselves even better.

This way of thinking flatters our pride and is very popular, but it is false, and God cannot endure falsehood. In being truthful with us, he helps us to see what is wrong with our self-perception and prepares the ground so that he can put it right in our lives. In his faithfulness to us he accomplishes what is needed and does what he has promised he would do. In his purity, he persists until the work is completed because nothing imperfect, however small and insignificant it may seem, can stand in his presence. It all comes back to his goodness in the end. It was his goodness that created us and provided everything we would need for sustenance in this life. It was his goodness that reached out to us when we were disobedient, and provided a means to reconcile us to him. And it is his goodness that does its best to make us fully aware of the reality of our fallen condition, not in order to condemn us with that knowledge but in order to persuade us to trust in his goodness for forgiveness and eternal salvation.

WHAT GOD LETS US SHARE WITH HIM

Most of God's attributes are proper to himself and cannot be shared with anyone or anything else, but one of the more amazing aspects of his sovereignty is that he is powerful enough to be able to extend some of his attributes to us, even though they are contrary to our human nature. Of these, the most important one is what we call his "holiness." As with his lordship, it is hard to see what this word could possibly mean inside God himself. The word "holy" basically means "separate," but God can be separate only if there is something for him to be separate from! It therefore makes no sense as far as his own being is concerned, but it does become meaningful when we talk about his relationship with his creation, which by definition is totally different from him and therefore completely "separate" (i.e., "distinct") from his being. God's holiness includes everything about him that sets him apart from the world, but over the years it has come to be understood primarily in relation to his moral and spiritual character.

In a world that has fallen into the grip of evil forces to which even human beings are subject, God stands out as someone who is not only completely different but whose demands on us run counter to what have now become our "natural" inclinations.[51] In practical terms, God's holiness is that aspect of his nature which makes it impossible for us, his disobedient creatures, to enjoy fellowship with him. For us to be holy does not mean that we must conform to his nature in every respect, since that is impossible. Even if we were perfect, we would not be invisible or omnipotent, nor would God expect us to be like him in ways that run counter to the way we were created. What he wants is for us to "have his mind in us," as the apostle Paul put it.[52] For us to be holy is to know what God likes and to learn to like it ourselves. Married couples discover what this involves as they work at their relationship, but being only human, they seldom succeed completely, and may end up merely tolerating their spouse's likes and dislikes when they cannot share them. This may be inevitable in a fallen human world, but in this respect our relationship with God goes beyond what we can realistically achieve with one another. Being holy does not mean learning to tolerate God's differences because we cannot change him, but rather being changed ourselves so that we are truly united with him in heart and mind. This is possible only as a fruit of love—our love for him, but even more, his transforming love for us which makes us children of God in a way that we could never otherwise be.

We have been given the privilege of being allowed to understand what God's purposes are, and to share in his way of thinking. We are holy because we have been set apart to serve him in all that we think, say, and do. Knowing the mind of the Lord does not automatically make us morally or spiritually perfect; on the contrary, it is more likely to remind us just how far short of the ideal we actually fall. But we also know that if we are holy in God's eyes, we have been given the divine power and protection we need to fight against "the lusts of the flesh," as the Authorized (King James) Bible so colorfully puts

---

[51]We must be careful here. The inclinations we now have are "natural" only in the sense that they reflect our fallen human condition. With respect to the way God created us, they are in fact *unnatural*, which is why God disapproves of them.

[52]See 1 Cor. 2:16; Phil. 2:5.

it.[53] Because of this, Christians can and do live in a way that goes against what the surrounding world expects and which it finds incomprehensible. Sooner or later, everyone who believes in Christ will discover that his or her thoughts are different from those of other people, and that those thoughts lead us to do things that make no sense to our non-Christian neighbors, who have no conception of the mind of God. This is what God's holiness means as far as we are concerned, but it is only partly and imperfectly related to what we normally think of as "morality."

There have always been Christians who have interpreted holiness as meaning that we must "deny the world" in the sense of avoiding or abstaining from certain clearly defined activities. To them, being holy means not doing certain things, such as dancing, drinking, smoking, and so on. The precise details change over time and may be quite different from one church to another—let us not forget, for example, that for the Roman Catholic and Eastern Orthodox traditions, celibacy is a mark of holiness, something that seems strange to most Protestants. In spite of differences like these, however, today we can probably say that thoughtful people of all traditions realize that our holiness as Christians is determined by what comes from our hearts and minds and not by things that are external to us, as Jesus himself taught.[54] There may be excellent reasons for not doing certain things, and Christians are called to use their freedom in a way that is edifying and profitable to others, but it is the love which that shows for our neighbors and not the abstinence or avoidance itself that reflects our holiness.[55]

Unfortunately, the fact that most modern Christians no longer interpret the concept of holiness as a series of taboos has often led, not to a deeper walk with God but to a different problem which is just as bad if not worse. Instead of recovering a biblical sense of holiness, the modern church is in danger of losing any clear idea of what holiness means or why it matters. The sad fact is that nowadays hardly anyone asks what they have to do in order to be holy, because they do not really want to be. There are people today whose parents would not have shopped on a Sunday because of the fourth commandment who now divorce and remarry almost as a matter of course, completely forgetting Jesus' teaching that those who do such things are committing adultery.[56] Worse still, ministers of the church are often just as bad as anyone else, and so are hardly in a position to exhort their flocks to more godly behavior! As a concept, holiness has virtually

---

[53] 2 Pet. 2:18.
[54] Matt. 15:10, 18–20.
[55] 1 Cor. 6:12; 10:23.
[56] Matt. 19:3–9.

disappeared from the Christian vocabulary, and we have to admit that the main reason for this is that it has also disappeared from the experience of many Christians.

And yet we cannot get away from holiness quite as easily as that. To be a Christian is not to pursue a life of moral perfection that is beyond our grasp, which can only lead to despair and failure. Holiness is a gift of God that forms an essential part of our relationship with him. If we know Jesus Christ as our Lord and Savior, we are holy whether or not we want to be. Therefore the task facing us is not to acquire holiness in some way but to manifest the holiness we already have by God's gift. What does that mean? We cannot leave the world, but must live in it as children of God.[57] Fortunately for us, God's sovereignty extends to this world and he is actively at work in it, so we are not being called to do something that is impossible. Rather, we are being asked to live in tune with the Lord of the universe and to enjoy his creation in the way that Adam and Eve were originally meant to. To be holy is to be world-affirming, not world-denying, but it is to be world-affirming in the way that God originally intended his creatures to be and not by giving in to the temptations that its desires can so easily lead us into.

This has to be said, because the Bible often uses the term "world" as a way of referring to the results of the rebellion of Satan and his angels, into which he has seduced the human race. The Devil is called the "ruler of this world," and we are told to flee him because we are holy.[58] What does this mean in practice? The apostle Paul knew that it would be impossible for Christians to cut themselves off completely from the world, and made it clear to the Corinthians that he did not expect them to try to do that.[59] At the same time, however, he also told them that they had a responsibility to govern their own affairs and to behave in a way that would reflect the holiness that God has given to us. By teaching us how to look at the world, God delivers us from its clutches and allows us to assert control over it.[60] The world itself is not evil, any more than the wood and stone that went into the making of idols in ancient times were bad in themselves. What is evil is spiritual submission to something created, whether it is an angel like Satan or a material object. To be set free from being controlled by worldly things is to be set free to do God's will in the world, which is the essence of true holiness and the way in which we are called to be like him.

Another divine attribute that God gives to us is his eternity. This gift is the

---

[57] 1 Cor. 5:10.
[58] John 12:31; 14:30; 16:11.
[59] 1 Cor. 5:9–10.
[60] Rom. 12:2.

supreme manifestation of his sovereign power, because it takes us out of our status as creatures who have been made in time and space and are therefore bound to them, and raises us to the level of his own eternal being. How this can happen is a mystery that has puzzled theologians through the ages, but it is God's promise to us and something that is within his capacity to fulfill. It is not very helpful to say that God will extend his own eternity to us, because that could be understood as a denial of our creation rather than a transformation of it. As far as we can tell, we shall still be finite creatures in eternity, more like the angels in that respect than like God himself. We have been promised a spiritual body and know that in that body we shall neither marry nor procreate (again like the angels), but beyond that not much has been revealed to us about it.[61] We have also been told that when we see God face-to-face we shall know and understand the mysteries currently hidden from our eyes, which presumably means that we shall see past, present, and future all as one, but we have no way of understanding that now.[62]

God's eternity is an eternal present, the mode that he uses to describe himself to us. The present is not a temporal concept, and yet it is the only means we have of distinguishing the past from the future. In popular speech we use the word "present" to describe what is really the immediate past and the foreseeable future, because strictly speaking, there is no "now." As soon as we utter the word "now," it retreats into the past and becomes "then." Yet in spite of this, we all live in the present and think of past and future time in relation to it. Furthermore, we carry our own present around with us through time, never abandoning it, however long we live on this earth. It is the most permanent reality in our lives, yet it does not really exist—at least, not in this world. To be present is therefore in some sense to be eternal. It is our concept of the present that allows us to connect with God and permits him to speak to us in time and space. Just as our notion of the present does not change, God does not change either, and neither does our relationship with him. Even in this world, we have a share in the firstfruits of eternal life because we are children of God. His eternity is present in us and there it remains, whether we are in the body or out of it. One day we shall leave this body behind, but God will not cease to be present in our lives. On the contrary, the eternal reality of his presence will shine out even more clearly than it already does and we shall be changed "from one degree of glory to another" as we contemplate and adore him forever.[63]

---

[61] 1 Cor. 15:35–58; Matt. 22:30.
[62] 1 Cor. 13:9–12.
[63] 2 Cor. 3:18.

This is the hope of the resurrection, the promise of eternal reward, and the fulfillment of God's purpose in and for our lives. To achieve this, he gives us what we need—first of all holiness, without which no one can see the Lord,[64] and then eternity, which will permit us not only to see him but to dwell with him in light forever.

---

[64]Heb. 12:14.

9

THE GOD OF THE OLD TESTAMENT AND THE FATHER OF JESUS CHRIST

THE GOD OF THE OLD TESTAMENT

The persons of the Trinity can be known only in the context of their mutual relations. It is not possible to know one or two of them without knowing all three, because they are inseparable and each of them reveals the others to us. But what are we to make of the revelation of God to his people in the Old Testament? The Israelites knew God as one, not as three, and the early Christians never denied the authenticity of their experience or dissociated themselves from it. Yet if we agree that the Israelites knew God, how can we explain the fact that not only did they not know him as a Trinity of persons but their descendants have consistently rejected the Christian doctrine on the ground that it is incompatible with a truly biblical monotheism?

Various answers have been given to these questions. The first and simplest is to deny the existence of a Trinity altogether. From an inter-faith point of view, this might have the advantage of bringing Christians closer to Jews and Muslims, both of whom suspect the Christian doctrine of being polytheistic. The word "Trinity" does not occur in the Bible, and so it is not an obviously biblical doctrine. It was elaborated in the early centuries of the church, and many theologians would argue that our doctrine of the Trinity reflects external influences from the Greco-Roman world more than the teaching of the New Testament. It is also easier to believe that Jesus was a great man than to accept that he was God in human flesh. That belief was the subject of long and bitter controversies in the church, which would have been avoided had the divinity of Christ never become an issue in the first place. It would not even be necessary for the church to alter its devotional practices, since there are already many Christians who pray to different saints, none of whom is regarded as being God. Could Jesus not simply be treated as the greatest of them and be venerated accordingly?

All these arguments have been made at different times, but none of them has succeeded in overturning traditional Christian belief. They have failed because the cumulative evidence of the New Testament points toward the divinity of Christ to such an extent that to deny it is to make the text incoherent. However close to Jewish monotheism we may be, Christians will always make claims about Jesus that will go beyond anything a Jew can accept as being compatible with his own faith. To put it another way, if we were to accept Jewish monotheism as definitive, we would cease to be Christians because we would find that Jesus' teaching about himself breaks the mold of traditional Jewish theology. If we were to stick to Judaism we would have no choice but to reject Jesus as our Lord and Savior.[1]

Another possible approach to this question is to say that the Jews experienced the persons of the Trinity in different guises, but they never developed a doctrine comparable to that of the Christian church because their knowledge of God was partial and incomplete.[2] Had they understood what we know thanks to the coming of Christ and the sending of the Holy Spirit, they would have come to the same conclusions that we have reached on the basis of a deeper revelation. As it is, we can look back into the Old Testament and find there indications of the Trinity that were hidden from the eyes of the ancient Israelites but have become clear to us now. Proponents of this view have read their Trinitarian interpretation of the Old Testament as far back as the creation story, where God says, "Let us make man in our image, after our likeness."[3] Similarly, after Adam and Eve succumbed to temptation, God said, "Behold, the man has become like one of us in knowing good and evil."[4] Who was he talking to when he said these things?

In the Old Testament, the name of God often (though not always) appears in the plural form "Elohim" instead of the singular "El." Furthermore, there are several instances where the Word of the Lord, the Spirit of the Lord, and the Wisdom of the Lord are personified, or at least described in ways that sug-

---

[1]See John 8:12–30.
[2]See Heb. 1:1.
[3]Gen. 1:26.
[4]Gen. 3:22.

gest they might be agents in their own right.[5] The apostle Paul even identified the rock that followed the people of Israel in the desert as Christ, even though there is nothing in the original text to suggest that the Israelites thought of it in personal terms, let alone divine ones.[6] Even more significantly, Jesus told his Jewish opponents that the Old Testament spoke about him, and after his resurrection he walked his disciples through the text, pointing out to them how that was the case.[7]

There is therefore some reason for Christians to believe that a notion of the Trinity is present in the Jewish Scriptures, even if it is nowhere clearly stated as such. But the fact remains that Jews have never read the Bible that way and have always rejected such interpretations of it. Is this blindness on their part, or are there good grounds for their unwillingness to accept such Christian readings of the texts? To answer this question, we must look at what Jesus meant when he accused the Jews of his day of failing to see him in the Scriptures, and compare that with the claims that later generations of Christians have made about them.

The teaching of Jesus was primarily concerned with the fulfillment of God's promises that he would redeem Israel from its sins, rescue it from its enemies, and establish it forever as a righteous nation reflecting his eternal glory. Most Jews who thought about how this would be accomplished had come to believe that, at the end of time, God would send the Messiah, or "anointed one," who would rally the people to his standard, expel the foreign invaders who had subdued them, and set up an empire in Jerusalem that would dominate the world. Messianic figures were not unknown in Jesus' day, though they were invariably discredited by their failure to do any of the things expected of them. Undoubtedly there were some who thought of Jesus in the same way, and had he openly proclaimed himself as Messiah, they would have assumed that he had come to fulfill their Messianic expectations and would then have been devastated by his failure to do so.[8] As we know, Jesus had a different conception of who the Messiah would be and what he would do, and most of his earthly ministry was taken up with his attempts to teach people about that. When he told the Jewish leaders to search the Scriptures, he expected them to see that the Messiah would come to Israel as the suffering servant, who would make the atoning sacrifice that would deal with the sins of the people once and for all. This pattern was clearly laid out in the Old Testament, but it seems that no one who looked for the coming of

---

[5]Prov. 8:22–36 is a particularly good example of this.
[6]1 Cor. 10:4. For the original story, see Ex. 17:6.
[7]John 5:39; Luke 24:25–27.
[8]See Luke 24:19–21.

the Messiah thought to connect their hope with what the law of Moses was essentially all about.

In the course of justifying his claims, Jesus had to explain what it was that gave him the authority to interpret the Scriptures as he did, and it is here that we find the revelation that he was God in human flesh. For a man to appropriate the biblical text to himself was blasphemy in Jewish eyes, because it amounted to a claim to be God. And as they saw it, that is precisely what Jesus did when he called God his Father.[9]

No one has ever doubted that the God of the Old Testament related to his people in personal terms. He spoke to his people, heard their prayers, and acted on their behalf. Although there was a strict prohibition against making idols of God,[10] and the notion that it is possible to see God was always firmly rejected, even in the New Testament,[11] there are many instances in which God is described as if he were a heavenly man. Phrases like the "arm of the LORD" and the "eyes of the LORD" are common in the Old Testament, and he is even portrayed as a king whose throne is heaven and whose footstool is the earth.[12] No one has ever taken this imagery literally, but the use of such phrases is enough to remind us that God is portrayed as a person in relationship with his people, not as an abstract power that determines their fate without any contact or interaction between them.

At the same time, however, the Old Testament picture of God is that he is one person, not three. The use of the plural form Elohim can be explained either as a plural of majesty or as a linguistic device used to describe a being who is too immense to be conceived of in the singular. In Hebrew, not only the name of God but words like "heaven" and "water" are plural, presumably because they are too extensive to be thought of as mere objects. The plural expressions attributed to God in the creation account are more promising for those trying to find evidence of the Trinity, but God may have been speaking to his angels, who also knew the difference between good and evil, and Jews have usually interpreted it in this way. We cannot rule out the suggestion that the Father was talking to the Son and the Holy Spirit in these verses, but that is not specified in the texts, and we must be cautious about drawing such a conclusion. Apart from anything else, there is no reason to suppose that the plural form that God used was restricted to only three persons. In any case, such possibilities are far-fetched when compared with the overwhelming evidence of the rest of the Old Testament, where God speaks in the singular and

---

[9] John 5:18–40.
[10] Ex. 20:4.
[11] John 1:18; 1 John 4:12.
[12] Isa. 51:9; Prov. 15:3; Isa. 66:1.

is clearly understood in that way. "The LORD our God, the LORD is one. You shall love the LORD your God with all your heart and with all your soul and with all your might."[13] This was the confession of Israel, and it was picked up by Jesus, for whom it was the essence of the law of Moses.[14] Later on, when speaking about the work of Christ, the apostle Paul made the same point, when he said that there is one God and one mediator between God and men, the *man* Christ Jesus.[15] Even in that context, where the Son is explicitly mentioned, the essential oneness of God was not to be compromised.

The Old Testament gives us no clear example of a prayer addressed to God as Father. The closest it comes to this is when Isaiah says, "But now, O LORD, you are our Father; we are the clay, and you are our potter; we are all the work of your hand."[16] Isaiah is acknowledging God as Creator, and using the term "Father" to express that, but although he goes on to plead for mercy to be shown to Israel because they are his people, he does not mention the concept of spiritual sonship. That concept does occur in the Pentateuch, both in Moses' challenge to Pharaoh to let the people of Israel go and later on when they were in the desert.[17] The only other instances where God is addressed directly as Father occur in Jeremiah 3, but the second of these is more hypothetical than real and the first is somewhat obscure, being more like a cry of desperation than a regular pattern of worship.[18] Israel's spiritual sonship was a collective term, not an individual one, and Jews did not normally think of God as their Father in a personal way or address him as such in their prayers.[19]

The great exception to the rule was the case of Solomon, the son of David. It was not Solomon who called God his Father, however, but the other way around. Furthermore, this statement occurs in verses where God is not speaking to Solomon but to David, promising that he would be a father to Solomon and establish his kingdom forever.[20] Solomon would have known this, but that knowledge does not seem to have influenced the way he prayed, nor is there any sign that Solomon was particularly close to God. On the contrary, toward the end of his life, Solomon turned away from God and was punished for his disobedience.[21] When Jesus came as the son of David to fulfill the promises originally made about Solomon, he knew what he was saying when he told

---

[13]Deut. 6:4–5.
[14]Matt. 22:37.
[15]1 Tim. 2:5.
[16]Isa. 64:8.
[17]Ex. 4:22–23; Deut. 14:1.
[18]Jer. 3:4, 19.
[19]John 8:37–59.
[20]2 Sam. 7:14; 1 Chron. 17:13; 22:10; 28:6; Ps. 89:26.
[21]1 Kings 11:1–40.

the Jews that someone greater than Solomon had come.[22] The promise made to David concerning Solomon is the only instance in the Old Testament of a father-son relationship between God and a man, but it was tied to an everlasting kingship vested in the house of David, and no member of that family, including Solomon, lived up to what was expected of him. By the time of Jesus, the whole thing had become a dead letter in practice, since the house of David had long ceased to reign and the rulers of the time had a vested interest in making sure that no member of his family would ever rise to prominence again.[23]

We can therefore understand why it was that, when Jesus spoke of his Father, the Jewish leaders were scandalized that he would dare to refer to God with such familiarity.[24] In their understanding, to call God "Father" was to claim to be divine, since a child has the same nature as its parent. Even Jesus' own disciples did not understand what he was talking about and wanted him to show them the Father, somewhat to his exasperation![25] We may therefore conclude that, however legitimate it might have been for an ancient Israelite to call God his Father, such language was not used in ancient Israel and would have provoked a negative reaction from anyone who introduced it. If some modern Jews are prepared to speak in this way, it is almost certainly because they have been influenced by Christians and have expanded their traditional language to accommodate an ingredient of the Old Testament revelation that was not appreciated by their ancestors.

When all the evidence is taken into account, it seems safe to say that God did not reveal himself to the Israelites as their Father, and he was never referred to in that way, except possibly as a synonym for "Creator." But Christians cannot leave the matter there. God spoke to the Jews as a single person and we know him as three. Does this mean that in the Old Testament, only one of the three persons whom we know, presumably the Father, spoke to Israel, or that all three spoke together with a single voice? To answer this question we have to turn to the New Testament, and especially to the teaching of Jesus. If we assume that when Jesus was talking about God he was referring to the God of the Old Testament, then it seems clear that Jesus identified him as the Father. The most famous example of this comes in the Lord's Prayer, where he teaches his disciples to pray, "Our Father in heaven."[26]

The disciples could not have distinguished the Father from Yahweh, and the same must be true of the other instances in the Gospels where Jesus spoke

---

[22]Matt. 12:42.
[23]This explains the behavior of King Herod in Matt. 2:16.
[24]John 5:18.
[25]John 14:8–9.
[26]Matt. 6:9.

of his Father in a way that clearly meant the Old Testament God. In contrast to this, he identified himself as the Son, and spoke of the Holy Spirit as one who was still to come.[27] It is obvious that when Jesus was praying to the Father, he was praying to another person, however closely connected to that person he may have been.[28] Put all this together and it seems clear that Yahweh and the Father are one and the same. Yet at the same time, Jesus also told his disciples that he was identical to the Father to such an extent that to see him was to see the Father also.[29] We are also told that the Son created the world, which makes it impossible to make a simple equation between "Father" and "Creator."[30] Since creation is the first and greatest of God's acts recorded in the Bible, and Israel's devotion to God was always closely tied to it, it seems that some allowance for the presence of at least a hidden Trinity must be made when speaking of Yahweh.

The best solution, and one which seems to match all the scriptural data, is that the one God of the Old Testament is to be equated with the Trinitarian God of the New, his oneness being accounted for by the fact that in the Old Testament he is speaking in the person of the Father, whose identity is fully revealed only in Jesus Christ. In support of this, we can mention two characteristics peculiar to the Father which are manifested by the Old Testament God. The first of these is his utter transcendence. At no point does the Father enter his creation or become visible in any way, a truth that is attested everywhere in Scripture. Second, Yahweh deals with his people through intermediaries and not directly. This is an aspect of his transcendence, but it has special importance, because in the New Testament it is the Holy Spirit who comes to dwell in our hearts and who gives us the ability to pray to God as our Father.[31] In the Old Testament, God speaks to his people through spiritual messengers (angels), by means of physical phenomena like fire and cloud,[32] and by visitations of his Spirit. No one ever saw him face-to-face, except Jacob and Moses, whose special roles in the life of God's people are underlined by that extraordinary fact.[33]

THE FATHER OF JESUS CHRIST

It is important to say that the Father of Jesus Christ is not to be understood as the personification of the divine substance. Many Christians, however,

---

[27]John 14:16–17.
[28]John 17:1–5.
[29]John 10:30; 14:8–9.
[30]John 1:3; Col. 1:16.
[31]Gal. 4:6.
[32]Ex. 13:21.
[33]Gen. 32:30; Deut. 34:10.

believe that he is, whether or not they say so openly. To their way of thinking, the Father is God in absolute terms, whereas the Son and the Holy Spirit are God only in a relative sense, because they supposedly derive their divinity from him. The Father is therefore considered to be the default person of the Godhead, which means that unless a biblical text specifies that "God" refers to the Son or the Holy Spirit, it should be taken as referring primarily to the Father. This position is supported by the fact that there is at least one instance where the word "God" is used along with the Son and the Holy Spirit, and it seems that it must be referring to the Father. This is the well-known text that reads, "The grace of the Lord Jesus Christ and the love of God and the fellowship of the Holy Spirit be with you all."[34] At first sight this argument sounds very persuasive, and we must not be surprised that it has convinced a great many people. Nevertheless, there are serious difficulties with this view that must also be taken into consideration before a final judgment is made.

First, as we have already noted, it is not possible to regard the Father alone as the sole Creator of the universe, as many of those who have identified Yahweh with the Father have done. The New Testament makes it perfectly clear that the Son is also the Creator, and the inference is drawn that the Holy Spirit is too, although that is not stated explicitly in the New Testament.[35] In other words, the Creator is God the Holy Trinity working together and not just one of the divine persons acting on his own. The history of the early church reminds us that identifying the Father alone as the Creator is risky because it opens the door to saying that the Son and the Holy Spirit must be creatures, and if they are creatures they cannot be God. There is no neutral ground here—the divide between the Creator and his creation is absolute, and one must be on one side or the other. If the Son and the Holy Spirit are truly God, as the New Testament tells us they are, then they must be co-Creators with the Father, who therefore does not (and cannot) stand in a creator-creature relationship to them.

Second, there are difficulties if we equate the covenant God of Israel with the Father alone, because however much that might seem to accord with the facts revealed to us in the Old Testament, we must bear in mind that Jesus told the Jews that Abraham knew about his coming and rejoiced in it.[36] Unfortunately, Jesus does not refer to any Old Testament text in support of this statement, which makes it hard to know what he had in mind when he made this claim. Perhaps he was thinking of the curious passage in Genesis

---

[34] 2 Cor. 13:14.
[35] For the Son, see John 1:3; Col. 1:16; Heb. 1:1. For the Holy Spirit, see what Paul says in Rom. 8:18–27.
[36] John 8:56–58.

18:1–21, where three men appeared to Abraham at Mamre but he addressed them in the singular as "Lord." The Jewish scholar Philo of Alexandria (d. A.D. 50) believed that this was an indication that some form of threeness exists in the one God, and a long Christian tradition has accepted it as a revelation of the Trinity in the Old Testament, though it was never mentioned either by Jesus or by his disciples.

It might be possible to argue that Jesus was saying that Abraham had a vision of the future, and if so, that might conceivably have been based on Genesis 22:8–14, but Jesus says nothing about that passage and appears to rule out such an interpretation by adding that he existed even before Abraham did. We are left to conclude that the God whom Abraham encountered was the Holy Trinity, even if he was not consciously aware of it at the time. If that is true, then the covenant God of Israel must be more than just the Father, even if the threeness of God is not mentioned or acknowledged in the Old Testament.

Third, the Father cannot exist on his own because he would not be the Father if there were no Son. The word is intrinsically relational and requires the existence of a child for it to have any meaning. If we take a human analogy and say that a man exists before becoming a father, we shall see immediately why this cannot be applied to God. If we were to say that God existed before becoming the Father, we would be locating the generation of the Son in time. That in turn would force us to say that either the Son is not God because he is not eternal, or that he is no more than a temporal manifestation of the divine and so not a person in his own right. Neither of these options does justice to the New Testament evidence, and both must be rejected.

Finally, we are told in the New Testament that it is the Son who has made the Father known. This he has done in the course of revealing himself as the Son who stands in a unique relationship to the Father.[37] Israel knew God, but it did not know that there was a Father-Son relationship in him, nor did it conceive of the Spirit as a distinct person. Jesus pointed out that the Old Testament spoke of him, but the Jews were not persuaded by his arguments, and in the end most of them rejected him. We can only conclude that such people did not know God as their Father in the way that Jesus meant them to, because if they had, they would have known and acknowledged the Son also. They could not be blamed for this as long as it had not been revealed to them, but when Jesus made the Father known, those Jews who rejected his message demonstrated by that rejection that they did not really know God at all.[38]

---

[37] John 1:18.
[38] John 8:19; 14:7.

Having said that, there are passages in the New Testament where it is clear that the word "God" refers both to the God of the Old Testament and to the Father of Jesus Christ. Hebrews 1:1–2 is a good example of this:

> Long ago, at many times and in many ways, God spoke to our fathers by the prophets, but in these last days he has spoken to us by his Son, whom he appointed the heir of all things, through whom also he created the world.

This verse neatly summarizes the three key things we have to say about the relationship between the Old Testament God and the Father of Jesus. The first is that the God who spoke by the prophets in the Old Testament is the same one who is now speaking to us through his Son. The difference is not that God has changed from one Testament to the other, but that now he is saying something more complete and more profound than anything he had said earlier.

What God said to the ancient Jews remains fully authoritative as his eternal Word, which is not canceled out or overturned by the coming of Jesus, but at the same time, the revelation of Jesus takes us to another level of perception. The first thing it does is enable us to recognize both the Son as God and God as his Father. Second, it restates the standard New Testament view that the Son is the Creator of the world, alongside the Father, and therefore is not a creature. Finally, it defines sonship in legal terms—the Son is the *heir* of all things, a position to which he is entitled precisely because he is himself God. Taken together, these three elements constitute the key ingredients of our belief that the God of the Old Testament is now revealed to us not as the Father alone but as the Father in fellowship with the Son and the Holy Spirit.

THE PERSON AND WORK OF THE FATHER

We have now seen why the God of the Old Testament must be the Trinity of the New Testament, and that although the name Yahweh indicates the oneness of his being, he does not communicate with us at that abstract level. God always speaks in and through one of his persons, and in the Old Testament that person is the one we know as the Father of Jesus Christ. From there we can deduce the following:

1. It is the particular task of the Father to reveal to us the *oneness* of the divine being. He did this at different times and in different ways, but the underlying message was always the same: "I am the LORD your God. . . . You shall have no other gods before me."[39] "The LORD our God, the LORD is

---

[39]Ex. 20:2–3.

one."[40] It is for this reason that the Son is described as being begotten from the Father and the Holy Spirit as proceeding from the Father—their divinity is expressed in relation to him. However, this does not mean that the Son and the Holy Spirit *derive* their divinity from the Father. Nor does it mean that the name "Father" is a personification of the divine being with no intrinsic value as a description of his personal identity and therefore can be abandoned or replaced by some other word. Because of its inherent uniqueness, the oneness of God's being surpasses definition and cannot be expressed in relational terms. It does not have a personal identity of its own, although it is the Father's role within the Trinity to express that oneness in relation to the other persons. He is not that oneness himself, but he represents it, and it is for that reason that the other persons are identified in relation to him.

2. The Father also shows us that the divine being is eternally transcendent and that it is not diminished, either by the incarnation of the Son or by the descent of the Holy Spirit. During the Son's incarnation on earth many people saw him, even if most of them failed to recognize who he was, and there is some indication that the work of the Holy Spirit may also be felt by people who do not understand who he is.[41] But the Father remains hidden and inaccessible, except to those who come to him by way of Jesus Christ, and no one can do that unless he or she is filled with the Holy Spirit.[42] The eternal transcendence of the Father and the intimate union between him and the Son are the guarantee that, when the Son "emptied himself" and took the form of a servant in order to become a man,[43] nothing was taken away from his divinity. At every point during his earthly ministry, the Son was in the same close relationship with the Father that characterizes his existence in eternity, and it was on that basis that he accomplished what he did for the salvation of mankind. Similarly, the work of the Holy Spirit who dwells in our hearts is possible and effective only because he too is anchored in the oneness of the divine being—which is expressed in and by his eternal procession from the Father.[44]

Every statement we make about the Son and the Holy Spirit must be interpreted in the light of their relationship with the Father, a relationship which is so close that it guarantees that there can be no contradiction between them. If someone claims to have received a word from the Holy Spirit which does not conform to the teaching of the Son, or which is not

---

[40]Deut. 6:4.
[41]John 3:8.
[42]John 14:6; 1 Cor. 12:3.
[43]Phil. 2:7.
[44]John 15:26.

supported by the revelation of the Father's will in Scripture, that word must be rejected—because to accept it would be to destroy the essential oneness of the divine being. Similarly, a spiritual experience that does not produce a deeper understanding of Christ and a more faithful obedience to the will of the Father cannot be regarded as valid, because the Holy Spirit cannot act in a way that denies the basic unity of the Godhead. Anyone who is a follower of Jesus and who is filled with the Holy Spirit will be submitted to the will of the Father, whose glory the other divine persons proclaim and to whom they are eternally united.

The Son and the Holy Spirit are not dependent on the Father for their divinity, nor are they subordinated to him because of it. At the same time, however, it is misleading to say that they have a mind or a will of their own, as we would understand this in human terms. The divine being is one because the love of the persons of the Trinity for each other is perfect. The Son does the Father's will, not because he is obliged to but because his love for the Father is such that he cannot do otherwise. For the Son to disobey the Father would be to lose his love for him, and if that love were lost, not only the unity of the divine persons but the being of God himself would dissolve. Divine love is not something added to the persons of the Godhead as if it were an external, controlling force. On the contrary, it springs from the inner desire of each of the persons of the Godhead to know the others in this way, and to relate to them in the manner appropriate to their identity and function. Because the second and third persons of the Trinity love the first and have given him the honor of precedence within their relationship, and because he has responded to their love by taking on himself the task of representing the divine being in its eternal transcendence and unity, the Son and the Holy Spirit, who are in every respect the Father's equals, defer to him in the way they do. That deference is not a sign of subjection but a recognition that what the Father represents is what they really are, and that to deny him would be to deny themselves and render meaningless everything that they are and do.

3. The Bible also reveals that, although the eternal plan and purpose of God is the joint work of all three persons, it is nevertheless announced by, and attributed to, the person of the Father, whose responsibility it is to ensure that it is accomplished. The New Testament tells us that it was the Father who sent the Son and that it was the Son's mission to do the will of the Father who had sent him.[45] The incarnation of Christ and the earthly work of Jesus of Nazareth that sprang from it was (and is) an expression of the eternal rela-

---

[45] John 3:16; 4:34.

tionship of the Father to the Son and vice versa. The Father gave everything to the Son so that the Son might glorify him during his earthly mission.[46] The death and resurrection of Christ were planned in eternity and were not an accident of history that emerged either immediately after the fall of Adam or in the course of the Son's earthly incarnation.[47] Jesus did not die on the cross by chance; he was the lamb of God, slain before the foundation of the world according to the eternal purpose of God.[48] Similarly, the work of the Holy Spirit is not aimless or open-ended; he has come into the world in order to bear witness to the Father and the Son, and to bring to fulfillment the plan of God for our lives.[49]

It is a failing common to human beings of every age to believe that the activity of God is a "work in progress" that can change or take a different direction depending on circumstances. In an extreme form, it becomes the belief that human beings can alter or deflect God's will by their own actions or desires. It is certainly true that we are rebellious creatures and do not want to do what God has told us to do, but that does not mean we have the power to prevent him from accomplishing what he has intended to do. When the Pharisees asked Jesus to restrain the crowds who were calling him "the King who comes in the name of the Lord" during his triumphal entrance into Jerusalem, Jesus replied that if the people were silent, the stones on the ground would cry out because the truth could not be so easily suppressed.[50] There have been many human attempts to thwart God's will, sometimes with the best of intentions and even (as in this case) by appealing to God himself to do it! But there is nothing we can do to turn God from his purpose, which will manifest itself however hard we try to prevent it from doing so.

The earthly ministry of Jesus offers some instructive examples of this. Right at the beginning, the Devil tried to cut it short by tempting Jesus to do things that would have nullified his long-term purpose by deflecting his attention to short-term manifestations of his divine power that would have had no lasting effect.[51] Toward the end, Jesus had to do battle with himself, as he sweated blood in the garden of Gethsemane the night before his crucifixion. He asked his Father to spare him the final suffering, but he knew that he had come into the world for that purpose. The result of the struggle was submission: "My Father, if this cannot pass unless I drink it, your will be done."[52]

---

[46]Matt. 11:25–27.
[47]1 Pet. 1:2.
[48]Eph. 1:4; Rev. 13:8.
[49]Luke 11:13; Eph. 1:13–14.
[50]Luke 19:39–40.
[51]Matt. 4:1–11.
[52]Matt. 26:42.

If that was the experience of Jesus, what can we say about ourselves? There are many examples in Scripture that confirm the overriding power of God, whatever human desires or appearances to the contrary might suggest. Jonah thought that he could prevent the Ninevites from repenting of their sins by running away when God told him to preach repentance to them, but he did not succeed. God intervened in a way that no one could have foreseen and made sure that his purpose for both Jonah and the Ninevites was accomplished. Jonah never really submitted to God's will, because even when the Ninevites listened to him and repented, he did not want to accept it. In the end, God had to deal with Jonah instead of with those who had sinned in ignorance.[53] Centuries before, Sarah had refused to believe God's promise that she would have a son because she was past the age of childbearing; when God overruled that obstacle, Abraham called the boy Isaac ("he laughs") as a reminder that human disbelief, even when based on apparently incontrovertible facts, cannot thwart God's will. Perhaps the supreme example of this is that the nation of Israel, which had rejected its inheritance by turning its back on Christ, will not be allowed to get away with its rebellion, and sooner or later will be turned back to God's will in spite of itself.[54]

The Son of God was put to death by angry Jews and fearful pagans, and the Holy Spirit's work can be quenched by disobedient and unspiritual Christians,[55] but the will of the Father cannot be undone. Death could not hold the Son captive, but instead saw its power overthrown.[56] The work of the Holy Spirit goes on, winning people for Christ and building his church, however much other forces try to prevent it, because the Father has determined that this should happen and there is no power in heaven or on earth that can separate us from the love of God.[57]

To sum up, it is the Father's special role to be the anchor person in the Trinity.[58] He is the one who rewards the obedient, to whom we must give thanks, and to whom all glory and worship must be given.[59] It is with that aim in view that the Son came into the world to reveal the Father, and that is what the Holy Spirit accomplishes by his indwelling presence in the hearts of believers. In assuming these responsibilities, the Father is not superior to the other persons of the Trinity nor does he dominate them. On the contrary, he has given them all that he has in himself and works together with them in

---

[53] Jonah 1:17; 4:1–4.
[54] Rom. 11:25–32.
[55] 1 Thess. 5:19.
[56] 1 Cor. 15:55.
[57] Rom. 8:38–39; John 6:37–39.
[58] James 1:17; Matt. 5:16, 45, 48; 1 Thess. 3:11–13.
[59] Matt. 6:1; 20:23; John 4:24.

everything that he does.[60] The authority he possesses is an authority given to him by the other persons of the Godhead, and he exercises that authority in collegiality with them.[61] This is the context in which we come to understand the person and work of the Father, and to honor him as he is revealed to us in and through his Son and his Holy Spirit.

"OUTSIDE" AND "INSIDE" GOD

Our understanding of the Old Testament God as Father makes sense only in the context of the incarnation of the Son, because it is in the Trinity that the term finds its meaning. Without the Son there could be no Father, and vice versa. To understand how we can hold both the biblical revelation of the one God and the existence of three divine persons without contradiction, we may perhaps venture to compare the picture of God that we find in the Bible with what we know of the atom. Viewed from the outside, an atom is one and indivisible. It cannot be reduced to anything else, and it exists in perfect simplicity and unity. The Jews understood God rather like this—they saw him, as it were, on the "outside." He dwelt in their midst, but in ways that made his presence inaccessible. He was a fire that could not be approached, a cloud that could be seen but not defined. He attached his name to the ark of the covenant, but anyone who touched that ark without authorization, however well-intentioned, would be severely punished, as the unfortunate Uzzah found out.[62] When the temple was built, the ark was placed in the "holy of holies," the inner room at its center that no one but the high priest was allowed to enter. Even he could go in only once a year, when he offered sacrifice to atone for the sins of the people.[63] Those who tried to sacrifice on their own initiative were severely punished, either by death or by being struck with leprosy.[64]

The coming of the Son changed all this and made the ancient sacrificial system redundant. When the Son offered himself as the sacrifice of atonement on the cross, the veil in the temple that separated the holy of holies from the people was torn in two.[65] The apostle Paul wrote that, in Christ, the barriers that had been set up in the temple to keep the people at the right distance from God were broken down.[66] As he put it, we now have access to the Father through the Son in the Spirit; we are "seated . . . with him [the Father] in the

---

[60]John 5:26; 10:29–30.
[61]John 13:3; 14:10–21.
[62]2 Sam. 6:6–8; 1 Chron. 13:9.
[63]Ex. 30:10; Heb. 5:1–5.
[64]Num. 16:5–40; 2 Chron. 26:16–21.
[65]Matt. 27:51.
[66]Gal. 3:28.

heavenly places in Christ Jesus."[67] This is not mere rhetoric. The symbolic language reflects the fact that the Old Testament experience of Yahweh, whom the people perceived from the "outside," has been replaced by a direct experience of God in Jesus Christ. To be seated with him in the heavenly places means that we have been integrated into the inner life of the Godhead. Where once God dwelt among us without dwelling in us, now he comes into our hearts by his Holy Spirit, adopting us as his children and enabling us to pray the words of the Son: "Abba! Father!"[68] To know the Father is to be united with the Son by and in the Holy Spirit.[69] When the atom was split, it revealed a world of energy that had previously been unknown. Similarly, when we enter into the inner life of God, we see him in a way that we did not previously imagine. Just as an atom seen from the outside has always contained the hidden energy that is its true life, so God has always been a Trinity of persons on the "inside," but one that presented itself to the "outside" world of the ancient Israelites in and through the person of the Father, whose mission it was to represent the divine unity.

TRANSCENDENCE

God revealed himself to Israel as utterly transcendent, and it was this belief, more than any other, that marked Jews out in the ancient world. In no way could God be identified with any created object, or tied down by the limitations of human understanding. In the Old Testament, this transcendence is communicated to us by the many prohibitions against idolatry. Today this does not strike us as exceptional, since very few people (other than Hindus) would think of making an image of their deity or be so crude as to imagine that a piece of wood or stone could have special divine power. But in ancient times that was the way most people thought. When Rachel stole the idols of her father Laban she thought she was removing the spiritual force that kept Laban and his family together, an offense that even Jacob believed was deserving of death.[70] When the statue of Dagon (the god of the Philistines) fell over, the incident provoked a major crisis, because it seemed to portend the loss of Philistine power.[71]

When secular rulers, from the Babylonians to the Romans, wanted to reinforce their authority, they built statues of themselves, which their subjects

---

[67]Eph. 2:6.
[68]Gal. 4:6.
[69]Eph. 2:18.
[70]Gen. 31:19–32. Fortunately for Rachel, although Laban searched Jacob's tents for the gods, he never found them.
[71]1 Sam. 5:1–5.

were expected to worship as divine.[72] The Israelites generally stood out against this, particularly after the Babylonian exile, although in earlier times they had by no means been immune from the same tendency. When Moses went up Mount Sinai to receive the Ten Commandments from God, the people left behind in the valley built themselves a golden calf to which they offered worship, an incident in which even Aaron the high priest was complicit and which very nearly destroyed the Mosaic covenant between God and his people.[73] Later on, the breakaway northern kingdom of Israel established shrines with golden calves, in order to deflect the people from the worship of the true God at Jerusalem, which had become the enemy capital.[74] Although this was understandable in political terms, it was an offense against God and it determined that the northern kingdom would never enjoy divine favor in the way that the southern kingdom of Judah did.

In condemning idolatry, the God of Israel was firmly countercultural, a fact often perceived as a weakness by Israel's neighbors. In the time of Elijah, for example, the prophets of Baal clearly felt that they had a superior form of worship, and it was only by a miraculous divine intervention that Elijah was able to save the day for the worship of Yahweh.[75] Transcendent monotheism had a hard time establishing itself, even in the Greco-Roman world, which prided itself on its intellectual superiority, and whose philosophers looked down on popular superstition with undisguised contempt. Despite that, Rome was unable to do away with idolatry, so ingrained had it become in popular religious consciousness. It was only after the triumph of Christianity that the worship of idols was gradually suppressed. Seen against that background, the Israelite insistence on the utter transcendence of God is all the more admirable and astonishing. When Egypt, Babylon, and Assyria were overthrown, their gods were trampled in the dust and people forgot about them because their power had been shown to be false. But when Israel's temple was razed to the ground and the people were sent into exile, it made no difference to God. He used the occasion to remind his people that, because of his overarching power and being, he could not be destroyed by human hands.[76] Israel returned from the exile diminished in political terms but greatly strengthened spiritually; after the exile, the temptation to relapse into pagan idolatry never again seriously reared its head.

The incarnation of Christ reinforced the transcendence of the Father,

---

[72]Dan. 3:1–7.
[73]Ex. 32:1–35.
[74]1 Kings 12:25–33.
[75]1 Kings 18:20–40.
[76]Jer. 29:1–29. Large parts of the book of Isaiah and the whole of the book of Ezekiel are also devoted to this theme.

who watched over the Son throughout his earthly life before finally vindicating him by raising him from the dead and taking him back into heaven. Jesus revealed the Father to his followers and made him accessible to them, but the effect of this was not to bring him down to earth in a way that might compromise his glory or diminish his power, but rather to take us up to heaven. God remained fully transcendent in his divinity, and he demonstrated that by triumphing over those who thought they could solve the problem of Jesus by getting rid of him. Like the Babylonians under Nebuchadnezzar, they could destroy the earthly temple but they could not touch God, who came back from destruction after three days and established a kingdom far greater than the one that had tried to eliminate him.[77] The power of the Father was never more visible than on that first Easter morning when the Son returned from the dead, and yet he remained as invisible as ever, working in the hearts and minds of the disciples of Jesus and bringing them to faith without ever stepping down from the throne of his sovereignty over all creation.[78] Even at that point, the Father's ultimate plan and purpose remained a mystery, which it was not given to the Son to reveal. When Jesus was asked by his followers after his resurrection when the kingdom of God would be ushered in, he replied that he could not tell them the answer, because the time was known only to the Father, whose plan would not be revealed until the final consummation of all things.[79]

---

[77] John 2:19–22.
[78] Acts 3:15; 4:10; 13:30; Rom. 4:24; 10:9; Gal. 1:1; Col. 2:12; 1 Thess. 1:10; 1 Pet. 1:3.
[79] Acts 1:6–7.

10

THE DIVINE SON
OF GOD

THE IDENTITY OF THE SON

At first sight, the identity of the Son may seem fairly easy to pin down. Is he not the man Jesus of Nazareth, who was proclaimed the Son of God at his baptism[1] and who has been worshiped as such at least since his ascension into heaven, and perhaps before?[2] The Christian church regarded Jesus as the Son of God even before the doctrine of the Trinity was fully developed, and it is safe to say that there would have been no Christianity without that belief. But it is also true that there were many people in Jesus' lifetime, just as there still are today, who respected Jesus as a great teacher but did not worship him as God. Instead, they looked for other explanations of his extraordinary influence. The objections raised against the divinity of Christ were many, but they can be classified into two main types.

The first type of objection was theological. Strict monotheists, as the Jews in Jesus' day undoubtedly were, protested that it was not possible to have a second person calling himself God, however much Christians claimed that he was "one" with the Father. Those who saw Jesus during his earthly ministry were impressed by his miracles, and some of the more open-minded ones were prepared to see him as a teacher who had come from God.[3] Jesus was regularly addressed as "Rabbi" during his earthly ministry in recognition of his teaching gift, even though he had not had a rabbinical education. His knowledge of the Scriptures was proverbial and his interpretations of them were frequently audacious, but it seems that no one dared to question the

---

[1] Matt. 3:17; John 1:29–34.
[2] See Matt. 16:16–17 for evidence of this.
[3] John 3:2.

truth of what he said.[4] Had there been no more to it than that, Jesus might have suffered persecution as the prophets before him had,[5] but after his death he would probably have been honored as one of the great teachers of Israel. Perhaps he would have been put on a par with Hillel and Gamaliel, two Jewish rabbis who were then laying the foundations of what would eventually become modern Judaism. But when Jesus went beyond offering novel rein-terpretations of the law and started calling God his Father, saying that the Scriptures spoke of him, and eventually telling his accusers that they would see him seated at the right hand of God, those who might have tolerated his prophetic challenge to the existing order were pushed over the edge and driven to denounce him for blasphemy.[6] It was not Jesus' claim to status as a teacher that got him into trouble but the content of what he taught. To those who agreed with him, his teaching made him far greater than any teacher or prophet could ever be. But to those who disagreed, he could hardly have been anything other than a messenger of the Devil who was determined to overthrow the nation of Israel.

The second kind of objection may be called "historical." This is based on the belief that no human being, however gifted, can possibly claim to be God. People who think like this cannot deny that divine attributes were attributed to Jesus by his devoted admirers, but even if they have some sympathy for that point of view, they cannot accept that it has any objective justification. Belief in Jesus may be more respectable, and certainly more enduring, than belief in someone like Elvis Presley, but essentially the two phenomena are the same—in both cases, a man has been idealized after his death and made "immortal" in the hearts and minds of his followers. Critics may accept this kind of devo-tion as a fact of life, or they may try to get rid of it as being groundless super-stition, rooted in the credulity of an earlier age, but either way they do not take it seriously as something based on objective historical fact. Charismatic figures like Elvis appear from time to time and attract a following that may continue for several generations, so we must not be too surprised if Jesus had a similar impact on people. In the eyes of their devotees, both men were "kings," but not even his most extravagant admirers would call Elvis "God," and in the eyes of many critics, we should not do that with Jesus either.

In between these two extremes there is a range of options, each of which has had its supporters at one time or other in the history of the church. At one end of the scale there are those who will accept that Jesus enjoyed a

---

[4]See, for example, Luke 4:25–29.
[5]Matt. 5:11–12.
[6]John 5:18, 39; Luke 22:67–71.

special relationship with God, but do not believe that he was identical with him. Some like Arius have gone so far as to say that he was a heavenly being, perhaps even a part of God, before he became incarnate in the womb of Mary, but his incarnation as a particular individual can only mean that he was essentially different from the God whom he called his Father, and therefore he must have been inferior to him. People who think like this will point to the many places in the Gospels where Jesus defers to the will of his Father, presumably because it was superior to his own will, and to those places where he openly states that the Father is greater than he is.[7] What can that possibly mean, they will ask, except that he recognized his own innate inferiority to the one who had begotten him? Others will allow that Jesus had a miraculous birth but will say that he was still no more than a human being who was adopted by God as his Son either at his baptism or by his resurrection, and so transformed into the Savior-figure that we know today.

In response to these criticisms and challenges, Christians generally adopt one of two approaches. Either they start with the man Jesus of Nazareth and try to show that he was indeed God in human flesh, or they begin with God's self-revelation and argue that if this were ever to lead to a true knowledge of him, he would have to appear in a form that would be comprehensible to us without denying or abandoning his essential transcendence. This is what we find in the doctrine of the Word of God made flesh.[8] The former approach is nowadays called a Christology "from below," because it starts with the human being and works up to God, whereas the latter is known as a Christology "from above," because it begins with God and explains how he accommodated himself to our understanding. Because modern liberal theologians all start with a Christology from below, it is often assumed that it is the standard liberal view and that a Christology from above is almost by definition more traditional and more orthodox. However, a careful examination of the New Testament evidence will show that things are not as simple as that, and that both approaches were used by those who first proclaimed the gospel message.

This double approach can be seen most clearly in the speech that the apostle Peter gave in Jerusalem on the day of Pentecost. Three thousand people professed faith in Christ that day and the church as we know it came into being. Notice how carefully Peter balances the human and divine perspectives in his preaching, which can be analyzed into a Christology from above and one from below, as follows:[9]

---

[7] John 14:28; Matt. 19:17.
[8] John 1:14.
[9] Acts 2:22–39.

1. Jesus was sent by God to perform miracles by his power (above).
2. These miracles were well attested and generally accepted as valid (below).
3. Jesus was sacrificed according to the definite plan and knowledge of God (above).
4. The people crucified him (below).
5. God raised him up from the dead (above).
6. The prophecy of King David was not fulfilled in him because he died (below).
7. The prophecy was instead fulfilled in Jesus (above).
8. Jesus inherited the kingdom promised to David (below).
9. The kingdom belongs to the risen, ascended, and glorified Christ (above).

The work of God and the witness of human beings are carefully intertwined, sometimes to such an extent that it is almost impossible to separate one from the other. Inevitably, there is a certain logical priority given to what we would call a Christology from above, since if God had not sent his Son there would have been no gospel at all. It is characteristic of the way the gospel was preached that it was by working back from generally accepted facts that the hearers were invited to conclude what had caused them. Christology from below is the method of scientific observation based on readily available evidence, whereas Christology from above is the explanatory theory to which that evidence points. Both approaches have their place, and if the church today worships the Son of God as the second person of the Trinity who became a man in order to save us from our sins and bring us back to God, it does so only because those events took place, were accepted as valid by those who saw them, and led them to understand that behind them lay the eternal plan and purpose of God.

The identity of the man Jesus of Nazareth can therefore not be fully understood in terms of his human origins alone. He was certainly a descendant of King David, though this was by no means unique in Israel; there must have been hundreds of people at that time who could have claimed the same thing,[10] just as there are many people today who can claim descent from William the Conqueror. Davidic descent was essential for the Messiah, but it was not enough. What really made the difference, as Peter pointed out on the day of Pentecost, was that this particular descendant achieved something that none of the others had or could claim to have done for themselves. Unlike David, who had died and been buried, and whose tomb was still extant, Jesus had not been abandoned to hell, nor had his soul seen corruption, because

---

[10]Matt. 1:1–17; Luke 3:23–38.

God had raised him from the dead and exalted him to his own right hand.[11] Jesus had gone from being *a* son of David to being *the* son of David because, fundamentally, he was more than that—he was the Son of God.

More than once in his sermon, Peter made it clear that God had planned the life, death, and resurrection of Jesus from the beginning. Other parts of the New Testament tell us that this was because Jesus had been with God all along.[12] In fact, he was himself God, which is what made everything else possible. This comes out most clearly in Philippians 2:6–11, where the apostle Paul explains what happened as follows:

1. In the beginning the Son was equal with God (the Father).
2. The Son chose to humble himself and become the Father's servant.
3. As a servant, the Son became a man, so that he could die in obedience to the Father.
4. In response to this obedience, the Father has exalted the Son.
5. The exaltation of the Son is the reason why we worship him.

These five points put the identity of Jesus as the son of David into a wider theological context. As the Son of God, he is eternally equal with the Father, although he also accepted a role in relation to him that makes him in some sense inferior. This inferiority is not one of substance or nature because it was voluntarily chosen by the Son and not imposed on him. Why did the Son agree to do this? The answer is that he did it out of love for the Father, and by extension out of love for the human race. We are so accustomed to think that Jesus died for our salvation that we forget that he also died to fulfill the Father's will. This becomes clear when we look at what he said on the cross. Of the seven words of Christ from the cross recorded in the Gospels, three are directly addressed to the Father. Matthew and Mark both record the famous quotation from Psalm 22:1: "My God, my God, why have you forsaken me?"[13] Two of the three statements found in Luke are, "Father, forgive them, for they know not what they do," and, "Father, into your hands I commend my spirit!"[14] The third statement in Luke is addressed to the thief on the cross next to him, after he confessed his belief in Jesus. In response, Jesus said to him, "Today you will be with me in Paradise," a statement that does not mention the Father explicitly but concerns him, because it is in his presence that Paradise is to be found.[15] Somewhat surprisingly perhaps, it is only the three

---

[11]Acts 2:29–33. The original prophecy is in Ps. 16:8–11.
[12]John 1:1.
[13]Matt. 27:46; Mark 15:34. Interestingly, Jesus cited it in Aramaic translation and not in the original Hebrew.
[14]Luke 23:34, 46.
[15]Luke 23:43.

Johannine words that are not addressed to the Father and do not contain any reference to him.[16]

The significance of these words for our understanding of who Jesus was cannot be overstated. The crucifixion takes us to the heart of his identity and mission in a way that nothing else does. Through it we see more clearly than anywhere else what he had really come to do. In dying for us, Jesus took on himself the curse of sin, which separated him from the Father, who cannot tolerate the presence of evil in his sight.[17] Yet, abandoned as he apparently was, the Son was still able to call out to his Father because the relationship between them was deeper than anything sin could do to destroy it. At no point did the Father renounce the personal link that he had to his Son; on the contrary, it was the existence of that link and its underlying immutability that made it possible for him to punish the Son's human body, which he freely offered as a sacrifice for our sin.[18] Had Jesus not been the Son of God, he would have had to make a sacrifice for his own sins and would not have had a sinless body to offer to the Father.[19]

The Lukan words underline the fact that, on the cross, Jesus was not spiritually cut off from his Father. The first one shows that his sacrifice was intended as a prayer for the forgiveness of those who had sinned against both him and the Father—the two being one. The relationship they had with each other within the Godhead made it possible for that ministry to begin even as he was dying. That it was not mere verbiage is demonstrated by his remarks to the thief being crucified with him, not only because his faith was enough to save him but because Jesus' sacrifice was sufficient to make it possible for him to offer the thief salvation. He already knew that his offering would be acceptable to the Father, and in speaking to the thief in the way he did, he gave his followers the assurance that the work of salvation had indeed been accomplished. Finally, as he breathed his last, Jesus gave himself up to the Father, knowing that he would see him through the pains of death and hell, and raise him up again. All this was the work of the one who had voluntarily chosen to become a servant, so that he could accomplish the Father's will and save those whom the Father had entrusted to him.[20]

In exalting the Son following his perfect sacrifice and death, the Father was not according him some new honor but restoring him to the glory that he had from the beginning. As Jesus himself put it,

---

[16]They are "Woman, behold your son!" . . . "Behold your mother" (John 19:26–27), "I thirst" (John 19:28), and "It is finished" (John 19:30).

[17]2 Cor. 5:21; Gal. 3:13.

[18]Heb. 4:15; 5:8–10.

[19]Heb. 7:26–28.

[20]John 17:12.

I glorified you on earth, having accomplished the work that you gave me to do. And now, Father, glorify me in your own presence with the glory that I had with you before the world existed.[21]

This statement is of the utmost importance for our understanding of the Son's identity. It excludes any notion that he was adopted by the Father because of his perfect obedience. His resurrection from the dead was not a reward for his successful sacrifice but the inevitable result of his being God in the first place. Death could not hold him because he was not subject to death. The resurrection of his body was the renewal of his human nature, not some kind of transformation into a divinity that he did not previously possess. In taking that body up to heaven, he took the sacrifice he made for our sins with him. He now uses it to plead with the Father for our forgiveness, but that is possible only because he has been given back the status of Son which was rightfully his from the beginning. In his heavenly glory he has received all power from the Father to work out his purposes on earth, and it is he who will come to judge the living and the dead in the Father's name.[22]

THE GENERATION OF THE SON IN ETERNITY

How should we interpret the concept of generation? There is no doubt that the Bible uses this language, which is inherent in the names themselves, to describe the relationship of the Father to the Son. Superficially it would appear that, however we interpret it, a good case can be made for saying that the Son is subordinate to the Father and therefore (in some way at least) is inferior to him. The difficulty is that, for a long time, the scriptural language was misinterpreted because it was put in the wrong category. To talk about birth is to talk about a process that occurs in time. If that is what we are talking about in the case of the Son, the logical conclusion must be that there was a time when the Son did not exist. If that were true, however, it would mean that he could not be God, because God is eternal. The theologians of the early church wrestled with this dilemma and eventually came up with the phrase that we now find in the creeds of the early church—the Son was "eternally begotten" of the Father. In one sense this is a logical contradiction, because the process of birth cannot occur outside time. The early Christians knew that, of course, and their intention was to remove any time element from the concept of generation, making it something different from what we normally imagine it to be. What they were doing was replacing a process by a relation-

---

[21]John 17:4–5.
[22]John 5:22.

ship in which the two persons of the Trinity regard each other as Father and Son and act accordingly. The key point is that they do so voluntarily and not because there is some inner structure inside God that obliges the Son to defer to the Father as being inherently superior to himself.

The importance of saying this can be seen from the fact that some people have pushed the language of generation used to describe the Son to the point of asking who his heavenly Mother is. The logic behind this question is that, whereas human generation requires both a male and a female, in divine generation as it has been revealed to us, there is only a male parent. If "generation" is a true analogy, the argument goes, then there must be a Mother. At least some of those who think this way have gone on to conclude that this Mother must be the Holy Spirit, a theory that has been supported on the ground that the word "Spirit" is feminine in both Hebrew (*ruakh*) and Aramaic (*rukho*). Even in modern times, this argument has seemed plausible to some people, who have gone in search of a feminine principle in the Godhead, quite apart from the generation of the Son. Unfortunately for them, the word "Spirit" is neuter in Greek (*pneuma*) and masculine in Latin (*spiritus*), which reminds us that grammatical gender has little to do with sex. It is certainly no reason at all for assigning motherhood, or even femininity, to the third person of the Trinity. That grammatical gender can be taken to such an extreme reminds us of the dangers of reading the Bible with the wrong intellectual framework as our guide. As the phrase "eternal generation" reminds us, we are not dealing with a process of generation inside God comparable to human birth, but with a different set of concepts altogether.

The framework within which we must understand the true meaning of "generation" with respect to the second person of the Trinity is established by the discipline of law, not by biology or grammar. As a legal principle, "generation" is fully consistent with the covenant principle and the structure of Old Testament revelation that provides the basic framework for understanding God's saving work. The relationship of the first to the second person of the Trinity is based on the concept of *inheritance*. The Son has been appointed the *heir* of all things, and it is in this sense that he is described as the first-born of all creation.[23] By the law of primogeniture, the firstborn is the one who receives the inheritance, as the story of Esau and Jacob reminds us.[24] In human affairs the language of inheritance is normally attached to the process of birth and human reproduction, but not always—it is quite possible to leave

---

[23]Col. 1:15–16; Heb. 1:2. See also Gal. 4:7.
[24]Gen. 27:18–35. Jacob (the younger son) stole his brother's inheritance by impersonating him in the presence of his blind father Isaac.

a legacy to someone totally unrelated to the donor, or to adopt others with the intention of giving them an inheritance, as God has done with us.[25] The concept is flexible and can be applied to different situations by choice, not merely by necessity, which makes it so valuable for understanding both our relationship to God and the relationship of the Son to the Father.

The use of Father-Son language serves the additional purpose of emphasizing the underlying unity of being that binds them together and makes it possible for us to say that the Son is the Father's natural heir, whereas we are heirs only by the grace of adoption. "Like father, like son" is a well-known popular expression that conveys the essence of this and reminds us that, just as a human child shares the nature of his parents, so the Son of God must share the nature of his Father if he is to be a genuine Son. The shared being and nature are inherent in the terminology used to describe them. It is true that angels, and perhaps other heavenly beings, are occasionally called "sons of God" in the Old Testament, but this refers to their spiritual nature, which is like that of God himself, and is not connected to any inheritance that might be reserved for them.[26] In that sense, the Son is the *only begotten*, as the prologue to John's Gospel specifies and as the creeds of the early church repeat.[27]

THE GENERATION OF THE SON IN TIME AND SPACE

The subject of the Son's generation is not exhausted by his relationship to the Father within the Godhead, because he was also begotten in time and space, in the womb of the Virgin Mary. It is the teaching of the New Testament that this birth was prophesied by Isaiah, some seven hundred years before it actually took place. As Matthew 1:23 puts it,

> "Behold, the virgin shall conceive and bear a son, and they shall call his name Immanuel" (which means, God with us).[28]

Whether this is the correct translation of the original Hebrew has frequently been disputed. It is argued that Isaiah used the word *almah* ("young woman") instead of *bethulah* ("virgin") in his prophecy. To this objection, three answers may be given:

1. There would be nothing prophetic or even remarkable about a young woman giving birth. It happens all the time, and if that were all that was

---

[25]Gal. 3:29; Eph. 3:6.
[26]Gen. 6:2–4; Job 1:6; 2:1.
[27]John 1:14.
[28]See Isa. 7:14.

involved, how would anyone know which young woman the prophet had in mind?

2. In many societies, "youth" is defined for all practical purposes by puberty and sexual experience, especially in the case of women. Those who have not reached that stage are regarded as "young" whereas those who have, and are no longer virgins, are considered to be "mature" or "adult." If that was the case in ancient Israel, then "young woman" and "virgin" would have been synonymous.

3. The pre-Christian Greek translation of the Old Testament (the Septuagint) uses the word *parthenos* ("virgin") here, showing that this is how *almah* was understood at least two or three centuries before the birth of Jesus. In no sense can it be regarded as a Christian interpolation or corruption of the original text.

Of course there have always been people who have denied the virgin birth (or more correctly, the virginal conception) of Jesus, and have preferred some other explanation of the unusual circumstances by which he came into the world. Often it is assumed that Joseph was his natural father, and occasionally it is suggested that Jesus may have been born out of wedlock, with the "virgin birth" story being an attempt to conceal this social disgrace. There is no way of testing theories of this kind, and in the end it comes down to a question of faith—either we believe that the New Testament accounts are trustworthy or we do not. In this case, it can be said in favor of the virginal conception that it is one of the few common elements in the two great birth narratives in the Gospel accounts.[29] Had the story been made up, it is hard to see why almost all the other details are completely different in the two accounts! It is also hard to see why anyone would have bothered to mention Joseph, whose existence would have been an embarrassment to someone who was trying to justify a virgin birth. The fact that Joseph is not only mentioned, but that his (perfectly understandable) negative reaction to the news that Mary was pregnant is given great prominence, also inclines us to believe that the account is true. If it were not, neither Joseph's nor Mary's family would have been happy to air their dirty linen in public, and the facts, whatever they were, would almost certainly have been suppressed by the relatives.[30]

From time to time various questions have been raised about the chronology of the events recorded in the birth narratives of Jesus, but as these are not strictly theological matters they need not detain us long. Jesus must have been born sometime between the announcement of the census carried out

---

[29]Matt. 1:18–25; Luke 1:26–38.
[30]Matt. 1:19.

when Quirinius was governor of Syria (9 B.C.) and the death of King Herod the Great (4 B.C.). In passing, we may note that the fact that he was not born in 1 B.C. or A.D. 1[31] is due to a computational error made by a sixth-century monk, Dionysius Exiguus, when he was trying to calculate backwards to the time of Herod and Augustus, and the mistake has no bearing on the subject one way or another. The biggest problem is that, if Jesus was still a small baby when Herod died, how could he have been born during the census taken by Quirinius four or five years before? The simplest answer is that in ancient times a census of the kind described in the Gospels would have taken several years to complete. The text does not say that Mary and Joseph were taxed while Quirinius was *still* governor of Syria, only that the process began at that time.[32] To appreciate what this might have entailed, we can perhaps compare the 1291 census of Pope Nicholas IV, in which he ordered that the clergy of the British Isles should be taxed. That census was still being carried out fifteen years later and was never completed, probably because the death of King Edward I in 1307 caused it to lapse. Nevertheless, it is still referred to today as the 1291 census of Pope Nicholas IV in spite of the fact that much of it is considerably later in date. In short, the chronological difficulties raised against the texts are by no means insuperable, and should not be used as evidence of untruthfulness.

From the theological point of view, the most important question about the virgin birth of Jesus concerns the nature of the conception of the fetus in Mary's womb. One way or another, this has been a point of contention since ancient times. From the strictly biological standpoint, parthenogenesis (the technical name for "virgin birth") is exceedingly rare in nature and unattested in humans, but it is not completely impossible. The problem is that, if it were to occur, it would produce only female offspring. Therefore, if Jesus was indeed born of a virgin, there must have been supernatural intervention for him to be a male, so we can rule out the possibility that his birth was a freak natural occurrence. The Bible, of course, makes it plain that his birth was planned by God, and that it occurred by the intervention of the Holy Spirit in Mary's womb.[33] Mary's role in this was entirely passive—she did not actively desire to be the mother of Jesus, and was in fact deeply disturbed when she learned what the angel Gabriel had to tell her.[34] But when she understood what was going to happen, she submitted to God's will and events took their

---

[31]Note that there was no year 0. When B.C. and A.D. dates are added together, it is therefore necessary to drop one from the total. Augustus Caesar, for example, reigned from 27 B.C. to A.D. 14, a total of forty years, not forty-one.
[32]Luke 2:1.
[33]Luke 1:35.
[34]Luke 1:29.

course.[35] There is no indication that her pregnancy was abnormal, though when she went to visit her cousin Elizabeth, who had become pregnant with John the Baptist, John leapt in Elizabeth's womb, and she was filled with the Holy Spirit to the extent that she could welcome Mary as "the mother of my Lord."[36]

Those words have had a remarkable history, because it was on the basis of them that subsequent generations came to venerate Mary as the "mother of God" or more precisely as the *Theotokos*, a Greek term which means "the one who bears God in her womb." That the fetus Mary was carrying was God in human flesh is orthodox Christian teaching and is accepted by all the major churches, but Protestants dislike the term "mother of God" because they say it is misleading. Mary gave the baby Jesus what she had to give—her human flesh—but in no sense can she be regarded as a source of his divinity. From the Protestant point of view, phrases that are open to such a misinterpretation are best avoided, even if they can be theologically justified. What happened in the womb of Mary is that the Son of God took on a human nature, including the attributes we normally associate with the "soul" (mind, will, conscience, etc.). Inside her body, he became a human being in exactly the same way that we all are, yet without sin.[37]

At a time when it was widely believed that sin was a congenital defect passed on from one generation to the next, it was natural for people to wonder how Jesus managed to avoid it. The answers given almost invariably focused on Mary. Some said that she was cleansed from her sin when the angel spoke to her, interpreting his words ("Greetings, O favored one, the Lord is with you!") to mean this, although nothing is said about this in the text itself.[38] Others have claimed that Mary was cleansed from sin when she was conceived in her mother's womb, and some theologians have even tried to trace her perfect humanity back to Adam and Eve, as if by some miracle a line of sinless people had been preserved until the coming of the Savior! A more moderate form of that belief has been official Roman Catholic doctrine since 1854, but it has no biblical support and is rejected by the other churches.

Roman Catholics also believe that Mary remained a virgin all her life, despite the fact that the Gospels explicitly mention that Jesus had brothers and sisters and even name them.[39] This is an example of popular piety uncon-

---

[35]Luke 1:38.
[36]Luke 1:43.
[37]Heb. 4:15.
[38]Luke 1:28. These words are well known today in their Latin version ("*Ave Maria, gratia plena*"), which have often been set to music and are frequently heard at weddings and on other solemn occasions, especially in Roman Catholic communities.
[39]Matt. 13:55.

trolled by the witness of Scripture, which in this case actually contradicts it. Sadly, the evidence of both Roman Catholic and Eastern Orthodox devotional practice demonstrates that Mary has often been given the kind of attention that ought to be reserved for her Son. Mary was a sinner in need of salvation just as much as anyone else, and the fact that she was privileged to carry the Savior in her womb gives her no special place in the kingdom of heaven. Jesus made that abundantly clear during his earthly ministry, when his mother and his brothers tried to gain access to him. The words are worth quoting in full:

> While he was still speaking to the people, behold, his mother and his broth-ers stood outside, asking to speak to him. But he replied to the man who told him, "Who is my mother, and who are my brothers?" And stretching out his hand toward his disciples, he said, "Here are my mother and my brothers! For whoever does the will of my Father in heaven is my brother and sister and mother."[40]

As far as devotion to Mary is concerned, there is nothing in the Bible to sup-port the Roman Catholic teaching that she is the "queen of heaven" or that she plays any part in the saving work of her son. All such ideas must be firmly rejected, not because we want to push Mary into the background or deny her importance, but in order to give her the honor due to the woman who submit-ted to God's will and became the means by which his Son entered the world for our redemption.

A side-effect of the excessive devotion given to Mary and the false asser-tion of her sinlessness is that it calls the nature of Jesus' humanity into ques-tion. If Mary was not a normal human being, how could she have passed on a normal human nature to Jesus? This matters, because it is all too easy for well-meaning people to make exaggerated claims for him that end up making him something less than what he really was. For example, the sinlessness of Jesus can be taken to mean that he was not tempted in the way that we are, even though the New Testament explicitly says that he was.[41] People are some-times shocked by the suggestion that Jesus was sexually tempted, but if he was tempted in the same way as everyone else, he must have been. Although the Gospels give us no details and we should not succumb to the imaginations of those who suggest that he was physically attracted to particular women (such as Mary Magdalene), the idea itself should not occasion any surprise. Jesus was not protected by his divinity from the stresses and strains of everyday human life, though we cannot say precisely what he may have suffered in the

---

[40]Matt. 12:46–50.
[41]Heb. 4:15.

course of it. Did he catch cold? Did he suffer toothache? Was he ever moody or depressed? We do not know the answers to such questions, but we must not exclude the possibility—even the probability—that he was. Certainly we can say that at the end of his life he bore our griefs and carried our sorrows, he was crushed for our iniquities, he was oppressed and he was afflicted—all for our sake.[42] Compared with that the rest seems rather trivial, and we should expect that he would have coped with whatever he came across during his lifetime much as we all do, and would not have taken refuge behind a protective divine covering that his human nature did not possess.

Finally, we cannot say why God chose to send his Son into the world when he did. The Bible tells us that the Son came into the world in the "fullness of time," but we know no more than that.[43] What we do know is that he had to come as a Jew of the house of David, and that it was prophesied of him that he would be born in Bethlehem.[44] We can also say that, given the Jewish context in which males were more significant as covenant-bearers than females were, he had to be a male himself and subject to the provisions of the Mosaic law during his earthly life.[45] This can be seen most clearly in the way in which he related to the Jerusalem temple, its priests, and its worship. Even though he had come into the world to replace the temple and its sacrifices, he never attempted to interfere with them during his lifetime; he regularly went up to Jerusalem for the Passover, as many pious Jews did.[46]

Jesus always recognized the legitimacy of worship in the Jerusalem temple, however much it had been corrupted by commercialization and the delinquency of the priests. He never succumbed to the temptation to set up a rival center of worship and was quite firm with the Samaritan woman who wondered whether her ancestral practices were a viable alternative to the temple rituals at Jerusalem.[47] We can probably also say that, in order to perform the task for which he had come into the world, the Son of God had to be a normally healthy adult—he would not have done much good if he had died in infancy, or if he had contracted some debilitating disease. That is not to say that he *could* not have suffered such things, but it would not have been expedient for his deeper ministry if he had. But we must always remember that, if he was spared those trials, it was only because something even more terrible had been reserved for him, and we cannot say that it was

---

[42]Isa. 53:4–7.
[43]Eph. 1:10.
[44]Matt. 2:6.
[45]Gal. 4:4.
[46]John 2:23; 12:1.
[47]John 4:19–24.

his divinity that kept him out of harm's way until the time for his supreme sacrifice approached.

JESUS' SELF-UNDERSTANDING

How conscious was Jesus of his divine nature and of his mission during his earthly life? This question has often been asked in modern times, and various answers have been given, though it probably would not have occurred to most people in the early church. Back then, it seems that almost everyone thought that the human Jesus was fully conscious of his divinity, even when he was in his mother's womb, and there were a number of stories circulating that claimed that he had performed miracles as a tiny baby. Today such fantasies are generally rejected, but in reaction to them many have gone to the other extreme, claiming that no real human being could possibly be conscious of being God at the same time, if only because the finite human mind cannot contain the infinite. To people who think like that, the divinity of Christ must be something that was attributed to him after his death, perhaps by a divine revelation connected with the resurrection, but more likely by a process of evolution within the early church whereby Christians came to believe that Jesus was God and gradually started working out the implications of that belief.

The picture we have of Jesus in the Gospels is not particularly helpful in answering this question because it passes over his early life almost completely. The only incident recorded for us from his childhood is the occasion when he went with his parents to Jerusalem at the age of twelve for what would nowadays be called his Bar-Mitzvah.[48] From this we learn that the boy Jesus was a child prodigy who knew far more about the law of Moses than someone his age would normally know, but that in itself does not prove his divinity. More significant is the fact that he was aware that he had to be in his Father's house and seemed surprised that Mary and Joseph were unaware of that.[49] They knew that Jesus was no ordinary child, but this incident shows that nothing he said or did revealed who he really was, even to them. The only other allusion to his childhood comes a bit later on, when he went back to Nazareth to preach in the synagogue after having begun his public ministry. No one in Nazareth thought that he was anyone special, despite the reputation he had already acquired elsewhere as a healer and miracle worker. They drove him out of town for his presumption.[50] All we can say for sure about Jesus' early

---

[48]Luke 2:41–51.
[49]Luke 2:49.
[50]Luke 4:16–30.

years is that, whatever he understood about himself and his future mission, he kept it to himself. Those who knew him best had little or no understanding of who he was or of what he had come to do. We are told that Mary reflected on the events surrounding Jesus' birth,[51] but how much she really understood about his destiny is unclear.

Once he began his public ministry, however, our information is much fuller. Particularly important are the accounts of his baptism, one of the few incidents in his life that is recorded in all four Gospels.[52] Like many godly people of the time, Jesus sought out John the Baptist in order to receive the baptism that John was preaching and administering for repentance, in preparation for the great work that God was going to do in Israel. But whereas everyone else who went to John was received and baptized without any apparent difficulty, Jesus was rejected. John initially refused to baptize him, not because Jesus was unworthy to receive his ministry but because John was unworthy to offer it to him. Given that John was a prophet sent by God to baptize, this can only mean that Jesus was important enough to overrule a divine mission, and only God himself could have done that. If John knew that Jesus was "the Lamb of God, who takes away the sin of the world" it would be very surprising if Jesus had not also known it, particularly as he did nothing to correct what would otherwise have been a false and even blasphemous assertion about him.[53] Instead, he remonstrated with John, insisting that he should be baptized, not because he needed to be but in order "to fulfill all righteousness."[54] This can only mean that Jesus knew that he had been sent to take the sins of the world upon himself, and that his baptism was intended to proclaim that the purpose of his ministry was to prepare the way for the atoning sacrifice he had come to make.

Deciding what to make of the witness of the Gospels is complicated by the fact that modern scholars who do not believe that Jesus had any divine self-consciousness are only too willing to dismiss anything in them that suggests the contrary. They say that such "evidence" represents what the early Christians were trying to put across and not anything that Jesus himself did or said. At that level, the argument can only be one of faith versus unbelief, and neither side can prove its point one way or the other. However, there is a compelling argument for accepting that Jesus must have taught his disciples that he was the Son of God, because if he had not done so, they would never have made it up or tolerated it if it had been suggested by others.

---

[51]Luke 2:19.
[52]Matt. 3:13–17; Mark 1:9–11; Luke 3:21–22; John 1:29–34.
[53]John 1:29.
[54]Matt. 3:15.

Christ's first followers were Jews, well-schooled in monotheism and temperamentally incapable of admitting the existence of a second deity. To them, Jesus would have been a great prophet, of whom Israel had known several in the past. That he had been put to death would not have surprised them in the least because that is the sort of thing that happened to prophets who told people truths they did not want to hear. Even resurrection from the dead would not of itself have proved his divinity. Elijah had not died an ordinary death,[55] and there were mysterious figures like Enoch who had apparently escaped it also.[56] Admittedly, there had never been a resurrection before, unless we count the resuscitation of Lazarus,[57] but it would have been possible to fit it into the career of an extraordinary prophet had no alternative explanation been forthcoming, and the ascension would have been no more than a repeat of Elijah's experience. Everything Jesus said and did could have been explained without recourse to the theory that he was God in human flesh, and no doubt it would have been—except that Jesus taught his disciples otherwise. In the end, the only plausible explanation of the church's subsequent worship of Jesus as God is that it was what he taught his disciples—in shadows and figures during his earthly ministry, but more clearly after his resurrection and before his ascension, when he helped them make sense of what had happened over the previous few years.[58]

Jesus verified his claim to divinity by the miracles he performed while still on earth, especially by his resurrection from the dead and subsequent ascension into heaven. But the claim itself was not based on those events.[59] The disciples interpreted those events the way they did because that was the explanation which Jesus himself gave of them. We have already seen that by calling God his Father, Jesus was making it clear to the Jews who heard him that he regarded himself as God.[60] If he had not intended them to understand him in that way, it would have been easy for him to have denied the inference they were drawing from his words, particularly if he could have escaped with his life by doing so.[61]

Furthermore, the strength of Jesus' claim to divinity is more immediately apparent in the Hebrew and Aramaic languages that he spoke than it was in Greek or would be in other Western tongues. Hebrew speakers used the expression "son of" in an adjectival sense. Thus the phrase "son of man"

[55] 2 Kings 2:11–12.
[56] Gen. 5:24. He is mentioned twice in the New Testament (Heb. 11:5 and Jude 14).
[57] John 11:44.
[58] Luke 24:44–49.
[59] John 10:37–38; 20:29.
[60] John 5:18.
[61] Luke 22:66–71.

meant simply "human being," as we see from examples of the term in the Old Testament.[62] Jesus also called himself the Son of Man, but in a more exclusive sense, tying the term to the eschatological figure who appears in Daniel and perhaps also to Adam, the "generic" human being.[63] In such a context, the term "Son of God" could only mean "divine being," and since there was only one God, the fact that Jesus claimed the title for himself indicates that in effect he was claiming to be God.

Another question often raised in this connection concerns Jesus' activity as God during the time of his incarnation. Does allowing that he was the eternal Son, who became incarnate in the womb of the Virgin Mary, imply that he was still acting as God in heaven, ruling the universe along with the Father and the Holy Spirit while at the same time crying as a baby in his mother's arms? Can we imagine such dual activity, or do we have to think of the Son taking a break from his divinity for a while, in order to allow him to be a normal human being for the duration of his incarnate life? The traditional answer to this question has been that the Son of God functioned simultaneously according to each of his two natures. As a human being, he lived in the way other human beings do, without drawing attention to himself or performing gratuitous divine acts simply in order to show everyone who he really was. But in his divine nature he remained united with the other persons of the Trinity, which means that he never ceased to rule the universe along with them. How he could do both at the same time is part of the mystery of the incarnation, when two essentially incompatible natures were joined together in a single person, who continued to live and work in each of his two natures according to their respective attributes.

This view, which is the standard one among Christians, has been challenged in modern times by some theologians who have tried to use Philippians 2:6–8 as the basis for a different understanding of the matter. Those verses read as follows:

> Though he was in the form of God, [Jesus] did not count equality with God a thing to be grasped, but *emptied himself*, by taking the form of a servant, being born in the likeness of men. And being found in human form, he *humbled himself* by becoming obedient to the point of death, even death on a cross.

The key words here are the ones in italics. In the original context, it seems that what the apostle Paul was saying is that the Son of God submitted himself

---

[62]It is particularly common in Ezekiel, where it occurs in almost every chapter.
[63]Matt. 9:6; 10:23; 12:8; etc. See also Dan. 7:13; Rev. 1:13.

to the authority of the Father, which led to his incarnation and subsequent humiliation, culminating in his ignominious death on a cross. Whether it also entailed a fundamental change in his divine nature is not explicitly stated, but it may be asked whether what transpired would have been possible otherwise. Do not the Son's acts at least imply that he must have surrendered something of his divinity in order to perform them?

The Greek words for "emptied himself" are *ekenōsen heauton*. From this theologians developed the noun *kenōsis*, or emptying, which they then used as the foundation for their new theory, known to us as "kenotic Christology." According to this theory, the Son of God voluntarily surrendered his divinity, or at least its prerogatives, in order to become a man. As Jesus of Nazareth, he therefore did not know everything, was not directly involved in ruling the universe, and could not call on his divine nature to get him out of trouble when the occasion arose. This last assertion is the most difficult one, because it is clear that Jesus did do things during his earthly ministry that a normal human being could not have done, but the explanation proposed for this is that in those cases God the Father came to his aid and worked miracles in and through his humanity. In support of the kenotic view, a theologian can point to the words of Jesus in John 17:5, where he says, "And now, Father, glorify me in your own presence with the glory that I had with you before the world existed." If the Son had never lost that glory nor laid it aside, the argument goes, why would he have prayed in this way?

There are also certain statements of Jesus which suggest that he was inferior to the Father, and these must also be taken into account. For example, in John 14:28 he tells his disciples, "I am going to the Father, for the Father is greater than I." Even more significantly, when the rich young ruler addressed him as "good teacher," Jesus challenged him and said, "Why do you call me good? No one is good except God alone."[64] Does this not amount to a denial that he is God in the full sense of the word? There are two difficulties in interpreting verses like these. In the first place, no one denies that *as a servant* the Son is "inferior" to the Father, because it is the Father's will that he has come to do. This does not mean, however, that he had to give up his divinity; on the contrary, it can be argued that it was precisely because he was divine and therefore equal to the Father that the Son could choose to become a servant. Had he been genuinely inferior, either in being or by having surrendered his divine attributes, the Son would have had no choice, and the nature of his submission would have been entirely different.

What Jesus did as the Father's servant he did voluntarily. To some extent

---

[64]Mark 10:18.

this may be compared with the way in which he washed his disciples' feet the night before the crucifixion.[65] It was not a sign of his inferiority to them but the opposite. Jesus showed the disciples that he was free to humble himself before them precisely because he was their Lord and master. As to whether or not he denied being good, it seems from the context that Jesus was challenging the rich young ruler's piety. The young man did not understand what true goodness was, and Jesus had to teach him. That he was able to do so shows that he was more than just the "good teacher" whom the young man was flattering with that title—he was God, the source and standard of all goodness. Statements of this kind must be read in their context and interpreted not as detracting from the divinity of the Son but as revealing it in a way that is more powerful than a mere statement of the fact could have achieved.

Kenotic Christology is best understood as an attempt to retain a Christology from above in the face of objections that the traditional belief that the Son of God came down from heaven has made it impossible to do justice to Jesus' full humanity. Those who have propounded the kenotic view know that the divine and human natures of Christ are mutually incompatible, and so they seek to minimize the former in order to do full justice to the latter. The picture they present is of a divine person who has exchanged his divine nature for a human one, instead of holding them both together. In that case, it is claimed, Jesus could have walked the earth as the Son of God and yet still could have been a normal human being, subject to all the limitations that affect the rest of us.

The theory has a certain attraction, but quite apart from the difficulty of accounting for the miracles that Jesus performed, there are serious flaws in it that make it ultimately untenable. The first of these flaws is that, while it is possible for a divine person to add a second nature, as the Son evidently did when he became incarnate, it is not so clear that he can dispose of his original nature in the process. If a divine person does not have a divine nature, or if his divine nature is somehow quiescent, what content does his personal divinity have? He could be truly divine only as long as he retained the ability to express himself in and through his divine nature. For that reason his humanity is an addition to his divinity and not a replacement for it. Second, if the Son's divinity were diluted in any way, his ability to save us would also be compromised. The Son of God was able to sacrifice his human nature for our salvation only because the death of that nature was not the end of his existence. In his divinity he remained who he had always been, and it was because of his remaining fully divine that death could not hold him captive.

---

[65] John 13:1–11.

As for the restoration of his heavenly glory, this must be seen in its proper context. When the Son of God took on human flesh, he did not lose his glory, even though it was revealed only to those who believed.[66] This should not be mistaken for wish-fulfillment on the part of his disciples, though, as the incident of Jesus' transfiguration makes clear.[67] Peter, James, and John were taken up Mount Tabor by Jesus, where "he was transfigured before them, and his face shone like the sun, and his clothes became white as light."[68] Then Moses and Elijah appeared on either side of him, and he was still speaking with them when "a voice from the cloud said, 'This is my beloved Son, with whom I am well pleased; listen to him.'"[69] And how did Peter and his companions react? "When the disciples heard this, they fell on their faces and were terrified."[70] Had the story been made up by the disciples in order to convince the early Christians that Jesus was really God, it is unlikely that they would have portrayed themselves in such a negative light! The importance of the incident should not be underrated, because years later, Peter referred to it as a key moment in Jesus' self-revelation:

> For we did not follow cleverly devised myths when we made known to you the power and coming of our Lord Jesus Christ, but we were eyewitnesses of his majesty. For when he received honor and glory from God the Father, and the voice was borne to him by the Majestic Glory, "This is my beloved Son, with whom I am well pleased," we ourselves heard this very voice borne from heaven, for we were with him on the holy mountain.[71]

At the time, Peter had wanted to erect shrines to Jesus, Moses, and Elijah in commemoration of this extraordinary event, but Jesus did not allow him to do so. Instead, he told the disciples to say nothing about it until an even greater manifestation of his divine glory should be given—his resurrection from the dead.[72] To those who understood what was going on, it was on the cross that the Son's glory was fully revealed, because it was there that the depth of his love for sinful human beings was shown in all its splendor and pathos.

When Pontius Pilate ordered his soldiers to put the inscription "Jesus of Nazareth, the King of the Jews" over Jesus' head, and when those soldiers organized a mock coronation with their crown of thorns, little did they realize that they were being used by God to preach the gospel. The crucifixion

---

[66] John 1:14.
[67] Matt. 17:1–11; Mark 9:2–8; Luke 9:28–36.
[68] Matt. 17:2.
[69] Matt. 17:5.
[70] Matt. 17:6.
[71] 2 Pet. 1:16–18.
[72] Matt. 17:9.

was indeed the moment of Jesus' coronation, when the kingdom he had proclaimed throughout his ministry at last came into being. We have a king who is our Savior because he has triumphed over sin and death and has united us to himself. It is by his wounds and the blood that flowed from them that we are made members of his kingdom, united to him in the deepest manifestation of God's love.[73] It is on the cross that we see how, in the depths of his humiliation before the powers of this world, the Son of God's divine glory shines out most clearly. When he ascended up into heaven to reclaim his throne, he took that glory with him, and now that he is seated at the Father's right hand, his wounds continue to plead for our salvation. It is this glory, inherent in the sacrifice, that the proponents of kenotic Christology do not understand, and which leads them to look for a solution that will avoid such an unacceptable paradox. What they do not realize is that, in bringing the mystery of Christ down to the level of human comprehension, they have lost him; the man they have put on the cross in his place is unable to save us as the Son came to do.

What it felt like for Jesus to be a human being and the Son of God at the same time is impossible for us to say, but perhaps we can begin to understand it if we think of someone who has two nationalities and lives in two different cultures. People like that sometimes think, speak, and act in one language and sometimes in another, without always realizing that they have switched. When they are asked what language they dream in, they often find it hard to say because it is only those who cannot shift subconsciously from one to the other who think there is a difficulty. Jesus must have been something like that during his time on earth. For him, it was natural to operate at some times in his human nature and at other times in his divine nature, and he may not have been fully conscious of switching from one to the other. As with bicultural people today, the problem occurs to outsiders but not to them, and they may wonder what it is like *not* to be able to change from one to the other more or less automatically.

Last but not least, only Jesus' claim to divinity can explain the emergence of Christian theology, which would not have come into being otherwise. Finding room in the one God for a Son to exist alongside the Father was the greatest single challenge that the early church faced. Only once that was accepted would questions about the nature of his incarnation become relevant. If Jesus was truly God, then how he could act both as God and as a human being at the same time would be of key importance in understanding him and his mission. If he were merely an extraordinary creature, however,

---

[73] Matt. 27:27–31; John 19:1–22.

that difficulty would not have arisen, since the difference between him and us would be merely one of degree rather than one of kind.

THE EARTHLY WORK OF THE INCARNATE SON

What indications did Jesus give that he was not just an exceptional creature, but the living God? One of earliest of them appears in the temptations that he suffered at the hand of Satan.[74] Temptation occurs when we are given the opportunity to do something that we have the ability to do but that we should have the strength and good sense to refuse. For example, I can be tempted to eat another piece of cake, knowing that I ought not to, but I cannot be tempted to turn the book in front of me into a cake; that is something beyond my ability. Yet Jesus was tempted to turn stones into bread, which must mean that he could have done it had he so wished. Who can perform such a miracle? Only God can do that, because he made both the stones and bread, and so he can change them into anything he likes. The inference must therefore be that Jesus was God, since otherwise the temptations he endured would have been impossible.

The second indication that Jesus was God is found in his ministry of forgiving sins. This comes out very clearly in the incident involving the paralyzed man who was let down through the roof in order to be healed.[75] Initially, Jesus did not heal him as the man desired, but told him that his sins were forgiven. This provoked the Jewish leaders standing by, who quite rightly objected that no one has the power to forgive sins except God. When Jesus heard that, he went on to rebuke their unbelief. In order to demonstrate that he had the power to forgive sins, he then told the paralytic to get up and walk away. It is very unlikely that the man had gone to Jesus wanting his sins to be forgiven. That thought had probably never crossed his mind, and he may even have been disappointed to discover that he was still disabled. Furthermore, there is no sign in the story that he repented of his sins, or was even aware that he ought to. Certainly Jesus never told him to change his way of life, as he told other people whom he forgave.[76] There is no reason to doubt that Jesus was deeply concerned for the paralytic's physical state, but it was his forgiving him that caused the real stir. Had that not been an act of God himself, it would have been an inexcusable presumption, and Jesus' miracle would probably have been regarded as a sign that he was possessed by the Devil.[77] Once again, Jesus was making a claim and backing it up with evidence.

---

[74] Matt. 4:1–11.
[75] Mark 2:1–12.
[76] See, for example, John 8:11.
[77] See Matt. 12:24.

It was when the fight against the Devil and the healing miracles came together that the issue of Jesus' relationship to God was brought to the fore in the most acute terms. This became clear when Jesus healed a demon-possessed man and those who saw it began to wonder whether he was the Son of David (who was the promised Messiah).[78] It seems that they were unable to think any higher than that, but, ironically, it was the Pharisees who came up with the explanation that Jesus was possessed by the Devil. That gave him a unique opportunity to reveal who he really was, and he took full advantage of it. Why, he asked them, would the Devil cast out his own servants? For what reason would he act against his own interests? That made no sense. The only other option, however, was that Jesus had cast out the demons by the power of God, since no human being, not even the promised Son of David, could have exercised such spiritual power on his own. This is indeed what Jesus told them, pointing out not only that it was by the Spirit of God that he cast the demons out, but that in doing so, the kingdom of God had come upon them. But the kingdom of God is present only where the king is, and the inference here is that Jesus was that king. His miracles were a test of faith, not in themselves, but in the one to whom they pointed, the Son of Man who had come down from heaven.[79]

It is perhaps worth remarking that these incidents occurred toward the beginning of Jesus' public ministry. His claim to be God was not something that grew on him gradually, nor was it the kind of megalomania that is often born of unexpected success. It was certainly not dreamed up from hindsight, after the resurrection and ascension had made his claims to divinity seem more plausible. Jesus *began* his earthly ministry with the assertion that he was God—the rest flowed logically from there. It was never really possible to follow him without acknowledging his divinity when the question arose. When Jesus asked his disciples who they thought he was, Peter confessed that he was the Christ, the Son of the living God. Jesus did not deny this statement, which would have been blasphemous if it had not been true. Instead, he replied that Peter's confession was not something he had deduced naturally from the evidence, but a revelation from God the Father to which he would not otherwise have had access.[80] After the resurrection, the unbelief of Thomas provided another opportunity for Jesus' true identity to be asserted. Thomas insisted that he would believe in the resurrection only if he could see and feel it for himself, but when that request was granted, he fell down and confessed,

---

[78]Matt. 12:22–32.
[79]See John 3:13.
[80]Matt. 16:15–17.

"My Lord and my God!"[81] That was the correct response, the true confession of faith. The supreme miracle and the ultimate victory over the power of the Devil had done their work, and future generations would be expected to believe as Thomas did, even without seeing what Thomas was privileged to witness.

WAS JESUS A MAN ADOPTED BY GOD?

The conviction that Jesus of Nazareth was the Son of God is the hallmark of true Christian faith, but there have always been people who have tried to deny it, sometimes by reinterpreting the meaning of the words in subtle ways. In the third century, a man called Paul of Samosata was accused of saying that Jesus had been adopted as God's Son at the moment of his baptism, when the heavens opened and a voice proclaimed, "This is my beloved Son, with whom I am well pleased."[82] According to this theory, until that time Jesus had been an ordinary man, the natural son of Joseph and Mary, but when God set him apart he received the indwelling power of the Holy Spirit and became something different—no longer an ordinary man but a man who had been adopted by God to be his Son. Whether or not he fully realized it, what Paul of Samosata did was to turn Jesus into the first Christian. In his way of thinking, Jesus was adopted as a child of God in baptism just as we are.[83] According to the adoptionists, the difference between Jesus and his followers is essentially one of degree. As the firstborn of all creation he received the honor that normally attaches to primogeniture. The rest of us look on as we see our older brother succeed to his inheritance, which is the throne of the kingdom of God. We do our best to follow him, so that we may share in his inheritance too, and if we are filled with the Spirit as he was, we shall get there in the end.

Adoptionism sounds too crude to be plausible, but it has proved to be immensely popular over the centuries and it is still widespread today, even though most people fail to recognize it. For example, those who ask, "What would Jesus do?" as if his behavior were a guide to what ours should be, may unintentionally fall into a form of adoptionism. Being a follower of Jesus does not mean copying his behavior or imagining what it would have been and doing that, because if that principle were to be pursued to its logical conclusion, we would also have to die for our sins just as he did. It sounds good to say that the aim of the follower must be to sacrifice himself in imitation of the leader, but such a goal is unrealizable for any number of reasons.

---

[81]John 20:28.
[82]Matt. 3:17.
[83]Rom. 8:15.

First, we must ask how far a literal imitation of Jesus can be pressed. Anyone who is not a single male Jew would be at an immediate disadvantage, because there are some things that Jesus did which would be difficult or impossible for anyone else to copy, such as preaching in a synagogue. Second, to become a carpenter and then embark on an itinerant ministry without special preparation or training is clearly out of the question for the vast majority of people, and it would be absurd if the church tried to impose such a norm on its members. Third, none of us can expect to be given the power to perform miracles, though some people have claimed that they have a healing ministry as part of their imitation of Christ. And of course, the fact that Jesus was celibate has occasionally been used as a justification for imposing the same discipline on his followers, or at least on those who take their discipleship seriously, which directly contradicts what the New Testament says elsewhere.[84] It is hard to imagine Jesus going to the wedding feast at Cana in Galilee if he were against marriage on principle, and it is noteworthy that it was there that he performed his first miracle.[85]

We could go on adding any number of things that would make a straightforward copying of Jesus impossible, absurd, or simply wrong, but from a theological standpoint the reason why this is not expected of us is that Jesus was not a Christian. A Christian is a sinner saved by grace through faith in Jesus Christ, and Jesus was obviously not a sinner saved by grace through faith in himself! The trouble with adoptionism is that it stresses the similarities between Jesus and his followers at the expense of the differences between them, which are just as important. However much he may have been a man like us, Jesus was also our Lord and Savior—God come to meet and to challenge us in human flesh. We can never relate to him by copying what he did for us, but only by submitting to his will and obeying him when he tells us what he wants us to do. At one level, what the Lord requires of us may be completely different from anything he himself did while he was on earth, but the link that unites us to him is that whatever we are asked to do, we must do in the same spirit of submission and obedience that he showed to the will of his Father.

It was that spirit of humble obedience that sent Jesus to his death on a cross for our salvation. We shall not travel the same road as he did because our calling from God is not to save the world. What we are expected to do is to bear witness to the one who has already saved it. We shall not die on a cross, but the cross we are called to take up and bear is nonetheless very real.[86]

---

[84]See 1 Cor. 7:1–7.
[85]John 2:1–11.
[86]Matt. 16:24.

Whether it involves pain and suffering or has some other physical resemblance to what Jesus had to endure, it will invariably lead to a life of self-denial and sacrifice that is the spiritual equivalent of dying and rising again. The apostle Paul made this clear when he wrote,

> Do you not know that all of us who have been baptized into Christ Jesus were baptized into his death? We were buried therefore with him by baptism into death, in order that, just as Christ was raised from the dead by the glory of the Father, we too might walk in newness of life.[87]

Adoptionism reduces an essentially spiritual demand to the level of physical imitation, and so ends up proclaiming a religion of good works and good intentions that can only lead to a form of self-salvation that is alien to the gospel of Christ.

WAS THE SON OF GOD A CREATURE?

A more sophisticated, but nowadays less credible, approach to the question of Jesus' divine sonship was developed in the early fourth century by Arius of Alexandria, who may have absorbed the ideas of Paul of Samosata at second hand. Arius shared Paul of Samosata's belief that the Son was not God in the full sense of the word, but he accepted that the Son had come down from heaven and was therefore not just a man whom God had adopted. The Son was the "firstborn of all creation,"[88] which Arius took to mean that he was the first and greatest of the creatures. According to Arius, when God determined to save mankind from its fall into sin, he sent this Son whom he had made and to whom he had assigned the governance of the universe, to become a man and die for the sins of the human race. From Arius's point of view, the advantages of this were several. First, it made it easier to explain how the Son could have suffered and died—things that are impossible for God but not for his creatures. Second, it made it easier to understand how the Son could become incarnate, since it meant no more than that one creature had transformed himself into another, not that the transcendent God had somehow become a part of his own creation. Finally, it protected the transcendent sovereignty of God from any suggestion that it might have been diminished or impaired by the saving work of the Son.

The difficulties with Arius's view were not easily discerned, and for a long time he swayed the greater part of the Christian world. But there were always some who saw the limitations of his approach, and in the end they prevailed.

---

[87]Rom. 6:3–4.
[88]Col. 1:15.

The bottom line is that if God sent a creature to save us from our sins, can we really say that we are saved by him? Even the highest creature stands far below God in the order of being and cannot do anything that goes beyond his creaturely limitations. Can a created being satisfy the demands of God's justice? If the Son were merely a creature, he could do no more than obey God's will. Even if he could somehow have paid the price for our sins, he would have had no power to forgive us, just as the sacrifices of the law could atone for sins without being able to offer the Israelites forgiveness for them. Moreover, a creature is not eternal. The stock accusation that Arius's opponents kept hurling at him was his statement that, "There was a time when the Son did not exist." If that were true, there would presumably also be a future time when he would cease to exist, and if he ceased to exist, he could no longer be our Savior and our salvation would come to an end. A being who does not possess eternal life cannot give it to us, yet it is eternal life that we have been promised in Christ.

Arius appears to have understood the concept of "mediator," which the New Testament applies to Christ,[89] as meaning "intermediary." This would mean that he was a creature higher than mankind and lower than God in the order of things, but similar enough to both that he could act as a go-between. That would mean that, in himself, he was neither God nor man, but had managed to become a man in his incarnation without being able to become God in his subsequent ascension. He may have gone back to sit at the right hand of the Father, but he was there as a servant admitted into the divine presence by grace, not as the Son who could commune with the Father as his equal. The servant Savior could have spoken only when he was spoken to, which would have compromised his ability to intercede for us and possibly even prevented him from ever doing so. What this would have meant in practice can be seen from the case of Nehemiah, who was cupbearer to King Artaxerxes I of Persia (465–424 B.C.). Nehemiah was a Jew who was deeply concerned for the welfare of his people and wanted the king to help him save them from their enemies. But it was only when the king noticed that he was unhappy about something and thought to inquire about it that Nehemiah was able to explain the situation and get the help he needed.[90] Had Jesus been in a similar position, there is a chance that he might have been given the same opportunity to speak as was given to Nehemiah, and help might have been forthcoming, but this would have been entirely dependent on the Father's good will and could not have been claimed as a right by those who are united to Christ.

---

[89]1 Tim. 2:5.
[90]Neh. 2:1–8.

For all these reasons, the interpretation of the Son's being that was proposed by Arius was inadequate and was therefore rejected by the church. In spite of that, though, it proved to be remarkably resilient. A form of Arianism survived for at least two and a half centuries after his death. Something akin to it survives to this day, and in fact it may be the majority view in most otherwise "orthodox" Christian congregations. To detect whether this is so, ask the members of your church whether Jesus is God. Those who hesitate on this point and answer that he is the *Son* of God (and therefore not really God) are Arian without knowing it. They have tried to reconcile their belief in monotheism with their belief in the divinity of Christ, and have come up with a compromise solution that makes Jesus divine but not fully God.

What they do not realize, and what the critics of Arius have always had to point out, is that such a solution is logically impossible. There is only one God, and so if the Son is divine in any real sense, he must be God. It is simply not possible to be *like* God without actually being God, because no creature can be like the absolute Creator. Either he is absolute or he is not—there is no compromise or middle way in this matter. We have to say that the Son is fully God, because anything less than that reduces him to the level of a creature and makes it impossible for him to bridge the gulf which separates us from the being of God.

We can really understand the importance of saying that the Son is fully God only in the context of the divine love. It was in love that the Father sent his Son to die for our sins and to reconcile us to him, so that we may live with him forever.[91] But what kind of relationship with God has this act of his love produced? It is well known in diplomatic circles, not to mention in many corporations and institutions of various kinds, that people are normally dealt with at the level appropriate to their status. An ambassador will be received by the head of state because that is whom he represents, but a trade minister will probably get to meet no one higher up than his opposite number in the country he is visiting. On the other hand, if an ambassador or trade minister is forced to deal with someone of a much lower rank than he is, he may legitimately conclude that he is being insulted—a not infrequent diplomatic practice. When we approach God we are approaching the ultimate "head of state," the king of the universe. At what level does he receive us? Does he admit us into his presence, or are we forced to deal with one of his subordinates because that is our place and we must stay in it?

When we put the question like that, we can see immediately what the answer must be. Inferior to God as we undoubtedly are, and not entitled to

---

[91] John 3:16.

any reception at all, we have nevertheless been called to sit in the heavenly places in Christ Jesus, to share with him in his filial relationship with the Father.[92] We are no longer servants but sons, given by adoption the inheritance that belongs uniquely to the one who is the Son by nature, because he is the true and living God.[93] The love of God is such that he deals with us not as subordinates but as children, a relationship that would not be possible if it did not already exist in him, in the eternal relationship between the Father and the Son. Arianism fails because it offers us only a distant God, who deals with our problems in an efficient but essentially impersonal way. In sending the Son to save us, however, the Father was not distancing himself from us but drawing us into himself, because the Son is one with him. He can stand in the Father's presence and act as our Mediator precisely because he is the Father's equal. This is our faith and our relationship with God, and when we experience his love at work, we can begin to appreciate that the Jesus who has given us eternal life is not just a heavenly creature but the eternal Lord and God himself.

---

[92]Eph. 2:6.
[93]John 15:15; Rom. 8:14–17.

11

THE
HOLY SPIRIT

THE IDENTITY OF THE HOLY SPIRIT

When we move on from the Son to the Holy Spirit we come to the knottiest Trinitarian problem of them all. To begin with, the Spirit's personhood and identity are less clearly expressed in the New Testament than those of the Father and the Son, and it is harder to see where he fits into the inner life of the Godhead. To start with his name, it is possible to argue that because the Father and the Son are also holy and spiritual, the designation "holy spirit" might equally well be applied to them. In John 14:16 Jesus tells his disciples that when he has gone away he will send them "another Comforter" to dwell with them forever, and the fact that this is the Holy Spirit has led many people to assume that Comforter (or *Paraclete* as he is known in Greek) is his personal name.[1] That, however, is not the case. First, Jesus tells his disciples that he will send them *another* Comforter, which assumes that he is one as well. But if the word "Comforter" can be used of both the second and the third persons of the Godhead, it can hardly be the Spirit's distinctive name. The second reason why "Comforter" cannot be the Holy Spirit's personal name is that the persons of the Trinity are named *in relation to each other and not in relation to us*. If the Holy Spirit is the Comforter, it is not because he brings comfort to the Father and the Son but because he brings it to us. The Father and the Son would recognize that in their own relationship to him, and so it cannot be his personal name within the Godhead.

Some have concluded that the Holy Spirit is anonymous and have explained this by saying that his function is to glorify the Father and the Son

---

[1]"Comforter" is the standard English translation for *Paraclete*, but other terms are also found, such as "Helper," "Advocate," "Counselor," and so on.

rather than to draw attention to himself. That may be true, but it is hardly a reason for him not to have a name of his own. After all, the angels draw attention to God and not to themselves, but those angels who are singled out as individuals have names like Michael and Gabriel, so why should the same not apply to the Holy Spirit? Yet the fact is that no such personal name is revealed to us in the Scriptures, where the third person of the Trinity is always referred to as the Spirit, often with some qualifying adjective or description like "Spirit of truth," which is a general term and not a personal designation.

Does the Holy Spirit appear anywhere in the Old Testament? This is a very difficult question to answer, not least because of the ambiguity inherent in the word "spirit." For example, when the Spirit of God hovered over the face of the waters on the first day of creation,[2] are we to understand this as a reference to the third person of the Trinity, or is it referring to the one God who is being described here, by focusing on one of his attributes? Lack of evidence makes it safer to assume that the passage is speaking of the one God, whom it describes as Spirit,[3] an observation that is more consonant both with Jewish monotheism and with the use of other phrases in the Old Testament, such as "Word of God" and "Wisdom of God," both of which could have been meant to refer to the Son but probably did not.[4]

THE RELATIONSHIP OF THE HOLY SPIRIT TO THE FATHER

What is the relationship of the Holy Spirit to the Father, and how is it best expressed? The Father represents the transcendence of divinity, and so the divine identity of the Son and of the Holy Spirit is expressed primarily in relation to him. To say that the Son is begotten of the Father and that the Holy Spirit proceeds from him is to confess that they both share the Father's divine nature and are equal to him. Jesus tells us that the Holy Spirit proceeds from the Father,[5] an assertion on which all Christians are agreed. What does the term "procession" mean? It is clearly different from "generation," and this cannot be an accident. We cannot give the impression that the Holy Spirit is a second Son, because that would risk making him an alternative Savior. On the other hand, while "generation" is a temporal term that cannot be interpreted literally when used in the context of eternity, the same is not so true of "procession." The Bible tells us that the Holy Spirit *proceeds* from the Father, and the use of the present tense implies that this is an eternal relationship.

---

[2]Gen. 1:2.
[3]See John 4:24.
[4]See, for example, 1 Kings 12:22; 1 Chron. 17:3; and compare with Luke 3:2, where the phrase "word of God" cannot refer to the Son.
[5]John 15:26.

The term "procession" underlines the divinity of the Spirit, because it speaks of a relationship with the Father that makes sense only in terms of a common nature. If that were not so, the Holy Spirit would be a creature and would suffer from the limitations of his inferior status. "Procession" also expresses the uniqueness of the Spirit's own identity. To proceed from the Father is to represent the Father as his ambassador, conveying his thoughts and character to the ones to whom he is sent. The first thing the Holy Spirit does is remind us that the Father (and therefore also the Trinity) is spiritual, not material. God cannot be portrayed in human terms, nor can he be defined by the creation that he has made. In the Old Testament this point was made by the multiple prohibitions against idolatry, which are reinforced by the Holy Spirit's own invisible working in and around us. Like the wind, he can be known and his presence can be felt, but he can never be tied down in time and space.[6]

The second great characteristic of God is his holiness, and this too is represented to us by the third person of the Trinity. For a creature to be holy is to be like God in both intellectual and moral terms. There are spiritual beings in the universe who are not holy, because they have rebelled against their Lord and Creator. The world in which we live has become subject to their influence and we too have fallen under their power, with the result that we are far more in tune with them than we are with God. To meet with the third person of the Trinity is therefore to be struck by how radically different he is from anything we have encountered before. When he first makes himself known to us, we are hostile to him because of that radical difference, but his task is to break our resistance down and bring us back to obedience to the Father who made us and who wants us to live in eternity with him. It is in this way that the ambassadorial role of the Holy Spirit is brought home to us—he is God's messenger in our hearts, telling us we have been adopted by the Father and giving us the means to make that adoption a reality in our spiritual experience.[7]

The first person to receive the Holy Spirit in this way was Jesus, on whom the Spirit descended at his baptism in the form of a dove.[8] As the eternal Son of God, Jesus did not need to receive the Holy Spirit, and his baptism should not be used to explain the way in which the Son and the Holy Spirit are related inside the Godhead. Some theologians (particularly in the Eastern tradition) have tried to do this by saying that the Holy Spirit proceeds from the Father and rests on the Son, as he did in the Son's baptism, making that event appear

---

[6]John 3:8.
[7]Rom. 8:14–17.
[8]Luke 3:22–23.

as a manifestation of the inner relations within the Godhead, but there is no evidence for this. It was as a man, sent "in the likeness of sinful flesh,"[9] that Jesus needed to be sealed with the presence of the Holy Spirit. This was a reminder that being filled with the Spirit of God is not impossible for us but is the norm to which believers are expected to conform. It is not just a matter of having our sins cleansed or removed, but of being united to God and set apart for his service in the world. Jesus was already united to God, but at his baptism he was set apart for his earthly ministry; in receiving the Holy Spirit, he expressed both his mission and his ability to do the will of the Father who had sent him. The Holy Spirit brought the Father's will into the Son's humanity, a point that is underlined by the biblical text which says that he descended on Jesus "in bodily form, like a dove," reminding us that our salvation is not just a spiritual experience but also a resurrection of the body to a new life.

THE RELATIONSHIP OF THE HOLY SPIRIT TO THE SON

The Father's relationship to the Son is rooted and grounded in love, and the descent of the Holy Spirit on the Son is an expression of that. On this point all Christians are agreed. Can we therefore say that the Son loves the Father just as much as the Father loves the Son? If we agree that their love for each other must be mutual in order for it to be perfect, then the answer must be yes. Unless the Son's love for the Father is equal and complementary to the Father's love for the Son, the love of God would be defective within the Godhead and we could not say that God is pure love. Furthermore, if the Son does not love the Father to the same degree as the Father loves him, would his work of redemption have any validity? Could we imagine that the Son went to his death in a spirit of resentment at what the Father was forcing him to do? Could we believe that we have been admitted into the Father's presence by a Son who does not really want us to be there, and who mediates for us only because he has been ordered by his Father to do so? That is absurd. The conclusion must surely be that everything the Son has done to redeem us he has done out of love for the Father. The Father's validation of that redeeming work, which he has shown in the resurrection, ascension, and heavenly session of the Son, is sufficient evidence of that.

Does the Son love the Father in the same way as the Father loves the Son? If he does, and if the Holy Spirit is the seal of the Father's love for the Son, he will proceed from the Son just as much as from the Father, because the love of each person for the other is the same. But if the Son does not love the

---

[9]Rom. 8:3.

Father in exactly the same way as the Father loves him, to say that the Holy Spirit proceeds from the Son is liable to be misleading and unhelpful at best, and erroneous and heretical at worst, because their relationships, though complementary, are not identical. It is on this point that Christians of East and West disagree. The Eastern Orthodox churches say that the nature of the Son's love for the Father is different from that of the Father's love for the Son because they are different persons. They love each other to the same degree but in a different way, so the term "procession" should not be used to describe the Holy Spirit's relationship to the Son as if it were identical with his relationship to the Father.

The Western churches, on the other hand, both Roman Catholic and Protestant, tend to sidestep this question and say that it is the degree of the love shown between the two that matters and not the precise nature of their mutual relationship. The degree of love the Father and Son show to each other must be equal because both are fully divine persons. Therefore, even if their love for each other is different because they are distinct persons, that difference does not invalidate the use of the term "procession" to describe the Holy Spirit's relationship to the Son as well as to the Father. Equality does not require absolute sameness, but can be expressed by different persons. In God the persons are fully divine and therefore equal to each other, however distinctive each one of them is in himself. Ultimately, it is argued, the fact of personhood is more universal and fundamental than whatever differences individual persons have or need in order to identify themselves. Therefore, the love of the Father for the Son is equal to that of the Son for the Father, and because each of them is fully God, that mutual love is one and the same.

Expressed in traditional theological language, the main question in dispute has been to decide whether the Holy Spirit proceeds from both the Father and the Son (the Western position), or whether he proceeds from the Father only (the Eastern position). If it is agreed that he proceeds from both, the next question is whether there is some difference in the way that he proceeds from each of them. Do the Father and the Son act together in the procession of the Holy Spirit, so that their roles cannot be effectively distinguished from each other, or does the Holy Spirit proceed *from* the Father *through* the Son, thereby maintaining a real distinction between the first two persons of the Godhead?

The Westerners hold to the so-called "double procession" of the Holy Spirit, which means that he proceeds from the Father and the Son, who work so closely together that it is almost impossible to distinguish them from each other. The Easterners reject this on the ground that it blurs the distinction between the persons of the Father and the Son and compromises the role of the Father as the unique source of divinity. They insist that when Jesus tells his disciples that he will send them the Holy Spirit who proceeds from the Father, his words must be taken in a way that excludes the possibility that the Son may also play a part in that procession.[10]

In 1439, the Council of Florence agreed on a compromise formula that was designed to unite the two branches of Christendom. It was there that the interpretation of the "double procession" as meaning "from the Father through the Son" was adopted, in the hope that the Eastern churches would accept that it avoids any confusion of the first two persons. The compromise did not work because it failed to affirm with sufficient clarity the Eastern belief that the Father is the unique "source of the Godhead," but it was accepted in the West and remains the official position of both the Roman Catholic and the main Protestant churches today.

This theological *impasse* is the result of relying on the "causal" model of the Trinity and it shows clearly the limits of that model. In the causal model, the Father is the "cause" of the other two persons, who are "caused," by generation in the case of the Son and by procession in the case of the Holy Spirit. If that way of thinking is accepted, those who opposed the "double procession" were probably right to insist that there could be only one cause in the Godhead, since otherwise the basic principle of monotheism would have been compromised. Of course, those who upheld the double procession denied that and argued that the Father and Son could act together as a single cause just as the Trinity acts together as the single cause of the created universe. Nevertheless, it is probably right to say that the double procession doctrine expounded according to the causal model jeopardizes the fundamental unity of God and ought to be discarded, if not actually denied, for that reason.

The question appears in a different light, however, if we abandon the causal approach and look at it in terms of relations. The evidence of the New Testament is that the Holy Spirit bears witness to the Son in the same way that he bears witness to the Father, representing each of them equally in the hearts and minds of believers.[11] To say that the Spirit has a relationship with the Father that is qualitatively different from his relationship to the Son introduces an imbalance in the Godhead, and the Eastern churches are just as opposed to that as the Western ones are. In a model based on mutual relations, the double procession of the Holy Spirit is not only admissible as a doctrine—it is essential if the equilibrium in the Trinity is to be maintained. If

---

[10]John 15:26.
[11]John 14:17, 23.

both sides in this debate can agree that causation must be transcended in favor of relations, as it was when the term "eternally begotten" was adopted for understanding the relationship between the Father and the Son, there should be no difficulty in accepting the double procession of the Holy Spirit, while recognizing that the historical objections to it were both understandable and justified in their context.

In fairness to the Western tradition, it has always recognized that the love of the Father and the Son for each other must take the particular identity of each of them into account. Given that this is so, the love that flows between them will be full and complete and yet bear the marks of the persons whose love it is. The parent's love for the child is just as strong and as valid as the child's love for the parent, and it seems unnatural for one to exist without the other. In the fractured world of fallen humanity, that kind of imbalance does occur from time to time, but in God it is inconceivable. At the end of the day, we must affirm that the Holy Spirit reveals the coequal and coeternal love of the Father for the Son and of the Son for the Father, and that it is into that mutual love that the Spirit integrates us.

Jesus told his disciples that, after his departure, the Spirit would come to dwell in their hearts, and that when that happened, both he and the Father would come to dwell in them.[12] When speaking of this indwelling presence, the apostle Paul did not hesitate to call the third person of the Godhead "the Spirit of the Son," making it clear that as far as we are concerned, he is the Spirit of the second as well as of the first person of the Trinity.[13] What are the implications of this for the Spirit's so-called "double procession"? In attempting to answer this, theologians distinguish between the *eternal origin* of the Holy Spirit within the Trinity and the *temporal mission* that he accomplishes on earth, in the hearts of believers. The Western church insists that experience of God in time and space must correspond to God as he is in his eternal self. If there is a difference between what we know about God and what he is in his own being, then our experience of him does not accurately reflect the reality and we may doubt whether (or to what extent) it is authentic.

The Eastern churches agree that, in his temporal mission, the Holy Spirit is the Spirit of both the Father and the Son, but they do not accept that this corresponds to the inner being of God. We live in a finite and imperfect world, and there are hidden depths of mystery in God that cannot be expressed in human terms. In speaking to us, God accommodates himself to the limits of our understanding, but if we assume that these limits are adequate to describe

---

[12]John 14:23.
[13]Gal. 4:6.

who and what he is in himself, we are not only mistaken but guilty of making an intellectual idol out of the one whose being goes beyond the bounds of human knowledge.

As so often in such controversies, each side is right in its own eyes and has difficulty comprehending the other point of view because it does not fit into its own system. In recent years many people have given up hope that a resolution of this difficulty will ever be found and have preferred to concentrate on the Spirit's temporal mission, partly because East and West agree about that and partly because it seems to be of greater practical significance. If we can agree about how the Holy Spirit works, they say, does it really matter how he is related to the other persons of the Trinity? Can we not leave that question to one side as a mystery that has not been revealed, and get on with the business of our everyday spiritual life? This line of reasoning appeals to many, but matters are not as simple as that. Both sides in the debate insist that what the Holy Spirit does reflects who he is, which means that if we do not agree about who he is, we shall not agree about what he does either.

To give an example of what this can involve, consider the question of the church. Both Eastern and Western Christians agree that the Holy Spirit animates and governs the people of God, but many Eastern theologians claim that the Western belief in the double procession of the Spirit means that he is subordinate to the Son, in practice if not in theory. This in turn means that the church is subject to the Son's representative on earth—the pope, who calls himself the "vicar of Christ." These theologians have even been known to accuse Protestants of being theologically inconsistent here, because they reject papal supremacy but not the double procession of the Holy Spirit that supposedly underlies it!

Given this intractable situation, it is perhaps worth summarizing the many points of agreement between the East and West, so that the relatively small area of disagreement, important though it is, can be seen in its proper perspective. All Christians agree on the following:

1. The Holy Spirit is the third person of the Trinity, fully God in every respect, and he proceeds from the Father.

2. He dwells in the hearts of Christians, where he acts as the Spirit of adoption, making us children of God. In this context he can be (and is) called the Spirit of the Son.

3. The Holy Spirit expresses the love of the Father for the Son, and the Son's love for the Father is of the same degree as the Father's love for him.

4. The Father's love for the Son differs in some way from the Son's love

for the Father because they are different persons, though both are equally perfect and divine.

Where we disagree is the issue of whether the differences of the two loves in God are sufficient to make it impossible (or at least very unwise) to use the term "procession" to describe the Holy Spirit's relationship to each of them indiscriminately.

Can this difference of opinion be resolved? Perhaps it can, if both sides in the discussion are prepared to look at the question objectively, with fresh eyes and a new spirit. Claiming infallibility for one's own position on the matter is a recipe for failure. If progress is to be made, it will have to be on the basis of a paradigm that avoids the pitfalls of the "causation" model of Trinitarian relations, which has dominated the field so far. On the other hand, we must humbly recognize that greater minds than ours have struggled with this question without success, and we may never find a solution that is satisfactory to both sides.

That will no doubt come as a disappointment to many who have labored in the field of ecumenical relations, but it may also be a sign from God that our experience of him cannot be tied down to a particular formula. As the apostle Paul said, now we see in a mirror dimly; only in the world to come will we see face-to-face. Now we know in part, but then we shall know fully, even as we are fully known by God.[14] If the resolution of this age-old difficulty has to wait until then, that may also be a sign from God that our theologies, however reasonable they may seem to us, can never fully grasp the mystery of his eternal and transcendent being. As Christians we are called to live with differences like these and admit that both sides have something to be said in their favor. In the final analysis, it is how we love one another in spite of these differences, and not how successfully we manage to prove to our own satisfaction that we are right and those who differ from us are wrong, that shows the world what it means for us to be children of God.

---

[14]1 Cor. 13:12.

PART THREE

GOD'S LOVE FOR HIS CREATION

12

WHAT GOD HAS MADE

THE NATURE OF CREATION

Why God created the universe is a question that the Bible neither asks nor answers. For the writers of Scripture, it was enough to know that God created the universe for his own purposes, but what those purposes might be remained a mystery. We can glean something about them from what God tells us about ourselves and from what he expects of us as the guardians of the created order, but beyond that we cannot go.

Many people have wondered what the meaning of the universe is and have sought answers based on their own speculations or desires. The ancient Greeks tended to believe that matter was eternal and had not been created at all. To their minds the visible world was the product of impersonal and unstable forces that brought things into being and then dissolved them. The only permanent realities were spiritual and invisible. According to them, the problem with the human race was that we are a combination of these two incompatible things. They believed that we are souls imprisoned in matter, a dilemma that makes us conscious of our true destiny but unable to achieve it, except by leaving the material body and returning to the spiritual realm from which we came. But reintegration into the eternal spirit meant the dissolution of our identity into the one supreme and all-embracing Being. The paradoxical result of this was that "salvation" and self-destruction were one and the same thing.

The biblical picture of creation is very different from this, so it should come as no surprise that the first chapters of Genesis were frequently commented on by the theologians of the early church, many of whom wrote specifically on the creation story.[1] Basil of Caesarea (d. 379) went into minute

---

[1] Which they referred to as the *hexaemeron*, the Greek term for "six days."

detail in describing the creation, revealing a knowledge of biology that is common enough among those who live close to nature and the soil but seems quite remarkable to urbanized people today. Most importantly, it was the biblical story which led Christians like Basil to find order and harmony in a universe that had seemed to their pagan ancestors to be capricious and unpredictable, and it was that discovery that laid the foundations for the eventual development of the natural sciences.

Christian theologians have always believed that God made the material world out of nothing (*ex nihilo*). This is not expressly stated in Genesis, where the earth is described as being "without form and void" before God started working on it,[2] but *creatio ex nihilo* is stated in the New Testament and is implied by the fact that God exercised complete control over matter from the beginning.[3] It is also implied by the New Testament assertion that God will eventually bring the created order to an end and put something else in its place.[4] We do not need to be told any more than this, and if we were, it would probably be beyond our understanding, which cannot transcend the limitations of time and space. Creation must have had a beginning just as surely as it will have an end, but to go back *before* the beginning and ask what God was doing then is to step outside the framework for which our minds were made. We know enough to understand that there is something out there that is beyond our grasp, but we can say no more about it than that.

The significance of this limitation should not be underestimated, because it is a constant theme of the Scriptures. The biblical writers do not hesitate to remind us that however hard we try, we shall never understand the mystery of the universe or plumb the depths of the mind of God.[5] One consequence of this is that any attempt to absolutize or worship a created thing or a figment of our imagination is not merely pointless but wrong. To bow down to an image carved out of wood or stone, as almost everyone in biblical times did, or to construct a philosophy of life out of the musings of our own finite minds and seek to impose that as a rule to live by, is an invitation to failure. In the modern world, there are relatively few people who practice idolatry in the traditional sense of the word, but there are many who live according to a worldview that another human being has invented or that they have pieced together. Man-made ideologies have struggled for power and have tried to impose themselves on human societies, first in the Western world and now everywhere. From the Christian point of view, it makes little difference

---

[2] Gen. 1:2. The original Hebrew is a rhyming expression meaning "topsy-turvy."
[3] Heb. 11:3.
[4] Rev. 21:1.
[5] Job 38–39; Rom. 11:33.

whether that ideology is repressive communism or liberal humanism, because each of them is a false gospel, promising an answer to life's problems that cannot be attained by purely material means.

To be a creature is to belong to a dimension in which things are relative, not absolute. The relativity of creation is the key to understanding what our relationship to it ought to be, and it is on this, rather than on the question of why there is a creation in the first place, that the Bible concentrates. The first chapter of Genesis is less an account of how the world came into being than an outline of how its different parts are interconnected. It presents us with a *cosmos*, an ordered universe in which everything finds its place. The story it tells is neither detailed nor comprehensive, but speaks in general categories and leaves many questions unanswered. For example, when God created vegetation, we are told that there appeared "plants yielding seed, and fruit trees bearing fruit in which is their seed,"[6] but that is all. There is not a word about the grass, nor about other kinds of trees or flowers. When were these created? We may assume that they were all part of the creation of "vegetation" but that is not specifically stated. We can hardly deny that they exist, but what we say about their origin must come from logical deduction, speculation, or scientific investigation. Those things do not contradict the biblical account but supplement it with information that is not essential for understanding the main point of the story.

The account in Genesis says nothing about the creation of spiritual beings, though they must have been created sometime before, because one of them, the serpent we know as Satan, plays an important part in the narrative.[7] Nor are we told anything about the rest of the universe beyond the briefest mention of the "stars," a term which presumably includes the other planets, comets, and so on.[8] What we are told is that God made everything that exists for a purpose. The sun and moon, for example, were made to be bearers of light. Light existed before they did,[9] but we would not experience it without them. We now know that moonlight is reflected sunlight, but although the biblical writer may not have understood that, the story hints at their interdependence—they were created together and appointed for complementary, though not equal, tasks. Scientists have since discovered how this works, but the basic framework for understanding it is already present in the Bible.

The emphasis in the Genesis account is on the immense variety of created things and their complex interrelationship. The story brings out their inner

---

[6]Gen. 1:11.
[7]Gen. 3:1.
[8]Gen. 1:16.
[9]Gen. 1:3, 16.

dynamic, and the creatures are portrayed as having what we might call "a life of their own." Far from being fixed in a static mode that cannot change or develop, we are told that many of them would spread, adapt, and reproduce themselves in different environments over time. Nothing is said about extinction, either natural or induced, but independent observation shows that it is part of this process and may have been intended by God from the beginning. As environments change and habitats are destroyed, some species disappear. Others have the capacity to adapt to new conditions and do so, but there are few if any clear examples of one species mutating into another. Whether new species can appear after the initial creation is complete seems to be ruled out by the assertion that God rested from his works on the seventh day,[10] but caution is required about this. We know that new varieties of plant life can be produced artificially, so it would be unwise for us to say that cross-breeding cannot happen in nature as well. It may be impossible to make something out of nothing, but we have not yet exhausted the potential of what already exists. Who knows what surprises may be lying in wait for us?

Much here depends on definition. We can suggest that entirely new species, of the kind that only a science fiction writer can imagine, will probably not now appear, but we cannot exclude the possibility that new forms of life may develop out of existing matter. Anything "new" that appears now will have a prehistory that shows its relationship to, and dependence on, something that already exists. We must not underestimate the created order's remarkable capacity for reproduction and internal development, which is one of the strongest arguments that can be made from natural science for belief in God.

Where does this inner potential come from and why does it act in such an amazing variety of ways? What is it that makes life so colorful and productive? Above all, how is it that so many of the relationships that keep our world in being are "fine-tuned" to such a degree that even the slightest change in the balance of forces would cause them to collapse and disappear? Perhaps one or two of these things could have come about by accident, or by trial and error, but it stretches credulity to suggest that this can be said of the entire universe. There are enough imperfections in the world to remind us that it is not mechanistically perfect, and surely it would have gone awry at some point if there were no overarching principle holding it together. Some people use the imperfections of the created order as an excuse to deny the existence of God, but if anything, they would seem to prove the opposite. The universe holds together despite such things, because, although the creation is interlocking,

---

[10]Gen. 2:2–3.

it is not self-contained. It has the capacity to tolerate "loose ends" here and there because God is in control of it, as the survival of what is less than the fittest testifies.

The relational interdependence of creation tells us that no part of God's world is intrinsically better or worse than any other part. It may be tempting to think that an animal is a "higher" form of being than a plant, which is in turn "higher" than a rock, and there is a sense in which that is true. To say that a horse is "better" than a rose, which in turn is "better" than a bar of gold may make sense if we think of human life as the highest form of existence, but which one of these would most people choose to have? The answer is not that obvious! In practice, our assessment of the value a thing has usually depends on the use to which it is going to be put and not on any intrinsic merit it may possess. Most city-dwellers would probably rather have a bar of gold than a horse, but would a gardener want a horse instead of an exotic variety of rose? Wealthy Arab sheikhs sometimes prefer to live in tents close to their horses and camels because they have been taught to value them more than mere oil, despite the fact that it is the oil that has given them the wherewithal to stock their stables. The value a thing has in our eyes is directly connected to the relationship which we have, or want to have, with that thing itself. In other words, it is an expression of love. As Christians we are called to love the created order, but not to value it above our relationship to the Creator himself. Other creatures have no choice and can only do what comes naturally to them, but human beings have a relationship to God that gives us a perspective and a responsibility to evaluate other created things and choose how we are going to relate to them.

The importance of this is brought out most clearly when we understand that creation is not a self-contained reality. Theories which claim that the world made itself and has no external reference point cannot be accepted by Christians because we believe that everything has a cause. It does not matter to us if the "system" is circular, in the sense that nothing within it can be singled out as the "first cause," because we do not expect to find that within the created order in any case. We are quite happy to accept the theory that there is no discernible "first cause" because the Creator is external to his creation. Only if a "first cause" were to be discovered within the created universe would we have reason to worry, because such a cause could not possibly be God.

The Creator stands outside what he has made, but we do not believe that the universe was set in motion by a God who now does little more than observe the chain reaction he started. On the contrary, it continues to function in direct dependence on him and could not continue to exist otherwise.

God is the absolute Being with respect to whom all created things are relative and on whom they depend. We can figure out how things fit together within the universe and explain their function, but their existence can be understood only in relation to the God who made them. This is especially important when we consider things that have no apparent function or use but which are nevertheless part of the created order. It is hard to see how a world that is self-created or totally interlocking could either produce or tolerate the existence of things that are purely decorative and serve no functional purpose. But in a world created by God there is no such difficulty. We may not know why hedgehogs or ragweed exist, but God does. He made them for some reason, whether we appreciate that or not. Whatever else they are meant to do, their chief purpose is to glorify him, and in that respect they are no different from the rest of the creation.

THE GOODNESS OF CREATION

Everything that God made is fundamentally good.[11] The systematic repetition of this affirmation on each day of creation in Genesis 1 is sufficient evidence of its importance. The word "good" indicates that God has made what he intended to make and it is therefore "perfect," not in some abstract way but in the sense that it is fully formed and equipped for the task(s) assigned to it. This "perfection" includes its undeveloped potential along with what we perceive to be its flaws and limitations. Human beings have been given dominion over creation in order to bring out its hidden capabilities. Just as a jigsaw puzzle is not defective merely because it comes in pieces, so the world is not "imperfect" either. It comes the way it does as part of God's purpose, and it is that which makes it "good."

It was in contrast to ancient Greek philosophical notions of matter that the biblical affirmation of the fundamental goodness of creation took on particular importance for the early Christians. Many ancient Greeks, and especially Platonists, believed that the things we see around us are pale and corrupt copies (or "forms") of ideas that exist in the mind of the supreme being. In the world we observe many different tables, for example, each of which has its own shape and size. But in the realm of ideas there is only the perfect table, a mental concept which all material tables aspire to imitate, with varying degrees of success. The basic reason why the tables we see in front of us are different from each other is that they are corruptions of the ideal that have occurred because of the limitations of mind and matter.

---

[11]Gen. 1:4, 10, 12, 18, 21, 25, 31.

The Bible does not endorse such a view. On the contrary, it tells us that what exists in the created order is what is meant to be; there is no hidden ideal compared to which the visible reality around us is inferior. This does not mean we have no mandate to develop the potential of things in order to get more out of them than we otherwise would. We are perfectly entitled to irrigate deserts, drain swamps, experiment with genetic modifications designed to produce higher crop yields, and so on. What we are not permitted to do is to *reject* any part of the created order on the ground that it is intrinsically evil. To be undeveloped or underdeveloped is not the same thing as to be useless or corrupt, and our primary task must be to look for the potential in what we have been given, not to reject it as if it were of no value.

The ancient Greeks tended to think that matter was evil and that any involvement with it was bound to lead to "sin." Their conception of this was not necessarily moral and often focused on ritual purity more than anything else, but whatever sin was, it resulted from contamination with matter. So strong was this feeling that in the early church there were some who refused to accept the idea that the Creator God could also be our Redeemer. To their minds, the function of a savior was to rescue us from the clutches of the material world, which has supposedly dragged us down and which now prevents us from being spiritual (and so automatically good). Christians have always rejected this idea and insisted that our Savior is also our Creator, but that has not always been enough to dispel the widespread impression that Christianity is somehow a "world-denying" religion.

What evidence is there for the belief that Christians are supposed to turn away from the material world? In the Old Testament, the Jewish people were given food laws that restricted what they were allowed to eat, and the words "clean" and "unclean" were employed to describe the difference. But the Jews were told to eat certain things and not others as a mark of their distinctiveness and of their consecration to God, *not* because the "unclean" things were bad in themselves. There is no correlation between what was forbidden and what is harmful to the human body—the Jewish food laws were not meant to be regarded as a "healthy diet"! Even so, it did not take much to conclude that there was something wrong with "unclean" things, and by the time of Jesus many Jews thought in those terms. Perhaps working on the assumption that "you are what you eat," they extended this clean versus unclean distinction to the Gentiles, creating a prejudice against them that was almost impossible to eradicate. But if there is one thing that is constantly reiterated in the New Testament, both in the teaching of Jesus and in that of his disciples, it is that the Mosaic distinction between clean and unclean food has no moral (or even hygienic) significance.[12]

This is why the first Christians were not bound to observe the Old Testament food laws, except when failure to do so might cause scandal and split the church. If there was nothing intrinsically wrong with "unclean" foodstuffs, there was nothing particularly "right" about them either. Christians were not to decide what to eat in reaction to the perceived inadequacies of Judaism, but in the context of what is right and proper in any given circumstance. In other words, Christians desacralized food and put it in its proper place as fuel for the body, to be used as and when it is most appropriate to do so, and not as a sign of spiritual achievement.

The same principle applies to everything else in the created order. A great deal of attention is paid nowadays to the "restrictions" placed on sexual activity in the New Testament, but these must be interpreted in the same way as the Christian reaction to the Jewish food laws. Sexual activity as such is neither good nor bad; it is a natural process which is an integral part of the preservation and propagation of the human race. Legitimate sexual intercourse is confined to lifelong heterosexual marriage, which is the context in which children are meant to be produced and brought up and which is therefore the basis for stability in the family and in wider societal relations.

But although sex is intended to be a part of marriage, it is not the only purpose for which marriage was instituted. It is just as wrong for Christians to marry for sexual gratification as it is for them to abstain from sexual activity within marriage for no reason. There may be times when a married person is called to devote special attention to his or her spiritual life, and at those times sexual activity may be a distraction that is best avoided.[13] There are also people who are called to a life of celibacy so that they can serve God more effectively, and that too is to be welcomed and honored in the church.[14] In neither case is anyone saying that sex is wrong or bad; it is simply that sometimes there are other priorities which demand that it should be set aside for the time being, just as there are times when it is right to fast in order to concentrate more fully on serving the Lord.[15] To do this is not to deny the world but to put the world in its place, as something made by the Creator for our use that is not to be idolized or abused in ways that lose sight of his primary claim to our allegiance.

Confusion about the goodness of creation arises because the New

[12]Acts 10:9–16. See also Matt. 15:17–20.
[13]1 Cor. 7:5.
[14]1 Cor. 7:8.
[15]Matt. 6:16–18; 1 Cor. 7:5.

Testament often uses words like "flesh" and "world" in ways that go beyond their literal meaning and indicate forces hostile to God. It is essential for us to appreciate that in these cases the biblical writers are not referring to the physical realities that the words stand for, but to a spiritual power that causes us to seek satisfaction from them rather than from God. To order our lives purely in terms of our bodily needs or our current circumstances is to misunderstand who we are and what God wants us to be. It is not that these things have no importance but rather that they are secondary. As Jesus taught his disciples, if God can feed and clothe birds and flowers, he can and will look after us too, and so we should not worry.[16] To be preoccupied with such matters is very understandable, but it is also deeply wrong. It mistakes the order of priorities that ought to govern our lives as Christians. That is why the "flesh" and the "world" are spoken of in negative terms—they are temporal distractions used by Satan to lure us from the service of God into some form of idolatry.

In the modern world, most people accept that there is nothing inherently bad in created things, although the use we make of them still affects both our physical well-being and our spiritual growth. However, there are still many who are inclined to regard some aspects of the created universe as evil because of the diseases and other "natural" disasters they can cause. This is an emotional issue, particularly when large numbers of people are killed by an earthquake, famine, or plague that they have done nothing to deserve or to bring about. But however much we must sympathize with the victims of such occurrences, we cannot say that the material forces that produced them are evil in and of themselves. Consider the case of fire. A fire can burn down a house, engulfing everyone in its flames, but fire is also essential for life and can be put to any number of good uses. In the Bible, hell is sometimes portrayed as a place of fiery torment, but God is also compared to fire,[17] and the fire that consumes the sins of mankind (represented by the sacrificial offerings) comes from heaven, not from hell.[18] Is fire good or bad? The answer has to be that it is "good" in the sense that all created things are good, but like anything else, it can also be used in ways that are harmful and destructive.

Natural phenomena cannot be wished away, but they can and ought to be recognized and treated with respect. Jesus tells us that a wise man builds his house on a rock, not on the sand.[19] This seems like an obvious piece of common sense until we look around us and see how many people choose to live on flood plains, in areas exposed to frequent hurricanes, and even on the slopes

---

[16]Matt. 6:25–34.
[17]Deut. 4:24; Ezek. 1:4; Heb. 12:29; Rev. 1:14.
[18]Lev. 9:24; Judg. 13:19–20; 2 Chron. 7:1.
[19]Matt. 7:24–27.

of volcanoes. Can we blame God if they then suffer the consequences of their own folly? Famines and epidemics are often the result of human incompetence, mismanagement, and uncleanliness, all of which can be corrected with the right guidance and motivation. The bacteria or viruses that cause disease are not to be blamed for doing what comes naturally to them. Rather it is we, who have been given dominion over the creatures, who must learn to control them so that they do not cause the harm they are capable of.

Do suffering and death have any legitimate place in the natural order? The Bible makes it clear that death entered the world because of sin,[20] but this must be interpreted in context. Sin is a spiritual rebellion against God, which means that the death it brings is also spiritual. Jesus told his disciples not to worry about those who kill the body—it is the danger of spiritual death that really matters, because while the body dies in time, the spirit dies in eternity.[21] That physical death is a part of the natural life cycle within the created order seems obvious, since if it were not, none of us would be able to eat anything. The "food chains" in the animal world remind us that many species could not exist without the death of other creatures, and there is no reason to think that this state of affairs came about as a result of the fall of man. Creation has suffered as a result of Adam's fall into sin, but much of the harm done to it has been caused by human neglect and destructiveness. When human abuse is brought under control, the natural order often reasserts itself and repairs the damage which we have inflicted on it, restoring the natural cycle of life and death in place of the destruction we have caused.

Physical death must therefore be regarded as a natural part of the time- and space-bound universe, and bodily suffering is a reminder of this. However healthy and active we may be, our bodies are material objects that grow and fade away just like everything else in creation. This process can be painful when the body starts to lose its ability to function properly, but of course there are "growing pains" as well! Change of any kind often involves discomfort, and the most painful suffering can be emotional or mental in ways that may or may not have physical effects. The message of the gospel is not that flesh and blood must be preserved at all costs, and that any harm done to them is evil by definition, but rather that flesh and blood cannot inherit the kingdom of God.[22] They must die, not to disappear but to be transformed into spiritual bodies whose nature lies beyond our comprehension. Creation is not destined to last forever in its present state, but is to be changed in a way that will make

---

[20]Rom. 5:12.
[21]Matt. 10:28.
[22]1 Cor. 15:50.

it possible for it to share in the inner life of God.[23] What exists now is not permanent. It is only a foretaste of the glory which is yet to be revealed and which will far surpass anything we can possibly imagine in our current state.

THE PURPOSE OF CREATION

The beauty and grandeur of this world is real, but it is not an end in itself. God has not put us in an ever-changing universe in order to taunt us with pleasures that do not last, nor does he want to destroy us along with the creation that he has made. Physically speaking, we are an integral part of the cycle of life and death that we see all around us, but in spiritual terms we have been created for something more permanent. God has a purpose for our lives which transcends the decay of the material order in which we now find ourselves but to which we do not fully belong. The fact that we are capable of lamenting the destruction of our surroundings and that we are able to question whether there is any meaning to life reminds us that in our heart of hearts, we know that there must be something better than what we now have. We have an inbuilt sense that life is greater than death, even if there is nothing we can do to prevent death, and we hope against hope that we shall somehow survive it. The will to live is a gift from God which bears witness that there is a purpose for us that can be fulfilled only beyond the grave.

In the wisdom of his all-embracing love, God has given us this world as a testing ground. Here we can work out our relationship to him and be made ready for a new order of being when the limitations imposed on us by time and space will be removed and we shall realize our full potential. We do not know why he has chosen to deal with us in this way, but the fact that he calls us his children may help us to understand it. Children have boundaries placed on their activities by their parents and other adults, not to restrict their growth but because they have to develop in a certain way and learn to appreciate the inheritance they have been given. Adulthood comes with a price tag of responsibility attached to it, and children must learn what it costs before they are able to enjoy the benefits of growing up. So it seems to be in the spiritual life also. We shall reign with Christ in his eternal glory, but that glory is a precious thing that we must learn to appreciate. In this life we are given a foretaste of it, but it then fades away, leaving us disappointed but also aware of how much we long to have it. By learning this now, we shall be in a better position to enjoy it when we enter into its fullness because then we shall appreciate it for what it is. Children who are given too much with little or nothing expected

---

[23]Rev. 21:1–4.

of them in return do not become healthy adults but spoiled brats. That is not what God wants us to be like in heaven.

What we shall one day be is held out to us as a promise, but in the meantime God speaks to us as we are now and reveals his purpose for us in ways that we can understand. It is precisely because we have a wonderful destiny ahead that much is expected of us in this life, as we prepare ourselves for it. God's words can seem harsh at times, but there is a reason for that. As the psalmist understood,[24] we must be told who we are and why we matter to God, but we must also be told how far short we fall and how we can be set free from the fears and doubts of our earthly existence. We have to realize that we are in our present state not because God intended it for us but because we have turned our backs on him and preferred to go our own way in the world. Like children who have run away from home, we have told ourselves that we are "free" when in fact we have fallen into a trap so deep that only God can get us out of it. We have done nothing to deserve rescue, but God's love is such that he has reached out to us poor, rebellious, and undeserving creatures who have dared to think that we know better than he does, and has brought us back to himself. The awful truth is that, although we are glad of it now, we never wanted that to happen. Bad though our sinful life may have been, we preferred to go our own way. To be stopped dead in our tracks, as Saul of Tarsus was, and then raised up again and sent off in a different direction hurts our pride, our self-esteem, and our desire for ease and pleasure.[25] In spite of ourselves, however, God's love overrules our innate rebelliousness and helps us to discover what true love is. In the process we come to know him in a new and more intimate way, and no power in heaven or on earth can take that knowledge away from us. It gives meaning to our existence and a sense of purpose to our lives, setting us free from fear and anxiety because we know that whatever happens to us will turn out for good.

THE BIBLE AND NATURAL SCIENCE

Today there are many people who claim that our ever-expanding knowledge, discoveries, and abilities make belief in God unnecessary and even impossible. Arguments that were used in earlier times to prove not only the existence of God but the need for the kind of Creator that the God of the Bible reveals himself to be are now often dismissed on the ground that the natural sciences have developed to the point where such a hypothesis is no longer required. Everything needed to explain the operation of the world can be discovered

---

[24]See, for example, Ps. 6:1–10.
[25]Acts 9:1–19.

within the natural order, leaving no room for an external force. Not surprisingly, Christians reject this conclusion, and some are even inclined to regard the whole scientific enterprise as hostile to their faith. There are many scientists who are Christians prepared to defend their belief in a Creator God, but all too often their voices are drowned out by highly vocal atheists on the one hand and naive "fundamentalist" believers on the other. A satisfactory middle ground seems to be difficult to find, and what we have ended up with are two different mental worlds which exist in conflict with and often in ignorance of one another.

From the Christian point of view, the first thing to say is that there can be no conflict between biblical revelation and natural science because both proceed from the mind and will of God. This was the belief that allowed the natural sciences to develop in the first place, since the God who had created man in his own image also gave him the rational capacity to understand and subdue the world over which he had placed him. The study of the natural sciences is an essential aid toward exercising dominion over the creatures, which is the human birthright, and for that reason it must be encouraged by every means at our disposal.

Second, the Bible is not a scientific textbook and was never intended to be. Its account of the creation is much too sketchy to be the basis for any scientific theory, and it is not really concerned with the origin of things at all. Genesis 1 is a statement about the *order* we see in the material world, and it is compatible with different scientific explanations of what happened. It cannot be claimed that the Bible supports one particular theory of origins to the exclusion of all others. There is nothing in Genesis 1 that obliges us to believe that the world was made in six twenty-four hour days, although some Christians have tried to insist on that interpretation. The creation of the sun and moon on the fourth day would seem to rule it out, as the original readers of the text would doubtless have realized.[26] Astronomy was a highly developed science in the ancient world, and even if the compilers of Genesis were not star-gazers themselves, they knew enough to understand that our concepts of evening and morning would be meaningless without the sun. Given that sun worship was widespread and popular, especially in Egypt, it may well be that putting its creation on the fourth day was at least partly meant to relativize its importance in the overall scheme of things, since something that was made so late in the process could hardly be considered the source of all life. The one thing we can be sure of is that the world is not the product of random forces adapting themselves to new circumstances and mutating over

[26]Gen. 1:16–19.

eons of time in what are essentially self-generated ways. The world is the way it is because God made it like that, whatever means he may have chosen to achieve his purpose.

Many early Christians understood this and had no problem interpreting the creation story in what we would call a "symbolic" way. The trouble was that pagan Greeks believed that matter was eternal and rejected any idea of a "young" universe, so some Christians concluded that they had to counter that denial of creation with an interpretation of the biblical account that went to the opposite extreme. Far from being ancient and eternal, they argued, the world was no more than a few thousand years old, as adding up the numbers of Genesis would demonstrate. What started out as a legitimate defense of the idea of creation (as opposed to the eternity of matter) ended up as dubious biblical exegesis, based on a literalistic understanding of the text that was probably not what the original writer intended. Such exegesis can be found as far back as Augustine of Hippo (354–430), was common for most of the Middle Ages, and still reappears from time to time today.

Having said that, the six days of creation are important because the fourth commandment gives them as the reason for sanctifying the seventh day as the day of rest.[27] The Sabbath rest indicates that once matter has been made by God, there will be no further act of creation, even if the inner potential of what already exists goes on developing. It is also a reminder that we are not justified or saved by our works but by our humble obedience to Almighty God. For this we must desist from our normal activities, however necessary they may be for our survival here on earth, and wait on him. Finally, the Sabbath rest is an indicator of what awaits us in heaven, when we shall enter not only into God's glory but into his eternal rest.[28]

For all these reasons, the observance of the Sabbath became central to the rhythm of Israelite life, eventually even to the point where it could be pushed beyond the bounds of reason and common sense.[29] The Israelites had to learn that the pattern of their life was meant to reflect the mind of God, which is why the Sabbath rest was called "holy." God's mind is eternal, simultaneously looking back to the origins of the existing creation and forward to the new creation in which everything will be brought to fulfillment, and therefore to rest, because there will be nothing further to achieve. God, as the perfect being, is at rest already, which is why it is peculiarly appropriate for us to set aside the day of rest in order to worship him.

---

[27]Ex. 20:11.
[28]Heb. 3:11; 4:9.
[29]Luke 14:5.

It is when we put the six days in this context that we can interpret the creation narrative as it was originally meant to be understood. Man has been given dominion over the creation, which has been designed to meet his needs and to support him in his God-appointed tasks. We are called to subdue the earth and to have dominion over the animals. At the same time we are dependent on what the Bible calls the "expanse" of heaven, the order of reality that assures the regular cycle of good and bad weather, of light and darkness, that is essential for our survival and over which we have no control.[30] By calling this order good, God tells us that it is designed for our benefit, and by placing it in heaven, he puts it beyond our reach. If the way in which we have treated the earth and its inhabitants is anything to go by, we would long ago have done great damage to the firmament if we had had the chance, and the result would surely have been even more catastrophic than the destruction we have wreaked on things that are within our grasp. It is one of God's greatest mercies, and a particular sign of his love toward us, that he has reserved the really important things for himself, so that in spite of our folly we shall not be able to destroy the basic framework within which we live, however hard we may try to do so. By telling us that God worked for six days and then rested, the Bible is reminding us that if we imitate him in this, we shall be fulfilling his purposes as he intended we should. That is the calling that is meant to shape the rhythm of our life, and it is for that reason that the creation is presented to us in the way that it is.

Third, just as the Bible is not a scientific textbook, so the theories of natural scientists are not divine revelation or even theological statements. It may be that the universe is 14 billion years old and has another 7 billion years or so to run before it gives out, but even if that is true, the really important questions about it remain unanswered. Why is there a universe at all? What happened all those billions of years ago to bring it into being, and where will its wreckage go to once it finally runs out of energy? The Bible has a clear and coherent answer to these questions which cannot be proved or disproved by any scientific argument. It says simply that God brought the world into being and that when the time is ready he will bring it to an end. This makes a lot more sense than saying that the universe appeared out of nowhere for no apparent reason—and then assigning a date to that remarkable event, which is what many modern scientists end up doing if they cannot bring God into the picture.

Christians are committed to the belief that behind everything we see and experience there is an "intelligent designer," to use a popular modern phrase. "Intelligent design" is a controversial scientific proposition, partly because

---

[30]Gen. 1:8, 14; 9:12–17.

it is often thought to be a form of religious commitment in disguise (even though its chief advocates deny that), but mainly because it appears not to allow for "random" selection and adaptation. If there is a God who made everything perfect, this objection goes, how is it that so many of these supposedly perfect things change and adjust themselves to new circumstances and that some of them die out because they cannot adapt? Would not a divinely ordered perfection preclude such possibilities? From the theological standpoint, the answer to this kind of reasoning is that, while God made the world "good," he did not make it absolute and immutable. The designer has built in the capacity for change, which includes decay as well as progress, because this universe is not an end in itself.

Moreover, the designer is greater than his design and is not bound by it. We can often figure out how the world works, and in doing so learn something about the plan and purpose of God for his creation, but we must never fall into the trap of thinking that these scientific "laws" are fixed in a way that they can never be transcended. Christians have always believed that the laws of nature are an indication of God's providential rule of the universe he has created, and that he maintains the world this way in order to give us confidence as we go about our daily tasks. We do not have to fear that something like the law of gravity will be arbitrarily suspended, leaving us (quite literally) dangling! Having said that, however, there is no reason why God cannot go beyond the "laws" he has made and perform what we call "miracles," like the ascension of Christ into heaven, when (in defiance of the laws of gravity) Jesus was taken up out of the disciples' sight. Who are we to tell the Creator what he can and cannot do with his creation?[31]

What we must insist on (and here there is a direct challenge to at least some theories of biological evolution) is that there is no such thing as a purely "random" occurrence. Randomness is a word we use to describe something that we cannot explain, and since it is likely that we shall never understand everything, there will always be a place for the concept in purely human terms. In the mind of God, however, nothing happens by accident. As limited and finite beings, we cannot expect to be able to understand everything, but that does not mean that there is no explanation. The apostle Paul tells us that "we know in part . . . , but when the perfect comes, the partial will pass away."[32] What we cannot figure out in this life will become clear when we see God face-to-face and understand his purposes for us, however mysterious and unfathomable they may be right now.

---

[31]See Rom. 9:20.
[32]1 Cor. 13:9.

Fourth, just as the Bible says little or nothing about the origins of the universe, so Christian theology cannot tie itself to any one theory of cosmic origins. To do so would be to give human speculation the same authority as divine revelation, and that would be a form of intellectual idolatry. The history of the church shows how foolish it would be for us to endorse current scientific theories as "truth." That is what previous generations did, with the result that when the theories were overturned the theology built on them was discredited. The classic example of this is the way in which medieval theologians adopted Aristotelian metaphysics and ancient Greek cosmology as an explanation of the physical universe and regarded it as just as authoritative as the Bible itself. When Copernicus (1473–1543) discovered that the earth revolves around the sun and not the other way around, he refused to believe it and kept quiet about his findings, because it was in conflict with what the church taught. He was wise to be cautious, because a century later Galileo (1564–1642) was tried for heresy and put under house arrest for teaching the Copernican system, which he believed was compatible with the biblical witness. The tragedy was that, as his view made headway, the theology which opposed it was rejected and the credibility of the Scriptures was undermined.

It is easy to portray the history of the past five hundred years as one in which the grip of a fanatical and misguided church was gradually broken in favor of the liberating doctrines of modern science, and this is what many secular historians of the subject do. However, it was not that simple. Not only have many of the most prominent scientists been believing Christians, as Galileo was, but scientists who reject biblical teaching have sometimes been led into making fraudulent claims on the basis of their so-called discoveries. For example, one of the offshoots of the development of evolutionary theories in the nineteenth century was the pseudoscience of eugenics, which purported to "prove" that the white races were further evolved than other branches of humanity. This belief conveniently justified Euro-American colonialism and racial segregation, and had a powerful impact on Adolf Hitler's ideology.

Nowadays eugenics has been discredited and so effectively suppressed that most people have never heard of it. If they think about racism at all, they are more likely to blame it on the church for having preached that Europeans were God's chosen people rather than on scientists of an earlier era. Admittedly, there were some theologians who defended racism, but they were a minority who were opposed not only by most of their contemporaries but by the entire Christian tradition, which has always insisted that all members of the human race are equal because of our common descent from Adam. In the traditional interpretation of Genesis, black Africans were regarded as the children of Ham, one of the sons of Noah. That made them distant cousins of Europeans, who were descended from Ham's brother Japheth, as well as of Middle Easterners, who were descended from Noah's third son Shem.[33]

Fanciful this may be, but racist it is not. Nor did this conviction remain at the level of theological theory. On the contrary, it impelled the church to evangelize the non-European world because Africans, Asians, and Native Americans were also children of God who needed to hear the message of salvation. So strong was this conviction that even churches that supported apartheid or racial segregation undertook missionary work to win the souls of supposedly "inferior" races to Christ.[34] The contradiction implied by this shows that they could never really accept a racist ideology, because they had to recognize those who were converted by their efforts as their brothers and sisters in Christ. We also have to remember that while this was going on, secular members of the scientific establishment had no qualms about using nonwhite people in medical experiments as if they were guinea pigs, nor did they hesitate for long before dropping atomic bombs on a non-European nation which they assumed was racially inferior to themselves.

The truth is that the conflict between "religion" and "science" is not about the supposed incompatibility of their respective methods and conclusions. It is a moral and spiritual disagreement about the nature of man's power over the rest of creation. In this debate, secularists swing from one extreme to another, sometimes favoring human development over everything else, and at other times opting for what we now call environmentalism. Christians, on the other hand, hold a steady position in the middle. In line with Genesis, we say that the human race has been given "dominion" over the earth, a term that implies both privilege and responsibility. It is a privilege, because to us alone has been accorded the freedom to examine, develop, and control the rest of the material creation. But this dominion is also a responsibility, because we have to answer to God for the way in which we exercise it. If we abuse it (as we frequently do) we shall suffer the consequences.

In the secular camp, we find scientists who have discovered new techniques of genetic modification and resent the social and legal restrictions which are often placed on their freedom to experiment. They argue that without trial and error there can be no progress, that a few eggs may have to be cracked in order to make the desired omelet, and that the benefits for the whole of mankind outweigh the inconvenience that may have to be endured

---

[33] This is why they are still known as "Semites."
[34] This was true of the Dutch Reformed Church in South Africa and of numerous denominations in the American South.

by particular individuals. It is also in their interest to define human beings as narrowly as possible—a fetus, for example, is not "human" (or at least not fully so), and someone who has slipped into a permanent and irreversible coma is no longer a "person" with an inherent right to life.

At the other end of the spectrum we find environmentalists and ecologists, who make the perfectly valid point that the world cannot go on burning up its nonrenewable resource and that we must seek ways of creating a sustainable environment. From there, however, some go on to conclude that human beings are no more special than rats or mosquitoes, who must also be protected in *their* environment. In other words, draining a malarial swamp in order to create new agricultural land, or drilling for oil in a national park, is a rape of nature which ought to be regarded as a criminal act. Most of the time, researchers and ecologists operate in different spheres and avoid conflict—few embryos contract malaria, for example—but their ultimate goals are incompatible, and when they do meet (as over the desirability of building nuclear power plants) they inevitably clash.

Once again, Christians are usually caught in the middle. We accept the importance of scientific progress and development, but not at the expense of human rights. We also agree that the environment must be protected, but not at the expense of human beings. In the end we take our stand on the need to protect the individual as well as communities from exploitation, whatever the cause or intention of the latter may be. We do this because we believe, as Genesis teaches us, that mankind has been given dominion over the creatures and that it is that mandate which has to be respected above all else.

CHRISTIANS AND THEORIES OF BIOLOGICAL EVOLUTION

To what extent should Christians express an opinion about particular scientific theories? Are there some that we cannot accept because of our beliefs? If there are, what should we do when we are confronted with them in the secular world? Let us begin with what might seem to be an extreme example. For many years, the idea that there was life on other planets belonged in the realm of science fiction, but recently it has been taken much more seriously within the scientific community on the ground that the chances of our planet being unique are statistically improbable. Space capsules carrying messages and even current popular music have been launched into outer space on the off-chance that some alien may pick one up and learn of our existence. It is not clear whether the said alien is meant to be attracted or repelled by such things, but for that we can only wait and see. The Bible says nothing about life on other planets, but if such life does exist, what relationship does it have to God? In particular, are there human beings (or equivalents) elsewhere who have *not* sinned, and if there are, are they enjoying the life of the garden of Eden that God intended for us?

In practical terms this does not matter very much, because even if there is life somewhere out there, the time it will take to find it and establish contact is so great that earth may well have vanished by then. We must certainly avoid the mistake of saying that such life cannot exist merely because it is not mentioned in the Bible. On that basis, America would not exist either! But we are fully entitled to point out that the resources being spent trying to find such life are disproportionate to any conceivable gain, and the whole subject is best left where it belongs—in the realm of speculation and science fiction.

Thinking about extraterrestrials may seem to be a long way from the main concerns of the church, and in one sense that is true, but it reveals something very important about the nature of the difference between Christian theology and the natural sciences. It is often said that the sciences are rooted in "reality" and are therefore incontrovertible, whereas theology is pure speculation and thus largely mythical, but as this example shows, the opposite is closer to the truth. The existence of alien beings is entirely speculative, based on the unproven assumption that the earth cannot be the only inhabited planet in the universe. No one has ever met such creatures, or even stumbled across a meteorite with strange markings on it that might point to their existence. There is no evidence to support the theory, and even if there were, it would remain unproven until such time as another inhabited world is actually discovered, which will probably be never.

In many ways the currently dominant theory of biological evolution is also a mental construct with evidence adduced to support it which may one day turn out to be misleading in the extreme. This is not to deny that there is a symbiotic relationship among the different creatures of the animal kingdom, including *homo sapiens*. There is no doubt that the genetic codes of gorillas, chimpanzees, orangutans, and humans are remarkably similar, or that whales are mammals, just as humans are. In terms of our physical life cycle, we are undoubtedly linked to these creatures, and no one has ever seriously questioned this. Children have always learned "where babies come from" by looking at animals, and anyone who feeds bread to birds knows that we often eat the same things as they do. Whether this interconnectedness points to descent from a common ancestor is less obvious, but it is certain that the theory of such common descent was being propounded long before there was any evidence to justify it. Since that time, new fossil discoveries have been fitted into the theory to make it more plausible, though there are still a large number of gaps in the record and much remains as uncertain as ever.

The real problem is not this, though. Theories of evolution get into difficulty when they try to explain how one species developed from another one. Interbreeding between species is sometimes possible, but it is not usually productive. A horse can mate with a donkey to produce a mule, but mules are sterile, and that pattern is replicated across the biological world. Adaptations within a species are very common and well-documented, but mutations (when they occur) tend to be defective and produce something inferior—the opposite of what evolutionary theory says is supposed to happen. If gorillas and human beings evolved from a common ancestor, it must have taken a very long time. The evidence of mutation suggests that the common ancestor was superior to what either of us is now, which cannot have been the case. On the other hand, despite the enormous variety that exists inside the human species, there is no doubt that headhunters in New Guinea, pygmies in Africa, and suburbanites in Western Europe and America are biologically identical. There can be problems when two very different kinds of people are thrown together, as the historically tortured relations between aborigines and settlers in Australia remind us, but not even the most myopic European colonizer ever seriously suggested that the Australian aborigines were subhuman. Attempts to treat them that way have always been resisted—for good reason. But if that is so, why did our prehuman ancestors vanish? Were they violently eliminated or did they just die out? Did this happen all at once, or was it a process spread over time?

We do not know the answers to such questions. Just as the search for extraterrestrials is speculation in space, so the search for prehuman ancestors is speculation in time. It would be unwise to deny their existence outright, because the Bible tells us that when Adam and Eve were created, they did not possess the moral awareness that we have now. That would make them somewhat different from modern human beings, though there is no evidence that they were biologically inferior to us. It is equally unwise, however, to make assumptions about what people without moral awareness were like when we have no evidence to go on. Biological evolution holds sway in the scientific community today but like any scientific theory it is falsifiable, and true scientists will look to see if and how they can replace it with something more satisfactory. A Christian theologian can no more endorse biological evolution than he can endorse any other form of speculation, because even if it turns out to be correct, it remains a form of fallible human perception and not a truth of divine revelation.

Modern evolutionism has created great difficulties for Christians, not so much because it tells us that we are genetically related to orangutans and chimpanzees, but because it insists that fundamentally we are not very different from them. In theory, say evolutionists, it would require only a few small genetic changes in those animals to turn them into human beings like us, and it is assumed that some millions of years ago all of us evolved out of a common ancestor. Without denying this possibility completely, Christians are obliged to make two observations about it. First, such an evolution was not and could not have been spontaneous. There is little evidence to support the theory that one species can evolve naturally into another by a process of random trial and error, and none to say that this happened to produce the human race. Orangutans, gorillas, and chimpanzees still exist, but how is it that all the intermediate species have died out, leaving little or no trace behind them? Logically, one would expect to find them around somewhere, but although it is sometimes claimed that proto-human bones have been dug up, the evidence is controversial and it must be concluded that such "missing links," as they are called, have never been convincingly identified.

The second observation is that even if there was a biological evolution of a particular animal toward humanity, that in itself would not have been enough to produce human beings as we know them today. This is because Adam and Eve were created not just out of the dust of the ground but also in the image and likeness of God.[35] This means there is something about humans that did not emerge from a purely evolutionary process and which is not susceptible to biological analysis. Christians cannot be happy with a natural, atheistic evolutionism, even if we accept that there may have been some form of biological evolution. There is something about men and women that makes them unique in the created order, neither purely material like animals nor purely spiritual like angels. We have many things in common with both of them, to be sure, but we are also different from them because we have an inbuilt relationship to God that cannot be reduced to (or explained by) those natural connections.

The image and likeness of God is mediated to us through the faculty of speech, which is common to God and to human beings, but to no other material creature. It is no accident that God not only created the world by his Word, but that when he determined to save us from our sins, it was his Word that became flesh in order to achieve that goal. Speech sets the human race apart, and studying it has some interesting lessons to teach us about how evolution might work. Strange as it may seem, some of the most complex human

---

[35]Gen. 1:26–27.

languages are those spoken by primitive peoples; as civilization advances, languages tend to simplify or disappear if they are too complex to master or too inflexible to be used in new situations. Anyone who has studied a modern Romance language, for example, knows that it is much simpler than its ancestral Latin, which is readily available for comparison.

Moreover, languages can contain some interesting coincidences that deceive the unwary and have important lessons to teach the scientifically incautious. For example, the English verb "have" is connected to the German *haben* but not to the Latin *habere*, even though all three words look alike and mean the same thing. Linguists tell us that the Latin equivalent of "have" and *haben* is not *habere* but *capere* ("seize"), which looks unlikely but is confirmed by the universal correspondence between "h" in the Germanic languages and "c" or "k" in Latin and Greek.[36] But if "have" and *habere* are unrelated, despite their apparent resemblance and synonymity, what about gorillas and human beings? Is it necessary to say that they *must* derive from a common ancestor just because they are so similar? Perhaps reality is more complicated than we have imagined, and one day clues will be discovered that will permit a different interpretation from the one that seems so obvious to most scientists now.

The biblical account of creation and the theologian's analysis of it are not subject to such qualifications. Many scientific atheists like to say that the natural sciences have dethroned God and put man in his place, which is where they think he belongs. In fact, however, the opposite is the case. By dethroning God, atheists have no way of understanding the uniqueness of man, except as the fruit of a long evolutionary process which is probably continuing and will eventually produce something even "higher" than what we are now. But if I am not much more than a highly developed orangutan, and if my remote descendants will be correspondingly superior to me, why should I bother doing anything? What is the point of thinking, speaking, and expressing myself in art, music, and literature if the animals cannot appreciate them and future generations will dismiss them as unacceptably primitive? Where does my moral awareness come from and why does it matter, if only the fittest are destined to survive? Somehow or other, the explanations offered by scientists, defensible though they may be within their own sphere, do not go far enough to explain human reality. There is something about us that cannot be analyzed in purely biological terms, and that something ultimately matters more than what can be explained by the natural sciences. The Bible tells us that we have

---

[36]Compare the following words in the four languages and you will get the point: head/Haupt/*caput*/*kephalē*, heart/Herz/*cor*/*kardia*, hundred/Hundert/*centum*/(*he*)*katon*, hound/Hund/*canis*/*kyōn*.

been created for a purpose and that we have rebelled against it. It is that rebellion which is the source of all our troubles, and unless it is put right, there will be no lasting solution to them.

But the Bible also tells us that God has provided the answer. It explains how the power of evil that binds us and drags us down has been overcome and will one day be eliminated entirely. This is an existential reality that confronts every human being. It is not some theory or speculation about what might have occurred, but a description of something that is—right here and now. How evil came about is important, but mainly because it helps us understand what has to be done to get rid of it. It is not enough for the Christian theologian to be able to explain how we have got to where we are; he must also show us what we must now do if the problems we face are to be resolved. This is not a matter of further evolution but of salvation, which is a different thing. Evolution, if it takes place, will almost certainly make a bad situation worse, whereas salvation is a new life built on a different basis. It is that fact, and the possibility we have of experiencing it now—and not having to wait for billions of years to watch it "evolve"—that gives theology its meaning and purpose, and in the process makes sense of the human race and its destiny.

STOP! 9/18/15

13

THE SPIRITUAL
CREATURES

THE NATURE OF ANGELS

The starting point for our understanding of creation must be the spiritual realm, because it existed before matter was created and will still be there when matter eventually disappears. It is the dimension of reality that corresponds to God's own nature and it is where he has angels to serve him forever. The Bible does not say much about the origin of the angels, but it is clear that they are creatures and therefore quite different from God himself. Although they are spiritual beings they are finite, and if they are spatially bound we may assume that they were also created in time, though what that means in heaven we cannot say. Perhaps time and space came into being in the spiritual world before its material counterpart was created and independently of it. If that is so, the destruction of the material universe will not bring time and space to an end, since they will continue to exist in the spiritual realm. In support of this theory, the Bible tells us that redeemed human beings will have spiritual bodies, which presumably means that they will be definable in spatial terms, though nothing is said about time.[1]

What we know is that the existence of spiritual creatures is presupposed in Scripture, even in the accounts of the material creation, so they must have been there before it was made. Perhaps the most important thing for us to remember about this is that the angels do not appear to have played any part in the creation of the material world. There is no sign that God delegated that responsibility or used his spiritual servants to create matter, and every reason to suppose that he did not. Had our world been made by angels (acting at God's bidding of course, but nevertheless made by them and not directly by

[1] 1 Cor. 15:42–49.

God), we human beings would be their creatures almost as much as we are God's. As such, we would be subject to them, albeit to a lesser degree, and perhaps we would even be made in their image as well as in God's. We would still be ultimately subject to God, but that subjection would be worked out in the context of an order in which the angels would stand between him and us and act as intermediaries on our behalf. For us to get to God would therefore mean going through the angels—something that is specifically ruled out in Scripture.[2] *we are not created by angels*

The evidence of the Bible is that, although God can and does sometimes use his angels as a way of communicating with human beings, it is never the only way in which he speaks to us nor is it the most common one. The appearance of an angel is usually a sign that something extraordinary is about to be revealed; such appearances have never been regarded as a "normal" part of our daily walk with God. Perhaps the most striking example of this occurs at the beginning of Luke's Gospel, where an angel appears to Zechariah and to Mary in order to announce the upcoming births of John the Baptist and of Jesus.[3] Mary would probably have thought that any communication from God to her was an extraordinary occurrence, although Zechariah may have been more prepared to accept the idea, given that he was a priest serving in the temple. It was when he was doing his duty in the normal course of events that the angel interrupted him with the news, but what we learn from Zechariah's reaction is that for him, serving God on a daily basis did not involve having a relationship with angels. More importantly, there is no indication anywhere in the Bible that we should seek to establish a connection with angels or try to use them as a means of getting closer to God. The angels take their orders from God, and so they cannot be influenced by us. At no point in the Bible is there any sign of a cult of angels that might be compared to the worship of a pagan pantheon of deities.

The Bible does say that we have been made a little lower than the angels,[4] which is a reference to our status as partly material (and not purely spiritual) beings, but the only thing it says about our relationship to them is that one day we shall judge them![5] The great paradox of humanity is that, having been made lower than a significant part of God's creation, we shall one day be raised higher than they are, because as creatures made in the image and likeness of God (something that is never said of angels) we shall be united to the Son in the fellowship of the Godhead and share in his kingly rule over the rest

are we not seated w/ Him high above all rule & authority?

---

[2] 1 Tim. 2:5.
[3] Luke 1:11–20, 26–38.
[4] Ps. 8:5; Heb. 2:7, 9.
[5] 1 Cor. 6:3.

of the created order. Having said that, though, this is a vision of the future, not of the present. In Genesis the human race was given dominion over the lower creation but not over the higher—we are not ruled by angels, but neither are they subject to us.   okay...

This is particularly important when we come to consider the place of the *fallen* angels in the created order and our relationship to them. If we had been made by Satan before his fall from grace, there might be some grounds for suggesting that the control he has over us now is no more than the natural continuation of the original state of affairs. If we had been subject to him at the beginning, it is only to be expected that when he fell, we would have been dragged down with him as his underlings. We know, however, that this is not the case. Satan does not rule over the world because he has some natural right to do so, but because he has deceived us and we have fallen into his trap. That is a very different thing, not least because one of the reasons why our present situation is so intolerable to God is that we were never meant to be subject to any angelic power, good or bad.

How many angels there are is unknown to us, though presumably there is a finite number of them that does not increase or decrease, since angels are not born and do not die.[6] It appears that they have names of their own and share the personal characteristics of human beings, but how they are related to each other is unclear. From what the Bible tells us, the impression we get is that they are an army, or series of armies (hence the term "Lord of hosts"), each of which is presumably headed by an archangel.[7] Both archangels and angels appear to human beings, but only two of them—Gabriel (an angel) and Michael (an archangel)—are known to us by name, the first because he announced the birth of Jesus to the Virgin Mary and the second because he waged war in heaven against Satan.[8]

Although we know virtually nothing about angels, we may nevertheless conclude that what happened among them has had a dramatic effect on the world as we know it. Why God made the angels is unknown, but we can safely say that he intended them for particular purposes and gave them the ability to fulfill them as and when they were expected to do so. What were those purposes? The first and greatest reason for their existence, and one which appears to be a permanent part of their activities, is that they were made to worship, glorify, and serve God. These activities are distinct, but they belong closely together. To worship God is to recognize who he is and

---

[6] Mark 12:25.
[7] This is a guess based on the meaning of the word "archangel," which is "chief of the angels."
[8] Luke 1:26; Jude 9; Rev. 12:7. Nonbiblical traditions also mention Raphael, who is thought to be another archangel, but whether he exists or not must remain uncertain.

what the worshiper's relationship to him ought to be, and that clearly must have come first for angels as it comes first for us. To glorify God is to accept this situation as the right one. Neither angels nor human beings are God's equals, but although we are allowed to have fellowship with him, the angels do not have that privilege. It would have been an act of rebellion for them to have tried to rise "above their station" and claim a kind of parity with God to which they were not entitled. Spiritual beings though they were, they had no right to saunter into God's presence, slap him on the back, and declare that he and they were all colleagues in the business of being spiritual and ruling the world!

On the contrary, it was the duty of the angels to serve and glorify God, which meant exalting him above themselves, and in so doing to provide an example of what is expected of us also. The angels were called to be available to God and ready to serve him in whatever way he chose. Service to God is the true mark of worship and glorification, because it is the proof that we mean what we say. The Israelites were accused of honoring God with their lips when their hearts were far from him, because although their outward ceremonies were impeccable, they had no intention of serving him in any serious or sacrificial way.[9] The angels were meant to show by their example that this was not true of them, and it is by observing them and experiencing the effects of their service to God that we learn most of what we know about them.

The name "angel" in the Greek is the word for "messenger" or "herald," and there are many occasions in the Bible where they are mentioned in that capacity.[10] At times they appear to be so much like God in what they do that it is difficult to distinguish them from him.[11] But because we know that God never appeared in visible form before the coming of Christ, we must say that the visions the patriarchs had were revelations of angelic messengers and not of God himself.[12] It is hard to generalize about the encounters different people had with angels over a long period of time, but certain features stand out as typical of them. The first is that angelic appearances were unexpected. Even when there is evidence that people were praying for God to do a special work in their lives, it still seems to have come as a surprise when it happened in this way.[13] The second thing is that angels appeared in human form, invariably as males and sometimes with the appearance of mighty warriors. But they could also be virtually *incognito*, so that it was not until after their departure that

---

[9]Isa. 29:13.
[10]Gen. 24:7; Dan. 3:28; Acts 12:8.
[11]See Judg. 13:21–2; Isa. 63:9.
[12]Gen. 18:1–3.
[13]1 Kings 19:5.

those who had met them realized that they had been conversing with angels unawares.[14] In those circumstances the angels must have looked fairly ordinary, though in every instance we know about, they came bringing a special word from the Lord that aroused curiosity about their identity.

Whether the apparent masculinity of angels has any significance is hard to say. As far as the biblical evidence is concerned it probably does not, because we are told that angels do not marry, which suggests that any sign of sexuality in them is superfluous. Perhaps the angels took on masculinity when they revealed themselves in human form because in the ancient world it would have been very strange if a woman had met people out of the blue and started speaking to them with authority. But if the masculinity of angels has no intrinsic significance in Scripture, it may have something to say to us today. Nowadays, the popular image of angels has become feminine and sometimes infantile as well. For several centuries now, angels have usually been portrayed either as young girls or as rather well-fed babies with wings, neither of which is remotely true to the biblical picture. The modern perception is romantic and attractive, but the biblical revelation is more likely to be one of fiery spiritual beings who are figures of terror and judgment. Certainly angels were beings of authority and power who were not to be trifled with, and the general picture we have today is in serious need of correction in this respect. To that extent, the masculinity of angels in the Bible may need to be recovered in order for us to respect them more and appreciate their significance better than modern popular piety has been inclined to do.

To say that angels appeared in masculine form also reminds us that there was an ancient tradition, which can be found in writers from the fourth to the seventeenth century and later, that said that at least some angelic apparitions were manifestations of the Son of God before his incarnation. The logic behind this was that the Son makes himself visible in a way that the Father does not, and that the knowledge which the New Testament says that Abraham and others had of Christ was due to their encounters with him in angelic form. Some have been tempted to think that the "angel of the Lord" who accompanied the people of Israel on their desert journey was the Son of God, but there is no evidence for this in the New Testament. The Bible makes it clear that the Son was not an angel, either in appearance or in reality, and so it is difficult to see how he could have manifested himself in that way without ceasing to be himself.[15] We must accept that angels are magnificent representatives of the Almighty and eternal God, but that they are also crea-

---

[14]Judg. 13:21–22; Heb. 13:2.
[15]Heb. 1:5–14.

tures, who speak in his name but who are not God himself in any form, not even that of the Son.

Another feature of angels is that they never speak on their own authority. The apostle Paul warned the Galatians not to believe anything contrary to the gospel proclaimed by Christ, even if it purported to come from an angel, because no true angel would or could say such a thing.[16] There is no evidence that the Galatians received angelic revelations, but the warning Paul gave them has longer-term consequences. Latter-day Saints and Muslims both place considerable emphasis on what they claim are angelic revelations, but these must be rejected on the same principle that Paul laid down in the case of the Galatians.

In the modern church, angels attract far less attention than they did in earlier times, when there were prominent theologians who tried to define the entire hierarchy of heaven and find a place within it for many different kinds of spiritual creatures. No one does that nowadays, and reported sightings of angels are so rare as to be virtually nonexistent. Those who claim to meet heavenly beings today usually say that they have had an encounter with one of the saints or with the Virgin Mary, apparitions of whom have become especially popular in the past two hundred years or so. Does this mean that angelic visions have ceased?

This is a hard question to answer. Angels never appeared very often even in biblical times, when there were only thirty or so encounters with them recorded over a two-thousand-year period. There is no indication in Scripture that an angel *cannot* appear nowadays, and there certainly is greater warrant for angelic appearances than for apparitions of Mary. The difficulty is that it is hard to see why God would send an angel now, or what the angel would say and do. One way or another, angelic appearances in the Bible were connected with ongoing divine revelation, which angels were sent to proclaim. Now that such revelation has ceased, that angelic function is superfluous and it is hard to see what new activity might have replaced it. But unlikely though angelic appearances now are, we have no scriptural authority for saying that they have ceased and we must remain open to the possibility, however skeptical we may (and ought to) be about them in practice.

ANGELS IN THE HISTORY OF SALVATION

In the Old Testament, angels appeared to particular individuals from time to time, usually to tell them that God had heard their prayer and would come to

---

[16]Gal. 1:8.

their rescue. The first and in many ways the most famous of these occasions was when three men appeared to Abraham at the oak trees of Mamre and announced that he would have a son by his wife Sarah, in spite of her great age.[17] The biblical text does not use the word "angel" but it does say that God spoke to Abraham, and that he addressed the men as "Lord," almost certainly recognizing by his use of this word that the men were somehow divine. For centuries theologians have interpreted this incident as a revelation of the Trinity to Abraham, because he spoke to the three men in the singular, but the New Testament does not pick up on this and we must be cautious before drawing such conclusions. On the other hand, there is no doubt that Abraham had a revelation of God in human form, and since only one person of the Godhead became incarnate, it seems clear that we must be talking here about angels. This impression is confirmed in the next chapter, where two angels are specifically mentioned as appearing to Lot and proclaiming to him the imminent destruction of Sodom.[18] The functions they perform are characteristic. On the one hand, they bring a word of promised blessing to Abraham and Sarah, but on the other hand, they also bring a message of judgment and destruction against Sodom and Gomorrah. In both cases it is their preserving role that comes to the fore. They promise Abraham an heir so that he would have descendants to be God's people in the future, and they prophesy the destruction of evil, which will not be allowed to pollute the earth indefinitely.

The protecting and preserving role of angels is also brought out very early on when an angel is sent to comfort Abraham's concubine Hagar after she bore him a son and incurred the wrath of Abraham's wife Sarah.[19] It was the angel who pronounced a blessing on the baby Ishmael, thereby assuring Hagar of God's ongoing care for her and her son. Later on that promise was fulfilled when, after Hagar and Ishmael were thrown out of Abraham's family because of Sarah's jealousy, an angel was sent to protect them from dying of thirst in the desert.[20] Angels also played an important part in the preservation of Isaac, Abraham's legitimate offspring. When he was still a young boy, God commanded Abraham to sacrifice his son, apparently as a test of his loyalty, but it was by sending an angel that he stopped Abraham from doing the awful deed and afterwards promised to bless him as a reward for his faithfulness.[21] This dual pattern of rescue and promise was also the experience of Jacob, as he recalled in his blessing of Joseph and his sons.[22] We are not given any

---

[17]Gen. 18:1–21.
[18]Gen. 19:1.
[19]Gen. 16:7–12.
[20]Gen. 21:17–19.
[21]Gen. 22:11, 15.
[22]Gen. 48:16.

details, but considering the fact that Joseph was Jacob's favorite son and that he mentions this at a moment of great solemnity, it is clear that the preserving activity of an angel played an important part in his life.

The next we hear of angels is when Moses found himself in the desert after fleeing from Egypt. When God spoke to him in the burning bush he saw an angel appearing in a flame of fire, another symbol of the purifying and empowering presence of the Lord.[23] Moses did not interact with the angel on that occasion, but later on, as the people of Israel journeyed through the desert, it was to the protection and guidance of an angel that God entrusted them.[24] The angel is not identified, but he was appointed to guide the people on their desert journey, and the promise was made that he would also drive out Israel's enemies when they arrived in the land of Canaan.[25] This angel of the Lord was so powerful and prominent in their lives that many have thought he was a preincarnate manifestation of the Son of God, but there is no scriptural justification for that view. The ancient Israelites did not perceive him in that way, and the New Testament is careful to distinguish the Son from any angel, however exalted the angel might be.

After the entry of the people of Israel into the Promised Land, angels seem to have appeared less often, but shortly before Joshua died and then for a time during the era of the judges, they were active once more. The first sign of their renewed presence occurs in a strange incident at a place called Bochim, where an angel appeared to the people and rebuked them for their disobedience.[26] He reminded them of the blessings they had received, both in their deliverance from Egypt and on their wilderness journey, but accused them of having forgotten those blessings once they had entered Canaan. For this, they would be obliged to suffer at the hands of the people of the land whom they had not succeeded in driving out. The Bible records that when they heard this, the Israelites repented and even offered sacrifice to God in an apparent attempt to receive forgiveness of their sin, but to no avail. The angel had no power to forgive them, but only to execute the judgment of God, which therefore stood.

Later we find an angel active in advising Gideon and also in choosing Samson.[27] In both these cases, the preservation of Israel was clearly at stake, and the role of the angel was primarily to further that cause. After the prophecy to Samson's parents, however, angels seem to fade out again, something

---

[23]Ex. 3:2.
[24]Ex. 14:19; 23:20.
[25]Ex. 23:20–23.
[26]Judg. 2:1–5.
[27]Judg. 6:11–22; 13:3–21.

that may have been linked to a general dearth of visions of the Lord during that period.[28] The next we hear of an angel is after David took a census of the people, which displeased God, and God sent one of his angels to punish David by destroying seventy thousand men.[29] It is a frightening reminder to us that God is not obliged to exercise his preserving power when dealing with his people. He is determined to punish sin, and even when he shows mercy as he did to Israel by stopping the slaughter before it did any further damage, the execution of his judgment against wrongdoing remains an essential part of the activity of angels.

After that, we find angels active again in the career of Elijah, who was protected by an angel when he fled to Mount Sinai in order to escape the wrath of Ahab and Jezebel, and then toward the end of his life when he was called to bear witness against the sins of the king of Israel.[30] After that, angels seem to recede into the background once more, making only very occasional appearances. A notable exception to this rule is Zechariah, where an angel appears to the prophet more than once and is one of the main protagonists of his vision. It can be safely said, however, that despite their rare occurrences, the activities of the angels are fully consonant with what we see of them earlier in the Old Testament, which indicates that their role had not changed significantly. Oddly enough, angels appear only twice in the Psalms, but on both occasions their behavior is fully consonant with what we have found elsewhere. In Psalm 34:7 we read that, "The angel of the Lord encamps around those who fear him, and delivers them," which is a clear affirmation of their protecting power, and in Psalm 35:5–6 we find the angel of the Lord driving David's enemies away as if they were chaff in the wind. Once again, the picture is one of the protection and defense of God's people.

After the time of Zechariah there is no mention of angels, which may have had something to do with the cessation of prophecy for four hundred years before the coming of Christ. It is always difficult to argue a case from silence, but the coincidence of the two things and the apparent parallel with the period of the later judges suggest that there may be substance in this observation. There is no doubt, however, about when angels made their reappearance. The birth narratives in Matthew and Luke contain no fewer than eighteen references to them, fourteen of which are in Luke. In Matthew's Gospel angels appear only twice, once to Joseph in order to reassure him that he should marry Mary even though she was already pregnant, and again in

---

[28] 1 Sam. 3:1.
[29] 2 Sam. 24:16–17.
[30] 1 Kings 19:5–8; 2 Kings 1:3, 15.

the context of the flight of Mary and Joseph into Egypt, where it was an angel who told them to go and when to return home.[31] In Luke's account, by contrast, angels play a major role. The birth of John the Baptist was announced to his father Zechariah by the angel Gabriel, as was the birth of Jesus to Mary.[32] Angels also announced the birth of Jesus to the shepherds in the fields near Bethlehem.[33] After that, they seem to have faded out again. Angels ministered to Jesus in the desert, after he had been tempted by Satan,[34] but apart from Luke's mention that an angel came to comfort Jesus in the garden of Gethsemane,[35] they do not reappear until the day of his resurrection, when they are seen as guardians of the empty tomb.[36]

Afterwards, there was considerable angelic activity in the Acts of the Apostles. Philip was told by an angel to go south to Gaza, and on the way he met the Ethiopian eunuch whom he led to Christ.[37] A little later, an angel told Peter in a dream to go to the Gentile Cornelius and minister to him even though he was not Jewish.[38] When Peter was thrown into prison he was delivered by an angel, and many years later when Paul was on the verge of shipwreck off the coast of Malta, an angel appeared to him to reassure him that the mission to Rome which he had undertaken would be accomplished because it was God's will.[39] From these and other indications of angelic activity we can conclude that, since the fall, God has used his angels for the following purposes:

1. They are there to protect us from harm.
2. They are sent to announce God's blessing and his judgment.
3. They appear most often when God is about to begin some new, great, and thitherto unexpected or unknown work.
4. They carry on their work of preservation even when they do not appear openly.

An ancient tradition says that each person has a guardian angel appointed to look after him or her, but although some people in New Testament times seem to have believed that,[40] it is not specifically taught by the apostles and so we must be cautious about affirming it or making too much of it. On the

---

[31]Matt. 1:20–24; 2:13–19.
[32]Luke 1:11–19, 26–38.
[33]Luke 2:9–13.
[34]Matt. 4:11.
[35]Luke 22:43.
[36]Matt. 28:2–7.
[37]Acts 8:26.
[38]Acts 10:3–22.
[39]Acts 12:7–11; 27:23.
[40]Acts 12:15.

other hand, John wrote his Revelation to the angels of the seven churches of Asia, so perhaps Christian congregations have angelic protectors assigned to them, although here again caution is required because of the highly symbolic nature of John's vision.[41] Nevertheless, the notion of angelic protection may help to explain what Paul meant when he told the women of Corinth to wear a head covering as a sign that they were under authority and added that it was "because of the angels."[42]

Why would the angels care about something like head coverings? The most plausible answer is that it was because they were the guardians of the church and expected its members to reflect the divine order of authority appointed for them. Paul does not say it, but it is possible and even probable when we consider what the angels did in other cases of open disobedience to God's commands, that the Corinthian women were not only honoring God by covering their heads but were also protecting themselves against his judgment, which his angels were appointed to execute. In this connection we must remember that the angels were not sent to decide cases but only to follow the orders they had received, and as the Israelites had discovered long before, even repentance and sacrifice would not be enough to deflect an angel from his appointed task.

The protecting role of the angels is the link between God and the fallen world that he preserves in existence. They are not his final word to mankind, nor is their task meant to continue forever. Rather, it is the expression of God's love for everything and everyone that he has made and that he loves, in spite of everything that has gone wrong. The fallen world is preserved by angels, but the children of God are redeemed by the Son. It is when we realize this difference that we can appreciate what the writer to the Hebrews meant when he makes such a sharp contrast between the glory of the angels and the much greater glory of Jesus Christ.[43] The difference is that we have been preserved in time by the angels but we have been saved in eternity by the Son of God.

OUR CONTACT WITH THE SPIRITUAL WORLD

What relationship do we have, or can we have, with the spiritual world? This is a difficult question and one that has been the subject of much speculation. On the one hand, the spiritual creatures are rational and personal beings, which makes a meaningful relationship with them possible, at least in principle. If

[41]Rev. 2:1; etc.
[42]1 Cor. 11:10.
[43]Heb. 1:5–14.

that were not so, God could not have sent his angels to the patriarchs because they would not have been able to communicate with them. What is true of the faithful angels must also be true of the disobedient ones, though it seems that in normal circumstances, the demons do not pretend to pass themselves off as human, but rather enter into human beings and possess them. That at least is the witness of the Bible, where there are reports of demons being cast out of people.[44] In contrast to that, there is no instance of a good angel possessing anyone, not even for the purpose of speaking God's word through them. Good angels appear to respect the identity of the human beings to whom they have been sent and deal with them as one person to another, relying on their innate authority rather than involuntary force to bring about acquiescence to their message. This in itself tells us something about the nature of the demonic. Rather than deal with us face-to-face, as God and his angels do, the Devil seeks to take us over and rule us by suppressing our natural capacities so that they become instruments of his will.

In neither case, however, can we speak of a genuine relationship with spiritual creatures, and there are many reasons for this. One is that such a relationship would have to be one of friendship, and friendship is possible only among equals. We have been created lower than the angels, and so cannot be regarded as being on the same level as they are. It is true that they can come down to us, but we cannot go up to them, which limits the possibilities for a real and lasting relationship. More importantly, though, angels are not authorized to enter into a personal relationship with us. Because they are faithful to their master, they do not want to do so. In some ways they are rather like civil servants doing their job. We may communicate with them and they with us, but we and they both know that our real relationship is with their master and not with them. We have fellowship with God as his children, but the angels are merely his servants, important in their way to be sure, but not on the same level of intimacy with the Lord that is our birthright and privilege. Nowhere in the Bible is there any suggestion that human beings can, do, or should pray to angels; the subject is simply never mentioned, in which case we have no authority either to do it ourselves or to encourage others to do it.

It is important to say this because films and television shows that would never dare mention God (or even the Devil) sometimes resort to angels and act as if communicating with them is not only possible but fairly normal, at least for some people. What should Christians say about this? The first point we have to make is that there is no evidence in the Bible for anything like this. The idea that an angel will suddenly appear to give me advice or help me

---

[44]Mark 9:38; Luke 4:41; 10:17; Acts 16:16–19.

out in difficult circumstances is unsupported by any scriptural evidence. The only thing in the Bible that is even remotely analogous to this is found when God sends an angel to someone, but then it is to tell that person to do God's will and not the other way around. Such occurrences cannot be interpreted as evidence that there is independent communication between human beings and angels, especially not if it bypasses or ignores God. No angel could possibly do that, because angels are servants of God, and when they come, it is as his messengers; they do not act on their own initiative or in their own right.

Here we come back to what for us must surely be the heart of the matter: we are children of God, no longer servants but sons of the Almighty. We have been put in a category different from that of the spiritual creatures and have been given a status which is so far above that of the angels that one day we shall judge them. If we are invited to visit people who have a lot of servants, we do not strike up a conversation with the servants as if they were the ones we had come to visit, nor would they expect us to do so. If we have been invited by the master of the house, we must certainly treat his servants with respect and not take them for granted, but we must also recognize them for who they are and behave accordingly. If that is true in earthly affairs, how much more will it be true in the courts of heaven? We do not seek to enter our Father's presence in prayer in order to dialogue with his servants, nor does he refuse to deal with us directly and delegate our affairs to them instead. Angels are servants of God who live with him in his heavenly home. We know that they are there, we may occasionally see them at work, and sometimes they communicate with us at their master's bidding, but we are not related to them and they are not part of the family of God's children to which we belong.

14

THE MATERIAL
CREATION

MATTER

Very different from the spiritual creatures are the material ones that we see
around us every day. It is the material world that most people think of when
they use the words "creation" and "creature," a tendency that is reinforced
by the Genesis account. It is important to emphasize this because the modern
secular world often likes to claim that Christianity is so opposed to material
things that anyone who values them is liable to come into conflict with religious people and their supposedly otherworldly beliefs. To understand how
this perception has arisen, we must go back to the ancient world, where almost
everyone worshiped matter in one form or another. Some people were devotees of fire, but many more had conceptualized the forces of nature as gods
and goddesses, whom they usually portrayed as superhuman or outlandish
figures. Because these deities were material, it was possible to make idols of
them, and their cults involved some highly material activities, ranging from
animal sacrifice to sexual intercourse with one of the deity's priests.

If there is one thing the Old Testament is against, it is idolatry and everything that proceeds from it. The prohibition against making images as objects
of worship was so important that it comes immediately after the confession
of monotheism in the Ten Commandments.[1] Elsewhere, the rituals associated
with idolatry are roundly condemned and sometimes mocked on the ground
that they mistake material objects for spiritual realities.[2]

To that extent there can be no doubt that both Judaism and Christianity
are opposed to materialism,[3] as they are opposed to anything that would

---

[1]Ex. 20:4–6. See also Deut. 4:15–31.
[2]1 Kings 18:27.
[3]Materialism in the philosophical sense, not modern consumerism!

exalt a creature above the Creator. Attempts to explain spiritual things in material terms can get very sophisticated, but they all fail in the end because matter is not spirit. Even if God can and does use material objects to convey spiritual truth, as he does for example in the water of baptism or in the bread and wine of Holy Communion, it is a gross error to confuse the one with the other and accord spiritual power to material things. Water, bread, and wine can never be anything more than the created things they are, however special the use to which they are put, and theories that claim they can be changed into spiritual substances and convey spiritual blessings in their own right violate their nature. They are means to an end, but they must never be mistaken for the end itself.

Having said that, it is a great misunderstanding to suppose that Christians undervalue matter or try to escape from it. Modern critics of Christianity do not seem to realize that that accusation can more accurately be laid at the door of a number of ancient Greek philosophers, who were disgusted by the immorality of the religious observances they saw around them, and who therefore sought to escape to what they saw as a higher, more spiritual plane. Some of them even accused the church of gross materialism, because it dared to proclaim the doctrine that God had become a man in Jesus Christ. Considering their context, it is easy to sympathize with the philosophers' point of view, and we can understand how converts to Judaism or to Christianity might have been motivated by similar feelings.

Understandable though it may be, however, the philosophical otherworldliness of the ancient Greeks was no more biblical than was the immorality of their religious cults. The Christian doctrines of creation, incarnation, and bodily resurrection all went against it, and the early church spent a lot of time defending those teachings for that very reason. It is true that Christians developed their own forms of asceticism and that some people went to extremes in their attempts to deny the world, but that was never the norm. Ordinary believers were expected (though not usually commanded) to fast and to refrain from sexual intercourse during special times of prayer, but these were spiritual disciplines that do not deny the value of matter any more than taking time out to concentrate on reading a book does.[4] Monasticism was a more rigorous form of asceticism, but it was intended for a minority who dedicated themselves to a life of prayer. It was certainly not anti-material as such. Many monks not only engaged in hard labor but were highly productive as farmers, businessmen, and artists. Their material resources were concen-

---

[4] 1 Cor. 7:5.

trated and redirected to a spiritual purpose, but they were not despised or rejected merely because of what they were.

The calling of the Christian is neither to worship matter nor to despise it, but to use it for the purposes for which God made it and in the way that will be most efficient and productive for our benefit. The accusation that Christians are more concerned with preaching a spiritual gospel than with relieving poverty and suffering in this life is belied by the facts. Christians have always been in the forefront of material progress and in many parts of the world social services would be much poorer, or even nonexistent, were it not for the churches. Christian aid agencies are just as prominent as their secular counterparts and often more efficient, and churches have long been in the forefront of movements for social justice. The difference between Christians and others is that, while we believe that such work is necessary and proper, we do not accept that it will solve the most basic human problems. Giving material help and comfort, valuable and necessary as it is, cannot meet the spiritual needs of the human race. If it could, then the rich would go to heaven and the poor would be left behind—a monstrous idea that is explicitly condemned in the Bible.[5] Material poverty can be alleviated but it can never be abolished because in the end it is relative. A poor person in Europe or America would be well-off in many parts of Africa, and almost everyone alive today is better off than the majority of people were in New Testament times. Jesus told his disciples that the poor will always be with us, but he saw this as potentially a positive thing. Often it is those who have the least in material terms who are the most sensitive and open to spiritual things.[6] Affluence is deadly in this respect, a truth that was perhaps more widely understood in ancient times than it is today.[7]

Matter is essentially good, as the creation account repeatedly insists, and every aspect of it has a purpose, whether we understand what it is or not. In spiritual terms, we need to be delivered from the material world's hold over us in order to make the most of it. The Bible bears witness to this when it warns us to flee the "lusts of the flesh," using the material flesh as the symbol for everything that attracts us away from the service of God. At the same time, however, it holds out to us the promise that the flesh will participate in the resurrection and that the whole material order will be re-created at the end of time.[8] It is not the flesh that is evil but our attitudes toward it that are wrong because they either make too much of it or too little.

The material creation is not immutably fixed for all time, but contains

---

[5]Matt. 11:5; Mark 12:42–43; Gal. 2:10; James 2:5–6.
[6]Matt. 26:11.
[7]Deut. 6:10–15.
[8]Rev. 21:1–2.

within it the potential for growth, change, and development. Some of this occurs spontaneously as the result of natural laws, and some of it is produced by human beings or even by animals, who also reproduce and some of whom can build things like nests or dams. The material creation is also divisible into distinct kinds of substance in a way that the spiritual creation is not. Some material objects are inert, like stones, some are alive but immobile, like plants and trees, while some are alive and mobile, like birds, animals, and human beings. These differences create a hierarchy in the material universe which is seldom remarked on but which is clearly visible and usually taken for granted. Plants and trees can grow on or around rocks and earth, even to the point of displacing them—as when the roots of a tree grow so strong that they split boulders—but not the other way around. Barring something like an earthquake or an avalanche, there is nothing a rock can do to a plant or tree, because a rock is not alive and cannot act on its own. Likewise, birds and animals feed off plants and trees, but not the reverse, apart from some flowers that trap insects and devour them. Birds and animals can also feed off each other, and in many instances must do so in order to survive. At this level human beings belong to the animal world, but although the exact nature of their relationship to other creatures is much disputed, virtually everyone agrees that humans are in a category of their own.

The inert creation is the most stable and enduring part of the material order. In ancient times it was common to break it down into four "elements"—earth, water, air, and fire. This division was naive and unscientific, but it encompasses most of the basic realities we encounter in everyday life, particularly so-called natural disasters. This four-element classification should not be despised merely because it has now been superseded by a more sophisticated approach. We could hardly exist if there were no earth to support us, and water is essential to life, even though it is not itself alive. Air is another thing that living beings cannot do without. Fire does not occur with the same frequency as the other three do and it usually has to be induced, but even so, it is of great importance in renewing the natural world, and our lives would be inconceivable without it.

Modern science has greatly expanded our knowledge of inert nature and has developed important skills for dealing with it. There were seven wonders in ancient times, of which only the pyramids survive, but the modern world has produced wonders by the thousands. In every sphere of human activity, from architecture to pharmaceuticals, enormous advances have been made and new achievements are constantly appearing. Matter has been analyzed in the periodic table of elements, and new elements have been produced artificially. Our understanding of energy has led to an electronics revolution, which has transformed the way we live. These things have led to debates about how far and how fast we should allow such developments to proceed, and there is no easy answer to that question. Technology is not immune to misuse, and there is no guarantee that it will not be abused by someone somewhere. The fear that nuclear weapons will spread to those who will be unscrupulous in using them is not groundless, and there is every likelihood that some terrible catastrophe will one day result from this. Similarly, the creation of new life forms or the modification of existing ones may have enormous benefits in certain circumstances, but it may also go horribly wrong. Cleaning up the damage once it has been done may be virtually impossible. Try as we may, there is no getting around this dilemma. As Christians, we are torn by our desire to improve the lot of the human race without destroying it in the process. It is impossible to lay down blanket guidelines that are applicable to every conceivable circumstance, but the Bible offers us important principles that can help us decide how to proceed when dealing with particular cases.

The first of these principles is that material development is not by itself evil or sinful. It may be wrong for practical reasons, but that is another matter. We must resist the temptation to believe that science is necessarily dangerous, and must allow scientists the freedom they need to conduct their research for the common good. Whether, or to what extent, this "common good" should include doing harm to other parts of creation (like guinea pigs, for example) cannot be resolved in a general way and has to be worked out on a case-by-case basis, but as long as we bear that *caveat* in mind, the principle that the world is there to be explored and developed remains valid.

The second principle is that true development must be for the *common* good and not solely for the benefit of a privileged minority. It is true that many advances in science, like the production of new drugs, will be available only to a few to start off with, but this disadvantage is balanced by the fact that the "lucky few" are also the ones who have to risk the unforeseen consequences that new and untested techniques may have. Over time it may be expected that a drug will become safer, cheaper, and more widely available, and so the initial restrictions put on it may be justified. But as always, great caution is required here. To develop a mind-enhancing drug that would only ever be made available to a limited number of people, with the intention that they would then go on to rule the rest of humanity, might be possible, but it would be an abuse of our scientific capabilities and so would have to be resisted. It is when the cost of a particular development outweighs any potential benefits that the real problems arise, and here we have to rely on consultation and judgment when making the decision whether to proceed.

In such matters, the Christian church cannot make dogmatic pronouncements but must accept that sometimes hard choices have to be made. An example of this can be seen in the need to make decisions about prolonging lives artificially. How long should a body be kept on a life-support machine when there is no reasonable hope of recovery? The commandment that we should not kill does not really apply in this case because if nature were allowed to take its course, the body would probably have died already. Some people will argue that although the purpose of modern technology is to save lives, it should not be used to create bizarre and unnatural situations that consume vast amounts of scarce resources for no very obvious reason. Others, however, will insist that as long as even a remote possibility of restoring normal life exists, it ought to be pursued, whatever the cost may be in other ways. Hard as it is to accept, and tempting though it may be to intervene and pronounce judgment one way or the other, the church has to leave decisions like these to the conscience of the individuals involved and work toward finding long-term solutions to such dilemmas that do justice to all sides of what are usually complex and emotionally charged arguments.

The basic principle we must cling to is that, as human beings, we have been given dominion over the earth and have been charged with developing it in ways that will be beneficial to human life. In general terms, preventing the spread of disease, increasing the productivity of the soil, and making the world a safer and more pleasant place to live in must be our priorities. At the same time, we have to be careful not to provoke unnecessary environmental damage and to conserve as much as we can of the natural order bequeathed to us by God. Sometimes the issues are clear, but very often they are not. Should a malarial swamp be drained? Is it all right to allow drilling for oil in a national park? Can animals or dead human beings be used for the purposes of scientific research? What about stem cell research? There is no simple or obvious answer to such questions, and good arguments can often be made on both sides. Inevitably, sincere Christians will disagree about these things and some will insist that their view is the only legitimate one. This we must resist. God has not told us what the right answer is, perhaps because it may vary from one situation to another and there is no blanket solution that will cover everything. What he expects of us is that we should use our rational judgment and our moral principles to come to the best decision in each case, accepting the limitations of our human perceptions and recognizing that, as long as we live in this world, perfection in these as in other things is beyond our grasp.

At the heart of the Christian understanding of matter is our belief that it has been made for time, and not for eternity. Within the framework of time and space we must use it and develop it to the fullness of its potential, but we must recognize that all such progress is a stage on the way to a higher purpose that cannot be fully realized in this life. Any notion that human effort, even if it is godly and devoted, will bring about heaven on earth must be firmly resisted. Social welfare may be a good and necessary thing, but the provision of universal health care and education has not produced a perfect society, and it never will. Mankind's deepest needs are spiritual ones, and these can never be met by material means. Here the church is in radical conflict with the world, not least in democratic countries where success at the polls often depends on promises that life can be made better by voting for a particular economic policy or political philosophy.

Even if improvements to our material well-being are possible and desirable, the idea that a real and permanent betterment of the human condition can be brought about by some form of human engineering is false. In the marketplace of ideas we must always remind the world of its limitations and of the relativity of every project that may be proposed for the improvement of human life. This is not to say that we must oppose such developments, many of which may be desirable, but we must refuse to sell ourselves to them as if they somehow provided the "answer" to all life's problems. That answer lies beyond the capacity of the material creation, and it is one of the church's most important functions to remind people of that. We are in the world but not of it, a balance that we as Christians have to maintain in all our many dealings with it.

NATURAL DISASTERS AND MORAL JUDGMENTS

The elements of nature are intended to be beneficial to us and usually they are, but we also know that they can act in ways that do great damage. An earthquake can destroy buildings and kill hundreds of people in just moments. A flood can easily have the same effect, and take much longer to subside. A hurricane, cyclone, or tornado can wreak havoc, and so can a fire that is out of control. In many ways we are at the mercy of the elements just as much today as our ancestors were thousands of years ago. Ironically, due to human progress, we may even suffer from them more than they did, as when large numbers of people are killed by falling buildings. The common factor in these disasters is that most of them occur naturally. There is not much that anyone can do to cause or to prevent extraordinary movements of earth, water, or air;

only fire tends to be the result of human action, though even fires can and do occur in nature.

News reports obscure this reality by their habit of blaming high wind, snow, and ice for causing human deaths, but in this context "blame" is a loose term with no real meaning. A natural phenomenon like a volcanic eruption is neither good nor bad in itself, and our judgment of it depends entirely on the effect it has. For example, in the year A.D. 180 there was a massive volcanic explosion in the North Island of New Zealand, which scattered red dust across the whole world—as was observed by both the Romans and the Chinese. No one was killed because there were no people living on the north island at that time, and today we are grateful to the explosion for having left us Lake Taupo, one of New Zealand's most beautiful places. On the other hand, the eruption of Mount Vesuvius in A.D. 79, only a century earlier, was one of the great catastrophes of the ancient world. Today we can visit the ruins of Pompeii and see human bodies covered in ash, frozen forever in the place where they were struck down, and still feel something of the panic and horror that the eruption caused. Are we then to conclude that the Taupo eruption was good and the Vesuvius one bad?

Oddly enough, no one at the time seems to have interpreted the destruction of Pompeii in moral terms, as punishment for the sins of the Roman empire, despite the well-known moralizing tendencies of ancient historians and philosophers. The early Christians could easily have claimed that it was a warning from God to the Romans, who had already begun to persecute them, but they did not do so. It was a different story, though, in the mid-fourteenth century when the bubonic plague struck Europe and killed about a third of the population. There were many people then who blamed this on the sins of the church, the clergy, or the world in general, and who sought to reform the offending institution (and occasionally even themselves) in the hope of avoiding a similar disaster in the future.

Some people still react to natural disasters like that, but they are usually regarded as eccentric, and their opinions are not taken seriously. Even so, natural disasters are a reminder that we are subject to forces beyond our control, and we can be struck down by them without warning. If God is sovereign over the universe and determines everything that happens in it, it is not unreasonable to suppose that a natural disaster may be his way of punishing our disobedience. But because it strikes indiscriminately and "the just and the unjust" suffer together, this explanation seems unfair. That fact is enough for some people to reject belief in God, because there is no obvious moral basis for the suffering he inflicts, but this is hardly logical. After all, if there is no

God, there is no reason to suppose that our moral principles have any validity outside our own imaginations, and the image of nature as "red in tooth and claw" may be right.

Having said all that, human beings are moral creatures, and so we tend to interpret natural calamities in moral terms. A volcanic eruption seen from afar can be a majestic sight, but for those who suffer the consequences, it is a different story. They may easily be tempted to call it "evil," giving it a moral dimension that it does not naturally have. As the Bible puts it, "[God] makes his sun rise on the evil and on the good, and sends rain on the just and on the unjust."[9] At the level of created nature there is no discrimination based on the moral character of individuals, and Jesus went out of his way to insist that disasters, physical disabilities, and the like do not indicate that the victims are any more guilty than those who were not affected. Mentioning an accident in which eighteen people were killed when a tower collapsed, he said, "Do you think that they were worse offenders than all the others who lived in Jerusalem? No, I tell you; but unless you repent, you will all likewise perish."[10] Similarly, when confronted with a man who was born blind, and asked whether this was his fault or that of his parents, Jesus replied, "It was not that this man sinned, or his parents, but that the works of God might be displayed in him."[11]

From these incidents we learn two things. First, death is a reality that will come to us eventually, and if we do not repent and turn to Christ, that death will be eternal and justly deserved. We cannot divide the world into "sinners" who can be recognized by their sufferings and the "righteous" who are by definition healthy, wealthy, and wise, because "all have sinned and fall short of the glory of God."[12] The second thing we learn is that human tragedy is an opportunity for the saving power of God to be revealed. The man born blind received his sight, but that was not the only possible outcome. There are many examples of people who have suffered terribly, yet who have overcome their misfortunes to reveal reserves of inner strength that would never have emerged otherwise. There are people whose compassion is stirred by the tragedies of others and who have responded with almost superhuman acts of self-sacrifice, which would never have happened without the circumstances needed to create them. Time and again we hear of heroic rescues, of people who perform extraordinary feats of endurance, of people who give away everything they have to help others. In sum, we discover the inner resources of love at work

---

[9]Matt. 5:45.
[10]Luke 13:4–5.
[11]John 9:3.
[12]Rom. 3:23.

in human lives. We do not wish misfortunes on people merely so that such wonderful responses will occur, but we are grateful when they do and feel a closer bond with those who have reached out to help us if we are the ones in need. We cannot explain tragedy, but we know that good can and does often come out of it, and that somehow this is all part of the plan and purpose of God for our lives.

Christians do not accept that natural disasters are an arbitrary judgment from God or that they occur in spite of him, because we uphold his sovereignty over all things. We do not know why some people suffer from particular catastrophes while others are spared, but we do know that death comes to us all sooner or later. There is no direct correlation between the sins we commit and the sufferings we endure, but in the bigger picture, the two things are connected and no one can opt out of the common lot of humanity. As Christians, we are not specially protected because of our faith but are given a faith and a hope that help us to accept our suffering as part of God's love for us, even when we cannot understand it.

The book of Job suggests that natural disasters can sometimes be the result of Satan's activity and that believers are not wrong to see them as tests of their faith.[13] It is particularly interesting to note that, although God gave Satan permission to inflict various calamities on him, Job himself never thought of them as being Satanic in origin. As far as he was concerned, the disasters that befell him came from God and had to be interpreted as acts of his sovereign will, not as the activity of the Devil or as punishment for something he had done. What stands out in Job's case is that each fresh catastrophe served to convince him even more that God was in control, that he knew what he was doing, and that in the end Job would be saved and vindicated.[14] Job's faith grew stronger as his troubles increased, not the other way around, which leaves us asking ourselves whether that might be God's underlying purpose in causing us to be afflicted as Job was.

The modern tradition of using natural disasters as an argument to disprove the existence of God goes back to Voltaire, who reacted to the devastation caused by the Lisbon earthquake of 1755 in that way. As Voltaire saw it, Portugal was an officially Christian country where prayers were offered to God on a daily basis, asking him for protection in this life and salvation in the next. And yet in this pious and Christian land, destruction on a massive scale occurred for no apparent reason. Even if Portugal had its dark side, it was certainly no worse than France or Italy and perhaps not as bad as they were,

---

[13] Job 1:6–12.
[14] Job 19:25.

and yet it was chosen to suffer whereas the other countries were spared. To argue, as many traditionalist Christians of the time were inclined to do, that the earthquake was a sign of God's wrath against the people of Lisbon made no sense to Voltaire. On that point at least, it is hard not to agree with him.

There is no discernible link between natural disasters and human sins, as if the former are invariably (or even frequently) the direct result of the latter. There are certainly cases where a natural calamity could have been prevented by timely human action, as in New Orleans, where the devastation wreaked in August 2005 by hurricane Katrina was aggravated by the city's lack of preparedness and slowness to react. No one would claim that New Orleans was a sinless place, and there were many who thought that it deserved its punishment, if only for the way in which it had blithely ignored all the warnings of impending disaster. Morally speaking, however, it would be hard to claim that New Orleans is any worse than Las Vegas or San Francisco, and they have both been spared, at least in recent years. We know that San Francisco has another devastating earthquake coming at some point, but it is hard to see what might happen to Las Vegas, other than destruction by a massive fire which someone would have to start. Its location makes it relatively immune to natural disasters, and yet on the moral scale it probably deserves one every bit as much as the other cities, and perhaps more.

It is our knowledge of this that must prevent us from making any causal link between natural disasters and moral retribution. We know that Japan is frequently struck by earthquakes, whereas Mongolia will never be inundated by a tsunami because our knowledge of geography tells us so. We also know that this is not because Mongolians are more virtuous than the Japanese, and we agree that any such assumption would be absurd. With the knowledge of geography that we now possess, we can often tell people what risks they are incurring when they choose to live near a volcano or on a flood plain, and if disaster strikes they really have no one to blame for it but themselves. Human beings have to take responsibility for their own behavior, and however sympathetic we may be to the victims of such occurrences, we must continue to remind them of that. At the end of the day we have to remember that the world we live in can be a dangerous place, and that life has its risks whether or not we invite them. Nothing in the physical universe is exempt from the law of suffering and death, which comes to us all. The Christian gospel is not a message of escape from pain but of victory over it by the suffering and death of Jesus Christ, who rose again to the newness of a life that was no longer subject to such things and that would continue forever.

We may never be able to control natural phenomena like earthquakes or hurricanes, but there is a real possibility that one day we shall be able to predict them with some accuracy and take steps to avoid the harm they can cause. We know that the next earthquake to hit San Francisco is unlikely to do the same amount of damage as the big one in 1906 did. This is because our understanding of quakes has improved, the technology needed to build structures able to withstand the shock is much better, and people know that they must be prepared for the inevitable, even if they cannot say for sure when it will happen. Today, the devastating effects of earthquakes are felt mainly in countries like Haiti which are too poor and underdeveloped to afford the structures needed to withstand such shocks, though they can also be the result of corrupt practices which affect more advanced countries as well. For example, the widespread flooding that has occurred in recent years in parts of Western Europe and North America has often been due to the willingness of land speculators to build on flood plains, or the greed of politicians who have diverted funds intended to shore up dams and levees—often with a short-term benefit to their own pockets. God can hardly be blamed for that!

Famine is another catastrophe that is largely preventable if a country is well governed. Joseph long ago showed the Egyptians how to do it, and in principle at least, his methods have been available ever since.[15] The problem has been that, until recently, few societies were sufficiently organized for that to happen. The terrible Irish famine of 1847–1850 made people realize that it could have been prevented with appropriate planning, and since then nothing comparable has occurred in economically developed countries. Today, famine takes hold only where such planning is unavailable or is obstructed by local governments, which may even encourage widespread starvation for their own nefarious purposes. Once again, God cannot be blamed, and even atheists have to admit that Christians are often in the forefront of relief efforts when such calamities occur.

The same is true of diseases and other health-related problems. Great advances have been made both in eliminating the causes and in curing the effects of disease, as we put into practice God's command to subdue the earth. Scourges like smallpox and polio have been wiped out, or virtually so, and there is nothing today to match the bubonic plague that killed a third of Europe's population in the mid-fourteenth century. The fight against leprosy, malaria, and a host of other diseases continues, as does the search to find cures for cancer, arthritis, and other bodily ailments. Once again, Christians have always been among the first to tackle such problems and they still pioneer new initiatives, such as the palliative care for the dying represented by the

---

[15]Gen. 41:33–57.

hospice movement—which has done so much to remove any justification for euthanasia. Christians do not blame God for human suffering; rather, they use their God-given gifts to make life easier and improve the world we live in, without denying the fundamental reality that we shall all die one day. Even the most miraculous cure or the greatest escape from disaster spares us only for a time, and we do not forget that physical deliverance in this life is never more than a foretaste of the spiritual deliverance awaiting us in the life to come.

Physical disasters are neither good nor evil in the moral sense, because morality is ultimately spiritual and not physical. But physical misfortunes serve to remind us that in spiritual terms we are *all* guilty in the sight of God, and deserving of the punishment we see meted out to some. If we are next in line, then so be it—we deserve what we shall get every bit as much as those who have already gotten it. Would these disasters and difficulties occur if mankind had not sinned against God? That we do not know. We like to think that a sinless world would not suffer natural calamities, but if something like congenital blindness is not the result of sin, how do we know that it would not have occurred without the fall? What we can say is that because of the fall we have no right to be here on earth at all, and so when disaster strikes we cannot protest our innocence and blame God for what has happened. The human condition is a serious one, but the fault lies with us, not with the world we live in and certainly not with God. No one is exempt from this, and when we see how badly things can go, we are meant to take it as a warning of what is coming our way if we do not repent and turn to God for forgiveness.

As Christians, we have been saved from our sins, but we have not been excused from the consequences of being children of Adam and Eve in this life. As the apostle Paul put it, "the whole creation has been groaning together in the pains of childbirth until now. And not only the creation, but we ourselves, who have the firstfruits of the Spirit, groan inwardly as we wait eagerly for adoption as sons, the redemption of our bodies."[16] Deliverance is at hand, but the final triumph must wait until the end of time and the consummation of all things, when "he will wipe away every tear from their eyes, and death shall be no more, neither shall there be mourning, nor crying, nor pain anymore, for the former things have passed away."[17]

Natural phenomena are disasters only when human beings get in the way of them and suffer as a result. The fleas that cause bubonic plague are not evil in themselves; they are merely living out their natural life cycle as that was ordained by God. A brain tumor can do great damage and even kill a per-

---

[16]Rom. 8:22–23.
[17]Rev. 21:4.

son, but it is not a responsible agent that can be blamed for doing something "evil"; indeed, viewed from another perspective, it is a natural outgrowth of the body whose brain it is harming. Words like "good" and "evil" cannot be used of such things without considerable qualification, because the mere fact that they have negative effects on us does not make them bad in themselves.

If that is so, do we have any mandate from God for trying to prevent natural disasters? For centuries many people, including Christians, believed that it was a sin to interfere with what they called "the workings of providence." The great Irish famine is a good example of this. On the one hand, there were the state authorities, almost all of whom were Protestants, who believed in a *laissez-faire* approach to economics and thought that famine was one means by which the natural balance of a population would be restored. To their way of thinking, there were too many people in Ireland for the land to be able to support, and a cull was inevitable. They were not necessarily heartless—many gave money to support emigration—but they saw no point in artificially preserving a situation which to them was unnatural.

The Roman Catholic Church, which was the spiritual home of most of those affected, tended to believe (and certainly taught) that the famine was an act of God which should not be interfered with. If people were dying, it was the church's job to help them on their way to heaven, not to hold them back from fulfilling God's will for them. Views like these were not thought to be as outrageous then as they would be now, but it is fair to say that the scale of the disaster was such that it forced both Protestants and Roman Catholics to rethink their views, an exercise that led to a massive change in the popular approach to natural disasters. The most lasting effect of the Irish famine was to make people realize that it was not only possible to do something about such disasters, it was morally necessary. Relief work, which had been sporadic and largely ineffective before that time, became a major preoccupation and has led to the situation we have today, where disaster relief seems to be almost as much a part of the natural order as the disasters themselves.

Of course, if all that is required is the feeding of starving bodies, no one should find any reason to object. In some cases, however, averting natural disasters means eliminating something God has created—the smallpox virus being an obvious case in point. This terrible scourge was eliminated in the late twentieth century, but the destruction of the last remaining stockpiles of the virus in 1993 was not universally welcomed. No one can foresee whether a time may come when the smallpox virus will be needed to deal with something as yet unknown. Interfering with God's creation is a risky business, and it would be most unwise to assume that the destruction of even such an apparently harmful thing as the smallpox virus is necessarily good. Once again we are dealing with complex matters to which no easy answer is possible, and we must have the humility to admit that, even as we decide which course of action is the best one to take in any given circumstance.

ECOLOGY AND CONSERVATION

Discussion of natural disasters inevitably raises the question of disasters that are man-made. These range from oil spills to the extinction of animal species, two emotive catastrophes that highlight deeper issues such as the wisdom of using nonrenewable sources of energy and the degree to which environmental damage can be tolerated. These things did not figure very prominently on any-one's agenda until the nineteenth century, when the effects of the industrial revolution were becoming manifest, and it is only much more recently that they have become matters of popular concern. People who, only a genera-tion ago, would have burnt oil and gas without thinking and who threw away mountains of rubbish are now learning the necessity of conservation and recycling, as competition for raw materials becomes more intense and waste disposal turns into a major problem.

The Bible does not address this issue directly, because when it was writ-ten there was relatively little danger of environmental degradation. About the worst that could (and did) happen was that Mediterranean forests were denuded for shipbuilding and the undergrowth was eaten away by goats, leaving the semi-desert appearance that we see today, but even that did not occur on a scale that caused serious alarm. Nevertheless, the Bible does make it clear that the human race has been given dominion over the material world and is therefore responsible to God for it. We have the right to develop natural resources and exploit their potential, but not to cause wanton destruction in the name of "progress." The kind of thoughtlessness that led European explorers and settlers, almost all of them at least nominally Christian, to exterminate the dodo and the carrier pigeon, had no justification and must be condemned. Similar tendencies today must also be firmly resisted. It dis-honors the gospel of Christ that so many of the offenders have claimed to be believers and that environmental concerns are often left to fringe groups who are derided as "tree-huggers" and the like. Even if it is true that some conser-vationists have strange ideas, that does not invalidate their main concern, and the church has only itself to blame if the creation mandate is usurped by those who do not honor and worship the Creator as we do. In the final analysis, conservation of the natural environment is just common sense and should be embraced as such by everyone who seeks to serve the God who gave us such wonderful resources in the first place.

ASTROLOGY AND DIVINATION

A question that sometimes arises is whether the physical world can have any influence over our destinies. Since ancient times, the sun, moon, and stars have been worshiped by many people because they have been thought to govern the fate of individuals on earth. There have even been rulers who professed to be Christians who have employed professional astrologers to tell them what to expect based on the movements of the heavens. The only instance in the Bible which suggests that there might be something to this is the story of the Magi, the "wise men" of Babylon, who came to visit the infant Jesus at Bethlehem because they had seen a star that indicated to them that he would become the king of the Jews.[18]

Babylonia was noted for its astrologers, who were great scientists and could predict such things as eclipses long before modern methods of observing the skies were invented. There were also many Jews who had remained in Babylon after the exile and who formed one of the most important Jewish cultural communities in Jesus' day. That these astrologers would have known of Jewish Messianic expectations should surprise no one, especially since they had a special interest in such predictions. Their ignorance of the true content of those prophecies can be seen in the fact that they went straight to King Herod, perhaps thinking that the future king would be a member of his family. They may not have realized that, in Jewish eyes, Herod was a usurper, and that the true king had to come from the line of David, who had been born in Bethlehem.[19] Had the Magi understood that, they probably would have gone straight there and said nothing to Herod at all. As it was, they were informed of the true nature of the prophecy when they reached Jerusalem and the Scriptures were read to them. That was how they discovered where to go to find the baby Jesus, although the star they had seen in the east reappeared to assure them that they were on the right track.

The question we must ask is whether this reading of the stars was objectively valid. Does God use stars to tell people what is going to happen? The Magi were responding to something that they believed in, and it seems that God used their belief to draw them to himself. Even so, they were still dependent on the Bible to tell them the exact details of what they were looking for, and it can be added that their spiritual blindness ended up causing

---

[18]Matt. 2:1–12.
[19]See Micah 5:2.

great harm. Herod did not take kindly what he perceived as a threat to his own rule. He was determined to use the wise men's naivete to snuff out any potential opposition to his rule. When the Magi were warned not to go back to Herod with the details of their discovery, Herod was furious and lashed out in a desperate attempt to protect himself. Not only did Joseph and Mary have to flee to Egypt, taking Jesus with them, but all male babies under the age of two in Bethlehem were slaughtered because of Herod's fear and jealousy. The role played by the star in the story of the wise men is ambiguous at best, and certainly cannot be used as a precedent to legitimate the Christian use of astrology. As far as we are concerned, the will of God is revealed in the Scriptures, not in the stars. We must avoid any temptation to resort to such methods to determine our conduct.

What is true of astrology is also true of other forms of divination, such as reading palms or tea leaves. Theologians and pastors tend to discount this kind of thing and seldom speak out against it, but this is a mistake. It is astonishing how many otherwise sensible people can be lured into such practices, and with no guidance from anyone in authority, they are left to their own devices. Even if not much practical harm comes from such activities, they are still wrong, and Christians need to be reminded that we have no mandate from God for them. The same thing applies to a superficially more "spiritual" form of divination, which consists of opening the Bible at random and picking out a verse as "guidance" for a particular day or situation. People who do that can at least claim that the Bible is the Word of God, but if it is misapplied or taken out of context, it is of no more value than tea leaves are. What would someone do, for example, if the verse he happened to read was that Judas "went and hanged himself"?[20] Would he take that as guidance for his own behavior? The foolishness of that is obvious, but unfortunately there are many people who do not see the consequences of their actions in advance and who are easily led into what looks like a pious practice but which is in fact the exact opposite.

DRUGS

What is true of the stars and of tea leaves is even more true of drugs and other hallucinatory substances or techniques that have the power to alter our consciousness but cannot bring us closer to God or give us any kind of genuine spiritual experience. The Bible does not explicitly condemn drugs, but if flesh and blood cannot inherit the kingdom of God or perceive spiritual realities unaided by his power, then we can safely assume that these things cannot and

---

[20]Matt. 27:5.

do not give us anything worthwhile in spiritual terms.[21] Any practice that does great harm to our bodies is most unlikely to be of spiritual benefit, because the God we worship is the Creator of both body and spirit, and wants the good of the one every bit as much as the good of the other.

In ancient times there was considerable awareness of the power that certain drugs had to alter consciousness and to kill people. The use of drugs for healing purposes was not unknown, but medicine was so little developed that a drug might easily end up killing the patient instead of curing him. So much was this the case that the German word for "poison" is *Gift*, so called because it was what the doctor *gave* to his patients! Nowadays medical science has progressed in ways that would have been scarcely imaginable even a century or two ago, though there is still a widespread distrust of doctors and hospitals in some quarters, and not entirely without reason. Misdiagnosis leading to wrong treatment and even serial killing disguised as medicine are not unknown. There have been times in the recent past, as in Nazi Germany for example, where doctors were encouraged to conduct dubious experiments in the name of "science" on people who were regarded as expendable. We cannot deny that these things have happened, but we must recognize that they are abuses and insist that when they are discovered, those responsible for them should be dealt with accordingly. Such abuses do not invalidate the science itself. There is no reason for Christians to fear or to refuse treatments that are not entirely natural if it is known or generally believed that they will be beneficial. For the same reason, research into the discovery of new medicines should be encouraged and every effort made to ensure that the resulting drugs can be made available as widely as possible to those who need them.

Having said that, we must also recognize that this is not the same thing as recommending the use of drugs for "recreational" purposes, which is what some people today advocate. There is no doubt that certain substances are capable of inducing hallucinations, and there are always those who think that this is some sort of "religious" experience, but Christians must deny that and combat such beliefs. Spiritual experiences can never be induced by a material substance because spirit and matter are completely different things. There are some people who have become addicted to drugs that have been prescribed to them, but this is relatively unusual, and when it occurs our efforts must be directed to weaning them off the addiction, not to encouraging it. Those who take such substances with no comparable excuse should be treated in the same way, under the supervision of properly qualified personnel. Under no circumstances should Christians encourage anyone to experiment with drugs or

---

[21] 1 Cor. 15:50.

use them for purposes unrelated to healing. Some people advocate legalizing marijuana and cannabis for "medicinal purposes," but even if there is some ground for believing that these drugs can help alleviate certain conditions, most of the arguments in favor of them are dubious and should be recognized as such. Certainly there is no use of the drugs that would justify making them freely available to anyone who might want them.

One of the complications here is that for many centuries, most countries have tolerated and even encouraged the use of certain drugs without calling them by that name. Leaving aside the scandalous behavior of early nineteenth-century British merchants and governments who tried to force China to accept shipments of opium, there has been a much wider acceptance of mild narcotics like *qat* in the Middle East and of peyote among North American Indians. Around the world, tobacco and alcohol have long been accepted as staples of everyday life, despite the harmful effects they are known to have. Tobacco was used in pre-Columbian America as a kind of drug, and for a quite a while it was believed to contain medicinal properties. In the eighteenth century it was often taken (usually in the form of snuff) for a variety of ailments, but we now know that it never did anyone any good. Smoking it is particularly harmful, and modern medicine has proved beyond any reasonable doubt that this habit has no matching benefits to counteract the damage it can do.

Alcohol is more difficult to deal with, not least because wine is prominent in the Bible; it is even recommended for health reasons.[22] It can also play a central part in Christian worship, since many Christian churches use wine (rather than unfermented grape juice) in Holy Communion. It is therefore wrong for Christians to seek to prohibit its use or to make total abstinence a criterion for church membership. Whatever benefit may be derived from not drinking, abstinence is not enjoined by Scripture and cannot be imposed on Christians as a matter of faith. Having said that, the Bible is clearly opposed to drunkenness, and Christians must resist the over-consumption and abuse of alcohol which is so destructive of human life.[23] The idea that drinking is an "adult" activity that ought to be tolerated, if not actively encouraged, in young people benefits no one except the merchants who sell the alcohol, and inebriation should be as unacceptable to us as it was to the ancient Israelites. The argument that people should be "free" to drink themselves unconscious if they want to ignores the fact that no one is an island; the behavior of one or two affects us all, as anyone affected by a death caused by drunken driving can testify. It is all very well to punish the perpetrators of such acts after the

---

[22]1 Tim. 5:23.
[23]Eccl. 10:17; Ezek. 23:33; Luke 21:34; Rom. 13:13; Gal. 5:21; 1 Tim. 3:3; Titus 1:7; 1 Pet. 4:3.

event, but the victims are justified in thinking that more could have been done to prevent the accidents in the first place, and here Christians should surely agree. It is never easy to find the right balance, and we must admit that in the past the church has gone too far in its opposition to alcohol—an effort which failed in its purpose and has had lasting negative effects. But now we are in danger of going to the opposite extreme, which is just as harmful and undesirable. Christians must not be cowed by the excesses of the past into making no protest against the wrongs of the present.

15

THE
HUMAN RACE

THE CREATION OF ADAM AND EVE

From the creation of the material world there is a natural and easy progression to the creation of the human race. In the Genesis account, the making of Adam and Eve is portrayed as the crowning glory of God's creative work. From this we may conclude that the earlier stages of creation were designed to prepare a universe fit for the human race to dwell in. Adam and Eve did not move into a half-built house but were placed in a garden that was already fully furnished to meet their needs. We are also told that they were formed "of dust from the ground," a reminder that we are physically connected with the animals and other material creatures and not with angels or demons.[1] The latter may be capable of appearing in human form, but they are not proto-humans, nor are we heavenly beings who have fallen into the material world and become trapped in it. That idea may seem far-fetched to most people today, but it was widely believed in the ancient world, with the consequence that the material aspects of human life were downgraded and regarded as corrupting influences on the soul. The Bible tells us without any hesitation that that is not true. When God made Adam he formed the flesh first (not last) and breathed into it the breath of life, which the Bible calls the *nephesh*, a word we normally translate as "soul."[2] In this respect, the biblical account of the creation of mankind is the exact opposite of the one most widely accepted in the ancient Greek world, a fact that Christians must remember whenever it is suggested that Christianity is closely related to a philosophy such as Platonism and has absorbed much of it into its own theological outlook.

---

[1] Gen. 2:7.
[2] Gen. 2:7. Note however that the ESV translates it as "living creature."

According to the biblical account, the human race first appeared as a single man, who is the remote ancestor of every one of us. Out of this man there was formed a woman, who became his companion and the means by which the human race could be procreated. How Eve came into being remains a mystery. If we accept that there was a form of biological evolution, there is no way of telling how a human couple emerged and began to reproduce. Theoretically it would have been possible for a male to appear in one place and a female in another, or for more than one of each to come into being at the same time. But how? The Genesis account says that Eve was taken from Adam's side. That is not a scientific account, and what it might mean in biological terms is hard to say. What we know for sure is that Eve was made of the same substance as Adam and was equal to him as a human being; at the same time she was dependent on him in a way that was not true in reverse. However it happened, Eve's humanity was derived from Adam's and reflects his, whereas his humanity came directly from God.[3] It is easy to read this account in terms of a hierarchy of gender that was intended to justify subordinating women to men, and many feminists have done so, but the focus of the story is quite different. The biblical emphasis is not on the woman's inferiority to the man but on her equality with him, as the statement that both were created in the image and likeness of God plainly indicates.[4]

There was an order in their creation, but that order does not imply a power play in the way that its critics claim. Adam was bound to Eve by a relationship of love for her that was natural and necessary because in the end loving her was the same as loving himself.[5] This may sound selfish, but it is not. Adam was expected to love the whole of God's material creation, but he was given dominion over it because he was superior to it. People familiar with rural societies will know how intimately farmers can know their animals, and until the invention of the automobile, men were often so close to their horses that they instinctively bonded with them. Even today this happens in urban environments with people who become closely attached to their pets. It is against this background that we must understand the relationship between Adam and Eve, which was placed on another footing altogether. The bond between them was not like that between a rider and his horse or between a man and his dog, but between equal human beings. Eve was just as much a child of God as Adam was and was entitled to share the same privilege of dominion over the created order that was given to him. But she did not hold this privilege independently of Adam or in competi-

---

[3]1 Cor. 11:7.
[4]Gen. 1:27.
[5]Eph. 5:29.

tion with him. On the contrary, she was granted it because she belonged to him in a way that was not true of any other creature.

Adam and Eve could not have lived independent lives if the human race was to expand and develop according to the divine commandment. Reproduction was part of their creation mandate, and the children born to them would be both male and female, in roughly equal proportion. Here too, we see how they belonged together. Statistically speaking, we know that slightly more males are born than females, but as males have a higher mortality rate, this imbalance is naturally rectified. All this may seem obvious, but we have only to consider the way that family planning has been imposed in a country like China, where biblical principles are not respected, to see just how important it is to be reminded of it. In that country there has long been a "one child only" policy, whose initial and primary purpose was to control the huge growth of population in what was already the world's most populous country. But the one-child policy had an unintended (and apparently unforeseen) consequence. Forced to restrict themselves to only one child, many couples preferred to have a boy, and were prepared to abort or kill baby girls in order to get what they wanted. The result is that, a generation later, there are too many boys and not nearly enough girls for them to marry, creating a tense social situation with potentially serious consequences for the future. Had biblical principles been followed and nature allowed to take its course, this imbalance would not have occurred and the problem we see today would never have arisen. People inclined to accuse the Bible of bias toward the male ought to consider this example, drawn from a nation that has a completely different outlook on such things, and compare it with the Judeo-Christian tradition, where the principle of equality at the point of procreation has always been taught and observed.

THE SURVIVAL AND GROWTH OF THE HUMAN RACE

The mandate to reproduce that God gave the human race is something we share with the animal world but not with the angels. This is significant because it means that we reproduce ourselves not only materially but also spiritually, which makes us unique. God cannot reproduce himself because he is eternal and absolute, and the angels do not do so. But we who are created in the image and likeness of God have the privilege of being able to bring new creatures like ourselves into being, and thus to increase the number of spiritual beings in the universe in a way that no one else does or can.

God also gave Adam and Eve the right to eat anything that is edible in the natural world and put no prohibition on consuming any kind of plant or vegetable.[6] After the flood, this vegetarianism was ended and Noah's descendants were permitted to eat meat, though with some restrictions.[7] This is important in view of what would be imposed on Israel by the law of Moses, when edible foods were divided into "clean" and "unclean."[8] We know that this distinction was abolished in the New Testament, though not without some difficulty and opposition from within the church itself,[9] but we do not always recognize that the basis for getting rid of the food laws is to be found in the original creation mandate. From the time of Noah it seems that everything edible could be eaten. It says a good deal about the way the Israelites understood the restrictions placed on them later on that they were prepared to admit this. Nothing could have been easier than for a Jewish scribe to have interpolated the food laws into the early chapters of Genesis as "proof" that the law of Moses reflected an eternal divine decree, but we find nothing of the kind. However much they clung to their traditions, at bottom the Jews knew that the food laws were not part of God's original intention, but a limitation on it. They did not foresee that the laws would one day be abolished, but when they were, most of those who accepted Christ as the fulfillment of the law accepted the change, and by the second generation of the church the problem had disappeared. This stands in sharp contrast to Islam, which claims to be an advance on Christianity comparable to the advance that Christianity is on Judaism, and yet has a system of food laws remarkably similar to that of the Mosaic law. Even Mormonism, an offshoot of the Christian tradition, puts some restrictions on what a Mormon can consume, reminding us yet again that the freedom to eat and drink whatever we want is not something to be taken for granted.

The food laws of the Old Testament do not apply to Christians because the purpose for which they were given has come to an end. Ancient Israel was told to distinguish itself from the surrounding nations in many different ways, of which abstinence from certain kinds of food was only one. Some people have tried to find hygienic reasons for the prohibition of things like pork, but there is no evidence to suggest that this was God's intention or that it corresponds to any scientific fact. There is no natural logic that determines what the Israelites could or could not eat; the rationale for the food laws was given by God, who wanted his people to understand that his holiness meant that they must be set apart from the rest of the world in every aspect of their lives. The coming of Christ

---

[6]Gen. 1:29–30.
[7]Gen. 9:3–4.
[8]Lev. 11:1–47. The distinction between "clean" and "unclean" is mentioned in Gen. 8:20, where it was applied to animals and birds offered up for sacrifice. It is not stated whether this distinction applied to the consumption of food at that time.
[9]See Rom. 14:14.

broke down those ancient barriers because he defined the principle of holiness in a new way. Material objects would no longer be used to determine or signify the sincerity of the people's dedication to God, and so the food laws passed into history, although the apostles made provision for a transitional phase to ease the consciences of Jewish converts who had been brought up under the old system.[10] For that reason, the church has always said that there is nothing wrong with observing the food laws, and it has been particularly tolerant of Jewish believers in this respect, but it has also insisted that such observance cannot be made a condition for church membership.

What is true of the Old Testament food laws is also true of any other form of diet. There may be good medical reasons for eating some things and not others, and Christians would be foolish to disregard the advice of those specially trained in the field, but that is a completely different matter. It is one of the curiosities of modern life that the word "sin" is often used in advertising particularly rich foods, as in "a sinful amount of chocolate cake," but there is nothing sinful about the cake, or even about eating it. Overeating is clearly a bad idea, but to use the language of sin to describe it is wrong. Christians are called by God to take care of themselves physically, because our bodies are temples of the Holy Spirit. Things likely to be harmful to the body should not be consumed, whatever they are. What our bodies can take will vary from one person to another, though excessive consumption of anything should be avoided. Physical fitness should be pursued as far as is reasonably possible as a means of subduing the body and of making us fit for the service of God, but it is not an end in itself and must never take the place of the service we owe to him.[11] The worship of the body is just as idolatrous as the worship of any other created thing, and Christians must learn to keep it in its place along with everything else that God has given for us to enjoy.

THE NATURE OF HUMANITY

To speak about God is to speak about his love for us and for everything he has made. But even before we are able to speak at all, we feel his love at work in the world we live in. It is present in and around us from the moment we are born, although it takes time before we can recognize and articulate it. If our parents are believers, they will tell us about God's love, but our conscious awareness of it does not stir until we realize how great the universe we live in is and how insignificant we are by comparison. As the psalmist said three thousand years ago,

---

[10] Acts 15:19–21.
[11] 1 Tim. 4:8; 5:23.

When I look at your heavens, the work of your fingers,
  the moon and the stars which you have set in place,
what is man that you are mindful of him,
  and the son of man that you care for him?[12]

Whether we look at the plants and animals around us or, like the psalmist, contemplate the distant heavens above us and beyond our grasp, we quickly realize that we are no more than tiny dots on a canvas of reality whose variety and extent surpass our imagination. Our first reaction is one of awe at the immensity of it all, and we long to find out more. For centuries, human beings have done what they can to penetrate the mystery of the universe, exploiting its resources, warding off its dangers, and trying to discover the best way to live in harmony with it. Sooner or later, however, the awe that initially overwhelms us gives way to fear. We till the soil and cultivate what we need to eat, but we are afraid that if the rain does not come, we shall lose the crops and run the risk of dying by starvation. Why do we have to worry about this? We build houses to live in, but one day the ground shifts under our feet and everything is consumed by an earthquake. What have we done to deserve that? We sail the high seas and marvel at the wealth of their marine life, but then the wind rises, the waves grow stronger, and suddenly we find that we are in imminent danger of death. How can water teeming with such goodness become a threat to our very existence?

The more we contemplate the power of "nature" to undo our petty creations and sweep us off our feet, often without warning, the more we tend to doubt ourselves. What can our place be in so vast a scheme? How can we possibly matter to anyone else or make a difference to anything when we can be blown away by a gust of wind? As we grow older, we realize that our time on earth is short, our opportunities few. Perhaps it is a mercy that most of us are forced to spend our days doing what we can to earn a living and seldom have the time or the energy left to ponder such things. We do our best not to think about whether anyone will remember us when we are dead, or what legacy we shall leave behind. If thoughts like these occur to us at all, we are likely to fear that our life will turn out to have been for nothing, that it is meaningless, and that when it is over we shall go back to the oblivion from which we sprang.

This sense of meaninglessness is our deepest fear, which gnaws at the heart of every human being, whether he is a "primitive" savage or a sophisticated intellectual. It is this that distinguishes us most clearly from other crea-

---

[12]Ps. 8:3–4.

tures that have a similarly circumscribed lifespan but lack the ability to reflect on it and therefore do not share our fear. Animals live and die in ignorance of such things and, for the most part, they appear to be indifferent to their fate. We human beings, on the other hand, live and die in self-awareness, and it is that knowledge which is the source of our anxiety. Can it really be that everything we have lived for or cared about will go back into nothing, leaving no trace behind? Will we all end up like the great Ozymandias, a stone statue staring blankly at the desert that was once his kingdom?[13] Even if our fame lasts for centuries, it will eventually come to an end, and a wilderness may be all that is left of our once flourishing kingdom.

Thoughts like these have been common to people in every age, but they did not trouble the psalmist. In answer to his own question, he went on to say,

> Yet you have made him a little lower than the heavenly beings
>   and crowned him with glory and honor.
> You have given him dominion over the works of your hands;
>   you have put all things under his feet.[14]

Human beings have been put into the world in order to subdue it and develop its potential. This is the essence of Christian anthropology. However much we have in common with the animal world, we are not naked apes. We are spiritual beings who have an in-built relationship to God and a mental capacity that outstrips any other living thing. In the spiritual realm we are at the bottom of the pile, being made "a little lower than the heavenly beings," or angels, but in the material creation we are on top, "crowned with glory and honor" and entrusted with "dominion over the works" of God's hands.

Paradoxically, this means we have a closer relationship to God than the angels do, because although as purely spiritual beings they are "higher" than we are, they have not been given any privilege or responsibility corresponding to ours in importance. The world we live in was created for our benefit and not for theirs. In many ways the world is fully functional in its original state, but it also contains unharnessed potential and natural phenomena that can be modified and improved. There is nothing wrong with deserts, and those who live in them are aware of how alive and varied they can sometimes be. At the same time, however, human beings are given the ability to irrigate them and make them bloom like roses.[15] This does not mean that we should do this to every desert, even if that were possible, but it shows that we can

---

[13]The reference is to the poem "Ozymandias," by Percy Bysshe Shelley, published in 1818.
[14]Ps. 8:5–6.
[15]Isa. 35:1.

develop technology to improve our environment for human use, and that this is a legitimate activity under the sovereignty of God. Similarly, we can drain swamps, eliminate harmful diseases, and exploit the natural resources of our planet for the common good. The divine mandate for development is not a license to abuse God's creation, but to use it in the way he intended and has equipped us for.

The great Albert Einstein is supposed to have said that the wonder of the universe is not that it is a mystery hidden from our eyes, but that so much of it can be understood and analyzed by mere human beings. What is it that gives us the ability to develop science in the first place? Christians say that it is because we are created in the image and likeness of God, but atheists have to rely on evolutionary theories to explain this phenomenon. But who or what set these evolutionary processes in motion, and why is it that some human beings become highly intellectual academics while others live in trees in tropical forests? We can demonstrate that humanity is the same everywhere, but we cannot explain why some people and societies are so much further advanced in these scientific pursuits than others are, when there is no innate genetic superiority to distinguish them. This matters, because ever since the beginning of European overseas expansion in the sixteenth century, there have been those who have tried to explain the more advanced development of some races over others by an appeal to innate differences. Nowadays most people regard this as horrific, and rightly so, but we have to remember that it was an atheistic worldview that made such thoughts possible.

Dozens of other questions also come to the surface once the idea of an orderly creation designed by God for a specific purpose is challenged. What right do human beings have to claim superiority over animals? It has recently been claimed that chimpanzees have undergone more beneficial mutations than human beings have since we split from our common ancestor, a statement that might conceivably be used to "prove" that chimpanzees are somehow superior to us. But whatever facts lie behind such a claim, it is clear to most people that we are superior to chimpanzees—after all, it is we who investigate them and not the other way around! Those who doubt the superiority of human beings over animals need only consider the following: would you rather be bitten by a dog or by another human being? From the standpoint of the potential damage inflicted, the human being is almost certainly the less dangerous choice, but we do not think that way. A dog that bites us may be a nuisance and would probably have to be put down, but we would not blame him for biting us in the way that we would blame a fellow human being. A man who bites us is clearly expected to be responsible for his actions, and we would all expect him to suffer the consequences for that reason. When it comes to situations like that, no one disputes that more is expected from human beings than from animals, but why should this be so?

We must also ask whether it is possible for a being higher than we are to emerge, either by natural evolution or by scientific experiment. Christianity says that man is the crowning glory of creation,[16] which suggests that no higher form of created life will ever emerge, though atheists have no way of knowing or determining whether this is so. Yet, if a race of superhuman beings were ever to appear, would we let them control us in the way that we dominate animals? Would any of us be content to be a pet in the household of such a being? This seems most unlikely, and the truth is that if superhuman beings ever did appear, we would be forced, if only in our own self-interest, to exterminate them before they became numerous enough to take us over. In other words, we have a vested interest in making sure that there is no further evolution, but would that not also have been true of our "missing link" ancestors? What stopped them from trying to do what we would do in self-defense? The genetic codes of human beings and orangutans are so similar that we might easily think of ourselves as biological cousins, but put the two of us next to a cat and it will soon be clear who the odd one out is. For however close we may be to certain animals, the gap between them and us is still enormous—and universal. In every way that matters—intellectual, spiritual, and social—human beings are a world apart from both cats and orangutans, which seem to us to inhabit a mental universe equally distant from our own.

To take another example, dolphins are now thought to be so intelligent as to be classifiable as "persons" in some respects, but what practical effect would such a classification have? Could we ever relate to a dolphin in the way that we habitually relate to other human beings? Could a dolphin be held responsible for its acts, which is part of the very essence of personhood? When we stop to think about these things, it is clear that the answer must be no, but if there is no God and no plan behind the universe, how can it be that animals genetically close to us are just as far away from us in this respect as those that are more distant from us genetically? When all is said and done, no animal comes anywhere near to human beings in intellectual or spiritual terms, and in the end these things matter more than any physical resemblances that there may be between us.

---

[16]Ps. 8:5.

PEOPLE WITH DISABILITIES AND SPECIAL NEEDS

Bodily health and strength are not given to everyone, nor are they given to different people in equal measure. Many are born with disabilities or other deficiencies, some of which are treatable but not others. In the past, and even today in some places, people suffering from such conditions were regarded as a liability and, in extreme cases, particularly when defects could be detected in newly born children, they were put to death. If they survived, they were often consigned to menial tasks like begging, and it was easy to assume that whatever the problem was, it was a mark of God's displeasure. Such opinions were also held in ancient Israel, as we can see from the story in the Gospels about the man born blind. He was brought to Jesus, who was asked to say whether the blindness was the result of the man's own sin (which hardly seemed possible) or that of his parents (which seemed unfair), but Jesus' reply took a completely different approach. He said,

> It was not that this man sinned, or his parents, but that the works of God might be displayed in him. We must work the works of him who sent me while it is day; night is coming, when no one can work. As long as I am in the world, I am the light of the world.[17]

It is true, of course, that this explanation does not apply in every case. Some people are born with disabilities that are the result of something their parents did, whether irresponsibly or not. It is well known that mothers who smoke or drink during pregnancy can harm their babies, and there have been cases of women who have taken fertility drugs (such as thalidomide) that have produced birth defects. Men are less directly involved in childbirth, but they too can pass on the effects of sexually transmitted diseases, and they cannot shirk their responsibility in this matter any more than women can. In rare cases, parents may have genetic or other disorders that make it inadvisable for them to have children. Many people become disabled after birth for a wide variety of reasons, some of which are not their fault. For example, small children can contract life-threatening diseases but survive with impairments of one kind or another. Others react badly to treatment and emerge from it scarred for life. Many more people have accidents for which they may or may not be responsible, and they are left blinded or seriously damaged in some other way. We cannot give one answer that will address every case, but even after allowing for the above possibilities, it is still true to say that there is no direct or necessary connection between sin and physical disabilities or defects, just as there is no

---

[17]John 9:3–5.

necessary, causal link between sin and illness, even if certain sins will almost certainly lead in that direction. Blaming those who suffer for a sin they may never have committed is no more helpful than promising believers that they will never experience any of these problems because of their faith. We do not know why some people and not others are afflicted with these things, but we can at least say that there is no physically perfect person and that even the healthiest among us will one day grow old and die.

What the Bible teaches is not that we have an entitlement to bodily health and welfare, but that whatever our condition may be, it is up to us to glorify God in and through it. If we are blessed with a sound mind and body, then we must use them to serve God and not defile them with things or activities that dishonor his name. If we are disabled, then we must seek to overcome that in the best way we can, and the church can rejoice that in recent times there has been great progress in this respect. The achievements of those who are disabled or who have special needs can be quite astounding. Thinking about their achievements, and the great hurdles they have overcome, and the great blessing that those who are not so disabled have thereby received, helps us glorify God and thank him for a goodness that we might otherwise take for granted. We know that this is not the ideal situation, but the world we live in is not ideal, and the promise is held out to us that one day the lame will walk, the deaf will hear, and the blind will receive their sight.[18] The gospel is a message of hope for physical restoration, if not in this life then in the resurrection from the dead, when all such disabilities will disappear. Occasionally we are given a foretaste of this glory in this life, either by divine intervention (as in the case of Jesus' healing miracles) or by the advances of medical science. We give thanks to God when this happens, but we remember that healing in this life is for a time only and is no more than a promise and shadow of the greater healing which is still to come.

A form of disability that is particularly difficult to deal with is the variety of conditions lumped together in the popular mind as "mental illness." This phenomenon was not understood for a very long time, and those who suffered from it were often locked away and mistreated in the most appalling manner. Even today, many people find it hard to deal with the mentally disabled and may treat them cruelly, not least by making fun of their disability. At the other extreme, though, some have regarded mental illness as a gift from God, and the word "blessed" can even be used in the sense of "touched in the head."[19] This does not happen very often nowadays, but it was fairly

---

[18]Matt. 11:4–6.
[19]Note that the word "silly" originally meant "blessed"; compare German *selig*.

common in biblical times, as we can see from the story of the unfortunate girl in Philippi, whose mental condition was exploited as an oracle of the gods.[20] That appears to have been a case of demon possession, but it is hard to say for sure, because the Bible speaks only of a "spirit of divination" without specifying that it was evil. It is quite possible that it was a form of mental illness or epilepsy, but the girl was cured by exorcism, and those who had sought to make money out of her misfortune were robbed of their ill-gotten treasure.

As far as the church is concerned, it is entirely right that we should respect disabled people and do everything we can to make their lives as rich and meaningful as possible. However severe their disabilities may be, they are human beings like us and we have no right to dispose of them merely because they seem to be an inconvenience. Of course we should encourage medical researchers to do everything they can to develop gene therapy and other techniques that may alleviate or remove the causes of their conditions, but those who suffer from them must not be regarded as second-class or inferior human beings for that reason. The only valid restriction, and one which was applied from ancient times in the worship of the Jerusalem temple, is that those called to Christian ministry and service in the church must be capable of performing the tasks they are expected to carry out. There is no justification for ordaining a severely disabled person out of sympathy for his plight when it is impossible for him to function in the role assigned to him. People already in Christian ministry who develop seriously debilitating conditions ought to be retired gracefully and looked after properly, not encouraged to continue in a task that they are clearly unable to perform. This is not discrimination but a sign of love for them and for the people of God, whose common worship must be conducted "decently and in order,"[21] and not in a way which can only embarrass all those involved.

WORK

Physical fitness is valuable because it helps those who are blessed with it to perform the tasks that God has assigned to them in the world. It is sometimes thought that human labor was a punishment laid on Adam and Eve as a result of their fall from grace, but this is not an accurate reading of the creation story. It is true that things were made more difficult for them after they were expelled from the garden, but the basic tasks God assigned to them in the beginning remained the same as before.[22] Work is part of the creation mandate given

---

[20]Acts 16:16.
[21]1 Cor. 14:40.
[22]Compare Gen. 2:15 with Gen. 3:17–19.

to us by God, and it must be developed in accordance with that. For many centuries, and still today in much of the world, men and women have had little choice but to work hard in order to survive. This was taken for granted almost everywhere until the nineteenth century, when the industrial revolution made it possible for large numbers of people to abandon menial tasks and look for more creative forms of work. Even in ancient times, however, when manual labor was so much more necessary than it is today, there were still those who were called and enabled to dedicate themselves to craftsmanship, to exploration, and to what we would now call "academic" pursuits. They may have been a minority, but in ancient societies people were more obviously interdependent than many of us are today, and we should not be surprised that Jesus, a carpenter's son, also found time to study the Scriptures. Many of his disciples were fishermen, but that did not prevent them from becoming preachers and teachers later on in life. The freedom to develop and use more intellectual skills that has become general in modern times has also come at a price; today we have to specialize and dedicate ourselves to only one major pursuit, whereas in former times it was possible to be a "jack of all trades" or a "Renaissance man" without being unemployable as a result.

Are there trades or pursuits that are not legitimate for a Christian, and should we prefer one kind of vocation over another? Jesus was a carpenter, so presumably that is a lawful occupation for his followers, but no one has ever suggested that all church leaders should take up carpentry. Nor has there been any great rush among Christians to become fishermen or tentmakers (as the apostle Paul was), although both of these callings have often been used as metaphors for Christian service. Jesus told his disciples that he would make them "fishers of men,"[23] and it is not uncommon today to hear people talk of having a "tentmaker" (or tentmaking) ministry, by which they mean working in a secular occupation in order to secure the funds for some kind of preaching or evangelistic activity. There are no rules laid down to determine what sort of work this should be, but certain principles are given to us in Scripture, and they must guide us in our choice of occupation.

First, whatever we do must be honoring to God, which means that it must be honest and above reproach. A man who proposed to take up armed robbery in order to use the proceeds to spread the gospel would be a hypocrite, but there are people in the world today who think that terrorist activities are fully compatible with their religious faith (and may even be *required* by it), so examples of immoral behavior being justified as service to God are not as far-fetched as they may seem. Even so, it is hard to imagine anyone advocat-

---

[23]Matt. 4:19.

ing that prostitution is a legitimate activity for a Christian, even if it is legal in some places, nor would we expect to find believers taking part in scams designed to fleece the unwary of their money, or engaging in professional gambling. These things compromise the moral integrity of those who do them and are designed to corrupt others. Even if they are not specifically condemned in the Bible, they are contrary to its general teaching about the way we should behave toward other people, and therefore must be ruled out as activities that a Christian can legitimately participate in.

But here the line between what is legitimate and what is not starts to become blurred. Churches may think it is wrong to operate a casino, but what about playing the stock market? That is a form of risk taking that may be considered gambling, and it is certainly possible to win and lose large sums of unearned money by doing so. Yet the world's economy depends on investment, and the corrections imposed by the stock market are a very effective way of ensuring that funds go to the right projects. Relatively few people are faced with the dilemmas posed by so-called "unethical investments," but almost everyone is employed by a company or institution that depends to some extent on funds generated by morally questionable means. Should a Christian invest in or work for a tobacco company, for example? What about a multinational corporation that exploits poor workers in underdeveloped countries? The list of potentially compromising situations could go on and on, and there is almost nothing that is not tainted in one way or another. Even Paul's tentmaking was not entirely innocent, since the main customer was the Roman army, and it was probably because his father or grandfather had been helpful to the Romans that the family acquired the Roman citizenship that came in so handy when he was put on trial in Jerusalem.[24] The complexity of economic life means that there can be no simple answer to this question, but the biblical evidence suggests that as long as it is possible to work with integrity at a task which is in itself legitimate, then Christians should be free to do so.

In modern times this question has been complicated by the phenomenon of people working and living under tyrannical governments who have found themselves doing the most appalling things because they were "only taking orders." There has been a considerable effort made to track such people down after the regime they had worked for was overthrown, but although the desire to see justice done to them is understandable, it is not always clear what that justice should be. Modern life is often too complex for individuals to be able to make the kind of responsible moral choice their judges expect of them, and even if they can, the options open to them may be far from clear. It is easy for

---

[24]Acts 22:25–28.

us to say that a prison guard at Auschwitz should not have done what he did, but was he not often just as much a victim as those whom he was forced to handle? Situations like this one are virtually impossible to resolve on a purely moral basis, and they remind us yet again that the world is a fallen place in which there are no true innocents, even if some people have a greater opportunity to incur guilt than others.

In the New Testament we find that Jesus and the apostles dealt with people as individuals, on a case-by-case basis. Cornelius was not rejected because he represented the power of an alien imperial force, nor was the Ethiopian eunuch berated for the misdeeds of his mistress, the queen of Ethiopia.[25] Matthew the tax collector was accepted as a disciple, but the rich young ruler was turned away, even though there was no such thing in ancient times as an honest tax collector and the rich young ruler had kept the Ten Commandments all his life.[26] In the end, the call of God does not depend on the worthiness of those who are summoned. When we turn to Christ in a spirit of obedience and submission to his will, the way we should follow will be made plain to us, but we should not be surprised if our way turns out to be different from the way opened up for others. We must refrain from passing judgment on those who have been led into doing things that we would find objectionable but which are not clearly condemned in Scripture.

EMPLOYMENT

Economic conditions today are very different from what they were in biblical times, and those who study the subject will probably also agree that the great turning point came with the industrial revolution in the late eighteenth and early nineteenth centuries. Before that time, and still today in parts of the world that have remained "preindustrial," the majority of people worked for themselves as farmers, artisans, or traders. It is true that they were often dependent on landlords and aristocrats, but even so they usually had a great deal of personal freedom in the work that they did. Paul made tents at his own pace, and the fishermen of Galilee did not have to reach a quota before they could go home, even if they normally expected to return with a reasonable catch of fish. Most of these people worked in households where every member was productive—it is no accident that the Greek word *pais* was used to mean both "child" and "servant," because small children did many of the menial tasks around the house, as they still do in some countries today. Big business, as we understand it, did not exist, although there were farms called *latifundia*

---

[25]Acts 8:26–40; 10:1–33.
[26]Matt. 9:9; 19:16–30.

which operated on a large scale, and there were also state-run enterprises like mines. In these and in many other places, most of the work was done by slaves, a feature which we find disconcerting and we wonder how the early church could possibly have tolerated it.

Up until about 1750 and even later, most countries in the world functioned in a way that was recognizably similar to what we find in the Bible. The Protestant Reformers had developed a philosophy of work based on the notion of "calling" or "vocation," which was derived from the medieval monasteries. The monasteries had developed what to them was a model Christian society, in which people bound together by a common faith and devotion parceled out the tasks of daily life in an ordered and purposeful way. Some monks did the chores, others farmed, while others engaged in creative tasks such as illustrating manuscripts. A few even became leading preachers and teachers whose writings are still studied today.

The Reformers took this pattern and threw it open to everyone. All members of the church—and in Europe that meant entire populations—were expected to show evidence of a calling to Christian service, which might be anything conducive to the welfare of society, as had been the case in the monasteries. Given the wide range of needs, it was possible for men, and sometimes also for women, to become artisans and traders in their own right. Tenant farmers could leave the land and seek their fortune in the cities if they had a marketable skill. Many did so, creating the first truly urban societies in Holland and England. Slavery was not a problem for them because it had disappeared in the Middle Ages, and the church forbade the enslavement of Christians. When it reappeared, it was in the overseas colonies generated by European expansion, and its victims were people from unevangelized places like Africa.

The industrial revolution changed all this. First of all, it created the means of mass production, which put many artisans out of business. Why have a shoemaker, for example, when shoes could be produced much more cheaply by machines? It also did away with many menial tasks that had previously been performed by children or servants, thus allowing the former to get an education and the latter to seek employment elsewhere, often in the colonies. Above all, it created a class of employed laborers who no longer worked for themselves but who toiled as cogs in a vast industrial machine that benefitted from, and was controlled by, the international market. There had always been economic cycles of boom and bust, but now for the first time, vast numbers of people were affected by them at the same time. They had no alternative means of earning a living that would tide them over until conditions improved.

Semi-independent laborers became wage-earning employees, with a different relationship to the work they were doing. Today that pattern has become the norm for most people, and we must interpret what the Bible says about labor in the light of that.

Industrialization caused a lot of damage, but it also had some good effects, one of which was speeding up the abolition of slavery. The church is often criticized for its apparent toleration of that institution, and modern Christians can be scandalized by what looks like the insensitivity of earlier generations to it, but this has to be understood in context. The truth is that neither Jews nor Christians approved of slavery, and both did what they could to control it. The Jews had been slaves in Egypt, and their national identity was closely tied up with their deliverance from it, so they could identify with slave populations more readily than we might think. The Israelites were constantly reminded of their humble beginnings (unlike other ancient peoples, who tended to see themselves as the offspring of gods and therefore greatly superior to others), and this memory was to guide them in the way they treated slaves. Slavery was never abolished completely, but Israel did not become a slave-dependent society, and the institution was confined to foreigners—Jews were not permitted to enslave each other for more than six years, unless the slave requested it.[27]

The Christian church inherited this situation and lived with it, not because it thought that human servitude was right in itself, but because its priorities were different. In first-century Palestine, Jews thought they were oppressed by the Romans and regarded their condition as a form of slavery. Jesus was under considerable pressure, even from his own disciples, to rise in revolt against it.[28] He refused, however, telling them that his kingdom was not of this world. This did not mean that he was indifferent to the problem of oppression, but that he taught that the way to resolve it lay in a spiritual transformation of hearts and minds and not in violent revolts that would only make the situation worse. From the very beginning, the apostle Paul insisted that converted slaves were members of the church on the same footing as free men were.[29] Later on he demonstrated what that meant in the letter he sent to Philemon, the owner of the runaway slave Onesimus. Paul sent Onesimus back to his master, but in a way that put the latter in a difficult position. Philemon could have used the force of the law to punish Onesimus, but Paul pointed out that to do so would be an offense against the principle of

---

[27]Lev. 25:39; Ex. 21:6; Deut. 15:17.
[28]Acts 1:6.
[29]Gal. 3:28.

Christian brotherhood, something which in his eyes ought to transform their relationship completely.[30]

Paul also gave instructions to both masters and slaves as to how they should relate to one another, and it is clear from those instructions that he saw the situation primarily in what we would now call employment terms. Slaves were to earn their keep, but masters were to treat them well,[31] a requirement that continues to govern the Christian approach to industrial relations today. Paul also pointed out that a laborer deserves his wages, a principle which, if applied consistently, makes slavery impossible.[32] Masters and slaves were to coexist in a mutual relationship that entailed responsibilities and obligations on both sides, rather than "rights," a principle that was extended to the life of the church as a whole. According to Paul, all human beings are slaves to the elementary principles of the world, whatever form this slavery might take.[33] Those who become Christians are set free from that slavery but only because they have become slaves of a new and better master, Jesus Christ. This kind of slavery is not the traditional kind of bondage but true freedom, and it applies equally to everyone. In the Christian vision, when masters realized that they too were slaves, their attitude to those under them would change and the economic institution of slavery would be modified and perhaps even formally abolished.

When Christianity became the official religion of the Roman empire, the church tried to limit slavery, and over time it succeeded. Ancient slavery evolved into serfdom, a form of indentured labor which concentrated on the economic aspect of the relationship between worker and master and did not give the latter the power of life and death over his serfs. Slavery in the traditional sense was restricted to the non-Christian world, which at that time included the Slavic tribes of Eastern Europe. This historical development has been preserved in our language, where the word "slave" is derived from "Slav." Later on, the Slavs accepted Christianity, and by the time of the great European expansion in the sixteenth century, slavery could flourish only in the colonies. Even so, the church made strenuous efforts to prevent the native Mexicans from being sold into slavery by their Spanish conquerors, though their success in that merely led the latter to turn to Africa instead. There, Europeans tapped into an existing slave trade that was endemic to African tribes and encouraged by the Muslim Arabs to the north and east, who still practice it today.

---

[30]Philem. 17–20.
[31]Eph. 6:5–9.
[32]1 Tim. 5:18.
[33]Gal. 4:3.

Modern slavery therefore developed along racial lines and produced vast slave economies in the New World of a kind that had never existed in Europe. There were always those who objected to this, but for most influential people in the seventeenth and eighteenth centuries, slavery was out of sight and therefore out of mind, and the powerful slave owners wanted to keep it that way. It was the religious revival known as the "Great Awakening" that stirred consciences again and led to the final battle against slavery in the Western world. Christians promoted abolition, but they also had to answer the charge that it would produce unacceptable levels of social unrest and economic dislocation. This was not merely a theoretical objection. Both of these things actually happened in the Haitian slave revolt that followed the French revolution. That revolt succeeded, but at a price so high that the country never fully recovered from it. It was here that industrialization came to the aid of the abolitionists; by changing the nature of the workforce, it made slavery uneconomical. Slaves might be fine in boom times but they could not be laid off in an economic downturn, when they became a major liability. In economic terms, it was better to set them free, pay them a wage, and leave them to their own devices in hard times. That was not an ideal solution, of course, but it did promote emancipation and put former slaves on the same level as other free members of the new working class.

If Christianity has failed in this sphere, it is not so much in its supposed toleration of slavery as in its failure to get to grips with the phenomenon of economic class struggle. In the nineteenth century, this issue came to the fore in a way that had not been true earlier on, but all too often the church found itself propping up the bosses and not their workers, who increasingly turned to non-Christian and even atheistic solutions to their problems. It is a tragedy that the early communists were often people who were fired by essentially Christian ideals but were alienated from the gospel because those who had a duty to proclaim it did not grasp its implications for the new world of employment relations. The church has not yet recovered from this terrible error, even though many Christians today are fully aware of it and do what they can to correct the mistake. One unfortunate result of this is that we now find ourselves in a situation where workers demand what they see as their "rights" and are much less willing to consider their responsibilities and obligations. Putting those responsibilities and obligations first is the correct Christian approach to economic as to all other relationships, and it applies to employers and employees alike. In the history of industrial relations there are honorable exceptions to the general rule, but on the whole, the church has still not come to terms with this problem and its message goes unheard in the workplace because of it. Churches can and should take the lead in emphasizing the importance of consensus and interaction in industrial and other employment relations. Workers should be encouraged to acquire a stake in the companies they work for, and the tendency to allow giant megacorporations to develop should be resisted if it can be shown that employer-employee relations suffer as a result. Churches should also support the claims of the disabled and encourage the retraining of the under-skilled, so that they can be gainfully employed and derive personal satisfaction from the work they do. Economic development has brought great blessing to many but there are always those who are left behind, and the churches have a special responsibility to seek them out and help them as much as they can.

LEISURE

One result of the industrial revolution is that it introduced leisure to the majority of people, for whom such a luxury had previously been unknown. That was unintended, because when machines were first invented, mill owners and the like thought that they could simply force their employees to work harder and longer than they had before. That was a disastrous policy, of course, and it led to widespread resistance among the labor force, which began to organize itself for the first time. Gradually, work conditions were improved, often as the result of campaigning by dedicated Christians, and the modern pattern of shift work and the forty-hour week emerged. Technological advances have made it possible for us to be increasingly flexible about how we apply these patterns, so that we can now have both round-the-clock production and a great deal of personal leisure time as well. In fact, in the modern world, leisure has become, for the first time in human history, a major industry in its own right and a social question scarcely envisaged in earlier times. It is true that the early Christians denounced circus games and the theater, both of which provided entertainment for the urban masses, but this was on a small scale compared to what we experience today, when literally billions of people watch the world championship (in the sport of their choice) at more or less the same time.

What should we do with our leisure? In the Bible, desisting from work meant taking time to worship God, as the provision of the Sabbath day makes clear. That is still a major preoccupation of Christians today, but we now find that it faces competition not so much from work that needs to be done as from leisure activities that compete for our attention. Sometimes Christians try to ensure that sports events, for example, do not interfere with public worship, but now that you can video anything or watch games being played on the other side of the world, this kind of control has become virtually impossible and has lost much of its meaning. When even the Olympic Games can be scheduled at times likely to attract the greatest television audience, banning football in the local park on Sundays is hardly worth the effort. Technology and communications have transformed the world we live in, and the church has barely begun to consider what this means for the way Christians ought to live their lives.

For many centuries, leisure was the privilege of a few but it was important because it provided the opportunity for them to sponsor what we now regard as the classical achievements of Western civilization. The church was a major patron of the arts, music, and literature as well as of architecture, law, and medicine. It was because of the basic Christian belief that human beings were endowed with creative instincts that this development was possible, and the only question was to what extent the fruits of such creativity could be used for the purpose of Christian worship. Here there was a divide between Protestants and Roman Catholics that is still visible today. Protestants supported music and literature, but they were less enthusiastic about the visual arts, especially if they depicted religious themes that might be used for the purpose of venerating Christ, the Virgin Mary, or the canonized saints. The Eastern church's use of icons was especially problematic in this respect, and it never caught on in the West, among either Protestants or Roman Catholics. The use of art for devotional purposes was unfortunate because it has cast a shadow over all art that has never been fully dispelled, but Christians have never objected in principle to the development of such human talents, regarding them as gifts of God.

In the modern period, however, this high culture has faded into the background. It still exists and can be very popular, particularly among those who have been educated to appreciate it, but it is seldom encountered in everyday life, where it is really only music, and that of a very different kind, that has made much of an impact. In recent years the church has accommodated modern popular music styles to a large extent, and guitars are now as frequent as organs in church services, but it is almost impossible to judge how much of this will survive the test of time. Inevitably, a good deal of what is being produced today is of indifferent quality, and works of lasting value are as uncommon now as they were in the past. Nevertheless, the church does not stand in the way of this creativity and even encourages it, even if the results are not as spectacular as one might hope.

The other major impact of mass leisure culture is in the field of sports, and here too there is an ancient history that needs to be taken into consideration. In biblical times, sports were mainly a Greek activity associated with pagan cults in places like Delphi and Olympia. When the church came to power in the fourth century, it closed down the Olympic Games and other similar festivals because of this association and never sponsored any replacement for them. For similar reasons, gladiatorial combats and the like were also suppressed, and when something like them later resurfaced in the form of knightly jousts, the church took a dim view of them as well. In contrast to the support given to the creative arts, the church has never shown much enthusiasm for games or athletics, which are now regarded as exclusively secular activities.

This might not matter very much, except that in recent years sports have become big business, and, in the eyes of many people, they are almost a substitute religion. One way or another, many churches have succumbed to this, and it would be hard to claim that Christians are markedly different from the rest of the population when it comes to their involvement in sporting events. There is nothing wrong with physical exercise, but it can be argued that the professionalization of sports has actually had a negative effect on it, as performance is restricted to a small elite and everyone else just watches. Unfortunately, one look at many of these spectators is enough to show that physical fitness is not their strongest point! Christians must face up to the fact that there is no encouragement given in the Bible to the cult of star athletes, and that there is something seriously wrong with a society that pays such people millions for doing nothing more than kick a ball across a field. That is not a sin, of course, but neither is it fulfilling the creation mandate. Christians should urgently consider whether this is really the best use of our leisure time and energy. Recovering genuine creativity for the glory of God is a challenge that faces us as our leisure opportunities for fulfilling it increase, and perhaps there is nothing quite as important for us to rediscover in our lives today as this great calling to use our creative imaginations in the service of Christ's kingdom. To do this effectively, we must recover a sense of what it means to be made in the image and likeness of God, and it is to that important subject that we now turn.

16

HUMAN
RELATIONSHIPS

THE IMAGE AND LIKENESS OF GOD

Our place in the created order is defined by the fact that we are made in the image and likeness of God, which distinguishes us from all other creatures, including the angels.[1] This is the reason why we have been given dominion over the material creation, and it places us in the relationship with God that we are meant to have. Modern atheists have tried to abolish the divine dimension of human life, but the result of this is not what they originally intended. Instead of putting man on the throne previously occupied by God as they claim to do, they have lost sight of what the human race is and so can no longer distinguish it effectively from the rest of the universe. If we are just highly evolved animals, how can we claim dominion over the rest of creation? That would be the ultimate case of might over right and the very essence of tyranny. Furthermore, if man is no more than an animal, moral and spiritual considerations have no real importance and we are reduced to the level of enlightened self-interest and the survival of the fittest—the law of the jungle in a sophisticated but unmistakable form.

If we are responsible to no one, we are guilty of nothing, and traditional codes of rights and obligations are replaced by claims of oppression and victimhood, which are no more than the cries of the weaker against the power of the stronger. Reverse the roles and this pattern is also reversed, as we have seen in Israel, where Jews discriminate against the Arabs in ways reminiscent of their own sufferings in the past, and among native peoples in Southern Africa, some of whom have sought to dispossess the Europeans whose ancestors once colonized them. These examples are particularly disconcerting

---
[1] Gen. 1:26–27.

because they involve people who claim to believe in the God of the Bible, but the same is true everywhere. Experience tells us that cries for justice and equality are unlikely to survive the experience of sacrifice and deprivation that may accompany the realization of such ideals, and that what usually happens is that one oppressive regime is simply replaced by another. Only the belief that we have been created in God's image is able to give us the sense of both our dignity as human beings and our responsibility to God and to one another. It is because we are made in the divine image and likeness that we are called to love God with all our heart, soul, mind, and strength, and in the light of that to love our neighbor as ourselves.[2] Without that belief, our Lord's summary of the law would make no sense, and our self-understanding as human beings would be distorted out of all recognition.

What the image of God really means has been the subject of widespread speculation since ancient times, when the general consensus was that it is to be found in the mind or rational soul that God gave to Adam and that distinguished him from the animals. In the Greek-speaking world, it was usually thought that the image and likeness were two different things, so that when Adam and Eve fell they lost the likeness of God but kept his image intact. Rather in the way that the queen's head on a coin is still clearly visible and unimpaired even after it loses its shine, the fathers of the church believed that, although human beings had lost the brilliance of being in God's likeness, they had retained the underlying image, which Christ came to restore to its original brightness. This was how they interpreted a verse like 2 Corinthians 3:18, where the apostle Paul writes that, ". . . beholding the glory of the Lord, [we] are being transformed into the same image from one degree of glory to another." As they saw it, even the fallen human race continues to reflect the glory of God, but with the coming of the gospel, those who receive it are being transformed from that glory into another which is higher and more perfect, which is also the glory that we were meant to have from the beginning.

That ancient view prevailed until the sixteenth century, when the rediscovery of Hebrew forced scholars to accept that the image and the likeness were a single entity and not two separate things. From that they concluded that if the likeness had been corrupted or lost at the fall, so too had the image, and this became the standard interpretation in post-Reformation thought. According to their way of thinking, because fallen human beings are corrupted in their minds and unable to understand the things of God or worship him correctly, his image and likeness in them has been effectively nullified, whether or not some remnant of it can still be detected in us. It therefore follows that only

---

[2]Mark 12:30–31.

if we are born again and filled with the Holy Spirit can the divine image and likeness in us be restored to what it was meant to be.

The difficulty with this view is that there is no indication anywhere in Scripture that the image and/or likeness of God was lost by the fall of Adam or even affected by it. In Genesis 9:6 there is a prohibition against murder, because man was created in the image of God. In James 3:9, we are warned not to slander other people because they are made in God's likeness. Neither of these verses would make much sense if the image and likeness had been lost or corrupted by the fall, and it is clear from the context that the biblical writers assumed that human beings still retained God's image. We must therefore start our examination of this subject by insisting that whatever the image/likeness of God is, the Bible assumes that it is still present in fallen man without any internal change or distortion. In this respect it can be compared with the nature of the fallen angels, who do not cease to be spiritual creatures merely because they have fallen. Just as they retain all their previous abilities and powers, which they now use to express their rebellion against God, so too human beings now use the image and likeness of God not to serve him but to reveal the extent and seriousness of their disobedience and rebellion against his will.

The biblical account does not define the divine image and likeness, but it does rule out two things that we might imagine would belong to it. One of these is immortality. Adam and Eve were protected from death in the garden, but they were still mortal beings and were not given access to the tree of life. That point is made very clear at the end of the story, when God, in order to prevent man from living forever, barred the way to the tree and expelled Adam and Eve from the garden.[3] The second thing ruled out is the knowledge of good and evil. This too was denied to Adam and Eve, but they obtained it by their disobedience and did not lose it again when they were shut out of paradise. The story tells us that by acquiring the knowledge of good and evil, Adam and Eve became like God. This knowledge was not part of the divine image in them, because God had given them that image before they succumbed to Satan's temptation. This does not mean that it is possible for us to function in God's image and likeness and be indifferent to moral questions, because now that we have moral awareness we have to take it into account, but it does tell us that they are not the same thing. Our knowledge of good and evil has become the context in which we work out the meaning of the image of God, but it must not be identified or confused with it.

The traditional definition of the image as the mind or rational soul

---

[3] Gen. 3:22–23.

appears attractive at first sight, but there are a number of problems with this idea. Not the least of them is the fact that if we accept it, we are liable to conclude that mentally ill people are worse off than others and may even be demon-possessed. That view was widespread for many centuries and led to great cruelty, as the mentally disabled were imprisoned and mistreated through no fault of their own. Today we have a greater awareness of these things, and that must make us more cautious about coming to wrong conclusions about the nature of the image. Equating the image with the mind would also suggest that very intelligent people are closer to God than the rest of us. The "tyranny of the experts" that would result if this view were accepted is by no means absent today—and it is particularly dangerous in an age where an "expert" is someone who knows a great deal about a very narrow range of subjects and may have little appreciation of anything beyond that.

It is enough to read the opinions of leading scientists on moral and spiritual questions to become aware of how foolish they can be once they step out of their own field of expertise. Of course, those whose minds have not been shaped by a biblical worldview may have some conception of a higher order of things, but even so, it is likely to be extremely vague, tentative, and even inconsistent. This is because they are extrapolating from something they know about to something they do not, but their intellectual prestige masks their ignorance of things outside the bounds of their own discipline. We tend not to pay much attention when sportsmen or movie stars pontificate on politics or something else they know nothing about, but our instinctive deference to the power of the mind makes us less cautious in the intellectual realm, which is far more dangerous for that reason. This is not to say that the mind has no function, or that it is irrelevant to the image of God in us. As with moral awareness, it is an important ingredient in the way in which we work out the meaning of God's image and likeness in us, but it must not be mistaken for that image and likeness itself.

We are nearer the mark if we link the image and likeness of God to the concept of personhood. Men and women are persons, just as God is three persons in one, and our personhood gives us the capacity to have a relationship with him and with each other. Our relationship with God is innate, and our relationships with each other are developed as we go through life. The most fundamental of them is the link we have with our parents, which is why the Bible uses genealogy as the principal means of establishing personal identity. Next in order come the relationships with our siblings and the wider household to which we belong. After that, there is the relationship with a spouse, which comes closest to replicating that between Adam and Eve, followed by relationships with in-laws, children, and so on. Beyond the family circle, we also establish links with other people which develop, change, and fade away over time. This relational capacity is of fundamental importance to our existence, not least because it is the channel through which we express the love of God in our lives.

Inter-human relations reflect the love of God in various ways and to varying degrees, and the Christian must work out what expression of it is appropriate in each case. We obey our parents, join our bodies to our spouses, and discipline our children because the nature of our relationship to these people determines what the appropriate response of love toward each of them is. Getting this wrong has serious consequences. For parents to obey their children would be folly, as would any attempt on the part of children to dominate their parents. Sexual intercourse with either is incest and is strictly forbidden. Yet each of these relationships is an equal manifestation of love and only in exceptional circumstances is one to be preferred above another. A married couple is called to leave father and mother and cling to each other, but that does not mean that they are free to abandon any responsibility for their parents, like the duty to care for them in old age. Nor do children usurp the place of a spouse in their parents' affections, because although both relationships are equal, they are also different. Relationality is not one-sided or univocal but has many possible manifestations, each of which is just as valid as any of the others and all of which can be held together in a harmonious whole.

Here, as elsewhere, the key is appropriateness—we must work out what kind of relationship we are meant to have with particular people and act accordingly. Love is the principle that governs my relationship to my neighbors, to my employer and employees, to my friends, and to complete strangers, just as it is the principle that governs my relationships within the family and my relationship to God. It is the nature of the relationship that is different in each case, not the quality of love, which stays the same and must guide and govern it in all circumstances.

Personhood is undoubtedly an important part of the image of God, but it is not an adequate definition of it because angels and demons are personal too. If we do not relate to them in the same way as we relate to God it is because of their status as his servants, not because they are incapable of relating to us in a personal way. Although angels and demons are personal, they are not created in God's image, so we must look for something more than personhood to explain it. The added ingredient which the angels do not possess is the dominion that we are given over the creatures, which entails both a function analogous to that of God and responsibility to him for fulfilling it. Studies of the meaning of the Hebrew words translated as "image" and "likeness" back up the idea that there is a royal dimension to them. Images and likenesses of their rulers were set up in Babylon and elsewhere as reminders to the people of their subjection to them. We bear God's image as a sign of our dominion over his creatures. As with moral awareness and rationality, personhood is a vital ingredient in the exercise of that image. It enables us to act in accordance with the image, but it must not be confused with the image itself.

Has the dominion God gave to Adam and Eve been lost as a result of the fall? There is nothing in Scripture to suggest that it has. The human race has certainly not been replaced by another species more worthy of the task originally assigned to it. Our first parents were expelled from the garden of Eden and told that they would till the soil and bear children in sorrow and heavy labor, but they were not told that their basic assignment had altered. On the contrary, it was the fact that they would now have to carry out their assigned work without the protection God had provided for them in the garden that was the essence of their punishment. Had they been reduced to a lower status, they would certainly have suffered the consequences of their sin, but they might have been unaware of that if they were no longer fully human. Fallen man is just as capable and just as responsible for the execution of the creation mandate as the pre-fallen Adam and Eve were, with the difference that the results are now harder to come by and more ambiguous. The achievements no longer come so easily, and the effects may have secondary consequences that are harmful, which presumably would not have been the case had the fall never happened. In spite of everything the fall entailed, however, human culture has continued to develop, the earth has been developed, and there have been many great human discoveries and inventions in which we must rejoice. Conditions have changed, but the image of God is alive and well in the human race and continues to function as best it can in the circumstances.

There is perhaps some ground for saying that Christian civilization has been more productive than others because we are aware of both our potential and our limitations, but whether that is true or not does not really matter. Many human achievements are admirable and highly beneficial to us all, and Christians have no need (or right) to reject them merely because they were produced by ungodly people. The mandate given to Adam and Eve was given to the entire human race and is being fulfilled by everyone, whether or not they realize this. In this respect, it is interesting to note that in the book of Revelation, the tree of life appears in the midst of the city (a sign of human creativity) and not in the garden (a product of nature), reminding us that human culture as well as created nature will be redeemed at the end of time.[4] It is important to understand this because there is a persistent tendency among Christians either to reject the science of the ungodly or else to succumb to it and abandon what seems like the unreasonable exclusivity of the Christian faith. There is no reason to suppose that a Christian will be better than anyone else when dealing with secular matters, and in fact, the Bible would seem to suggest the opposite. Jesus told his disciples, "The sons of this world are more shrewd in dealing with their own generation than the sons of light."[5] And the apostle Paul told the Corinthian church that God had chosen the foolish things of the world in order to shame the wise.[6] Given this situation, Jesus' advice was to make friends of the ungodly, in order to benefit from their cleverness, but of course without falling into their ungodliness.[7]

The main difference between Christians and others in this respect is that others tend to believe that "man is the measure of all things," as the ancient proverb expressed it, whereas Christians say that it is God who sets the standard. The non-Christian world mistakes the image for the reality and behaves as though "man" is sovereign, even though this is self-evidently nonsensical. What, after all, is "man"? There is no such thing as a generic human being, nor is there a single individual who acts as the ultimate arbiter of the creation mandate. People who talk this way are almost always trying to claim an authority for themselves that allows them to do more or less whatever they like. This is particularly obvious in the field of scientific research, where some people demand the right to do whatever they are capable of without any regard for moral or spiritual issues that might oblige them to refrain from doing something that is possible but unethical. If there is no standard above and beyond what I happen to think or want to do, why should I be stopped from doing it? Of course, if this principle were universally applied there would be chaos. Sovereign freedom of this kind could not possibly be granted to 7 billion people at the same time, not to mention the countless numbers of former generations and those yet unborn, who will presumably have the same "rights" as we claim to have. Those who think like this almost always end up promoting the cause of a small minority, which they then impose on everyone else, whether they want it or not. Individual sovereignty cannot be exercised without dominion, and in the nature of things, that dominion will end up as domination over the weak and disadvantaged. The creation mandate is not a license to do whatever we want to; it is a privilege given by God, to whom

---

[4]Rev. 22:2.
[5]Luke 16:8.
[6]1 Cor. 1:27.
[7]Luke 16:9.

we are ultimately accountable for its exercise and who will judge us if we fail to observe the limitations placed on it or if we take undue advantage of the opportunities it offers.

THE PURPOSE OF HUMAN SEXUALITY

The creation of Adam and Eve gives us a picture of what God intended for the human race from the beginning—one couple united to each other for the purposes of companionship and procreation. The first of these is more fundamental to the relationship, because it provides the context in which a newborn child can receive the security he needs to grow and develop in a balanced way. It also outlasts the childbearing years and can provide the couple with comfort and security into old age. The bond thus formed is for this life only, leaving a widowed partner free to find another companion if he or she wishes to do so and other factors permit it. In the case of widows under the age of sixty, remarriage after the death of a husband is positively encouraged by the apostle Paul, and even after that it is by no means forbidden.[8] He does not say anything about widowers, perhaps because there were fewer of them in ancient times, but probably also because they would most likely seek another wife without being prompted. It was easier in ancient times for a man to choose whether or not to marry, and more acceptable for him to wed a woman considerably younger than himself. The Bible places no restrictions on this, either for men or for women, but most of the time common sense prevails and it has always been unusual for married couples to have extreme differences of age between them.

Sexual intercourse for pleasure is acceptable within the bond of marriage but not otherwise, and it is here that the greatest challenge to Christian values comes. In ancient times, prostitution and concubinage were prevalent, often with the backing of fertility cults in which temples served as brothels. It was both easy and socially acceptable for men to seek sexual encounters wherever they could find them, although women had much less freedom and could often be stigmatized if they lost their virginity outside marriage. Today this ancient tendency is reinforced by a powerful pornography industry, an intellectual culture that regards sexual activity as both normal and desirable in itself, and greater freedom given to women, which often has the effect of making them more willing to indulge in such activities than they once would have been. The sexualization of children has been so strong that it has become a matter of public concern, particularly when it leads to sexual experimenta-

---

[8]1 Cor. 7:39–40; 1 Tim. 5:9–16.

tion among the very young. Christians must be opposed to this, not because we are against sexual activity but because we value it and want to see it preserved within its proper context. We must also insist as much as we can that sexual behavior, even within the context of marriage, ought to be honoring to God. Sadomasochistic practices, for example, have no place in a Christian marriage, nor does anything that is not acceptable to one or the other of the partners. Sexual intercourse is, after all, an expression of love, and love begins in the heart and mind of those involved, not in merely physical desires. If that rule is followed, then the rest will fall into place.

Until recently, it was considered indecent even to mention such things in public, but the sexual revolution of the past generation has made that attitude no longer realistic. As Christians, we have to be forthright about the importance we attach to sexuality, but we must also insist that it is not the most important thing in life, that many other kinds of relationship are both possible and desirable, and that the human body is not to be regarded as an object of lust. This is particularly important for single people, who can easily be pressured into adopting expressions of sexuality that are dishonoring to God. The kind of man who is forever chasing women (or talking about it), and the kind of woman who flirts with every male who walks by and sees nothing wrong in wearing revealing clothing, may be doing nothing more than responding to this kind of pressure, but it is important for the church to create a space where such behavior is neither acceptable nor necessary to attract attention. In particular, Christians should remember that church activities are times for fellowship across the entire spectrum of the body of Christ and not substitute dating agencies. Of course, it may be desirable for people to meet their future spouse in such a context, but that should not be regarded as one of the main purposes of Christian worship. God has not called church leaders to be matchmakers, and such conduct is unbecoming of those in Christian ministry, especially when many people are already under considerable pressure from the secular world. The great challenge facing us today is to create and promote nonsexual friendships and fellowship, where God is glorified and no one is excluded for failure or unwillingness to participate in sexual or potentially sexual activities.

One of the most harmful aspects of the modern obsession with sex is that suspicion and fear of it tend to corrupt other kinds of relationships. It is now much harder than it used to be to maintain friendships, not only between members of the opposite sex (which has always been difficult) but among those of the same sex as well. We now live in a society where older men dare not go near children for fear of being accused of having predatory intentions.

Nudity, which was once common in same-sex situations (locker rooms, public baths, and so on) is often no longer accepted even there, and people are subtly encouraged to jump to unwarranted conclusions if they come across it. The net effect, unfortunately, is that such hypersensitivity is more likely to create the situation that it is trying to avoid by making people aware of things they would otherwise never have thought of. Nowhere is a healthy sense of perspective more needed than in matters like these, and the church has a duty to be as straightforward and honest about them as it can be.

A major element of any discussion of human sexuality in biblical times, and still important today, is the question of procreation. This was one reason why it was often more acceptable for older men to marry younger women than the other way around, and there have always been potential problems when a marriage proves to be childless. If the marriage has not been consummated at all, the church has usually been willing to annul it, but things are more complicated when biological factors make childbearing unlikely or impossible. In the past, this was sometimes used as an argument for permitting polygamy or concubinage, but it was never considered an adequate ground for divorce. The rights of a married woman were protected in both Jewish and Christian circles, and if she was barren, the promise was held out to her that one day that affliction would be taken away.[9] In the final analysis, a man and a woman are bound to each other in marriage, and that bond is valid whether children are born of it or not.

At the same time, procreation must not be downplayed, because it is fundamental to the survival of the human race. Although some couples cannot have children and others choose not to have them, the church has always tried to encourage couples to reproduce so that our species will be propagated. There is such a thing as overproduction, of course, and it is permissible for married couples to practice forms of birth control that do not involve killing a fetus. Family planning is perfectly reasonable and in no way forbidden by the Scriptures. Some Christians have tried to ban artificial means of birth control, but there is no biblical justification for this, and we should be free to make our own choices in the matter according to circumstances. Natural means of birth control may be safer and healthier than artificial ones, but that is not a justification for forbidding the latter, which may often be the more practical course to follow.

Abortion is another matter. No Christian should seek or perform an abortion without good reason because it is the termination of a life. The Bible is clear that life begins at conception, and that God knows us and cares for us

---

[9]Isa. 54:1; Gal. 4:27.

in the womb as much as he does in the world.[10] Nevertheless, we cannot make an absolute rule about this, because there are some circumstances in which an abortion may be the lesser of two evils. This will probably be the case when the life of the mother is in serious danger, and it may also be true when the fetus is irreparably damaged. Each situation is different, and it is impossible to make a general rule that would be applicable to all circumstances. As Christians we are basically pro-life, but we must acknowledge that there are hard cases where a choice has to be made about whose life is to be saved, and allow those most directly involved to act according to their consciences.

The modern difficulty is that abortion on demand is now the effective rule in most developed countries, which creates problems of its own. How late in a pregnancy should abortion be allowed? Should the father have any rights in the matter, or must it be exclusively the mother's decision? What about cases of rape, where a healthy child's life may be threatened by something that is no fault of his? There is also the problem of the gynecologist and his or her conscience. Medical doctors are pledged to save lives, not to terminate them, and many refuse to perform what are otherwise perfectly legal abortions. Should they be allowed to do this, or are they obliged to perform an abortion as a public service to anyone who wants one within the bounds of the law? There are no easy answers to these questions, but the principle that life should be saved wherever possible ought to guide Christians as they try to work out the best solution. No medical practitioner should ever be forced to violate his or her conscience, and here the church must be prepared to stand up in defense of those who take a principled stand on the matter. The church should also try to persuade those who seek abortions to reconsider their decision, and offer alternatives like adoption, which would allow the child to have a normal life in a family willing to take it. Abortion is seldom the best and almost never the only possible solution, and Christians have a duty both to point this out and to make other options viable and attractive to those whose decision it is.

GENDER EQUALITY

The innate equality of every human being also applies to the differences between male and female, though here there is a complication that has to be acknowledged and accounted for. In the sight of God and with respect to eternal salvation, there is no difference at all between men and women, who are equally loved by God and chosen by him for eternity.[11] At the same time, however, there are important differences between males and females that are

---

[10]Jer. 1:5; Luke 1:41.
[11]Gal. 3:28.

fundamental to the nature of the human race and to its survival. Failure to recognize this, and insistence on an exaggerated form of "equality" that seeks to abolish this legitimate distinctiveness (often by comparing it to the artificial and quite illegitimate barriers that have been erected between different races or to the exploitation inherent in slavery) is one of the great errors of our time and threatens our very existence as a species. It is therefore not something that the church can ignore. As with everything else to do with sex, we must listen to what the Scriptures teach us on this subject and seek to apply it in our lives.

The first thing the Bible says is that male and female are complementary and that neither can exist for long without the other. Of course there have always been "all-male" and "all-female" activities, which vary from one culture to another, and the Christian church has often promoted single-sex religious communities with the aim of serving God and spreading the gospel. But neither an all-male nor an all-female religious community can exist entirely on its own, and both are ultimately dependent on a wider society in which men and women live together and interact with each other. Christian religious communities are deliberately and consciously countercultural, and are in no sense intended to be models for society at large. The apostle Paul preferred celibacy for those who (like himself) were engaged in full-time Christian service, but he did not impose it on everyone nor did he encourage it for its own sake.[12] Contrary to popular legend, Paul had nothing against women and worked happily with people like Lydia and Priscilla.[13] He understood that an interactive community of male and female is essential to human survival, and such a model of community has always been defended and promoted by the church.

The image and likeness of God is given equally to both males and females, a point made explicit in the Genesis account of creation.[14] There is a difference, however, in the way each of them receives it. That is implicit in the creation story and is brought out specifically by Paul when he discusses the question in the course of his pastoral ministry.[15] The difference is that Adam received the image directly from God whereas Eve received it from God through Adam. That this distinction remains valid can be seen from the context in which Paul mentions it. Women must relate to men in a way that reflects the fact that Adam is the source of Eve's life. This relationship gives the man both an authority over the woman and a responsibility toward her. These two things are complementary and go together in equal measure;

---

[12]1 Cor. 7:6–7.
[13]Acts 16:14–15; 18:1–2
[14]Gen. 1:27.
[15]1 Cor. 11:3–16.

to overemphasize the one is to distort the other, just as to ignore the one is to nullify the other. The archetypal male-female relationship is that between husband and wife, because this comes closest to replicating the situation of Adam and Eve, but the same principle must be reflected in all male-female relationships, as Paul implies.[16]

A wife is expected to be submissive toward her husband, accepting his authority over her and doing what he says.[17] This submission is not merely intended as something to be observed within the privacy of a marriage but is also for public demonstration, as Paul reminds us when he tells women that they must cover their heads (a sign of their submission in the ancient world) so that their modesty will be observed by everyone, including even the angels.[18] Here we have a curious but important reminder that we all live in a context of fellowship much wider than ourselves, which extends even into the spiritual realm where such things might be thought to be irrelevant. Obedience is never optional; it is the foundation of all our relationships because everything we do is ultimately done in submission to the Lord. The outward sign of this is different for the male, but the inward spirit is the same and may be even more demanding. For if a wife is told she must submit to her husband, the husband is reminded that he must sacrifice himself for his wife, giving himself up for her in the way that Christ gave himself up for the church.[19] Both husbands and wives have to make concessions for the other, and if the man is to be regarded as the head of the wife, then for him to justify that honor, his concessions to her must be even greater than hers to him.

There have been times in human history and there are still many human societies today where men have used their authority to assert an unwarranted superiority over women that has led to great injustice and oppression. We have only to look at Islamic societies where women are forced to veil themselves and are restricted from living independent lives to see what the effects of this can be. Christians have sometimes been guilty of similar behavior, though it is fair to say that it has seldom, if ever, gone as far as what we see in Islam. Women in Victorian times led lives more restricted than women today, but they were never forced into seclusion. Many of them were highly successful within the spheres that were thought to be appropriate for them. This is not to say that the restrictions were right, but merely that compared with some things that we see today, they were not nearly as bad as they are often made out to be.

---

[16]1 Cor. 11:7–16.
[17]Eph. 5:22–24.
[18]1 Cor. 11:10.
[19]Eph. 5:25–28.

Today in the Western world, the pendulum has swung so far in the opposite direction and women's rights have been elevated to such an extent that they now invade, more or less as a matter of course, spheres properly reserved to men. This is very evident in education, where some mothers have started to express alarm that their sons are being demasculinized by a system in which they are exposed to all-female teachers and are forced to engage in activities deemed suitable for both sexes, just so that the principle of equality is observed. In practice, of course, this almost always means forcing boys to do "girlie" things like drawing or making cardboard cutouts because boys tend to be more aggressive and harder to control. The idea that boys and girls are different and that in some respects they ought to be brought up separately is occasionally acknowledged, but it often suffers from the feeling that it is a cover for discrimination against girls. The result has been a measure of discrimination against boys instead, who often do less well at school than girls do because schooling is biased toward the feminine, and they feel left out.

How widespread a problem this really is, is a matter for debate, but the fact that concerns of this kind are now being expressed by mothers (more so than by fathers) ought to alert us to its seriousness. In adult society, male bonding is now more difficult than it used to be, and men who want to associate with each other are often restricted to spheres like sports, where their physical prowess makes an obvious difference. But not all men are interested in sports, and the projection of that image of masculinity can be very damaging, not least to women who find themselves being sacrificed to the game or the team!

It also seems very probable that the apparently high incidence of homosexuality in our modern culture is due in part to a failure to distinguish between the sexes properly. There are certainly effeminate men, but there are also ultra-masculine ones in the homosexual community, and the same is true of lesbians (with the roles reversed). The unisex environment in which we are increasingly forced to live is not what the Bible prescribes for us, nor is it consonant with human nature. We can and must respect one another's differences without falling into the trap of domination of one sex by the other, and biblical counsels about this are as sure a guide now as they were two millennia ago.

CELIBACY

Abstinence is the first and most universal approach to sexual relations, and all human beings are called to practice it at some point in their lives. The time between the onset of puberty and marriage will vary enormously from one individual to another, but whether it is long or short, sexual abstinence is required of Christians during this period. Given that it is a time of great emotional and physical intensity, this can be very difficult, but it must be seen as an act of love—love for God, for self, and for a potential spouse. We are called to present our bodies as a living sacrifice, and part of this means keeping it pure in every respect, since an acceptable sacrifice must be spotless.[20] Abstinence in these circumstances is both a service to God and a reassurance to a future spouse that we do not regard sexual gratification as an end in itself and intend to commit that part of our lives to build up a lasting marriage. Within a marital relationship, sexual abstinence also finds its place. It may be practiced deliberately in order to make time for special fasting and prayer,[21] but it may also occur circumstantially, as when spouses are separated for business or other legitimate reasons. It may become necessary if one of the marriage partners is ill or otherwise unable to engage in sexual activity. Finally, when a marriage ends in separation or death, sexual abstinence once again becomes the expected norm unless and until a second marriage takes place.

Abstinence of this kind affects everyone one way or another, but it must be distinguished from celibacy as a dedicated way of life. True celibacy is not the result of physical incapacity for sexual activity, nor is it the accidental by-product of circumstances that may be beyond our control. On the contrary, it is a conscious commitment to a life of abstention in this area with the deliberate purpose of serving God more fully. It is perfectly possible for people who find themselves single more or less by accident to adopt a celibate lifestyle, but there are no grounds for insisting on celibacy as a precondition for full-time Christian ministry. Having said that, celibacy is held up to us in the New Testament as a spiritual gift which is to be gratefully received both by those to whom it is given and by the wider church.[22] This has to be said because, all too often, celibate people are subjected to pressures from people who think that celibacy is unnatural, and in some cases they may even become the victims of salacious gossip. Christians must remember that Jesus was celibate, as was Paul, who was not afraid to tell the church that it was a blessing given to him for the benefit of others, and who recommended it as the best option for those able to accept the discipline that goes with it.

Celibacy is not intended to be the norm for Christians, but when the gift is given it should be respected and honored and not looked down upon as a sign of failure or as the mark of a less valuable lifestyle. Paul preferred it,

---

[20]Rom. 12:1.
[21]1 Cor. 7:5.
[22]1 Cor. 7:32–35.

not because he disliked marriage but because he saw that a married couple were bound to each other and therefore not free to serve the Lord in the way that a celibate person could be.[23] He warned Christians to take this into consideration and not to expect that married people would be able to devote themselves as fully to the work of the church as single people can do. For that reason, someone who is called to an itinerant or unusually solitary ministry probably should not get married because the other partner in the relationship will be forced to pay too high a price for it. Unfortunately this kind of situation is far from unknown in the modern church, and it has contributed to a number of marital breakdowns. People called to full-time Christian service ought to consider very seriously whether they should remain celibate for the sake of their ministry and not allow themselves to be pressured into an unfortunate and unhappy marriage.

MATRIMONY

Celibacy has an important place in the life of the church, but it cannot be the norm for everyone, or even for any large number of people. Sexual relations are essential for the propagation of the human race, and it is important to regulate the context in which they may legitimately take place. This is necessary for the greater good both of individuals and of societies, where unbridled promiscuity is almost certain to lead to disaster and the disintegration of the community.[24] In essence, matrimonial regulations are a form of love for one's neighbor because they make it clear what the relationship is, and as such they belong at the very heart of the Christian life.[25] When legalized matrimony began is unknown. The principle of monogamy would appear to have been laid down in the story of Adam and Eve, and the earliest generations recorded in Genesis also seem to have been monogamous. Yet in many ways matrimony as we now understand it is a social construct and not something inherent in the original creation. Whatever else Adam and Eve did, they did not pledge lifelong faithfulness to one another in a ceremony conducted in the presence of witnesses, which reminds us that marriage is primarily an agreement between two individuals that is valid in itself. The legal and ceremonial superstructure that now surrounds marriage developed as the human race grew and diversified, but it was many centuries before it became fixed in what we would recognize as the "biblical" pattern.

Some indication of the variety of forms that matrimony might take can

---

[23]1 Cor. 7:7.
[24]1 Cor. 7:2.
[25]See Gen. 20:1–7.

be seen in the lives of the three great patriarchs of ancient Israel. Abraham was monogamous, but also childless, which encouraged his wife Sarah to suggest that he should take a concubine. He eventually had children by several other women, but never married them, with the possible exception of Keturah.[26] Isaac was also monogamous, and as far as we know he remained so. Jacob however was bigamous, though this was not entirely by his own choice, and he had children by concubines as well, who were apparently supplied to him by his wives. What is most interesting about this is that the sons borne by these women were all recognized as ancestors of Israel. They were not categorized or stigmatized according to their official legitimacy or illegitimacy but were all treated alike, as table 16.1 illustrates.[27]

Leah (wife)	Rachel (wife)	Bilhah (concubine)	Zilpah (concubine)
Reuben	Joseph	Dan	Gad
Simeon	Benjamin	Naphtali	Asher
Levi			
Judah			
Issachar			
Zebulun			
(Dinah)			

TABLE 16.1

Leah, Jacob's first wife, was the mother of half of his sons, including the eldest (Reuben) and the two who would be most important in the nation's later history—Levi, ancestor of the priests, and Judah, ancestor of the kings. Leah was also the mother of the only daughter of Jacob who is mentioned by name. Joseph, the son of Jacob's second (and preferred) wife, received a double blessing and became the ancestor of the tribes of Ephraim and Manasseh. The tribe of Benjamin, the second son of that marriage, remained loyal to the Judaic kings when Israel was divided after the death of Solomon, and it was therefore part of the remnant that was to form the Jewish people as we now know them. There is no discernible difference, however, between the sons of the two wives and the sons of the two concubines, so we can only conclude that matrimony was not the determining factor in their inheritance, as it would have been later on in Israel's history.

After Jacob's time it would seem that, although monogamy was probably the most frequent form of matrimony in Israel, it was only one option among others available to and tolerated among God's chosen people. Odd as it may seem to us, some of Israel's greatest leaders were polygamous (Moses, David, and Solomon), but there were also humbler folk who had more than one wife,

---

[26]Gen. 25:1.
[27]Gen. 29:31–30:24, 35:18.

like Elkanah, the father of Samuel.[28] None of these men was criticized for having more than one spouse, although some modern commentators have suggested that the family difficulties encountered by David were a subtle hint that monogamy would have been preferable even for him. With 700 wives and 300 concubines, Solomon was in a class by himself, but he was still the man who built the temple, and as the son of David, he was the prototype of the greater Son of David who would come as Jesus Christ.[29] His wives caused trouble, but he was not rebuked for having so many women around. The problem with Solomon's wives was not their number but the fact that many of them were *foreign* women, who persuaded him to set up shrines to their native gods and thus polluted the pure worship of Yahweh.[30] This was essentially the same criticism later applied to Ahab, who was monogamous but married to a foreign queen who did everything she could to make Israel accept the worship of her native gods.[31]

Monogamy seems to have become increasingly the norm in post-Solomonic Israel and Judah, but along with this there was a greater emphasis placed on the undesirability of marrying outside the nation. We have no way of knowing how widespread such intermarriage was, but we do know that a custom which had been tolerated in the days of Ruth, who was herself a foreign bride, was forbidden after the exile, when it had become quite common and had to be formally suppressed.[32]

As time went on, Israelite marriage practices became increasingly strict, and, by the time of Jesus, they had settled into a pattern which we still recognize today and which was broadly similar to the rest of the Greco-Roman world. Monogamy imposed itself for a number of reasons. Theologically speaking, the most important of them was that the Bible commanded a man to leave his father and mother and cling to his wife, so that the two would become "one flesh."[33] A marriage was the start not just of a new relationship but of a new family unit, which could not have come into being in the same way had polygamy and concubinage been the norm. Union of husband and wife in one flesh was of great practical benefit to the woman especially, because it underscored her basic equality with her husband and made it clear that she would not have to share her position in the household with anyone else.

It is perhaps because neither Jews nor Gentiles had to change their

---

[28]1 Sam. 1:2.
[29]1 Kings 11:3. See also Matt. 12:42.
[30]1 Kings 11:8.
[31]1 Kings 16:31–33.
[32]Ezra 10:14–44.
[33]Gen. 2:24.

inherited practices to any significant extent when they became Christians that no particular form of matrimony is prescribed in the New Testament. The church did not perform weddings, and the only thing it tried to insist on was that Christians should marry other believers.[34] Apart from that, there is no indication of how Christians entered into marriage, and we must assume that people continued to do whatever they had been doing before, and that they made their domestic arrangements in a basically secular context, though there were clear restrictions on whom Christians could marry.[35] Even when Christianity was legalized and then became the state religion in the fourth century, the church accepted the existing legal framework and did virtually nothing to impose any matrimonial discipline of its own. It was only after the fall of the Roman empire in the West that the church became deeply involved in matrimonial matters, largely because there was no other means of registering a marriage once the Roman law courts had ceased to function.

The church found that it did not like certain aspects of traditional matrimonial law, and it tried to introduce changes that would make it more compatible with Christian principles. The most important of these was the right of each of the parties to a marriage to give their consent to it. This meant that the woman as well as the man had the right to refuse a marriage partner. Although this principle was frequently observed more in the breach than in practice, it nevertheless set a new standard and gradually changed the way that matrimony was perceived. What the church wanted to insist on was that marriage was a solemn commitment between two equally consenting adults, and not a family arrangement decided by the parents for reasons of their own. This seems obvious to us now, but in an age when a marriage was as much a business contract as anything else, it was extremely difficult to persuade families not to put their financial interests before the happiness of the couple. Despite many failures and lapses, the church's insistence on the right of consent transformed the basis of marital relations in Western Europe and paved the way for the freedom of choice that we now take for granted. As Christianity has spread around the world, it is this concept of marriage that has gone with it, often having the same transforming effect on inherited matrimonial traditions as it had in medieval Europe.

The medieval church also transformed matrimony into a sacrament, to be celebrated by a priest in the church. That gave it a holy character which it had not previously had and made it indissoluble, since once the grace of God had been given, it could not be rejected or despised by anyone who claimed

---

[34] 2 Cor. 6:14.
[35] 1 Tim. 3:2; 5:9; Matt. 19:3–6.

to be a faithful Christian.[36] At the same time, however, the Western church also withdrew matrimonial privileges from the clergy, who after 1123 had to be celibate. The Eastern churches did not follow this pattern but continued to permit a married priesthood, subject to the proviso that, if a priest's wife should die, he could not remarry. Bishops, however, as in the Western church, had to be celibate. This system still operates in the Eastern churches today, as of course does the celibacy rule for both priests and bishops in the Roman Catholic Church.

It was the Protestant Reformation that challenged this pattern in the West. The Protestants realized that Peter and many of the early church leaders had been married, and saw no biblical reason why celibacy should be imposed on the clergy.[37] They also rejected the idea that matrimony was a sacrament, because it was not a special rite instituted by Christ as a sign of the gospel but was a universal human practice. They did, however, retain church weddings and attempted to impose some rules about who could and could not marry. In the medieval church there had been an arrangement whereby individuals who were within the proscribed degrees of kindred and affinity (originally seven but later restricted to four) could not marry one another. In practice it could be very hard to prove this and the prohibition was often ignored, but it came in handy if the marriage failed to work out, because it could then be annulled relatively easily on the ground that the couple were within the prohibited degrees and had therefore contracted an illegal marriage in the first place. In a medieval village everyone was related to everyone else, and so the "prohibited degrees" operated as a safety valve for terminating unhappy marriages. Perhaps not surprisingly, the Reformers saw this as an abuse and adopted the table of kindred and affinity laid down in Leviticus 18 as the basis for deciding who could and could not wed, and with some modifications in the years since then, that is the pattern which prevails in most Western countries today. The big difference is that nowadays restrictions on who can marry whom tend to be based on genetic considerations, so that close blood relatives cannot marry each other because of the dangers inherent in incest. In earlier times "affinity" played an important role as well, so that a man could not marry his mother-in-law, for example, even though she was not a blood relative, nor could he marry his godmother, who would probably not have been related to him at all. Today such restrictions have been increasingly abandoned, though for other reasons cases of such marriages are by their nature very rare.

The church still marries people, although in some countries a couple must

---

[36]See Matt. 19:6.
[37]See 1 Cor. 9:5.

register their wedding with the state beforehand, and most of the ritual surrounding modern weddings is Christian in origin. Whether we like it or not, the church is more deeply involved in matrimonial affairs today than it was in biblical times, and despite major shifts away from traditional Christian values in recent years, it still does what it can to uphold and enforce them. Whether this can be called biblical is an open question, but the fact of the matter is that those churches which cling most tenaciously to the Scriptures are also usually the ones that are most determined to uphold traditional marriage customs, which can be done only by claiming and exercising as much control over the institution of matrimony as possible. The basic New Testament principle that a Christian should not marry an unbeliever is usually retained as far as it can be, but to that is often added a number of other things generally lumped together as "marriage preparation." Many churches and Christian groups also offer marital guidance and counseling services, neither of which was known in the early church, but both of which can be justified by the stresses of modern life, where newlywed couples are less likely to go on living with or near relatives than was the case in the past.

The big difference that Christianity made to the institution of matrimony, however, and the thing that underlay the other reforms that were eventually put in place, was the belief that marriage should be a love affair. The apostles did not understand this in the way that is so common today, when it is assumed that a couple will fall in love and then get married. On the contrary, it was more usually the other way around. A couple would be betrothed for marriage and then be expected to love each other.[38] One of the reasons for this was that it was not often that young girls mixed socially, and certainly not with prospective husbands, because it was important to protect their reputation and the family's honor. As a result, it was far from uncommon for a couple to be complete strangers to each other until they were betrothed, and sometimes they did not meet until *after* they had been married—by proxy! But it was also because the early Christians saw love as a command from God and not as a human response to physical attraction. They knew about falling in love but regarded it as potentially dangerous. Emotions wear off sooner or later and beauty fades, but a marriage is meant to last a lifetime. This is why, when the church developed its own forms of marriage service, it asked both the bride and the groom to promise to give themselves totally to one another "for better and for worse, for richer and for poorer, in sickness and in health, till death do us part." These words and the promise that lies behind them are not taken directly from the Bible, but the thought underlying them most

---

[38]See 1 Cor. 7:36–38.

definitely is, and the standard expressed here remains the ideal and the norm for Christian marriage to this day.

It should be said in passing that the Bible knows nothing of "sex before marriage" because in its terms, sexual intercourse *is* marriage, whether or not there has been a ceremony to record this fact. This principle continues to be upheld by many churches in two ways. The first is that if sexual intercourse does not take place after a wedding, the marriage can relatively easily be annulled because it has never been consummated according to the promises made in the ceremony. The other is that those who have decided to live together have effectively married each other, whether or not there is formal evidence of this. Witnesses and formal documents are valuable but not absolutely essential, and the reality of cohabitation takes precedence over legal niceties or church services.

The Bible says nothing about a minimum age for marriage, though for many centuries it was fixed in Roman (and subsequently in church) law as twelve for girls and fourteen for boys—approximately the age of puberty. This sounds very low to us, but in an age when people seldom lived beyond forty and it was customary for parents to marry off their children, or at least betroth them, almost as soon as they were born, the prescribed marriage age operated as a kind of restraint that was not felt to be too onerous. In the modern world, the minimum age is almost always higher that this, but may be as low as sixteen, with parental consent, and eighteen without it. It hardly need be said that marriage at such a young age, even if it is legal, is not to be recommended because maturity and life experience count for so much more in a world where married couples are less likely to live near their parents or extended family than was once the case, and where the problems inherent in living together are ones that the couple are expected to work out for themselves. Childbirth can also have lasting negative effects if the woman is too young, and so care should be taken to avoid this as much as possible.

Is matrimony a specifically Christian institution? Or should the church today accept that it became one for historical reasons that no longer apply, and so there should be no objection to letting it go back to being the largely secular affair that it was in New Testament times? Marriage cannot be defended as a sacrament in the way that baptism is, but, for Christians, it has a holy character because it is a symbol and prototype of the relationship between Jesus Christ and the church. It is perfectly true that there will be no marriage in heaven, but this is because we shall all be "married" to Christ. Jesus himself used this imagery in the story he told of

the wise and foolish virgins. It was a theme well known to Paul and finds
its greatest expression in the grand finale of the book of Revelation, the
great wedding feast of the Lamb.[39] Because of this, Christian matrimony
is a witness to what is to come. Those who commit themselves to it in the
right spirit have the inestimable privilege of getting a foretaste of the glory
of heaven. For that reason it must be honored and protected as a gift from
God, and maintained until death brings it to a natural end. At that point
the surviving partner is free to marry again, and is encouraged to do so if
young enough to make a new life. There is no compulsion in this matter,
however, and on the whole Paul thought it was better for the widowed to
remain as they are and devote their time to the service of God in the same
way as celibates are expected to do.[40]

DIVORCE

With higher expectations placed on marriage has also come a higher rate of
failure. This has always been a problem, but for centuries the options available
to Christians were essentially one of two—separation from bed and board
(*a thoro et mensa*), a solution that maintained the marriage as a legal fiction
but allowed incompatible couples to part; or annulment, which declared that
no marriage had ever taken place. In the former instance, the marriage was
not dissolved and the children, if any, were considered legitimate. That was
important, because only legitimate children had a right of inheritance. In the
latter case, the marriage was obliterated from the public record and any children from it were automatically bastardized and disinherited. Complex rules
and an enormous body of case law were developed to deal with every—or
almost every—conceivable situation. One of the few things not decided in the
Middle Ages was whether a person could lawfully marry a great-grandparent
or great-grandchild, because that relationship was beyond even the very broad
reach of the table of kindred and affinity. The Roman Catholic Church finally
banned such marriages in 1917, but the Protestant churches have never done
so, and it is presumably still legal among them, though it must be exceedingly
rare in practice. But again, unlikely though it may seem, in a society where
marriage is mostly about property and inheritance, a man could marry his
great-granddaughter and then leave everything to her, thereby cutting out the
generations in between.

The medieval church facilitated annulments but did not recognize divorce
in the modern sense, because of the indissoluble character of matrimony as

---

[39]Rev. 19:6–9.
[40]1 Cor. 7:8–9.

a sacrament. Jesus, however, had permitted divorce in the case of adultery, because when that occurred the marriage bond was violated and effectively negated.[41] The medieval church had great difficulty with this "Matthean exception" (so called because it is recorded in Matthew's Gospel) and, in spite of divine authority, did not allow it. However, it was accepted at the time of the Reformation and would now be recognized by most Protestant churches as valid grounds for divorce. Some people might also want to argue that, just as Jesus "expanded" the force of the other commandments to include the intentions of the heart as well as the actions of the body, he would also have considered a number of other things as coming within the purview of the commandment against adultery. Desertion, for example, could be seen as a form of adultery, since it involves putting something else ahead of the relationship. Cruelty to a spouse might also be so regarded, because it is a violation of the other person and therefore of the integrity of the marriage.

There will obviously be differences of opinion about whether such extensions of the "Matthean exception" are legitimate, not least because, in an age of increasingly easy divorce, it is possible to justify almost anything in such terms. We must be alive to this danger, but at the same time we must also be open to discussing what the acceptable limits of divorce are and not rely on a rigid legalistic formula which virtually forces people to allow themselves to be caught *in flagrante delicto* before they can obtain a divorce, as was the case in many places until relatively recently. Finding the right balance is never easy and perfect solutions are seldom possible, but love for one another compels us to treat each case separately and seek to determine what the best way forward should be in that particular situation.

A Christian marriage can be contracted only by the willing consent of the parties to it, but divorce by consent, even if it is possible in law, cannot be so readily accepted by the church. This is because marriage is a public commitment which may well affect other people, especially the children of the married couple, and it is also a witness to the eternal plan and purpose of God. The practical consequences of this are that the church performs weddings but does not dissolve marriages. It has to accept civil divorce (as well as civil marriage) as valid within the sphere of competence reserved for the state, but not in matters reserved for the church. This is of particular significance in the case of divorced people who remarry within the lifetime of the former spouse. The church cannot perform that kind of wedding because it is a breach of the vow taken at the time of the first marriage to remain faithful until death. A divorce in the eyes of the state is not a divorce in the eyes of God, and the church has

---

[41]Matt. 19:9.

a duty to declare publicly which of those two it must serve. Jesus made it quite clear that anyone contracting such a marriage is committing adultery, and attempts to "reinterpret" this for the sake of convenience are unworthy of Christians. Admittedly this is a very hard saying, but Jesus' own disciples thought the same and he told them they had to accept it whether they liked it or not![42] At the same time, adultery is a sin that can be forgiven, and people who have genuinely repented of their past failure can and should be restored to the fellowship of the church.

Having said that, there is a price to be paid for remarriage after divorce, and that price is exclusion from the preaching and teaching ministry of the church. Those who have remarried during the lifetime of a previous partner ought not to be ordained in the church or admitted to any teaching or administrative role that involves the pastoral care of others. Christian ministers must lead by their example, and those with a checkered marital history cannot command the moral authority they need to do this effectively. Paul insisted that a church leader should be the husband of "one wife," [43] and given the fact that polygamy had died out in the Greco-Roman world of his time, his command cannot be interpreted exclusively in that sense. It must also apply to remarriage after divorce, especially given the words of Jesus on this subject.

Complications arise when a person who has never been married or divorced marries someone else who has been. Considering the widespread occurrence of divorce nowadays, many Christians are prepared to admit such people into pastoral positions, especially if they were uninvolved in their spouse's previous divorce and may even have been used by God to bring psychological healing to him or her. Whether this sort of flexibility is a good thing is hard to say. In some cases it may be a sign of genuine compassion, but in others it may just be opening the door to further corruption by setting a precedent that can then be used to extend the indulgence still further. Some kind of compromise in areas like this may be almost inevitable in modern society, but it is at least arguable that, as divorce becomes more common, the church's discipline should become stricter and lean further in the opposite direction, in an attempt to set an example of faithfulness and stem the tide of marital breakdown. There is no easy answer to this problem, except perhaps to raise the bar for marriage by insisting on serious preparation courses before a wedding and discouraging people who have no real commitment to Christ from seeking a church ceremony to endorse their marriage.

---

[42] Matt. 19:10–12.
[43] Titus 1:6.

POLYGAMY

Lifelong heterosexual monogamy is the pattern laid down for marriage in the Scriptures, but it must be acknowledged that in the course of human history this ideal has often been compromised in different ways, and by no means always by divorce. The most frequent form this has taken is polygamy (or more rarely, polyandry). A polygamous relationship is one in which a man takes more than one woman to himself and establishes an equal, or near-equal, relationship with all of them. (In polyandry, a woman does the same thing with a number of different men.) Polygamous societies have existed from time immemorial, and as we have already seen, in the Old Testament there are many examples of polygamous practice, which were not condemned, even among godly people who are held up to us as examples of faith.

Polygamy died out in ancient Israel, and over the centuries it has not been much of a problem for the church, although it is tolerated in Islam and is also found among some Mormons.[44] The main context in which it is relevant today is in sub-Saharan Africa, where there is both a significant number of polygamous households and widespread conversion to Christianity. The general policy of the church nowadays is to phase the practice out over a generation, allowing what has been done in the past to remain but forbidding people who are already Christians from contracting a polygamous marriage. This is a reasonably fair solution, because for a man to send his many wives away on becoming a Christian might lead to serious (and quite undeserved) problems for them. A girl who is married off by her parents as the third wife of a local chief could not easily return to her family, which might not be Christian, and she could find herself a penniless outcast through no fault of her own. In such cases the wisest and most compassionate thing to do might well be to keep her in the man's household and respect her for the role she has been assigned in it.

At the present time there is widespread consensus that polygamy is unjust, perhaps because of an emphasis on women's rights which underlines the equality inherent in monogamy, and even in Muslim and Mormon communities polygamy is increasingly frowned upon, at least in official circles. Certainly there is no Christian church that is actively prepared to encourage it, and although there will undoubtedly always be people somewhere who are willing to practice it, we can probably say that, on the whole, it is a thing of the past that is unlikely to become a major problem in the foreseeable future.

---

[44]The main body of Latter-day Saints has banned it, but some individuals and breakaway groups continue to practice it unofficially.

HOMOSEXUALITY

Another area where the original divine intention is breached with increasing frequency is that of homosexuality, which stands in sharp contrast to polygamy. The Bible contains many examples of polygamous unions, which it generally passes over without comment. It seldom mentions homosexuality, but when it does it is negative in its assessment of it.[45] Modern Western society, on the other hand, while disinclined to accept polygamy, seems to be increasingly willing to embrace homosexuality as an alternative lifestyle.

In the Bible, same-sex friendships are common and occasionally celebrated, as in the well-known case of David and Jonathan, but there is no mention of any sexual intercourse between them, and the very idea seems alien to biblical culture. Homosexual orientation is a complex issue, and the church has never made any pronouncement about it one way or another, but homosexual practice is unacceptable whether or not those who engage in it are "oriented" that way. Homosexual people are as welcome in the fellowship of Christians as anyone else, but they have no mandate to engage in that form of sexual practice and the church cannot endorse it. Same-sex "marriages" are completely foreign to the biblical concept of matrimony and can never be more than an attempt to legitimize immorality. It may be true that civil society in Western countries has become more tolerant of such things, but although the church has been strongly encouraged to follow suit, it must stick to its principles and resist something that is a denial of procreation and therefore ultimately a message of death. The church already has (or tries to have) a stricter discipline in matters of divorce than the one accepted by the state, and so there is no reason for it not to be out of step with the law on this matter either. Christian principles are not determined by popular opinion but by the Word of God, and if (as seems to be the case at the present time) the two things diverge on the issue of homosexual practice, then it is the Word of God and not current intellectual fashion that must take precedence and claim the allegiance of believers.

THE FAMILY

Closely tied to the principle of matrimony is that of the family, which is the basic social unit recognized in the Bible. The long lists of genealogies found in Genesis and in 1 Chronicles testify to the importance of the family, not least because the genealogies demonstrate that nations are really just extended families and that ultimately all human beings are related to one another. In

---

[45]Lev. 18:22; 20:13; Rom. 1:26–27.

the Bible, the family unit is important for several reasons. First, it gives us our identity as individuals. I am who and what I am because I am the child of particular people who are in turn the children of other people stretching right back to the beginning of time. My genetic makeup, my inheritance, and a large part of my temperament comes from them. Many people are proud of their family background and like to trace their ancestry back as far as they can, because it gives them a sense of who they are. This is not necessarily a bad thing, and the genealogies of ancient Israel were certainly used to reinforce the people's sense of their heritage and of their obligation to maintain it. At the same time, digging into family history may not produce the results we are looking for. To take a well-known example, Queen Elizabeth II is a highly respected woman, but you do not have to go very far back in her genealogy to find much less savory characters. We know about them because they were royalty, but if there are skeletons in the closet of the most highly placed people, how much more likely will this be true of humbler individuals, whose genealogies remain mercifully untraced? Ultimately of course we are all descended from Adam and Eve, and the Bible makes it quite clear what a mixed blessing that is. Going in search of one's ancestors may be an interesting pastime, but if it teaches us anything at all, it must surely be that boasting of our human inheritance is not the best way of honoring God in our lives today, even if it has left us an important and irreplaceable legacy.

The second reason that the family matters is that it is the primary context in which we are formed and developed as human beings. Some aspects of this may be delegated to other authorities, especially the school and the church, but the principal responsibility for the upbringing of children remains with the parents, who set the standard for their offspring. In actual fact, this is often a mutual thing, although the children do not realize it at the time. Many people do not understand the need for discipline in the home until they become parents and have to exercise it themselves. The workshop that is the family thus offers a steep learning curve for parents as well as for children, a point which Paul underlines in the advice he gives to each of them.[46]

The third reason the family is important is that it provides the emotional stability and security that is such a basic part of our lives. People who come from broken homes can perhaps acquire that stability in other ways, but this is not guaranteed. Most of us readily acknowledge that coming from an unstable family background is a serious disadvantage. Statistics bear this out in the disproportionate numbers of criminals and other socially maladjusted people who have been the childhood victims of broken homes, and the church

---

[46]Eph. 6:1–4.

must do whatever it can to promote harmonious family relationships to help reduce the incidence of that kind of thing.

The fourth and final reason the family is important is that it is to the family unit that we most naturally turn in times of trouble. The family is there to help us when we need to be helped, and to take us in with no questions asked. Even in an age of widespread public welfare, it is the family that bears the brunt of caring for the elderly and the disabled, and the social services would collapse if that safety net were no longer available to help. Families can be hard to live with but they are almost impossible to live without. They are God's provision for us in what might otherwise be a lonely and hostile world.

Defining what the family is can be more problematic than it sounds. At its heart there is the basic unit of mother and father, along with their natural children, the so-called "nuclear" family that is regarded as the norm in most places. Variations on this basic theme do of course arise, and taken together they may outnumber the traditional family unit, but they are anomalies and it is important to understand this. For example, one of the parents may be missing because of death, divorce, or desertion. A second marriage may bring other children into the household who are either not biologically related or share only one parent. There are also frequent cases of adoption, where the biological parents are replaced by others who play the emotional and spiritual role that the biological parents cannot or will not play. None of these variations alters the basic structure of family discipline, nor do they diminish the importance of the family unit. On the contrary, by extending it to cover a variety of different circumstances, they confirm the importance of the family, and the church must support it in the face of all the pressures that would weaken and destroy it.

Every church welcomes families and expects them to worship together. This can sometimes be difficult, particularly if the parents come from different backgrounds, and especially if one of them is not a believer. This is one reason why the church must warn its members not to marry outside the faith and should be prepared to back up its warnings with a refusal to perform the wedding of someone who disobeys them.[47] The precise details of how families should be integrated into church life are not set out in the Bible, and there is a variety of practice, depending on local traditions and circumstances. Some churches admit families as a unit and count their membership by head of household. Children are treated differently, sometimes being admitted to full membership, more often being given a kind of intermediate position comparable to their citizenship status (where they enjoy the benefits of

---

[47] 2 Cor. 6:14.

membership without exercising the rights or performing the duties associated with it), and sometimes being regarded as nonmembers until they make their own profession of faith. Some people feel strongly about this one way or another, but the emphasis in Scripture is that children should be brought up in the knowledge and fear of the Lord, which is what really matters. The form this takes will vary, but as long as the end result is the same we should not quarrel too much over the different methods used to obtain it.

First, the head of the family is the husband or father. He is told to leave his own parents in order to start a new household and to exercise the kind of authority and discipline needed to make that household a model of divine governance.[48] The first task here is that he must define his position with respect to the wider family circle, which consists of the so-called "in-laws" on both sides. It is one thing for a married couple to leave father and mother, but if the latter tag along anyway they are asking for trouble. Married children always have a duty to respect their parents and to care for them if necessary, but they cannot submit to their control. Sometimes this is very difficult, particularly when there is an inheritance waiting and the parents are in a position to revoke it if their children refuse to obey them. Often grandparents will want a say in the upbringing of their grandchildren, even though they are not primarily responsible for them. In most cases grandmothers are more of a problem than grandfathers, perhaps because they are usually more family-oriented to begin with and generally live longer. A man who is under his mother's thumb is unfit to be the head of an independent household, and a woman who cannot leave her mother is practically inviting her husband to leave her. For the sake of a healthy marriage, this kind of situation has to be resolved at the start, however painful that may be. Most family feuds of this kind do not last, and it is usually better to establish the position up front at the start, so that everyone knows where they stand and has the time to adjust accordingly.

Second, the head of the family has to establish his authority over his wife. In theory this should not be too difficult if she accepts the principle of submission, but it can often cause problems in practice, especially if she has her own career or interests that are very different from his. There may be cases where it is best for him to sacrifice his ambitions and let her become the main breadwinner, but these are exceptions to the rule and must not be regarded as the norm. It is the man who is expected to provide for the family and to represent it to the outside world, not least to his wife's friends and relatives. Sometimes there will be serious disagreements within a marriage and difficult decisions will have to be taken, and then it is the considered judgment of the

---

[48]Matt. 19:5.

husband which must prevail. This is not to say that he should not discuss the matter thoroughly with all those who are involved, and it certainly is not an excuse for him to do what he wants regardless of the feelings of others. At the end of the day, however, the decision and the responsibility for it rest with him, and this must be respected.

Finally, it is the father who is chiefly responsible for discipline in the home.[49] It is primarily up to him to decide how to teach and correct his children, and for that he has to take a serious interest in their welfare and activities. Mothers are usually more closely involved with the children at the day-to-day level, and they need to be able to rely on a more distant authority that will permit them to fulfill their own calling more effectively. Behind the scenes, the father will often have to rely on his wife's advice and moderate his disciplinary actions accordingly, but from the children's point of view it is his voice that carries the greater weight, and she must be prepared to back him up. If children learn that they can play one parent off against the other, the task of disciplining them becomes virtually impossible and the family unit is seriously weakened. Every member of the family is called to play his or her part to create a happy and godly home.

Just as matrimony is a sign of the kingdom of heaven, so too the family is a model of the church. In Christ, all believers belong to a single spiritual family and are called to treat one another as brothers and sisters.[50] This is particularly important when it comes to sexual matters, because it is all too easy for a congregation to be severely disrupted by love affairs illicitly conducted between members of the church, often between the pastor and a woman in the pews. In biblical terms, such behavior is nothing less than spiritual incest, and it should be avoided with the same sense of horror that its physical counterpart would provoke.[51] At another level, brothers and sisters often fight with one another but at the end of the day they stand united against external threats. Whatever differences we may have with our brothers and sisters in Christ, they belong to us and we to them. The outside world perceives this immediately, and wonders why we find it so hard to see it for ourselves. Of course there are always false believers, who need to be exposed for what they are and expelled from the community,[52] but those who share a common heavenly Father and who are joined together in his Son must demonstrate the unity of the Holy Spirit that is given to them as their common inheritance. Family life is not always easy, but that is how God has chosen to reveal himself to us.

---

[49] Col. 3:20–21.
[50] 1 Tim. 5:1–2.
[51] 1 Cor. 5:1–2.
[52] 2 John 7–11; Jude 4.

The lessons we learn in the church and in our families will stand us in good stead both in this life and in the life of the world to come.

RACIAL AND ETHNIC EQUALITY

The genealogies of the Old Testament remind us that all nations are interconnected at some level and that all belong to a universal human family. The implications of all this are many and varied. First of all, it cannot be stressed too strongly that every human being on earth is equal in terms of his or her humanity. This is now a standard assumption in Western countries and in international organizations, but we have to remember that until quite recently that was not the case, and even now it is denied, in theory or in practice, in many parts of the world. When the Spanish conquistadores reached the New World they found natives who were living in what to them was a vastly inferior social and cultural state, so much so that they debated whether or not they were fully human. Much of the slave trade that followed was predicated on the belief that Africans were a lower species than Europeans, and as late as the mid-twentieth century there were still people conducting experiments trying to prove that some races were genetically superior or inferior to others. The excesses of the German Nazis have put a stop to that, at least for the time being, but the possibility that the idea may one day be revived must not be ignored.

To this, the Christian church is resolutely opposed. Cultural differences may be very great, and undoubtedly some societies are, or seem to be, more primitive than others in their development, but that does not make the people involved any less human than those living in more advanced societies. The theory and practice of Christian mission is to take the gospel to everyone, whatever their social or cultural level may be. Experience has shown time and again that the most "primitive" tribes are just as capable of receiving Christ as the most advanced Western societies—perhaps even more so, because their relative lack of sophistication allows them to perceive good and evil more clearly than Westerners often do. Above all, there can be no excuse for mistreating others on the ground of some alleged inferiority on their part, and the fact that this has happened on a wide scale within living memory must make Christians all the more determined to insist on this principle.

That is the theory, but the reality is more complicated. The growth and spread of the human race has produced a diversification that is real, even though it has in no way affected our basic humanity. We perceive these differences and classify them in terms of "race" and "ethnicity," though very often it is hard to say precisely what those things are. There is no doubt that Norwegians are white and Ugandans are black, but although we can say that someone with fair skin and red hair is more likely to be Irish than Portuguese, this is a much less scientific observation and can fairly easily be contradicted by producing specific counterexamples. Americans are made up of a vast array of different ethnicities, but the rest of the world sees them coming and recognizes them as a distinct group, regardless of their individual ethnic backgrounds. On the other hand, Westerners will easily confuse Chinese with Koreans, Japanese, and Southeast Asians, but those nations do not usually make the same mistake with each other.

How is it that they see something that passes us by? Race is a hard category to define, which is probably why strictly racial conflicts, despite some well-known examples, are relatively rare, but it exists at some level and we have to take it into consideration in certain contexts. For example, it is known that sickle-cell anemia affects African-Americans more than other racial groups, and pretending otherwise accomplishes nothing. Conflicts that have a racial component usually arise for other reasons, especially when vastly different social groups suddenly find themselves forced to live together and compete for the same space.

This, rather than racial difference as such, is what ultimately explains the conflicts that have occurred in the United States and in South Africa. Prejudice against black people in America has its roots in the history of slavery, which was confined to them. This may explain why some white people disapprove of marrying blacks but are quite happy to accept intermarriage with Asians, which on the surface would appear to be hypocritical. In South Africa, racial conflict is also very much tribal conflict, conducted within the black community (and even between Afrikaners and English-speakers within the white community as well). It is made worse because the Europeans who settled there in the seventeenth century became to some extent an African tribe of their own and not just colonial overlords. Race has helped to define the nature of the struggle, and perhaps it has had the effect of uniting tribes against a perceived common threat in a way that is not true in other parts of Africa, but even so, the underlying problem is cultural, not racial.

The church has never officially accepted race as a classification that determines either membership or authority roles within it, although circumstances in places like South Africa and the United States have produced race-based congregations and even denominations that in theory ought not to exist as separate entities within the body of Christ. The trouble is knowing what to do with them once they have appeared and established themselves. In America, for example, there is no doubt that the black churches have a creative culture of their own and have provided a sphere in which black people have been able to rise to positions of high leadership. In terms of music, black churches have probably contributed more to the Christian world than white American churches have. If these churches were to be integrated with white ones, the distinctive black voice would become a minority and would probably be submerged to a large extent. Does anyone want that to happen? It is not necessary to be a racist to believe that black churches have their own distinctive contribution to make and that it would be a great shame if this were to be lost because of some well-meant but ultimately misguided drive toward integration. Perhaps the best answer is to say that in this case God has brought good out of evil. As long as individuals are free to do what they wish and there is no bar erected to keep minorities out of any of these churches, this need not be a cause of scandal and may even help to enrich our understanding of the many-splendored body of Christ.

Much harder to deal with is ethnic division based on language and culture. In the United States there are many ethnic heritage denominations which are clearly recognizable as such, even if they have formally dropped adjectives like "Swedish," "Dutch," or "German." They began as congregations of immigrant groups speaking their own languages, but although that has now changed, their original identity continues to be enshrined in an institutional form. It is even possible for Americans to create home-grown heritage churches, as the existence of a Southern Baptist Convention demonstrates. Occasionally someone suggests that it is time to drop the word "Southern" but this always meets with resistance, for reasons one can only imagine.

In other countries, things are often much worse. The Eastern Orthodox churches, for example, have become so closely identified with different national groupings that many people do not realize that they are all part of the same church. Attempts to create an American Orthodox church have come up against this problem, because the Russians and the Greeks cannot unite with each other, to say nothing of the Ukrainians, Serbs, Romanians, Lebanese, and so on. Even when there is no obvious language barrier, nationalism can easily get in the way and cause division. A little-known but telling example of this can be found in the English-speaking churches of Western Europe, where congregations belonging to the American Episcopal Church sit alongside chaplaincies organized by the Church of England. They speak the same language and are in communion with each other, but one is for the Americans and the other for the British, and they go their separate ways.

What can or should the church do about this? Language differences are a major problem and are almost impossible to overcome unless people are bilingual. That is the case in Wales, for example, where, strictly speaking, there is no need for Welsh-language church services at all. But the Welsh language has survived on the strength of its religious tradition, and those who worship in it are determined to preserve it, however unnecessary and "divisive" that may seem to others. In multiethnic African states the problem of linguistic diversity can be solved only by using a common language, which is usually that of the former colonial power and therefore equally foreign to everyone. Oddly enough, this African solution is probably the one closest to what existed in the early church, where Greek was the common language of worship even though it was not the mother tongue of many Christians, including most (if not all) of the apostles.

Over the centuries many solutions to the problem of ethnic diversity have been tried, but so far none has been entirely successful. For more than 1,500 years the Roman Catholic Church worshiped in Latin, even though it was not even understood by many of its congregations. That practice has now been abandoned, but not without considerable loss. The Protestant churches opted for the vernacular at the time of the Reformation, but what this meant in practice was that standardized forms of English and German advanced at the expense of local dialects, creating a national tongue as much as reflecting one that was already in existence. Modern Bible translators have a similar dilemma in many tribal areas. Do they translate the Scriptures into every local form of speech, thereby creating a number of distinct languages, or do they look for a middle form that can serve as a link dialect and unite groups instead of dividing them? In some cases the decision may rest on linguistic considerations, but it may also be the result of politics, especially if there are rival Christian missions at work in the same area.

What biblical principles are there to guide us in this? The first thing we can say is that the church is not an ethnic community in the way that Judaism was and still is. There is no Christian language or Christian homeland to which we are longing to return. In the early church there were those who wanted Gentile converts to become Jews because they thought of Christianity as a fulfillment and extension of Judaism, but this was rejected, and before long the distinctive Jewish Christianity that we can see in the pages of the New Testament had virtually disappeared. Paul occasionally met people on his missionary journeys with whom he could not communicate, but he never seemed to bother about trying to translate the gospel into their languages, and he certainly never wrote to anyone in anything other than Greek. Sensitivity to ethnic groups was not his primary concern, nor does it seem to have worried the early Christians very much. When the apostles got up to preach on the day of Pentecost, they were given the gift of tongues, so that all who heard them thought they were being spoken to in their own languages, but this miracle was not repeated in the same form and did not lead to any cross-cultural mission attempts. Even Aramaic, the mother tongue of Jesus and his disciples, was reduced to a subordinate status, apart from a few words like *abba*, which managed to get into the New Testament.[53]

What we can say for certain is that ethnic origin did not constitute a barrier to church membership. From the beginning, it was the aim of the apostles to preach the gospel to the ends of the earth, so that every nation should hear its message. Eventually this would require translation and the cultural adaptation that went with it, but that was never a priority, and perhaps the history of the church gives us some idea why. When the Bible is translated into a new language it tends to create a sacred tongue which then acquires a status that it never previously had. This has happened even with Greek, the original language of the New Testament. Its authors wrote in the ordinary speech of their day, but over the centuries their words acquired a religious aura which now makes translating them into modern Greek extremely difficult. The same was true of Latin for many centuries and it is true of Old Church Slavonic, which was developed out of a Macedonian dialect in the ninth century and is still going strong today. Even in the English-speaking world there is a tension between those who want to preserve Tudor English in worship and those who believe that we must change with the times. In its passage through time, the gospel has become embedded in many languages and cultures, but it can never be contained by any one of them. Translations and cultural contextualizations have their place, but they are never an end in themselves. In the end the only way to ensure that the church remains a truly multiethnic community is to refuse to canonize any particular nation, language, or culture. The church is open to all, and the gospel will transform everyone it touches, turning them into the new and transcultural people of God.

HUMAN COMMUNITIES AND GOVERNMENT

Every human society requires some kind of organization and government if it is to grow and prosper as it should. That is clearly true of the family, and as we have already seen, tribes and nations are at bottom no more than extended family structures. In the sixteenth and seventeenth centuries there was intense debate about whether human government was part of the creation

---

[53] Mark 14:36; Rom. 8:15; Gal. 4:6.

order intended by God from the beginning, or whether it was something that emerged only after the fall and was therefore part of the disorder which that entailed. At one level, this debate was purely academic and insoluble, because there were no human communities in the garden of Eden. Its practical importance lay in the issue of what attitude Christians ought to take toward secular authority in their own day. A number of the more radical Protestant Reformers believed that state and class structures were inherently sinful and would be abolished in the perfect society. Their attitude was neatly summed up in a popular rhyme of the time:

> When Adam delved and Eve span
> Who was then the gentleman?

Anarchism, as this view is now known, has occasionally resurfaced on the far left wing of politics and at times has been influential in countries like Spain, which were prone to dictatorship and therefore suspicious of authority. The impracticality of anarchism is obvious, however, and it has never gotten very far. More insidious and much more widespread is the notion that all government is corrupt and to be avoided as much as possible. It must be admitted that, after the fall, no system of human authority is going to be perfect, but that it would not exist at all in an ideal world is far from certain. For Adam and Eve to have exercised dominion over the creation as God intended them to do would have required organization, and that in turn would have been some form of government. Beyond that, we cannot go. Whatever God intended for his people was cut short by their rebellion against him, which produced a new situation. God would continue to watch over his creatures in love, but that love would henceforth be exercised in a context in which the recipients would be more inclined to resent and reject it than they would be to embrace it in the spirit in which it was given.

PART FOUR

THE REJECTION OF GOD'S LOVE

17

THE REJECTION OF GOD'S LOVE BY ANGELS

THE NATURE OF THEIR REBELLION AGAINST GOD

Rebellion against God is the rejection of his love. Why did it occur first among the spiritual creatures, who saw God face-to-face and knew—as they still know—exactly what they were doing?[1] Who would choose to live in conscious opposition to the will of God, and why would God allow them to do so? Here we find a mystery that is insoluble in purely human terms. If we cannot understand the deepest motivations of our own hearts and minds, we have little hope of probing those of an angelic being. Yet the rebellion of the angels is not something that we can ignore on the ground that it is beyond our understanding, because even if it is a mystery to our minds, we have been caught up in it. The evil we experience is not self-generated but has been brought upon us by Satan, who has seduced us into joining his rebellion. We have to make some attempt to find out why he turned away from God, in order to understand the predicament into which we have fallen.

At some point and for reasons unknown to us, one of the angels led a rebellion against God. The Bible does not say what motivated Satan to revolt against his divine Master, but Isaiah 14:12–15 may offer a clue as to what happened:

> "How you are fallen from heaven,
>   O Day Star, son of Dawn!
> How you are cut down to the ground,
>   you who laid the nations low!

---

[1] James 2:19.

You said in your heart,
  'I will ascend to heaven;
above the stars of God
  I will set my throne on high;
I will sit on the mount of assembly
  in the far reaches of the north;
I will ascend above the heights of the clouds;
  I will make myself like the Most High.'
But you are brought down to Sheol,
  to the far reaches of the pit."

Isaiah did not write this about Satan but about the king of Babylon's pretensions to divinity and the retribution that he had suffered (or would suffer) as a result. There is a similar passage in Ezekiel 28:2–10 about the king of Tyre, which may also be an allusion to the fall of Satan. Ancient monarchs often claimed to be gods, and in the New Testament Satan is referred to as both the god and the ruler of this world, which suggests that there is more than just a passing connection between the fall of Satan and the fall of these two kings.[2] The kings of Babylon and Tyre were claiming an authority that belongs to God alone, and as they were servants of the ruler of this world, it would be logical for them to have followed their master's example. Isaiah may have been mocking the king of Babylon by using the absurdly exaggerated titles he claimed for himself, but the tone of the passage makes it clear that the king was engaged in a spiritual rebellion against God, and that God's punishment of them was also spiritual. Sheol and "the far reaches of the pit" sound very much like hell, and it is not unreasonable to conclude that eternal damnation was the king's ultimate reward for his temerity. If that is so, it does not seem at all fanciful to suggest that there is behind these verses an allusion to Satan's fall, which gives us at least some insight into what happened to him.

The details of Satan's fall may elude us, but there are some things about it that we can affirm with some confidence. First, we know that he must have had free will. Although he was created to be a servant of God, he was not an automaton who had no choice but to do whatever God wished. This is important because it reminds us that although the relationship between God and his angels is a hierarchical one, it is a relationship of love. The angels do God's bidding because they want to, not because they are forced to do so. They are servants of their Lord, but they obey him with a whole heart. Satan's rebellion, whatever prompted it, must have begun as an expression of his free will. Even before he did anything to demonstrate it, he had already turned

---

[2] 2 Cor. 4:4; John 12:31.

away from God in his mind, and God must have known that. Satan's behavior manifests his rebelliousness; it is the result and not the cause of it, which can be found only in the hidden recesses of his heart and mind.

Satan chose to rebel against God of his own free will, and he did so in full knowledge of what he was doing. It can perhaps be argued that he could not have known what evil was because he had not experienced it, but this is misleading and it certainly does not excuse or mitigate the seriousness of his rebellion. He knew that disobedience was not what God wanted, but in spite of that he chose it willingly. There was no other power or influence to tempt him in the way that he was later to tempt others, so the decision was entirely his and sprang from hatred in his heart toward God. Did God know when he created Satan that he would turn out this way? This is a question impossible to answer. By giving his angels free will, God created the possibility of rebellion, but that can hardly have been his intention. The angels were meant to use their free will to enjoy eternal fellowship with God, which reached its perfection in the service and worship they displayed toward him. As far as we can tell, most of them have been perfectly content with their status and have never thought of rejecting it. Satan's rebellion must therefore have been the result of an unwillingness to serve his Creator that was unique to him and not something that his status as a creature made highly probable or inevitable.

Isaiah suggested that the king of Babylon wanted to dethrone God, but whether this was also true of Satan we cannot say. He must have known that it would have been impossible for him to do so, and so perhaps he did not try. But what he did want was his independence, and God let him have it, just as the father in the parable of the prodigal son let his younger son go his own way.[3] Satan was free to make his own choice, but he could not escape the fact that he was a creature. If rebelling against God was the only way he could demonstrate his freedom, then perfect freedom would have been self-annihilation, and Satan did not choose that. It seems that he wanted to have it both ways. He wanted to exercise his will independently of God, but at the same time he also wanted to go on living in a universe he had not made and with a nature that he had been given, not one of his own choosing. Satan's rebellion against God was a revolt against his own condition; his hatred of the Creator was a hatred of the creation, and of himself above all. The paradox of Satan's rebellion is that, while he could offend God by his behavior, he could do nothing to harm him, whereas he could and did harm himself. Satan's life is one of constant frustration because of its inner contradictions. He can get what he wants only by destroying himself, but his unwillingness to go that far

---

[3] Luke 15:12.

ensures that he can never satisfy his desires. Unable to achieve his own goals, he takes out his frustration on anyone he can, and it is here that human beings come into the picture.

Whether the angels who fell along with Satan made the same free choice that he did is not clear. Perhaps they did, and were attracted by the same desire for freedom that he had. In that case, they also exercised their free will and fell because of it. Perhaps they were subjected to Satan as one of the archangels, and when he fell, they followed him out of loyalty. We cannot be sure of this, but if their rebellion was an act of loyalty to Satan, it would explain why they are subject to him now and have not gone their own way. It would also mean that the hierarchy of the fallen angels has the same internal structure as the hierarchy of the unfallen ones, since they were originally one and the same. The kingdom of Satan is not anarchic but has its own organization that allows it to function as a force for evil in the world. Jesus himself tells us that the demonic world is not a house divided against itself but a realm of evil spirits who are united in their opposition to God, which strongly suggests that their original rebellion was a joint revolt and not a series of discrete and independent acts.[4] If that conclusion is right, it is both a strength and a weakness. Looking at it from Satan's point of view, it is a strength because the demons do not work at cross-purposes to one another. But it is also a weakness, because if Satan is defeated, it means that the lesser demons subject to him are conquered as well. That, of course, is the reason why Christians are confident that, when Jesus overthrew the kingdom of Satan, we were delivered from all evil powers, and not just from him.

What we can say for sure is that Satan did not rebel on his own and is not without supporters in his fallen state.[5] We do not know why they listened to him, but perhaps he was originally an archangel like Michael, and when he fell he took the angels under his command down with him. Whether the number of fallen angels is smaller than the number of those still in heaven is impossible to say, but it makes little difference. The fact is that there is a considerable number of fallen angels who serve Satan in his rebellion, with whom we must deal whether we want to or not.

The fallen angels are in revolt against God but they are essentially the same type of spiritual creature as the faithful ones are. This means that they are not born, do not marry, and cannot die. They retain the knowledge of God that they had before their rebellion, which was in no sense the result of their ignorance. The fallen angels also retain the capacities inherent in their

---

[4]Matt. 12:24–26.
[5]2 Pet. 2:4.

spiritual nature, which they now use to oppose God rather than to serve him. The retention of their created nature also means that, in spite of their rebellion, they are still subject to God's will. What they do, they do only with his permission, hard as it is for us to understand why God would give it to them.[6]

For us, the most important practical aspect of their ongoing subjection to the will of God is that Satan and his agents can be cast out and controlled by God's divine power, which may also be given to human beings as the gift of exorcism. There is no reason for Christians to be afraid of the Devil, because the spiritual power given to us is greater than anything he can muster. It may be added that, in this respect, the fallen angels are different from the loyal ones because the latter are God's messengers and must be obeyed. We cannot ignore or exorcize them, because they come with the power and authority of God.

THE RULE OF LAWLESSNESS

Did the fall of Satan and his angels occur before or after the material world was created? The Bible tells us that Satan is the ruler of this world, but by what right does he claim that distinction? Why should he be present and powerful among us now that he has fallen from God's grace? If he was not the ruler of the world before his rebellion, why was he allowed to take charge of it afterwards? Can we say that Satan was rewarded for his revolt by being given an authority that he did not previously have, making his possession of the world something of a consolation prize for being expelled from heaven? That would go against everything we know about God, who rewards us according to our works and not in complete contradiction to them.[7] One answer to this problem is to say that the "world" refers to the state of spiritual rebellion against God and is not to be identified with the material creation. There is a good deal of truth in that, of course, but it is not the whole story. Without being evil in itself, the physical universe is nevertheless used by Satan to inflict harm on human beings, something he would not be capable of if it were not in some way subject to him. It therefore seems possible that God gave Satan the task of governing the world *before* he fell. His position as the ruler of this world is not something that he acquired as a result of his rebellion but was a divine gift that his rebellion is not enough to cancel out. This seems strange to us, but it fits very well with the standard pattern by which God operates. When the nation of Israel rebelled against him and put his Son to death, God did

---

[6]See Job 1:12.
[7]Matt. 16:27; 2 Tim. 4:14.

not crush or abandon it, nor did it lose its status as his chosen people. As Paul explained, this was because "the gifts and the calling of God are irrevocable."[8]

If this conclusion is correct, the "world," or at least matter, must have existed in some form before Satan's rebellion. Evidence to support this theory comes from the creation account in Genesis, which says that before God spoke, the earth was "without form and void," which is meant to translate the Hebrew *tohu wa-bohu*, a phrase that has no meaning in itself but which says it all, rather like "topsy-turvy" in English.[9] Genesis 1 does not say that the earth did not exist before God got to work on it, but that it was dark and disorganized.[10] Did God make it that way? Perhaps he did, but it seems strange that he should have made a universe so unlike himself and so like Satan. Might it be the case that everything was dark and in disorder because Satan and his angels, who had been given the responsibility for taking care of the world, had failed in their task and let things go to rack and ruin? Here we can only speculate, but since we know that Satan was already present in the garden of Eden when Adam and Eve were created and that evil could have been known at that time, the theory is not as odd as it may sound. Furthermore, it is reinforced by the common Old Testament habit of describing Satan's rule as "confusion," echoes of which are found in the New Testament as well.[11]

The absence of law and order is a particular characteristic of the Satanic, as the dramatic description of it given by Paul clearly indicates:

> Let no one deceive you in any way. For that day [of the Lord] will not come, unless the rebellion comes first, and the man of lawlessness is revealed, the son of destruction, who opposes and exalts himself against every so-called god or object of worship, so that he takes his seat in the temple of God, proclaiming himself to be God.[12]

There is an obvious resonance here with Isaiah's words about the king of Babylon, quoted at the beginning of this chapter, and the scenario is comparable—once again, we have a powerful man who wants to rebel against God and take his place. In describing this Satanic desire as "lawlessness," Paul does not mean that the rule of Satan and his agents has no inner coherence of its own. Those familiar with lawless parts of the world know that, while normal

---

[8]Rom. 11:29.
[9]Gen. 1:2.
[10]This is one reason for doubting whether Genesis 1 is really about "creation" in the strict sense of the word.
[11]This theme can be seen most consistently in the Authorized (King James) Version. See, for example, Lev. 20:12; Ps. 35:4; 44:15; 109:29; Isa. 45:16; 1 Cor. 14:33; James 3:16.
[12]2 Thess. 2:3–4.

standards of law and order may be absent, there is almost always a local mafia that administers its own "law of the jungle," sowing fear in the hearts of those forced to live under its rule and maintaining its authority by arbitrary killings and the like. This is how Satan operates among us. There is no telling when he will attack or what instruments he will use to further his designs. He even tried to bend Jesus to his will, but although he failed in that, he was successful with one of Jesus' disciples, who then betrayed his master and led him to his death.[13] No one is more deceived than the person who thinks that he is safe from such maneuvers, and the Bible warns us that we must always be on our guard against Satan.[14]

Lawlessness is arbitrary, and as Paul reminds us, it is destructive as well. There is a well-meaning saying that advises us to practice "random acts of kindness" as a way of spreading good will across the world. Although the intention of that saying may be good, the method it advocates is not. Kindness can never be random because, if it were, it would have no context and no purpose, both of which are essential to its true meaning. A mother who fed her baby every once in a while as the mood took her would not be showing kindness toward that child, and the same principle applies by extension to everything else. Evil, on the other hand, can be lawless because it has no order to uphold and no purpose to fulfill. All that it can achieve is the destruction of what God has given, which it sees as an end in itself.

In this context, however, "destruction" is a relative term. Satan cannot undo the created order or subvert the laws of nature. The natural world has not been corrupted or infected by his activity because he lacks the power to affect it in any substantial way. What he can do is more subtle than that, and therefore more dangerous. Satan takes what God has made and uses it for purposes for which it was not originally intended. The destruction he brings comes about because what is good is used for the wrong ends and is therefore discredited. A gun, for example, is a lethal weapon that can be put to good use in circumstances where the health and safety of the population is at risk. But if it falls into the wrong hands and is used for terrorizing people instead of protecting them, the good it can do is easily lost sight of. In some countries, theoretically legitimate law enforcement agencies are used by dictatorial regimes to shore up their power. When that happens people lose confidence in the law, sometimes to the point of taking up arms in what they see as necessary self-defense against the state. A country that has been through such an experience can find it very difficult to restore law and order once the evil

---

[13]Matt. 4:1–11; Luke 22:3.
[14]1 Pet. 5:8.

regime has been overthrown, because those who are supposed to uphold the law can no longer be trusted. This is the kind of confusion and destruction Satan does his best to encourage.

Those who live in countries that have been spared such a fate may be grateful, but Satan is present and active in them too. Even in the most successful democracies, people are easily persuaded to vote for "peace," "prosperity," and "justice." When the politicians who promise these things fail to deliver them, the result is often widespread cynicism coupled with a kind of popular despair that is ready to believe that any change would be an improvement. Furthermore, such democracies often do their best to suppress any mention of God, partly on the assumption that all problems are man-made and can be solved by purely human means, and partly because it is claimed that "religion" is a divisive force in society. They do not see that failure to deal with spiritual issues in spiritual terms condemns all proposed solutions to failure and undermines the entire social order in the process. The result is that liberal democracies preach a "freedom" that offers no escape from the spiritual bondage of the human race, but the delusion is so powerful that most people fall for it and willingly enslave themselves to a system that can only deliver permanent frustration. Seen in that light, the appearance of liberal democracy may well be Satan's biggest triumph so far in the history of mankind.

THE PROBLEM OF EVIL

The created order, which God made for his glory, has been corrupted by the self-will of those spiritual creatures who have turned against him and have used their gifts and abilities to destroy as much of his work as they can. It is a sad tale, and no one would be surprised if God had responded to this rejection of his love by wiping out what he had made and starting again. But God did not do that. Even when his creatures disobeyed him and went their own way, he did not retaliate by using his power against them. This is not because he was not entitled to do so. As the sovereign Lord of the universe, God can do what he likes with his creatures, and we are in no position to criticize him or complain about that.[15] From a purely logical point of view, it seems only right that he should eliminate anything that goes against his own character, and if he does not do so, we may think there is some inconsistency in him. The prophet Habakkuk wrestled with this very problem many centuries ago. As he put it,

---

[15] Rom. 9:20.

You who are of purer eyes than to see evil and cannot look at wrong, why do you idly look at traitors and remain silent when the wicked swallows up the man more righteous than he?[16]

Centuries later, Paul confronted the same dilemma when he wrote, "What if God, desiring to show his wrath and to make known his power, has endured with much patience vessels of wrath prepared for destruction?"[17] Paul went on to argue that it was all part of God's purpose to redeem what he calls "vessels of mercy," in contrast to those "vessels of wrath," but even though we understand that there must be a purpose in what God has done, it still seems strange that he should somehow suspend the execution of his justice. Yet that is exactly what he has done. Logic and justice demand the appropriate punishment, but God's love and mercy are greater than they are. In spite of everything his rebellious creatures have done and everything they so richly deserve, God has reached out to them and allowed them to remain in existence as a sign of his great love for them and of their continuing importance to him as beings he has made and over whom he remains fully sovereign.

The preservation of Satan and his angels, and the limited but still significant authority given to them, is the greatest mystery in the world. If God had eliminated them after their revolt, there would be no problem now because they would not have been able to tempt Adam and Eve to fall away. The spiritual warfare in which we are engaged would not exist and the human race would presumably be fulfilling its God-ordained purpose in a world that did not know the power of evil. But this paradise was not to be. By allowing Satan to survive, God acquiesced in a situation in which a force opposed to him would hold sway over an important part of his created universe, and would be free to tempt the first humans into following him. Why did God do this?

The existence of evil in a world made and governed by a good God is the paradox known to theologians as "theodicy," and it has never been satisfactorily explained or resolved. In the final analysis, we do not know why God has done this and we do not understand why he allows evil to continue when it is against his revealed will for his creatures. And yet this is the situation we must live with, whether we like it or not. We might wish things were otherwise, but there is nothing we can do to change them and so our main task must be to try to come to terms with the situation. If theodicy presents us with an insoluble philosophical dilemma, however, it also provides the perfect challenge to our pastoral calling, as we seek to apply what we know

---

[16]Hab. 1:13.
[17]Rom. 9:22.

about God's will to circumstances that we know are (in some sense at least) contrary to it.

We should begin by accepting that the problems associated with theodicy are insoluble within the limitations of God's revelation to us in this life, but that does not preclude us from seeking to define the proper context of the debate. The first thing that we need to establish is what evil is. Augustine and others in the early church believed that evil was essentially "nonbeing." This is because they interpreted God as both the Supreme Being and the Supreme Good, thereby conflating the notions of "good" and "being" in what is essentially a Platonic synthesis. A man who turns away from what he knows to be right ceases to be good because he ceases to be what God has made him, and so his being is diminished. The more this happens, the less of a being he is, so that in the end pure evil amounts to "nonbeing."

This way of thinking raises a number of difficult problems. First, it means that Satan cannot be pure evil, because if he were he would not exist. But if Satan continues to exist, in what way has his being been diminished? He has not ceased to be a spiritual creature enjoying all the capabilities of those who are spiritual. He is able to act anywhere at any time, apparently unhindered by barriers of time and space. He has the power to appear as an angel of light, which suggests that he can still do whatever he could have done before his fall.[18] His relationship to God may have changed, but the nature given to him by his creation has remained the same, so the idea that evil is "nonbeing" must be false. The difference between the Christian and the Platonic approach is that for Christians it is possible to be a good, *created* being, made as such by God for a particular purpose and not condemned to evil by the mere fact of being finite.

Having said that, there are still theologians today who argue that evil is a diminution or deprivation of good. They say that it cannot be described in personal terms because personhood is essentially good. Therefore, whatever evil is, it must be sub-personal, and its effects on human beings are to corrupt and enfeeble our personal character. No one will dispute that evil has harmful effects on those it touches, but whether it can really be described like this is less clear. Some of the most obviously evil people in human history have been extremely gifted and do not appear to have been diminished in any significant way. It will doubtless be objected that, although these people may have been brilliant in intellectual terms, they were morally and spiritually deficient, although that is a subjective judgment that is not open to objective verification. Suffice it to say that such a definition of evil is at best debatable and lacks clear biblical support.

---

[18]2 Cor. 11:15.

Evil is not a reality in its own right but is always parasitical on what is good and cannot exist without it. It is a denial of what is, not an alternative form of being that stands in competition with the universe made by God. That idea is known as "dualism," a theory that can be found in some ancient religions like Zoroastrianism, and which was embraced in different guises by a number of early Christian heretics. The ancient Greeks also tended to be dualists, but of a slightly different kind, seeing spiritual things as good and matter as evil, but this seems simplistic when compared to the teaching of the Bible. In ancient Greek dualism, evil and its consequences are unavoidable because they are inherent in us. Nor can evil be regarded as a spiritual problem because it is thought to stem from matter, making it possible to escape from it by escaping from the body. The Greek mind could not conceive that a purely spiritual being could be evil, because if it had any concept of "spiritual warfare," it thought of it as the soul's struggle to overcome the pull of matter. Asceticism was therefore the path of spiritual growth, which by its very nature could not be brought to fruition as long as we are tied down by matter in this life. Self-destruction was the only escape, but the ancient Greeks seldom took this to its logical conclusion and therefore they remained incapable of finding a solution to the basic dilemma of the human race.

Dualism in any form is rejected by Christians, partly because it is inherently incapable of solving the problem of evil, or even of defining it. After all, if "good" and "evil" are equal and competing forces, why should we prefer one over the other? If Satan were a power equal to God, why should he not appear as good in the eyes of his followers, and be equally attractive to the undecided? To choose one over the other would be mere prejudice. Christians reject dualism because we cannot accept that there is any power, even a potentially good one, that can compete with the sovereignty of God, who alone can bring harmony and order to the universe. If there is a rival power capable of independent existence, why does the world not simply split up into respective spheres of influence where each of them can be sovereign in its own right? If spirit and matter cannot get along with each other, why do they not just go their separate ways and live in peace? The reason of course is that God created both, and each of them is fundamentally good. That does not solve the problem of evil, but it reshapes it because we are forced to ask what evil is, if it is not an independent reality? And if a good God really is sovereign, why does evil continue to exist?

As presented in the Bible, the essence of evil is not the absence or diminution of being but rebellion against God. Evil does not produce any objective change in the nature of the one who rebels, but ensures that the rebel will use his powers in a way that both reveals and promotes his disobedience to God. The forces of evil ranged against us are not weak and declining as they become more alienated from the source of their being, but are formidable powers in their own right, capable of engaging in serious combat against the people of God. No Christian can be unaware of this, because spiritual warfare against the Devil and his legions is part of our calling in this world to bear witness to our faith in Christ. Anyone who denies this simply has no idea of what it means to be a Christian.

To combat evil is to combat Satan, and to destroy it is to destroy him. Evil is therefore both personal and spiritual. It is highly organized and aggressive, and its existence is tolerated by God. He did not create it as such, but he does not destroy it either, because at some deep level beyond our understanding, he loves the one whom he made who has brought it into being by his revolt. The question of theodicy is first and foremost the question of why God gives Satan permission to operate within the created order.

The second principle is that, although Satan now acts in ways that are in opposition to God, God has set clear boundaries to his activities and he cannot transgress them. For example, Satan cannot create, destroy, or alter the nature of matter. He has no power to bring things into existence, nor can he wipe out things that God has created for his glory. He cannot turn base metals into gold, as ancient alchemists tried to do, nor can he turn men into frogs or make them fly. Nor does Satan have the power to force anyone to do his will. He can tempt us, as he tempted Adam and Eve and as he later tempted Jesus,[19] but he cannot compel us to submit to him. We can always say no, a fact that puts limits on Satan's authority and gives us a spiritual freedom that we only have to claim in order to make effective.[20] Whatever power God has given to Satan, the power he has given to us is greater, and we have no reason to fear that we shall ever be defeated if we cling to God and trust in his love.[21]

The third principle is that Satan is truly evil, and not a good angel who has been tragically misunderstood. This needs to be said because there are some people and some religions (such as Hinduism) that tend to think that evil is a matter of perspective. Just as rain may be a blessing to a farmer but a curse to people trying to enjoy a holiday, so it will be argued that behavior which appears harmful to us may be seen by others in a different light. A classic example of this is connected to the biblical command not to murder, the fifth of the Ten Commandments.[22] Later on in the Old Testament, God com-

---

[19]See Matt. 4:1–11.
[20]1 Cor. 10:13; James 4:7.
[21]Rom. 8:38–39; 1 John 4:4.
[22]Ex. 20:13.

manded King Saul to kill the Amalekites, a pagan tribe that threatened both the political and the spiritual integrity of Israel, and to destroy all their possessions.[23] Saul defeated them, but rather than destroy their goods, his army plundered them and captured their king alive. This was not what God wanted, and Saul was punished for his leniency by being told that the kingdom would be taken from him.[24]

From a modern point of view, Saul's moderation seems almost humanitarian, though armies in ancient times were not usually squeamish about what they did to their enemies, and so we probably should not credit Saul with such high-minded motives. More likely he wanted to enrich himself with Amalekite treasure and show off the captured king as a trophy of war! Leaving that aside, the fact remains that God ordered Saul to kill, in apparent violation of the fifth commandment. How could that be? The answer is that "good" is not an abstract concept defined by a moral code, even if that code has the authority of the Ten Commandments. Most of the time and in most circumstances, murder is wrong, but God can overrule his own orders, and when he does so, we must obey.[25] This was the lesson that Saul failed to learn, and it showed that he was not the child of God that a proper king of Israel ought to be. But if goodness is not reducible to a fixed moral code, is evil similarly flexible? Was Satan wrong, for example, to attack Job within the limits prescribed by God, when God had given him express permission to do so?

Here the answer must be that everything Satan does is evil, even if it results in good.[26] This is because he is in revolt against God, and it is that which constitutes the evil. It is conceivable that Satan might do some good things in order to ingratiate himself with others, but if he does, those things are still wrong because they are done in the wrong spirit. Evil is an objective reality in the person of Satan, whose broken relationship with his Creator makes the evil what it is. There is no reason to believe that it is simply a matter of perspective, or something that can be adjusted according to circumstances.

The next point we must bear in mind is that, in the end, justice will be done. God is righteous and will not allow his honor and sovereignty to be compromised. Satan may be given some leeway for the time being, but he has already been condemned and punished for his rebellion, and that punishment will not be mitigated or revoked. God's people may suffer at Satan's hands, but in the end he will be judged and they will be vindicated. However hard it is for us to understand why God permits Satan to do the things he does, he

[23] 1 Sam. 15:3.
[24] 1 Sam. 15:26–27.
[25] 1 Sam. 15:22.
[26] 2 Cor. 11:14.

is not unjust in doing so, and when the final judgment comes we shall understand how God's apparent tolerance fits into his overall plan for his creation
and for mankind.

Finally, odd though it may seem, if Satan were to be eliminated now, most
of the human race would be destroyed along with him. The destruction of the
Devil would imply the annihilation of his kingdom, of which we are native-
born subjects. In the passage from Romans 9 quoted above, Paul surmised that
God was tolerating the "vessels of wrath" prepared for destruction for as long
as it took to rescue the "vessels of mercy" whom he had chosen for salvation.
Satan is tolerated for as long as it will take God to gather in his chosen people,
and then he will be destroyed along with all the other vessels of wrath. Until
that happens, Satan cannot be uprooted without taking his servants with him,
and they include those who are destined for redemption but who have not yet
been redeemed. Hard though it may be to accept, we must try to appreciate
that this is the better way in the present circumstances. If God had chosen to
destroy Satan before we were converted, we would have gone down with him,
and surely we would not have wanted that to happen!

THE NATURE OF EVIL

We have to understand the rebellion of Satan because of what it tells us about
the nature of evil. It is certain that Satan did not revolt out of ignorance. Finite
though he may be, he is nevertheless fully aware of who God is and of what
his own limitations are as a creature. The fallen angels, or demons as they are
often called, know full well who God is and they shudder because of it, but
that knowledge is not enough to cause them to repent.[27] There is something
about the nature of evil that flies in the face of the facts and that refuses to
yield to rational argument. If anyone could be cajoled into the kingdom of
heaven, it should be the fallen angels, but the fact is that they are more resis-
tant to reconciliation than any other creature. To know God is not a work of
the intellect alone but something that only the Holy Spirit can produce. Why
he does not work on the fallen angels is a mystery to us, but that he must do
so if they are to be saved from their folly is certain.

It is also clear that evil is not part of nature, not even of Satan's nature.
He was not made that way. As far as God's creative act is concerned, Satan
was just as "good" as any other creature and had no inherent bias or defect
that might lead him to rebel. It is important to understand this because there
is always a temptation to blame wrongdoing on something innate in us that

---

[27] James 2:19.

is beyond our control. Some people say that because we are finite beings, we shall inevitably go wrong sooner or later, and that will separate us from God. Satan was also a finite being, but there is no suggestion that he was structured in a way that made it inevitable that he would fall away. He could have continued to serve God in the same way that Michael serves him, but he chose not to. Even now, if he were somehow to be redeemed, he would presumably be restored to his original state, though there is no promise or expectation of that held out in Scripture. The picture we are given is that Satan's rebellion is definitive and that the tolerance that God now shows toward him will one day be withdrawn.[28] Whether that means he will be annihilated or that he will be confined to eternal punishment is hard to say, but that makes little real difference. Either way, Satan's residual power will be cut off, and the world will be delivered from his embrace, whatever happens to him as an individual.

It may ultimately be due to his goodness as a creature that Satan was not cut off from the presence of God when he was cast out of heaven. The traditional picture is that he was sent to hell, a place of punishment for rebellion against God. What or where hell might be is impossible to say—the only thing we know for sure is that it is not under the earth, as many people imagine it to be. As always when we are dealing with spiritual things, we must be careful not to mistake symbolic imagery for the reality it is trying to convey. The Bible uses words like "heaven" and "hell," and the biblical writers picture them as being "above" and "below" the earth, but this language is not meant to be taken literally. The creation account in Genesis refers to the physical heavens that are above the earth, but it does not specify that they are the dwelling-place of God, and there is no mention of any underworld. The symbolism is intended to make it easier for us to understand the spiritual concepts that lie behind it and is not to be used as an excuse for locating heaven or hell in different parts of the created order.

The Bible tells us that God is present in hell, which should not surprise us since he is omnipresent,[29] but the notion that Satan might be wandering freely across the earth and might be found even in the courts of heaven strikes us as strange.[30] Whether or not it makes sense to us, the Devil can prowl around like a roaring lion, seeking people to devour and deceiving even the children of God, but all this activity is pointless in the end.[31] His so-called achievements will be overturned, his kingdom will be wiped out, and he himself will ultimately be thrown into "the lake of fire," a vivid term that evokes

---

[28]Rev. 20:10.
[29]Ps. 139:7–9.
[30]Job 1:6–12.
[31]1 Pet. 5:8.

the power of God to whom he will be subject.[32] The message to us is that joining with Satan in his rebellion against God is a waste of time, because those who do so will also be cast into the lake of fire and will suffer the same punishment as their master. God will not destroy them any more than he will destroy Satan, but in his love for what he has made, he will keep them in existence in spite of themselves and exercise his sovereignty over them, which from their perspective will be the ultimate humiliation and punishment.

The spiritual creatures, whether obedient or rebellious, are ontologically on a par with each other. This is shown by the fact that, in the battle against Satan, God does not get directly involved but sends the archangel Michael to lead the heavenly hosts in battle against their peers. This is an acknowledgment of the reality that Satan is a spiritual creature, but it is also a great humiliation for him. He wanted to be like God, which is why he rebelled, but God dealt with him by leaving him to the judgment of his peer, who is mockingly named *Mi-cha-el*, "Who is like God?"[33] The answer to that question is clear—not Satan!

Michael did battle with Satan for the body of Moses, an obscure incident which probably indicates that Satan was trying to claim the Mosaic legacy, including the law and the sacrificial system of Israel, and had to be beaten back.[34] Michael also appears in the book of Revelation as the one sent to wage war with the Devil on God's behalf.[35] In the book of Daniel, the same Michael appears as the guardian and prince of Israel who acts as the chief assistant to the Son of Man and protects the people in times of trouble.[36] In the figure of Michael we see two things coming together. First, he is God's deputy and messenger, sent by him to execute his will. Second, as the protector of God's people, he comes alongside them and gives them the strength to resist their enemies and overcome them. He is a reminder to us that the battles we wage as Christians are spiritual ones and that it is only by the Spirit of God that we can win them.[37]

By treating him like the creature he is, God puts Satan in his place. In doing this he reminds us that, however powerful evil is, it is not nearly as powerful as God. There can be no equation of these two things, no suggestion that God would ever honor evil by granting it a status similar to his own. The struggle between good and evil is one in which the two forces are unequal. However difficult we may find it to resist the pull of Satan, we must know that

---

[32]Rev. 20:10.
[33]Rev. 12:7.
[34]Jude 9.
[35]Rev. 12:7.
[36]Dan. 10:13, 21; 12:1.
[37]See Zech. 4:6.

his power over us is as nothing when compared to the power of God, who will vindicate his elect and deliver them from evil no matter how long it may take or how difficult the task may seem to us.

THE POWER OF SATAN

What is astonishing about Satan is the fact that God not only continues to tolerate his existence but allows him a degree of independence and authority. Far from obliterating him at the first sign of rebellion, God has permitted the Devil to operate more or less freely within a sphere of power that may be restricted in some ways but is still very broad. Why this is so is beyond our understanding, but it is a fact that we must reckon with. When Satan tempted Job, he did so by divine permission, although it is noteworthy that God did not allow him to take Job's life.[38] That was not always the case, however. When God determined that the wicked King Ahab would die in battle at Ramoth-Gilead, in fulfillment of a prophecy given to the king by Elijah,[39] he did not destroy Ahab himself but asked for a spiritual being to come forward and do what was necessary. In response, it was an evil spirit, who may have been Satan himself (or if not, then certainly one of his followers) who took up the challenge, and God allowed him to proceed with his plan of destruction.[40] Ahab went to his death because he listened to the lies put in the mouths of his prophets by the evil spirit, but the Bible makes it clear that this was done with God's permission and ultimately at his command.

Satan cannot act otherwise, and however hard it is for us to accept, we must remember that when he attacks us, he is able to do so only because God has allowed it. Paul learned this the hard way. Satan attacked him with what he called a "thorn in his flesh," but despite praying to God for deliverance, Paul was told to put up with it. God's grace was stronger than any Satanic attack, and Paul would be sustained through it if his faith and obedience remained constant.[41] We cannot say that every Satanic attack is authorized by God for this purpose, but since it was true in the case of Job and of Paul, we must consider the possibility very seriously. The Christian life is a challenge to engage in spiritual warfare against the schemes of the Devil, and we must not confuse deliverance from his power, which we have been promised in Christ, with freedom from his attacks, which has not been given to us.[42] For us to be united with Christ is to be protected from the power of Satan, but it is also to

---

[38] Job 1:12.
[39] 1 Kings 21:19.
[40] 1 Kings 22:19–23.
[41] 2 Cor. 12:7–9.
[42] Eph. 6:11.

be called to engage in battle with him as Christ did. We have been given the whole armor of God to aid us in that fight, but there is no safe haven for us this side of heaven and we must not pretend that there is.

Once Satan got the independence he wanted, he revealed what he was capable of and the lengths to which he would go to maintain his newly won freedom. Unable to bear the truth, he turned to lies in order to extend his sway. Incapable of giving life, he preferred to take it away instead. As Jesus put it, from the beginning he was a murderer and a liar, or as the name "devil" indicates, the great deceiver.[43] He beguiled Adam and Eve by offering them something desirable and lying to them by the clever device of telling them a half-truth. It is a good thing to want to be like God, especially if you have been created in his image and likeness, and Satan promised them that they could attain that desirable goal simply by eating the fruit of the tree of the knowledge of good and evil. Adam and Eve hesitated at first because they knew that the fruit was forbidden to them, but in the end they succumbed, and Satan's promise to them was duly fulfilled—they became like God.[44] But because this happened in the wrong way, Adam and Eve did not enjoy its benefits and instead fell into Satan's power and were thrown out of the garden of Eden. The deception was very clever, and Satan was the only one who gained anything from it. This pattern has not altered, and those who are deceived by Satan today often have a similar experience. For a brief moment they may get what they have been promised, but it soon turns to dust and ashes and the latter state is worse than the first.[45]

Perhaps the greatest deception of Satan is that he appears as an angel of light who equips his followers to present themselves as servants of righteousness.[46] This was a major problem in the early church, where false teachers and apostles did all they could to discredit men like Paul and overturn their teaching. What was true then is still true today. The greatest enemies of the Christian faith are not those who openly reject it but those who claim to accept it while denying everything it stands for. Sometimes this takes the form of hypocrites who preach one thing and do another, but bad as they are, they usually harm no one but themselves. Far worse are those who teach that the Bible does not mean what it says or that it is no longer authoritative for Christians because it is an ancient book written by people who had no understanding of modern life. These people claim to be enlightened and to have shaken off the superstitions of past ages, but in reality they have betrayed

---

[43] John 8:44. This is the meaning of the Greek word *diabolos*, from which "devil" is derived.
[44] Gen. 3:22.
[45] 2 Pet. 2:20.
[46] 2 Cor. 11:14–15.

the gospel of Christ and exalted their own minds at the expense of God's revealed truth. The modern church is full of such blind guides, and we must be constantly on our guard against their false teaching. Anyone who claims to be a Christian teacher but who denies the existence of Satan and regards the Bible's teaching about him as outdated and mythological must be avoided, because Satan likes nothing better than to persuade people that they have nothing to fear from him.

Satan is also the zealous protector and defender of his flock. Having duped the human race, he is unwilling to let go of it. Whenever he gets the chance, he prevents us from hearing and receiving God's Word. He cannot defeat the power of God, of course, but where the Word has been preached and has failed to take root, he quickly removes whatever influence it may have had and makes any further move in its direction impossible.[47] It is this Satanic activity that explains what the writer to the Hebrews meant when he wrote,

> It is impossible, in the case of those who have once been enlightened, who have tasted the heavenly gift, and have shared in the Holy Spirit, and have tasted the goodness of the word of God and the powers of the age to come, and then have fallen away, to restore them again to repentance, since they are crucifying once again the Son of God to their own harm and holding him up to contempt. For land that has drunk the rain that often falls on it, and produces a crop useful to those for whose sake it is cultivated, receives a blessing from God. But if it bears thorns and thistles, it is worthless and near to being cursed, and its end is to be burned.[48]

One of Satan's favorite ploys is to accuse us before God, pointing out that we have no righteousness of our own and therefore no right to stand in God's presence. Once again, we are faced with a half-truth that can easily lead us astray, if we are not careful. As a statement of fact, Satan is right to say that we are unworthy to stand before God, but in saying this he is not reckoning with God's grace and mercy, to both of which he is a stranger. A classic example that illustrates this occurs in Zechariah 3:1–2, where the prophet has a vision of the high priest who is clothed in filthy rags and is therefore unworthy to perform the all-important task of making atonement for the sins of the people. But the high priest, who was called Joshua, is saved by God, and Joshua's atoning sacrifice is accepted because he has taken the sins of the people on himself. His filthy clothing is not a sign of his character but of the sins of the people for whom he is making atonement, and the fact

---

[47]Mark 4:15.
[48]Heb. 6:4–8.

that the high priest takes this on himself reveals a deeper righteousness than anything Satan can grasp.

The vision of Zechariah was fulfilled in the sacrifice of Jesus, when he became sin for us in order to take it away and make it possible for us to share in the righteousness of God himself.[49] We who are filthy inside and totally unworthy of God's grace have been covered by a cloak of righteousness dyed in the blood of the one who was slain in our place. It is because of that covering that we who have no merit of our own have been made acceptable to God. Satan has no right to accuse those whom Jesus has chosen and united to himself—because we have been set free from the condemnation that we would otherwise deserve.[50] That does not stop Satan from trying, of course, and it is here perhaps more than anywhere else that we must be constantly on our guard, so as not to fall into the trap that he wants to set for us.

As well as trying to accuse us of what we have already done, Satan continues the work of temptation by which he brought Adam and Eve down. A clear instance of this occurs in the Old Testament, where we are told that he persuaded King David to take a census of Israel.[51] It seems strange to us that such an activity would be seen as Satanic, but the context suggests that David was proud to have so many fighting men at his command and wanted to boast of his strength. It is a constant temptation for men in his position to rely on human power for success, but in doing that, David was denying God. As God's chosen people, Israel had never prospered by being physically strong, and it never would. As Zechariah later said to Zerubbabel, when he was trying to reorganize Israel after the exile, "Not by might, nor by power, but by my Spirit, says the LORD of hosts."[52] Spiritual people must rely on spiritual strength, not on material power, even if the latter appears to offer a surer hope of success in this world. Something very similar to this happened to Jesus when he was tempted by Satan at the beginning of his earthly ministry.[53] Satan promised to give him an earthly empire in return for his soul, but Jesus knew that his kingdom was not of this world and so he turned on Satan, exposing his false pretense and driving him off. From this example we learn that Satan cannot withstand resistance to his will, and if he encounters it, he runs away. This is a promise explicitly given to us later in the New Testament, and our ability to stand up to Satan is one of the most powerful weapons we possess.[54]

Along with his work of deception and temptation, Satan is also our great

[49]2 Cor. 5:21. Note that "Jesus" is just the Greek form of "Joshua."
[50]Rom. 8:31–39.
[51]1 Chron. 21:1.
[52]Zech. 4:6.
[53]Matt. 4:1–11.
[54]James 4:7.

tormentor. We see this most clearly in the case of Job, but it also appears from other instances that he can and does inflict diseases and hardships of various kinds on God's people.[55] This does not mean that all forms of suffering are Satanic in origin, but that Satan is capable of employing such means is a possibility that we must bear in mind, given the fact that he will do everything he can to attack us and drag us down.[56] He can also possess people, and there are several instances in the New Testament where Jesus or his disciples cast him out of particular individuals.[57] However, there is no example in Scripture of Satan possessing a Christian, and the indwelling presence of the Holy Spirit in our hearts must rule that out. Jesus was accused of being possessed by an evil spirit,[58] so we should not be surprised if Christians are also accused of this, but just as Jesus appealed to his acts as evidence that the claims made against him were false, so we should be able to do the same. The presence of the Holy Spirit in our hearts produces the fruits of the same Spirit in our lives, and if these are present, we have no need to fear that we might be possessed by the Devil.[59]

More subtle than outright possession, though, is the way in which Satan can enter people's hearts and minds and get them to do his will, even when they think they are doing the opposite. This happened to the unfortunate Peter when he refused to accept that Jesus had to suffer and die.[60] Peter's concern for Jesus' safety was perfectly understandable and natural, but that was the problem. Jesus had not come to lead an ordinary human life but to sacrifice himself for the sins of the world, and to try to stop him from doing that, however well-intentioned the motivation, was to do the work of Satan. If Jesus had been spared suffering and death, the world would not have been saved, and Satan's rule would have continued unaffected. Very clever! Later on, Satan made another bid to capture Peter, but Jesus protected his disciple and Satan got nowhere.[61] That was not the case with Judas, however, whom Satan managed to take over with great success.[62] Later on, he did the same thing with Ananias, whom he persuaded to lie to the Holy Spirit.[63] In both of these instances, however, Satan's triumphs were pyrrhic victories. In capturing Judas and Ananias he led them both to their destruction, and once they were dead his power over them was meaningless.

---

[55] Luke 22:31; 2 Cor. 12:7; 1 Thess. 2:18.
[56] 1 Pet. 5:8.
[57] Matt. 9:32; 12:22; Luke 10:17–20; Acts 10:38.
[58] Matt. 12:24.
[59] Gal. 5:16–26.
[60] Matt. 16:23.
[61] Luke 22:31–32.
[62] Luke 22:3; John 13:27.
[63] Acts 5:3.

One of Satan's favorite activities is to stir up trouble in the church, and he can do this in any number of ways.[64] For example, he can tempt people sexually, especially if they are trying to ignore their marital responsibilities.[65] A church plagued with broken marriages and divorce is denying the gospel of Christ and is just what Satan wants. Unfortunately, it is also what he has got in many parts of the Western world today, where even church leaders have often succumbed to this evil and so have no authority to prevent its spread in others. We are expressly warned in Scripture that before the return of Christ and the end of time, there will be a great rebellion in the church itself, as a lawless power hostile to God takes over and tries to bend it to his will.[66] Satan will not let us go until he is forced to, and if he can make the church do his bidding, then so much the better from his point of view.[67] As a curious but revealing footnote to this, we may recall that Paul did not hesitate to turn people over to Satan if there was no way they could be satisfactorily disciplined inside the church.[68] It seems that the only hope of salvation for some people is a spell in Satan's clutches, so that they will learn the hard way what that feels like and will repent before having to spend eternity in that state. That was not what Paul wanted, and in one sense it went completely against the purpose of his ministry, which was to turn people from Satan to God and not the other way around,[69] but he also understood that unless and until a person comes under conviction of sin and genuinely wants to repent of it, there is nothing much that can be done to turn him around. Sad though it is, sometimes the hard way is the only way to learn.

The other demons do the work of Satan. Like him, they can also possess people and speak through them, giving the impression that those who have been possessed are divine oracles, but in reality using them to deceive people as Satan their master does.[70] There was some controversy in the early church about whether the gods of the pagans were demons or merely imaginary characters. It was an important issue in determining whether meat sacrificed to idols had been sacrificed to demons, because in that case, the meat might have been exposed to some demonic power. The response of Paul to that idea suggests that he thought that the pagan gods were purely imaginary, but that does not mean that they were not also a trick of the Devil or that he did not send his servants to work through pagan cults of various kinds.[71]

---

[64]2 Cor. 2:11.
[65]1 Cor. 7:5; 1 Tim. 5:15.
[66]2 Thess. 2:9.
[67]Rev. 2:9; 3:9.
[68]1 Cor. 5:5; 1 Tim. 1:20.
[69]Acts 26:18.
[70]Acts 16:16–19.
[71]1 Cor. 8:1–13.

Similar considerations may be applied to the rites of other religions. Few people would want to suggest that these are inspired by the Devil, but it is perfectly possible—indeed, it is highly probable—that he uses them for his own purposes. After all, if Satan appears as an angel of light, it is only to be expected that various means of enlightenment will bear his imprint. Much the same can be said of deviant forms of Christianity, including cults like the Jehovah's Witnesses, the Mormons, and Christian Science, which also claim to be special revelations from God but deny basic elements of the Christian faith. Nor should we forget that Satan can use perfectly orthodox truths for his own purposes, either by taking them out of context or by giving them an importance that they do not deserve. For example, Christians are called to be baptized, but if we equate water baptism with spiritual rebirth or make it so central to our understanding of Christian fellowship that we cannot accept those who disagree with us about how it should be administered, then we have fallen into the trap of Satan by dividing the body of Christ instead of holding it together. The moral of this and every other example like it is that there is no end to Satan's trickery, and we must be constantly on our guard against it.[72] As long as his rule over this world continues, Satan will not give up trying to seduce us, even though he knows that he is doomed to destruction in the end. He wants to take us down with him, and we must do our utmost to avoid that.

DEMON POSSESSION

Fallen angels can have a kind of relationship with us, but it is very different from the one that God wants us to have with him. Satan does not recognize us as his children, however much he may try to flatter and seduce us. For him, only one kind of relationship is possible—total control, extending even to the point of outright possession. In countries where the Christian church has been strong for a long time, demon possession is relatively rare and is not talked about much these days. This has led some people to deny that there is any such thing, and to treat the biblical accounts of it as records of epilepsy or mental illness recorded at a time when such things were not properly understood. Yet demon possession has not faded out completely, even in the Western world, and in places where the gospel has not penetrated or where it has taken root only recently, it is still found on a considerable scale. The scoffers are inclined to explain this as ignorant superstition, but it is not that simple. People who only recently have been liberated from evil powers are more sensitive to their presence, especially if they live around others who are still in their grip. The

---

[72] 1 Pet. 5:8.

relative absence of such phenomena from Christianized societies may be evidence that the prayers of Christian people have the power to banish demons from our midst. If that is true, we must be warned that if we cease to pray for this protection we may no longer receive it, and demon possession may become a more frequent occurrence than it has been in the recent past. It is sometimes said that Satan's most effective trick is to persuade people that he does not exist, and a culture which is heading that way is more likely to suffer the consequences of such myopia than one that is alive and alert to the danger he presents.

Satan and his demons may seek to possess us, but they cannot do so if we are Christians, because the indwelling presence of God's Holy Spirit in our hearts rules that out. Someone who is not a Christian may want to strike a bargain with the Devil, as the legendary Doctor Faust is supposed to have done, but this is an illusion. On Satan's side there is no deal to strike because, as the ruler of this world, his aim is to dominate and destroy us. There is no halfway house, and we are fooling ourselves if we think that we can give only a part of our lives to him. There were people who sought to make such a deal with Jesus, promising to follow him when they had settled their affairs on earth, but he rejected them.[73] The Devil merely laughs at people who try that on him, because he knows that he has them in his power already. They may think they can keep a part of their lives free of his influence, but they cannot, because he is the great deceiver. He has no problem letting us think that we are in control of our lives, because his deception consists in just that—making us think that we are our own masters. The rest is just a matter of degree and owes more to perception than to reality.

At the same time, we must recognize that, because the Devil is the ruler of this world, all human beings are in bondage to him and there are some who actively serve him, whether openly or covertly. The most obvious example of this is the practice of the occult, which is found in many cultures and is far from dead, even in countries that have a long Christian heritage. Witchcraft and sorcery have often been discounted in rationalistic Western societies and treated as if they were no more than absurd, folkloristic survivals of an earlier age of superstition. This may be true in some cases, but not in all, and dabbling with the demonic is strictly forbidden to Christians, as it was to Jews in ancient Israel. This includes attempts to contact the dead, for whatever purposes. There is a famous instance of this in the Old Testament, when King Saul sought out the witch of Endor and asked her to conjure up

---

[73] Matt. 8:18–22.

the prophet Samuel.[74] According to the story, Samuel returned from the grave in ghostly form and told Saul what his fate would be, an incident that caused grave alarm among the early Christians. Is it possible, they wanted to know, for people on earth to call back the dead in this way? Will we be subject to such manipulation by evil powers once we have passed beyond this life?

To this, the answer must be no. A Christian who dies goes to be with Christ in heaven and is protected from any earthly or demonic interference with his eternal happiness.[75] We are not told what happens to unbelievers, but we must assume that they cannot be called back either, since if that were possible, we would know who has been saved and who has not. Hebrews 11:39–40 says that the saints of the Old Testament were held back from entering their eternal rest until Christians could join them, but whether this left them exposed to demonic forces is unclear. The witch of Endor was apparently able to conjure up Samuel, though some have argued that this must have been a deception. We can only suspend our judgment about this and accept that God may have permitted Samuel to return from the dead in order to condemn Saul. Whether or not that was true, we can say with complete certainty that such a thing cannot now happen to us. Anyone who thinks they have met a dead person through some form of spiritualism has been deceived, however realistic the deception may appear to have been.

THE END OF SATAN'S REBELLION

The rejection of God's love is a serious thing, and its consequences have been far-reaching. The rebellion of the angels led to the seduction of the human race and the spread of sin to every aspect of our being and life. The preservation of the fallen angels does not extend to their redemption, however. We do not know why this is so, but it may be because they are servants and not children of the Father. Perhaps it has to do with the fact that not all the angels fell, so that heaven is still populated with angelic beings, which would not be the case with humans if none of us were to be redeemed. Here we are in the realm of speculation, and must accept what we know to be true without trying to probe into the mind of God beyond what he has revealed to us.

Can Satan repent and be saved? Logically there is no reason why he cannot, because he was created good and was condemned for his rebellion, not because his nature is fundamentally evil. Perhaps for this reason, there have been some people who have speculated, on the basis of God's absolute sovereignty and equally absolute goodness, that even Satan will be redeemed

---

[74]1 Sam. 28:7–25.
[75]Rom. 8:38–39.

in the end. Against this, however, must be set the testimony of Scripture, which holds out no such hope for him or for the angels who fell along with him. In 2 Peter 2:4 we read that "God did not spare angels when they sinned, but cast them into hell and committed them to chains of gloomy darkness to be kept until the judgment." Of course, statements of this kind have to be interpreted spiritually and not physically. There is no dungeon lying underneath the earth's surface where Satan and the fallen angels will be bound, but the image shows us what separation from the presence of God will feel like. Satan is seen as ruling over "this present darkness,"[76] which explains why the fallen angels are described as being chained in darkness, but we know that they are active in Satan's service and not languishing in some forgotten prison, doing nothing and unable to move. There will be a judgment for the angels just as there will be for us, the main difference being that we shall sit with God in judgment over them.[77] We shall be able to do this only because we have been redeemed by Christ and united to him; this strongly suggests that the angels will not be so privileged.

Scripture also indicates that neither Satan nor any of his followers has shown any desire to repent and be forgiven, and there is no indication that they will ever do so, despite the fact that they know the gospel inside out.[78] Instead, the Bible tells us that God will crush Satan under our feet, his works will be destroyed, and after the final judgment, he will be dethroned and cast into the "lake of fire," where he "will be tormented day and night forever and ever."[79] Even allowing for the fact that this is a physical description of a spiritual reality, there are no grounds for supposing that Satan will either repent or be annihilated. As far as we can tell, he will be sent along with those who have followed him to suffer the eternal punishment that he deserves. Furthermore, it seems that this will happen *before* we sit in judgment over the angels, because as far as we know, our judgment will take place after Satan's power has been destroyed.[80] As always, we must be careful about how literally we interpret these spiritual phenomena, but it seems safe to say that there will be no opportunity for us to plead for God to show mercy on Satan and his angels, even if we were inclined to do so. Our participation in the divine judgment will therefore be to confirm what God has already done, not to deliberate with him about what he should do.

---

[76]Eph. 6:12.
[77]1 Cor. 6:3.
[78]James 2:19.
[79]Rom. 16:20; 1 John 3:8; Rev. 20:10.
[80]Rev. 20:7–15.

ETERNAL PUNISHMENT OR ANNIHILATION?

This brings us finally to the question of whether the judgment against Satan and his angels will lead to eternal punishment in some kind of prison, or whether they will be simply extinguished, either immediately or after a certain interval. In recent years we have become familiar with this question in relation to human beings who are condemned to eternal damnation, but it is more logical to discuss the question in the context of Satan. This is because the Devil is the ruler of the kingdom of darkness, into which condemned human beings will be plunged, and what happens to him will presumably happen to them too. Looking at the matter from the opposite end, it is hard to see why God would annihilate human beings after a time in hell but not Satan and his angels, since by what logic would he want to keep them in being? If suffering is to be ended, surely it should be ended for demons as well as for human beings!

We have already indicated that eternal punishment is the more likely outcome on the basis of scriptural testimony, so it is important to consider on what the annihilationist case is based. As far as biblical testimony is concerned, annihilationism relies mainly on the testimony of Revelation 20:10, which says that the Devil "was thrown into the lake of fire and sulfur where the beast and the false prophet were, and they will be tormented day and night forever and ever." That does not sound like annihilationism, but the response to this is that the words have to be taken figuratively. There is no literal lake of fire and therefore no literal eternal torment. What is meant by this vivid description is that Satan and his followers will be destroyed, and that is what we call annihilation!

We must agree that the lake of fire is to be understood in a figurative or spiritual sense. Physical fire can have no effect on a spiritual being, so that interpretation makes no sense. Having said that, however, there is nothing here or anywhere else in Scripture to suggest that Satan and his angels, not to mention those under his rule, will be annihilated. The argument that lies behind this suggestion is not drawn from Scripture but from the moral sense that endless suffering is pointless and therefore unworthy of God. If it had some redemptive purpose it would be understood and could be accepted, but as it does not, it seems monstrous to suppose that it will go on forever with no positive outcome. To put it in human terms, what the annihilationists are advocating is a kind of euthanasia after death. Euthanasia is also justified on the ground that pointless suffering should be terminated, and annihilationism merely extends that principle to life beyond the grave.

What the annihilationists overlook, however, is the love and justice of

God. Most people would agree that a life sentence in prison is a milder form of punishment than judicial execution and would probably prefer it if faced with the choice. Someone imprisoned for life might one day be proved innocent and set free, which an executed criminal could not be, but even if there is no chance of reversing the verdict in the case of a person who has been condemned to hell, there is something in us which says that life is better than death because where there is life, there is hope. To this feeling we may add the consideration that God will not destroy what he has made because, however far it may have gone from his original will and purpose, he still loves it. Even if Satan does not want to live and desires his own destruction, God will not permit it because of his deep love for him and for those who serve him. Their disobedience has not turned him to hatred, even if he must punish them for it. For all eternity they will still be his creatures, and their continued existence will bear witness to his glory and power at work in them just as much as in everything else that he has made.

18

THE REJECTION
OF GOD'S LOVE
BY HUMAN BEINGS

WHY ADAM AND EVE REBELLED

The greatest of Satan's achievements was his deception of the human race, the effects of which we still feel and will continue to suffer from until the final judgment at the end of time. Adam and Eve had been created as both spiritual and material beings, which made them a little lower than the angels, because they were physically limited in ways that the angels were not.[1] But their spiritual side gave them the ability to communicate with God and with the other spiritual creatures in what we would now call "personal" terms. At the same time, they had been denied access to the knowledge of good and evil, not because that knowledge was too great for them to bear or incompatible with the limitations of their being, but in order to protect them from exposure to the forces of rebellion against God represented by Satan and his followers. The principle seems to have been that what they did not know would not hurt them, and we must assume that if they had obeyed God's command and had exercised the dominion entrusted to them according to God's original will and plan, they would have prospered. Unlike Satan, Adam and Eve did not fall spontaneously but were tempted away from God by a power thitherto unknown to them. They did not invite Satan into their lives, nor is there any sign that he was particularly welcome when he appeared. We are told that Adam and Eve initially resisted him, because they knew that what he was asking them to do was forbidden. Their fall, when it came, was not the poisonous effect of the fruit they ate. It was their disobedience that cut them

[1]Ps. 8:5; Heb. 2:7, 9.

off from God, and everything else flowed from that. Adam and Eve did not become "free" or "independent" after choosing to go their own way, but were enslaved to Satan and trapped in a rebellion which they had not initiated and over which they had no control. What made them choose such a fate?

The traditional answer is to say that the fall of Adam and Eve was due to their pride, because pride is the root of all evil. That may well have been true in Satan's case, and to the extent that Satan's rebellion is what Adam and Eve were caught up in, it is a valid explanation of human sin as well. However, it is not clear that pride was the immediate cause that impelled Adam and Eve to listen to the serpent's tempting words and follow him. Pride can exist only where there is self-awareness, and the Bible tells us that Adam and Eve acquired that in and through their fall.[2] The Genesis account gives the impression that they were motivated by something more positive and appealing than selfish pride. They wanted to be like God.[3] Adam and Eve knew that they had been created in God's image and likeness, and they wanted to be more like him than they already were. They were not trying to go beyond the bounds of their created nature and become like the angels. The tree of the knowledge of good and evil was readily available to them, and it had always been possible for them to eat its fruit. The problem was not that the moral awareness they acquired was beyond their capacities as human beings but that they had been forbidden to obtain it. After their fall, they did not become either more or less human than they had been before, nor did they lose the knowledge of good and evil when they were expelled from the garden as punishment for their disobedience. We still have that knowledge today, and there is no indication that we shall forfeit it when we are finally caught up into glory. It seems that our moral awareness is here to stay and that it is a good thing for us to have, even if Adam and Eve acquired it in the wrong way.

The explanation for the sin of Adam and Eve seems to be that they wanted something that was good in itself, but they wanted it in the wrong way. They were not forced to submit to Satan, and they could have rejected his blandishments, but temptation got the better of their curiosity and they fell. The cost to them far outweighed any benefit they may have received, and from that perspective their sin made no sense at all. Disobedience to the Creator is an essentially irrational act. The only way we can come to terms with it is by looking into our own hearts and asking ourselves what we would have done in their place. Would we have resisted the forbidden fruit in a way that they did not? If we are honest, we shall admit that the

---

[2]Gen. 3:7.
[3]Gen. 3:5.

temptation to eat what had been denied us would have become too much to deal with and our resistance to it, however principled and well-intentioned it might have been at first, would eventually have crumbled. We cannot explain why this is so because it makes no sense. We know in our hearts that such a surrender is an act of our free will and not something forced on us by God or made inevitable by our finite human nature. To pretend otherwise is to fail to understand ourselves.

THE RESULTS OF ADAM AND EVE'S FALL

Once it was acquired, the knowledge of good and evil could not simply be rejected. Adam and Eve could not apologize for their mistake and put the fruit back on the tree where it had come from. In this sense it may be compared to something harmful or unpleasant that we find out about by mistake, perhaps by reading a letter that has been inadvertently left lying around. We may wish we had never seen it, but we cannot erase it from our memory. In the same way, Adam and Eve had to live with the consequences of their act, and so did God. What was done was done, and there could be no going back to their earlier state.

The immediate result of obtaining the forbidden knowledge was that Adam and Eve acquired self-awareness, and they did not like what they saw. As the Bible puts it, "The eyes of both were opened, and they knew that they were naked. And they sewed fig leaves together and made themselves loincloths."[4] The story is well known, but it has often been misunderstood, with disastrous consequences that continue to affect us today. As elsewhere in the creation narrative, God uses physical symbols to express spiritual truths, but nowhere has this fact been less appreciated than here. Nakedness is not by itself a sin. If it were, we would be doing something wrong every time we took a shower or a bath. Strange as it may seem to us now, for centuries there were many devout Christians who never washed themselves for precisely that reason, convinced that the "odor of sanctity" was superior to personal hygiene. That is absurd, of course, and if there were no more to it than that, we could just laugh it off and move on. Unfortunately, and far more seriously, this verse has also been used to claim that there is something tainted about human sexuality, a mistake which has led to gross distortions that range all the way from castration at one end of the spectrum to orgiastic libertinism at the other. Because of this, a favorite accusation against Christians and the church is that we have misunderstood sexuality, and therefore nothing we say

---

[4]Gen. 3:7.

about it has any validity. The Devil got more out of that piece of fruit than even he could have imagined!

What the nakedness of Adam and Eve points to is not the wickedness of the body and its desires, but our weakness. Cut off from the protecting power of God that we were given at creation, we are now exposed to danger on all fronts—physical, moral, and spiritual. To be naked in the world is to be defenseless, and that is what the loincloths symbolize. Our sexual organs are precious to us because they are the means by which we reproduce the human race. They are delicate and easily tampered with, so we must take great care of them in order to preserve ourselves. If they are harmed, we suffer at the most basic level of our existence. It is for this reason, and not because we are ashamed of our sexuality, that we take such care to make sure that our most vulnerable parts are the ones least exposed to harm.[5]

The persistent notion that sexual intercourse is tainted with sin, which is passed on from one generation to the next as a kind of congenital defect that is sometimes referred to as a "stain on the soul," has had some mischievous effects. It was but a short step from there to regarding the "flesh" as inherently sinful and interpreting all biblical references to it in that light. The Bible tells us that the flesh is weak, that it is mortal, and that it encourages us to desire things that are contrary to God's will, all of which are factors that contribute to using the word as a term for rebellion against God, but nowhere does it say that the flesh is evil in itself. Adam and Eve were created as mortal beings, but in the garden of Eden they were protected from the consequences of their mortality. When they fell, that protection was removed and they died. What would have happened to them had they not fallen is not known, but presumably they would have remained mortal beings in a mortal universe. If they had lived a normal physical life and had children, there would have been a process of growth and decay, at the end of which their earthly life would have been terminated. Whether this would have been by death as we know it or by some kind of transmutation into another life, such as happened to Enoch and Elijah,[6] we cannot say.

What persuades us that our first parents were naturally mortal and not immortal? There are two things that point us toward this conclusion. The first is a comparison between what happened to them and what happened to the fallen angels. The angels were immortal by nature, and so after their fall they went on living—death did not come into the world as a result of their disobedience. This explains why Satan and his fellow demons are still with us.

---

[5]1 Cor. 12:23.
[6]Gen. 5:24; 2 Kings 2:11.

But when human beings sinned, they died, because the protection from which they had benefitted in the garden of Eden was removed. The second thing is the presence in the garden of the tree of life. After Adam and Eve disobeyed God, there was a brief moment when it would have been possible for them to have eaten of the tree of life as well, and if they had done so, they would have lived forever.[7] Had they been immortal, a tree of life would not have been necessary. Like the knowledge of good and evil, eternal life is not incompatible with human nature, and acquiring it is one of the great promises made by the gospel of Jesus Christ. At the same time, eternal life is not intrinsic to human nature either, because if it were, we could not lose it any more than we can lose any other part of our human nature.

Some will object that in Genesis 2:17 God says to Adam and Eve that "in the day you eat of it [the tree of the knowledge of good and evil] you shall surely die," and they interpret this to mean that Adam and Eve were immortal before the fall. This, however, is to misinterpret the text. First, it is obvious that Adam and Eve did not die on the day that they ate the fruit. According to Genesis 5:3–4, Adam lived to be 930, and at least 800 of those years must be placed after the fall. If death was supposed to be the immediate result of their transgression, it was a long time in coming. Second, Adam and Eve *did* die when they ate the fruit because their disobedience cut them off from God, but their death was spiritual and not physical. All human beings are born spiritually dead, even though they are physically alive, and those who are born again in Christ have no fear of physical death, although they must still experience it. The one does not automatically entail the other, and it is clear from the context that, if we are to understand it literally, then it must be spiritual as well as physical death that God was warning Adam and Eve about. That makes perfect sense, since it is hard to see how physical death alone could be adequate punishment for what was clearly a spiritual offense.

The implications of this for our understanding of human beings, as well as of the material world, are far-reaching. Some people have thought that physical death did not exist before the fall, but there is no statement to that effect in Scripture and it goes against what we know about the life cycle of plants and animals. If natural death is the result of sin, why does an oak tree live far longer than a rose, or some kinds of tortoise survive ten or even twenty times as long as a dog? Restricting ourselves to human beings, can we say that the improved life expectancy in modern developed countries means that people living in them are somehow less sinful than others, or than earlier

---

[7]Gen. 3:22.

generations? That is a monstrous idea, but it is the logical consequence of such a theory of the results of the fall.

Here we are dealing with what is primarily a spiritual matter, and everything we say about sin and death must be understood in those terms. Given that human beings are both spiritual and material creatures, it is only to be expected that what touches us spiritually will have material consequences. But there is no simple correlation between the two, and to use evidence from the material world (such as disease, for example) as an index or guide to the spiritual state of a particular individual or group is to misunderstand the nature of the fall. The material world we live in is the common inheritance of every human being, and the exposure to its dangers to which we are subject is the same for us all. In this life, it is possible to be born again spiritually and enjoy the firstfruits of eternal life in fellowship with God, but we cannot so easily escape from the world of sin and death. For that to happen, our physical bodies must die and be raised again to a new and heavenly life which we have been promised. That life is real, but because it remains outside our experience, it is largely beyond our understanding.[8]

ORIGINAL SIN

Theories of sin which treat it as an inherited physical defect are wrong, but they do point to something very important. The fall of Adam and Eve had consequences for the entire human race that are no less serious now than they were then. It is not true to say that children are born without sin and that they "fall" into it at some point in their early lives, but that belief is remarkably widespread, whether or not it is openly acknowledged. The problem it creates can be seen most clearly in the questions that arise about the spiritual state of those who die in infancy or who never acquire the mental capacity to sin in a way for which they can be held responsible. Many people have a strong desire to believe that a child who dies before reaching the age of accountability is sinless and will automatically go to heaven, and the temptation for a pastor to offer this assurance as a consolation to bereaved parents can be overwhelming. Even people who believe that only those who have made a personal decision for Christ will get to heaven would not be so heartless as to tell the grieving parents of a stillborn child that it has gone to hell, although the supposedly necessary decision has not been made.

Very few people pause to consider that, if this way of thinking were correct, there would be a distinct advantage in dying young, and those who

---

[8] 1 Cor. 15:35–57.

reached an age where they were likely to fall into sin would be in serious trouble. Yet only a mentally deranged parent would put his or her children to death in the hope of ensuring that they would go to heaven before losing their innocence, and no Christian church can accept such an interpretation of human sinfulness. From a more positive standpoint, it would presumably be possible to shield children from sin and have them grow up with no need of a Savior, but that never happens and is against the plain teaching of the Bible.[9] Whatever the explanation is, there has to be more to sin than the mere choice of each individual that he or she makes upon reaching the so-called age of discretion.

Do children have any spiritual advantage over adults? Jesus told his followers to let them come to him, because "to such belongs the kingdom of heaven," and he warned his disciples that unless we come to him with the same absolute confidence and trust that we find in little children, we cannot be saved.[10] It should be noted, however, that he says this to adults whom he expects to adopt that attitude, and not to the children to whom it comes naturally. Nor can a verse like this be used by Christians as an excuse not to grow to maturity in the faith as adults.[11] Childhood is a precious thing, and little children can have a living relationship with God just as much as a grown-up can. But it is also a stage on a journey toward adulthood and a preparation for the life we are meant to lead, not a golden age after which there can only be decline. As Paul said, "When I was a child, I spoke like a child, I thought like a child, I reasoned like a child. When I became a man, I gave up childish ways."[12] In his eyes, that was a good and necessary development, and it was what he was recommending to the Corinthian church. Exactly the same principle holds good for us. Elsewhere Paul tells us that the Old Testament law was a schoolmaster that leads us to Christ, the implication being that when Jesus came, the children of Israel were meant to become adults in their faith and understanding of the gospel.[13]

There is therefore no reason to believe in the spiritual innocence of children or in their superiority to adults in this respect, even though it is obviously true that a newborn baby has not committed any actual sin. Can the baby be blamed for what its parents or remote ancestors have done? This question takes us to the heart of what we call "original sin." Many people believe that, because Adam and Eve sinned, all their descendants have inherited a

---

[9]Rom. 3:23.
[10]Matt. 18:3.
[11]Matt. 19:13–14; Heb. 5:11–14.
[12]1 Cor. 13:11.
[13]Gal. 3:24–25.

propensity to sin, which they will exercise as soon as they get the chance to do so. According to their way of thinking, the only real difference between a baby and an older person is that the baby has not yet had the opportunity to demonstrate its innate sinful tendency. In a general sense, this is true enough, but if we think about it more carefully, we shall soon see that it is inadequate as an explanation for human sinfulness. Adam and Eve disobeyed God in a deliberate action that went against his revealed will, and in that way, they broke their relationship with him.

It is that broken relationship which we have inherited from Adam and Eve, and that is more serious than a mere sinful tendency that has not yet been activated. The first human beings were not sinners until they actually sinned, but we are not so privileged. The wrong relationship with God that we have inherited is a fact of life that we must live with, whether or not we have done anything to deserve it. To those who think this is unfair, consider how many other things we have inherited from our ancestors. Our very humanity goes back to them, as does almost everything we have in this life. I am a white man because my parents were white, but when I lived in an African village there were times when I regretted my skin color because it made me stand out in a crowd even when I did not want to.

Unfortunately there was nothing I could do about it. I am forced to live in the body I was given at birth, whether I like it or not. At the physical level, everyone accepts that we have inherited talents and tendencies which may be used for good or ill. We have to come to terms with these things and we discipline ourselves so that we get the best out of our inheritance and avoid the worst. Why should anyone object when we say that the same is true at the spiritual level also? In fact, the spiritual dimension to this is much fairer than the physical one is, because in spiritual terms we are all identical. Physically speaking, I may inherit brittle bones or a rare blood deficiency from my parents and may suffer in ways that do not apply to most other people. Alternatively, I may be musically or athletically gifted to a degree that most other people are not, and win fame and fortune as a result. In spiritual terms, however, I am just as sinful and in need of salvation as anyone else is, because at that level all human beings have inherited the same condition, which is a broken relationship with our Creator. Furthermore, whereas physical matters require attention to individual needs and conditions, so that there is seldom one solution that can be applied on a general basis, our spiritual problem can be dealt with by the act or acts of a single individual, as long as he is someone qualified to do what is necessary. To quote Paul,

> For as by a man came death, by a man has come also the resurrection of the dead. For as in Adam all die, so also in Christ shall all be made alive.[14]

What one man did wrong, another can put right. That this has actually happened is the glorious message of the gospel, which is the ultimate and only cure for the problem of what we call "original sin."

Original sin is not something we acquire but is part of the package called "humanity" that we are born with. We cannot wish it away, nor is there any treatment or exercise that will cure it or make it less debilitating. Spiritual problems can be dealt with only in a spiritual way, and it is here that we hit the glass ceiling that prevents us from rising up to the level of God. For original sin is not just a defect inherited from our first parents; it has also led to a commitment—a relationship, in fact—which the Bible refers to as being "enslaved to the elementary principles of the world."[15] These "principles" are not abstract ideas but evil spirits, of whom Satan is the chief. In other words, just as the goodness of Adam and Eve did not come from anything they did but from the relationship in which they were created, so our sinfulness does not come from anything we have done but from the relationships into which we have been born. One of these is a broken relationship with God, and the other is a dependent relationship with Satan. The former cannot be healed unless and until the latter is broken, which is why the message of the gospel of Christ cannot be expressed exclusively in terms of individual salvation, important as that is. I can and must be saved as an individual, but for that to happen, the power of Satan must first be broken. In other words, I can be saved by being included in God's victory over the powers of evil, but I cannot be saved without it.

Why are we held responsible for original sin, when it is clear that we did not bring it upon ourselves? Here there has been great disagreement among theologians, the effects of which are still apparent today. On the one hand, it is rightly said that we cannot be held guilty for sins we have not committed, even if we have derived some benefit from them. I am not responsible for the fact that my remote ancestors practiced slavery and amassed fortunes that to some extent are still the basis of the prosperity of much of the Western world. I have a responsibility to do what I can to correct the injustices that have resulted from this situation, but that is not the same thing as emptying my bank account and sending its contents to someone in the West Indies whose equally remote ancestors were enslaved. If restitution for real and imagined

---

[14]1 Cor. 15:21–22.
[15]Gal. 4:3.

wrongs were a cumulative legal obligation imposed on all the descendants of particular sinners, each new generation would be worse off than the one before it, and by now every one of us would be so overloaded with inherited guilt that we would hardly know which way to turn.

In the ancient world, however, and still today in many places, it was assumed that not only the consequences of sin but the responsibility to atone for particular wrongs is passed on from one generation to the next, creating the phenomenon that we call the "vendetta," as one tribe or gang seeks to avenge the harm inflected on them by members of another tribe or gang, even if those immediately responsible are long dead. The prophet Ezekiel dealt with this issue very firmly when he wrote,

> You say, "Why should not the son suffer for the iniquity of the father?" When the son has done what is just and right, and has been careful to observe all my statutes, he shall surely live. The soul who sins shall die. The son shall not suffer for the iniquity of the father, nor the father suffer for the iniquity of the son. The righteousness of the righteous shall be upon himself, and the wickedness of the wicked shall be upon himself.[16]

In the sense that sin is an act or series of acts committed by particular individuals, we can say that in God's eyes there is no inherited guilt, and that on the day of judgment each person will have to answer to God for his own deeds and/or misdeeds. As we have just seen, however, original sin is not an act but a broken relationship, and that is something we have inherited. Whether we call this "inherited guilt" or not is largely a matter of definition. It might be better to make a distinction here between "blame," which cannot be inherited and "responsibility," which can be. If we think of sin primarily in terms of "blame," it is misleading to say that we are guilty of original sin, because "guilt" suggests that we have done something to deserve it, which we have not. In that case, the words of Ezekiel would apply to our situation and there would be no inherited guilt at all.

Unfortunately, original sin is deeper and more serious than that. If it were the result of a sinful act on my part, I could offer to put it right by some form of compensation. If I had stolen something, for example, I could return it, and if I had offended someone I could apologize. Even if specific restitution were not possible, as it would not be if I were to eat a stolen piece of fruit, I could at least offer to pay for it or find something just as good to replace it. It certainly need not lead to a fallen world or an eternity cut off from God. The trouble

---

[16]Ezek. 18:19–20.

with original sin is that it is not something we have done but a condition we have inherited, so there is nothing we can do about it. At the same time, we cannot just accept it and get on with life because it entails a relationship of slavery to Satan, which is not what God wants for us. Whether or not we use the word "guilt" to describe it, the fact remains that we are in the wrong relationship with God and are responsible for that. The only way out of it is to put the relationship right, and that we cannot do because we have neither the power nor the freedom to do it. Unlike sinful acts, which have defined effects, a sinful condition is all-embracing. Even the good we do is done within that context and is quite unable to change it.

Broken relationships are different from sinful acts, and this difference must be taken into account in any discussion about whether we should be held responsible for them. I cannot be blamed for sins committed long ago by people I have never heard of, but I can be held responsible for repairing the damage they may have caused. If broken relationships have resulted, I may well be implicated in them whether or not I choose to be. Let us take a few well-known examples which will help to illustrate this. In the United States there is a long-standing bad relationship between white and black people which goes back to the days of segregation, which are still within living memory, and of slavery before that. No one alive today can be held personally accountable for that past, but everyone recognizes that for many centuries the white majority oppressed the black minority, and that the burden of responsibility for putting matters right lies mainly with the majority. This is something that all sides agree on, and although it would be an exaggeration to say that everything has now been corrected, it is fair to say that real progress toward reconciliation has begun.

In the United Kingdom, on the other hand, there is a long-standing rift between the (mainly Protestant) British and the Irish Catholics, which, like slavery in the United States, cannot be blamed on anyone living today. But in this case, it is less clear where responsibility for the problem lies, and the insistence of many on the Catholic side that all the blame lies with the Protestants has been a major factor in making the situation worse. Unless and until both sides accept that they share responsibility for what has happened, real progress toward a lasting reconciliation is unlikely to be made. In yet another example, the establishment of the state of Israel in 1948 was to some extent the result of guilt feelings in the Western world following the Holocaust in which 6 million Jews lost their lives. A Jewish homeland in Palestine was seen by many as a kind of compensation for that tragedy, but no one noticed that it was bought at the price of displacing thousands of Arabs, who had lived in the country for centuries and were in no sense guilty of causing the Holocaust.

For hundreds of years, Jews and Arabs got along tolerably well, but for the past two generations they have been at daggers drawn for reasons that originally had nothing to do with either of them. In this instance it is not at all clear who is to blame for what, nor is it easy to see how the wrongs of the past can be rectified, even though they have happened in living memory. Sadly, all the signs are that this situation will only get worse, as the list of atrocities committed by both sides against each other lengthens and their ability to understand each other's position diminishes with the passing of time. These three examples, and many more like them that could be cited, demonstrate how serious broken relationships can become and how hard it is to put them right once things have gone wrong. Yet they also show us that we must try to do something, since otherwise the brokenness will only continue to fester and become even more intractable as time goes on and the original causes fade from view.

In the case of the fall of Adam and Eve, the apportionment of blame is clear. The fault lies entirely with the human race, which must take full responsibility for the need to effect a reconciliation, even if achieving it is beyond our grasp. Unfortunately, many people refuse to accept this and think that God must bear at least some of the blame for what has happened to us. There are even those who would accuse him of being entirely responsible for the human condition, on the grounds that he could (and therefore, in their eyes, *ought to*) alleviate it immediately. The reasoning behind this is that if God is a God of love, he must be unable to tolerate suffering, whatever the cause of it might be. The idea that we might be responsible for our own misfortune is completely unacceptable to those who think this way, and they love to cite instances of so-called "innocent suffering" to prove their point. A baby who dies has done nothing wrong, so its death must be unjust. Here we are back to the concept that sin is wrongdoing, and therefore (in principle at least) avoidable. It is deeply offensive to human pride to have to accept the truth that our sinfulness is an inherited condition, and even worse when we realize that there is nothing we can do about it.

Original sin puts us out of fellowship with God. It is not a choice but a fact of life that we have to deal with, and for that we have no remedy at our disposal. We are not born innocent only to sin later on when we reach the so-called "age of discretion" and become aware of what we are doing. We are born like fish in an aquarium where we can swim around and perhaps even see something of the world beyond, but we cannot alter the fundamental limitations placed on our lives. If a fish manages to leap out of the aquarium and experience the wider world, it will die, because it cannot live outside the water it was born in. The same is true, spiritually speaking, for us. If we were somehow able to escape this life and experience God "face-to-face" we would also die, because we cannot live in his presence without being like him.[17] The miracle of salvation is not that we are spared death, but that (unlike a fish that jumps out of the aquarium) we are brought back from it to a new life which is capable of surviving in the changed conditions of the kingdom of heaven.

Being locked into the world of rebellion against God, we inevitably take on the characteristics of that world and live according to its principles, because if we did not adapt to our environment, we would not be able to live in it. Far from being a modern Darwinian concept, the "survival of the fittest" was well known to Jesus, who not only said, "The sons of this world are more shrewd in dealing with their own generation than the sons of light," but even commended them for their wisdom in this![18] He did not say that they were right to do what they did or that their intelligence would save them, but he recognized that, within the parameters created by sinfulness, they were doing their best to make the world work for them.

Once we understand what "original sin" is, we can begin to address the pastoral problems that arise when people who have not consciously sinned die. We cannot say that they are "sinless," because whether or not they have done anything wrong, they are born into the sinful state that affects us all. Perhaps in an unfallen world they would not have been born handicapped or died young, but we must be careful about this, because we cannot say that such things are the result of sin. When Jesus healed a man who had been born blind, he made it clear that the blindness had nothing to do with sin, but that it was intended to demonstrate the glory of God, and so it may have occurred even without the fall of Adam and Eve into sin.[19] Original sin cuts us off from God and creates the conditions under which we do things that are wrong, so it makes no difference how many actual sins we have or have not committed. Even if everything we do in this life is good, we are still sinners in God's eyes, because the fundamental relationship we have with him is broken. In this connection, babies and mentally handicapped people are in the same situation as the rest of us; it is not what they have done or not done, but who they are that counts in the sight of God.

Does this mean that we must condemn such people to hell because there is

---

[17]Ex. 33:20; Deut. 4:33; 5:26.
[18]Luke 16:8.
[19]John 9:1–3.

no evidence that they have repented? Not at all! Quite apart from the fact that it is God who judges and not us, we have no way of knowing why God deals with particular individuals in the way he does or what his ultimate purpose for them is. Christian parents understand that their children are a gift from God, and if they lose one, they know that God has taken that child to himself. They trust him for the child's salvation. God knows what he is doing even if we do not, and those who die in abnormal circumstances are in his hand. We grieve at their loss, but we do so with the spirit of Job:

> Job arose and tore his robe and shaved his head and fell on the ground and worshiped. And he said, "Naked I came from my mother's womb and naked shall I return. The LORD gave and the LORD has taken away; blessed be the name of the LORD." In all this Job did not sin or charge God with wrong.[20]

Here perhaps more than anywhere else, we must walk by faith and not by sight, praying to him for those whom we love and trusting him to do what is right for them, as he surely will.[21]

THE SPREAD OF SIN

When Adam and Eve were expelled from the garden of Eden, Adam was told that he would have to struggle to make a living, and Eve was warned that she would suffer pain in childbirth. She was also told that her desire would be for her husband, and that he would rule over her. Modern Christian feminists have interpreted this statement as a curse, and claim that it has been removed by the coming of Christ.[22] Is this the right interpretation? If it were, then the curse laid on Adam would also have been removed by the coming of Christ, but earning a living today is no easier than it was back then. Likewise, the pangs of childbirth are just as severe today as they ever were, although modern medicine can relieve the worst of them. Given this wider context, it would be strange if the only aspect of the curse that had been removed was Eve's subjection to her husband, and so we must conclude that, whatever it means, it remains just as valid now as it ever was.

Is it right to interpret Eve's desire for her husband and his rule over her as a curse? Eve was told that she would want to cling to her husband, and that his rule over her would not go against her will. It was Adam who bore the brunt of the punishment, and in comparison with that we should perhaps see

---

[20]Job 1:20–22.
[21]Gen. 18:25.
[22]Gen. 3:16.

Eve's destiny as something positive. In their adversity, the first couple were called to draw closer together and work out their relationship in a mutually beneficial way. Her desire for him was meant to be balanced by his concern for her, which is what "rule over" means. A good ruler does not tyrannize his subjects but takes care of them and furthers their well-being. If he abuses or exploits them, he suffers the consequences just as much as they do, and so it is not in his interest to do that. In the world outside the garden, Eve's task would be to love and care for her husband, and Adam's would be to guide and protect his more vulnerable wife from harm. After the fall, the different needs and gifts of men and women would no longer be taken for granted but would be exposed and come under increasing strain as they battled together against their common enemies. That is why their bonding could not be assumed, but it was nonetheless essential if they were to survive in a climate where sin would become increasingly dominant and oppressive.

As human beings multiplied, their relations with one another became more difficult, and they were soon at each other's throats. Even Adam and Eve's son Cain murdered his brother Abel, a chilling example of what the disruption of God's plan for human life could lead to.[23] Once murder entered the world, it would multiply and spread, as Cain himself realized. The ground that had been difficult for his father Adam to cultivate now became almost impossible, and Cain was reduced to the life of a nomad. He understood what it would mean to be homeless, and was afraid that, as a stranger, he would be killed on sight by anyone more powerful than himself. To prevent this, God put a mark on Cain so that he would be left alone. As with so much else in the story, this "mark" must have been symbolic, though it was clearly something that others would recognize. How? If it was something like a birthmark on his face, it would have been easy to see, but who would have known how to interpret it? In the ancient world, physical blemishes were usually taken as a sign of God's displeasure, not as evidence of his favor, so it seems very unlikely that it was anything like that. But if it were something less tangible, like superior intelligence, other people would have to get close enough to Cain to appreciate it, and he would probably have been struck dead before that could happen. The same would presumably have been true if it were a mark like circumcision, which would not be immediately apparent on first meeting and would probably have been discovered only after it was too late.

Precisely what this mark was is therefore impossible to say, but whatever it refers to, it is clear that God was protecting the human race from the consequences of their actions. This is the first instance of what we now call

---

[23]Gen. 4:1–16.

"equity," the procedure by which justice is mitigated in order to make life bearable for those who deserve a harsher punishment. The awful truth is that Cain could have paid the price of his wrongdoing only by being annihilated, which would have removed the restorative aspect of retribution. He could survive only by receiving God's mercy, but that meant that justice was not properly satisfied. The blood of righteous Abel still cried out for vengeance, and the file on him would not be closed until that need was met.[24]

The story of Cain and Abel teaches us that violence is an inescapable fact of fallen human existence. Disobedience to God is the rejection of the source of our life, which can only lead to death, a punishment which our sense of justice demands. If a sin has been committed, we believe that it must be paid for, and if that sin leads to death, then ultimately death is the only acceptable payment for it. This is made clear in the story of Cain and Abel even before Cain kills his brother. We tend to think that Cain was wicked and Abel good, but the story is not as simplistic as that. Both men knew that they were cut off from God because of their parents' sin. They also knew that they had to offer a sacrifice to God in order to demonstrate that they understood the need to put right their broken relationship with him. The difference between them was that Cain offered fruits and vegetables, whereas Abel killed a lamb and offered its blood in sacrifice. By doing that, Abel showed that he understood more deeply than Cain did the violent effects of sin and the nature of the sacrifice needed to deal with it. Sin had brought death into the world, and one death could be expiated only by another.

It is a constant temptation of well-meaning people to underplay the dire consequences of sin. Those who have had a fairly comfortable life and who have not suffered from the violence of others are often easily persuaded that blood sacrifices are barbaric. Cain's sacrifice seems more acceptable to them than Abel's because it was nonviolent and eco-friendly, whereas Abel felt that he had to do even more harm by killing an innocent lamb. People who think like that are more inclined to condemn Abel and exonerate Cain, and the fact that God did the opposite suggests to them that the ancient Israelites had a primitive view of God that we ought to abandon.

From a purely human point of view this reaction is understandable, but those who think that way have not understood how serious sin and our sinful condition are. Those who have suffered violence often demand retribution, which to them is nothing more or less than simple justice. There is considerable debate about whether the state is justified in imposing the death penalty, but there are plenty of instances where people take matters into their own

---
[24]Matt. 23:35; Heb. 11:4; 12:24.

hands and kill offenders without further ado. Nor is there much doubt that many of those directly affected by violence would not object to the death penalty being applied in their case, if not more generally. Such people have a greater understanding of Abel's sacrifice because they have experienced the horror of sin and violence for themselves and know what is needed to deal with it effectively. Abel was not a better man than Cain, but he was declared righteous by God because he understood the extent of his own sinfulness in a way that Cain did not. As the writer to the Hebrews put it, "By faith Abel offered to God a more acceptable sacrifice than Cain, through which he was commended as righteous, God commending him by accepting his gifts."[25]

Most telling in this respect is Cain's reaction when his offering was rejected. Instead of imitating his brother, which would have been easy for him to do, he killed him instead, thereby revealing not only that his understanding of sin was inadequate but that rather than correct it, he preferred to eliminate the man who set him the right example. Abel had slaughtered a lamb to satisfy God, but Cain killed his brother to satisfy himself, an observation that sums up the difference between the two men.

The story of Cain has provoked as much debate as that of his parents, and possibly more, because there are things about it that are even harder for us to understand. For example, if Adam and Eve were the first and only human couple, how could Cain have met strangers? Surely they would have been his brothers! And from where did he get his wife, if she was not his sister? These questions have puzzled interpreters since ancient times, and they continue to stretch our imaginations today. On the one hand, it is important for us to say that we are all descended from a single couple, because there is only one human race and we all share the same legacy of original sin. On the other hand, the biblical story gives the impression that there were other people around, but it does not explain who they were or how they were related to Adam.

There is a mysterious verse at the beginning of Genesis 6 which reads, "When man began to multiply on the face of the land and daughters were born to them, the sons of God saw that the daughters of man were attractive. And they took as their wives any they chose."[26] What can this possibly mean? Adam could not have multiplied without producing daughters, so presumably there was a considerable number of them before the "sons of God" came onto the scene. Who were they? They cannot have been angels, as some have thought, and the most natural interpretation, supported by the genealogy in the previous chapter, is that they were the direct descendants of Adam. The

[25]Heb. 11:4.
[26]Gen. 6:1–2.

implication is that by mingling with inferior stock (the "daughters of man") they diminished themselves and became even more corrupt than they already were. Where that stock came from we are not told.

This theme would return in later Israelite history, when marriage to foreign wives was forbidden for exactly this reason, and Christians too are advised not to marry outside the faith.[27] It is not improbable that the lesson we are meant to draw here is that if believers take unbelieving spouses, the likelihood is that it is their faith that will give way and not their partner's unbelief. The curious thing about these early chapters of Genesis is that if we consider them in the light of what we now experience, we have no problem with them—the world they describe is the world we live in, with all its interconnectedness and complexity. But if we try to work out how it got that way, we run into difficulties and come up against mysteries that we cannot solve. There is much that God has hidden from our eyes, and we must be humble enough to admit this. At the same time, we must also recognize that he has concealed some things from us in order to clarify others. What we understand from his Word is more than enough to tell us how serious our present condition is and how much we need to be reminded that God has reached out to save us from the fallen world we live in.

Particularly important for this are the genealogies, of which the one in Genesis 5 is the first and most detailed, giving not only the names of the patriarchs but also their ages. Fascination with the study of ancestry and numbers is still common today, although we normally go about studying them in a different way and would not usually connect the two as Genesis does. The great ages to which the ancients supposedly lived have been the object of much criticism, and it is not unusual for people to dismiss them as purely mythological. This is a great mistake. The ancients thought differently from us about such things, but they gave their calculations a great deal of importance, so it is no exaggeration to say that Genesis 5 was just as important and in some ways perhaps even more meaningful for them than the rest of the creation narrative. They connected with these genealogies and their high numbers in ways that made perfect sense to them, and if the latter no longer speak to us in the same way, the problem lies with our inability to understand them rather than with the original compilers or readers.

However we interpret the genealogies, certain things stand out clearly. The first is that the problem of sin and death was not resolved. However long an individual patriarch lived, in the end he died, with the sole exception of

---

[27]Ezra 10:2–5; 1 Cor. 7:39.

Enoch, who "walked with God, and he was not, for God took him."[28] Hebrews explains that because of his special relationship with God, Enoch was taken up to heaven without having to go through the ordinary process of dying.[29] In other words, even in those ancient times, salvation was possible, but it was highly unusual. It must be of some significance that Enoch lived on earth for a much shorter period of time than the others. He was only 365 years old when he was taken up, and it is tempting to think that this age was not accidental, since it is precisely the same as the number of days in a calendar year. Whether there is a connection between the two and what its significance might be if there is such a connection is unknown to us now, but this is a good example of the kind of question we should be asking of the text, which uses these figures for symbolic purposes, whatever their relationship to historical time may be.

Another thing that is clear from Genesis 5 is that the human race multiplied at a great rate, though our precise knowledge of this is confined to the line of patriarchal descent. The most significant thing for us to notice is that all of the patriarchs were made in the image and likeness of God, just as Adam had been. In terms of our fundamental humanity, there was neither improvement nor decline as the generations went by, and in terms of our nature, we are all what Adam and Eve were when they were created. It is also plain that the lifespans recorded overlap to a considerable extent, so that the succession of generations was not a transition from one historical epoch to another but a continuous process which enabled the traditions of the ancestors to be passed on without interruption. The extent of this interlocking can be seen from chart 18.1, on page 393, which shows dates from creation rather than in the more familiar "B.C." numbering.

According to this reckoning all the patriarchs except Noah were born before Adam died, and most of them were still living when Noah was born. This means that the connection between Adam and Noah, though not direct, is very close, with no fewer than six men living long enough to bridge the gap between them. Notice too that when Enoch was taken up to heaven, only Adam had died, and all the others, except Noah and his sons, had already been born. Notice in particular that Methuselah, the longest-lived of them all, died in the year of the flood. There is no indication that he was one of the wicked people who was drowned in it, so we may assume that the flood came immediately after his death, which marks the close of the prehistoric age. The fact that Methuselah died at 969, just short of his millennium, may also be significant, especially given the importance of that length of time elsewhere

---

[28]Gen. 5:24.
[29]Heb. 11:5.

in Scripture.[30] Note too that the timespan from the creation to the death of Noah is roughly the same as that from Abraham to Jesus, which may also be of some significance in helping us to understand how they are related to one another.

As shown in the chart, the chronology of Shem's descendants continues after the flood (see Gen. 11:10–32). Once again, the extraordinary thing is that all the patriarchs from Noah onwards were still alive when Abram (later Abraham) was born, and that he apparently set out for Canaan only five years after Noah died. It is also noteworthy how two of the patriarchs outlived Abraham and no fewer than six were still alive when Isaac was born. As with the pre-flood patriarchs, it is extremely difficult to know what to make of these numbers. The overall lifespans are considerably shorter than the ones before the flood, but they are still not down to the levels we would recognize today. There is no sign of any personal interaction between the people mentioned, other than the normal pattern of descent. We are not told, for example, whether Abraham went to visit Noah, or even whether he knew that Noah was still alive when he was a young man.

This stands in sharp contrast to the later patriarchs, who constantly interact on a personal level and whom we feel we know as human beings— Abraham, Isaac, and Jacob, along with their wives and children. Ancient lineage and contemporary reality meet and mingle in this genealogy as we make the transition from the prehistoric era into what we can reasonably call "historical times."

The significance of this for theology is that we are reminded of the close interconnections that exist between Noah, the man who, according to his father Lamech, would bring his people "relief from our work and from the painful toil of our hands,"[31] and Abraham, to whom God gave the covenant promises that would undergird the nation of Israel. The message is that, from the days of Adam, God had not left himself without a witness. There was always someone alive who knew him and who had been sent to do his will on earth, in spite of the general sinfulness of the human race. At the same time, the persistence of this ongoing witness was matched by a growing sense that conditions were getting worse. As time went on, knowledge of the one true God became rarer, people ceased to be able to communicate easily with one another, and mutual suspicion and hostility became a normal part of everyday life. Things got so bad that God sent the flood in the days of Noah, and it is noticeable how Noah's life separates what went before that from what was to come

---

[30]Ps. 90:4; Rev. 20:2–7.
[31]Gen. 5:29.

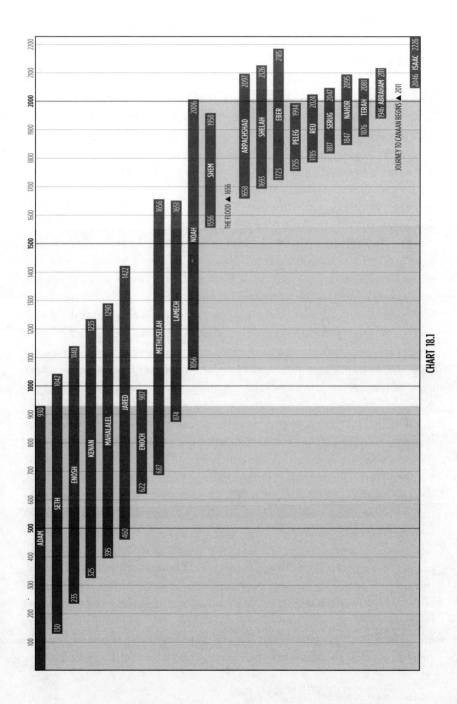

CHART 18.1

afterwards. There were men who bridged the gap between Adam and Noah, but the flood was a cesura. No one apart from Noah and his family survived it, and whatever connection later generations had with the world that had existed before the flood had to pass through him.

The flood was God's response to the spread of sin, but it did not bring human sinfulness to an end. As soon as the flood was over, it was back to business as usual as far as mankind was concerned. We see this in Noah's own family. After the flood, Noah turned to farming and planted vineyards, but he drank the wine to excess and got drunk.[32] Drunkenness was (and still is) regarded as shameful in the Middle East, and readers of this passage would have understood that this was a sign that Noah was exposing himself to sin. Sure enough, one of his sons, Ham, saw that his father was not only drunk but naked as well, but instead of doing something about it, he told his brothers. It was they, Shem and Japheth, who came to the rescue, and because of that, Ham and his son Canaan were cursed. This all sounds very strange to most people today, but in a society where family honor was paramount, the episode is very telling. Ham saw his father's faults but had no feeling of filial piety toward him, whereas his brothers knew that their first duty was to protect Noah and shield him from the disgrace he had brought on himself. When Noah realized what had happened to him, he put a curse on Ham as a reminder to future generations of how they should respond in such circumstances. It is no accident that Ham's son Canaan should be specifically mentioned as well, because the curse was not limited to Ham but would continue to do its evil work from one generation to another. The Israelites were the descendants of Shem, and many of the northern peoples, like the Hittites and Persians, were descendants of Japheth (we now call them Indo-Europeans). Between them, they would come to dominate the Middle East in later times, and the Hamites would lose out. The Canaanites in particular would later be conquered and effectively annihilated, and this story is told to explain why such a fate would befall them.

When God told Adam and Eve to be fruitful and multiply, he did not predict that entire nations would be destroyed in this way, but as sin spread, this became one of its inevitable consequences. The Bible makes it clear that all human beings are related to one another but that it is often the closest relationships that prove to be the most difficult. We are not told that Shem and Japheth fell out with Ham, though that is the clear implication of the story, but in later times enmity between brothers became almost the norm.

---

[32]The story is told in Gen. 9:20–27.

Abraham had to send Ishmael away because of the threat he posed to Isaac,[33] and the twins Esau and Jacob were rivals from the start.[34] Their conflict was prophesied even before they were born, and it continued for many generations. Esau became the ancestor of the Edomites, who were close enough to the Israelites to be assimilated to them (Herod the Great was an Edomite), but they were deadly enemies at the same time.[35] Jacob's sons even sold their brother Joseph into slavery in Egypt, an act which had the double effect of saving them from famine in the short term but in the long term enslaving their descendants in a foreign land and exposing them to persecution there.[36]

Sometime after Noah, mankind began to urbanize, a process symbolized by the construction of the Tower of Babel.[37] Rural and nomadic peoples tend to speak the same language and seldom get into serious conflict. But city-dwellers rub up against each other to a much greater extent, and their attempts to improve themselves by cooperative effort can easily lead to trouble. Urban life demands compromise and tolerance, and it soon becomes clear that people do not see eye to eye and therefore do not speak the same language. The confusion of tongues at Babel was a foretaste of things to come, as organized nations fought each other for dominion over the earth. Today we see how the spread of civilization is also the spread of weapons of mass destruction, and the ability to communicate with virtually everyone shows us just how little we agree on. Without a common foundation, however, we cannot live together in a functioning society. The great dilemma of the modern world is that we want everyone to live together in peace and harmony, but we also want everyone to be free to be themselves. Ultimately, these two goals are incompatible, but the architects of modern society prefer to ignore this. The lesson of Babel is there to remind us of the consequences of this willful blindness, but it is a lesson that sinful people will not and perhaps cannot learn.

To sum all this up, instead of spreading a blessing, the growth and expansion of the human race across the face of the earth brought a curse, and man's exercise of his dominion over nature became a tale of abuse and destruction, sometimes on a massive scale, of the beauty and resources that God had provided for him. Over time, whole species would be exterminated, and in some places the landscape would be altered beyond recognition by the greed and mindless exploitation of natural resources. People would fight each other for food and riches, as well as for territory, and in the course of history nations

---

[33]Gen. 21:9–14.
[34]Gen. 25:22–23.
[35]Obad. 10–14.
[36]Gen. 46:1–4; Ex. 1:8–22.
[37]Gen. 11:1–9.

would rise and fall without a trace. Eventually the world would become the armed camp that it is today, with a handful of people holding the power to blow up everyone else in a matter of seconds. The development of scientific technology has revealed the capacities of the human mind, but at the same time it has also provided the means for ever greater and more ruthless destruction. It is a sobering thought that the twentieth century, the period of the greatest human progress so far, which began with the widespread hope that the world would be won for Christ in a single generation, saw the spread of mass mur-der, genocide, and religious persecution on a scale thitherto unimaginable. Christians are as horrified by this as anyone else, but we are not surprised. It springs directly from the fall of man and the spread of human sinfulness, the consequences of which are still far from having been fully worked out.

THE FALLEN HUMAN MIND

The fall of Adam and Eve in the garden of Eden darkened the human mind. God is light, and to turn away from him is to prefer darkness, where evil deeds can be concealed.[38] Darkness facilitates concealment and deception, both of which are typical of rebellion against God. The evidence of the Bible seems to suggest that the descent of the human race into darkness was a gradual one, which makes perfect sense if we stop to think about it. Even though Adam and Eve were thrown out of the garden, they still had a knowledge of God which they could pass on to their descendants. As Paul put it, the problem was not that they did not know God but that they did not respect him as their Lord by obeying his commands.[39] Over time, the knowledge that was passed on diminished and was corrupted, leading to ever greater deviations from the belief and worship that the earliest generations knew. Eventually the situation became so bad that people were no longer able to recognize the truth, and rejected it when it was presented to them.[40] That is the world we live in, where the chief obstacle we face as Christians is the unwillingness of most people even to talk about God, let alone consider his claim on their lives.

The process by which this descent into darkness occurred is sketched for us in the Bible, but there are few precise details and there is much that we have to infer from experience. In the first stage after the fall, genuine knowledge of the true God continued to exist although the number of people who possessed it progressively narrowed. By the time of the flood it seems that only Noah was still worshiping God, even though he did not enjoy the kind of fellowship with

---

[38] John 3:19.
[39] Rom. 1:21.
[40] See Luke 16:27–31.

him that Adam and Eve had known in the garden.[41] How Noah expressed his faith we do not know, but it is clear that it rested on a personal relationship with God who guided him "in spirit and truth"[42] without any formal teaching. Noah did not have God's law in a written form, which presumably means that he had no detailed understanding of sin, but he obviously knew from the behavior of those around him that the world was in deep trouble because of mankind's ignorance of God.[43]

What we can say is that Noah knew enough about God to be saved from destruction, though it should be noted that no promise of eternal life was held out to him. He was preserved from death in the flood, but whether he eventually obtained eternal life is not clear. Perhaps he did, but it was not part of what God revealed to mankind at that stage. The New Testament tells us that after Jesus died he went to preach to the souls of those who had been imprisoned in the days of Noah, which may indicate that he and his believing contemporaries were eventually saved, but it also reminds us that the people of Noah's time did not know anything about the gospel of forgiveness and salvation.[44]

The next stage in the progressive fall of mankind seems to have occurred after the flood. There were still people like the children of Noah who knew about the true God and understood something of his plan and purpose for the human race, but it appears that they were no longer in personal contact with him in the way that Noah had been. The knowledge of God that they had was no longer based on a personal relationship with him but on the fact that, because all human beings are created in God's image and likeness, they have some innate idea of their Creator.[45] Our moral awareness reflects our knowledge of God's moral standards, and our conscience reminds us of what we should and should not be doing. But because human beings no longer know God personally, these things can easily get distorted. We all have an understanding of good and evil, but because we obtained it in the wrong way, the content we give to these words is not necessarily what God intends. Our idea of what is "good" may amount to no more than enlightened self-interest, although that is not always the case. Many people can testify that there is pleasure to be derived from doing the right thing, and making sacrifices often produces a sense of achievement in which we can take pride and which we can offer to God as evidence that we are sincere in our desire to please him.

---

[41]Gen. 6:9.
[42]See John 4:24.
[43]Rom. 7:8 says that sin was dead without the law.
[44]See 1 Pet. 3:18–20.
[45]Rom. 1:19–20.

Even today, there are people all over the world who justify themselves in this way. They try to do good and to stay out of trouble, and believe that if they succeed in sticking to their own standards, God will endorse their conduct and admit them to heaven when they die. Such people may not be particularly "religious" or have much time for things like theology and worship, but they feel that if God exists and is the God of love that Christians say he is, he will be fair to them on the day of judgment. By that, of course, they mean that he will recognize their good intentions and let them into heaven on the strength of them. Meanwhile there is no need for them to think too hard about it or to put themselves out unduly because that would be hypocritical and God does not want hypocrites. What we have here is the best and cleverest form of Satanic deception, and the hardest one to crack. Lots of good, decent, kind human beings doing their best to lead honest and respectable lives without worrying about God is a "win-win" situation as far as the Devil is concerned. The world these people live in is a pleasant environment, where no one gets fanatical or unpleasant about what they believe and everyone ends up in heaven. From Satan's point of view, what better example of concealment and deception could there be than that?

Once this mentality takes hold, it is only a short step from holding beliefs about God that are essentially true, to modifying them in subtle ways that ultimately falsify them. For example, we may say that God is love but then interpret "love" in a way that excludes the God of the Bible. If the God of love we want to believe in is incapable of sending anyone to hell, then we have created an image of God that goes against what we find in Scripture and is false, however much we might want to believe it. It is difficult to find clear examples of this tendency in the Bible itself, but it is a common phenomenon nowadays, when many people have been persuaded that the traditional view of God is outdated and needs to be replaced. Accusations against God include claims that he is a misogynist, a child abuser who tortured his own Son, and a killjoy tyrant whose main aim is to make everyone miserable. It is therefore hardly surprising when people feel that we need a more user-friendly deity today. Others may be less negative in their assessment, but they still think that the picture of a God who saves some people but not others must be wrong. They do not believe that God revealed himself in that way and they put the blame on ancient Israel's chauvinism instead, but whatever line they take, the end result is the same. The traditional image of God must go and be replaced by something more to the liking of what they like to call "modern man."

There are several things wrong with this sort of approach. First of all, it creates a deity who reflects our contemporary value system, whether it is right

or wrong, and ignores that of both past and future ages. Can we be so confident that our generation has a better grasp of these things than other ages had
or will have? Second, it causes controversy when modern ideas are unsettled
or in conflict with one another. For example, does God favor euthanasia or
oppose it? People today differ on this question, but does that mean that God
is undecided about it? Third, it risks creating different gods to suit different
human cultures. The "needs" of Western suburbanites may be nothing like
those of tropical rain forest dwellers, but can our picture of God be adjusted
to fit these different markets? What if there is a clash of values between them,
as there may well be over something like women's rights or homosexuality?
But most seriously of all, it is a view of God that denies the objectivity of his
being and of his self-revelation. There is no reason why human beings who
have fallen away from God should find him comfortable to live with, and every
likelihood that the exact opposite will be true. If we are no longer in tune with
God, we have to expect that our understanding of what he is like will probably be faulty. Refusing to accept this, and insisting that we have some right
to refocus the traditional image of God in order to suit our own priorities and
prejudices, is basically a denial of the fall and its effects. Once again, the truth
is concealed and we are deceived. Even worse, we become agents of our own
self-deception, colleagues of Satan and not merely his servants or his victims.
What a victory for him that is!

Once false beliefs start to control the human mind, it becomes increasingly difficult to recognize the true God, even if some vague acknowledgment
of the existence of a "great spirit" persists in some quarters. When things
reach this stage, the human mind starts to look for other ways of describing
divine or transcendent power and how we gain access to it. It is interesting to
reflect on how Satan handles this situation. Men and women are ultimately
in his grip, but for some reason he has never compelled or even encouraged us
to worship him instead of God. Satanism does exist, but it is a minority pursuit and cannot be said to have attracted a broad following. There was much
debate in the early church about whether pagan idolatry was devil worship
or just a human invention with no substance, but in a sense it does not really
matter one way or the other. The Devil is much too clever to invite people to
worship him openly and is quite happy that those who do so should continue
to be regarded as eccentric. As the source and archetype of all sinfulness, his
natural preference is for concealment and deception, and this extends to his
relationship with us. If he cannot persuade us to worship the true God in the
wrong way, then he will get us to channel our spiritual energies into creating

gods or ideals for ourselves that will take God's place and fill the spiritual vacuum thus created.

It has been said that those who do not believe in God are not people who believe nothing, but people who will believe anything. In the officially atheistic Soviet Union superstition was rife—and was often encouraged by the authorities who saw the need to fill the void left by the abolition of religion. Many people in Western countries have abandoned Christianity only to turn to so-called "new age" cultism, with its absurd collection of irrational beliefs. This is exactly what Paul says when he writes, "Claiming to be wise, they became fools, and exchanged the glory of the immortal God for images resembling mortal man and birds and animals and creeping things."[46]

In ancient times the innate human need to come to terms with the spiritual world took the form that we now call idolatry. People made gods for themselves, projecting their moral and spiritual values onto inanimate objects and sometimes even creating elaborate divisions of responsibility which were parceled out among the different deities. They came up with a god of war, a god of love, a god of rain, and so on, each of which did what he or she was supposed to do when asked or propitiated in the right way. Failure to obtain the right results meant that the gods were angry, and that in turn led to further acts of worship and propitiation in the hope of changing their minds. That kind of behavior is foolish, and even in ancient times it was denounced by intelligent people who saw through it, but it had a powerful hold on the popular imagination. So strong was this way of thinking that after the rise of Christianity, much of it drifted into the church, where it was "baptized" by being turned into the cult of saints and relics, which still flourishes today.

In this form, ancient idolatry has once again become very subtle. Attached as it now is to Christianity, it can claim to be linked to the worship of the true God, whereas in reality it is often in direct competition with it. Yet rather than try to suppress it, large parts of the church have preferred to regulate and control it, hoping thereby to channel popular piety in a Christian direction. Pagan gods have been assimilated to Christian "saints," and pagan shrines have been turned into churches. Rituals that go back to pre-Christian idolatry have been quietly "Christianized" and allowed to continue, often with little or no change. It is a trap into which not only simple believers but sophisticated church leaders have fallen, and its Satanic character is betrayed by the way it deflects people away from God by getting them to concentrate on those who are near to him instead, like the Virgin Mary and the officially canonized saints.

---

[46]Rom. 1:22–23.

Praying to Mary or the saints for help instead of going directly to God can even be made to appear humble and pious, because rather than disturb the Master, his lowly servants bring their petitions to the courtiers, who can then intercede with the Lord on their behalf. It is a diplomatic approach, well suited to an oriental court, but Jesus invited people to come to him without hesitation, and rebuked his disciples when they tried to "protect" him from the masses.[47] We are told in the New Testament that there is only one mediator between God and man, the man Christ Jesus,[48] and to create a hierarchy that blocks direct access to him is to deny the essential foundation of our relationship with God. Getting people to turn away from God by persuading them that they are too insignificant to relate to him directly, and at the same time offering to provide alternative channels to attract his attention is yet another, very clever trick of the Devil, who will turn us away from God even as he promises to give us access to him.

Idolatry, as it was known in the ancient world, has now largely disappeared, and even in its Christianized form, the cult of saints and relics tends to appeal mostly to the uneducated. But if its cruder forms have either vanished or been sidelined, the spirit that brought them into being is alive and well. The essence of classical idolatry was the worship of a creature instead of the Creator. The impulse to shift attention from the subject to one of the objects came from the belief that it is man and not God who is the measure of all things. Instead of looking up to his Creator and honoring him as the source of human prosperity, man sought to improve his own lot and claim the credit for whatever successes he might have. In the process, the certainty of God's revelation was exchanged for the vagaries of human imagination.

Thinking that his own ideas were not only wise and sensible but sufficient to meet any need that might come along, man sought to create his own version of heaven. The snag was that, by definition, this could not surpass the limits of his own mind, and those limits were determined by the framework of the created order. In the Old Testament, we see this at work in the pattern of divine self-revelation, where God tells us what he is like by using created things as pictures to help us understand him. There, even a concept like "heaven" has a double meaning, referring to the sky above us which is basically part of the material world, but also to the spiritual realm of God's presence which is hidden from our eyes. You can take God out of the picture and the physical heaven is still there, but it will no longer point to anything beyond the created order. The man who has abandoned belief in a transcendent God fills

---

[47]Matt. 11:28; 19:13–14.
[48]1 Tim. 2:5.

this space with his own ideas, which take the place of the divine and acquire a comparable status.

At the most basic level, we see this happening when the reproduction of human life is elevated to the level properly reserved for the creative power of God. Human sexuality is deified, either in a fertility cult (as was common in antiquity) or in the glorification of sexual intercourse that we see everywhere in the modern world. Even the word "love" has now been thoroughly perverted in the interest of sex, so much so that it is hard for some people to imagine how there can be love without it. The curious thing about this is that the more sexuality is deified, the more it tends to distance itself from the reproduction of the species, even though that remains its fundamental biological purpose. Contraception, abortion, and homosexuality all restrict or deny reproduction, and when sexual activity is glorified as an end in itself, it is no accident that such things acquire great prominence. In this cult of sexuality, promiscuity is presented as a form of liberation and physical satisfaction is regarded as the highest good. The reality, of course, is that sexual distortion and excess lead to sterility, disease, and death, not to the increased happiness and fulfillment which the Satanic promoters of sex-based lifestyles claim will be the result. Once again, concealment and deception are the order of the day, and the Satanic character of the whole thing is cruelly exposed.

Freedom of speech and information has become an excuse for the dissemination of pornography, and things that earlier generations would have regarded as shameful are now offered to us as a matter of course, with even young children being exposed to premature sexualization on a frightening scale. So-called sexual liberation has led to widespread relationship breakdown, with all the heartache, loneliness, and cynicism that comes with it. All too often, what is presented as freedom has degenerated into another form of slavery, and those trapped by the false promise of blessing have reaped the inevitable curse instead. This plague appears everywhere, because it is in the heart of man and will resurface wherever human beings are allowed to express themselves naturally without restriction. The "permissive society" in which we live is one in which immorality is not only legal but popular and often encouraged as an expression of personal "freedom," when in fact it is the very opposite.

More sophisticated than this, but just as harmful, is the elevation of human ideas to a quasi-divine status, with the inevitable consequence that people are trapped into serving those ideas as intellectual idols. The links between the erotic and the intellectual have been apparent ever since the time of Plato, who saw homosexuality as a means of sublimating the lusts of the former to the demands of the latter, so we should not be surprised to find the same connection being made by Paul.[49] Students of our contemporary world have also recognized that the development of modern ideologies has often been accompanied by an explosion of violence and a lust for domination that have close parallels in the erotic sphere and may well be a sublimation of it. Moreover, it does not really matter what the ideology is. Fascism and communism were quite different in the way they analyzed and sought to manipulate human society, but the practical outcome was virtually identical and there was almost nothing to choose between them.

The same is true, though in a much more subtle and sophisticated way, of the liberal humanism that now dominates most Western (and supposedly "post-Christian") societies. Whether the context is fascist, communist, or liberal humanist, belief in God is relegated to the private sphere and is generally discouraged. People are told that religious faith is regressive and harmful to human development. Different reasons are given for saying this, but it does not really matter what they are. This is because, on the one hand, they can all be refuted without much difficulty, and on the other hand, they are not the main factors motivating the suppression of religion. The deification of human reason is not in itself rational; pretending that it is misses the point. If "reason" really were the standard by which everything else must be measured, then not only would it have to be a faculty present in every human being (which it is, barring exceptional cases of mental handicap and so on) but it would also have to operate in exactly the same way in everyone, and it is by no means certain that it does.

Rationalists will argue that, in principle, the human mind is the same in every individual, although they are usually prepared to admit that not everyone is sufficiently skilled to be able to employ it without distortion. As they see it, the human brain is like a computer which processes the data fed into it in clearly defined (and definable) ways. If that does not happen, then there is probably something wrong with the computer, which then has to be dismantled and rebuilt in order to find and eliminate the defect. The human brain, as our inbuilt computer system, also has to be put right in the same way, which is why brainwashing, as this process is called, is such an important part of the process. A liberal humanist society does this in a more sophisticated way than either a fascist or a communist state is capable of, but it does it all the same. God has no place in the system and so he is edited out, not by force perhaps, but by other, more subtle means.

The end result of this process is that today it is no more acceptable to

---

[49]Rom. 1:24–27.

speak seriously about God in Western democracies than it was in the Soviet Union. Those who do so are regarded as being socially divisive and potentially dangerous. Religion has now been identified with so-called "fundamentalism," and that in turn is widely thought to encourage terrorism against modern multicultural and pluralistic democracy. Commentators who draw this kind of conclusion usually make no attempt to distinguish between Christian students preaching the gospel on a university campus and Islamic jihadists seeking to bomb Western embassies in Third World countries—and in the popular imagination, these two very different phenomena have become one. The only difference is that it is much easier to discipline students than it is to eliminate terrorists, and thus Christianity is gradually being eliminated from serious public discourse, even if it is still tolerated as a cultural heritage or a private eccentricity.

Perhaps the worst manifestation of this tendency is the demand of the liberal establishment that we should be tolerant of those whose lifestyle is radically different from ours, but that we need not tolerate those who disagree with generally held opinions such as the belief that religion is purely subjective. This means that no religious position can claim to be uniquely true, and therefore all must be treated equally. At one level there is nothing objectionable about this, and we must certainly accept the right of everyone to worship (or not) as they wish. At the same time, however, we cannot accept that all religious views carry equal weight. No expert in any other branch of knowledge would take seriously the opinions of those who know nothing about it, but in spiritual matters, the modern mind tends to assume that there is a level playing field, because spirituality is merely the expression of an inner experience of life and cannot be challenged by any objective criteria. If that is the case, Christian beliefs are no more or less valid than any others, and there is no compelling reason why anyone else should accept them. Proselytization or evangelism must therefore be ruled out on the ground that it infringes on the rights of others to think whatever they like.

No Christian can agree with this. We cannot define tolerance as a willingness to accept opinions about spiritual matters that differ from what is revealed in Scripture. We do not countenance the persecution of such people, but we do believe that we can and must try to persuade them that they are wrong, and we must warn other people not to listen to their message. The human mind has fallen away from God and is incapable of finding truth on its own. Anyone who claims to have done so must be resisted by those who have received the truth revealed in Christ.

The paradox of our current situation is that we now live in a world where "religious freedom" is more widespread than ever before, but at the same time the rule of Satan and his accomplices is also more powerful and more far-reaching than ever. It is perfectly true that there is no compulsory religion among us (as there is in Saudi Arabia or Iran, for example) and that even in countries where there is a state church, no one is forced to belong to it or to support it financially. Any kind of heresy or blasphemy can be expressed in the public sphere, the only constraint being the tendency of so-called "public opinion" to reject statements that are obviously false, offensive, or obscene. But even these conventional restrictions are breaking down. A generation ago it was still shocking to suggest that Jesus and his disciples might have been homosexual, and those who did so could be prosecuted with popular backing. But although this view is still regarded as highly improbable and is not accepted by any reputable scholar as historical fact, it is no longer inconceivable that some people will promote the idea as ancillary to their own agenda and get away with it, because such opinions are no longer regarded as obscene and the assumption is that only those who are homophobic will be offended by them.

But if religious freedom in terms of belief and doctrine is now virtually absolute, it is highly restricted in other ways. In the United States, hardly anyone would now dare to pray openly in a public place, although what harm that does has never been explained. In the United Kingdom, nurses have lost their jobs for offering to pray for patients, even if the patients themselves have no problem with this. Even worse, people have been dismissed for giving even the slightest hint that they are Christians, for example, by wearing a cross around their necks. Elected representatives of the people can express religious convictions if they wish, subject only to ridicule by the media, but academics have to be more careful. Anyone who tried to write a history that referred to God as a providential cause of events would be severely criticized and possibly dismissed, and for a scholar to refer to the resurrection of Jesus as a plausible historical event is almost out of the question. Denying it, on the other hand, is perfectly acceptable and not regarded as a legitimate cause of offense. Things have gotten so bad that even supposedly "Christian" publishers now put out books using the so-called "Common Era" dating system, which is nothing but a secularization of the (politically incorrect) Christian calendar. Even something as apparently trivial as this has become the object of concealment and deception, since there is no explanation given as to why our current dating system should be what it is, let alone be regarded as "common."

Today we live in a world where most people are "free" in any number of trivial or perverse ways, but where thought control on a global scale is more pervasive than ever. What is more, we are taught to believe that this is "progress," and so effective is the brainwashing we have received that most of us actually believe that it is. For example, does anyone nowadays really think that life was better a hundred years ago? Objectively speaking, we could say that in many ways it was. Among other things, local communities were more cohesive than they are now, family life was more stable, and it was possible to travel almost anywhere in the world safely and without a passport. But the technological advances that have occurred since then have been so great that it is easy to present a counterargument, and because we have become so attached to our electronic devices that we cannot imagine living without them, we are easily persuaded to believe in the march of "progress." What did people do before television was invented? A foolish question, one might think, but one that puzzles those who cannot remember that far back. It reminds us of the power technology has to shape the way we perceive reality.

The truth is that the freedom of the modern world is a deception, and may well be the most effective one that Satan has so far managed to inflict on us. The popular belief that things can only continue to get better conceals the fact that in many ways they are getting worse. Certainly the profligate and irresponsible way in which we are using up irreplaceable resources like oil and gas is bound to come back and hit future generations, as is the debt mountain that we are creating to finance our current excesses. We live quite happily as if there were no tomorrow and prefer not to think about it, which is a deeply irresponsible stance, but one that suits our contemporaries very well. Any attempt to bring a spiritual dimension to bear on this issue is rejected from the start, so that Satan does not even have to hide—public opinion as shaped by the media conceals him from us and does his work for him. We have come a long way since the days of Adam and Eve, but the current state of the fallen world is no better now than it was then. Sin has spread more widely and taken root in ways that would have been unimaginable in the days of Noah, and if that has been the pattern in the past, we can only assume that it will get worse (and doubtless also more subtle) in the future. The spiritual battle that we wage in the name and service of Jesus Christ has not diminished over the years but has grown more intense, and the struggle seems set to increase even more as the end of time approaches. The only consolation we have is that when the final judgment comes, the secrets of our hearts will be laid bare, and it will become plain to everyone who are the sheep who will enter into the joy of the Lord because they have been faithful in spite of everything, and who are the goats who will be cast out because they have served God with their lips only, while their hearts have been far from him.[50]

SPIRITUAL DEATH

The most severe effect of the fall of the human race, and the thing that makes everything else pale into insignificance, is the fact that we have been cut off from the tree of life.[51] Adam's disobedience was spiritual, and the death which has spread to everyone as a result of it is spiritual also. Spiritual death is the reality that governs the lives of everyone born into the world since the time of Adam.[52] It does not mean that we have ceased to be spiritual beings, nor does it imply that our spirits are somehow dormant. In one sense they are alive and active, but not in the way that God originally intended. We are spiritually dead, not because we have ceased to exist but because we are in subservience to Satan. It is for that reason that everything we think, say, or do belongs to the realm of spiritual death. The knowledge of God that remains in us no longer gives us life but condemns us by revealing the true nature of our spiritual state. Even God's law is a sentence of death because it is too holy for us to be able to keep, and the more we know about it the more desperate we become.[53]

Spiritually dead people are not troubled by their condition because they are unaware of it, just as people who live in the dark do not realize it until the light appears. When that happens, however, they are not automatically transformed into obedient children of God. Instead, they are blinded by the light because in their fallen spiritual condition they cannot bear it. Paul's description of this is both telling and chilling:

> We know that the law [of God] is spiritual, but I am of the flesh, sold under sin. I do not understand my own actions. For I do not do what I want, but I do the very thing I hate. Now if I do what I do not want, I agree with the law, that it is good. So now it is no longer I who do it, but sin that dwells within me. For I know that nothing good dwells in me, that is, in my flesh. For I have the desire to do what is right, but not the ability to carry it out.[54]

Paul is speaking not as a man who is spiritually dead but as a child of God who has been enlightened by his Word. He not only understands what is right but he accepts it and wants to do it. The trouble is that he cannot do what he wants because there is a law of sin and death at work in him that has a mind

---

[50]Matt. 25:31–40.
[51]Gen. 3:22–23.
[52]1 Cor. 15:22.
[53]Rom. 7:10–11.
[54]Rom. 7:14–18.

of its own and acts according to its own principles. This is what Paul calls the "flesh" because it is the sum total of our human inheritance from Adam and Eve. The spiritual life that Paul has received in Christ is not a resuscitation of his Adamic spirit but the life of Christ that has come to dwell in him.[55] Paul does not deny that he has to go on living in the flesh and dealing with the spiritual death that he has inherited from Adam, but he lives by faith in Christ and not by some inner transformation that has given him a renewed ability to respond to God. Christian faith is not a self-help technique that empowers believers and allows them to develop their hidden potential. On the contrary, it is death to self, because as Paul says in this passage, nothing good dwells in us by nature.

Some people want to say that Paul is here describing the spiritual struggle of *unbelievers* before they come to Christ, as if such people are constantly frustrated by trying to do the right thing and failing. That interpretation is mistaken because it goes against the plain words of the text and contradicts our experience of spiritual life and death. A spiritually dead person does not suffer from any such inner conflict. Even if he knows what good is and wants to do it, he is not frustrated by his inability to achieve his aim for the simple reason that he adapts his goals to what is achievable. This is what the Pharisees were doing in Jesus' day, and it is why he condemned their good intentions so severely. It is only the spiritually alive person who knows what spiritual death really means because he understands that he cannot modify his goals in order to make them attainable. If God is present in our lives, then we have to accept that his standards must be ours, and that in our fallen state we cannot do what we know is right. We did not struggle with this until we discovered Christ, and we started to understand the problem only when Christ "discovered" us. It was then that we came to realize that we must cling to him for salvation because, without him, we could never have done the right thing on our own.

It is when we become spiritually alive that we understand that the spiritual death of our "flesh" is permanent and irreversible. There is no going back to the garden of Eden, however hard we try or however much we want to. By being united with Christ, we die spiritually with him and come back to a new life, which is at odds with the life we have inherited in this world. Some people go to be with Christ soon after believing in him, but most of us are called to continue living in our earthly state for some time. As long as we are still here we have to struggle against our human inheritance. It is only when this life comes to an end in our physical death that the effects of our spiritual death

[55]Gal. 2:20; Phil. 1:21.

in Adam finally disappear. When we are resurrected it will be to a new kind of existence in which our present physical bodies will be replaced by spiritual ones that are not infected by sin or subject to the disadvantages of the fall.[56]

Until that happens, we have to go on living in a world whose inhabitants have no understanding of this, and the closer we get to Christ, the more of a problem it becomes. New Christians are frequently overwhelmed with the joy and wonder of their new life and want to share it with others. It can come as a shock to them to discover that not only do many people have no idea what that is, but they do not want to find out either. Being spiritually dead, they cannot grasp what Christians are talking about. To them, death is purely physical and is a subject they often prefer to avoid because, although they know that it is coming, they cannot come to terms with it. Christians are not afraid to tackle the subject because we do not have to worry about it. We know that physical death is the great reality that stares us in the face every day that we live on earth. We understand that it is the basic truth that relativizes all our human achievements and negates our worldly claims to wealth and fame. "You can't take it with you" is a phrase often heard on the lips of people who are not believers, yet how many of them spend their lives laying up treasure on earth as if it were somehow a worthwhile thing to do?[57] There is surely no one more tragic than the rich fool who said to his soul,

> "Soul, you have ample goods laid up for many years; relax, eat, drink, be merry." But God said to him, "Fool! This night your soul is required of you, and the things you have prepared, whose will they be?"[58]

Too late, the rich fool found out the truth, but by then he was trapped in the vise of Satan. In the depth of his torment, we can imagine, he could see Abraham in heaven, and the poor beggar Lazarus, and he called out to them,

> "Father Abraham, have mercy on me, and send Lazarus to dip the end of his finger in water and cool my tongue, for I am in anguish in this flame." But Abraham said, "Child, remember that you in your lifetime received your good things, and Lazarus in like manner bad things; but now he is comforted here, and you are in anguish. And besides all this, between us and you a great chasm has been fixed, in order that those who would pass from here to you may not be able, and none may cross from there to us."[59]

---

[56] 1 Cor. 15:35–58.
[57] Matt. 6:19–21.
[58] Luke 12:19–20.
[59] Luke 16:24–26. It is not clear that the rich fool of Luke 12 is the same as the rich man of Luke 16, but as neither is identified and the principle is the same, I have taken the liberty of conflating them for this purpose.

From this we learn that spiritual death is absolute. Men and women who in eternity are alive in Christ cannot minister to those who have been condemned as this rich man was, even if they want to do so, and there is no "second chance" for the lost—because spiritual rebirth is not man's choice but God's. It is a hard saying, but there is no community of interest or even of understanding between those who have been redeemed and those who have not been. Death and life are radically incompatible, and those who have been condemned to the one or rewarded with the other must go their separate ways. This does not mean that we have no sympathy or understanding for those who have not come to eternal life. After all, Christians are people who once were just as dead in their sins as anyone else, and we have no reason to think that we are superior to them in any way. As Paul puts it,

> You were dead in the trespasses and sins in which you once walked, following the course of this world, following the prince of the power of the air, the spirit that is now at work in the sons of disobedience—among whom we all once lived in the passions of our flesh, carrying out the desires of the body and the mind, and were by nature children of wrath, like the rest of mankind.[60]

Knowing this ought to make us humble and give us a special concern for those who have not yet come to the knowledge of Christ. We pray for their salvation and do all we can to share the good news of the gospel with them in the hope that God will use our message to show mercy and turn their hearts to him in faith. We know that this is possible because it has happened to us, but we also know that it is a work of God which only he can do. As Paul goes on to explain,

> But God, being rich in mercy, because of the great love with which he loved us, even when we were dead in our trespasses, made us alive together with Christ—by grace you have been saved—and raised us up with him and seated us with him in the heavenly places in Christ Jesus . . .[61]

As Christians, we have been set free from spiritual death even though we still have to deal with its effects in this life. In spiritual terms, we have been seated with Christ in the heavenly places, an assurance that transforms our outlook and makes it possible for us to understand what our mission and our destiny are. Although our place in heaven is secure, however, we are still engaged in spiritual warfare because we are not yet free of the legacy of spiritual death

---

[60]Eph. 2:1–3.
[61]Eph. 2:4–6.

that we have inherited. Even knowing the truth does not stop us from fearing for our earthly future, and the temptations of this life continue to assail us until the day we die. Reason, common sense, and spiritual conviction are not enough to take this away, and we are liable to pursue the mirage of earthly well-being even when we know that God holds us in the palm of his hand and has promised to take care of us.[62] There is no logical explanation for this other than to say that Satan's powers of deception are at their most potent in his ability to keep us preoccupied with the cares of our earthly existence, even when we have the assurance that we are safe in the arms of our heavenly Father.

We fight not against flesh and blood, said Paul, but against spiritual forces.[63] Our human problems are basically spiritual ones, just as God's response is. It is in the spiritual realm that we live and move and have our being, and it is with spiritual strength that we are equipped to combat the evils ranged against us. Spiritual death is the enemy we face and the power that we do battle against. It is the fate we have been delivered from, but it remains the destiny of those around us, to whom we are called by God's love to preach the gospel of grace and the promise of eternal life that it contains.

---

[62]Matt. 6:25–34; Rom. 8:38–39.
[63]Eph. 6:12.

19

THE ORIGIN OF RELIGION AND ETHICS

REFLECTING ON THE MEANING OF LIFE

Some people go through life taking everything for granted, but those who stop to consider why things are the way they are will almost inevitably turn to contemplating whether there is a mind with a purpose behind it all, and if there is, what that mind might be like. In every tribe and nation in the course of history, men and women have pondered the mystery of our existence and have developed ways of understanding it. Not everyone has reached the same conclusions, but it would be fair to say that virtually every human culture has (or once had) some notion of what we call the "divine." All thoughtful people know that behind the world of sense perception there lies something more powerful than we are, which influences us in ways we do not fully grasp. To many people this is our "fate," and as far as they can see, there is nothing we can do about it. Others are less pessimistic and believe that we can at least try to persuade this hidden power to act in our favor, if we display the right degree of humility toward it and make the appropriate sacrifices to propitiate it. Whether that will be enough to do the trick is impossible to predict, but if something occurs to indicate that the higher power has been satisfied, the sacrifice that supposedly did this will probably be repeated. In time it will become a ritual that both those who perform it and those for whose benefit it is performed recognize and accept.

The assumption undergirding this logic is that, if it has worked before, it can work again. If the desired result is not forthcoming, the failure can be blamed on some inadequacy, either in the sacrifice or in the one making it.

If it is the sacrifice that is found wanting, the ritual will most likely be made more elaborate and demanding, in the hope that it will work better in the future. If it is the sacrificer who is thought to be at fault, he may be subjected to some further humiliation, often in the form of ritual purification, so that he may become worthy to offer the sacrifice. If that fails, he may be replaced by someone more suitable. Finally, there is always the possibility that the people on whose behalf the sacrifice has been made are themselves unworthy to receive its benefits, and in that case it is they who will be further humbled and "cleansed" of their faults. It does not take much imagination to realize that it is in the interest of the sacrificers to shift the blame for failure onto the people for whose benefit the sacrifices have been made, and that is usually what happens. The result is that the society in question will be governed by a respected (and feared) priestly caste protected by legal and other forms of immunity, while the majority of the people do what they are told and hope for the best.

Readers of the Old Testament will recognize these phenomena in the life of the people of Israel. The similarities between Israelite religion and the practices of other human cultures are well known, but the reasons for these similarities are hotly debated. Among secular historians and anthropologists it is often assumed that Israel's religion was pretty much the same as that of the surrounding peoples, and that things like animal sacrifice must be rejected as "primitive." Nowadays there tends to be greater respect shown for the customs of so-called "primitive" peoples, and this allows some anthropologists to be less negative in their assessment of ancient Israel, but they are no more inclined than their predecessors were to see Israel's religious practices as fundamentally different from those of its neighbors. Before the exile to Babylon in 586 B.C., it seems that Israelites often worshiped the same deities as other Canaanite peoples did and that the cult of Yahweh, the God of Israel, had to compete with them for supremacy. To the minds of many skeptical modern scholars, the Old Testament is the account of the victors in that struggle, who were naturally predisposed to believe that Yahweh was destined to win out in the end.

We cannot deny that the similarities observed by historians and anthropologists are there, but as Christians we put a different construction on them. At the most basic level, Israel and the other nations were grappling with real problems that cried out for a solution. They both knew that something was wrong in human life that could not be put right merely by changing people's behavior. Even with the best laws in the world, the fundamental flaw would continue to manifest itself and the only hope of dealing with it lay in appealing to a higher power. That this would require both humility and sacrifice in regard to that power was also universally agreed. The kind of religion practiced by the peoples of the ancient Near East, which has many structural parallels in other parts of the world even today, is easy to criticize for its polytheism and for rituals such as child sacrifice and temple prostitution, which seem to us highly immoral, but even in the most depraved of these cults there was a glimmer of truth. When Paul and Barnabas went to Lystra (in Asia Minor) to preach the gospel, they were welcomed as gods and, had they not protested, sacrifices would have been offered to them.[1] They corrected the mistake, of course, but in their preaching to the Lystrans they spoke about God the Creator as follows:

> In past generations he allowed all the nations to walk in their own ways. Yet he did not leave himself without witness, for he did good by giving you rains from heaven and fruitful seasons, satisfying your hearts with food and gladness.[2]

When speaking about pagans to the Romans, Paul described them in these words:

> What can be known about God is plain to them, because God has shown it to them. For his invisible attributes, namely, his eternal power and divine nature, have been clearly perceived, ever since the creation of the world, in the things that have been made. So they are without excuse. For although *they knew God*, they did not honor him as God or give thanks to him, but they became futile in their thinking, and their foolish hearts were darkened. Claiming to be wise, they became fools, and exchanged the glory of the immortal God for images resembling mortal man and birds and animals and creeping things.[3]

The picture is hardly flattering, but these two passages tell us something of great importance about so-called "primitive" or pagan religious practices. The pagans knew God in their hearts, and God continued to speak to them by the providential care that he lavished on them. They went wrong because they had no access to spiritual knowledge and found themselves looking for substitutes within the material universe. The result was absurd, but these people were neither atheists nor agnostics who were indifferent to the claims of faith. They knew there was a problem and were looking for the answer; what they needed was someone who could remove their blindness and show

---

[1] Acts 14:8–18.
[2] Acts 14:16–17.
[3] Rom. 1:19–23.

them what they were ignorantly looking for. They had invented gods and given them names, but they had little idea of how these gods were related to one another or whether there was some overarching principle that held them together. Sacrifice to one deity might not work, either because he (or she) was the wrong one to propitiate or because some other god might have the power to intervene and spoil it all. Their omnipresent spiritual world was chaotic and unpredictable, but they understood that they needed help from it. In his love for them, God had preserved enough awareness of that so that when the gospel came to them, they were ready and able to respond to it. The Lystrans may have been comically wrong to think that Barnabas was Zeus (Jupiter) and that Paul was Hermes (Mercury), but at least they understood that they were welcoming men with a message from heaven, and so despite their ignorance, they were closer to God than those who denied his existence altogether.

Israel was different from its neighbors because it was a nation formed by a man who had been called and chosen by God, but who also shared much of the background and outlook of his pagan contemporaries. There is no attempt in the Old Testament to deny this. Abraham came from Ur of the Chaldees, his nearest relatives lived in upper Mesopotamia, and several of his children became the founders of other pagan nations, a process that was repeated in the next generation with Esau. The genealogies preserved in the Old Testament make it clear that Israel's neighbors were also its cousins, and it was even possible for them to be rebuked for not coming to Israel's help in time of need.[4] What set Abraham apart from them was the fact that he had received a promise from God in return for his undivided obedience.[5] The written record tells us that it was Yahweh, the God of Israel, who had spoken to Abraham, even though he did not know that at the time.[6] God did not tell Abraham that the other nations were wrong to think about the human condition in the way they did. Perhaps this was because in many ways their instincts were right, although they did not know how to resolve the basic problem.

This is where Yahweh stepped in. By revealing himself to Abraham as the one true God, he brought order to Abraham's understanding of the spiritual world and gave him a focus for both his acts of self-humiliation and his sacrifices. But he did more than that. God required submission and sacrifice from Abraham and his descendants, not because he wanted to oppress them but because he intended to rescue them from their plight. Ritual activities, which in other societies were a kind of guesswork designed to impress unknown and

---

[4]Obad. 10–14.
[5]Gen. 12:1–3.
[6]Ex. 6:3.

capricious spiritual powers, were in Israel designed to explain what was wrong with the human race, how it had to be put right, and (most importantly) why no one on earth would ever be able to do that.

Israel's sacrifices were not intended to propitiate an angry deity; in fact, they were not meant to achieve anything in and of themselves. What God did with his people was to take the sacrificial principle with which they were already familiar and which was valid in itself, and restructure it into a pattern consistent with his love for his chosen people. Rather than being hit-or-miss attempts to achieve the right relationship with some fundamentally unknown higher power, the sacrifices of Israel were picture lessons meant to tell them how God would someday reconcile them to himself. This was made clear to Abraham when he was told to sacrifice Isaac, his only legitimate son and heir.[7] Abraham demonstrated the depth of his faith by obeying God, even though the command went against everything that he had been promised when his heir was born.[8] At the last minute, just as Abraham was about to plunge his knife into Isaac, God stopped him and pointed to a ram caught in the bushes, which he was to take and sacrifice instead. The story tells us that what God wanted from Abraham was not sacrifice but obedience, and when he saw that Abraham loved him more than his own flesh and blood and was prepared to obey him even beyond the limits of his own understanding, he was satisfied.

In due time God would sacrifice his own Son and do for us what we cannot do for ourselves. One day Jesus would humble himself and go to his sacrificial death in obedience to his Father's will, paying the price that had to be paid for our sins and that only he could pay. But essential as that sacrifice was, it was not by itself the ultimate foundation of our salvation. That foundation was love—God's love for his people, which led him to reveal himself to them in the first place, and the Son's love for his Father, which gave him the strength and the courage to do the Father's will, however painful and uncongenial to him it must have been. The meaning and the power of Christ's sacrifice lay not in the quantity of blood that he shed or the degree of pain that his body endured, but in the quality of his relationship to the Father. That principle was not new in Jesus' day but had been well understood for at least a thousand years before his time. As King David put it, "The sacrifices of God are a broken spirit; a broken and contrite heart, O God, you will not despise."[9] Israel was different from the other nations because instead of the fear that lay at the heart of their religions, Israel knew

---

[7] Gen. 22:1–18.
[8] Gen. 17:19.
[9] Ps. 51:17.

the love of God, which gave another meaning to their outward rituals, making those rituals both incapable of achieving the result for which they were originally designed and at the same time essential for showing what it was that God himself would one day do for them in love.

RITUAL AND MORALITY

The development of specific rituals is the basis of what we call "organized religion," and we can see this process at work in both the pagan and the Israelite worlds. We know too little about most pagan societies to be able to chart developments in detail, but there is no reason to suppose that they differed in any fundamental way from what we can see in the history of Israel. What seems to have occurred is that at some point, an unstructured religious culture developed fixed norms, or laws, usually centered around the worship of a particular deity. A god like Marduk, Aten, or Apollo became the focus of a cult which had its own places of worship and its own officers, or priests as we now call them. These priests were responsible for keeping the god happy by worshiping him in the right way and with the appropriate sacrifices, and the cult attracted devotees who practiced and over time developed ritual observances connected with it. Eventually, the cults of the different gods (and goddesses) were drawn together and some attempt was made to apportion spheres of responsibility among them. At that point, a pantheon emerged, often with one of the gods acting as "king" over the others, but without replacing them. Sometimes, as in ancient Greece and Rome, there was a designated "lawgiver," who more often than not was a larger-than-life but still historical character to whom this development was attributed. Once that happened, a polytheistic society could accommodate a wide range of religious practices, some of which might be mutually incompatible (such as sacred virginity and temple prostitution), but all of which could be embraced in the overarching pantheon.

The priests normally remained assigned to a particular deity, but their functions might extend to the publicly recognized pantheon, and as they did, they tended to become agents of civil government. As this happened, the rituals they performed took root and created bonds of human community that extended to every aspect of life. A cultic code was then elaborated that defined not only the nature of public worship and the position of those who conducted it, but also the behavior of the entire community. Failure to fulfill the requirements of the code was regarded as "sin" and created ritual impurity, which in turn required further sacrifice in order to propitiate the god or gods who had been offended by such transgressions. The more elaborate the system was, the more sophisticated this connection would be, until it reached the point at which every conceivable sin was provided with a corresponding sacrifice that had to be offered in order for it to be taken away.

In the modern world, it is customary for us to assume that the ritual observances of a religion will be tied to some form of morality, but that is not necessarily so. The pagan gods might easily demand that their adherents should propitiate them in ways that would not have been acceptable in ordinary life, the justification for this being that the gods are not ordinary. Thus we find that the gods might demand prostitution, murder, or even incest. In such a religion, immorality cannot be regarded as ritual defilement or equated with it, but it does have something else in common with the Christian notion of sin: disobedience. The person who goes against what is commanded by the gods is punished for his transgression and must try to find a way to atone for his temerity. At this level, even the most primitive religions reflect something that is true about the relationship between human beings and God, although they do not know how to express it properly. Sin is rooted in disobedience, and that disobedience must be atoned for, because the power that has issued the broken commandment has to avenge such an open attack on his authority, or else that authority will be lost.

Once again, we see how the development of ancient Israel often paralleled what was customary elsewhere. We know that the transition from an unstructured religion to a carefully regulated pattern of ritual observances occurred immediately after the escape of the people of Israel from their slavery in Egypt, and that the law which they were given was attributed to Moses, their great lawgiver. The cultic code contained in this law has a carefully worked-out pattern of ritual requirements, which is balanced in turn by a graded system of punishments designed to indicate and match the heinousness of particular offenses. The pattern of the sacrifices, the role of the priests, and the demands laid upon the people are all spelled out and the lawgiver's successors, who are not themselves part of the cultic system, are given the task of supervising it and ensuring that everyone does what is expected of him. In Israel, the succession to Moses passed to Joshua, then to a series of judges whose rule was spasmodic and unsatisfactory, and finally to a line of hereditary kings that lasted until the fall of Jerusalem in 586 B.C. On the surface at least, it would appear that Israel followed the standard pattern of the surrounding nations, with the exception that instead of worshiping a pantheon of gods, it focused on only one.

It would be idle to deny that there were resemblances between the cultic system of Israel and that of its neighbors, but once again, we must note that these similarities are superficial and deceptive. God worked with his people in ways that they would understand, and we should not be surprised to discover that Israel emerged as a religious state that is recognizable in terms of its historical environment. But the key difference is that Israel worshiped only one God, who would not tolerate any associates or rivals.[10] Neither would he accept any visual representation of himself, and when he finally permitted the erection of a temple and the establishment of a hereditary monarchy, it was only with the greatest reluctance that he did so. Such things are represented in the Old Testament as demands that came from the people who wanted to imitate their neighbors and who were even prepared to rebel against God in order to get their way.[11] In spite of this, however, the monarchy and the temple were integrated into God's purpose for his people, and in the end they both found their fulfillment in Christ, who (it would be fair to say) transformed them out of all recognition and broke whatever lingering connection there may have been in people's minds with the cults of the neighboring states.

Another important difference between Israel and the other nations of antiquity is that its human lawgiver was no more than the messenger of God, who was the law's true author. Because of this, the law was never just a functional arrangement for the good government of the state; it was from the very beginning a reflection of the divine character, and in that respect it transcended whatever political arrangements Israel might have or be subjected to. The laws of Hammurabi, Solon, and Lycurgus vanished with the states that recognized them, but the law of Israel has survived to the present day and is still regarded as fundamental by both Jews and Christians. This has been possible because Israel's law is basically moral and spiritual in nature. To break the law is not merely to harm a human victim, it is to offend God, whether or not there is a human victim involved.

Israel's law also differed from the ritual practices of the surrounding nations in the degree to which it can be regarded as moral. This is a controversial subject because not everyone has the same idea of morality to begin with. There are many people today who are appalled at the level of animal sacrifice demanded by the Mosaic rituals. There are also cases where God specifically directed his people to kill their enemies, which is likewise distasteful to most people today.[12] The problem is that all morality is related to behavior and therefore relative to the circumstances involved. Ancient Israel's primary

---

[10]Ex. 20:2–3.
[11]1 Sam. 8:1–22.
[12]See 1 Sam. 15:9–23; Ps. 137:9.

duty was to protect itself against being corrupted by the paganism of its neighbors, which had to be stamped out of the land promised to them by God. The destruction of their enemies was not mindless personal vengeance but a carefully planned exercise with specific goals in view. The same might be said in the case of animal sacrifice. The animals bore the sins of the people, and were put to death because the cost of sin was death. The rituals had a very specific and limited purpose, whose ultimate goal was the salvation of human beings. In the final analysis, the morality of the law of Moses is not an abstract concept tied to some ideal norm but a working out of the principle of love— love for God, in the first instance, and then love for neighbor. This is the way the Ten Commandments are set out for us, the first four relating primarily to our worship of God and the last six explaining the way we should treat other people. Viewed in that light, they are indeed moral, and as such they continue to exert a powerful influence on generations that have known nothing of the circumstances in which they were originally given to God's people.

One of the functions of law is to make sure that the punishment fits the crime, and Israelite law does this with respect to offenses committed against other people and their property. But behind that there lies something deeper— the offense such behavior gives to God, which cannot be so easily rectified. This dimension was unknown to Israel's pagan neighbors, because they lacked a unified vision of the spiritual world and did not know that they were answerable to a single all-powerful God. Their notion of propitiation did not include atonement, because they had no conception of having a relationship with God and so did not know that reconciliation with the spiritual power that controlled their lives was possible. Here again the Israelites were different because they believed that restoring the relationship they already had with God would provide a permanent solution to the problem of sin. Their temple sacrifices covered a wide variety of transgressions, but although the sacrifices were repeated on an annual basis (if not more frequently), that was not strictly necessary. During the seventy-year period (586–516 B.C.) when the temple lay in ruins, God did not abandon his people but used that experience to teach them that he loved them and cared for them, even though they were in exile and could not perform the sacrifices that the law prescribed. The truth was that God did not need or want sacrifices for their own sake; what he wanted was the love and obedience of his chosen people:

> If I were hungry, I would not tell you,
>   for the world and its fullness are mine.
> Do I eat the flesh of bulls

or drink the blood of goats?
Offer to God a sacrifice of thanksgiving,
 and perform your vows to the Most High,
and call upon me in the day of trouble;
 I will deliver you, and you shall glorify me.[13]

To sum all this up, because religion is a human response to a perceived problem in human life, we must not be surprised to discover that, despite the great variety of ritual and emphasis that we find in different cultures around the world, there are a number of common themes that recur. As long as the higher power being worshiped is undefined, propitiating it is bound to be a hit-or-miss affair, since it is impossible to know whether the sacrifices are on target. The uncertainty endemic in such a system makes its adherents particularly sensitive to the charge that it is inadequate, and when more highly organized systems challenge them, followers of undefined religions are liable to embrace them with enthusiasm. History shows how easily many tribal peoples have been won over to Christianity or to Islam for essentially this reason. In the Middle Ages the barbarian peoples of northern Europe, and in modern times the tribes of Africa and America, were largely Christianized (or in parts of Africa Islamized) in a generation or two, even if aspects of their former religions survived in different guises. Sometimes they were simply absorbed by the new religion, so that (to take one example) ancestor worship was transformed into prayers for (and to) the departed, but often the influences have been more subtle. The need to propitiate an offended deity carries over from one religion to another because it is more basic than either of them. The result is that the sacrificial system of the earlier religion may simply be restructured by the new one, which will impose a much stricter form of control on it but also guarantee its efficacy, giving believers a sense of assurance that they could not otherwise have had.

The danger for Christianity is that it can be subconsciously paganized by people who think they have found a better way of appeasing the gods than they had before, but who have not understood that their newly adopted faith takes a different approach to the whole problem. This happened to a large degree in medieval Europe, when Christian rites and symbols which pointed to the saving work of Christ were held to have magical powers in their own right. Christian language continued to be used, but the pastor who broke bread with his congregation was turned into a priest who sacrificed Christ

---

[13]Ps. 50:12–15.

on the altar for the sins of the people—a form of "baptized paganism" which denied the work of Christ even as it superficially honored it.

MORAL SYSTEMS AS SUBSTITUTE RELIGIONS

Explanations of what the spiritual world is like may take many different forms. In some cultures, like the Chinese, there has been little attempt to develop a traditional religion. Instead, there has evolved a complex ethical and legal system which depends in a general way on the "mandate of heaven" but which in practice relies on one or more lawgivers, such as Confucius and Lao-tzu, the chief exponent of Daoism (Taoism), who long ago imposed a code of conduct on society that still provides a system of ethics. For many centuries this worked remarkably well, but the failure to develop an inner spirituality produced a pattern of outward conformity to a set of social norms. Those who fell short of this were subjected to "loss of face," a form of public shame which could be severe enough to drive the unfortunate victim to suicide. It is this fear, rather than any pangs of conscience, that determines what is good or bad and makes it difficult for those brought up in a theistic tradition to appreciate it. It also makes it hard for Confucianists or Daoists to absorb the teachings of Christianity, whose outward forms (including moral behavior) stem from inner convictions dependent on a well structured understanding of the spiritual world, rather than being based on an external system of imposed social conformity.

Conversions from this type of background to Christianity do nevertheless take place in significant numbers, perhaps because Christianity addresses a dimension of human experience largely neglected or suppressed in Confucianism and Daoism, but among these converts there is often a noticeable disconnect between their theological convictions (which are new) and their ethical behavior (which is ancient but governed by different principles.) The result is that the rightness or wrongness of stealing, or even the definition of what "stealing" is, may be decided not in terms of one's relationship to God and obligations to him, but according to non-Christian social norms.

One of the odder features of the modern world is that, although there are many converts to Christianity from cultures imbued with Confucianism, there are also many people from a traditional Judeo-Christian background who have to all intents and purposes gone the other way. While very few of them have adopted traditional Chinese ethics, many have reduced their understanding and practice of Judaism or Christianity to a similarly moralistic level. This problem is not new, and was already apparent in New Testament times, as we can see from the behavior of the Pharisees, who were so strongly criticized by Jesus for just that reason. The Jewish law that the Pharisees upheld was much more than a moral code, but too many Jews were limiting it to superficial observances and missing the spiritual message that underlay it.[14] Similar criticisms have been voiced down the ages by would-be religious reformers, who have not hesitated to condemn what in the nineteenth century came to be called "bourgeois morality" for its similar propensity to substitute formal observances of a legalistic ethical code for fundamental theological principles.

In more recent times, however, a different and more positive stance toward morality has emerged and has been accepted by many as being not far short of the essence of Christianity. The cause of this seems to have been the decline of belief in miracles and therefore in the revealed nature of the Christian faith, a decline that characterized the eighteenth-century Enlightenment. That might have spelled the end of Christianity altogether, had it not been for the fact that even many of the skeptics who attacked its doctrines understood that it provided a moral foundation that was necessary for any society to survive. For that reason, many people who saw themselves as enlightened skeptics when it came to theological matters continued to support the church as a social institution which they felt was needed in order to inculcate moral principles. Popular religious belief was less affected by the Enlightenment, but for social reasons of their own many people readily embraced the call for morality, and by 1900 things like "Sabbatarianism" and "teetotalism" had become powerful forces in many places.[15]

The aim of those who advocated such policies was to improve society by enforcing strict codes of moral behavior. This reached its apogee in the United States in 1920, when the sale of alcoholic beverages was prohibited by constitutional amendment. Prohibition failed, and today most people would agree that it was a huge mistake, but the link between Christianity and "morality" remained strong in the popular mind. Rather than try to enforce morality by law, people increasingly privatized it, believing that as long as they themselves led a decent, moral, and law-abiding life, their Christian values would permeate society and gradually improve it. Dissatisfaction with the obvious lack of success in that area has in turn produced what might be called a public, or activist theology, which advocates social policies designed to promote what is assumed to be the common good—"equality" and "justice" being terms in vogue today.

---

[14]Matt. 23:23–24.
[15]Teetotalism is a term used mainly in the United States for a movement that advocated total abstinence from alcoholic beverages.

Those who adopt this approach can point to the words of Jesus, some of which appear to support their cause, such as, "You shall love your neighbor as yourself,"[16] and, "So whatsoever you wish that others would do to you, do also to them, for this is the Law and the Prophets."[17] The latter in particular has come to be known as the "Golden Rule" and is widely quoted by many people as being the essence, not just of Christianity, but of all religion everywhere. It so happens that this verse comes toward the end of the Sermon on the Mount in Matthew's Gospel, which is often used to ward off any more serious interest in the claims of Christ. "My religion is the Sermon on the Mount" is a phrase that trips easily off the lips of people who are thereby indicating their unwillingness to discuss the matter any further—and perhaps hinting that people who want to delve more deeply into doctrinal matters are somehow hypocritical and have missed the point of their faith.

The difficulty in dealing with this misunderstanding of Christianity is that it contains an important element of the truth. No Christian has any right to lead an immoral life, and those who do are severely castigated for it by Paul.[18] Moral behavior of the kind enjoined in the Ten Commandments is a good thing, and Jesus never suggested that his followers had any right to kill, steal, or commit adultery as if the law did not matter.[19] The notion that a sinner saved by grace could go on sinning in order to promote the spread of divine grace is an absurdity that the Bible rightly condemns.[20] In upholding the Commandments, however, Jesus launched a fierce attack on those who upheld the letter of the law but denied its spirit. "You shall not murder" appears to be clear enough, and in one sense, it can be said that very few people have ever disobeyed this command. Most of the time it is relatively easy to avoid killing people, and only a small minority of the population have ever done so.

But Jesus takes that commandment and interprets it by saying that anyone who has ever been angry with another person, even privately, has killed that person already![21] If that is the standard required, how many of us can truthfully claim to be innocent? Certainly not anyone who has ever driven a car in heavy traffic! The point Jesus was trying to make is that moral behavior, good and necessary as it is, can never get to the heart of the problem, which is fundamentally spiritual. Outward observances have their place and may indeed be necessary if society is to function the way it should, but they are no substitute for a living relationship with God. When morality leads to moral-

---

[16]Matt. 22:39; cited from Lev. 19:18.
[17]Matt. 7:12.
[18]See for example 1 Cor. 5:1–3.
[19]Matt. 5:18–19.
[20]Rom. 6:15.
[21]Matt. 5:21–23.

ism, it creates a simulacrum of Christianity which resembles the real thing about as much as a wax figure at Madame Tussaud's resembles the human being it represents. From a distance we can easily be fooled, but the closer we get to it the more we see that what appears to be vibrant with life is in fact a mute object incapable of fulfilling the promise it seems to hold out to those who pass by.

20

THE RELIGIONS OF
THE WORLD

GRECO-ROMAN RELIGION AND PHILOSOPHY

Like China, the Greco-Roman world offers another instance of a great civilization in which legal and ethical norms outstripped spiritual development, but there it took a different path. Greco-Roman culture is of particular importance to us, not only because it is the context in which early Christianity developed but also because it is still widely admired today. Despite the decline of classical studies in schools and universities, it is not uncommon to find people who believe that the triumph of Christianity over ancient Greece and Rome was a disaster that led to what has been called the "closing of the Western mind," a process by which theological dogma is supposed to have replaced rational enquiry as the intellectual basis of society. Greece stands out in the ancient world, because when the inadequacy of its religious life was perceived by its leading thinkers, they turned to the power of human reason and developed various kinds of philosophy to account for the nature of things. Some of these philosophies, notably Platonism, could be described as monotheistic, in the sense that they believed in a supreme being, which they sometimes referred to as "god." This "god," however, was a rational construction, not a revealed being, and although its existence could be plausibly defended, there was never any question of being able to enter into a personal relationship with it. The ancient Greeks had no concept of the "person," and the term was not used in their philosophy. As for the traditional deities of Greek religion, the philosophers dismissed them with contempt. Zeus, Apollo, and the other gods were personifications of natural forces, but none of them was the supreme being. On the contrary, it was the very things that identified them as "personal" that were the limitations which prevented them from having the absolute quality essential to the philosophical concept of the supreme being.

Today it is noticeable how even the greatest admirers of ancient Greece pay little attention to its religion, regarding the Delphic Apollo or the Venus de Milo[1] as great works of art rather than as potential objects of worship. It is the secular aspects of that culture that claim the attention of the modern world, but we tend to forget that those aspects were only one part of a bigger whole. Ancient Greece and Rome were split between a religion that was widely recognized as being vulgar and immoral and an ethic based on philosophy and law, in which they excelled. Ultimately, however, this dichotomy, which ran through the whole of society, was unsustainable. The early Christians had no difficulty in condemning paganism, not least because the more intellectual elements in the Greco-Roman world often agreed with them. The various philosophical alternatives also lacked coherence, and had little to offer beyond an arid rationalism, as Christians pointed out. Christians generally admired Roman law, which held the empire together in a way that neither religion nor philosophy could do, but they also believed that the Christian faith provided an underpinning for it that nothing in the pagan world could match. In their view, what was good in classical civilization would survive only to the extent that it was compatible with Christianity.

Nowadays it is commonly said that ancient Greek philosophy combined with Judeo-Christian religion to produce what we now call "Western civilization," but this is not how matters were perceived at the time. Paul warned the Colossians not to be deceived by the vanities of philosophy, which he perceived as the enemy of true faith.[2] Ancient Christian writers did not admire the philosophers nearly as much as many people today do, and a man like Justin Martyr (100?–156), who is usually thought to have been more open to Greek influences than most of his contemporaries, was perfectly happy to describe Plato as a man groping for truth in the dark who occasionally stumbled across it without recognizing what it was.[3] A generation or two later, Tertullian of Carthage (160?–220?) uttered his famous quote, "What has Athens got to do with Jerusalem?" a question which continues to provoke discussion today.[4]

It is true that Christians felt free to use philosophical terminology to develop their theology, but they gave it a different (and generally more strictly defined) meaning. Furthermore, when philosophical terms were incapable of

---

[1] A statue of the Greek goddess Aphrodite (Venus) that was found on the island of Melos and is now in the Louvre Museum in Paris.
[2] Col. 2:8.
[3] Justin Martyr, *Apologia* I.20, 59–60; II.13.
[4] Tertullian, *De praescriptione haereticorum* 7, 9.

expressing what they wanted to say they came up with new words, "person" and "Trinity" being the most obvious examples of this theological creativity. The pagan philosophers, for their part, were scarcely more accommodating. Men such as Celsus (second century) and Porphyry (fourth century) wrote bitter polemics against Christianity, and the triumph of the new religion did little to make them think again. On the contrary, the philosophical schools of Athens were among the last holdouts against Christianity in the ancient world, and it was because of that opposition that they were finally closed down in 529.

The belief that Christianity was Hellenized by its development of a systematic theology, or that pre-Christian Greek philosophies were somehow more rational than the religion of the Bible and therefore superior to it, is false and results from a distorted reading of history. Christianity triumphed over Hellenism because it was richer and more comprehensive in its scope than anything the ancient Greek world had to offer. Its leading thinkers showed that they could answer the questions posed by the philosophical schools (which often differed radically among themselves as to what the answers should be) and could integrate the spiritual and the rational dimension of human life in a way that had not been possible before.

The superiority of Christianity to both the religion and the philosophy of ancient Greco-Roman civilization is clear to anyone who has studied the transition from one to the other with an open mind. Yet such is the hold that the latter has on some people that they are still prepared to argue that philosophers like Plato were right to banish religion from their ideal republic, agreeing with him that religion is an irrational force that can only harm a society governed by the rule of law. These people assume that Christianity is really no different from ancient paganism, and that Plato would have banished it also if he had known about it. Like the other Greeks of his time, Plato had no concept of a philosophically grounded religion. He knew that his beliefs would appeal only to a small minority, but he was glad of that fact, because they were the enlightened ones who would escape the vulgarity of the masses by embracing it. Abstract intellectual principles have only ever appealed to a minority, who have usually not hesitated to proclaim themselves superior to everyone else. The fact that so much modern secularization has been guided by principles ultimately derived from Platonism ought to be a warning to us that it will almost certainly succumb, as ancient Platonism eventually did, to religious forces which have a deeper grasp of the true meaning of life than any form of rationalism does.

Would Plato have rejected Christianity had he known about it? Generations of Christians have argued that he would have appreciated its integrative power and adopted it as the basis for the laws of his ideal republic, and there are many today who take a similar position. There is no way that we shall ever know this for sure, but we should at least remember that, for every thinker who has had the idea that Christianity and Greek philosophical ideas are incompatible, there has been at least one other who has said the opposite. Some ancient Christian writers even maintained that the philosophers were the prophets of the Gentiles, whose ideas pointed them toward the coming of Christ although they did not realize it at the time. When he was in Athens, Paul did not hesitate to quote pagan authors in support of his message, and even Tertullian claimed that the Stoic philosopher Seneca often said things that were perfectly compatible with Christianity.[5] But whether their assessment of ancient philosophy was basically negative or positive, all Christians were agreed on one thing: it was not enough for salvation. The most it could do was point people to Christ, who would save them by the shedding of his blood and not merely by the power of his mind.

HINDUISM AND BUDDHISM

In the modern world, the closest thing we can find to ancient Greek religion is Hinduism, which is also polytheistic and may be historically related to its ancient Greek counterpart through a common Indo-European source. Whether or not that is true, however, Hinduism is open to all the objections leveled against Greek religion both by Christians and by their own philosophers. None of its many gods can claim to be uniquely supreme, which means that propitiating one may have no effect on the others, who may even be jealous and try to wreak revenge on worshipers for devoting so much attention to one of their rivals. Hinduism is closely connected to India and its culture, which makes it hard for Christians to reject it out of hand. There are many things about Indian culture that are admirable, although we would insist that they could exist perfectly well without Hinduism to shore them up and would be even better if they were Christianized. As with the conversion of Europe from paganism to Christianity, the difficulty in India is knowing what aspects of its traditional culture can be kept and what must be discarded, either because it is compromised by its association with pagan religion or because it is innately wrong.

Ultimately, this is something that Indian Christians must decide for themselves, and then do what they can to absorb legitimate features of traditional Indian life into their own practice of Christianity. What is certain, however,

---

[5]Acts 17:27–29; Tertullian, *De anima* 20.

is that Hinduism contains features that cannot be reconciled with Christian values, and those things must certainly be discarded by those who come to Christ. The caste system is an obvious example of this, as is the doctrine of reincarnation. Also repugnant to Christians is the ancient Hindu custom of *sati* (suttee), according to which a widow casts herself on her husband's burial pyre. *Sati* was abolished in British India but there are reports that it has recently been revived in some places, making it more necessary than ever for Christians to be wary of elements in Hindu religious tradition that contradict the Christian view of God, man, and creation.

Like ancient Greek religion, Hinduism also produced internal opposition movements, of which Buddhism is the best-known example. Buddhism is essentially a nontheistic "religion" of contemplation, in which the "believer" is expected to rise through different states of consciousness until finally reaching the desired goal of nirvana. This is not to be confused with heaven in the Christian sense, because nirvana is reintegration with the universal spirit, which means the loss of individual self-consciousness. As such, it is close to Platonism, especially the mystical form of it known to us as Neoplatonism, which may be one reason why some intellectuals brought up in the Western tradition have been attracted to Buddhism. It has a form of morality, but not one that would be easily recognized by Christians, as its attitude to human sexuality demonstrates. Buddhists think that the human body plays a part in the spiritual quest, and are therefore open to forms of sexual expression, including homosexuality, that Christianity rejects. As in Platonism, these things are not ends in themselves but steps on the way toward a higher state of being. When the goal is transcendence, the means used to get there are relatively unimportant because they are no more than passing stages on the way to enlightenment.

Buddhism is not a philosophy in the Greek sense, but it has spawned a number of different strands of thought whose interrelationships and rivalries recall those of the Greek philosophical schools. These resemblances were noted in ancient times by the few people who had contact with both the Greek world and India, and there are scholars who believe that one may have influenced the other at different times in history, even after the rise of Christianity. For example, yoga and the Greek monastic practice of hesychasm are so similar that it is tempting to think that there was some connection between them.[6] Insufficient evidence means that we shall probably never be able to answer this

[6]Hesychasm is a form of mystical contemplation, derided by its opponents as "navel-gazing." It did not become prominent in the Greek world until the fourteenth century, but it is almost certainly much older than that.

question, but that it can be asked at all reminds us that when a polytheistic religion is confronted by the demand for a unity of truth deeper than any of its known gods can provide, the search for a mystical experience of that truth is liable to result in the emergence of a more spiritual and more intellectually satisfying synthesis.[7]

ISLAM

Islam presents a different picture. It is the only major world religion that appeared after the coming of Christ and that explicitly rejects his claim to be the Son of God incarnate.[8] Like Judaism, Islam does not have a theology in the Christian sense, and its teaching about God (Allah) is closer to Judaism than it is to Christianity. The Islamic God is totally transcendent, and never appears in any visible form, human or otherwise, so the possibility of an incarnation of God is ruled out from the start. The message of its great prophet Muhammad is a form of law, and must be studied in that way. As with the Jews, the great interpreters of Islam are jurists rather than theologians in the Christian sense. Islam is also an attempt to reconcile the principle of universalism with that of nationality, though in a way that is quite different from Judaism. In theory at least, Islam constitutes not a church but an *ummah*, a sacred "nation" that embraces all Muslims regardless of their ethnic origin. Islam relegates both the Old and the New Testaments to its prehistory, claiming to be the third and final stage of God's revelation. In a sense, Muslims regard Christianity much as Christians regard Judaism, as a true but now obsolete form of their own religion. However, whereas Christians treat the Old Testament as history and see themselves in continuity with it, Islam's appropriation of the Christian Bible is more mystical and impressionistic than historical. Biblical characters appear in the Qur'an, the sacred text of Islam, but they are presented in ways that are hard to reconcile with the historical record.

Of no one is this more true than of Jesus, who is regarded as semi-divine, having been born of the Virgin Mary, but who could not have died on the cross because his divine nature made such a disgraceful death unworthy of him. The man whom Muslims say died in his place was the one who deserved the punishment—Judas Iscariot! Assertions like these not only go against everything we know about what actually happened, but they show ignorance of what Christianity is. The whole point of Christ's death is that the innocent gave his life for the guilty, paying the price for human sin with the blood of

---

[7]The early Christians sensed this. See Acts 17:22–23.
[8]Judaism does this only implicitly.

the incarnate Son of God. Muslims are right to claim that Jesus was too good to die such a death, but to make that a reason for denying that it happened destroys the gospel message. As Christians, we are happy to agree with them that Jesus was "too good" to die, but that is precisely what makes his death so meaningful to us! If Jesus had deserved death, he could not have been our Savior. What Muslims cannot grasp is that God "loved us and sent his Son to be the propitiation for our sins."[9] As Paul put it, we live by faith in the Son of God, who loves us and gave himself for us.[10]

It is Islam's failure to accept the person and work of Jesus Christ as presented in the New Testament that makes it impossible for Christians to regard it as a true revelation from God. Jesus told his followers that no one could come to God except through him,[11] and the New Testament says that there will be no further revelation before the final consummation of all things.[12] It is therefore impossible for Christians to recognize the prophetic claims of Muhammad that Islam is a further (and by implication higher) revelation from God. This refusal is not new, but goes back to the prophet's own lifetime, when the Christians he encountered rejected his message for precisely that reason. Muhammad could easily have become a Christian himself, but he did not. Why not? The reason must be that he believed that he had received a revelation from God that overruled the claims of Jesus and made them redundant.

From the Christian standpoint, Islam is a regression from the saving message of Jesus Christ to something altogether more limited. It is a religion of justice rather than of love, of fate rather than of forgiveness and restoration to new life. Like Judaism, it is a religion of law more than of salvation by grace, and so from the Christian point of view it is a regression from the gospel of Christ, not an advance on it. In some ways it is virtually a retreat into the Old Testament, where God cannot be known directly and all communication between him and us comes through intermediate beings, such as angels or *jinn*.[13] Shorn of such doctrines as the Trinity and the divinity of Christ, Islam can justly claim to offer its followers a simpler form of monotheism than Christianity does, but the price it has paid for this is the loss of any personal relationship with God and the abandonment of the good news that we have been saved from our sins by the shed blood of Jesus. Islam claims that Muhammad was a prophet who was closer to God than any human being before or since, but Christianity claims that Jesus Christ was (and still is) God

---

[9]1 John 4:10.
[10]Gal. 2:20.
[11]John 14:6.
[12]Heb. 1:1–4.
[13]In Islam, *jinn* are spirits, known to us as "genies."

himself. You cannot believe that Jesus was a great teacher and then deny that he is God, since that is what he taught his disciples to believe.[14] To deny his divinity is to deny his greatness as a human being, since it would make him a liar and a deceiver. "What do you think of Christ?" remains the touchstone, and it is the answer Muslims give to that question that reveals the width of the gulf that separates them from Christians.

We cannot deny that Islam has many good points, and it is often close to Christianity on matters of social justice (though less so when it comes to moral issues like monogamy), but insofar as it sees itself as supplementing and replacing Christianity, we have no option but to regard it as false. The fact is that although it originated several centuries after Christianity and in contact with it, Islam has a less profound grasp of sin than Christianity has. According to Muslim tradition, Adam and Eve did not pass their sinfulness on to their descendants, who are not born in sin and so are at least theoretically capable of avoiding it. This is a complete contradiction of Christian belief and demonstrates once again how Islam is not true to the biblical account, even when it refers directly to the Bible. Similarly, the Islamic picture of heaven is a caricature of the biblical vision of eternal life in the presence of God, and its notion of how to get there is based on works, not on faith in a loving and forgiving Savior. Islam also has some strange teachings that derive from a very primitive paganism, the most famous example being the prominence given to the black meteorite in Mecca, known as the Ka'ba, which is a major site of Islamic pilgrimage. No Christian could turn such an object into a focus of veneration, and the contradiction between superstition like that and the spiritual message that Islam is supposed to convey is readily apparent to anyone who tries to harmonize them.

The one area where Islam is more like Christianity than like Judaism is in its commitment to proselytization, which has marked it from the beginning. But whereas Christian expansion did not begin until after the death and resurrection of Jesus, the meaning of which formed the main content of the message the apostles preached, Muhammad was himself the head of an army which spread his teachings across Arabia at the point of the sword. His immediate followers quickly conquered a worldwide empire, which gave its pagan subjects the choice between conversion and death. The contrast with Jesus could hardly be more striking, and it is fair to say that the two religions expanded by very different means. From the Christian point of view, a religion of peace (which is what Islam claims to be) should be spread peacefully, and if it is not, its validity must be called into question.

---

[14]Matt. 16:16–17.

Muslims like to claim that they are tolerant of the "people of the book," that is to say of Jews and Christians, who are fellow monotheists, and there is some truth in this. There certainly have been times in the past when Muslims were more accepting of other monotheists than contemporary Christians were, but the nature of that tolerance should not be misunderstood. Jews and Christians were acceptable in Muslim states only as second-class citizens, and they were not allowed to participate fully in public life. There was often pressure on them to convert to Islam, and once that happened, there could be no going back to their earlier faith, even if their conversion was artificial or forced. Nor could there be any question of allowing non-Muslims the freedom to preach their own views, as anyone who tried to do so would discover to their cost. Even today, very few Muslim countries do anything more than tolerate the existence of religious minorities, who are seldom allowed to express themselves publicly, let alone proselytize. In many Muslim countries conversion from Islam to another religion is still punishable by death, something that would be unthinkable almost everywhere else.

Islam sends out conflicting messages here, and while there is no reason to doubt that the vast majority of Muslims are peace-loving and nonviolent, it may be asked whether this is really an integral part of their religious beliefs. The question is particularly important in the modern world, where Islam is making itself felt in a way that it has not done for several generations. Muslim governments build huge mosques in non-Muslim countries, even when there is hardly anyone to attend them, but they do not permit Christians to put up churches in their countries. These mosques have sometimes become centers of radical Islam where terrorists are recruited and trained to spread their faith, and it is not clear how or by whom such activities can be stopped, not least because it is hard to say whether they are really contrary to the spirit of Islam (as opposed to the inclinations of the majority of Muslims). On the other hand, it can safely be said that no modern Christian would ever dream of preaching the gospel in that way, if only because the contradiction between the means and the end would be too obvious to be tolerated. Hard as it may be for them to accept, Islamic spokesmen must face the fact that their faith is open to criticism in this area and that (so far at least) there does not seem to be much inclination on their part to do anything about it.

Christians have to approach Islam differently from Judaism, despite the fact that it is equally monotheistic. We are much closer to Jews because we share the same Scriptures, identify ourselves spiritually with ancient Israel, and believe that our Savior is their Messiah. None of this applies to our relationship with Islam. Muslims honor the Bible but do not put it on the same level as their own Qur'an, nor do they see Islam as an outgrowth of Christianity in the way that Christianity can be said to be an outgrowth of Judaism. They recognize that they have an affinity with the "people of the Book" as they call Jews and Christians, but this is not nearly as close as the Christian self-identification with Israel. It also involves a distortion of the evidence which makes the honor Muslims show to Jesus, Mary, and other biblical figures questionable and problematic. From a Christian point of view, it is not the real people they are honoring but their own reconstruction of them, which is not fully in accord with the known historical facts. It must also be said that although Muslim-Christian relations have been even more unhappy than Jewish-Christian ones, the responsibility for this is more evenly balanced and Muslims are probably somewhat more to blame than Christians. Both religions proselytize to gain converts, but although there are roughly twice as many Christians in the world today as there are Muslims, over the course of history far more Christians have become Muslims (often by force) than the other way around. All of this must affect the kind of "dialogue" Christians can have with Islam and the sort of evangelism that we must undertake with regard to it. There is no biblical promise that faithful Muslims are God's chosen people and will be saved at the end of time, and therefore we have no reason to regard them as any different from other non-Christians. Missionary work among Muslims has never been easy and it may well prove to be fatal for those who engage in it, but it is part of the Great Commission to go to the nations with the gospel,[15] and Islamic monotheism is not an excuse for Christians to renounce or downplay this divine imperative.

A PREPARATION FOR THE GOSPEL?

Do Christians have anything good to say about other religions? The ancient Israelites were surrounded by tribes and nations that practiced different forms of idolatrous polytheism, which were all equally unacceptable to God. Attempts to introduce the worship of Baal into Israel were met with fierce resistance, and the name of Queen Jezebel, who was a particularly zealous advocate of paganism, passed into Hebrew legend as the archetypal "wicked woman."[16] The early church was in a similar situation and took much the same attitude, but when it began to evangelize the Gentiles, it had to say something about their previous religious inheritance.

The Gentiles did not have the law of Moses and so could not be blamed for their failure to keep it. But God had not left them entirely bereft of any

---

[15]Matt. 28:19–20.
[16]Rev. 2:20. For the historical Jezebel, see 1 Kings 16:31–2 Kings 9:37 *passim*.

knowledge of him. He had given them a law written on their hearts, and it was by that law that they would be judged.[17] The only question was to what extent that law was reflected in the religious practices of the Gentiles before the coming of Christ. Here, Paul was less encouraging. He recognized that the Gentiles knew God, but because they were rebellious children of Adam, they had turned away from God, suppressed the truth, and made gods for themselves out of created things. The result was that they had brought condemnation on themselves and could not possibly appeal to their invented religions as an excuse for their behavior.[18] Elsewhere, Paul appealed to ancient Greek writers in support of his claims for the gospel of Christ, pointing out that some of them had been aware of the Creator and of their dependence on him, but his words had little effect on those who heard them.[19]

Even so, as the mission to the Gentiles spread and gathered momentum, Christian evangelists sometimes appealed to the wisdom of the ancient Greeks, which they interpreted as the residue of a God-given truth that had been obscured by idolatrous practices. But however much Christians resonated with some pre-Christian Greek and Roman writers, there was never any thought of creating a "pagan canon" comparable to the Old Testament, and if some pagan ideas slipped into their thinking it was because they had been successfully "baptized" and recycled as the thoughts of other Christians.[20]

When we look at other religions today, the same principles must be applied to them that the early Christians applied to the Gentile beliefs of their day. God has not left himself without a witness, and we must expect that non-Christians, who have never heard the gospel through no fault of their own, nevertheless have an innate moral and spiritual sense which tells them that there is a difference between good and evil, and that the world is governed by a higher spiritual power whom they do not know as they should and whom they have offended. In every religious culture there are some who are genuinely seeking the truth, and we believe that when the gospel is preached to them they will respond to it for that reason. As Paul told the Athenians, God will not condemn them for what they did in ignorance, but now that they know what is right, they must repent and believe.[21]

We may therefore conclude that, in his love, God left his rebellious creatures enough light for those who took it seriously to understand how far

---

[17]Rom. 2:12–16.
[18]Rom. 1:18–32.
[19]Acts 17:22–34.
[20]The most famous example of this was the appropriation of Neoplatonic philosophy by a sixth-century monk, who passed himself off as Dionysius the Areopagite, who had been converted in Athens during Paul's ministry there (Acts 17:34).
[21]Acts 17:30.

short of the ideal they fell. But by an even greater love he has now sent his Son to save them, and thus has brought more light into the world.[22] Just as the Jews had no reason to cling to their ancient law once it had been fulfilled, so Gentiles had no excuse to appeal to the light they had previously received after the true light had come, because the true light is given to everyone in order to make the right pathway plain to all.[23] In other words, not all non-Christian religions are entirely bad, and most of them contain elements of the truth, but none is adequate to save its followers. In his great love for them, God has provided something better—the gospel of his Son Jesus Christ. Once that is understood and accepted, there can be no going back to what went before. In New Testament times, converted Jews might continue to live according to the law of Moses, and the same may still be true today, though it is not compulsory for them to do so. Gentiles, however, had to make a clean break with their past when they came to know the one true God, and that principle still applies. What is good from the past will survive, but it will do so in the light of Christ, who alone is "the way, and the truth, and the life."[24]

---

[22] John 1:9–10.
[23] John 1:9–12.
[24] John 14:6.

21

CHRISTIANITY AND RELIGIOUS SYNCRETISM

THE UNIQUENESS OF CHRISTIANITY

When faced with the claims of other religions, the Christian response is to proclaim that everyone needs to have a personal relationship with God in Jesus Christ. That is the only thing that can offer the peace of mind and spirit they are all looking for but that none of them has found. As Christians, we assert that in Jesus Christ we have met the God who made us, who has delivered us from our sins, and who has promised us deliverance from the troubles we suffer in this world. We proclaim that the way of salvation has been found, not because someone has invented it or discovered it, but because it has been revealed by God himself. The Son of God, eternally begotten of the Father and fully equal to him in every respect, became a man so that he could unite us to himself, pay the price for our sins, and bring us back to God. No other religion makes such a claim, and none of them penetrates so deeply into the heart of the human condition or resolves it in the way that the Christian gospel does. Christianity is not a national or cultural expression of human spirituality but a universal faith revealed by God and freely available to all without distinction or preference. It is true that it is also exclusive, but only in the sense that there is no other way in which people can be saved.[1]

To put Christianity alongside another religion or philosophy, to think of it as one spiritual option among others, or to mix it with beliefs and practices drawn from elsewhere is not merely to diminish it but to deny it altogether. Both the universalism and the exclusivity of Christianity are acts of God's love,

---

[1]John 14:6; Acts 4:12.

because Christianity's availability to all means that no one is excluded from the possibility of coming to him and no one is forced to accept something that is only second-best. If Christianity were not universal, it would not be possible to offer it to everyone, and if it were not exclusive, it would not be necessary for everyone to accept it. Other ways to God would be viable alternatives, even if they were not equal to Christianity in every respect. Given that eternal salvation would have to be the promise offered by any religion or belief system that wanted to be an adequate substitute for Christianity, the chances are that either the substitute faith would be superior, in which case there would be every incentive for Christians to abandon our faith and look to it instead, or else it would be inferior, which would make followers of other paths second-class citizens in the kingdom of heaven and give us a reason to evangelize them. Complete and unambiguous equality could only be reduplication, and what would be the point of that?

In spite of this logic, however, for many people the Christian faith is just one religion among many, attractive in some ways but not in others. Even among those who profess to believe in it, it is not uncommon to hear, for instance, the claim that Christians have a less reverent attitude toward the natural world than the adherents of other religions do, and that we could learn a lot about respect for the environment from Hindus, Buddhists, and so on. Much of this is a matter of perspective and the result of subjective value judgment, rather than a rigorous analysis of the claims that different religions actually make. It is sometimes tempting to take one aspect of another religion and detach it from its context, giving it a higher value than it would deserve if it were seen as part of the wider whole to which it belongs.

An obvious example of how our perspective will affect our judgment can be seen by comparing the Christian insistence on monogamy with the Muslim acceptance of polygamy. Are we to prefer Islam on the ground that it is more tolerant in this respect, or Christianity, because it treats women as fully equal to men? Both views have their defenders, and we should not assume that one of them is so obviously superior to the other that all right-thinking people will automatically accept it. Some people say that the choice is usually not as stark as this and that it is possible to take what is good in different religions and put them together in an eclectic mix. This sounds good, and some individuals have done it to their own satisfaction, but probably they have made a selection which they feel free to modify as their tastes change or as their circumstances may require. Unfortunately, there are two big problems with syncretism, as this approach is called, which make it highly questionable as a method and impossible to implement consistently.

The first problem is that syncretism is parasitic. It depends on the preexistence of clearly defined religious systems, which are "raided" for material that looks congenial to whoever is selecting it. But no religion is a collage of discrete beliefs, and to borrow one or two elements of a religion without taking on the rest distorts it. For example, Christians believe that God is love, but we reject the practice of polygamy because it goes against the story of creation, where it is clear that the fundamental human relationship was to be between one man and one woman.[2] A Muslim, however, might easily conclude that, if God is love, then the more wives a man has the better, because to their minds it is a way of protecting women who might otherwise be left alone in the world.[3] A Buddhist might argue that because sexual intercourse is a stage on the way to experiencing the supreme love of God, it should be encouraged without any reference to matrimony, as long as ultimate union with the divine is what is desired. For Christians, however, such an approach is even less acceptable than polygamy, though for much the same reason: it devalues the human person. Can we then say that someone who has taken the Christian principle that God is love and applied it in a Muslim or Buddhist way has successfully fused one religion with another? Is it not more likely that he has adopted a practice that is alien to Christianity but used Christian language to justify it and in the process emptied that language of its meaning? Christians say yes to that second question, and regard anyone who thinks along such lines as ignorant of the true meaning of the Christian faith. In other words, eclecticism of this kind is fundamentally incoherent and does not work.

The second problem with syncretism is that the freedom which individuals have to pick and choose what they like is not available to an organized religious group, which is forced to come to common (and preferably consistent) decisions if it is to have a logically coherent identity. Deciding what elements to take and what to reject is not easy, and the potential for conflicts of interest is enormous. In the above example, how could a single congregation tolerate the coexistence of monogamy (the Christian view of sexual love), polygamy (acceptable to Muslims), and sexual intercourse outside marriage? Even if all three were regarded as possible manifestations of the love of God, to allow them to function side by side would be no easy matter. How would a woman who prefers monogamy cohabit with a polygamous man? It is true that many men have sexual intercourse outside of marriage, but this does not mean that their wives approve of it, and still less that they regard it as a spiritual exercise

---

[2] Gen. 2:18, 21–25.
[3] This argument is actually made by some Muslims, who claim that it avoids the loneliness and rejection that single women can often feel in Western society.

that is helping their husbands get closer to God. Yet there are some extreme religious groups which advocate such practices for precisely that reason, and the members have little choice but to go along with whatever the leadership has decreed. The result is anything but "freedom," and when such groups are exposed to the glare of publicity, it is often full of horror stories about sexual slavery and the like. The track record of religious eclecticism on a mass scale is not good, and as this example demonstrates, the potential for abuse is enormous.

The most fundamental reason why syncretism cannot work is that every religious group needs a leader who can determine what its beliefs and practices should be. The leadership may be collective or dispersed, but there has to be some principle that guides the group's decision making (consensus, or majority vote) that will ensure that the group stays together. Who can claim the authority to determine what is acceptable and what is not? Election of such a leader by members of the group is unlikely to work, because the person so chosen would then owe his authority to the community, and be badly placed to dictate to them. Some kind of supernatural spiritual claim is required for such leadership to be effective, but when that happens a new religion is born. However syncretistic it may be to start off with, and however dependent on the teachings and practices of others it is, it will nevertheless be a new system, operating on its own principles and devoted to the teacher who brought it into being. In other words, religious eclecticism is a transitional phase in the establishment of a new religious identity, not a position that a religious community can hold indefinitely. The real choice is between accepting an existing religion or inventing a new one. Existing religions have all had a checkered history and carry considerable baggage, but for all their faults, there are millions of people who have found them satisfactory. Inventing a new one escapes the burden of history but it is also untried and lacks any authority. If this is the choice, it is surely better to go with something that has credibility because it has been tried and tested, rather than make up something that is ultimately no bigger than our own imagination.

CHRISTIANITY AS AN EXPRESSION OF WESTERN CULTURE

If Christianity were just a particular form of an underlying religiosity common to all human beings, it could be practiced and admired for what it is, but it could hardly be promoted as inherently superior to, or fundamentally different from, any other religion. There are some people, mostly in countries that have been historically Christian for many generations, who take that view, and it is more or less the official line of secular governments in Europe, North America, and Australia. According to their way of thinking, Christianity is a religious phenomenon which may contain any number of truths but which cannot be regarded as the Truth in an absolute sense, because in the final analysis it is just an expression of traditional Western spirituality which is no better than any other human spiritual tradition. These people tend to see Christian missionary work among people of other cultural backgrounds as a form of Western imperialism and are against it for that reason. At home, they may join and support a local church in the way that they may belong to the public library or subscribe to a concert series, but they dissent from Christianity's more exclusivist claims and are suspicious of those who take their faith too seriously. The concept of conversion is generally anathema to them, except perhaps in the case of people who are rescued from a life of crime or alcoholism. In those cases, however, it is the moral reform that appeals to them and makes the idea of "conversion" seem respectable, not any intellectual conviction about the nature of ultimate truth.

Despite the popularity of this view, culture is not what Christianity is about. It came into being as a living faith centuries before it developed a higher culture, and in recent times it has spread across the world to embrace peoples who have little understanding of, or contact with, Western civilization—at least in its more refined form. Propping up medieval cathedrals is the last thing on the minds of Christians in the developing world, and the great works of art, music, and literature that past generations of (mainly European) Christians have produced are alien to them. Yet Christians in Africa or Asia can have a vibrant faith that puts those from traditionally Christian countries to shame. What makes these people tick is not an alien cultural heritage. The heart of our faith lies elsewhere, in a spiritual experience accessible to people of any race, language, or nation. It is a universal faith that proclaims a universal truth. The similarities that Christianity shares with other religions are due to the universal human condition to which all religions must respond, but these similarities are deceptive. Unlike most religions, Christianity is not an attempt to deal with mysteries beyond our understanding, getting them to work for us instead of against us, as they so often seem to be doing. Far from groping in the dark to propitiate an unknown higher power, Christianity claims to be a message from God, whom it reveals as a personal being who identifies himself as the creative and sustaining power behind the universe.

This message speaks as powerfully to people in Africa and Asia as it once did to Europeans. The only difference between them is that people in traditionally Christian countries, most of which are European or of European origin, have had the Christian revelation for such a long time now that it has taken on some aspects of the folk religion that it originally replaced. Christian festivals like Christmas and Easter are notorious for this, with figures like Santa Claus and the Easter bunny representing a non-Christian substratum that has been integrated into the celebration of the life, death, and resurrection of Jesus Christ to such an extent that many people no longer notice it. More recently, the appalling carnage of two world wars and the threat of worse to come have created an unofficial (but often state-sponsored) cult of remembering the sacrifice of dead combatants that is secular in origin and orientation, but that has often been overlaid with the trappings of Christianity. We may argue whether this is a deformed kind of Christianity or "baptized paganism," but either way it has nothing to do with biblical faith and often the churches do what they can to downplay it, even if they find it hard to get rid of it altogether. Here the living witness of the newer churches of the developing world comes to the rescue of the West, by reminding us that what we believe transcends such cultural manifestations and by challenging those who have inherited Western civilization to rethink what their core values really are—or should be.

THE "RELIGION(S) OF ABRAHAM" AND BAHA'I

Judaism and Islam hold beliefs about God that are similar to those of Christianity, but traditionally at least, all three religions have rejected each other's claims. In spite of this, however, there is a persistent current in Western society, dating from the eighteenth-century European Enlightenment, which wants to put the three great monotheisms together as the "religion(s) of Abraham." According to this theory, monotheism is a higher form of religion than polytheism is, and it originated in the ancient Near East. The biblical account tells us that Abraham, to whom the honor of being the first monotheist is usually attributed, had many children, of whom Isaac was only one. The account we have was written from the perspective of Isaac's descendants, so it is naturally skewed in their favor, but even they admitted that Isaac was not alone. In particular, he had an older half-brother, Ishmael, who was also blessed by God and became the ancestor of a great nation.[4] From the very beginning, the Arabs who propagated Islam claimed descent from Ishmael (Ismail), and this claim was implicitly recognized by Christians, who often referred to them as "Hagarenes," after his mother Hagar. Nowadays, few people pay much attention to this concocted genealogy, but it may have some

---

[4]Gen. 21:12–18.

basis in historical fact, since we are told that the descendants of Ishmael went into the desert, where they formed various tribes that must have intermarried dozens of times in the 2,500 years that separate Ishmael from Muhammad.[5] Can Muslims therefore claim the blessing from God that was given to Ishmael, and if so, does that mean that Christians should accept them as half-brothers, whose common ancestry has been obscured by the cultural accretions that have accumulated over time?

It is a tempting vision and is often advocated by well-meaning people who have little time for the details of theology but believe that those who agree on the essentials, which for them seem to consist mainly of belief in one holy and transcendent God who has revealed himself in the words of a sacred book, ought to be able to make common cause. Anything more than that—such as the fact that the sacred books in question say different and even mutually incompatible things—is a complication and therefore a disposable addition to the pure faith of Abraham (who of course did not have any sacred book himself). In their view, we should all aspire to that model as the best way to reconnect with our spiritual roots and bring peace to the world today. Before examining this claim, it must be pointed out that in all three religious traditions, thinking of this kind has usually been the preserve of an intellectual elite. Jews who have held views like these have usually been assimilated into the surrounding Christian or Muslim environment, if only because they are too few in number to remain distinct from them. Christians and Muslims can usually stay within their own communities, where they constitute a liberal (or in the case of Muslims, Westernized) element. However, there has been at least one serious attempt to create a generically Abrahamic religion, and interestingly enough, it has come from an Islamic background.

In the middle of the nineteenth century a young Iranian Persian by the name of Mirza Ali Muhammad claimed to have received a revelation from God to the effect that Moses, Jesus, and Muhammad were all prophets who reflected God's glory and came bearing a message from the Great Creator. Mirza saw himself as the gateway (*bab*) to heaven and prophesied that after him there would come a man who was chosen by God to be the last and greatest of the prophets. This was anathema to the rulers of Persia (present-day Iran), whose Shi'ite form of Islam is more militant than the more common Sunni version, and on July 8, 1850, they sentenced him to death by firing squad.[6] That might have been the end of the story, but Mirza's mantle was taken up by one of his followers, Mirza Husayn Ali, who took the name

---

[5]See Gen. 25:12–16.
[6]Ironically, those chosen to shoot him were not Muslims but Armenian Christians!

Baha'u'llah ("glory of God") and in 1863 announced that he was the prophet whom the *bab* had promised would come. He preached the essential unity of all mankind and the need for a religion that corresponded to that reality, which he proceeded to construct by merging the elements common to Judaism, Christianity, and Islam and discarding the rest. Among other things, this meant rejecting Christ's claim to be God and the doctrine of the Trinity, both of which are fundamental tenets of Christianity. He died in Haifa on May 29, 1892, and is buried in a shrine that is now the center of the Baha'i faith.

Haifa was then part of the Ottoman empire, but in 1918 it came under British control and since 1948 has been part of the state of Israel, so that the Baha'is can claim that, despite their short history, they have already gone from Muslim to Christian to Jewish rule![7] Today their beliefs have been spread worldwide but they have attracted only a few followers, many of them intellectuals or marginalized social groups to whom the call for unity especially appeals. They have been severely persecuted in their original homeland of Iran, though this has not received much publicity outside Baha'i circles. Over the years, their originally monotheistic syncretism has expanded to take in other world religions as well, making Baha'i theologically incoherent, except as a message of human brotherhood from the Baha'u'llah, whose own status is now equal (and for practical purposes, superior) to that of the founders of the other great religions of the world. Baha'i is a fascinating reminder of what can happen when a charismatic personality founds a new religion. What started as a message of "unity" trying to overcome differences has ended up creating a new difference of its own, a contradiction that seems to be the inevitable result of trying to attempt the impossible.

---

[7] Note that the order in which the Baha'is have experienced this is the exact opposite of the historical sequence in which the great monotheisms first appeared.

22

DEVIATIONS FROM CHRISTIANITY

THE CONCEPT OF HERESY

In addition to attempts to relativize Christianity or to merge it with other religions, there have been a number of deviations from it which have resulted in the emergence of satellite religions, or "cults," that sometimes claim to be Christian but that have denied something fundamental about the Christian faith and have therefore diverged from the core beliefs of orthodox Christianity. Often they have substituted other beliefs of their own, and this has merely increased the gulf that separates them from the main body of the church. This pattern is known to Christians as "heresy," and it has existed in one form or another since New Testament times.[1] In the early church there were a number of self-appointed charismatic teachers who formally accepted the teaching of the apostles but transformed its substance into something incompatible with the gospel. One of the best known of these was Marcion (d. 144?), who tried to abolish the Old Testament and cut the church off from its Jewish roots, something that would have made the life and work of Christ incomprehensible.

A number of such teachers have been loosely grouped together by modern scholars, who have labeled them "gnostics" because they created a hierarchy of being and of spiritual awareness that the newly initiated believer was expected to master before he could attain to true knowledge. These "gnostics" were imbued with a spirit of Platonism that denied the goodness of matter and postulated a world of forms and ideas as the true reality. No "gnostic" could accept the incarnation of the Son of God, a doctrine which went

---

[1] 1 Cor. 11:19; Gal. 5:20; 2 Pet. 2:1. It is not clear whether the New Testament use of *hairesis* involves doctrinal deviation, though the last of these verses seems to come close to that (see ESV "heresies"). Otherwise, it may just mean "factionalism" or "party strife," which could have many different causes.

completely against their basic worldview, and so their way of thinking had to be expunged from the church. Today they are known mainly from the writings of their opponents or from manuscripts that have been discovered in recent times. In the fourth century the great heresy of Arianism, which denied the full divinity of Christ, created its own church that survived for a few centuries, but it seems to have died out by A.D. 600 at the latest.

Other heresies have come and gone over the centuries, but almost all of them eventually died out. The ones that exist today do not go back any further than the sixteenth century, although in some cases they have picked up ideas that are much older and have integrated them into their own systems of thought. For example, it is often said that modern Jehovah's Witnesses are latter-day Arians because, like them, they also deny the divinity of Christ, but this resemblance is best seen as a coincidence rather than as a conscious attempt to revive fourth-century Arianism.

UNITARIANISM

In modern times, the oldest and most lasting deviation from Christianity has been unitarianism. It began in the sixteenth century, when some humanist scholars questioned the authority of the church and began to doubt the truth of the doctrine of the Trinity. A famous early representative of this tendency was Michael Servetus (1511–1563), who was burned at the stake in Geneva for his beliefs, but Servetus left no lasting movement.[2] That was the work of Lelio Sozzini or Socinus (1525–1562) and his nephew Fausto (1539–1604). Lelio developed ideas similar to those of Servetus, though he died without being condemned for them, but Fausto had to flee to Hungary and then to Poland in order to escape persecution. In 1605 their followers issued the Racovian Catechism, which was soon circulating all over the Christian world.[3] Socinianism, as this heresy was known, attracted a following among some elite intellectuals, but although it was regarded as a serious danger by the leading theologians of the time, it never got very far.

Toward the end of the seventeenth century, however, anti-Trinitarianism revived in the form of deism, which maintained that the world had been created by a God who then left it to operate according to its own inner laws. Deism was widespread in intellectual circles throughout the eighteenth cen-

---

[2]Even at the time, there were attempts to put the blame for Servetus's execution on John Calvin, the leading preacher and reformer in Geneva, and this view is widely held today. However, as modern scholars have shown, it was the town council that demanded his execution, which Calvin actually tried to prevent. It is also true, of course, that Servetus would have suffered the same fate anywhere else in Europe at that time, and he seems to have gone to Geneva hoping that it would be more accepting of him than most other places.
[3]It was named after the Polish city of Raków, where they had found refuge.

tury, and some deists left the churches they formally belonged to because of what they called their unitarianism. This unitarianism was associated with radical politics in the eighteenth and nineteenth centuries and attracted a considerable following, but it has declined in importance since then. Today it is a fringe movement, sometimes known as "Unitarian Universalism," which maintains its reputation for radical social activism but has virtually ceased to exist as a coherent theological system. It appeals to some people who have been involved in conservative Christian churches but who have subsequently left them, perhaps over issues like divorce or homosexuality, and have found a home for their views among the Unitarians. As a result, unitarianism sometimes has a bitter edge to it, as disillusioned refugees from more orthodox churches use it as a platform from which to berate the Christianity they have rejected.

Another form of unitarianism is Christadelphianism, whose beliefs go back to John Thomas (1805–1871). Christadelphians are more orthodox than Unitarian Universalists are, but like them, they also deny the deity of Christ and the Holy Spirit. They do, however, affirm that the Bible is the infallible Word of God, but they interpret it in a minimalist way, apart from putting a great deal of emphasis on the return of Christ and the millennial reign of the saints. Though not a numerous body, Christadelphians have done some missionary work around the world and can be found scattered across Asia and the South Pacific in particular.

QUAKERISM

Another seventeenth-century movement that has continued to exist as a minority group on the fringes of the Christian church is Quakerism. The Quakers are the remnant of a number of similar groups that sprang up in the religious confusion of the English civil war in the seventeenth century. Among others, there were the Levelers and the Diggers, both of whom practiced a form of primitive communism, and the Muggletonians, who followed a man called Ludovic Muggleton and his brother, who claimed to be the two witnesses whose coming was prophesied in the book of Revelation.[4] Most like the Quakers were the Ranters, so called because of their ecstatic utterances. They denounced all forms of law and government, and advocated a return to primitive anarchy. Since the seventeenth century, most of these groups have gone the way of all flesh, but the Quakers have survived, having successfully transformed

---

[4] Rev. 11:3–12. The last of the Muggletonians died as recently as 1979, leaving the sect's archives to the University of Sussex.

themselves from being a radical mystical sect into a quietist movement noted chiefly for its pacifism and dedication to works of practical charity.

Most Quakers have claimed to be Christians and have been accepted as such, but there is a serious theological difficulty in accepting their creed as truly compatible with Christianity. Quakers believe in the "inner light," the voice of the Spirit who speaks to them as they sit and wait for him to come, making them "quake" when he does. What the Spirit tells them is regarded as a word from God, and as such it can be shared with other believers for their edification. The problem is that there is no prior insistence that these words attributed to the Spirit must conform to the teachings of the Bible, nor is there any necessary reason why they should glorify Jesus Christ. Quakers who are conscious of their Christian heritage can certainly interpret things in that way, and many of them do, but this is their choice, and not something imposed on them by the nature of their faith. It is here that orthodox Christians must dissent from them. We may believe in the inner witness of the Holy Spirit and accept that he can and does speak to individuals, but not in a way that ignores or contradicts the revelation of God found in Holy Scripture. Unfortunately, in recent years secularization has made inroads into Quakerism as it has elsewhere, with the result that the Christian context of the inner voice has often been obscured or has disappeared entirely. Modern Quakers are therefore likely to be closer to Unitarians than to orthodox Christians in their beliefs, and if that is so, they must be regarded as having departed from true Christianity.

Similar to the Quakers but of later origin are the Shakers, whose inspiration came from Ann Lee (1736–1784), an Englishwoman who emigrated to America in 1774 in order to escape religious persecution. Shaker theology is similar to that of the Quakers, but they place greater emphasis on gender equality, which in their case is interpreted as total abstinence from sexual relations. As a result, the Shakers can only increase by attracting new members, but these tapered off in the twentieth century and there are now hardly any Shakers left. They are remembered, however, for their unique and beautiful furniture and admired for their primitive, frontier-like lifestyle.

FREEMASONRY

The origins of freemasonry are obscure, but in its present form the phenomenon can be traced back to the seventeenth century. It exists today in a number of different forms, but all of them require their members to affirm belief in a supreme being, known as the "great architect of the universe," and most also display what they call a "volume of the sacred law" at their meetings and in their lodges. In Christian countries, it is generally understood that the "supreme being" is God and that the sacred law is the Bible (usually in the Authorized or King James Version of 1611), but there is nothing in the constitution of freemasonry that insists on that, and freemasons who belong to other religions are at liberty to substitute their own beliefs and sacred texts for those used by Christians. The fact that freemasonry constitutes a brotherhood to which allegiance is sworn and which takes precedence over any theological differences the brothers may have is enough to make it clear that it is incompatible with Christianity, which insists on the uniqueness of Christ and the exclusive nature of the biblical revelation. It is also true that Masonic ritual incorporates a number of pagan and other alien elements, which Christians cannot readily accept as valid, even if most of them seem harmless. That it is a highly select group of men (no women are allowed to join) is a further indication of its remoteness from Christianity, which is open to both sexes without distinction. Freemasonry has been closely connected with some Christian churches in the past, but in recent years there has been growing unease about this and there are now denominations which officially forbid or strongly discourage their members from becoming masons. It may technically be possible for a Christian to be a mason as well, but it is hard to see how he could be loyal to freemasonry and maintain the integrity of his Christian witness at the same time.

SEVENTH-DAY ADVENTISTS

Once regarded as a cult, Seventh-day Adventists are now more widely recognized as a genuinely Christian denomination, though there are still points of controversy concerning their beliefs that have not been fully resolved. The church began in mid-nineteenth-century America and was undoubtedly more extreme and eccentric than it is now. Over the years its edges have softened and it has become more like a conservative Protestant church, though one with special emphases of its own, such as the foot-washing ceremony which is an integral part of their celebration of Communion.[5] The main barrier to their full acceptance as a Christian denomination is their insistence on Saturday as their day of worship. For Adventists this is not a matter of indifference, but an essential part of their faith, which they claim brings them particularly close to the love of Christ. Most Christians do not worry too much about which day is set aside for worship, although Sunday has been all but universal since ancient

---

[5]Other churches sometimes do this, particularly on Maundy Thursday, when the Last Supper is recalled in a special way, but it is not an integral part of the Communion service as such.

times and it seems odd to change it deliberately, particularly when it means falling out of step with the rest of the Christian world. The deeper objection to Saturday worship is not to the observance but to the significance attached to it, particularly because this was evidently a problem in the early church, when Jewish Christians tried to insist on keeping the law of Moses even when it had been superseded by the coming of Christ.[6] Paul mentioned the Sabbath specifically as something that was not to be imposed on Christians.[7] Seventh-day Adventists have made a minor issue primary and a mark of their identity, and for this reason other Christians hesitate to accept them as fully orthodox.

In recent years there has been a tendency among some Adventists to move into mainstream Protestant evangelicalism, but other members of the church remain more closely wedded to its legalistic origins. Which of these two will triumph, or whether there will be a split, is not yet clear, but it seems safe to say that the closer the church moves toward other Christians, the less likely it is to stress or even to practice the distinctive traits that brought it into being in the first place.

JEHOVAH'S WITNESSES

Another group with a strongly Old Testament flavor is the Jehovah's Witnesses. They originated in the late nineteenth century, thanks to the teaching and preaching of Charles Taze Russell (1852–1916), and settled on their present name in 1931. From the beginning they have been characterized by an overly literalist reading of the Bible, which they also believe to have been corrupted in certain key places. As a result, they are one of the very few Christian or semi-Christian bodies that has produced its own translation of the Scriptures, which is designed to reflect their particular views. Somewhat oddly, they deny the divinity of Christ but at the same time expect his imminent return, which they have even been prepared to forecast.[8]

As their name indicates, they put great store on what they believe to be the "true" name of God, which they accuse both Jews and Christians of having hidden and distorted. Russell knew that the Hebrew name for God was YHWH, which had no vowels because Hebrew is written with consonants only. This name was never pronounced, and even before the time of Christ it had been replaced in speech by substitutes, especially "Lord" or "my Lord," a practice reflected both in the Greek translations of the Hebrew text and in the New Testament. Russell insisted that the traditional English reconstruction

---

[6] Gal. 4:10; Rom. 14:5–6.
[7] Col. 2:16.
[8] The years 1914 and 1975 were both popular at one time.

of this Hebrew name, which is "Jehovah," was the "true" name of God, even though it has almost certainly never been used in that form, and most scholars today reconstruct it as Yahweh.[9]

Objections of this kind to traditional Christianity are naive and characterize a movement that draws much of its strength from uneducated people who resent what they see as the condescension of the church and its scholars. This aspect has been especially popular among working-class people in Roman Catholic and Eastern Orthodox countries, who often feel alienated from the official church, and in whose eyes Jehovah's Witnesses are frequently regarded as evangelical Protestants. In Protestant countries they are more marginal, being known nowadays mainly for their aggressive proselytizing, which they undertake in the belief that it will make them one of the 144,000 who (in their understanding of the Bible) will be privileged to rule over the world with Christ when he returns at the end of time.[10]

The Jehovah's Witnesses' reading of the Scriptures cannot stand up to serious scrutiny and must be rejected. No serious scholar adopts or defends their interpretations of the Bible, and Jehovah's Witnesses remain for the most part an anti-intellectual and working-class movement for whom zealous activism and theological simplicity are an attractive combination.

CHRISTIAN SCIENCE

Christian Science is the name given to what is essentially a religious philosophy invented by Mary Baker Eddy (1821–1910) in nineteenth-century Boston. It is highly Platonic, in that it denies the reality of matter and claims that only spiritual things are real. This in turn means that there is no pain or disease, which are illusions of the material world and can be banished with the right understanding of the spirit. Mrs. Eddy propagated her beliefs in her book *Science and Health with a Key to the Scriptures*, which remains the movement's basic text. Christian Science has always exerted a curious appeal among wealthy people, who have funded its missionary efforts and support its flagship newspaper, *The Christian Science Monitor*, a highly respected journal of news and public opinion. Christian Scientists also maintain "reading rooms" in many cities, where interested people are invited to read and consider their doctrines. The fact that Christian Science denies creation and claims that evil is a delusion makes it impossible to recognize it as either Christian or science, and it has never been taken seriously by theologians or

---

[9]Yahweh is usually regarded as a form of the Hebrew verb "to be." Jehovah is a Hellenized form of this, with the vowels of "adonai" ("my Lord" in Hebrew) inserted. It first appears in the Septuagint and is found four times in the King James Version of the English Bible (Ex. 6:3; Ps. 83:18; Isa. 12:2; 26:4).
[10]Rev. 7:4.

intellectuals, nor has it been able to attract a popular following, in spite of its many efforts to do so.

THE LATTER-DAY SAINTS (MORMONS)

In a category all its own is the Church of Jesus Christ of Latter-day Saints, founded by Joseph Smith (1805–1844) in the early nineteenth century and propagated by his followers ever since. It originated in the northeastern United States, but after being persecuted there, members of the church migrated westward, eventually settling in the desert of what in 1896 would become the state of Utah. They are still dominant there and in parts of the neighboring states, and have developed a worldwide presence through their extensive and sometimes aggressive missionary efforts. The Latter-day Saints are unique among the deviant forms of Christianity in that they are the only ones who have made a serious attempt to justify their beliefs in scientific terms. Most outsiders believe that Joseph Smith had a vivid imagination and a charismatic gift for story-telling, which he put to good use. His claim that he received golden plates from heaven on which a divine revelation was written, and which he transcribed as *The Book of Mormon*, has never been given any credence outside Mormon circles, not least because the plates have miraculously disappeared and no one but Smith himself has ever seen them.

There is a strong Old Testament flavor to their beliefs, as can be seen in the centrality of temple worship and their deep interest in genealogy, which has made the Mormons world leaders in that field. They even claim that the ten lost tribes of Israel migrated to America, and Mormon archaeologists have gone looking for their remains, so far without success. In relation to Christianity, the Latter-day Saints claim to have received a revelation that complements, and therefore basically supersedes, the one already given in the Bible. In some respects their beliefs are similar to Islam, though they pay more attention to the Christian Scriptures than Muslims do and give Jesus Christ a more central place in their worship.

The relationship of Mormon theology to orthodox Christianity is sometimes hard to pin down, as its doctrine of the Trinity demonstrates. The Latter-day Saints generally reject the ancient formula of "three persons in one substance," not so much because they disagree with it as because it was elaborated by church councils and not received from God by direct revelation. Instead of accepting the historic creeds of the church, they prefer to claim that their own prophets have revealed that God is "three beings, united in purpose and separate in person." In classical Christian theology, however, "being" and "substance" are synonymous, so that by that standard, the Saints would appear to believe in three gods, although of course they deny this. Probably the best evaluation of their beliefs is to say that they are naive and tend to fall into traps that could have been avoided if they had paid more attention to the Christian theological tradition.

In other matters, the Latter-day Saints appear to have evolved somewhat since their early days, when the practice of polygamy was encouraged and black people were excluded from their number. It is hard to say whether (or to what extent) these earlier beliefs have persisted in an unofficial way. There are certainly still many polygamous Mormons, most of whom conceal the fact because polygamy is against the law in most Western countries. In other respects, the church of the Latter-day Saints resembles a very conservative form of American Protestantism, which is what it wants to be, although it continues to be rejected by orthodox Christians of every kind.

OTHER DEVIANT GROUPS

There are many other, smaller groups that can be regarded as deviant forms of Christianity, and from time to time some of them come into prominence for various reasons. One of them is the Church of the New Jerusalem, more usually known as Swedenborgianism, after its founder, Emanuel Swedenborg (1688–1772). Swedenborg was a gifted if somewhat eccentric genius who dabbled in the science of his age, seeking to invent new contraptions of various kinds. He was a friend of kings and traveled around the courts of Europe, but in 1745 he claimed to have received a vision from God which settled his course for the remainder of his life. For several years he received a stream of visions, mainly connected with prophecy and the coming of the New Jerusalem, as the name of his church suggests. Swedenborg interpreted his religious awakening as the second coming of Christ, and wrote a large number of books trying to demonstrate the truth of his teaching. The Swedenborgian church is a liturgical body similar to the Anglican or Lutheran churches, but its doctrines are very different. Swedenborgians deny the Trinity and interpret salvation as a kind of spiritual enlightenment. Though few in number, they are active in publishing, and their writings circulate far beyond their own congregations. Orthodox Christians do not accept their beliefs, but on the whole they are too small and esoteric to present much of a threat to the wider Christian church and so they have been generally ignored.

Another movement is the Unification Church of the Korean Sun Myung Moon (1920–), popularly known as the Moonies. This had a certain vogue in the 1970s but now seems to have retreated to its native Korea, where it continues to attract followers. Essentially, it is a syncretism of Christianity, Buddhism, and Korean folk religion, which has little appeal outside its native milieu.

Yet another such movement is that of the Kimbanguists in the Democratic Republic of the Congo (Kinshasa), named after its founder Simon Kimbangu (1887–1951). Kimbangu became a Baptist preacher in 1915 but after a few years came to see himself as a prophet with miraculous healing powers. After a short public ministry in 1921, during which he claimed to have performed numerous healings, Kimbangu was imprisoned by the Belgian rulers of the Congo and died in jail thirty years later. His church was subsequently legalized and run by his son (until his death in 1992), and now his grandson heads it. The Kimbanguist church was admitted to the World Council of Churches in 1969, probably because it was regarded as an authentic expression of African resistance to colonialist oppression, but its veneration of Simon Kimbangu as the incarnation of the Holy Spirit clearly puts it outside the bounds of what can legitimately be regarded as Christian.

One of the difficulties with groups like the Moonies and the Kimbanguists is that it is hard to know whether they will last, or whether they represent a transitional phase in which traditional religious beliefs are confused with the recently arrived Christianity and will disappear once the latter is more firmly implanted. Some of them may survive and develop into distinctive religions, as has happened with the Latter-day Saints; others may draw closer to orthodox Christianity and eventually merge with it, as seems to be happening with Seventh-day Adventism; others may simply vanish, as did the seventeenth-century Ranters. Only time will tell which of them, if any, will have staying power and how far they will be able to expand their ministry and influence.

Another intriguing sect is that of Scientology. Scientology is the invention of Lafayette Ron Hubbard (1911–1986), and its main teachings are found in his book *Dianetics: The Modern Science of Mental Health*, published in 1950. Its beliefs amount to a complete denial of Christianity, and in that respect it is much more radical than Christian Science. It is polytheistic, and regards the "Christ legend" as an eternal myth which has been mistakenly attached to Jesus. It denies any form of sin or hell, and promises a life of happiness to those who follow its self-help ideology. It has attracted some prominent followers but has also been dogged by criticism of its financial and other operations, which has led to investigations by a number of secular governments. In particular, scientologists have been accused of kidnaping and brainwashing wealthy young people whom they seek to lure into their sect. It is hard to know how long Scientology will last now that the founder is dead, but it shows some signs of developing into a "church" and it may eventually become a theosophical religious body not unlike Christian Science.

Finally, something should be said about Russia, which along with England and the United States has historically been one of the great homes of sectarian Christianity. From the seventeenth to the early twentieth century, the Russian Orthodox Church had to deal with breakaway groups, most of which rejected its elaborate liturgy and close involvement with the state, preferring simple and even extreme forms of ascetical piety. Most of them have disappeared over time, but one group which is still active and widely known is the sect of the Doukhobors ("Spirit-wrestlers"), whose origins go back to the seventeenth century. They regarded matter as evil and rejected Russian Orthodox theology and rituals, putting them at odds with the state, which persecuted them. In the late nineteenth century their sufferings became the object of widespread international protest, supported by the famous Russian novelist Leo Tolstoy, who wanted the Doukhobors to be granted religious freedom. In 1899 they were allowed to emigrate to Canada, where many of them still live. Over the years they have declined in numbers thanks to their progressive assimilation into the wider community, but they are still capable of making headlines by marching naked through the streets when they feel that their freedom of worship is being jeopardized. On the whole, though, their eccentricity and unwillingness to proselytize have kept them away from public notice, and most Christians now have little to do with them.

THE NATURE OF CHRISTIAN SECTARIANISM

Many theories have been proposed to explain the emergence of Christian sectarianism, but the sects themselves are so diverse that it is doubtful whether any one of these explanations can cover every case. Nevertheless, it seems that the phenomenon is due to one or more of the following factors, which emerge or combine in particular circumstances to produce any given deviation from orthodox Christianity.

1. Dissatisfaction with the perceived worldliness of the mainline church(es). This was a powerful factor in ancient times and also in the seventeenth century, and is still a factor to be reckoned with today. For a variety of reasons, institutional churches are often seen as having compromised with non-Christian forces and having been corrupted as a result, so that the forming of a particular new sect is seen as a return to the purity of primitive Christianity.

2. Objections to Christian theology. Most of these objections have cen-

tered around the doctrine of the Trinity and of the divinity of Christ, which are interpreted as unnecessary accretions to a "pure" biblical faith.

3. Mysticism. It is notable how many sects have been started by charismatic individuals following a vision or visions that they claim to have had. Orthodox Christians have always rejected such claims because of the finality which they accord to the New Testament revelation, but this has not deterred the visionaries, who have gone on to proclaim their beliefs to anyone prepared to listen. The result has often been the formation of a new community, which after initial excesses and perhaps persecution from the state authorities has then settled down to a much more socially respectable existence.

4. Independent-mindedness. Some people simply do not like being told what to do, particularly in spiritual matters, and have pushed what they see as their right to freedom of religion to the point where they effectively make up their own. The individualism of this approach is often so great that no communities can be formed, but occasionally enough people share a common vision that they are able to constitute a form of church.

Whether sectarianism has much of a future is impossible to say. The conditions which produced most of the deviant groups that now exist have changed dramatically, and it may be that they will decline and die out in the next couple of generations, as happened with the heresies that flourished in ancient times but have long since disappeared. On the other hand, based on one or more of the factors mentioned above, it is also very likely that new sects will emerge, bearing new names and professing a different mix of beliefs. What these sects will be like and how many followers they will attract obviously remains unknown, but one thing is certain: orthodox Christianity will continue to flourish and be the standard against which all of these sects will rebel—and will be judged. In the end, heresies come and go, but the word of our God stands forever and its greatness is enhanced, not diminished, by those who do it the honor of rejecting it with such evident determination.

23

CHRISTIANITY AND ATHEISM

THE ORIGINS OF MODERN ATHEISM

So far we have been talking within the parameters of religion, explaining why we believe that Christianity is superior to its rivals, and why its orthodox expression is to be preferred to any deviant versions thereof. However, many people nowadays reject the religious way of thinking altogether, whatever form it takes. In their own self-understanding, instead of trying to influence some supernatural power whose existence cannot be proved, they rely on rational enquiry and claim that human science can control and shape the universe in ways that will obtain the results that older civilizations sought and failed to get by religion. Some of the advocates of modern scientific thought suppose that they have outgrown all forms of religious belief, but in some ways what they prefer is more like some primitive forms of paganism than they realize. If modern scientists try to solve the world's problems by material means, then they are acting rather like witch doctors who do much the same thing in a less sophisticated way. The difference between them is that scientists analyze and test the means they use by experiments designed to achieve consistent and reliable results. That is perfectly valid in itself, of course, but if it is used to address problems that cannot be resolved in that way, then the proposed solutions will be as useless as any magical potion would be. Searching for an "evil" gene, for example, and trying to modify its behavior is a pointless exercise, because evil is not something located in our physical makeup. It is here that atheistic materialism not only falls short but becomes evil in itself, because not only does it promise something that it cannot deliver, but it attacks as unscientific and therefore dangerous, those who point this out and offer another way.

Those who adopt the modern atheistic worldview almost invariably see it as superior to Christianity because it appears to promise eventual success in overcoming life's problems in a way that Christianity cannot do. Christians may seek relief from earthly troubles but we cannot promise to eradicate them, and the hope that research may eventually help the human race overcome poverty, sickness, and death is one that we do not share.[1] For Christians, guarantees of health, wealth, and eternal life belong to another dimension of being.[2] Many "modern" people do not believe that dimension exists outside the imagination of religious believers, and they accuse the church of having preached a message that has tolerated and even encouraged the spread of evil in this world by claiming that there is a reality higher and more real than the life we are now living on earth. They can point with some justification to places like Latin America, where a corrupt church has allied itself with the local aristocracy to exploit the peasant masses, or to South Africa and the American South, where some conservative Protestants have defended racism by appealing to obscure verses in the Old Testament.[3] The fact that Christians have long been in the forefront of charitable work around the world, that missionaries have brought education and health care along with the gospel, and that even today it is the church that stays in deprived inner-city areas when everyone else has departed, is conveniently overlooked or else dismissed as "imperialism" or "paternalism."

At the heart of modern atheism there is *anger* at the plight of the world. Instead of blaming this on people, atheists prefer to ascribe it to abstractions like "religion" and the "socioeconomic system" that religion appears designed to prop up. Anger was what motivated Karl Marx and Friedrich Engels as they witnessed the injustices of nineteenth-century industrialization, and their legacy continues to haunt atheism to this day. While Christians like Lord Shaftesbury were doing all they could to change social conditions for the poor, Marx and Engels were merely campaigning against the "system." Where Christian philanthropy did its work, their rhetoric fell on deaf ears, but in places where the churches appeared to be propping up social injustice, their followers brought about revolution. Unfortunately, they then went on to prove that when scientific atheism was put into practice, the result was just as bad as, if not worse than, the evil it was trying to rectify. But despite this obvious and catastrophic failure, modern atheists continue to campaign for what they see as "justice" while Christians work behind the scenes and often below

---

[1] See, for example, Matt. 26:11.
[2] Matt. 6:19–21.
[3] A particular favorite has been the so-called "curse of Ham" found in Gen. 9:20–27. Needless to say, the text says nothing that could reasonably be used to defend racism.

the radar to bring it about as far as they can. Modern atheism was and still is largely propaganda, in which specific cases of injustice (such as *apartheid* in South Africa) are generalized into universal victimhood and made the excuse for obliterating both belief and believers in God who stand in their way.

For Christians, accepting the revelation of Jesus Christ gives us the key to seeing the mysteries of life in their proper perspective, but it does not necessarily "resolve" them. Pain and suffering continue to exist in spite of the healing power of Christ's message, and evil is still present in a world that is by nature fundamentally good. Christians do not know why this is so and cannot claim exemption from the effects these things cause, but they do believe that they are in contact with the God who is in control of what is going on, and who protects his people in their earthly struggles. We cannot make sense of this within the limitations of our earthly life, but we have a perspective on an eternal and spiritual world that gives us the hope that one day we shall overcome our current troubles and finally come to understand what is now still hidden from our eyes. No other religion can promise this in the way that Christianity does. Islam comes closest perhaps, but Islam means submission to an all-powerful and hidden deity, not fellowship with the Father, Son, and Holy Spirit in the inner life of God. Or to put it a different way, Muslims can never see themselves as anything more than servants of God, whereas Christians affirm that we are his children, a difference of status that makes all the difference in the world.[4]

THE CHRISTIAN ANSWER TO ATHEISM

How should Christians tackle modern scientific atheism? We cannot offer the sort of proof for spiritual reality that a scientific atheist would accept on his own terms, because spiritual things cannot be reduced to material forms. We may believe that the spiritual realm exists and act on that belief, but there is no scientific proof that would put its existence beyond any reasonable doubt. However much the material world points to a reality beyond itself, and however satisfactory an explanation for what we can see based on what is invisible to us may be, concrete and irrefutable proof that the spiritual world exists is not forthcoming because its very nature precludes that possibility. To the scientific atheist, therefore, the existence of such a spiritual world is irrelevant, because even if it is there, he can neither know it nor say anything meaningful about it. The only way for a Christian to tackle scientific atheism is to examine its presuppositions and demonstrate, if he can, that they are inadequate

---

[4]John 15:15; Rom. 8:16–17.

and unable to account for the data or to perform the tasks that its adherents claim it can do. As a matter of historical fact, Christians have been doing this ever since scientific atheism made its appearance in the seventeenth century, and although they have certainly not eliminated it, they can reasonably claim to have demonstrated that the atheist case is not nearly as compelling as its proponents think it is. The truth is that atheism is a belief that is (quite literally) in denial. There is no objective evidence that points in its direction, and there is a good deal of evidence that makes it harder to believe than theism. It is one thing to say that science cannot demonstrate the existence of a personal God, but was it ever meant to? The natural sciences examine material reality but cannot explain where it came from, why it is there, or what will eventually happen to it. Christianity has an answer to all these questions: material reality was made by God out of nothing, it stays where it is because God is in control of it, and it will eventually be transformed into a spiritual reality at his command.[5]

Atheists dismiss these claims as mythical, but what alternative can they provide? They may agree that matter came out of nothing, but how? Current scientific theories prefer the explanation known as the "big bang" theory of cosmic origins, which states that about 13.7 billion years ago the material universe exploded into being—but out of what? This the scientists cannot answer, beyond saying that it seems to have come out of nothing at all. The irony is that Christians have been saying this for centuries, even without the benefit of modern scientific knowledge, and now it appears that they were right all along. But if scientists have trouble explaining how the big bang took place, they are completely unable to tell us *why* it occurred. Here the Christian claim is that natural science will never be able to account for this, because it is outside its purview. The only answer they could possibly come up with is that somewhere there is an intelligent mind that wanted this to happen and was powerful enough to bring it about, though why it did so will forever remain a mystery. Once again, this is exactly what Christians have always said, with the important difference that the "it" is known to us as a "he"—a personal being with whom we are in relationship, and who created us out of love, a concept that lies well beyond the competence of the scientific world to investigate.

So much for the origin of the world. Atheists also have to agree that the universe is kept in being by operating according to set "laws," but where does this order come from? Is it really plausible that the entire universe should have developed so complex a rational order without a controlling mind behind it? It is sometimes claimed that because there is a natural "randomness" in the

---
[5]Rev. 21:1.

world that makes things unpredictable, it cannot be held together by the will of a God who is sovereign over it. Whether or to what extent such randomness really exists is controversial. It is true that there seem to be degrees of uncertainty in certain procedures, which might be considered random, but the fact that this kind of uncertainty can be artificially produced and injected into a system (of computer analysis, for example) makes it highly unlikely that it is an example of true randomness. Similarly, it can be argued that throwing dice will produce random results that cannot be predicted, but the range of possibilities is limited and statistical analysis will show that there is a probability that any one combination will turn up in a measure proportionate to what that range allows for. There may also be what are known as "hidden variables," factors that we are not aware of that have determined a particular outcome. Mathematicians and other scientists refer to this sort of thing as "pseudo-randomness" because it exists only within carefully defined parameters.

True randomness is more than the belief that certain phenomena are unpredictable. An insect, for example, may fly in a bizarre pattern in order to escape its predators, but although we cannot say where it will go, we can understand the phenomenon and explain it. If it were truly random, there would be no such explanation because there would be no rational framework within which the insect operates. It is at this level that the debate about the existence of randomness takes place, and where the greatest objections to accepting it occur. As far as Christians are concerned, we do not have to worry if it turns out that there are some things in the world than cannot be explained or predicted by natural laws. This is fully compatible with our belief in a Creator God who sustains what he has made by his own will, which is not bound to observe preconceived "laws." We believe that, although God does not negate the nature of his creatures, he is free to guide and direct them in ways that go beyond our understanding and that may not be reducible to fixed axioms.

Some people might be tempted to argue that God is the ultimate "hidden variable." Although Christians have some sympathy with that suggestion, we do not accept it, for the simple reason that hidden variables are part of the created order, whereas God is not. In the end, all that this "uncertainty principle" does is show that the complexity of the universe goes beyond the ability of the human mind to understand, which is not the same thing as saying that disorder lies at the heart of it. The truth seems to be that even uncertainty is governed by laws, which (if true) is an argument *for* the existence of a transcendent mind, not against it. It is probably not too much to say that, with every advance of science, the case for atheism gets weaker, which is the exact opposite of what "scientific" atheists claim.

Nor can scientists tell us exactly where the universe is headed. They know that it is constantly expanding, a fact which in itself almost necessitates an external mover, but how long this will go on and where it will all end is impossible to say. What will happen to matter when energy eventually runs down? We know that the sun will have burned up all its hydrogen in about 5 billion years, but what will happen when it finally gives out? If life on earth still exists at that time, it will presumably come to an end, but can we keep going that long? It is easy to sound alarmist about the prospects for the next few centuries, and perhaps the apocalyptic scenarios sketched by climatologists and others are exaggerated, but who can say? Even if their details are wrong, their warnings of disaster have to be taken seriously, if only because the human race cannot go on growing and consuming irreplaceable natural resources indefinitely. Sooner or later it will all come to an end, which Christians not only expect, but for which they eagerly pray and wait. We do not know when that end will come, but science confirms our belief that it will. Once again, atheists have no answer to give.

ATHEISM AND HUMAN MORAL RESPONSIBILITY

Atheists believe that we must solve the problems we face within the material context of this world, and they are fond of pointing to religious people who do irrational things—like pray or sacrifice to some divine being in the hope that he or she will intervene on their behalf—as evidence that religion is both false and harmful. If there were no more to it than that, and if religion were merely an excuse for avoiding the use of our intellectual capacities, then it would be hard to disagree with atheists on this point. Christians do not believe that religious exercises are supposed to allow us to avoid serious thought and practical dedication to resolving material problems. We are just as critical of these things as atheists are—perhaps even more so, because we believe that such behavior, while it may appear to be devout and pious, is dishonoring to the God who gave us our minds and commanded us to use them to rule over his creation.

Christians part company with atheists, however, when it comes to the deeper questions of where these problems come from and why we bother with them to the extent that we do. Physical difficulties are known to the animal world, and we marvel at the way in which birds travel vast distances to find their winter quarters, or salmon seem to know what stream to return to in order to lay their eggs. Human beings also have to face the challenges posed by their environment and resolve them, but it is remarkable that, although we may do some things out of a basic instinct for self-preservation, we normally inject an element of thoughtful deliberation into our decision making that is unknown to animals. Furthermore, the thought we give to things may lead us to act against our instincts and even against our own self-interest, which seems irrational.

When we come to moral questions of good and evil, it quickly becomes apparent that we are in a different league from the animals. It is true that there are some people who say that all human morality is ultimately a form of self-preservation, but the mere fact that the great moral teachers of mankind have spoken out against this and condemned it is a reminder that we are different from animals in this respect. Has anyone ever tried to reason that way with a dog or a snake? The very idea makes us smile, but we do this with other people all the time. Indeed, intellectual atheists are often among the most moral people around (at least in their own self-understanding) and do not hesitate to criticize religious believers, especially Christians, for the hypocrisies and moral lapses they perceive in the church and elsewhere. But what warrant do they have for doing this? Christians have a standard of goodness which we admit we cannot live up to, and the message of our faith is that we can be forgiven and restored to spiritual health by the grace of our loving God. To claim moral superiority over other people or to judge them for their failings is anti-Christian, because it denies the basic premise of the gospel of Christ, which is that all have sinned and fall short of the glory of God.[6] It was as sinners that the Son of God loved us and came to rescue us from the consequences of our own behavior, and those who do not understand that have no hope of ever entering the kingdom of heaven.[7] To condemn others is to condemn ourselves, which we readily do because in our hearts we know that it is the truth, and that the truth will set us free.[8]

Atheists who make moral judgments have no fixed principles by which to measure those judgments, and consequently they are forced to take their own behavior as the norm. Even if they do not say this explicitly, it is clear from the way they speak and act that this is what they believe, and given their presuppositions, it is hard to see how they could think otherwise. Their judgments are not based on an objective standard, which they confess they are incapable of attaining. Instead, they make their judgments from a standpoint of implied

---

[6]Rom. 3:23.
[7]Matt. 9:13.
[8]John 8:32.

moral superiority that is not justified by the facts. We can all criticize other people for doing things that have never crossed our minds or that we would be unlikely to do ourselves, but can we really claim to be morally superior to them?

Attempts to blame antisocial behavior on a bad background or poor economic conditions may have some plausibility, but they cannot provide a universal answer to every criminal act, since some of the most vicious and effective offenders are perfectly normal, even privileged, in this respect. Besides, who decides what is evil anyhow? What principles ought to govern our conduct in particular cases? Every once in a while we hear of someone who has killed an innocent person because he was afraid of a possible attack and acted in self-defense. Is this right or wrong? A jury that convicts such a person of manslaughter is almost certain to provoke a backlash among the general population, where many people will feel that their life and liberty have been potentially threatened by the verdict. Yet to acquit him without further ado opens the door to people who would use the plea of self-defense whether or not there is any justification for it. In such a situation, what is good and what is evil?

The Christian answer is to distinguish morality from the law, which can only be an approximation of it. Legally, it may be necessary to weigh the facts of the case and decide what punishment, if any, is appropriate in the circumstances. But morally, there is no question at all, because in God's eyes there are no innocents, and even the person who kills in self-defense has committed a sin for which he must repent and seek forgiveness. Such killing may be necessary in the context of a fallen world, and it is often lawful in certain contexts. Regrettable as it is, there are times when we are forced to go to war, for example, in which there is bound to be killing. Some people will argue that the death penalty is the appropriate punishment for certain crimes, but Christians can only do so with a heavy heart, and recognize that this is not what God originally intended for his creatures. Rather than call such lawful killing "good," we prefer to say that it is the lesser of two evils and justify it on those grounds. In the sight of God, it is still wrong, and Christians are right to remember that we too are part of a fallen world, in which every act is tainted with our sinfulness.

It is a hard lesson to learn, but Christians do not let their standards be determined by legal norms alone. The atheist, on the other hand, has no other option because he has no logical place for a standard higher than that of the law. It is only the fact that the laws of most Western societies have until recently been governed by Christian norms that gives the atheist case a semblance of righteousness. Once the religious foundation is removed, the law is no defense. In the twentieth century we saw the consequences of this in the Soviet Union and in Nazi Germany, where laws were made to fit the reigning atheistic ideology, with dire consequences. Academic atheists will say that such examples are false because the Communists and the Nazis turned atheism into a religion and used it to stir up a religious-like fanaticism in their followers, which of course these academics would never do themselves. But this argument is fatuous. Neither the Communists nor the Nazis had any trouble finding intellectual atheists to support and justify their behavior, even as the dirty deeds they authorized were carried out by less refined members of the human race. Where there is no fear of God there is no fear of anything, except perhaps the knock on the door that tells us that it is now our turn to be liquidated.

ATHEISM AND THE ABSOLUTE

Whatever an atheist thinks the point of living is, he must recognize, as we all do, that death is inevitable. Living on earth forever may be an aspiration for some, but it is not a reality, nor is it ever likely to be more than science fiction. There are some noble souls who believe that it is worth sacrificing themselves for the sake of future generations, but their sense of commitment has no foundation in logic. What is the point of working for a better future if we are not going to be there to see it? Should others benefit from our labors, and is it really good for them not to have to learn life's hard lessons for themselves? What basis can there be for morality if there is no fundamental absolute? The fact is that most modern atheists are living in a historically Christian culture and have taken over the moral standards of the Bible without the devotion to God that undergirds it. Their beliefs are fundamentally parasitical because they make sense only as a denial of the God whom they insist does not exist. Atheists claim to have no notion of any divine being, but in fact it is the God of the Bible that they are rejecting, which becomes clear as soon as they start to defend their position.

Very few atheists will bother denying the existence of the different Hindu gods, for example, because they are obviously personifications of natural forces and not beings that exist in their own right. Their target is the Christian God, without whom atheism as we know it would not mean anything. In a backhanded way, the self-definition of atheists is evidence that the God of the Bible is really there, since no one would reject a phantom with the passion that they direct against him. Compare their attitude toward what they insist is a nonexistent God with something else, and the oddity of their position will be obvious. For example, I do not believe in fairies or leprechauns, but I would never think of writing books or giving lectures trying to prove that they do not exist. I know that there are people who do believe in them and who are convinced that they have great influence over their lives, but I do not care very much about that. I have no great desire to persuade them to share my unbelief, because in the end I know that it makes no difference. Why do atheists make such a huge effort to attack religious believers, if they really think that God falls into the same category as fairies and leprechauns? If believers are just fantasizing, why worry about it, especially since most of them are praying for good things to happen, not bad ones? The truth is that God is dangerous because he is not a fantasy, and in their heart of hearts, atheists know it. At the end of the day, they have to rebel against God because if they simply ignored him, their own existence would have no meaning.

AGNOSTICISM

Many people try to avoid the risks of claiming absolute certainty by calling themselves "agnostics" instead of atheists. An agnostic is a person who does not want to deny the existence of God categorically, but who is not prepared to affirm it either. This position of noncommitment is popular with people who want to hedge their bets or who recognize that outright atheism is just as impossible to prove as any form of religious belief is. But in practical terms it makes no real difference whether one is an atheist or an agnostic, because at bottom an agnostic is no more than an atheist who does not want to commit himself—the unbelieving equivalent of a Christian who does not go to church. If anything, he is even further away from God than the atheist is, because he is determined to avoid the issues by never letting himself be confronted with the need to make a decision about them. In this sense, indifference is worse than hostility because it is impossible to get to grips with it in any serious way. Those who are openly hostile to God are usually only too willing to talk about it, and where there is dialogue, conversion is at least a theoretical possibility. But when the door is shut and dialogue cannot take place, the chances of conversion are reduced, making agnosticism the last refuge of the truly determined atheist.

THE PERSISTENCE OF ATHEISM

If atheism is parasitical by nature and unlikely to be true, why is it so widespread and dominant in Western countries today? The main reason for this is that Christians believe that everyone who does not know God in Jesus Christ is effectively an atheist, whether or not they realize this. It may seem wrong to put Jews, Muslims, and nominal Christians in this category, since they so obviously profess the contrary, but that is nevertheless where they properly belong. This is because belief in God is not just an intellectual exercise. Of course we must believe that he exists, but we must also have a relationship with him that accepts his self-revelation in Jesus Christ and submits to the obedience which that relationship demands of us.[9] Failure to do this is to be "without God in the world,"[10] which is the state of everyone who does not know Christ.

To be without God is to be an atheist in practice, even if not in theory. If we go back to the sixteenth century, we find that this is how the term was used then—an atheist was defined as someone who disobeyed the commandments of God, even if he never questioned God's existence. In a society that has been shaped by Christian values to the extent that "belief in God" is generally understood to mean "belief in the God of the Bible," we cannot be surprised if those who reject him fall naturally into the atheist (or agnostic) category, because there is really nowhere else to go. Intellectual atheism is a highly sophisticated manifestation of this more basic unbelief, which is widespread among the population. In a typical Western country, a majority of people will claim to believe in God, but far fewer will act on that belief to any significant extent. Secular humanists know this, of course, and promote their atheistic agenda with the tacit support of a large number of theoretical "believers" whom they quite rightly count as allies. Christians know it too, and put little faith in what people tell pollsters about their "faith." As far as we are concerned, there is no substitute for knowing God, or being "born again," as Jesus said.[11] The only real alternative is a practical atheism, whether or not it is expressed in such terms. The rejection of God's love may be concealed under many different guises, but this is what it comes down to in the end.

---

[9]Heb. 11:6.
[10]Eph. 2:12.
[11]John 3:7.

PART FIVE

GOD
SO LOVED
THE WORLD

24

GOD'S LOVE FOR THE MATERIAL WORLD

THE PRESERVATION OF THE HUMAN RACE

God's willingness to preserve the fallen spiritual creatures in spite of their rebellion is matched by his desire to keep the human race in being. This is a mystery that can be explained only by his deep love for his creatures. Looked at in a purely rational light, it would not have been surprising if God had decided to wipe us out and start again. A master potter does not tolerate a flawed vase and will either smash it or rework it. The Bible reminds us that we are pottery in God's hands and that he has made us without consulting us first.[1] After the fall of Adam and Eve, it would been natural for God to have concluded that his experiment in creation had gone wrong, and that it was best to terminate it. That is probably what we would have done in his place, and had he done so, there would have been no further problem, since none of us would have been around to object. The Bible tells us that God did react to the spread of evil and decided to wipe it off the face of the earth by sending a flood to destroy it.[2] Even then, however, the destruction was not total. Instead of destroying the human race completely, he preserved it in the family of Noah and revealed that he would never resort to such punishment again. Even in our fallen state, God respects us as his creatures and has done nothing to alter or diminish the nature he gave us at the beginning. It is yet another reminder of how different God's thoughts are from ours, and how little we understand or appreciate his love for us.

That God did not destroy the fallen human race is clear, but it is hard to explain why he gave us the ability to disobey him in the first place. Did he

---

[1] Rom. 9:19–23.
[2] Gen. 6:5–8.

know what Adam and Eve would do when he put them in the garden of Eden? Was their fall planned from the beginning, and therefore not really against his will at all? If God had not wanted us to fall away from him, our minds think, surely he could have prevented it by making us incapable of doing anything like that. Adam and Eve were not obviously flawed when they were created, but if God made them "perfect" in the sense that they were what they were meant to be, did he intend for them to respond positively to Satan's tempting? If we follow that logic to its natural conclusion, we must conclude that their transgression was part of God's plan, hard as that is to understand. There was a school of thought in the Middle Ages which argued precisely that, calling the sin of Adam a "happy fault" (*felix culpa*) because by it mankind was set free from the limitations of an earthly paradise and the way was opened up to an inheritance of eternal life in heaven instead. In this respect, the fall might be compared to something like teething troubles. We suffer the loss of our first set of teeth, but only because a better set is on the way, painful though the transition from the one to the other may sometimes be.

The *felix culpa* argument was an ingenious attempt to solve a real problem. We cannot believe that God would have created something that was less than perfect, because that would contradict his own nature. But neither can we believe that the fall of Adam and Eve thwarted the plan of a sovereign God for his creatures. Seeing the fall as internal to that plan resolves this dilemma by making it part of the overall divine perfection, even if we do not experience it in that way to begin with. Nevertheless, and despite its apparent logic, the *felix culpa* argument never got very far. It seems odd to think that the pain and suffering of mankind, not to mention the sacrifice of Jesus Christ for us on the cross, was all part of a preordained plan for improving our lot. There must have been an easier way of accomplishing that! Why would God inflict such cruelty and devastation on his beloved creatures, if all he wanted to do was to give them a better life than the one they already had?

There is also a serious moral objection to this solution to the problem. We can understand that if someone sins, he or she must suffer for it, and that sometimes people learn their lesson and improve their behavior, but we would prefer that they had learned this without going to all that trouble. We also know that that is possible, because not everyone has to learn the hard way. Surely that was what God intended for his creatures, and it seems monstrous to suggest that he made them with an inbuilt inclination to go astray. But the biggest objection to this way of thinking is that, if sin had been an innate tendency in Adam and Eve, they could hardly have been held responsible for it, since it would have been what God had planned for them all along. If I drive my car off the road and land in a ditch, I am to blame, but if I can prove that the car's steering was fixed in such a way that it would go off the road whether or not I wanted it to, it would not be my fault, and I could claim compensation. But the preservation of mankind is a gift from God that we have not deserved and are not entitled to—it is certainly not compensation for something that we are not responsible for. However we try to explain it, we have to say that Adam and Eve did not have an inbuilt propensity to sin, given to them when they were created, that the fall is entirely our own fault, and that by responding to it in the way that he has, God has revealed a depth of love that we would not otherwise have seen.

We therefore cannot accept the *felix culpa* argument as the solution to the problem of the fall, though we can affirm with it that we have been shown a greater love and have been promised a higher reward than fallen human beings have any right to claim. A horse will be put down if it breaks a leg, and a car will be written off if it suffers too much damage in an accident, but human beings remain precious in God's eyes. However much harm we have done to ourselves, we are still salvageable. In this respect, we are different from the fallen angels, who cannot be rescued after their rebellion. That ought to make us appreciate just how deeply God cares for us. We have betrayed his trust and sold ourselves into slavery to the Devil, but God has not let us slip out of his grasp. His plan to redeem the human race began with Adam and Eve themselves, who were promised his protection after they were expelled from the garden, and were promised that at some future stage, the "offspring" of the woman would bruise the serpent's head.[3] The wrong done by the serpent would be avenged, though precisely how that would happen was not made clear. A natural interpretation might suggest that human beings would hunt down serpents and try to kill them, but while that may be true at one level, it seems somewhat pedestrian to be the substance of a divine promise, and it is hard not to believe that there must be more to it than that. Christian exegetes have often interpreted this verse as a prophecy of the coming of Christ, and the fact that the man who is to come is described as the son of Eve, not of Adam, is particularly suggestive of this because he did not have a human father.[4] That may be the right interpretation, though the context is too vague to make it certain, and it is not referred to in the New Testament as a prophecy that had been fulfilled.[5]

On the other hand, there is no doubt that Paul saw the coming of Christ

[3] Gen. 3:15.
[4] Normally he would have been described as the offspring of the man, as in Rom. 1:3, where Jesus is said to have descended from David according to the flesh.
[5] But see Gal. 4:4.

as God's answer to the sin of Adam, and he was not slow to draw a parallel between the two men: "As in Adam all die, so also in Christ shall all be made alive."[6] And more explicitly still,

> As one trespass led to condemnation for all men, so one act of righteousness leads to justification and life for all men. For as by the one man's disobedience the many were made sinners, so by the one man's obedience the many will be made righteous.[7]

Adam did not sin because of some flaw in his nature, but because he chose to follow the tempting of the serpent and disobey God. God could have destroyed him as punishment, but that would not have put the sin right because it was a broken relationship and not a natural defect. Natural defects can be cured by going back to the drawing board and remaking whatever it is that is flawed, but a broken relationship is not healed by ending it and starting again. The preservation of Adam was therefore necessary for the promise to be fulfilled, since if he had been destroyed there would have been no relationship with God to be put right, and the Son of God would have had nothing to come into the world for. Christ's relationship with Adam by descent is fundamental to his work of reconciliation. For that reason even the sinful Adam was allowed to go on living.

Does this mean that Adam was saved in the end? The Bible is silent on this question, which is an indication that we do not know the answer. It is clearly stated that every human being is now a sinner because of Adam's fall; in quantitative terms, his transgression has extended to the entire human race, and there is no one who has managed to escape its influence. It is equally clear, however, that not everyone is saved in Christ, even though his death paid the price for Adam's sin and in some sense reversed its effects. How can we say, as Paul does, that Christ's achievement was greater than Adam's sin when it is less far-reaching? To put it bluntly, more people are lost than are saved, even if those who are saved are better off than they were before or than they would have been had they not fallen in the first place. The only way to understand what Paul is saying is to think in terms of quality and not quantity. Adam sinned by his disobedience, which in physical terms was painless and insignificant, but Christ's obedience was very painful and involved making the supreme human sacrifice. The effort he expended to save us was far greater than anything Adam had done, and so we should expect that its effects will be greater too.

---

[6] 1 Cor. 15:22. See also Rom. 5:14–16.
[7] Rom. 5:18–19.

The human race comprises many millions of people who have either never heard the gospel or who have heard it and rejected it. It can certainly be said that Adam was in the first category, since the gospel was never preached to him. He is even omitted from the great catalogue of Old Testament saints in Hebrews 11. Can a case be made for saying that he heard the gospel at some point? Perhaps he heard the gospel preached to him when Christ went down to hell. He may have accepted it then and been set free, but this is not stated in the Bible and we do not know whether or not he did.[8] But whatever happened to Adam as an individual, we can say that he was not saved in his representative role as the head of the human race. If he had been, the Bible would surely say so, but it does not. Furthermore, if he had been saved as our head, all his followers and/or descendants would have been saved in him, which is not the case. The teaching of Jesus, the preaching of the gospel, and the reality of the church as a faithful remnant in a hostile world combine to make it impossible for us to affirm that Adam, the archetypal human being, was saved, and it is probably for this reason that nothing is said about it in the New Testament. The promise made to him after the fall was that he would be protected, not that he would be saved, and there we must leave it.

GOD'S COVENANT WITH NOAH

Although the protection that God gave to Adam and his descendants continued through the generations until the time of Noah, it was not a general or absolute promise that would never be revoked. As conditions on earth worsened and sin became more of a problem, God's anger grew stronger and his determination to do something about it became correspondingly greater. The destruction that Adam and Eve had been spared was eventually inflicted on their descendants, all of whom (except Noah and his family) were wiped out because of their sinfulness. It would be nice to think that the flood purified the human race from sin, but it did not. Noah and his family were preserved from destruction, but they were not cured of their rebelliousness. Before long, mankind was back where it had been before. The only difference was that because Noah was faithful and offered the right kind of sacrifices after the flood waters had subsided, God made a covenant with him that renewed and extended the creation mandate given to Adam.[9] Its exact provisions were as follows:

> Be fruitful and multiply and fill the earth. The fear of you and the dread of you shall be upon every beast of the earth and upon every bird of the

---

[8]See 1 Pet. 3:18–19, where there is no mention of Adam.
[9]Gen. 9:1–7.

heavens, upon everything that creeps on the ground and all the fish of the
sea. Into your hand they are delivered. Every moving thing that lives shall
be food for you. And as I gave you the green plants, I give you everything.[10]

The basic command to exercise dominion over the earth that was originally
given to Adam is repeated, but now God tells Noah that the other creatures
will live in fear of human domination and give way to it. He also gives Noah
permission to kill and eat animals, birds, and fish. Before the flood, mankind
was vegetarian, but not now. It is true that there are some Christians who prefer a vegetarian diet, either on health grounds or because of religious scruples,
or both. Some have principled objections to the way animals are processed
for food, and abstain from meat for that reason. If there are good biological
reasons for not eating meat or fish, then of course we must accept them, and
there have always been living creatures that we have not killed or eaten for a
variety of reasons. Even Noah was told not to eat meat with the blood still in
it, so we must not be surprised if we find that there are restrictions imposed
on us, if only by custom or a sense of revulsion at the prospect of devouring
certain types of animal. But we cannot accept that there is any reason for
Christians to become vegetarians on purely religious grounds, and anyone
who advocates that is going against the covenant God made with Noah.

It is because of God's covenant with Noah that we are still here, enjoying the inheritance bequeathed to us from Adam without fear that we shall
be suddenly wiped out by a stroke of divine justice. What happened to those
who were destroyed in the flood is unclear, though there is a curious verse in
the New Testament that suggests that they were imprisoned in hell, and that
Jesus went to preach to them after his death and before his resurrection.[11] If
that is so, then those who perished in the days of Noah were given a chance
to hear the saving plan of God, though whether any of them responded to it
is unknown.

The importance of the preservation of Noah as a manifestation of God's
love can hardly be exaggerated. Human beings have performed every act of
cruelty imaginable and have wreaked untold havoc wherever they have gone,
yet God has allowed us to go on living in the world. Men have tried to destroy
whole races and tribes, and sometimes they have succeeded—there are no
more Beothuks in Newfoundland or native Tasmanians—but this kind of
genocide has not been decreed by God as a sign of his avenging justice. If it
has been permitted by him, it is as an example of human sinfulness that will

---

[10]Gen. 9:1–3.
[11]1 Pet. 3:18.

one day be judged, and we may be sure that those who committed such atrocities will be punished for their crime unless they repent. Despite its almost endless catalogue of follies, however, mankind after the flood has established governments, developed systems of law and order, encouraged education and health care, and done myriad other things that help to maintain and improve the quality of life for everyone on the planet. In these activities, Christians work alongside people of all beliefs and none and recognize that we share a common goal with them, which, as we understand it, is the preservation of humanity according to God's covenant with Noah.

Those who believe in God have cause to be grateful for this situation, as a number of biblical references testify. The covenant God made with Noah has created conditions in which the truth of God's Word can be preached and disseminated, even when those who have made this possible have had no idea what they were doing. It was the pagan King Cyrus of Persia who allowed the Jews to reestablish their homeland in Palestine, though he could not have known what importance this would have in later years.[12] It was the pagan Romans who created a Mediterranean empire that sent Mary and Joseph back home to Bethlehem for the birth of Jesus and later permitted the apostles to travel far and wide, proclaiming the gospel and building the church as they went. Even today, there are secular people with no interest in religion who nevertheless sit up and take notice when an initiative proposed by Christians produces an effect that they desire for other reasons. This has happened, for example, with a prison ministry called Inner Change, which has led to the conversion of many inmates and—most important from the secular point of view—a discernible drop in their number. As a result, Inner Change is respected by people who have no desire to hear or preach the gospel, but who approve of it for reasons that belong essentially to the covenant God made with Noah. The emperors and others who have done these things did not understand what the consequences of their actions would be, but they inadvertently made possible the spreading of a message in which they themselves did not believe, and so played their part in spreading the Word of God.

THE ROLE OF CIVIL GOVERNMENT

Paul recognized the providential role of secular governments when he told the Roman Christians to pray for their rulers because they were God's agents, appointed by him for the good of society as a whole.[13] Paul was writing in the context of the Roman empire, most probably during the reign of Nero (54–

---

[12]Ezra 1:1–4.
[13]Rom. 13:1–10.

68), popularly (if somewhat unfairly) regarded as one of its more vicious and dissolute emperors. Whatever Paul thought about that, he must have known that Rome was not a model of freely chosen popular government and that it was quite capable of perpetrating gross injustices for which no one was held accountable. The crucifixion of Jesus was a miscarriage of justice brought about by the craven surrender of Pontius Pilate to a Jewish mob, and although it was part of God's eternal plan for the salvation of the world, no Christian could forget that aspect of it. The pagan Pilate is the only human being other than the Virgin Mary to have made it into the creeds of the church, precisely because he was the government official who wrongly authorized Jesus' death.

Yet despite the many obvious abuses, Paul recognized the benefits of civil government and regarded it as a blessing sent by God. This is not a theme emphasized in the Old Testament, although there were clearly what we would call civil governments to which the Jews were subject. The situation before the time of Joseph is unclear, but once Israel went down to Egypt, God's people were under the secular authority of a state whose religious beliefs were alien to theirs. This does not seem to have made much practical difference, however, perhaps because Israel's religious life had not been organized at that point. The Egyptians, like many polytheists, were generally tolerant of other peoples' gods. Later on, during the time of the judges and the kings, civil and religious authority in Israel and Judah were closely connected to one another. It was no accident that it was King Solomon who built the temple and not the high priest, who despite his exalted office was little more than a member of the royal court. When the kingdom was divided after Solomon's death, it was not long before the northern kings set up their own places of worship because it was politically difficult for them to allow their subjects to go to Jerusalem.[14] But the idea that the division of the state should necessitate the division of that state's religion did not go down well in Israel. The Bible is clear that this was the beginning of a corrupt form of worship which would eventually become the cult of the Samaritans, with whom the Jews of later times would have no dealings.[15]

After the fall of Jerusalem to the Babylonians in 586 B.C., the question of how Jews should relate to the religiously alien state systems to which they were subjected came up from time to time but was never really resolved. The Persians were friendly to them, and that was greatly appreciated, but the Hellenistic rulers of Syria were not. Eventually, the Jews rebelled and established their own independent state, which was governed by priests who

---

[14]1 Kings 12:25–33.
[15]John 4:9.

made themselves kings, a combination unknown in ancient Israel. That state survived for about a century, and then was conquered by the Romans, who established a series of client kingdoms as well as a province of Judea that was under their direct rule. After A.D. 70 the client kingdoms were abolished and the Jews were deprived of the last remnants of their national government, which would not be restored until 1948. In general, in ancient times, the Jews did not get along very well with the secular authorities, not least because the two were religiously incompatible. Every ancient state had its own gods and its official religion, to which Jewish monotheism was fundamentally hostile. In exile, the Jews could come to terms with the local rulers, but they never lost sight of the land promised to them in Palestine, and the restoration of their independent statehood was always their principal aim. In this connection, we must remember that when Jesus came to proclaim the kingdom of God, this was how many Jews interpreted it, and even after his resurrection, his disciples were still wondering when he would "restore the kingdom to Israel."[16]

It was Jesus who first recognized the importance and legitimacy of civil government in its own right. When he was asked whether Jews should pay taxes to a foreign power, he replied that what belonged to Caesar should be given back to him, but that what belonged to God should be kept separate.[17] Today we hear this as an acceptance of Roman rule on his part, in contrast to the hotheads among the Jews who were forever preaching revolt and whose excesses would lead to the destruction of Jerusalem in the next generation. That was part of it, of course, but it was only one side of the story. The other side was that Rome made its own religious claims. The emperor was supposed to be worshiped, if not as a god then as the son of a god, since his predecessors were routinely deified after their death. By telling people to give to God what belongs to him, Jesus was establishing what we would now call a separation between church and state, each of which was legitimate in its own sphere, but neither of which ought to intrude on the competence of the other.

It was the business of the state to take care of the temporal needs of earthly government and the business of the church to proclaim the kingdom of God and prepare its members for the life of heaven. Normally, these two should not overlap, but if there was a conflict between them for some reason, Christians had no choice but to put their allegiance to God first. Since the pagan Roman empire claimed the spiritual allegiance of its subjects, conflict was inevitable and led to the persecution of Christians. The problem was resolved only in A.D. 313, when the emperor legalized Christianity and

---

[16]Acts 1:6.
[17]Matt. 22:15–21.

effectively renounced his own claims to divinity. When that happened, Christians could (and did) give their loyalty to the empire without reservation, but imperial attempts to interfere in the life of the church were never popular, and if they led to the promotion of heresy, they were stoutly resisted. When Christianity was made the official religion of the Roman state on February 27, 380, it was not so much the empire that took over the church as the other way around. The empire soon disappeared, at least in the West, but the church still exists and is much larger and stronger than the Roman empire ever was or could have been.

The remarkable thing about this is that, through all the changing patterns of church-state relations in ancient times, the fundamental principles laid down in the New Testament remained the same. The state had a legitimate role to play, even if it was officially pagan and its rulers persecuted the church. At the same time, the church remained the spiritual home of believers, whose loyalty to the state was always marked by a certain emotional detachment from it. The fall of Rome, when it came, was not welcomed by Christians, but neither was it greatly lamented (as it was by the surviving pagans.) The New Testament had accepted the empire but had not prescribed it as the ideal or only legitimate form of human government. Christians have never attached themselves to a single state, nor have they officially advocated any one system of government. Most Christians today would probably agree that democracy is the best form of secular government, if only because it provides a peaceful way of getting rid of unacceptable rulers, but we are not blind to its faults, nor do we insist on it as a matter of faith. For us, the important thing is not whether or how we choose our rulers, but whether those rulers are conscious of their responsibilities toward God and faithful in carrying out their duties. To put it another way, it is the responsibilities of those who hold public office that concern us more than the supposed rights of the citizens who may or may not have elected them.

This is important because Christians are called to accept the government in power whether we like it or not. In a democracy, we can work for peaceful and orderly change, but if people sympathetic to our views and values do not win elections, we must accept that and get on with what we are primarily called to do. At the same time, the state must not seek to interfere in matters properly reserved for the church, and it is here that conflict most often occurs today. As an example of how difficult it can be to decide what to do on the basis of the New Testament alone, consider the question of matrimony. In the Roman empire, that was a secular concern, regulated by the courts and regarded as part of property law, because of the dowries that were involved.

There is no suggestion anywhere in Scripture that this system was inappropriate for Christians, although they were advised not to marry outside the faith.[18] On the other hand, they were not to desert an unbelieving spouse, although if the unbeliever left, the Christian was to accept it and move on.[19]

After the collapse of the Roman empire, the church found itself more and more involved in matrimonial affairs, and it was then that it sought to impose Christian standards on the institution. In practical terms, that meant obtaining the consent of both of the parties (as opposed to the arranged marriages common in the ancient world) and forbidding divorce.[20] For a thousand years or so, that was the standard pattern in Western countries—which began to break down only in the nineteenth century when civil marriage (and civil divorce) were introduced. The church was forced to accept civil marriage but not civil divorce, which meant that it could refuse to recognize the remarriage of a divorced person during the lifetime of his or her previous spouse. In practical terms, this made it possible for churches to refuse to perform the remarriage or to ordain or employ such people. As time went on and instances of this became more common, the lines got blurred, and the church's internal procedures for dealing with divorce gradually crumbled.

Much more recently, this growing problem of matrimonial indiscipline has been accompanied by another one that is even more serious—the union of same-sex couples. No Christian can enter such a union, but where they are legal in the eyes of the state, there has been pressure put on the church to bless them, if not actually to perform them. People in such unions cannot legally be discriminated against, which causes problems for churches that do not want to employ them. A church or a Christian organization can now be sued for discrimination against people who openly reject the standards of Christian marriage that are laid down in the Bible and have been practiced for most of the past two millennia. Is this a case of the state overstepping its bounds and entering a sphere reserved for the church? Or has the church historically invaded territory that traditionally belonged to the state, and is now paying the price for that as the state subtly redefines what it means by a "marriage"? What should we do if a person in a legalized same-sex relationship becomes a Christian? And how do we deal with people in the church who approve of such unions and even encourage them?

The basic problem is that, while church and state are no longer as clearly separate as they were in New Testament times, neither are they as closely

[18] 1 Cor. 7:39.
[19] 1 Cor. 7:12–16.
[20] Matt. 19:6.

linked as they were for much of Christian history. We are in uncharted waters here, with the result that the church is divided between those who insist that we must conform to whatever the state decides is legal, and those who say that we must resist legally recognized forms of marriage that are incompatible with Christian teaching. It is this second group that has the Bible on its side, but making the biblical norm stick in modern church life is by no means as easy as it may sound, and there is no guarantee that the state will simply sit back and let the church operate according to its own principles in this matter.

The problems related to matrimony are but one example of the difficulties that can arise in church-state relations. Another, which has a long history, is that of conscientious objection to military service. Very few churches are officially pacifist, but many individual Christians are. Should the church support them, or does giving Caesar his due include accepting the legitimacy of compulsory military service? The problem here is not so much between the church as an institution and the armed forces of the state, since even in New Testament times there were soldiers who became Christians, and no one suggested there was anything incompatible between their profession and their faith.[21] The issue is rather one between the individual conscience and the demands of the state. The church can support the right of individuals to freedom of conscience without necessarily endorsing what that conscience feels strongly about. A precedent for this can be found in the tolerance shown by Paul to the "weaker brethren" who did not eat meat sacrificed to idols because of their tender consciences. Paul did not agree with their reasoning but he respected their scruples and told the Corinthian church that it must do the same.[22]

Another area of potential conflict arises in the sphere of education. In modern times, the state has imposed universal education on children but does not always allow for the religious conscience of those whom it subjects to that law. Should the state permit religious education in accordance with the beliefs and wishes of parents, or should it rule it out as something that is superfluous and outside its sphere of competence? If religious freedom is accepted in principle, to whom should it be granted? It is one thing to say that Protestants and Roman Catholics should have their own schools, but what about Muslims, who do not believe in giving girls the same education as boys? What about people who might even invent their own religion (as many so-called "neo-pagans" have done) and demand equal rights for their manufactured beliefs? The result of these complications is that we now find ourselves in a situation

---

[21]See Acts 10:1–2.
[22]1 Cor. 8:4–13.

where Christians are being denied the right to educate their children because the state cannot tolerate the sort of discrimination imposed by Muslims, and since all religions have to be treated alike, Christians must submit to the same restrictions as those imposed on others.

None of these questions arises in the New Testament because church-state relations were not as developed then as they are now. But in the modern world it seems virtually certain that the potential for conflict between the two institutions will grow, and so Christians have to be clear about what their basic principles are. These can be discerned in the Bible, even if the situations in which they must be applied are peculiar to our own times. The first principle is that both church and state are legitimate entities. Neither has the right to take over the other, and each must protect its own rights and responsibilities. The primary task of the state is to preserve law and order. This requires the possession, and occasionally the use, of force to which the church must submit, as long as it is not being abused. If people are arrested without warrant or are arbitrarily dispossessed, the church cannot accept that the state is acting legitimately and it must protest. But such protests must also be nonviolent because the church has no right to use the sword to avenge the wrongs done to its members or to others.

The state has an interest in ensuring certain levels of education, especially now that life has become so much more complex than it once was. No one can reasonably object to state-imposed driving tests, for example, and the state must be supported in its efforts to regulate and improve services of that kind. But although the state has a right to impose certain standards for the common good, it has no business interfering with the conscientiously held beliefs of its citizens. If abortions are made legal, for instance, those who object to them must not be forced to perform them. A citizen's "right" to choose should not be more important than a medical specialist's right to refuse if his or her conscience so dictates. A neutral state cannot assign some rights to particular people if it means depriving others of their freedom. As the old saying goes, "What's sauce for the goose is sauce for the gander," and a policy of true equality must recognize that.

In terms of matrimony and its equivalents, the church does not have to claim the right to perform weddings or register marriages, but it does have to be able to discipline members who do not live up to its standards, even if they are still within the law. The state does not have the same moral and spiritual obligations that the church has and can be broader in what it permits, but it must not expect that the church will simply go along with whatever is legal. The church will always be more restrictive than the state on matters of divorce and same-sex unions, and it must retain its freedom to practice what the Bible teaches in these areas, whether or not that is accepted as the norm in wider society.

CIVIC RELIGION

Can civil society exist for long without some acknowledgment of the existence of God? This question was not asked in biblical times because it was self-evident to everyone that it could not. When a man like Socrates (469–399 B.C.) appeared to question the existence of the gods, he was condemned to death because it was universally believed that if his ideas gained currency, society would descend into anarchy and fall apart. Similar opinions were almost universally held until the eighteenth century and even later. The United States was the first secular state in the modern sense, but it was deistic rather than atheistic. In early America there was a kind of civic religion based on the principle that human reason postulated the existence of a supreme being. This civic religion had a strongly Judeo-Christian coloring because that was the tradition recognized by the vast majority of the citizenry, but it was based on different principles. Instead of submitting to divine revelation as this was contained in the Bible, it grounded its morality on rational calculation and analysis. In practice, this produced conclusions that were very similar to and largely compatible with Christian ones, and since most people believed that Christianity was the highest expression of rational religion that had so far appeared on earth, there was no conflict between them. Not until the mid-twentieth century was this synthesis seriously challenged, and only now is it in the process of disintegrating.

Other countries came to secularization by different routes. In some cases, as in France and Russia, the process was violent, and an openly atheistic state found itself persecuting religious believers of all kinds, the Christian church in particular. In those countries, a secular ideology replaced Christian theology in an openly antagonistic way, but elsewhere things were generally more peaceful. Most European countries preserved a state church and the outward forms of public religious observance, but no longer enforced conformity to Christian teaching, which became the preserve of a respectable but increasingly marginalized minority. By the early twentieth century it was possible for an ideology like National Socialism in Germany to come to power and institute a radically atheistic social program without seriously disturbing the church at all. There was some opposition from a theologically alert minority, but for the most part the institutional church went on as before and survived the debacle more or less intact. State churches continue to exist and even to enjoy certain privileges in many countries, but the majority of the population is alienated from them, and their leaders generally conform to the prevailing secular norms in the belief that this is the only way to preserve any kind of voice in modern society. To the extent that civic religion still exists, it is pomp and ceremony rather than substance, a reminder of the past more than a portent of the future.

The demise of civic religion as a serious intellectual force does not mean that Christianity in public life is dead. In many ways, it is alive and well, but as a counterculture in Western society and not as the dominant belief system. In the collapse of civic religion, Christians have often recovered a sense of the supernatural character of their faith and now understand better than they used to that it cannot be reduced to rational principles or made to conform to popular ideologies. At the same time, Christianity's traditional opponents have reasserted their claim that human reason can stand on its own and does not need the support of religion in any form. They dislike the remnants of civic religion but reserve the main force of their wrath for revived Christianity, which they see as a threat to the social order and not as a support for it. In between these extremes, there is the indifferent majority, which either has little interest in spiritual questions or else looks to alternative lifestyles for answers that neither the traditional churches nor the militant atheists seem able to provide.

The divorce between faith and rationalism is now virtually complete in the Western world, but they cannot simply go their separate ways. Christian faith has always expressed itself in rational terms, and while it has never exalted the human mind to the level of an absolute authority, it has never ignored or underestimated it either. For their part, rationalists need to explain not just the existence but the persistence of religious and spiritual phenomena. Most of them accept that there is such a thing as morality based on a distinction between good and evil. There is also the inescapable fact that in the non-Western world, religious influences are very strong and seem to be getting stronger. It is hardly reasonable to dismiss all non-Western people as nitwits or savages, and so the claim of religion to represent something real has acquired a new force, as the often vicious and sometimes desperate attacks on it testify. Where all this will lead is hard to say, but persecution and conflict have usually been healthy for the church because they force people to decide what it is that they really believe. Those who stand up for Jesus in the face of opposition generally have more conviction and more credibility than those who simply go with the flow, whether or not that flow is sympathetic to Christianity.

COMMON GRACE AND HUMAN CULTURE

Civic religion continues to exist because the knowledge of God is innate in every human being. Theologians sometimes call it "common grace," because this knowledge is a form of divine revelation planted in the hearts and minds of us all. The Bible says that the ordinary person knows there is an order in the universe that is too complicated to be purely accidental.[23] He also knows that there is a difference between right and wrong, and that human beings have abilities and characteristics that distinguish us from other creatures and enable us to manipulate, control, develop, and subdue them. Furthermore, the ordinary person has a conscience to tell him that our superiority in these respects carries both privileges and responsibilities. Even if he does not use the language of "dominion" found in Genesis 1, he will still recognize the validity of what that chapter is trying to convey. Without articulating it, he will agree that human beings can do things with the world that no other creature can do, and it is in everyone's interest that we treat it with respect and take care of it as best we can. He should be able to see that this situation depends on the existence of a superior power, evidence for which can be seen in the laws of nature without the need for any special revelation from God.

That, at least, is what the Bible says *should* be possible. In practice, there are many people who do not hold such views or at least do not articulate them very clearly, either because they have never heard anything about them or because they have deliberately rejected them. The more sophisticated may even have elaborated competing theories of reality that rule out what the Bible regards as self-evident truths. Others may add further items to the list, as did the framers of the American Declaration of Independence, who thought that a God-given right to "life, liberty, and the pursuit of happiness" was also "self-evident," though that idea reflects a certain enlightenment ideology, and it would be difficult to find any warrant for it beyond their own imaginations. Either way, we are faced with a world where truths that the Bible says should be obvious to everyone often are not, and what is regarded as self-evident does not always coincide with biblical notions of truth.

Because of this, Christians must be careful when they appeal to common norms shared by all human beings as evidence for the existence of the Christian God. Even when the teaching of the Bible is generally agreed upon

---

[23]Ps. 19:1; Rom. 1:18. See also Job 38–39.

(as sometimes happens in countries with a long tradition of Christian teaching), there is nothing in nature to prove that God is a personal being, that there is a Trinity of persons, or that Jesus Christ is the Son of God incarnate. We realize this most clearly when we meet people who respect Jesus as a great teacher, leader, and even philosopher, but reject the supernatural claims made for him. People like that may be seen (and may see themselves) as allies of the Christian church, but in fact they are among its greatest enemies, because they have accepted a caricature of the Christian faith and decided that the caricature is an acceptable substitute for the real thing. Far from being prepared for receiving the gospel, they have been inoculated against it and are liable to think that those who take things further than what their natural theology will allow are religious fanatics.

That fear is a real one, because the Christian message does divide people, and only some will accept it in its entirety. That the truth is available to everyone but will not be universally accepted is one of the hardest claims that the church has to make, and it raises serious questions about the church's place as a unifying force in human society. Can the church ever truly embrace an entire population? How should it act toward those who reject all or part of its message? Can it subscribe publicly to a minimalist version of its own creed while tolerating those who believe it all as a somewhat unwelcome minority within it? That is the situation today in most Western countries, resulting in tensions within the church that are often the source of great conflict and that reduce its credibility in a fundamentally hostile world. How can the gospel be true, critics argue, when church members who profess it disagree among themselves about what it really is? Of course those church members see things rather differently—for them, the gospel is betrayed by those within the church who claim to be preaching it but who have no idea what it really means.

For all these reasons, Christians are often unhappy to accept the idea that there are people outside the church whose belief in a God is the same as theirs. God can be known only as he reveals himself to his people, not as his works are studied by those who have no idea who he really is. But even if belief in God is problematic, there would seem to be a general consensus that there are moral norms by which human society ought to be governed. At the most basic level, virtually everyone agrees that murder and theft are wrong, if only because they are liable to propagate more murder and theft and so end up doing as much harm to the perpetrators as to their victims. But can an ethic based on such self-interest really coexist with the Christian one, which bases its moral norms on an unselfish love for God and for our fellow human beings?

In practical terms, the answer would seem to be yes. Christians coexist with others in many different human societies and share with them a sufficiently large body of common values to make peaceful coexistence possible much of the time. This is clearly easier in countries where an explicitly Christian ethic has provided the moral compass for determining the fundamentals of civil law; in such cases Christians can easily appear to be representatives of the secular establishment. The banning of polygamy in all Western societies is a good example of this. There have been groups that have advocated polygamy (notably the Mormons) and there are Muslim minorities who might claim that banning it is an infringement of their freedom of religion, but the social consensus is such that the Christian view prevails and therefore most people think that it is equivalent to the natural law.

That was also the case until recently with homosexuality. Christians were against it, but so was the rest of society, mainly because it was believed to be a "sin against nature." But in recent years there has been increasing support for the idea that homosexuality is an unavoidable physical condition and that those who have it should no more be discriminated against than people who are left-handed. This view has prevailed in secular circles to the point that anyone who refuses to accept it is liable to suffer legal sanctions if their views affect their behavior in any public way. The church has been divided on this issue, but only between those who are Christians in the true sense of the word and those who are theists with a Christian cultural heritage. At least this division has revealed what many have suspected all along, which is that the common values supposedly shared between Christians and secularists are not really common at all. Where they coincide, they do so for historical reasons or from perceived self-interest, and when either of these factors changes or disappears, the superficial alliance between believers and others is liable to crumble, dividing the institutional church as it does so.

Nevertheless, Christians continue to maintain that fallen human beings have an innate sense of right and wrong to which we can appeal. From the evidence we possess, it seems that this was especially effective as an evangelistic tool in the Roman empire, where many were disturbed by the gap between the ideals of their culture and the realities of everyday life. Lofty concepts of morality proclaimed by philosophers were openly denied by the devotees of religion, who often indulged in absurd and immoral practices as part of their worship. This gap was a favorite theme of the early Christians, who used it to great effect to undermine the truth claims made by the ancients.[24] Their argument was basically that if right-thinking people wanted to see truth applied in everyday life, they should become Christians, because only Christians had

---

[24]See Tertullian, *Apologeticum*; Augustine, *The City of God*, I-V, and so on.

achieved the correct balance between truth and falsehood, and between right and wrong. Of course, they generally added that they had achieved this, not by their own efforts or by trying to turn philosophical principles into religious practice (as the Neoplatonists often did), but because they had accepted the truth of God's revelation in Scripture and in Christ. In the end, therefore, even the noblest of the ancient pagans was little more than a blind guide, groping in the dark to discover something that was obvious to the Christian believer.

Christians are spiritually distinct from those who live in the world, but when common interests throw us together, it is right for us to cooperate and play our part in furthering what we believe in. We must recognize that worldly people are often wiser in their own domain than Christians are, and their realism can be a blessing to us.[25] For example, many Christians are inclined toward pacifism and unilateral disarmament, because they (rightly) believe that war is a bad thing. What they fail to see is that being well armed is often the best way to prevent the outbreak of conflict. The hardheadedness of some unbelievers may be what the Bible calls the wisdom of serpents,[26] but in its own context it works better than the naive idealism of so many Christians. Similar considerations apply to helping the poor—what is right in principle may be done in entirely the wrong way because of a misplaced compassion that fails to take the realities of human sinfulness into account. For example, huge sums of money are often poured into helping Third World countries with little visible result, and collections for disaster relief often do not reach the intended victims because of theft and fraud. Christians are right to show compassion, but often this needs to be channeled by worldly wisdom in order to be effective. In this sphere, unbelievers can sometimes be more realistic (and therefore more successful) in achieving their aims than believers are.[27]

Christians can cooperate most successfully with others when we are engaged in tasks related to the dominion over creation that we have been given. Even when we do not have the same motives and may not share the same moral principles or goals, we often have enough in common to make it possible for us to work together. Broadly speaking, these areas of overlap and agreement may be classified either as work or as leisure. Work includes what we do for a living and the wider questions of economic, social, and technological development. Leisure covers what we often think of as "culture"—music, the arts, literature, and so on—and of course, sports. For people who work in the leisure industry there will obviously be no clear distinction between these

---

[25]Luke 16:8.

[26]Matt. 10:16.

[27]In fairness, this is not always the case. Many unbelievers are idealists and many believers have a thoroughly realistic appreciation of the nature of fallen humanity.

things, but even they will specialize in one aspect of leisure and treat the rest in the same way as everyone else does.

To deal with economic, social, and technological development first, Christians have a common interest with others in maintaining law and order and in developing the resources needed for progress and prosperity. The principles undergirding economics are the same for everyone, whether they are Christians or not, and there is nothing to prevent us from engaging in commerce with people who do not share our beliefs. Even Paul was a tentmaker, as were his friends Priscilla and Aquila.[28] From what we can tell, it seems that the churches he founded were often composed of merchants who earned their living by trade. This was of great benefit to Paul because they had connections all over the world that he was able to use as he traveled around preaching the gospel, but their occupations were lawful and honest in themselves and Paul never suggested that they should give them up in order to preach the gospel or to form exclusively Christian communities. From the beginning, Christians mixed freely with others around them and did not go in for the sort of ritual or social exclusivism that marked out Jews and prevented many God-fearing Gentiles from joining the synagogues.

Christians are not barred from joining social organizations that have been established to further legitimate causes. They may belong to craftsmen's guilds, trade unions, political parties, community associations, conservationist groups, and so on. Indeed, a case can be made for saying that Christians ought to support such things, both because of the good such groups can do and also because the presence of believers in them can help to ensure that they stay honest and focused on their primary purpose. In this respect, Christians are called to be "the salt of the earth" and "the light of the world."[29] Belonging to organizations of these kinds may or may not offer opportunities to share the gospel, and they may require certain compromises. For example, as Christians we would prefer not to meet or work on Sunday, but it may not be possible to persuade others of this, and we may have to accept a majority decision to which we are in principle opposed. It is extremely difficult to say at what point compromises of that kind are no longer tolerable; this is a matter that has to be worked out in each individual circumstance. There will always be differences between those with a robust conscience and the so-called weaker brethren who find it harder to negotiate the kind of delicate balancing acts that involvement with the world may require.[30] In our fallen state, no

---

[28] Acts 18:3.
[29] Matt. 5:13–16.
[30] Rom. 14:1–2.

situation is entirely free from sin, and there are many cases where we would impose standards on ourselves that would be irrelevant or inappropriate for the wider community. Paul dealt with this when he said,

> I wrote to you in my letter not to associate with sexually immoral people— not at all meaning the sexually immoral of this world, or the greedy and swindlers, or idolaters, since then you would need to go out of the world. But now I am writing to you not to associate with anyone who bears the name of brother if he is guilty of sexual immorality or greed, or is an idola- ter, reviler, drunkard, or swindler—not even to eat with such a one. For what have I to do with judging outsiders? Is it not those inside the church whom you are to judge? God judges those outside. "Purge the evil person from among you."[31]

Here the boundary lines appear to be very clear. People who make no pretense of being Christians are not to be judged by Christian standards, but those who claim the name of Christ must live up to it. This sounds straightforward, but many complications arise. First of all, if a Christian is engaged in busi- ness with someone else who does some or all of the things mentioned above, should he tolerate it? Can we really say to potential business clients that we cannot have a meal with them because they are not Christians? It is here that things become more difficult. For example, I may have to have lunch with col- leagues at work, but I do not have to join them if that involves excessive drink- ing, sexual impropriety, or the misuse of expense accounts. In these areas, even non-Christians usually respect those who have conscientious principles. Taking a stand and refusing to be "one of the gang" is often a more demand- ing and a more telling witness to our faith than outright preaching of the gos- pel. Christians who work in alien environments have a duty to be exemplary in their attitude to their work and in their behavior toward others, because in our hearts and minds we are serving God and not men.[32] If we think and act that way, we may not have many opportunities to share our faith, but when we do we shall be listened to with greater respect because others will realize that we practice what we preach.

There is no reason to suppose that believers are more intelligent, gifted, upright, or successful than others, and we must respect those who are supe- rior to us in these respects, whether or not they share our faith. Their gifts have been given to them by God, even if they do not acknowledge him, and we are privileged to benefit from them, knowing whose servants they are.[33]

[31]1 Cor. 5:9–13.
[32]Col. 3:23.
[33]See Rom. 13:4.

Sometimes it is possible for Christians to set up their own businesses or schools and to operate them along Christian lines, but that is not an excuse for rejecting the wisdom of the world if it is a genuine contribution to our understanding of God's creation. No one should reject computers, for example, merely because those who invented them were probably not believers!

Another complication that arises may be one of the problems created by success. There are many companies in the world today that started as family businesses owned and operated by Christians who applied the principles of their faith to their working practices. Over time, these businesses have grown and become "impersonal" in the sense that they are no longer run by the people who founded them or even by others who share their principles. In many cases they will have been sold to or merged with bigger corporations, and only the name of the original founder remains. Along the way, it is very likely that compromises will have been made that Christians who now work for those companies are uncomfortable with. What should a believer do about this? There may be situations when he or she will have to resign because company policies go against individual conscience, but these are relatively rare. Much more common will be instances where the issues are unclear, and it is difficult to know what to do. For example, a company's pension fund may be invested in stocks with a high rate of return, but that rate may be boosted by dubious or illegal practices on the part of the businesses whose stocks they are. Can anything be done about this?

One of the more encouraging signs in recent years has been the growing interest in business ethics, which seeks to deal with precisely these kinds of problems. Increasingly, there are watchdog bodies that encourage people to report bad practice so that standards can be maintained and corruption brought under control, if not eliminated altogether. Christians must welcome these developments and not be afraid to make use of them, if the need arises. Taking a stand is seldom easy and may be costly to the individuals involved, but God is our witness, and he will not let us down if we do what we know to be right.

Issues in the workplace can be difficult and complex, but they often pale into insignificance beside the problems created by what we have called the "leisure" category. Very often the compromises demanded in business are pragmatic and somewhat technical in nature. People may be irritated by those with scruples, but they usually have a grudging respect for them and may well back down, especially if there is a risk of getting caught. It is a different story with the arts, however. Music, painting, and literature deal with the higher senses and are therefore both more refined and more easily corrupted. There can be no doubt that some of the most outstanding monuments of higher culture in the world have been produced by Christians or by people who accepted Christian norms and values. People debate what William Shakespeare actually believed, but no one would call his plays obscene or immoral, even though they often deal with sin in its various guises. Truly great works of art will generally both celebrate the glory of creation and decry the tragedy of the fall, because art is a mirror of life, and that combination of glory and tragedy is the closest imitation of life that art can achieve. We must not reject or ban a great book merely because it talks about unpleasant subjects that we would normally seek to avoid. As long as it is faithful to its calling as art and gives us a deeper insight into why murder or sexual immorality (to take two obvious examples) are so bad, there is no reason not to affirm it as a voice of truth. If something turns our stomach we may wish to avoid it, but if the circumstances are such that our stomachs ought to be turned by the very real evil being depicted, we should recognize that it is our weakness and not the artist's immorality that lies at the root of our negative reaction.

Christians are called to be the salt of the earth and the light of the world in this as in every other sphere of human activity. It is interesting to reflect that most people want their novels to have a "happy ending" and expect a "cops and robbers" drama to end with the victory of the cops as the good guys, even if that is not always true to life. The innate desire for the triumph of right over wrong is very strong, and if that does not always happen in fact, then at least it should be the case in fiction! Entertainment is not morally neutral, and in a world where leisure is increasingly common, it is more important than ever before to consider the kind of diversions we provide. In our audio-visual age, there is constant pressure to shock the public with ever more outrageous spectacles, and Christians have a duty to emphasize what great artists have always known—that restraint and subtlety are often the most powerful and effective forms of communication. Vulgarity for its own sake is not art and is seldom enduring; people are shocked by it at first, but the shock quickly wears off and the pointlessness of it is the only thing that anyone remembers.

Another area of great importance in the modern world is sports, which in some circles have almost become an alternative religion. In theory, sports are meant to be bodily exercise that is a useful and enjoyable way of staying healthy and fit. As long as that end is not lost sight of, there would seem to be little reason to object to sports, although the Bible is not as encouraging in this respect as we might wish.[34] Sports were a major activity in the ancient world, as events like the Olympic games bear witness, but Christians never

---

[34]See 1 Tim. 4:8.

got very involved with such things. Partly that was because sports were closely connected with pagan religious rites, and partly because much so-called sports were bloody and cruel. Christians who were thrown to the lions in the Roman coliseum were objects of entertainment to the masses, but it is easy to see why they would not have appreciated that, and we cannot blame them if their attitude to sports was less enthusiastic than ours might be.

Today, however, it is in sports that we see most clearly the challenge that all Christian engagement with the world presents. On the one hand, most of what we do is not wrong in itself. Indeed, the presence of believers on the tennis courts, on the football fields, and in the swimming pools has been used by God both to maintain the standards of the sport itself and to show the world that Christians can have a positive attitude to the human body and the benefits of good health. On the other hand, however, nowhere else in the modern world is it so obvious how something essentially good can be corrupted and become a force for evil.

This tendency can be seen at many levels. First, there is the distraction from other things that sports can entail. So important is it to train for excellence that those deeply involved in sports can sacrifice everything, including their own health, for the sake of winning a competition. When that happens, the benefit that bodily exercise is meant to bring becomes the exact opposite, and healthy young people are burnt out before their time. It is also the case that although a few stars may make enough money to set themselves up for life, many others find themselves in debt and without the means of earning a decent living because they have sacrificed their studies to their sport. Worst of all, it is the easiest thing in the world to give up the worship of God for athletic exercise, especially when Sunday is a free day for so many, and unbelievers see no reason why anyone should want to go to church. The temptation to give up everything for the game is a great one, and Christians must do all they can to resist it.

Second, there is a lot of money tied up in sports, along with fame and prestige. This means that corruption is almost inevitable, and scandals are now a regular occurrence. Olympic medals have been won by people taking illegal steroids, and the fantastic sums that very young players can sometimes earn do nothing to encourage respect for hard work and the value of money. The idolization of sporting heroes is such that they become role models, opinion shapers, and even politicians, whether or not they are qualified for such things. The ability to kick a ball around a field is not to be despised, but why should it make someone a millionaire and social trendsetter? As activities, sports are unproductive and essentially meaningless, yet they have become the dream of youth the world over. To the extent that they can unite people across the divides of class, race, or religion, they may be a good thing, but ultimately the unity is superficial and is an enemy of truth and salvation because it dulls the appetite for spiritual things and makes them seem both unimportant and unprofitable.

We see the corruption of earthly things most clearly in the realm of sports because they are so prominent and popular, but the same principles apply to every other aspect of human culture as well. Great art is very beautiful, but if it becomes an object of worship, as it has in some parts of the Christian church, it is abused and becomes harmful in spite of its many attractive qualities. Music can also be moving and uplifting, but if it takes people over, and they begin to be ruled by it, then it too is harmful. Certainly, the immoral lifestyles of so many leading pop idols is an unedifying commentary on what can happen when it is abused. Literature too can be very satisfying to the mind and the spirit, but if it is allowed to become a god, it will lead us astray. This is a particularly difficult area for the Christian, because a book is at the heart of our faith. Is the Bible great literature or not? Can it be read in that way at the expense of its spiritual message? Some have tried to do this, and there are even courses in the Bible as "literature" at secular universities, but ultimately it is a futile exercise. If there are parts of the Bible that can be called "great literature," that is accidental; its real purpose is quite different. To try to read it without the theology is to abuse it, and if it were not a life-changing message of salvation, it is unlikely that many people would study it as a serious contribution to human civilization.

The sad truth is that art can become pornography, literature can be obscene, and music can be demonic in its hold over people. All these things are abuses against which Christians have to struggle, and it is to avoid letting these potentially good things fall into such traps that we are called to be engaged in cultural pursuits. Similarly, it is for the benefit of mankind as a whole that we are expected to play our part in economic and social affairs, bringing our presence and values as children of light to bear on them. If we are successful, then we give thanks to God, and if not, we can still offer what we have to him. The fame and achievements of this life are fleeting and ultimately of no lasting significance. Once again, this is most obvious in sports, where the peak of perfection is reached early and fame has usually vanished by the time a person reaches middle age. In other areas, recognition may be a long time coming and is occasionally only posthumous. Christians are called to remember this and to remind others that what ought to be an obvious truth is frequently derided and resented. As Paul put it in a different context, but one which is applicable here as well,

Though our outer nature is wasting away, our inner self is being renewed day by day. For this slight momentary affliction is preparing for us an eternal weight of glory beyond all comparison, as we look not to the things that are seen but to the things that are unseen. For the things that are seen are transient, but the things that are unseen are eternal.[35]

Before leaving the subject of common grace, we must look briefly at an aspect of it that has frequently troubled the church. To what extent can the goods and achievements of this world be used in the service and worship of God? Is it right to decorate our churches with pictures? What place should music have in our worship? Do things like drama and fiction have any role to play in our common Christian life?

There is no simple or straightforward answer to this question. The Bible says very little about it, although it is clear that the early Christians sang in the course of their worship.[36] What they sang and how has been controversial, especially when it has been appealed to as a model for worship today. Some Christians have insisted that only the psalms (and possibly also the New Testament canticles) should be sung in worship, and others have banned the use of musical instruments as "unbiblical." There is no reason not to respect these options when they are the conscientious choice of particular groups of Christians, but they cannot really be defended as the teaching of the Bible. The early Christians sang hymns and "spiritual songs" in addition to the psalms, and there is no indication that musical instruments were forbidden. They were certainly used in the Old Testament and may have found a place in early Christian worship as well, though the evidence is sparse. By the end of the ancient world, there had developed a lively and robust *a cappella* tradition of singing that still survives, but this has not led to a rejection of musical instruments and today both kinds of music coexist in the church.

As for artwork, there are whole sections of the church that have made icons and even statues central to their worship, but although there is nothing wrong with these things in themselves, there is every reason to suggest that this tendency has gotten seriously out of hand and gone astray from its original purpose. Those who first promoted the use of pictorial images in the church's devotional life did so because they wanted to affirm the reality of Christ's incarnation. If God had truly become man, then he had made himself visible in Jesus of Nazareth, who could certainly have been painted (or photographed, if the technology for that had existed in those days). But there is no indication anywhere in the New Testament that such pictures ought to

---

[35] 2 Cor. 4:16–18.
[36] Col. 3:16.

be made, nor did they play any discernible part in the worship of the early church. All that we know for certain is that there were Christian frescoes painted in the catacombs of Rome. It does not seem that they were the objects of veneration, however, and there is no biblical warrant for such a practice.

Finally, the use of secular literature in worship is possible, but it must be kept under control and subordinated to the demands of the gospel. When Paul went to Athens, he quoted some of the Greek poets in order to further his evangelistic purposes, [37] but he never regarded their words as divinely inspired, nor would he have countenanced using them instead of Scripture in church worship. The early church did not normally go in for inspirational fiction, possibly because the existing examples of it had the taint of heresy about them, but there have been remarkable examples from later times which have been greatly used by God, such as John Bunyan's *Pilgrim's Progress*. Bunyan knew what he was doing, of course, and so did his readers, and neither of them would have seen his work as a replacement for Scripture. His allegorical novel was a vivid application of biblical principles to the spiritual life of the believer, and its purpose was to take readers back to the sacred text, not to distract them from it.

The tendency in some churches to substitute readings from poets and novelists for passages from the Bible has no justification. The Bible is the Word of God, and all these other writings are words of men. Good and uplifting though they may be, they must be kept firmly in their place. As aids to illuminate the truth, they can be useful and helpful, but they are not substitutes for it. Here as elsewhere, the products of human genius have their place, but their temporal character must be recognized and respected for what it is, and the works themselves must never be confused with the eternal Word of God, which alone is able to save and comfort the soul.

DEALING WITH OUR OWN FALLEN STATE

If Christians are called by God to be the salt of the earth and the light of the world, it is vitally important that we make sure that the salt does not lose its taste, because as Jesus famously reminded his disciples, if it does, it is good for nothing.[38] In practical terms, this means that Christians are soldiers waging a spiritual battle and have to keep themselves fully armed and well trained in order to be of service to the Lord. We are still sinners, even though we have been born again in Christ. As long as we live in this world we shall have to deal with that basic reality.

---

[37] Acts 17:28.
[38] Matt. 5:13.

The first problem we have to deal with and overcome is that of temptation. It is often thought that temptation plays on our weaknesses, but that is not necessarily so. Very few of us would be tempted to strive for an Olympic medal or a Nobel prize, not because we are strong enough to be able to resist such temptations but because we are too weak even to enter the competition! The reality is that it is often our greatest strengths that provide the most fruitful soil for temptation to take root, because it is there that we imagine that we are least exposed to danger. Someone with a gift for making money may easily be tempted to exploit that talent beyond what is legitimate and succumb to the temptation of greed. Another person who is naturally charming and persuasive may be tempted to use that gift for selfish purposes or to sell things that in normal circumstances no one would want to buy. A very intelligent person may be tempted to use his brain to devise any number of dubious schemes, either to avoid obligations like paying taxes or to exercise power in ways that are not legitimate. The list of possibilities is virtually endless, but Paul sums it up nicely when he reviews the sad history of the Israelites in the desert and concludes with the following warning to the Corinthian church:

> Let anyone who thinks that he stands take heed lest he fall. No temptation has overtaken you that is not common to man. God is faithful, and he will not let you be tempted beyond your ability, but with the temptation he will also provide the way of escape, that you may be able to endure it.[39]

Our strength is not in ourselves but in the Lord, who makes sure that we can resist whatever temptations come our way, as long as we put our trust in him and not in ourselves.

This is not to say that we do not have genuine weaknesses, and recognizing what they are is very important. It is easy for Christians to fall into the trap of thinking that we must not have any trials in our lives, on the ground that, if we do, it is a sign that we are not fully dedicated to God's service. That is false. Paul was plagued by a "thorn in the flesh," which he prayed to be relieved of, but after three tries, God replied, "My grace is sufficient for you, for my power is made perfect in weakness," after which Paul concluded, "Therefore I will boast all the more gladly of my weaknesses, so that the power of Christ may rest upon me."[40] Note, however, that although we know that Paul had his weaknesses, we are not told what they were. Here we should follow his example and admit our imperfections both to ourselves and to one another, but not make a public display of them or spend so much time talking

---

[39] 1 Cor. 10:12–13.
[40] 2 Cor. 12:9.

about them that we lose sight of the grace of God. Our weaknesses are given to us in order to keep us humble and dependent on God, not as an excuse to become self-absorbed. Paul did not expect the Corinthian church to feel sorry for him, and neither should we expect that of others today. Boasting in our weaknesses is meant to be boasting in the grace of God, not drawing attention to ourselves.

The next thing we have to bear in mind is that, although we are never tempted beyond what we can bear, there will be times when we sin, either consciously or unconsciously. There is no way of avoiding this. Those who preach that it is possible to attain sinless perfection in this life are not only wrong, they are deceived—which is even worse. Repentance is not a one-time thing that we do when we come to Christ, but a daily discipline in which we ask God to forgive not only those sins that we know about but also those which have escaped our notice. None of us is fully aware of our thoughts and actions, and we all sin in many ways.[41] Christian spiritual growth entails movement not toward a higher degree of perfection but toward a greater degree of self-awareness.[42] It is not our business to pass judgment on others but rather to take heed to ourselves, to make sure that we do not fall into the same sins that we so easily detect in other people.[43] There is nothing easier or more damaging to our standing before God than to see what is wrong in everyone else but to fail to put right what is wrong in ourselves. As Jesus said,

> "Why do you see the speck that is in your brother's eye, but do not notice the log that is in your own eye? Or how can you say to your brother, 'Let me take the speck out of your eye,' when there is the log in your own eye? You hypocrite, first take the log out of your own eye and then you will see clearly to take the speck out of your brother's eye."[44]

Self-awareness is an important reality check that will inevitably turn us back to the grace of God in all our dealings with others. This is particularly important when it comes to the way we handle our affairs as Christians in fellowship with one another. It often happens that believers think that they do not have to abide by the ordinary rules of human life because they have been delivered from its limitations by the Holy Spirit. Some Christians refuse to take an oath, for example, because they think that it is contrary to Scripture,[45] when in fact it is just a reassurance to the outside world that we are committed to telling

---

[41]James 3:2.
[42]Note, for example, Paul's expression of self-awareness in Eph. 3:8.
[43]Matt. 7:1; Luke 17:3.
[44]Matt. 7:3–5.
[45]See Matt. 5:34–37; James 5:12.

the truth, the whole truth, and nothing but the truth. We may think that we do not need extra encouragement to do that, but we have a responsibility to demonstrate our honesty in ways that will be meaningful to others, and that is why oath-taking in a court is lawful and necessary for Christians, as much as for anyone else.

It is also important for us to arrange our affairs in ways that are publicly accountable and above suspicion. A Christian couple can cohabit and call this "marriage," but in the eyes of the world the situation is unclear, and it is important for a marriage to be publicly acknowledged. We have only to think of Abraham, who passed his wife Sarah off as his sister on two separate occasions, neither of which turned out well.[46] In both cases it was because he was afraid to tell the whole truth, thinking that he could play it safe by telling only half of the truth. Abraham is our father in faith, and we are not superior to him. His temptation, which in the circumstances was perfectly understandable and led him to adopt what he thought was a reasonable course of action, led him into deeper trouble and into situations where it became impossible for anyone to trust him. Christians who find themselves heading down that road must stop themselves and realize that the salt is rapidly losing its taste and that their witness is of no value in spreading the gospel. Quite the contrary, it is liable to do great harm and to discredit everything they claim to stand for.

Christians must also make sure that they follow acceptable procedures when dealing with each other. These will vary from place to place, but every society and institution has norms to which its members are expected to conform, and Christians have no right to claim exemption from those norms merely because of their faith. They must keep proper accounts, employ people in ways that are legal, and make sure that no one can accuse them of substandard behavior in their dealings with others. In a church or other organization, they must operate the same checks and balances and the same monitoring procedures that would be expected anywhere else; if they can, they ought to go even further. Christians who indulge in sloppy business practices or who cut corners are not witnesses to their faith but embarrassments. There is nothing worse than when a prominent figure or organization in the Christian world is convicted of some crime that could have been avoided if proper procedures had been in place and observed. The world likes nothing better than to accuse the church of hypocrisy, and when there is substance in the charge, it can only bring shame and disgrace on God's people.[47]

Another issue that Christians have to deal with is the proper relationship

---

[46]Gen. 12:10–20; 20:2–14. Sarah was his half-sister.
[47]Rom. 2:17–24.

between what is private and what is held or shared in common. The goods of the church are not the property of a single individual, and care must be taken to ensure that church funds are not misappropriated for the private use of the pastor or some other member of the congregation. At the same time, it is usually better for individual Christians to handle their own financial affairs, making generous provision for the church and its needs, but not surrendering total control of their assets to it. In the early days of Christianity, there was an experiment in primitive communism in the Jerusalem church, but it failed because of the selfish behavior of Ananias and Sapphira, who pretended that they had given all their goods to the community when in fact they had kept back a substantial amount for themselves. They were punished for their sin, and the experiment was subsequently discontinued.[48] Over the centuries there have been monastic and semi-monastic communities that have revived this kind of communism and made it work on a limited scale, but it has never become the norm. Spontaneous attempts to do this in modern times have usually ended in tears. Human selfishness is deeply rooted, and although we must do all we can to combat it, we must also recognize that we shall never be able to eradicate the desire of people to have their own property. As the early church discovered, it is better to allow this and encourage generosity than to take it away and deprive individuals of the sense of responsibility that ought to accompany ownership.

The Bible warns us that there are things that God will not tolerate among his people. It is essential for the health of the church that we should bear them in mind and do our utmost to make sure that we are not guilty of them. Unfortunately, this means that we must keep on teaching about such things, not because we want to take some perverse pleasure in contemplating them but so that we shall be better equipped to spot them when they arise and deal with them before they get out of hand. In the Old Testament, we find the following list in Proverbs:

> There are six things that the LORD hates,
>   seven that are an abomination to him:
> haughty eyes, a lying tongue,
>   and hands that shed innocent blood,
> a heart that devises wicked plans,
>   feet that make haste to run to evil,
> a false witness who breathes out lies,
>   and one who sows discord among brothers.[49]

---

[48] Acts 5:1–11.
[49] Prov. 6:16–19.

When we read a list like this in the abstract, we are likely to recoil from it and think that we are not guilty of any of the things mentioned, which may well be true. It is unlikely, for example, that many of us would have shed innocent blood at a prayer meeting! But we must remember how Jesus interpreted things of that kind. He taught his disciples that if we have anger or hatred toward someone else in our hearts, we have committed murder already, and that can happen in church as much as anywhere else. If we judge ourselves by that standard, we shall soon see that we are not as innocent as we might think.[50] All of the things mentioned in the Proverbs list can easily surface in Christian circles if we let our guard down, and we must do our utmost to make sure that that does not happen.

In the New Testament, Paul also gives us a handy checklist of things to avoid:

> Now the works of the flesh are evident: sexual immorality, impurity, sensuality, idolatry, sorcery, enmity, strife, jealousy, fits of anger, rivalries, dissensions, divisions, envy, drunkenness, orgies, and things like these. I warn you, as I warned you before, that those who do such things will not inherit the kingdom of God.[51]

This list is more generic than the one in Proverbs, and therefore more directly applicable to a wider variety of situations, though most of us would probably think that idolatry and drunkenness were not common in church circles today. In the literal sense that may be so, but if we think in terms of obsessive preoccupations with things of secondary importance that distract us from our main purpose, then it is easier to see how these things also crop up in our midst. As always, we must be on our guard against tendencies that can catch us unawares. Self-discipline remains the fundamental requirement for Christian service, and as long as we live in a fallen world these are the things that we must be most on our guard against.

OUR RESPONSIBILITY FOR THE FALLEN MATERIAL WORLD

God's preserving power is also seen at work in the natural, material world, and Christians have as much responsibility as others for sustainable conservation and development. The laws of nature have not been suspended because of human sin. In fact, after the flood, God promised Noah that natural laws would continue to function to the end of time.[52] The benefit of this is so great

---

[50]Matt. 5:21–22.
[51]Gal. 5:19–21.
[52]Gen. 8:22.

that we often fail to notice it or to realize how dependent we are on the continued functioning of these laws. This indifference has begun to change in recent years as concerns about the effects of global warming have reminded us that even a slight change in temperatures can have enormous effects on climate and geography. Global warming is a highly controversial subject, and the data used to support it have been severely criticized, but it is certain that whole islands in the Pacific Ocean will disappear if the polar ice caps melt, and highly populated low-lying areas will be flooded. It is uncertain how much changes like these are due to human activity and how much they are the result of forces beyond our control, but either way, we are dependent on the material world for our survival and must do what we can to ensure that it is maintained in good working condition.

The preservation of the natural order for the benefit of all is a vital part of the Christian message and of the service of Christians to the surrounding world. God loves every human being, and we are called to do the same. It is true that we have a special responsibility to our fellow believers, but that is not because we care only for their well-being and not for that of others. Rather, it is to show the world that we are a family of faith united by bonds of love that transcend the barriers that separate and divide us. It would not be much of a witness to the wider world if the church did not look after its own members, and we must see the priority we give to them in that light. But priority for our brothers and sisters in Christ does not mean that we ignore everyone else. In many cases, such as famine relief and disease prevention, it would make no sense to confine our activities to other believers because the nature of the problem is such that it cannot be resolved in that way. Just as the gospel must be preached without fear or favor to the entire human race, so the Christian relief work that accompanies it must also be given freely to everyone. Christians have a duty to be actively involved in trying to improve the lot of mankind in every sphere of normal human activity. Needs of health, housing, and education must be recognized and attended to wherever they occur, and we cannot discriminate against those who are not of our faith. Nor should we use such humanitarian aid as a pretext for winning converts. The aid is worth giving for its own sake, and we should not expect anything in return. This selflessness is an important aspect of Christian witness because it shows that we care for the world as God's creation, and not because we want something out of it for ourselves.

On the whole, the church has done rather well in this sphere. All over the world there are hospitals, schools, and housing projects associated with Christianity, and wherever missionaries have gone, they have taken these things with them. The importance of such activities for our faith should not be underestimated. Jesus himself told his disciples that he would admit them to the kingdom of heaven at the last judgment because,

> "I was hungry and you gave me food, I was thirsty and you gave me drink, I was a stranger and you welcomed me, I was naked and you clothed me, I was sick and you visited me, I was in prison and you came to me."[53]

He then went on to add that the righteous would respond to this by asking him when all these things had happened, and he would reply, "As you did it to one of the least of these my brothers, you did it to me."[54]

The humanitarian contribution that Christians make is generally welcomed, but we must always bear in mind its limitations. Feeding the body is important and cannot be neglected, but converting the soul is more important still. Some Christians are tempted to believe that social action is all that is needed, and there are forces in the world that would conspire to keep it that way. We often find that while Christian material aid is welcome, the spiritual message that accompanies and underpins it is not. In some countries, this resistance to the gospel may even prevent the church from doing its humanitarian work. Here we have to walk a fine line between fulfilling our humanitarian tasks and remaining faithful to the gospel of Jesus Christ. Any ideology that promotes affluence and prosperity in this life at the expense of proclaiming salvation in the next falls short of the Christian message and cannot be embraced by the church. However much it may want to reach out to the wider community with material assistance, the church must not neglect or downplay its spiritual mission. We are not helping people if we protect their mortal bodies but do nothing for their immortal spirits, because in that case all we are really doing is postponing the day of reckoning. It is not a case of either/or but of both/and, and we must always bear that in mind as we set our goals and priorities for mission.

In modern times, the inability of the church to do its social work because of its unwelcome spiritual mission has been mainly associated with countries like Saudi Arabia or North Korea, where the local religion or ideology sees such activity as a threat. Recently, however, the problem has begun to surface in traditionally Christian countries, where changing social norms are incompatible with Christian beliefs. For example, a Christian hospital will not want to offer abortion on demand, even if it is legal in the country in which it is located. Similarly, church adoption agencies will not want to place children

---

[53]Matt. 25:35–36.
[54]Matt. 25:40.

with homosexual couples, even if they have the legal right to adopt them. In some countries this has already forced Christian agencies working in these fields either to close altogether or to abandon their church connections. This is regrettable, but it is the fault of an intolerant state. The church cannot be browbeaten into compromising its principles by a tendentious appeal to humanitarian need. If we lose our commitment to the gospel, our salt loses its taste, and anything else we might do is compromised as a result.

At a practical level, Christians show their love for others by adapting to their cultures and customs as far as they are compatible with our faith. The disciples of Jesus did not expect their Gentile converts to become Jews, but reached out to them as they were.[55] In the history of Christian mission, however, this principle has not always been followed—the most notable example being the Christianization of Western Europe in the Middle Ages, when Latin was adopted as the universal language of the church, even though hardly anyone could understand it. More recently, it has not been unknown for Western missionaries in Africa or Asia to impose European or American forms of worship or foreign denominational identities on native populations, some of whom have been only too willing to adopt them. Yet that approach is not true to the gospel, which, as the day of Pentecost made clear, everyone heard "in his own language."[56] The unity of the church was based on the message of the gospel and not on a shared cultural frame of reference. Today, in an increasingly globalized world, we must be particularly careful about this and resist the tendency to homogenize everything into a single pattern that does not allow for the legitimate diversity of human culture.

At the same time, the church must also resist being assimilated by the forces of tribalism or nationalism. This is a major problem in many parts of the world, where the identification of religion and nationality is so strong that it is virtually impossible for some people to become Christians. If they profess faith in Christ, they have to keep it secret because the social and legal pressures they face are too great for them to bear. In the Muslim world especially, there are many secret converts who are officially forbidden to change their religion and may be living in fear for their lives. Christians must do whatever we can to alleviate this situation, but we must also recognize that, in some cases, the ban on proselytism stems from a not unreasonable fear that Christian missionary work has some connection to a potentially hostile foreign power. It is hard to change such false perceptions, but we can at least try to make sure that we do nothing to encourage such views.

---

[55] 1 Cor. 9:20–21.
[56] Acts 2:6.

On another level, Christians show their love for others by treating them with respect as individuals, whatever their religion or social standing may be. God is no respecter of persons, and those in the early church who were inclined to favor the richer over the poorer members of their congregations were severely rebuked for their attitude.[57] Everyone is equal in the sight of God and deserving of equal consideration, whatever their status in human terms may be. This is not a matter of bringing everyone down to the lowest common denominator but of raising them up to the highest level by making each person special in our eyes. Treating people with respect also means dealing honestly with them. In many parts of the world, it is taken for granted that bribery and other forms of corruption are the norm and are essential in doing business. Christians must resist this, not only because it is wrong in itself but also because it is disrespectful and demeaning to the other person. We must never accept bribes ourselves, and we must remember that if we offer someone else a bribe in order to get what we want, we corrupt them. Admittedly, it is not always easy (or even possible) to avoid this, but at least we should be aware of the problem and challenge those who take such things as the norm to examine their own consciences. The sad fact is that the poorest people and countries of the world are often in that state because of the corruption of a few who make it impossible to establish a normal economy. Christians must do what they can to correct this terrible scourge in the interests of everyone involved.

THE FINAL TRANSFORMATION OF THE MATERIAL WORLD

What will happen to the material world in the end? That it will not go on forever is a fact that can be confirmed by natural scientists, who predict that it will wind down in about 7 billion years or so, even without divine intervention. Is there some sense in which God will redeem it? What will happen to the human race if and when he does? As far as we can tell from the biblical evidence, the created order will be done away with and will be replaced by something else, which the Bible calls "a new heaven and a new earth," in which there will be no more sea.[58] When that happens, sorrow and suffering will be abolished, because the conditions that create them now will have ceased to exist. Another feature of this new creation is that it is presented to us as a city—the New Jerusalem.[59] Cities are the product of human creativity, which suggests that our creativity too will be caught up in the transformation of all

---

[57] Acts 10:34; James 2:1–7.
[58] Rev. 21:1.
[59] Rev. 21:2.

things. It would be idle to speculate about what this will involve in practice, and people who say that they cannot wait to get to heaven to enjoy their favorite foods or listen to their favorite music are speculating about something that has not been revealed to us. What we are told is that, in the New Jerusalem, God will dwell with mankind. We must assume that we shall be so preoccupied with him when that happens that we shall have no time to give our attention to anything else.

As far as human beings are concerned, people who have died will be resurrected with a new spiritual nature and those who are still alive will be transformed into that same new nature.[60] Some indication of what we may expect is given in 1 Corinthians 15, where the apostle Paul talks about the resurrection of the body. The key point is that "flesh and blood cannot inherit the kingdom of God."[61] The material world as we know it does not carry over into the spiritual realm, where it is incompatible. This world is temporal and mortal, whereas the spiritual world is eternal and immortal. Therefore, if we are going to be material beings in that world, the matter of which we are made will have to change so that it can survive in those conditions. According to Paul, the process by which this occurs is one of death and rebirth. He compares our bodies to seeds that must die in order to give birth to plants that look nothing like the seeds, but which are nevertheless intimately bound up with them. There can be no plants without the sowing of the seeds, yet we cannot tell from the seeds what the plants will look like.[62] The analogy is imperfect, of course, as all analogies are, but it gives us a picture of how we might look at the end-time transformation. The bodies we have now will be changed into spiritual ones by a mysterious process that will involve the renewal of the entire created order.

We can hardly imagine that our transformed bodies will have nowhere to put themselves, and as we have seen, we are promised a new heaven and earth. Presumably these will be adapted to the transformed body's needs, but beyond that we cannot say what our new nature will be like. In particular, we have no idea how we shall recognize one another. Will we look young or old? We know that there will be no marriage in heaven, and so possibly no sexuality either, but that we cannot say for sure.[63] The precise details are hidden from our eyes, and we shall have to wait and see what happens when the time comes.

It is important to remember that the resurrection will be universal. All human beings who have died, from Adam until the return of Christ, will be

---

[60]1 Thess. 4:13–17.
[61]1 Cor. 15:50.
[62]1 Cor. 15:36–38.
[63]Matt. 22:30.

brought back to face judgment. Those who are united to Christ will go to be with him in eternity, but those who are not will be condemned to the same destruction as that reserved for Satan and the fallen angels.[64] There is no sign that they will be annihilated, but rather that they will suffer eternal punishment, being kept in existence as Satan and his angels will be, because God will not destroy anything he has made.

However we conceive of God's plan of salvation, we must remember that it is designed and executed in love. God saves us because he loves us and wants us to live with him forever. We know that the world which he has prepared for us is one in which we shall be eternally secure and enjoy the best of what he can offer us in close fellowship with him. In the midst of the city that comes down from heaven will be the tree of life that was originally planted in the garden of Eden.[65] That tree of life is Christ, whose leaves will heal the nations. All sorrow and suffering will be banished from that heavenly existence, as of course will death. The forces that so insistently attack us here below will be defeated, and there will be no room in our thoughts for anything but the love and power of God at work in our lives. It is a powerful vision, and one that constitutes the hope to which we have been called. Even if we cannot understand it all now, it is held out to us as the reward for our faithfulness. That faithfulness may be very costly, and there are many sorrows we may have to endure, but in the end we shall enter into that eternal kingdom which he has prepared for us from before the foundation of the world.[66]

---

[64] Matt. 25:33–41; Rev. 21:6–8.
[65] Rev. 22:2.
[66] Eph. 1:4.

25

GOD'S
COVENANT PEOPLE

THE LOGIC OF RECONCILIATION

God's response to the rebellion of his creatures was not confined to keeping them alive. He went further than that, and in his deep love decided to bring fallen human beings back into fellowship with himself. Restoring the broken relationship between God and man was to be a long, slow, and painful process, which would take many generations before being fully accomplished. Those whom God reconciled to himself had to understand what had gone wrong and why it mattered, since otherwise they would never have appreciated what they were being given. Their knowledge of good and evil had to be established on the right footing so that they would come to desire what God wants and not what they might prefer. Above all, the death they had inherited had to be overcome by a new and eternal life that would be immune to Satan's temptations.

By disobeying God, Adam and Eve condemned themselves to spiritual death. We have inherited that death, and if we want to live with God in eternity, we have to get rid of their legacy. The only way we can do that is by dying, because our human nature is unable to regenerate itself. The dilemma we face is that if we die, we shall destroy ourselves and achieve nothing. Compare this with the way our physical nature works. If we have a gangrenous limb, we can cut it off and go on living, but if the cancer has spread to our whole body, how can we get rid of it without dying? In spiritual terms, sin is like a cancer that has affected every part of us, leaving no untouched remainder that can begin the process of restoring us to health. We understand the consequences of this in our relationship with the natural world, and act accordingly all the time. If we have to deal with a diseased tree or a physically broken animal, we do not hesitate to cut the tree down or put the animal to death because we know that that is the only viable solution to the problem.

Logically speaking, God ought to do the same with us. If he were to destroy the cancerous evil in his creation, there might be a chance that the healthy remainder could go on living as he originally intended. In the angelic world, such a policy would mean destroying only some of his spiritual creatures (those who rebelled against him). In the material order, however, it would entail the elimination of the entire human race because we have all sinned and fall short of the glory of God.[1] If that had happened, the created order would be quite different from what it is because its crowning glory would have been cut off and there would be nothing to replace it. The rest of creation would still exist, but the link between God and his world that he wanted mankind to be would be cut off. The miracle is that God has not done this. Instead of following the dictates of logic, his love for us has led him not only to rescue us from the consequences of our folly, but to invite us to share his eternal life in heaven.

In order to do this, God had to eliminate our sinfulness without destroying us in the process. But how? There were basically two ways that God could have chosen to deal with our sin. He could have demanded full retribution for the wrong that has been done to him, or he could have excused it and told us to forget it because it does not matter. The first of these options is logically justifiable, and many people would want something similar for themselves if they were the victims of wrongdoing. To them, anything less than full retribution seems to be unjust, even if the consequences only cause further damage. In some societies, this has led to the vendetta or blood feud, which carries on through the generations and wreaks untold havoc on everyone involved. To limit the destructive effects of this, most human societies have introduced a system of fixed penalties, which can be exacted from the offending party as payment for his misdeeds. When the penalty has been discharged, the wronged party must accept that the demands of justice have been satisfied, and that he has no further claim against the offender, even if the original problem remains unresolved.

God did something like this when he instituted the system of sacrifice for sin. In the law of Moses, he told his people that there was a price to be paid for every wrong they committed. That could be done by offering specific things in compensation. If those offerings were acceptable to God, he would write off the debt incurred by the sin in question, and the offender would be discharged. In ancient Israel this led to an elaborate and comprehensive system

---

[1] Rom. 3:23.

of sacrifices, which culminated in the great offering of a spotless lamb once a year. That offering was made by the high priest in the temple at Jerusalem and was meant to cover the sins of the whole people.

As a system this worked reasonably well, but there were problems with it that remained insoluble. First of all, the high priest had to sacrifice for his own sins as well as for those of the people. He did what the law prescribed, but he himself remained a sinner and therefore spiritually unworthy to make the offering. Considering that the sacrifice itself had to be spotlessly pure, the inadequacy of the priest inevitably called the effectiveness of his action into question. Second, the sacrifice was only an animal, which lacked the spiritual dimension found in human beings. Given that our sinfulness is a spiritual problem, it is hard to see how the blood of bulls and goats, or even spotless lambs, could take away sins that they could not have understood, let alone committed.[2]

Third, the sacrifice had to be performed every year. When the temple was destroyed or the office of high priest eliminated, the system could not function. From 586 to 516 B.C. the temple lay in ruins, although the priests survived and the sacrificial system was eventually restored. After the destruction of Jerusalem in A.D. 70, however, both the temple and the priestly caste disappeared, making the sacrificial system inoperable. Even before that, though, the danger that the sacrifices might be interrupted made it desirable to look for something that would remain effective regardless of what might happen to the temple and its priests.

The second option that God could have chosen was to forget it all and carry on as if nothing had happened. Nowadays we normally call this *forgiveness*, by which we mean an act of mercy that goes beyond the demands of justice and makes retribution redundant. In this scenario, the offended party accepts his loss and decides that it is better (and possibly more rewarding) to seek reconciliation with the offender rather than pursue his claim. Forgiving and forgetting is hard at the best of times, but it may be the wisest policy, especially when both sides in a dispute bear some of the responsibility for it. Not only can attempts to exact justice or revenge become self-destructive, the passage of time often removes both the cause of the original hurt and any means of restitution. What has gone beyond recall is not worth remembering (especially as it is unlikely to be remembered accurately), and forgetting about what can never be put right is surely the best course to follow. As Christians, we teach that forgiveness is more than a form of enlightened self-interest. It is a sign of the compassion and love for others that we are

---

[2]Heb. 10:4.

expected to demonstrate in our dealings with them, and to do this without counting the cost to ourselves is a measure of our spiritual maturity.[3]

It can therefore come as a shock when we discover that God demands retribution for the sins we have committed against him and is not prepared to excuse them in the way that we are expected to forgive one another. Some people find this apparent "double standard" so repellent that they use it as an excuse not to believe in God at all. To their minds, if God exists, he ought to manifest human virtues to an infinite degree. If he is as all-powerful as his followers claim, what stops him from letting bygones be bygones and wiping our sins from his mind? If revenge seldom achieves its object and forgiveness is what God expects of us, why should he not practice it himself? Does God demand a higher moral standard from us than the one he himself lives by? Skeptics are well aware that in human affairs, those in authority often expect a higher performance from their subordinates than they apply to themselves, but we regard that as an abuse of power, not as a prerogative of high office. Is that what God is like?

At first sight this kind of argument sounds very plausible, and it has certainly led many people to reject the God of the Bible, whom they regard as an immoral tyrant. Christians respond to this accusation by saying that it is a false conclusion that ignores the fundamental differences between God and man. When one human being wrongs another, the offended party cannot claim to be totally innocent because neither of them is morally perfect. The fact that we all make mistakes is a powerful reason for limiting the extent to which justice should be pursued. At some stage, the finger of the accuser may be pointed back at him. As Jesus told his disciples,

> Judge not, that you be not judged. For with the judgment you pronounce you will be judged, and with the measure you use it will be measured to you. Why do you see the speck that is in your brother's eye, but do not notice the log that is in your own eye?[4]

None of us is so pure that we can smugly pass judgment on the wrongdoing of others, even when that wrongdoing is confessed and the demands of law and order oblige us to punish it.[5] For us there is always a sense of "there but for the grace of God go I," and humility must be our watchword when we seek to administer justice. But in the broken relationship between God and man, there is only one guilty party—man. God is not at fault, and he bears

---

[3]See Ps. 15:3–4.
[4]Matt. 7:1–3.
[5]Ps. 14:3.

no responsibility for what has happened. Even to suggest that he might be responsible is a sin because it amounts to saying that God is not perfect any more than we are.

Nor are we God's equals. An employee is subordinate to his employer, but only in the context of his employment. As human beings they are on the same level, and no employer has the right to mistreat those who work for him (or vice versa).[6] But we cannot argue with the one who made us and whose rights over us are unchallenged. It is only because he tolerates our existence that we are here at all; we have no bargaining chips to use in our dealings with him.[7] For us to expect God to forgive and forget what we have done is not only presumptuous but is a denial of his nature. At the same time, God cannot just walk away from our wrongdoing and pretend that it is not there, because his being is incompatible with the existence of evil.[8] From God's point of view, our sin is spoiling his creation and he cannot ignore it. It must be dealt with, and that means getting rid of it as we would get rid of any rot or pest that is spoiling our home or garden. The only question is how God can do that without destroying us in the process.

Second, although it is easy for us to forget about Adam and his sin because it all happened so long ago, God does not dwell in time and cannot forget a past which for him is the same as the present. Human sin is always present in his mind. From his perspective we are all "in Adam" and are just as responsible for our fallen state as Adam was. To put it another way, the tragedy of our separation from God remains as real and as damning for us as it was for Adam and Eve. Reconciliation cannot be achieved by forgetting the past, but only by facing up to it and putting right what has gone wrong.

Third, the fact that God takes our sin so seriously is a measure of his great love for us. This is paradoxical, but when the Bible speaks of God's punishment, it does so in the most intimate terms. Just as a human father disciplines his son, so God disciplines his children because of his great love for them.[9] There are people today who do not believe that punishment is a form of love and who even want to make it illegal for parents to spank their children. To them, even a slap on the wrist is a form of abuse that ought to be banned. They see banning every form of corporal punishment as an act of love, but wiser heads know that they are wrong. A child who is allowed to get away with whatever he wants is liable to feel unloved because those who are expected to discipline him apparently do not care enough to do so. Some

---

[6]See Col. 3:22–25.
[7]Rom. 9:21.
[8]Hab. 1:13.
[9]Deut. 8:5; Prov. 13:24; Heb. 12:6–7.

children even provoke their parents into punishing them, just to see whether the parents notice what they are doing and care enough about it to take action.

Our heavenly Father notices everything that we do and objects very strongly when we disobey him. If we provoke him, he will not let us get away with it. Every sin that we commit must be accounted for and put right because he will not allow us to stand in his presence if we do not measure up to his standards.

The snag is that we have no way of satisfying God's demands. We cannot undo the sin of Adam and return to his original righteousness, nor can we make up for what has gone wrong because everything we do is defined and limited by the sinfulness we have inherited from him. If God really wants us to live with him in eternity, he must do what is necessary to make that happen because we cannot do it for ourselves. It is not for us to speculate whether God could have achieved the reconciliation he wants in some other way. God does not ask us whether we think that his plan for our salvation was the best or the only one available to him. Instead, he presents us with what he has done and asks us to accept it as the only means of overcoming the barrier separating us from him.

What God did was to bring a second Adam into being, a man who was not encumbered by the legacy of the fall, but who was nevertheless a real human being who shared our nature. In order to bridge the gap between man and God, this second Adam also had to be divine, since no creature has the right to stand in the presence of the Creator and be heard. In order to save us from our sins, God opened himself up by sending his Son into the world. He shared with us the deepest love that one person can have for another—he gave his life on earth for us in order that we might live forever in heaven with him.[10]

When the Son of God came into the world, he did so as a man who was in the likeness of Adam, but who had not inherited Adam's sin. Because this man was also the second person of the Trinity, he had a relationship with the Father that could withstand whatever pressure might be put on him, including the weight of human sinfulness. The Son was therefore able to pay the price for our broken relationship with God by taking both that brokenness and its cause on himself. In a supreme paradox, the sinless man became sin, and the immortal God endured human suffering and death in order to destroy them and deliver us from their power.[11] When the Son of God came back from the dead, he did not return to the human life that he had shared with us, in the

---

[10]John 3:16.
[11]2 Cor. 5:21.

way that Lazarus did.[12] That would have been a miracle, but it would not have achieved our salvation. Instead, he came back to a higher form of existence that stands in continuity with what went before but is no longer bound by the same limitations. Those whom he has chosen for salvation will also share in that new and transformed life. As Christians we know it as a spiritual experience here and now, and when we die it will become our new life in the kingdom of heaven, where we shall stand forever in the presence of God.

Should we describe this new life primarily as an individual experience or as something bigger than we are, in which we shall participate along with others? When the Bible speaks about sin and salvation, it does so primarily in individual terms. Adam, Eve, and Jesus Christ were all individuals whose actions and decisions had far-reaching and long-lasting effects. In biblical times, the call of God came to individuals—to Noah, Abraham, Moses, and so on. These men became the ancestors and leaders of a nation, but they themselves were identifiable persons, as indeed was Jacob, to whom the name Israel was given.[13] The pattern of salvation revealed in the Bible starts with individuals and proceeds from them to the group, which is created and shaped by their teachings and actions and identifies with them. Just as Israel was an extension of Jacob, so the church is the body of Christ, reaching out across continents and generations to draw all those who have been called and to unite them with him.

Today the message of the gospel is still proclaimed by and to particular individuals who respond to it either by accepting or by rejecting its claims. The proclaimer may represent a group, as Peter did when he stood up to preach on the day of Pentecost, but he is still a particular individual. Having said that, what is proclaimed by individuals is not private or isolationist. Peter preached to a large crowd and over three thousand people responded to his message, thereby creating the first Christian church.[14] No one who receives the gospel can keep it to himself; he will immediately seek to communicate it to others and join in fellowship with those who share his convictions. Groups are created by the witness of individuals, and they provide the support and nurture that other individuals need to carry on the work. Both individuals and groups have their place, and if priority is given to the former, it is only in order to promote the more effective development of the latter.

The fellowship of believers, which we call the church, is the result of the proclamation of the message of salvation. The church would not exist

---

[12]John 11:44.
[13]Gen. 32:28.
[14]Acts 2:41.

otherwise, and if it ceases to preach the gospel, it will wither and die. As a visible presence in the world, the church attracts some people and repels others, but it is not by this reaction that the gospel must be judged. Those who are attracted to the church must be challenged by the message it proclaims and be convicted of its truth. The fellowship of believers is only as strong as the commitment of individual believers themselves, and when the church admits adherents who do not share that commitment, it is weakened and compromised. At the same time, the gospel has never been the possession of only one person, and true believers cannot operate outside the community of those who share their beliefs. We are all parts of the body of Christ, and we need one another if we are going to function properly within it.[15]

The Bible tells us how God began to reveal his plan of salvation by speaking to Abraham, Isaac, and Jacob. Through them he chose a people and trained them to understand what had to be done to repair the broken relationship between man and God. One step at a time, God taught them who he is, what he is like, and what standard he requires of those whom he has chosen to live with him. He began by showing them the seriousness of their own predicament as fallen human beings who did not deserve what he was prepared to do for them. After that, he not only set out in detail how every sin they committed had to be paid for, but he showed them that there is an underlying sinfulness in us that cannot be corrected in this piecemeal way.

The New Testament then tells us that when the time was ripe, God the Father sent his Son to accomplish the task of reconciliation, although many who belonged to his chosen people did not accept him.[16] If the Israelites were thrown into confusion, however, there were large numbers of other people who understood what the Son had accomplished and believed in him. They were integrated into the chosen people, while Jews who rejected the Son were cut off from their promised inheritance. That things should have turned out like this seems strange to us, but it was part of God's plan from the beginning. His choice of those who will serve him in eternity is a spiritual one, determined entirely by him.[17] It is manifested and proclaimed on earth by a particular group of people, but no human being can claim to have been chosen by God merely because he or she was born into that group or joined it in order to reap its benefits.

Those who had received the training that had prepared the way for the coming of the Son had a certain advantage, but there was no guarantee that

---

[15]1 Cor. 12:12–30.
[16]John 1:11.
[17]John 15:16.

they would necessarily benefit from it. On the other hand, lack of previous training was not an insurmountable barrier for those who believed, because the gift of God is essentially spiritual, and they received it on the strength of their faith. God's purpose was not thwarted or modified in any way. On the contrary, it was revealed for what it had been all along—a personal relationship of love restored by the work of the Son, who cleared away the barriers that had prevented our reconciliation with the Father and opened the way for us to dwell with him forever.

THE PEOPLE OF GOD

It was God's decision to reconcile fallen human beings to himself that led to the emergence of both Israel and the Christian church, neither of which would have come into being otherwise. To this day their respective identities are determined by the fact that God has called them to live in eternal fellowship with him. At the deepest level, Israel and the church merge into one another because each of them is the people of God. Although they share a common spiritual vocation, however, in most other ways they remain quite distinct from one another. Israel was a tribal nation that traditionally propagated itself by natural growth rather than by proselytization, whereas the church is a mixed body that has actively sought to embrace people from every tribe and nation. Historically speaking, Israel and the church are different because Israel was chosen to be God's people before his Son came into the world, whereas the church was formed out of those who followed God's Son, in order to spread the good news of what he had accomplished. In that sense, Israel and the church complement one another, and it is possible to belong to both of them simultaneously, as the apostles and most of the first generation of Christians did. Since the day of Pentecost, Israel and the church have lived together side by side, though this coexistence has seldom been harmonious. They are bound together by a common inheritance but divided by their different ways of understanding it, and, sadly, it is that which has governed their relations through most of the past two millennia. At the end of time, we are promised that this historical division will be overcome and the people of God will be reunited, but precisely how this will happen remains hidden from our eyes.[18]

There has been much speculation about the final redemption of Israel and considerable disagreement about what that will involve. One reason for this uncertainty is that when we talk about Jews today, we tend to think

---

[18]Rom. 11:25–27.

about ethnic Judaism and the state of Israel, whereas the New Testament's perspective is more inward and spiritual. We can all agree that, at the end of time, spiritually minded Jews will be united with spiritually minded Christians to form the one eternal people of God, but what this will mean in visible or institutional terms is unclear. Are we to expect that all ethnic Jews will profess faith in Christ, whether or not they practice their religion? There have been times in the past when misguided church authorities have tried to force Jews to convert to Christianity, partly for their own good but partly also in order to hasten the end of time; the results were disastrous. We must wait and see how God will fulfill this particular prophecy. Although we do not know how it will happen, we can certainly say that the conversion of the Jews will be a spiritual movement among them and not the result of coercion on our part.

We can also say that the Bible teaches that the physical and spiritual realms of Israel are distinct from each other. Not everyone who belonged to the historic Israelite nation was a child of God, and it seems probable that the majority of them were not.[19] Statistics can be contentious and misleading, but if there were originally twelve tribes in Israel and ten of them were "lost" by being deported and dispersed among alien peoples, it seems reasonable to suggest that the two remaining tribes were a remnant of the original nation. This assumption is borne out by 2 Samuel 24:9, where we are told that the fighting men of the ten northern tribes numbered 800,000 whereas those of Judah (presumably including Benjamin) numbered only 500,000. However, it is worth noting that if these statistics are correct, Judah must have been by far the largest single tribe, accounting for about a third of all Israelites instead of the twelfth that one might expect, so the "remnant" was far from insignificant.

We must also remember that there were non-Israelites in ancient times, like Ruth and Naaman the Syrian, who were believers.[20] They may have been few in number, but they existed, and mention of them in the Bible serves to remind us that we cannot use ethnic origin as the criterion for deciding whether a particular individual belongs to God's people. Despite its physical existence as a nation among other nations and its tendency to reproduce itself almost exclusively by natural means, Israel remained a spiritual community whose membership was determined not by man but by God. Those who fell away from it, like the ten tribes just mentioned, lost their ethnic identity as well as their religion, and the few outsiders who submitted to the

---

[19]Rom. 3:21–4:25. See also Luke 4:24–29.
[20]Ruth 1:16; 2 Kings 5:17–19.

stringent requirements of the law were admitted into fellowship, though no one could say that that was actively encouraged.

How Israel should be defined became a matter of great importance in the early days of Christianity, when believers in Christ had to work out what their relationship to Judaism should be. There were some who took the historical nation as the norm and insisted that Christians must integrate into it by taking on board the ritual requirements of the Old Testament law, especially circumcision. It seems that these people were quite influential at first, but before long they were being combated by Paul, who regarded their teaching not only as false but as a complete perversion of the gospel of Christ. In a stinging letter to the Galatians, and in his great epistle to the Romans, Paul defined Israel as a spiritual nation, insisting that it is on that basis that Christians belong to God's chosen people. We claim Abraham as our ancestor, not because we are descended from him in the physical sense but because we share his faith and have inherited his relationship to God. On the other hand, Jews who do not share Abraham's faith cannot appeal to their physical descent from him as evidence that they belong to Israel because without Abraham's faith, they are cut off from God and cast out of the nation.[21]

On the basis of Paul's teaching, Christians have appropriated the spiritual inheritance of Israel without feeling obliged to follow the legal prescriptions laid down in the Old Testament. It is true that there have been periodic attempts to use those laws as models for the behavior of Christians, but this has always been piecemeal and inconsistent. The medieval church tried to apply to Christian ministers the tithe regulations originally designed to support the Israelite priests, by claiming that ministers were the equivalents of Jewish priests and Levites and were therefore entitled to the same compensation and privileges. But the same church contradicted this by enforcing a rule of priestly celibacy in order to prevent the emergence of a hereditary priestly caste, although heredity had been the basis of the priesthood in ancient Israel.

There have also been attempts to regard modern states as "Christian nations" and to expect them to adopt laws drawn from ancient Israel, like those governing the observance of the Sabbath. Such an approach can only be haphazard and inconsistent, since not even the strongest defenders of strict Sabbath observance would insist on keeping the Jewish food laws, or on stoning women caught in adultery. One of the beneficial results of modern biblical scholarship is that it has made us more aware of the processes of historical development. This allows us to respect ancient Israelite laws in their context without having to apply them directly to our very different circumstances.

---

[21]This is a summary of the case made in Romans 2–4 and 9–11.

Today it is fair to say that the spiritual understanding of Israel that is found in the New Testament is all but universal in the Christian world.

Many Christians are prepared to regard the modern state of Israel as the legitimate descendant of the Old Testament kingdom, but even they have to admit that Israel today operates very differently from what is prescribed in the Bible and makes no attempt to revive either the Davidic monarchy or the Aaronic priesthood and its attendant sacrifices. Circumcision survives, as do most of the traditional food laws, though there is some laxity in practice where these are concerned. Modern Judaism stands out in many ways, most of which can be traced back to the Old Testament, but even Jews will usually agree that theirs is a spiritual faith, manifested in particular practices but no longer defined by them in the way that was common in the time of Jesus. The modern state of Israel is not identical with the Jewish "nation" (the majority of whom do not live there), nor does it regard itself as the physical embodiment of the people of God. It offers Jews a homeland if they wish to take advantage of that, but does not try to force itself on all Jews as an integral part of their faith, nor does it exclude non-Jews from citizenship, as its ancient forbear did.

In one respect, however, modern Israel stands in continuity with its biblical prototype, and remains profoundly different from the Christian church. Jews still do not customarily proselytize, though they are prepared to receive outsiders into their faith if they wish to join it, whereas Christians actively seek to win others to Christ. Since the day of Pentecost, the Christian church has prided itself on the fact that it contains men and women of every race and ethnic background. Not only can God's people be found everywhere, the church makes it its business to go out and look for them, so that they can be integrated into the visible fellowship of Christ's body on earth. To this end, it has no holy land, no sacred language, and no privileged racial group in its midst. It may be true that the church has sometimes slipped from this ideal in practice, as when it tried to impose Latin as the universal language in the Middle Ages, or when it acquiesced in apartheid and other forms of racial discrimination in the nineteenth and twentieth centuries, but theological justifications for these things (such as they were) were never universally accepted, and, in the end, even those who once promoted them rejected them as aberrations.

Today it can safely be said that Christians are highly conscious of their calling to embrace all mankind, and they are very often in the forefront of globalization. As tribal communities break up and small nations disappear, it is Bible translators who preserve their languages and respect their identity, while at the same time seeking to connect them to the worldwide fellowship of the gospel. In this respect, the modern church has been outstandingly faithful to the Great Commission of Jesus and puts the message of universal equality into practice to a degree unmatched by any other religion or ideology.

Although the Christian message has gone out to the whole world, and the ancient barrier that divided Jews from others has been broken down, it cannot be said that everyone on earth now belongs to God's people. There are still people who have never heard the gospel, and large numbers who have rejected it, either explicitly or implicitly (by adhering to another religion, for example). Even within the bounds of the Christian church, there are many who are spiritually dead, just as there were in ancient Israel and still are in modern Judaism. The distinction between what is outward and physical on the one hand, and what is inward and spiritual on the other, is as real today as it has ever been, and the biblical principle that only the spiritually minded are truly members of God's people remains as valid now as it was in ancient times. Furthermore, it is God who puts his Spirit into our hearts, not we who choose to believe in him. As Jesus said to Nicodemus,

> That which is born of the flesh is flesh, and that which is born of the Spirit is spirit. Do not marvel that I said to you, "You must be born again." The wind blows where it wishes, and you hear its sound, but you do not know where it comes from or where it goes. So it is with everyone who is born of the Spirit.[22]

GOD'S CHOICE

The differences between Israel and the church are easy enough to see, but there are profound similarities as well. The most important of these is that God has chosen each of them. Neither Israel nor the church came into being spontaneously, a truth that is meant to keep us humble and to reassure us that God's purpose for our lives cannot be thwarted by our inability to do anything to please him.[23] Is there any way of knowing why he has chosen us and not others? The simple answer to this question is that we do not know. Even the Israelites seem to have been puzzled by it, as the Old Testament indicates:

> The LORD your God has chosen you to be a people for his treasured possession, out of all the peoples who are on the face of the earth. It was not because you were more in number than any other people that the LORD set

---

[22]John 3:6–8.
[23]Deut. 7:6b–8a; John 15:16; Eph. 1:4–6.

his love on you and chose you, for you were the fewest of all peoples, but it is because the LORD loves you . . .[24]

It was God's love, not our fame or fortune, that motivated his choice and that binds us together as his people. Love is its own explanation, because God is love. Those who have experienced it know what it is and respond to it accordingly. They do not ask why God has not extended the same love to everyone else, just as we do not ask those who love us why they do not relate to everyone in the same way. The relationship that God's love creates and sustains is the source of our life in him, and that is all we need to know. We share God's love with others who have received it because we are bound together in a single spiritual reality, and we are called to reach out to those who have not known it. But much as we may yearn for them to come to know God's love in Christ, the truth is that unless and until they do, we cannot have fellowship with them. There is nothing we can do to change that, other than to pray to God, asking him to have mercy on those whom we desire to see be born again. We know that he has promised to hear our prayers, but he will answer them in his own time and in his own way. As Paul said to the Corinthians, when they were quarreling over who had first preached the gospel to them, "I planted, Apollos watered, but God gave the growth. So neither he who plants nor he who waters is anything, but only God who gives the growth."[25]

Do those whom God has chosen possess any moral or spiritual qualities that set them apart from others and might justify God's choosing them? It is easy to imagine how a small and unlucky nation would compensate for its misfortunes by claiming some kind of moral and spiritual superiority over its enemies, but Israel did not do that. The biblical texts are unsparing in their condemnation of their own people and their leaders, neither of whom comes out of the story at all well. Even the greatest national heroes, like Abraham, Moses, and David, are portrayed as men with deep and sometimes fatal flaws, and we have to search long and hard to find anyone who could be regarded as a role model for future generations to imitate. Joseph is perhaps one such person, but his invitation to Jacob to bring his family down to Egypt eventually led them into slavery, which was not what Joseph intended. Or Jonathan, who never seems to have done anything wrong, but who ended up being killed along with his wicked father Saul—and there was no one of his stature to take his place.[26] In the Bible, the archetypal example of a truly righteous man is

---

[24]Deut. 7:6b–8a.
[25]1 Cor. 3:6–7.
[26]2 Sam. 1:23–26.

Job, who was certainly not an Israelite and may never have existed at all.[27] It is necessary only to glance at the classical literature of other oppressed peoples with historical grievances to see how totally different Israel's self-understanding was from theirs. At times it even seems that the Israelites regarded their special spiritual status as a burden they would gladly have been rid of, and not as a blessing that made them superior to their neighbors.[28]

Another question often asked is why God chose some people for salvation but not others. The very smallness of Israel reminds us that God has saved very few people compared to the number of human beings that have lived on the earth. Why is this so? Every human being is a child of Adam and has inherited his broken relationship with God. At that level we are all equal, and none of us can claim to be better or worse than anyone else. To many people, it seems outrageous that, for no obvious reason, God picked out a tiny minority whom he reconciled to himself while abandoning the rest to their fate. Even many Christians are embarrassed by this and do their best to explain it away. Some have said that Israel was chosen not so much for salvation as to bear the sins of the whole world and purchase universal redemption by suffering on behalf of others. Many have claimed that the number of those eventually saved will be far greater than the number of the damned, although how they reach that conclusion is unknown. Not a few relapse into a form of universalism, according to which virtually everyone will be saved in the end unless they have been particularly wicked. They seem to believe in what might be called damnation by works—in other words, those who do little or nothing will go to heaven and only people who work hard at doing evil, like Adolf Hitler for example, will miss out in the end.

Unfortunately, views of that kind are based more on sentiment and wishful thinking than on anything the Bible says. Whether we like it or not, the gospel came first to Israel and spread out from there, but it took many centuries to reach the ends of the earth. It is only in our own time that almost everyone has had an opportunity to hear it. Why is it that Greeks had the chance to turn to Christ within a generation of his appearance, whereas the Germanic tribes of northern Europe had to wait several centuries for the same opportunity, and most of Africa and Asia were held back for nearly two millennia? Can we really say that God loves the people of Denmark more than those of Sri Lanka or Laos because more Europeans have heard the gospel than others? Can it really be true that the English have remote

---

[27]It is not clear from the text whether Job was a historical person, or whether he and the other characters in the story were created by the author to represent certain "types."

[28]See, for example, 1 Sam. 8:1–9.

ancestors in heaven whereas the Chinese and Indians do not? In a rapidly globalizing world, these questions have acquired a new urgency, not least because many people reject the Bible's teaching for precisely this reason. They think that if there is a God, he cannot possibly have practiced such blatant discrimination, and they blame Jews and Christians for preaching a message that has produced racism and injustice instead of the universal peace and harmony that they supposedly proclaim.[29]

Answering this accusation is not easy, and there are many things about God's plan that remain mysterious to us. The first thing we must understand is that if God had not reached out to us, no human being would have been saved. Modern people find this very hard to accept. We live in a world that has been programmed to think that everyone is entitled to receive benefits of one kind or another, and so we think it is unfair if some people are (or appear to be) excluded from them. When it comes to eternity, the default position for us is salvation, not damnation, and we are puzzled (if not offended) to be told otherwise. In our mental universe, heaven is presumed to be the final resting place of everyone who dies, even if some people do not believe in an afterlife and many speak of "heaven" in a vague and noncommittal way. All that really matters to them is that those who have died have been released from pain and suffering, and to that extent at least, they are better off than they were before. The one thing we do not want to hear is that we are going to hell, a place which many people prefer to think does not exist.

The trouble is that if we think like this, we cannot even begin to understand the Bible. From its point of view, the default position is not heaven but eternal death, and the fact that anyone is saved from that is a miracle of God's grace. The Bible gives no comfort to people who want to think that everyone is saved. It is not those who believe that God has chosen only a few who weaken the church, but those who believe that he has chosen everyone—because they have no gospel to preach. After all, what is the point of talking about sin, righteousness, and judgment if you think that everyone will be saved?

At the opposite extreme, those who believe that God has chosen only some go wrong if they try to identify who the chosen ones are, or if they sit back and do nothing on the assumption those who are saved will get to heaven whether or not they do anything about it. The Bible tells us that Jesus was sent to the lost sheep of the house of Israel, the main point being that although they were sheep, they were still *lost* and had to be found.[30] There was never

---

[29]Isa. 11:6–9.
[30]Matt. 10:6.

any question of rounding up the goats and including them, but as long as even one of the sheep had gone astray, the Good Shepherd had a duty to go out and bring him back to the flock where he belonged.[31]

To use a modern analogy, the world is like a plane that has crashed, leaving only a few lucky survivors. When that happens to a plane, our immediate reaction is to be amazed and grateful that anyone has come out of it alive. We do not stop to ask why those who survived should have been the lucky ones, nor do we think that everyone on board ought to have been rescued and look for someone to blame because that has not happened. On the contrary, we assume that when a plane crashes everyone in it will probably be dead, so if there are any survivors we regard it as a miracle. That is how we should look at our world. Such a perspective does not explain why only a few have been saved, nor does it give us any way of determining why it should have been those particular few and not others. Were they the only ones whose seatbelts were tightly fastened? Probably not. Were they sitting in some particularly safe part of the plane? Perhaps, but they almost certainly did not choose their seats with that in mind. There is usually no simple answer that will explain it, only the glorious fact of deliverance, and it is on that, not on the tragedy of the enormous loss of life, that we rightly fix our gaze and for which we give thanks.

Of course, people who have been delivered from a disaster of that kind often (and quite rightly) wonder why they have been spared, and reflecting on this should make them feel both humble and grateful to be alive. They also ought to be more aware of the value and precariousness of life and feel deeply sorry for those who did not escape. There is no cause for boasting or rejoicing at the misfortune of others, and anyone who indulged in that would rightly be regarded as grotesque. At the same time, however, the blessing of being rescued cannot be denied either. However "unfair" it may appear to be, it has nevertheless occurred, and complaining about the injustice of it will come across sounding like base ingratitude, not like the righteous indignation the complainer himself may think he is manifesting.

Why God decided to save only some people is unknown to us, but whatever the reason was, it remains the supreme manifestation of his love. If God were a God of justice and nothing more, he would never have saved anyone because no one has deserved it. As the apostle Paul put it, "All have sinned and fall short of the glory of God and are justified by his grace as a gift."[32] Everything to do with our salvation is an act of God's love, manifested in the free grace and

---

[31]Matt. 18:10–13.
[32]Rom. 3:23–24.

mercy that temper the natural effects of his justice. It is by his grace that he has made our salvation possible, and in his mercy that he has forgiven us, allowing us to share in the blessings that his grace has provided. The importance of this double action of grace and mercy can be appreciated by comparing the salvation of those who have been chosen in Abraham with the preservation of Noah and his descendants after the flood. That was also an act of divine grace but it lacked the mercy of forgiveness because Noah and his children were held accountable for their sins and died because of them. The salvation that God grants to those whom he has chosen is not just an act of preservation in and for this life, but one of restoration, which enables those who receive it to live with him in eternity.

As far as the nature and numbers of those chosen are concerned, all we can say for sure is that God has chosen them of his own free will, without any action on their part that might explain or justify his choice. The history of Israel shows us that being called by God does not entail any special privileges in this life, and may well mean the exact opposite. The ranks of the chosen ones have never contained many rich or famous people, nor can anyone claim that worldly success is the natural outcome of having been called by God to eternal salvation.[33] Much more likely than that is the path of martyrdom, as Jesus reminded his followers when he told them they must take up their cross if they wanted to be his disciples.[34] God's freedom to choose whomever he wishes may seem arbitrary to us, but actually it is very liberating because it means that we have no right to look down on anyone else or to exclude those whom we dislike from hearing the gospel. God can save anyone, and so we have no right to ignore those whom we regard as hopeless cases. Our task is to preach the Word of God and offer the promise of salvation to anyone who will listen, accepting those who respond to the call whether we like them or not. As far as God's chosen people are concerned, Israel has survived and made a mark on human history out of all proportion to its numerical significance. Even if many of them refuse to admit it, their achievements remain outstanding evidence of the faithfulness of God in keeping his promises to his rebellious (but still chosen) people.

It is clear that God chose Israel as a nation and not just particular individuals within it. Everyone born to the descendants of Abraham, Isaac, and Jacob was in some sense a member of this chosen people, regardless of his or her individual destiny. At the same time, the evidence of the Bible is that only a remnant of the nation was saved in the end. How should we interpret

[33] 1 Cor. 1:26–31.
[34] Matt. 16:24.

this apparent discrepancy between the calling of the nation and the saving of only a few within it?

Basically, there are two lines of approach we can take. The first is to say that it is possible for people to be chosen by God yet not to be saved. The most obvious way in which that might happen would be if individual members of the chosen people had the right to opt out, just as people today can renounce their citizenship if they choose to do so. A variant of this would be to say that the choosing of a nation does not automatically imply that everyone in that nation enjoys the same rights and privileges. That sounds undemocratic to modern ears, but it has been a fact for most of human history and would not have surprised the biblical authors unduly. Nevertheless, that is not the picture that we are given in the Scriptures. As Paul puts it,

> I do not want you to be unaware, brothers, that our fathers were all under the cloud, and all passed through the sea, and all were baptized into Moses in the cloud and in the sea, and all ate the same spiritual food, and all drank the same spiritual drink. For they drank from the spiritual Rock that followed them, and the Rock was Christ.[35]

The calling and the blessing that accompanied it, which Paul tells us was an experience of Christ, was given without discrimination to the entire nation of Israel. Yet Paul goes on to add, "Nevertheless, with most of them God was not pleased, for they were overthrown in the wilderness."[36] When we look at this in greater detail, it seems that the reason for this was that many of these people had no understanding of God or of his purposes. Paul summarizes the Old Testament account by reminding the Corinthian church that, not only were they rebellious, they were idolaters, which was the ultimate denial of God. The historical facts are not in doubt, but they raise serious theological questions about the power and sovereignty of God. Did his chosen people have the freedom to rebel against him and get away with it? Or was he always in control of the situation, quite deliberately choosing people whom he never intended to save?

This brings us to the second option, which is to say that God never envisaged that there would be an exact correspondence between the physical nation of Israel and those he has chosen for salvation. Though the spiritual people belong to the physical nation, they constitute a remnant within it and have always done so. According to this explanation, the historical nation of Israel was intended to be a home for God's people, a protective human community

---

[35] 1 Cor. 10:1–4.
[36] 1 Cor. 10:5.

within which they could flourish, but which ultimately they would leave behind. This distinction between the (broader) ethnic community of Israel and the (narrower) spiritual fellowship of God's chosen people was there from the beginning, but it came out in the open after the death and resurrection of Christ. At that time, those who were truly chosen accepted him and gradually abandoned their historic Judaism, which they did not impose on new believers who entered the church from outside the ethnically Jewish nation.

A solution along these lines is more consonant with the biblical evidence and must be preferred to any theory which suggests that God said one thing and did another, although it does not resolve every difficulty. At the end of the day, it remains true that ancient Israel was chosen by God as a community, and we must see it primarily in that light. Its ritual observances were commanded by him and performed by all the people, even by those who were clearly unworthy to do so. The blessing of the Promised Land went to everyone, whether or not they deserved it. The great events of Israel's history touched them all, whether it was the empire-building of David and Solomon or the Babylonian exile.[37] Yet at the same time only a remnant truly understood the nation's calling, and only they were ultimately saved.

In trying to express this in theological terms, we must focus on the substance of the matter first and then look for the best way to describe it. Let us begin by asserting that the Israelites were chosen by God for a special purpose. They received the law and the promise that God would redeem them and establish them forever as his chosen people. Exactly how this would happen was unclear, and the Jews of Jesus' day disagreed about the precise details, but they all believed that whatever God was planning to do would affect them primarily, if not exclusively. Nevertheless, and at the same time, the process of separating out the good from the bad *within* the chosen nation was already well established before Israel entered the Promised Land, and the theme recurs with great frequency throughout the Old Testament. Individual Jews had no reason to suppose that they would be saved merely because they were members of the ethnic community that constituted the chosen people. It was because many Jews did think that, that Paul criticized them so severely in his letter to the Romans.[38] Paul did not reject the outward trappings of Judaism, but he understood that they were meant to convey a spiritual reality which, if it were not present, would make the outward rituals useless and perhaps even blasphemous.

---

[37]Not everyone was exiled to Babylon, but the destruction of Jerusalem and its temple affected the entire nation.
[38]See Rom. 4:1–25.

In the New Testament, many of the tensions and ambiguities inherent in the identity of ancient Israel as God's people were resolved. Non-Jews were admitted as heirs to the covenant blessings formerly reserved for Israel, while ethnic Israelites who did not believe that God had fulfilled his promises to them in the life and death of Christ were excluded as long as they persisted in their unbelief. More importantly, no new nation was created by the emergence of the Christian church, which from the beginning was a supranational community in both the physical and the spiritual sense. There has often been some question about whether, or to what extent, the families and children of believers are included in this community, but however we answer that, the bonds that unite Christians do not enroll their dependents into the church in a binding way. If they subsequently choose to leave it, they are free to go, and there is nothing to remind them or anyone else that they have rejected their family background.

The church is the fellowship of those who believe in Christ and not an ethnic community. In the Christian church there can be no special nation or family because, whatever advantages may be given to those who have been born and brought up among Christians, in the end it is the commitment of the individual that is decisive. No one is guaranteed a place in heaven simply because of his inheritance, and those who come to faith from a totally alien background are not discriminated against on that account. As Paul put it,

> There is neither Jew nor Greek, there is neither slave nor free, there is no male and female, for you are all one in Christ Jesus. And if you are Christ's then you are Abraham's offspring, heirs according to promise.[39]

Because of this, if Christians have a concept of being chosen by God, it must apply primarily to individuals and not to social groups. What by the end of the Old Testament is the remnant of two tribes from one nation, in the New Testament becomes the company of the redeemed drawn from every tribe and nation, but not specifically identified with any one of them.

In other respects, the spiritual reality underlying the Old Testament remains the same in the New. Like ancient Israel, the church has both an external and an internal aspect to it which cannot be denied or ignored. In its visible and institutional aspect, the Christian church is called to be God's people on earth but it is no more "pure" than ancient Israel was. Belonging to it is not the same thing as believing what it teaches, and there are many people who associate themselves with the church who are not true members of the body of Christ. On the

---

[39]Gal. 3:28–29.

outermost fringes are those who would call themselves "Christian" because they were born and brought up in a "Christian" country and have not opted out of that. Closer to the center are those who attend church from time to time but see it mainly as a social occasion and have little interest in what it is all about. Then there are those who are signed-up members of a congregation who have chosen to identify with the institutional church, even though their levels of involvement may vary enormously from one individual to another. It is among these that the true believers are most likely to be found, not because membership leads to commitment but the other way around.

Whatever else it does, the visible church must never teach that belonging to it is a guarantee of salvation. We must not make the mistake of assuming that those who are most deeply involved in the institution are those who are closest to God. Institutionalization must never be equated with spiritual growth. When ritual observance takes over from genuine spiritual commitment, the witness of the church suffers. Those who are truly called and chosen will know of this danger and will guard against it, even as they participate actively in the life of the institution itself. The families of believers benefit from their presence in much the same way as the people of Israel benefitted from the remnant among them who preserved the faith, but there is no promise given to them that if they turn away from God, they will preserve their identity as Christians in the way that nonobservant Jews have preserved their Jewish identity.

At the same time, men and women who have come to Christ will naturally want to join in fellowship with others and, in normal circumstances, that will mean being members of the visible church. There is no excuse for opting out of this. In the Old Testament, those who were saved were for the most part already members of God's chosen people, and the exhortations to belief and commitment were directed almost exclusively to them. This is not true of the Christian church in the same way, but even if the message of salvation is not confined to church members, they must also be challenged and exhorted to believe and to follow Christ more deeply and more fully than they already do. As Christians we are urged not to be complacent about our salvation but to go out and find lost sheep among nations and communities that have never heard the Word of God.

The church is a missionary organization in a way that Israel was not. Unlike Israel, it obliges its members to make a personal profession of faith in the gospel message and urges them to proclaim that message to others. We accept those who respond by professing faith in Christ as members of God's chosen people and recognize them as our brothers and sisters, but we also know that they are children of God and are ultimately responsible to him. Only he knows for sure whose profession of faith is genuine because he knows the deepest secrets of the heart. Just as it was possible to belong to the nation of Israel without being a true believer, so it is possible to join the visible church and participate in its rituals without being transformed by the spirit of faith that brought them into being.

At the same time, we are told that we can have assurance of our salvation by putting our faith in Christ and experiencing the indwelling presence and power of his Spirit in our lives. It may seem paradoxical to say that we can have assurance of faith without a visible guarantee of our salvation, but this paradox reflects the relationship between spiritual and physical reality and is necessary for the health of the church as a whole. Each of us needs to know that we are safe in the arms of God's love, and the presence of his Spirit in our hearts bears witness to that.[40] But we cannot rely on our own profession of faith and church membership as proof of our spiritual standing before God, nor can we use such external criteria to pass judgment on others. God knows who belongs to him, and we must not pretend to understand better than he does who will and who will not dwell with him in eternity. Humility, not pride, is the mark of a true believer, and it is inward obedience to the Spirit of God, not outward conformity to the rites of the institutional church, that is the key that opens the door to the heavenly kingdom.

THE PROPHETIC COVENANT GOD MADE WITH ABRAHAM

The first person to whom God promised the blessing of eternal salvation was Abram, who was told to leave his home (in what is now Iraq) and migrate westwards. There he would be given a land where he and his descendants would prosper and become a great nation.[41] Abram was an unusual choice for this mission in that he was seventy-five years old and childless, but he believed the promises that God made to him and obeyed the instructions he was given. That act of trust and obedience was to become the foundation stone of the new nation his family was called to establish. As a sign of his faith, Abram was given the mark of circumcision, which was to be passed on to his male descendants through Isaac as evidence that God's promise extended to them as well.[42] Time would produce a large number of people who could claim physical descent from Abram, but although they would all be circumcised, they would not all necessarily inherit the promise to which their circumcision

---

[40]Rom. 8:16.
[41]Gen. 12:1–3.
[42]Gen. 17:10.

bore witness. Abram's true heirs would be those who shared his faith and his commitment, and eventually they would be far more numerous and varied than his physical descendants would be. In recognition of this, God changed his name from Abram, which means "exalted father," to Abraham, "father of a multitude," which is how we know him today.[43]

Unable to have children by his legal wife, Abraham had a number of off-spring by other women. The most prominent of those children was Ishmael, the son of his wife Sarah's handmaid Hagar.[44] Abraham loved all his children, and ensured that they received a portion of his goods as their inheritance, but there were limits to this generosity. When Sarah was finally enabled to conceive a son by divine intervention, it was he who was to be the chief beneficiary of his father's will and the sole heir to the promise God had given his father.[45] To ensure that this would happen, Sarah insisted that Ishmael, whom she perceived as Isaac's chief potential rival, and his mother should be sent away, a decision to which Abraham reluctantly agreed.[46] The significance of this is that it shows that although Abraham had other children whom he loved and provided for, they were not children of the promise and so did not become heirs of eternal salvation. That privilege was reserved for the son who had been born against all expectations and in defiance of natural law.

God did not establish his covenant with Abraham all at once. It progressed in stages, beginning with the call to leave his homeland. Only after he had done that was he told that he would have an heir to succeed him, and only after he had shown his willingness to sacrifice that heir in obedience to God's command was the covenant finally confirmed.[47] God moved one step at a time in his dealings with Abraham, and there was still much left unfulfilled when he died. Abraham had seen the land that was promised to him but he had not been able to occupy it, and his title to it remained somewhat tenuous. It would be many centuries before his descendants would be able to claim that the land was truly theirs, and even then their possession of it was not to be permanent. God's covenant with Abraham was a beginning that would be foundational for everything that followed, but it was not the last word on the subject. God had more to do for his people, as even the Old Testament writers recognized. Today we look back to him with gratitude but do not try to revive his covenant in its pristine purity, since it was never intended to remain in its original state.

The covenant God made with Abraham is the foundation of Christianity

---

[43]Gen. 17:4–5.
[44]Gen. 16:15.
[45]Gen. 18:9–10; 21:1–7.
[46]Gen. 21:9–12.
[47]Gen. 22:15–18.

just as much as it is of Judaism.[48] Although both Jews and Christians trace our roots to this covenant, however, we interpret it in different ways. For the Jewish tradition, the Abrahamic covenant is a spiritual promise meant to be worked out in both spiritual and physical terms. The circumcision given to Abraham as a sign of his faith continues to be the mark of the male Jew, and the multitude of Abraham's descendants is interpreted as referring to the Jewish people, whose historical existence and influence on the world is regarded as the fulfillment of the covenant promise. Christians, however, believe that the promise made to Abraham was always primarily spiritual and is now exclusively so. Everyone who shares Abraham's faith is an heir to the promises and can claim spiritual descent from him. Circumcision is not imposed on Christians, though it is not forbidden either. What counts for us is the "circumcision of the heart," an idea that is present in the Old Testament but has been given greater prominence among Christians than among Jews.[49]

Abraham's covenant is based on the faith by which he was united to God and chosen to accomplish his purposes. Faith is both the key to our union with Christ and the ultimate assurance of our salvation. It restores the relationship with God that was broken by the fall of Adam and Eve. Everything else flows from that faith, and the covenant promises make no sense without it. This has a special significance for Christians because Jesus said that Abraham foresaw his coming.[50] He did not elaborate on this, but the context implies that Abraham must have recognized Jesus as the one who would fulfill the covenant promises. But what does that mean in practice? Forming a chosen people and dwelling in a Promised Land were great blessings, but Jesus could not have meant that Abraham saw him as the one who would bring those things to fruition in the literal sense because that had been accomplished long before his coming. Jesus made no attempt to play the part of a national savior in the way that Jewish patriots of his time expected. If that is what Abraham had imagined the fulfillment of the covenant promises to be, Jesus would probably never have mentioned him, nor would the early Christians have recorded something that was obviously not true.

Perhaps it is the mysterious figure of Melchizedek that provides the clue as to how Abraham regarded Jesus.[51] Melchizedek was the king of Salem,[52] who appears out of nowhere and is described only as "the priest of God Most High." He was a king with no known genealogy (an anomaly in the

---

[48]Rom. 4:1–16.
[49]Deut. 10:16; 30:6; Jer. 4:4.
[50]John 8:56.
[51]Gen. 14:18–20.
[52]"Salem" means "peace" and was the city we now call Jerusalem.

ancient world) and was unrelated to Abraham, yet Abraham was prepared
to offer him a tenth of all the spoils on his return from the so-called "battle
of the kings." The payment of a tenth clearly resonates with the tithe that
the Israelites later paid to the priests in the Jerusalem temple, and since
Melchizedek was a priest, we may assume that what Abraham did had a religious significance. But if Abraham had paid a tithe to a pagan priest it would
hardly have been recorded and celebrated as it was, nor would the blessing of
such a priest have been taken seriously. Melchizedek's priesthood must therefore have been recognized by God, even though he was not a priest in the line
of Aaron (whose birth was still several centuries in the future). That this was
indeed the case is made clear by Psalm 110, which is attributed to King David.
In that psalm, David says that the Lord God has told his Lord, whoever that
is, to sit at his right hand, and then goes on to describe this second Lord as "a
priest forever after the order of Melchizedek."[53] This mysterious statement
was later picked up by the writer to the Hebrews, who used it to claim that
Melchizedek was a prototype of Christ, who is further described as a priest
forever in Melchizedek's order of priesthood, picking up the words of Psalm
110 and applying them as a prophecy directly related to Christ.[54] It therefore
seems probable that when Jesus spoke of Abraham rejoicing to see his coming, it was the priestly work of Melchizedek that he had in mind.

If that is so, it ties in very well with another theme that we find in the
story of Abraham, which is the sacrifice of Isaac, the son of the promise.[55]
The Genesis account makes it clear that God respected Abraham's willingness
to sacrifice Isaac and responded to it by confirming his determination to fulfill
his covenant promises to Abraham. We must therefore regard this incident as
central to Abraham's calling and as the supreme manifestation of the faith
that made him righteous in God's eyes. When God initially made his covenant
with Abraham, nothing was said about human sinfulness or the need to do
something about it. God had promised Noah after the flood that he would
never again destroy mankind because of its disobedience, but the idea that
the problem could somehow be put right was not mentioned. Abraham was
rewarded for his obedience to God's calling, but he did not receive a promise
of eternal salvation. Even the sacrifice of Isaac is not portrayed in that light,
though the implications are clear, because sacrifice was the only way to deal
with sin.

The connection between Melchizedek and sacrifice is not made in the

---

[53]Ps. 110:1, 4.
[54]Heb. 7:1–16.
[55]Gen. 22:1–18.

Old Testament and had to wait until the writer to the Hebrews brought it out, but the reason for this is plain. Jesus, our great high priest in the line of Melchizedek, was also the offering that atoned for our sins. What was hinted at in the covenant made with Abraham was brought to fulfillment in Christ. Instead of demanding the sacrifice of Abraham's son, God would offer up his Son instead. Not only would that be a better sacrifice but it would be the best and most effective one possible. The death of Isaac would have demonstrated the faithful obedience of Abraham, but Isaac would have had no power to save people from their sins. Only the death of the Son of God could do that, as the priest who made the sacrifice and the offering that was slain merged into one.

Isaac inherited his father's covenant without challenge, but its future was called into question when his wife Rebecca gave birth to two nonidentical twins. Esau, the older one, was legally entitled to inherit, but God chose Jacob, the younger one, instead. Once again, we see that God's choice does not follow human patterns of inheritance. More significantly still, we also learn that it does not depend on human values either. By human standards, Esau was superior to Jacob in every way. He was the hunter, the man's man whose physical prowess was universally admired. He was straightforwardly honest, though he was also incautious and apparently unable to appreciate the true value of his inheritance. When he was tempted to sell his birthright for the immediate satisfaction of his hunger, he did so, apparently assuming that there would be no serious consequences of his action. Jacob was less well-endowed physically and was openly dishonest in his dealings with his brother. Not only did he persuade him to sell his birthright, he later stole his father's blessing by an act of impersonation (which would never have worked if Isaac had not been blind, and which even then was implausible). Jacob tricked both his brother and his father, and although he had to pay for his behavior by spending many years in exile (where he was in turned tricked by his uncle Laban), he nevertheless became the one who inherited the promise made to Abraham. The extraordinary tale of Jacob reminds us that God's choice has nothing to do with a person's physical ability or upright moral character. As Jesus put it, God does not want to save the righteous, but to bring sinners to repentance.[56] He has chosen us in spite of our failings, in order to show the world that we have been saved not by our own merits but by the grace that he has bestowed on us in love.

Abraham, Isaac, and Jacob were to become the ancestors of the people of God. It was when he was returning from exile to face the possible wrath of Esau that Jacob was confronted by a spiritual being who wrestled with him.

---

[56]Luke 5:32.

Jacob did not know who he was, but he withstood the test and was given the name Israel, meaning "he strives with God." This name became permanent when God confirmed it at Bethel, the place where he had first appeared to Jacob when he fled from Esau many years before.[57] That confirmation had a special significance because Jacob had gone to Bethel and built an altar to God on the site where he had received his first revelation, thereby reinforcing the centrality of sacrifice to Israel's knowledge and worship of God. It is also significant because it was at Bethel that God revealed his identity to Jacob in a way that he had not done on the earlier occasion. Jacob had raised his altar to El-Bethel (the "God of Bethel") as a token of his spiritual experience, but now God revealed himself as El-Shaddai, "God Almighty," a divine name higher than any that Jacob had previously known that expressed the power and universal sovereignty of the one who had spoken to him. Jacob lived in a world where there were many gods and many lords, but there could only ever be one Almighty, and it was he who had made the covenant with Abraham and given the promises to Isaac and Jacob.

The covenant made with Abraham and his descendants was essentially prophetic. He was actually called a prophet, though he never prophesied in the way that the later prophets did.[58] The reason must be that he was a sign of God's presence, whether or not he said anything about that. Neither he nor his son Isaac lived to see the covenant promises fulfilled. Isaac's son Jacob even led his people out of the land God had given them and took them into Egypt because it seemed to be the only place where they were likely to survive and prosper. It would be hundreds of years before they would see the promises fulfilled, but they never gave up hope and, in the end, God's call to Abraham bore fruit. Summing up the historical experience of the patriarchs, the writer to the Hebrews said,

> These all died in faith, not having received the things promised, but having seen them and greeted them from afar, and having acknowledged that they were strangers and exiles on the earth.[59]

This was the essence of God's covenant with Abraham and it became the classic description of God's people before the coming of Christ, who would give them the things promised in a way that most of Abraham's descendants could hardly have dared to hope for.

---

[57]Gen. 32:28; 35:9–10.
[58]Gen. 20:7.
[59]Heb. 11:13.

THE PRIESTLY COVENANT GOD MADE WITH MOSES

The nation of Israel was reconstituted by the escape of Jacob's descendants from Egypt. Having originally gone there at the behest of Joseph, who had miraculously been preserved and raised to the level of first minister of the Egyptian crown, the people of Israel were gradually reduced to slavery and spent several centuries in that condition. Eventually they became too numerous for comfort and the Egyptians began a campaign of genocide against them.[60] That was the signal for God's next act of deliverance, which he planned and executed in the person of Moses, who had been rescued from destruction by the cleverness of his mother and the compassion of the king's daughter.[61] Moses was brought up at the Egyptian court, but an accidental murder forced him to flee to the desert, where his spiritual preparation began.[62] It was there that God met him in the burning bush and revealed himself as both the only true God and also as the God of his ancestors, Abraham, Isaac, and Jacob.[63] That incident proved to be the true beginning of Moses' career, which would eventually take him from leading his people out of Egypt to shaping them into a viable society by the laws that he gave them in the desert. These laws were to be the basic constitution of later Israelite society, and to this day they still form the earliest and most fundamental layer of Judaism.

It is true that Jesus looked back to Abraham as a more fundamental figure in Israel's history than Moses was.[64] The priority of Abraham emerged in Christ's debates with the Jewish leaders of his time and was later taken up by Paul, who states that Moses came along several hundred years later because Abraham's descendants could not live up to the high standards of faith set by their increasingly remote ancestor.[65] Having said that, however, the covenant God made with Moses had its own importance and could not simply be brushed aside.

The law of Moses set Israel apart from the other nations and established the norms by which its society was to be governed. It was accepted by Jesus, who was born into it, lived under it, and died to fulfill it. His life and career can be understood only in reference to the law, but at the same time, his relationship to it made him fundamentally different from the other Jewish leaders of his day. The priests, scribes, and Pharisees all believed themselves to be subject to the law and therefore bound to fulfill its provisions. That they

[60]Ex. 1:8–22.
[61]Ex. 2:1–10.
[62]Ex. 2:15.
[63]Ex. 3:4–15.
[64]John 8:39–59.
[65]Gal. 3:17.

interpreted these provisions in ways that often evaded their full force does not alter this fact but merely demonstrates that it was impossible for any sinful person to do everything the law commands. Jesus, on the other hand, felt free to reinterpret the law in thitherto unheard-of ways. Unlike the Jewish leaders, who softened its provisions, Jesus made the law much harder to observe, but he also did everything it commanded. In essence, he was above the law, not in the sense that he could disregard it at will, but in the sense that the law spoke about him and revealed him, albeit only in partial and inadequate ways.[66] An important part of Christ's mission was to reveal the law's inadequacy, thereby undermining the Jewish sacrificial system and replacing it with a better sacrifice of his own.

The principle of sacrifice lay at the heart of the Jewish law. There were many different kinds of sacrifice for different types of sin, but the most important and solemn one was the yearly sacrifice of atonement for the sins of the people.[67] On that occasion, the high priest went into the inner sanctum of the temple and offered a pure, spotless lamb as payment for the sins of the people during the preceding year. This ritual had to be repeated on an annual basis because without it the people's sins could not be pardoned.[68] When there was no tabernacle or temple, as there was not during the Babylonian exile and has not been since the destruction of Jerusalem in A.D. 70, the solemnity of the day of atonement (Yom Kippur) was still observed, as it continues to be today, but no actual sacrifice could be made. Because of that, for the past two thousand years it has been impossible for Jews to fulfill their covenant obligations to God according to the law of Moses. This obviously raises big questions about the validity of the Mosaic covenant today because, if there are no sacrifices, it would seem that the rest of the covenant lacks a meaningful context and is therefore invalid.

This is a problem for Jews, but Christians are not bothered by it because a generation before the temple was destroyed, Christ's sacrifice had made the rituals of the temple redundant. Assuming the role of the high priest, Jesus offered himself as the spotless lamb and paid the price for the sins of all his people. When he ascended to heaven, he took that finished sacrifice with him and presented it to his Father as an everlasting atonement.[69] Once that was done, there was nothing left for the Mosaic law to accomplish, and in Christian eyes it faded into the background.

The need for sacrifice is difficult for many people to understand, espe-

---

[66] John 5:39; Heb. 1:1.
[67] Ex. 30:1–10.
[68] Heb. 9:1–14.
[69] Eph. 4:8; Heb. 9:11–28.

cially since there are now few religions that practice it in the way that was common in ancient times. Some people actually condemn Christians for clinging to the idea and believe that it should be discarded as an outdated and inferior metaphor for the work of Christ in our salvation. How, they ask, can something as barbaric as death on a cross possibly be what God demanded of his Son as payment for the sins of the world? Was there no better way than this for God to save his people? In extreme forms, this kind of criticism insists that belief in the atoning sacrifice of Christ makes God the Father guilty of cosmic child abuse because the innocent Son was made to suffer for the guilt of others. The moral outrage provoked by this doctrine is misplaced, not least because it ignores the fact that Christ's sacrifice was a *voluntary* act of love.[70] Such outrage is by no means new. Ancient pagan philosophers were just as appalled by it as their modern descendants are, and for many of the same reasons. Yet in spite of the opposition it has provoked over the years, the atoning death of Christ remains central to our understanding of his earthly mission, and the cross is still the most revered and universally recognized symbol of our faith. Why is this?

To the question of whether God could have provided another way of salvation for us, there is really no answer. It must have been possible for him to have done so, since otherwise he would not be the Almighty God. But this is a theoretical conclusion divorced from the reality of the situation. In mandating the necessity of blood sacrifice, God is making us understand the seriousness of what has gone wrong in human life and what will happen to us if proper atonement for our sin is not made. If the cure does not get to grips with the disease, the disease will only get worse and end by destroying us. Sin brought violence and death into our lives, and therefore violence and death must be overcome if sin is to be forgiven. To claim that God is a sadist for inflicting unnecessary pain on his Son is to misunderstand what happened. We human beings brought this on ourselves by sinning against God in the first place. It was not his will to send his Son to suffer and die merely for the sake of suffering and dying; he came to do that because it was necessary to cleanse us from our sins. The horror of it does not reflect on God but on us. If we fail to understand that, then we have not grasped the depth of the love that God has shown to us.

God could not just wipe away our sins as if they did not matter, for the simple reason that they *do* matter, not because of what *they* are but because of who *we* are. A dog who bites a human being has not sinned, and we do not blame him for that, even if we have to put him down because of it. If a

---

[70] See Phil. 2:6–7.

man wounds another man, however, we take it very seriously because a man is supposed to know better and is held accountable for his actions. It is this accountability that makes our actions significant and dignifies us as human beings. The fact that God the Father sent his Son to die for us shows us just how important we are to him. It is a sign of his love for us, not of his sadistic tendencies, that he went to such apparently extreme lengths on our behalf. To understand his acts is to understand ourselves and how important we are to him.

It is in this context that we must interpret the meaning of the Old Testament sacrifices. They were a preparation for Christ's atonement and demonstrated the extent of human sinfulness. Every aspect of life was touched in some way by the fall of Adam and Eve, and therefore everything had to be atoned for. Some sins were more serious than others and demanded a greater sacrifice, but the underlying principle is the same.

The beauty of the Mosaic covenant is that, in it, the great principles of sacrifice and law were united and reconciled. Moses was the lawgiver, but his elder brother Aaron was the high priest, who made the atonement that the law prescribed. The Pentateuch makes it clear that it was the law that governed the sacrifices and not the other way around, and when Aaron (or others) tried to sacrifice apart from Moses there was trouble. Even before the law was given, Aaron succumbed to the demand of the people for sacrifice and created his own god, the famous golden calf, to which he then proceeded to offer worship.[71] Sacrifices made without the governing authority of the law lost their proper focus on God and were prone to idolatry, one of the most serious sins that God's people can commit. At the same time, the law was never just a moral code that people were expected to keep. That was the mistake of the rich young ruler who is mentioned in the Gospels.[72] He had kept the commandments all his life but that was not enough. What was missing was any notion of sacrifice, and when Jesus told him to sell everything he had, he turned away in sorrow because he could not bring himself to do that. Obeying the law is a good thing, but it can only restrain evil, not cure it. The law of Moses was holy, just, and good, a point emphasized even by Paul, who was vehement in his denunciation of those who were trying to force it down the throats of Gentile Christians.[73]

While the law could clarify what was wrong, however, it could do nothing to right that wrong. Only sacrifice could do that, but for it to work

---

[71]Ex. 32:1–35.
[72]Matt. 19:16–22.
[73]Rom. 7:12–16.

properly, it had to be performed in accordance with the demands of the law. A sacrifice that did not fulfill the legal requirements was not valid. The abiding importance of the law for Christians is that it shows us both what God requires and what Christ has achieved on our behalf. His fulfillment of the law's provisions means that what was once an external law written on tablets of stone is now an internal law, written on the "tablets" of the heart. Because of that, we no longer offer dead animals as sacrifices for sin but present our bodies as a living sacrifice, determined to use them in whatever way we can for the glory of God.[74] The conjunction of law and sacrifice found in the Old Testament is still with us today, but as with everything else, it has also been internalized and now operates by the power of the Holy Spirit working in our hearts by faith.

Sacrifice was at the heart of the Old Testament law, but there were many other features of it that also prepared the way for the coming of the Messiah. The word "Messiah" means the "anointed one," and in Israel there were three offices that qualified for this anointing: the prophet, the priest, and the king. It was the duty of the prophet to proclaim the Word of God, the duty of the priest to perform what it commanded, and the duty of the king to maintain law and order so that the others could go about their business unhindered. In Israel it was possible for a priest or a king to be a prophet (Habakkuk and David come to mind) but no one was allowed to combine the offices of priest and king. The closest we come to that is the case of Samuel, who grew up in the tabernacle and later judged Israel, which made him functionally similar to a priest-king, even though he was neither one nor the other. The Messiah, however, would be all three, and in a way that would make the traditional offices unnecessary. The Old Testament prophets received a word from God and proclaimed it, but Jesus proclaimed himself because he was the Word incarnate. The Old Testament priests sacrificed a spotless lamb, but Jesus sacrificed himself because he was the Lamb of God. The Old Testament kings ruled over a people distinct from themselves, but Jesus united the people to himself because the kingdom is his body. After his resurrection, Jesus appeared to the men on the road to Emmaus and opened up the Hebrew Bible, pointing out all the things in it that referred to him. We do not have a definitive list of what those things were, but the establishment and outworking of the three great covenant offices must surely be a central ingredient of the Old Testament proclamation of Christ.[75]

To summarize this, the law of Moses was a gift from God to Israel

---

[74]Rom. 12:1.
[75]Luke 24:13–35.

designed to show just what the love of God means to those of us who believe in him. The law tells us that we are not good enough for God as we are, and that we can never improve ourselves to the point where we might become acceptable to him. The law also tells us that the only solution to our dilemma is sacrifice, and it lays out the many different kinds of sacrifice that there are. Just as sin affects the whole of life, so law and sacrifice touch on everything. This is a sign of God's love because in the law he shows us the comprehensive nature of our failings and of his provision for them. The law reminds us that we cannot and will not be "half-saved" but will be totally redeemed for God's glory. Finally, by its own built-in obsolescence, the law reminds us that no earthly or human activity can do what is necessary to put right a problem that is essentially spiritual. Even keeping the commandments to perfection is not enough. This sounds negative, but in reality it is a great blessing to us. God does not dwell in temples made with hands, so even if these are destroyed it makes no difference to our salvation.

Christ's sacrifice and death fulfilled the law, but they also abolished it by going beyond it and opening up for us a world of which the law is but a distant shadow. The law shows us the way to go and begs us to look beyond the limited benefits that it can offer to the one of whom it bears witness—Jesus Christ, the Son of God and the only mediator of the new covenant made for us in his blood. At its heart, the law was a priestly covenant built around the principle of sacrificial atonement for the sins of the people. By fulfilling it in his suffering, death, and resurrection, Jesus transformed it from something limited by the constraints of time and space and made it an eternal offering available to all who call on him for salvation.

THE KINGLY COVENANT GOD MADE WITH DAVID

Ancient Israel had two major institutions through which the law given to Moses was preserved and applied—the priesthood and the monarchy. But unlike the priesthood, which was specifically instituted by God in the covenant made with Moses, the Israelite monarchy was initially established as an act of rebellion against him. For some time after their arrival in the Promised Land, Israel was ruled by a succession of judges, who were charismatic figures raised up from time to time in order to govern the people and deliver them from their enemies. As time went on, however, the Israelites began to think that they would be better off with a hereditary monarchy similar to the ones possessed by the surrounding nations. They thought that a king would be better able to protect them from their hostile neighbors and would eliminate the risk that, in times of danger, there might be no charismatic leader forth-coming. Rather than take that chance, they preferred to have a permanent leadership structure in place, ready to take action when needed. They asked Samuel, who was then their judge, to appoint a king to succeed him.[76]

From a purely human point of view, their request made good sense. Samuel was growing old, and his sons were not up to the task of govern-ment. A credible successor had to be found. The people saw no reason why they should not organize themselves along the same lines as the surrounding tribes because then they would have a better chance of competing with them on equal terms. The problem was that Israel was not a nation like the others, but God's chosen people. It was he who was their king, and they depended on him for their survival and prosperity. A human king would impose a central-ized administration, which would involve heavy taxation and great sacrifice of lives and labor on the part of the population. Whatever protection a king might offer them would come at a high price, a point which God told Samuel to make before acceding to their request. But the people were not to be per-suaded by such arguments. Their minds were made up, and they insisted on having their way. The remarkable thing is that God agreed to go along with them. Their rebellion would not thwart his purpose but instead would be used to further it. At God's direction, Samuel went out to look for a suitable king, and he found what he was looking for in the person of Saul.

Saul was tall and handsome, but he had little else to commend him. He was from Benjamin, the smallest and least important of the tribes, and from the humblest elements in that tribe to boot.[77] He had no experience of govern-ment and could not even find his father's donkeys when they got lost.[78] Yet this was the man whom God chose to be the first king of Israel, almost cer-tainly in order to show that whatever greatness Saul might eventually aspire to, he would owe everything to the Lord who had chosen and appointed him. Saul was duly acclaimed king, and for a while things went reasonably well. As Saul grew in power and authority, however, his willingness to submit to the will of God gradually weakened. Pressed into battle against the Philistines, who were technologically more advanced than the Israelites and therefore more dangerous, Saul refused to wait for Samuel to come and make the burnt offering that would ensure victory, and instead performed it himself.[79] That was enough for Samuel to declare that Saul had forfeited his right to be king, and it was all downhill from there. Saul grew increasingly disobedient to the

---

[76] See 1 Sam. 8:1–22 for the story.
[77] 1 Sam. 9:21.
[78] 1 Sam. 9:3–4, 20.
[79] 1 Sam. 13:8–14.

will of God, and when he was told that his kingdom would be given to someone else, he became paranoid. In the end, he and his son Jonathan (who would
have made a much better king, if he had been allowed to succeed) were killed
by the Philistines. The throne passed to David, another man from nowhere
who had been chosen by Samuel, once more at God's direction.[80]

Like Saul, David was an unlikely candidate for the kingship, though his
origins were not as humble as Saul's were. David was from the large tribe
of Judah, his father Jesse seems to have been wealthier and more prominent
than Saul's father Kish, and David had talents that Saul lacked. Even as
a young man, he was a gifted outdoorsman who could use a slingshot to
devastating effect, as he did in single combat against the Philistine giant
Goliath.[81] He was also a talented poet and musician, an accomplishment
that was unusual in a warrior and highly prized because it was through song
that the epic deeds of the people were recorded and God was worshiped.
Unlike Saul, who was anointed king in a public assembly of the whole
nation, David was anointed privately by Samuel and the proceeding was
kept secret.[82] David did not rebel against Saul, whom he always regarded
as the rightful king, but Saul's increasing paranoia soon made it clear to
him who his successor would be. Despite the fact that David was invited to
court and was co-opted into the royal family by being given Saul's daughter
Michal in marriage, the true nature of Saul's relationship with him could
not be hidden. Before long, David was on the run, and it is a measure of
Saul's incompetence and loss of authority that in spite of many close calls,
David was consistently able to evade capture.

When Saul was killed, David was still an outlaw, and the throne passed
to Ishbosheth, one of Saul's surviving sons.[83] The tribe of Judah refused to
accept this, however, and the result was a long civil war between the house
of Saul and David, which did not end until Ishbosheth was murdered and
his remaining followers submitted to David's authority. David did what he
could to show respect for his dead rival and took the lame Mephibosheth,
Jonathan's son and Saul's grandson, under his wing, but real reconciliation
was never achieved. Mephibosheth remained a rallying point for those who
disliked David's rule, and David could never shake off the feeling of many
Israelites that he was Judah's king, who had been imposed on the rest of
Israel by force. That feeling would resurface in the time of his grandson
Rehoboam, when the united kingdom of Israel would be permanently

[80] 1 Sam. 16:1–13.
[81] 1 Sam. 17:1–49.
[82] 1 Sam. 16:1–13.
[83] 2 Sam. 2:8–10.

divided.[84] Yet when that happened, it would not be the majority kingdom of the north but the kingdom of Judah that would carry the mantle of Israel's destiny, so much so that in due time the northern kingdom would be wiped off the map and Judah would become identified with Israel as a whole, as is still the case today.

This is because God not only chose David to be king in place of Saul but he also made a covenant with him, promising him that his descendants would reign over the nation forever. The circumstances in which God made that promise are of special interest because David had decided to build a temple at Jerusalem which would house the ark of the covenant and be the focal point of Israel's worship.[85] He thought he had God's approval for this plan, but he was soon told that he did not. God explained to David that he did not need such a temple because he did not dwell in a building made with human hands, a lesson that Israel constantly had to relearn.[86] But just as Israel was eventually given a king that it did not need, so it would also be provided with the unnecessary house of God, not by David but by his son and heir. Furthermore, just as the monarchy was transformed from being a sign of the people's rebellion into an instrument for the fulfilling of God's promises to them, so the building of the temple would be transformed into a confirmation of the continuity of that monarchy in the Davidic line:

> I will raise up your offspring after you, who shall come from your body, and I will establish his kingdom. He shall build a house for my name, and I will establish the throne of his kingdom forever. I will be to him a father, and he shall be to me a son. When he commits iniquity, I will discipline him with the rod of men, with the stripes of the sons of men, but my steadfast love will not depart from him, as I took it from Saul, whom I put away from before you. And your house and your kingdom shall be made sure forever before me. Your throne shall be established forever.[87]

The Bible makes it abundantly clear that the promise of an eternal kingdom was not due to David's innate virtues, nor was there any suggestion that his son would be perfect. David was more talented than Saul had been, but with greater achievement came greater sin, and David's uncontrollable lusts cost him the loyalty and unity of his own family, on which the fulfillment of God's promise depended.[88] David's last years were a tale of civil war in his

---

[84] 1 Kings 12:16–24.
[85] 2 Sam. 7:1–3; 1 Chron. 17:1–2.
[86] See Isa. 66:1; John 2:19–21.
[87] 2 Sam. 7:12b–16; compare 1 Chron. 17:11b–14.
[88] 2 Sam. 12:10–12.

own household, and even on his deathbed the succession of his chosen son Solomon was far from assured.[89] Solomon reigned for forty years, a time that later generations would look back on as Israel's golden age, but the military and financial exertions needed to affirm his glory took their toll. Solomon himself compromised with the religions of the surrounding nations, with whom he established marriage alliances. By the end of his reign, Israel was in a crisis from which it would not recover.[90] After Solomon's death, his kingdom fell apart. The northern kingdom of Israel survived for another two hundred years or so, but its kings were all bad and it was internally unstable most of the time. A number of different dynasties rose and fell, and none of its rulers was a descendant of David.

Judah was better off in this respect, though not by much. The throne remained in the hands of the house of David until the fall of Jerusalem in 586 B.C., more than three hundred years after the death of Solomon. A few of its kings were quite good, though none was flawless. In the end, the Davidic monarchy perished just as definitively as its northern cousin had more than a century earlier. The history of the Israelite monarchy was inglorious, but this had been foreseen in the original promise, and the failure of the kings would not cause the divine promise to be withdrawn. As with Israel in general, so with its monarchy—the call and promise of God rested not on human merit or achievement but on his steadfast love, which remained pure and powerful regardless of what might be done to test it.

David's legacy is still discernible today in the survival of Judah as Israel, but what has happened to the promises God made to him? There is no possibility nowadays that any descendant of David could become king of Israel, if only because his descendants can no longer be identified. There is no pretender to the Jewish throne, and even if there were, his claims could not be tested. There have been great rabbis and other Jewish leaders who have claimed descent from David, but recognition of such pretensions by the Jewish people says more about the greatness of the person concerned than it does about any historical link with him. In short, God's promise to the house of David of an eternal throne in Jerusalem cannot now be realized in a physical sense.

Credible lines of descent from David were, however, maintained among the Jews until the destruction of Jerusalem in A.D. 70, a generation or so after the time of Jesus, when continuity with the Davidic monarchy was finally broken. This means that the claims of Jesus to Davidic ancestry have a validity that cannot be matched by people living in later times. If the promise made to David

[89] 1 Kings 1:1–2:27.
[90] 1 Kings 11:1–40.

is to be regarded as unbreakable, Christ's claim to his inheritance has no rival. The New Testament makes it quite clear not only that Jesus was a descendant of David but also that this was of central importance to his ministry and mission. Jesus had no legal right to the priesthood, which is why he is described as a priest forever after the order of Melchizedek and not of Aaron.[91] But he did have a legal right to the kingship, a point which is frequently made in the New Testament, and which underlines the claim that he was the promised Messiah, who was expected to come from the house of David.[92]

In support of this, there can be no doubt that Jesus preached the message of the kingdom of God, and that he was perceived, at least by Pontius Pilate, as the one who claimed to be "king of the Jews."[93] Pilate and the Roman soldiers who mocked Jesus at his crucifixion believed that they were executing the unsuccessful leader of a potential insurrection. Jesus, of course, never had any intention of rising in revolt against the Romans and did everything he could to dissuade his followers from thinking he might. When he was asked about the legitimacy of paying taxes to Caesar, he simply took a coin and asked whose head was on it. When told that it was Caesar's, he said that the people should give Caesar what was owed to him, a statement that showed his fundamental loyalty to the secular state.[94] In his interrogation by Pilate, when he was asked whether he was the king of the Jews, Jesus replied,

> My kingdom is not of this world. If my kingdom were of this world, my servants would have been fighting, that I might not be delivered over to the Jews. But my kingdom is not from the world.[95]

Even after his resurrection, when his disciples felt sure that the moment had come to "restore the kingdom to Israel," Jesus simply told them,

> It is not for you to know times or seasons that the Father has fixed by his own authority. But you will receive power when the Holy Spirit has come upon you, and you will be my witnesses in Jerusalem and in all Judaea and Samaria, and to the end of the earth.[96]

The promised kingdom will come at the end of time, when earth and heaven will pass away and a new spiritual creation will take their place.[97] The eternal

---

[91]Heb. 7:11–17.
[92]Matt. 9:27; 12:23; 21:9, 15; John 7:42; Rom. 1:3; Rev. 3:7; 5:5; 22:16.
[93]Matt. 27:37; John 19:12–16.
[94]Matt. 22:21.
[95]John 18:36.
[96]Acts 1:6–8.
[97]1 Cor. 15:24–28; Rev. 21:1–4.

kingdom which Jesus has inherited as the son of David is a spiritual reality in which his disciples are called to take their place. The kingdom of God is within us, we are seated in the heavenly places in Christ Jesus, and we shall reign with him as kings and priests forever and ever.[98] That is the true fulfillment of the covenant made with David, and everything that Jesus taught about the coming of his kingdom points us in that direction.

THE BLESSING OF THE LAW

The law was given by God as the means by which Israel would learn what kind of nation it was meant to be and would be protected against the danger of syncretism. Without the law and its prohibitions against eating or doing certain things, Israel would almost certainly have been submerged by the surrounding peoples. It was not distinguished from them by having a distinct language (Hebrew is closely related to the other Semitic dialects spoken in the region), nor did it enjoy a separate economy, since it was closely connected to a trading network that extended across the Middle East. Even in religious terms it was exposed to the forms of paganism prevalent in the region, and on more than one occasion it nearly fell victim to those who were trying to integrate it into the common value system of the time.[99] Yet against all the odds, Israel survived, not because it was blessed with good rulers—on the whole it was not—but because faithful men and women kept the covenant alive, often at great personal cost.[100] The force that kept the faithful Israelites alive and held them together as a community was the law. The temple at Jerusalem, where the sacrifices were performed, the rituals of family devotion, and the countless provisions that touched every aspect of their lives, served to remind them of the purity and holiness of a God who watched over their every move and who guided and protected them at all times and in every way.

The law established clear boundaries between what was right and what was wrong. It provided a benchmark for human behavior that was both challenging and overwhelming. As Paul put it, the law draws attention to our failings and forces us to face up to them. When we do not know it, we are not bothered by its provisions because we have no understanding of them. But as soon as we hear the words of its commandments, we realize that we have failed to live up to them, and stand condemned for our own misdeeds.[101] At first sight, it might seem that this is a very negative situation, and that the law is anything but a blessing to those who have received it. But that is not how

[98]Luke 17:21; Eph. 2:6; 2 Tim. 2:12; Rev. 5:10.
[99]See 1 Kings 11:1–8; 12:25–33; 18:20–40; 2 Kings 17:7–23; 21:10–18.
[100]1 Kings 19:10; Heb. 11:32–38.
[101]Rom. 7:7–13.

Paul understood the matter, nor does it correspond to what we read in the Old Testament. Like the psalmist, Paul tells us that he takes delight in the law of God, but as he says, "I see in my members another law waging war against the law of my mind and making me captive to the law of sin that dwells in my members."[102] It is this struggle between the two kinds of law, the one that is spiritual and the one that is worldly, that turns the believer to Christ, who is the only one who can resolve this conflict inside us.[103] As Paul says elsewhere, the law is like a schoolmaster or guardian who points us to Christ and keeps us in its power until we are set free by him.[104] Those in the grip of the law of God may feel it as a constraint, but it is far better than to be in the grip of the law of sin, which is the case for those who do not know Jesus Christ as their Lord and Savior. For that reason, the Jews of the Old Testament were better off than their Gentile neighbors, who had nothing but their own consciences to rely on to tell them what they should and should not do.[105]

In essence, the law was a blessing because it taught the people to love God with all their heart, soul, mind, and strength, and because it taught them to love their neighbors as themselves.[106] This pattern is clear from the Ten Commandments, which can be divided according to these criteria. The first four commandments speak primarily about the love we should have for God, while the last six concentrate on the love we should show to one another.[107]

I am the LORD *your God, who brought you out of the land of Egypt, out of the house of slavery.* You shall have no other gods before me. From the very beginning, the people's relationship with God was rooted in the great act of deliverance that had reconstituted their nation and given rise to the need for the law. Like them, we must put God first in our lives and let no one else take his place. This is the foundation of everything else and the only way that the rest of the law makes sense. It is the practical outworking of a relationship that God designed in order to prepare his people for eternal life in heaven with him.

You shall not make for yourself a carved image. . . . for I the LORD *your God am a jealous God.* Again, the lines are clearly drawn. To make an image of God is to diminish him by reducing him to the level of a creature that we can control and manipulate. Nothing could be further from the truth, or show a greater ignorance of his true character. The commandment goes

---

[102]Rom. 7:22–23. See also Ps. 1:2; 19:7–11; 119:1–176.
[103]Rom. 7:24–25.
[104]Gal. 3:24–25.
[105]Rom. 2:12–29.
[106]Matt. 22:37–39. See Deut. 6:5 and Lev. 19:18.
[107]Ex. 20:2–17.

on to state that God will punish those who despise him in this way, but will show his steadfast love forever to those who love him and keep his commandments.

You shall not take the name of the LORD your God in vain. The name of God is his glory and his power, and we must treat it with the greatest respect. We must never despise God or take him for granted, because his power is the source of our life and his glory should be the aim of everything we do.

Finally, we are told to *remember the Sabbath day, to keep it holy. . . . For in six days the LORD made heaven and earth, . . . and rested on the seventh day. Therefore the LORD blessed the Sabbath day and made it holy.* As God's creatures, we must respect his work of creation, recognize our place in it, and live in harmony with the world that he has given us. To abuse it is to abuse the trust that he has placed in us as the guardians of what he has made, and to bring destruction on ourselves. It is often said that imitation is the sincerest form of flattery, and if that is true, then our stewardship of creation is the closest that we can come to imitating God our Creator. As such it is the supreme evidence of our service to him and the ultimate guarantee that we acknowledge and respect who he is and what he has done for us.

Once we understand all that, we must treat our fellow human beings as we would want to be treated by them.[108] This means that we must first of all respect our parents. *Honor your father and your mother, that your days may be long in the land that the LORD your God is giving you.* It is easy, and sometimes very tempting, to throw over our inheritance and pretend that we know better than generations gone by. The achievements of modern technology lend a specious credibility to this tendency and make it easy to claim that we know better than our parents did. But what we owe them is life itself, and what we achieve is built on the shoulders of giants. To forget this is to lose our way and disintegrate as a people.

Nor are we permitted to turn on one another. *You shall not murder.* To take the life of another human being is to destroy ourselves because we all come from the same human stock.

Nor are we permitted to violate their persons. *You shall not commit adultery.* When two people marry, they become one flesh, and to commit adultery is to destroy the integrity of that relationship.[109] No human bond is so consistently defended in Scripture as the bond of matrimony, starting with Adam and Eve and culminating in the great bridal feast of the Lamb and the church at the end of the book of Revelation. To break that bond for any rea-

---

[108]Matt. 7:12; Luke 6:31.
[109]Gen. 2:24.

son other than sexual infidelity is to commit adultery, a sobering truth that Jesus' disciples, then as now, have found hard to bear.[110]

You shall not steal. Just as we are not to violate the person of another, so we are not to seize his or her possessions. So much of the law is ultimately concerned with this because the right to personal property is so fundamental to our sense of self-respect and responsibility. We are called to be stewards of God's creation, but we do that best when we protect what we call our own. The law teaches us to be kind, generous, and fair with what we have, to help the poor and needy as much as we can, but not to resort to theft as a means of doing it. Robin Hood may have been a legendary folk hero, but he was not a Christian because robbing from the rich, even if it is to be given to the poor, is not the way prescribed for God's people.

You shall not bear false witness against your neighbor. We must not tell lies about other people because to do so is to sin against the God of truth and to corrupt our relationship both with him and with our fellow human beings. Where there is no truth there is no trust, and the foundation of human society is undermined. It is no accident that social breakdown is most rampant in countries where truth-telling is rare and unexpected, and Christians must not fall into that sometimes very tempting trap.

Finally, *you shall not covet . . . anything that is your neighbor's.* What we have been given is ours, but what others have been given, whether it be wealth, fame, long life, good looks, intelligence, charm, or what we call "lucky breaks," is theirs, and we must not be jealous. No one person can have everything, and how do we know what we would do with the gifts given to others if we should suddenly acquire them? There are people who rise from rags to riches overnight, and often their lives end in tragedy because they have no idea how to cope with their "good fortune." As Paul said, we should be content with what we have, live within our means, and glorify God with the resources and opportunities that have been given to us.[111]

Working all this out requires great self-discipline, and it will affect different people in different ways. Some aspects of it will come more readily than others, and we shall all fail at one point or another. But at least the law points us in the right direction and gives meaning to our actions, even when it condemns them. We know where we stand, and hard though that may be to accept, it is the necessary starting point for change and improvement. In that respect, the law is indeed a blessing, and it continues to direct and inspire us even though we are no longer under its power.

---

[110]Matt. 19:9–10.
[111]Phil. 4:11; 1 Tim. 6:8.

THE CURSE OF THE LAW

The blessings of the law are clear, but the Bible tells us that the law is also a curse. That aspect of it is not mentioned in the Old Testament, nor is it to be found in the teaching of Jesus, who had come to fulfill the law and who reserved his criticisms for those who twisted it to suit their own convenience.[112] The notion that the law is harmful as well as good is stated most clearly in the letters of Paul, and it was a major theme of his evangelistic activity. Like the Old Testament writers and Jesus, Paul believed that the law itself was good and holy.[113] The problem lay elsewhere, as he explains:

> What then shall we say? That the law is sin? By no means! Yet if it had not been for the law, I would not have known sin. For I would not have known what it is to covet if the law had not said, "You shall not covet." But sin, seizing an opportunity through the commandment, produced in me all kinds of covetousness. For apart from the law, sin lies dead. I was once alive apart from the law, but when the commandment came, sin came alive and I died. The very commandment that promised life proved to be death to me. For sin, seizing an opportunity through the commandment, deceived me and through it killed me.[114]

Here Paul is describing, in dramatic fashion, something familiar to us all. If no one tells us that we are forbidden to do something, it may never occur to us to do it. But if we discover that something is forbidden, then there is a desire inside us to do it, simply because we are not allowed to. This feeling has nothing to do with the prohibition itself, which may well be designed for our own good, as the Ten Commandments are. What the law does is awaken in us sinful desires that spring from our innate sinfulness. Paul's rhetoric here is very colorful, but he did not mean to leave the impression that before he became aware of the law he was perfect. We know that he did not think that, because only a couple of chapters before he referred to the sin of Adam that had extended to the entire human race, bringing spiritual death along with it.[115] Rather, Paul was saying that "ignorance is bliss." We cannot be condemned for something we have never even thought about, let alone done, even if the potential for wrongdoing lies dormant in us.

The trouble with the law of Moses was that it made wrongdoing clear and specific, thereby giving us the perfect blueprint for detecting all kinds of sin in ourselves. The paradox of this is that the better and more complete the

---

[112]Matt. 5:17–20; Mark 7:9–13.
[113]Rom. 7:12.
[114]Rom. 7:7–11.
[115]Rom. 5:12.

law was, the more sin it produced because those who found out what it said became that much more aware of their own sinfulness. When Adam and Eve ate the fruit of the tree of the knowledge of good and evil, not only did they sin against God but they became aware of the sinfulness that resulted from it. Whereas previously they had walked naked and unashamed, just as the animals do, now they had to cover themselves because they had become aware of their guilt and vulnerability.[116] In our fallen state, says Paul, the law is a curse because its perfection constantly reminds us how far short we come and how hopeless our situation is. For although the law can point out what is wrong, and in a perverse way even tempt us into doing it, it can do nothing to save us from it once we succumb. The law has no healing or restorative power and can do no more than what it is meant to do, which is to condemn those who disobey it. Even in our modern, secular world, laws and regulations have no power over us if we obey them because that is what we are expected to do. It is only when we contravene them that we feel their force and realize why they are there. Only then do we understand what a curse they can be, holding over us only the threat of punishment without any promise of redemption.

Paul develops the same theme in his letter to the Galatians, where he explains what our relationship to the law is, and why it has to be changed:

> All who rely on works of the law are under a curse; for it is written, "Cursed be everyone who does not abide by all things written in the Book of the Law, and do them."[117] Now it is evident that no one is justified before God by the law, for "The righteous shall live by faith."[118] But the law is not of faith, rather "The one who does them shall live by them."[119] Christ redeemed us from the curse of the law by becoming a curse for us—for it is written, "Cursed is everyone who is hanged on a tree"[120]—so that in Christ Jesus the blessing of Abraham might come to the Gentiles, so that we might receive the promised Spirit through faith.[121]

This simply restates everything we have just said about the passage in Romans 7. Those who do not keep the law are cursed, which means that every one of us is in deep trouble, since there is no one who can keep it fully. Furthermore, even if we could obey it all to perfection, we would still not be justified in the sight of God because justification comes by faith in him and not by what we manage to do on our own. This is so because the law is confined to this life,

---

[116]Gen. 3:7.
[117]See Deut. 27:26.
[118]See Hab. 2:4.
[119]See Lev. 18:5.
[120]See Deut. 21:23.
[121]Gal. 3:10–14.

so that, even if we keep it, we are doing no more than ordering our affairs in this world in the right way. That is fine as far as it goes, but it can do nothing to restore the broken relationship with God that we have inherited from Adam and Eve. For that, faith is required, but this faith is more than a simple belief that God exists. Our faith must also believe that God has dealt with our sin, and that he has done so by sending his Son to become sin for us, to take the curse of the law on himself and die to it. The curse will not just vanish; it has to be lifted, and only God can do that.

In the end, therefore, the curse itself becomes a kind of blessing in disguise. Its existence is evidence that there is a standard of goodness that is expected of us. Had that not been the case, there could have been no salvation because there would have been nothing to be saved *for*. The conditions of our sinful state would have seemed perfectly normal, and we would have had nothing to regret or complain about. It is only because we know that there is something better that we feel our current situation as a curse from which we have to be set free. In that sense, the curse may be compared to the pain we feel when something goes wrong in our body. If there were no pain, our bodies might decay without our noticing it and we would accept our disintegration as normal. But because we feel pain, we are roused to take action against it, and by doing that, to seek the remedy that can restore us to health and soundness. This is the role played by the curse of the law in our spiritual lives. It bears down on us, not in order to crush us but in order to drive us to seek help. This does not make the curse "good" any more than pain is good in itself, but it does show us how the love of God works on our stubborn hearts in order to turn us from an otherwise inevitable (if painless) death, to the promised blessing of eternal life in Christ.

ISRAEL'S DESTINY

All Christians agree that the law and the promises given to Israel belong to the inheritance of those who profess faith in Christ and rely on him for their salvation. We know that not all the Jewish people did this, and that there is still a large body of Jews today who keep the law of Moses as best they can. Have these people ceased to be children of God, or is there some purpose reserved for them in his plan that has not yet been revealed? The Jews themselves are divided as to the purpose of their existence. Most of them probably give the matter very little thought. The founders of the modern state of Israel were quite irreligious on the whole, and had no intention of creating a theocratic state run along Old Testament lines. At the same time, they would have had no claim to a Palestinian homeland had it not been for the promise that God had originally made to Abraham. Thus we have the curious situation in which even atheist Israelis have to appeal to God's covenant to justify the existence of their state.

There are, however, other Jews who believe in the coming of a Messiah who will do what Christians claim Jesus has done, but in a more material way. The future Messiah, they believe, will redeem Israel and transform the conditions of Jews everywhere, though it is less clear what will happen to the rest of mankind at that point. Some believe that Jews will rule over them, but most probably think that God-fearing Gentiles will benefit from the reign of the Messiah just as much as Jews will. The irony is that Jews who think this way often have little time for the state of Israel and do not believe that its establishment represents a fulfillment of Old Testament prophecy. There are even Jewish communities in Jerusalem who refuse to recognize the state they live in for precisely that reason!

Christians have to appreciate this because the church is also deeply divided about what the prospects for the Jewish people are. At one end of the spectrum are those who believe that, in restoring an independent Jewish state in Palestine, God has fulfilled the promise made to Abraham that his descendants would possess the land. They believe that the ingathering of Israel has already begun and that when it is complete—about a third of the world's Jewish population now lives there—Christ the Messiah will return. It is important to understand that, although this view is clearly "pro-Israeli," it is not held by any significant body of Jewish opinion, nor is it the official policy of the state of Israel. In other words, pro-Israeli Christians do not correspond to any significant group within the Jewish world itself, even if elements of what they believe can be found among different (and often mutually antagonistic) Jewish circles.

The view just sketched above is usually associated with Christians whose interpretation of the Bible is literalistic, but a variant of it can be found among more liberal Christians as well. These are the people who think that it is wrong to try to evangelize Jews, either because God has made a separate covenant with them or (more commonly) because the Jewish people has its own way of discovering and worshiping him. To them it is wrong to preach the gospel to Jews because to attempt to turn them into Christians is a sign of disrespect for the authenticity and ongoing validity of their own beliefs. The obvious problem with this view is that the early Christians were Jews themselves, and if they had shared this opinion they would never have evangelized their coreligionists. The preaching of Peter and Paul would have made no sense if they were not meant to convert anyone to their beliefs. We must therefore conclude that however attractive such an idea may be to modern liberals, it finds no echo in the New Testament and by its very nature contradicts the teaching of Jesus.

At the other end of the spectrum are those Christians, historically the vast majority, who claim that although Jews may have some advantage over Gentiles, they cannot inherit the promises made to Abraham in any way other than by having faith in Christ because he is the fulfillment of those promises. Jews who receive Christ will doubtless feel that their previous beliefs have been fulfilled and will not have the sense that those beliefs must be abandoned in the way that pagans and adherents of other religions must abandon their previous convictions. The end result is the same. In the final analysis, Jewish Christians are saved on the same basis and in the same way as anyone else.

Between these two positions, there are various forms of compromise, all of which insist that, although Jews can get to heaven only in and through Christ, there is still a divine promise to them that in the end they will all be redeemed. Paul wrote that "a partial hardening has come upon Israel, until the fullness of the Gentiles has come in, and in this way all Israel will be saved."[122] He seems to suggest that the final conversion of the Jews has been delayed until the gospel has been preached to all the Gentiles, and that when that has happened, the Old Testament covenant will come into play once more. Whether that is the right interpretation of these verses must remain uncertain until the end of time arrives because only then will we know for sure what God's plan for the historic people of Israel will be. Whatever the case, it is certain that the salvation of the Jews can only be in and through Christ, who is their Messiah. The Gentiles have benefitted from Christ's work on their behalf, but they have not taken him away from Israel. Converted Jews do not leave Israel behind when they become Christians, but enter into the true Israel for which they were predestined and have been prepared by God to inherit as children of Abraham, Isaac, and Jacob.

---

[122]Rom. 11:25b–26a.

26

THE SENDING OF
THE SON

THE PREPARATION FOR HIS COMING

Why did God choose to fulfill the promises made in the Old Testament at the time he did? This is a divine mystery to which there is no definitive answer. We can look at the circumstances of the time and surmise that it was appropriate for the Messiah to appear shortly before Jewish society was convulsed by revolution and crushed by the Romans, but that is a view from hindsight and things could have turned out differently. We can say that the Jewish diaspora gave the first followers of Jesus a network they could use to spread the gospel all over the Mediterranean world, but why the message should have gone west and not east, where there were far more people and where large Jewish settlements had thrived since the exile, is unknown. All we are told is that when the Son became a man, the "fullness of time" had come; the right moment had arrived.[1] God had certainly prepared it beforehand, and perhaps external factors like the ones just mentioned were signs of that preparation, but the Bible does not elaborate on this and so we cannot say for sure one way or the other.

We do know, however, that the Son of God did not come into the world completely unannounced or unexpected. God had been preparing the hearts of men like Simeon and women like Anna, who prayed and waited devoutly for the fulfillment of the Old Testament promises. When the baby Jesus was brought to the temple to be circumcised, they recognized that God had heard and answered their prayers, even though they did not live to see the outcome.[2] What we do not know is whether they were typical of pious Jews of their time or exceptional. Anna seems to have been widowed at a young age and to have

---

[1] Gal. 4:4; Eph. 1:10; compare Heb. 1:1–2a.
[2] Luke 2:25–38.

spent her entire life in the temple, which must have been fairly unusual and may even have been unique. On the other hand, there is nothing to indicate that either Simeon or Anna belonged to a Messianic sect or were any different from their fellow Jews, so it would seem that their piety was conventional. We know that Messianic hopes were high in first-century Judaism, and we should probably conclude that Simeon and Anna give us a picture of what that meant for ordinary people of the time.

What we know for certain is that God prepared the way for Jesus by sending his cousin John to baptize people and call them to repentance. John's birth was just as miraculous as Jesus' was, and in both cases it was the angel Gabriel who announced their coming.[3] There were, however, significant differences between the two. In the case of John, the angel appeared to his father Zechariah, not to his mother Elizabeth, and told him what was about to happen. Elizabeth was beyond the normal childbearing years, but she became pregnant in the usual human way, not unlike what had happened to Sarah and Hannah.[4] The birth of Jesus, on the other hand, was announced to his mother Mary and not to her husband-to-be, Joseph, who had to be reassured by a separate angelic visitation that her pregnancy was of the Lord.[5] Furthermore, unlike Elizabeth, Mary was not too old to have children but too young, because she was still an unmarried virgin. In terms of childbearing capacity, she resembled Hannah more than Sarah, which may explain why her song of rejoicing at the news is borrowed from Hannah's in similar circumstances.[6]

We know nothing about John's upbringing, but it must have been in and around the Jerusalem temple. Whether he ever served as a priest there in the way that his father did is unknown, but as no mention is made of it, it is unlikely that he did. When we next hear of John, he was a preacher in the desert who had broken whatever links he had once had with the temple establishment. The year was A.D. 28 or 29, when he would have been in his mid-thirties.[7]

There had not been a prophet like John in Israel for at least four hundred years, and his appearance caused a sensation. There had been times in the earlier history of Israel when the voice of prophecy had been rare, and it is possible that God had permitted such a time of dearth in preparation for the coming of Christ just as he had apparently done before calling Samuel.[8] Four centuries

---

[3]Luke 1:11–20, 26–38.
[4]Gen. 17:15–21; 1 Sam. 1:12–20.
[5]Matt. 1:18–25.
[6]Compare Luke 1:46–55 with 1 Sam. 2:1–10.
[7]Luke 3:1 tells us that it was the fifteenth year of Tiberius Caesar, which ran from August 18, 28 to August 17, 29.
[8]1 Sam. 3:1.

was roughly the length of time that the people of Israel had spent in Egypt before being delivered from slavery there, and the lapse of prophecy for a similar time may have been intended to reflect that. It may be that God had caused prophecy to cease before sending John so that when he finally did appear, people would sit up and take notice. After all, had there been hundreds of prophets wandering around, as there were in the days of Elijah and Elisha, it might have been hard for the average person to discern why John was different from the others. Whatever the truth of the matter was, John's uniqueness did not lie in the fact that he appeared so many centuries after the supposed end of prophecy, but in the content of his message and the way in which he understood his own career.

John was conscious of being the forerunner of the Messiah in a way that the earlier prophets had not been. He took his cue from Isaiah, who had spoken of a voice crying in the wilderness, "Prepare the way of the Lord," but Isaiah was speaking about someone who would come in the future, not about himself.[9] Unlike the earlier prophets, John baptized those who came to him as a sign that they had repented of their sins. This was specifically done as a preparation for the Messiah's coming, the implication being that those who were baptized by him would not have long to wait. Ritual cleansing with water was an ancient practice in many cultures and can be found in the Old Testament law, where it was expressly prescribed in a number of specific situations.[10] That John should have adopted it is hardly surprising, but he stands out because he made it central to his ministry. Those who came to him were not baptized for particular types of ritual defilement in the way that the law had ordained. John's baptism did not look back to sins committed in the past but forward, to the new life that would be marked by the fruits of repentance. It is this eschatological dimension that set him and his ministry apart from anything that had gone before or that was practiced elsewhere in his time.

As Luke tells the story, John's preaching was full of condemnation for the sorry state of the Israelites of his day. He rejected their claims to special spiritual status based on their descent from Abraham and warned them, in language similar to that used by Paul in Romans, that just as a tree that did not bear good fruit would be chopped down, so the Jewish people would be uprooted and rejected if they did not live the kind of life expected of them as Abraham's children.[11] John seems to have laid particular stress on the need for believers to have fair and honest dealings with other people, and not to abuse

---

[9]Luke 3:4–6, quoting Isa. 40:3–5.
[10]Lev. 11:24–40; 15:5–27; Num. 19:17–20.
[11]Luke 3:8–9. Compare Rom. 11:16–25.

their status or position for the sake of personal gain.[12] This problem was evidently widespread, not least because of the Roman habit of farming out tax collection to the highest bidder, which made the collectors (and the soldiers who protected them) especially prone to extortion. Jesus had an approach similar to John's, and it is no accident that tax collectors are lumped together with harlots and other notorious sinners in the Gospels.[13]

John clearly anticipated much of what Jesus would later teach, but in one vital respect Jesus was very different from his predecessor. John knew that he was not the Messiah, and he also knew that Jesus was—and he said so.[14] When he saw Jesus coming to be baptized by him, John recognized that the purpose of his mission had been fulfilled, and he was neither surprised nor resentful when people started following Jesus rather than himself.[15]

John's ministry evoked both positive and negative responses. He had his faithful disciples and was popular among ordinary people, who noticed that there was something different and authentic about him and his message, but he provoked both the priestly establishment and Herod the tetrarch.[16] John was a direct threat to them because he pointed out their weaknesses—the hypocrisy of the priests and the immoral behavior of Herod, who had John arrested for his temerity.[17] Herod was too weak politically to risk putting John to death, but his wife Herodias was determined to get rid of him, and, in the end, she managed to trick her husband into ordering John's execution.[18] In other circumstances, that might have led to serious trouble, or at least to the formation of a cult around the memory of John, but that did not happen. John left no organized group of followers, which is the final confirmation that, despite their many similarities, he was fundamentally different from Jesus. The death of Jesus, with the connivance of this same Herod, was far from being the end of his career! On the other hand, we hear no more of John. His mission had been accomplished, and the world was ready for the appearance of its Messiah.

THE BIRTH OF JESUS

The Messiah came into the world as the son of Mary, a virgin engaged to Joseph, a carpenter from the town of Nazareth in Galilee, who was a descen-

---

[12]Luke 3:11–14.
[13]Matt. 5:46–47; 9:11; 11:19; 18:17; 21:31–32; Luke 18:10–13.
[14]Luke 3:16–17; John 1:19–34.
[15]John 3:25–30.
[16]A title given to a member of the Herodian family who ruled over part of Judaea at that time.
[17]Luke 3:19–20.
[18]Matt. 14:3–12.

dant of the great King David.[19] Many of the Jews settled in Galilee had been encouraged to go there from Judaea about two generations before Jesus was born, and this may have been the case with the family of Joseph, who seems to have been considerably older than Mary and already well established as a carpenter in Nazareth when Jesus was born. Even so, it is clear that he still had links with Bethlehem that were sufficiently strong for him to go there to register for the census of Quirinius, but also distant enough that he needed public accommodation when he went there. He did not stay with relatives, which he probably would have done if his connections had been closer.[20] This census has been the subject of considerable controversy because it is not certain when it took place or what it consisted of. Quirinius became governor of Syria in 6 B.C., so the census could not have started before that, but there is no extrabiblical record of it. Probably what happened is that Quirinius brought into effect a policy developed by the Emperor Augustus, which was that Roman taxation should be extended to cover "all the world," meaning the client kingdoms under Roman rule as well as the provinces the empire controlled directly.[21] If that was the case, the census would have been administered locally, which would explain why Joseph and Mary went to their ancestral home in Bethlehem in order to be registered for it, following a Jewish custom which the Romans would neither have known nor cared about.

The two accounts of the birth of Jesus that are preserved in the New Testament, in Matthew and Luke, are quite different in many ways, but on one point they both agree—the conception of Jesus took place by a miraculous intervention of the Holy Spirit in the womb of a virgin.[22] If a virgin birth were to take place in nature, the child would be female because no male chromosome would have been present in conception. From the biological viewpoint, the fact that Jesus was born as a male supports the claim that the event was miraculous. Of course, Jesus' contemporaries would not have known that, but it is good for us to know that the maleness of Jesus has a biological significance as well as a theological justification in the revealed "masculinity" of God.

We know that Jesus was born before the death of Herod the Great, which occurred sometime between March 13, 4 B.C., the date of a lunar eclipse, and April 10, which was the start of Passover. By that time, Jesus may have been as much as two years old, since when Herod heard the news of Jesus' birth, he decreed that all the boys in Bethlehem who were two years and less should

---

[19]Matt. 1:16, 20; Luke 3:31.
[20]Luke 2:1–5.
[21]Luke 2:1.
[22]Matt. 1:20; Luke 1:35.

be put to death —basing his calculation on what the wise men from the east had told him.[23] There is good reason to suppose that the "star" they had seen was a constellation that appeared at different times during the course of 5 B.C. We know that Jesus cannot have been born before 6 B.C. because that is the earliest date that the census of Quirinius could have been announced, but if Mary was pregnant when she and Joseph set out from Nazareth, a birthdate for Jesus sometime in 5 B.C. does not seem improbable. It is true that Luke says that Jesus was "about thirty" when he began his ministry,[24] which cannot have been before A.D. 29, but the term is vague and may simply mean that he was in his thirties, which was undoubtedly true. An additional factor that may be relevant here is that, if Jesus was crucified in A.D. 33, as seems most probable, he would have been a few years short of his fortieth birthday, which may also be significant. Forty was a sacred number to the Jews, and had Jesus been crucified at that age something might well have been said about it in the New Testament.

The fact that Jesus was born so many years before the supposedly "correct" date of A.D. 1 has nothing to do with the Bible. It is the result of a series of chronological errors made by Dionysius Exiguus, a sixth-century Roman monk, who tried to calculate the birth of Jesus by counting back through the Roman emperors, but who managed to miss some in the process. He therefore came up short and was never corrected.[25] As for the date, December 25 was chosen as a date for celebrating Christ's birth in order to replace the Roman festival of Saturnalia, which was held at that time of the year. Christmas Day is the first time that it is possible to measure the return of daylight in the northern hemisphere following the winter solstice, and so it was thought to be an appropriate symbol of Christ, the light of the world. He cannot have been born on that day, however, because the shepherds who were watching their flocks would not have been out in the fields in mid-winter. Jesus must have been born sometime between March and November, but we can say no more than that. The important thing is that he *was* born on a particular day, and as December 25 is now the universally accepted date, there seems to be little point in trying to change it for the sake of an unattainable "accuracy."

The genealogies of Jesus in Matthew and Luke present other difficulties which cannot be so easily resolved. Matthew begins with Abraham and continues to Jesus, schematically dividing his list into three groups of fourteen men each. There is a difficulty with the last of these groups, which

---

[23] Matt. 2:16.
[24] Luke 3:23.
[25] As noted in chapter 10, there was no year 0. January 1, A.D. 1 was the day after December 31, 1 B.C., so that in adding A.D. and B.C. dates together, it is necessary to subtract 1 in order to get the correct length of time.

contains only thirteen names, and it is not clear why this should be so. Either Jesus and Christ are treated as two, or King Jechoniah (Jehoiachin) is counted twice, once as a king and again as a private individual, since after his deportation to Babylon he was replaced by Zedekiah on the throne in Jerusalem and was no longer king. It is generally surmised that Matthew's list represents the covenant and royal succession from the time of Abraham. There are certainly some names omitted from the list, but we cannot say for certain why that is so.

Luke's genealogy starts with Jesus and works back to Adam, and even to God. It has seventy-seven names, compared with Matthew's forty-one, or fifty-seven if only the generations back to Abraham are counted. This genealogy may represent the actual line of physical descent as opposed to the legal line of inheritance, but that is a guess that cannot be substantiated. What is certain is that because the ancient Jews paid great attention to genealogies, the arrangement is not accidental. Luke's can be subdivided into eleven groups of seven names. David heads the seventh group and Abraham the ninth, which may be significant as both seven and nine (as three threes) were regarded as special numbers. We cannot say whether the arrangement is Luke's own or comes from another source, but it is clear that both genealogies bear witness to an ordered and ancient succession, even if the intricacies of its details are now partially hidden from our eyes.

To understand just how complex genealogies can be, we need look no further than that of the British royal family. Queen Elizabeth II can trace her ancestry back more or less directly to the accession of George I in 1714, but there is not a straightforward succession from father to son.[26] When we go back to the Tudors (1485–1603) and Stuarts (1603–1714), we find that of the twelve rulers they produced between them, the present queen is descended from only two—Henry VII (1485–1509) and James I (1603–1625). Ironically, although she cannot claim the first Elizabeth as her ancestor, she *can* include Elizabeth's great rival, Mary Queen of Scots, whom Elizabeth I executed for her pretensions to the throne of England! Legal and physical descent are very different, and if we do not know the details, we might easily think that one (or both) of the competing genealogies had been made up. We do not have the background information we need to decide what the different genealogies of Jesus mean, but the British example is a warning that we must be careful not to draw conclusions that may seem obvious on the surface but that are actually quite mistaken.

---

[26]Of the eleven monarchs since 1714, George II was succeeded by his grandson (1760), George IV by his brother (1830), William IV by his niece (1837), and Edward VIII by his brother (1936).

THE HUMANITY OF JESUS

More important than dates or genealogies is the question of whether the humanity of Jesus was genuine. Was the uniqueness of Christ's person and birth such as to make it impossible for him to be truly one of us? The Bible tells us that the Son of God was conceived by the Holy Spirit in the womb of the Virgin Mary, which means that he overruled the normal process of procreation and caused it to occur without the intervention of a male.[27] But what kind of being did such a conjunction produce? One possible answer is that the Holy Spirit took the place of a human father, and that the baby Jesus was conceived by the divine equivalent of *in vitro* fertilization. If that were the case, he would be no different from anyone else, despite his rather unusual origin. Another possibility is that the Holy Spirit combined with Mary's flesh to produce a creature who was neither fully man nor fully God, but a mixture of the two, similar to what happens when people of different races marry and have mixed-race children. Was Jesus a fusion of God and man without really being either?

Both of these possibilities were canvassed in the early centuries of the church, but neither one carried conviction. The belief that Jesus was an ordinary human being with an unusual relationship to God did not do justice either to the claims he made to divine authority or to the mission he was meant to accomplish for the salvation of the human race. As an example of the former, we may cite his claim to be able to forgive sins, which was a divine prerogative.[28] As for the latter, Jesus claimed to be able to give people eternal life, and prayed that, in his passion, the Father would glorify him with the glory that he had before the world existed.[29] Neither of these things would have been possible if Jesus had been just an unusually conceived human being, and so that theory had to be rejected.

The idea that Jesus was some kind of mixture, part-God and part-man, had longer life, and was occasionally justified by appealing to 1 Timothy 2:5: "For there is one God and one mediator between God and men, the man Christ Jesus." This conclusion hung on the interpretation given to the word "mediator," which was taken to mean an "intermediate being" who stood somewhere between divinity and humanity and who could therefore link up with both. In the end, however, this theory was also abandoned because it did not do justice to either component of Jesus' being. On the one hand, it is impossible for anyone to be only partly God. The being of God cannot be

---

[27]Matt. 1:20; Luke 1:35.
[28]Mark 2:7–12.
[29]John 17:3–5.

divided or diluted, so if Jesus is God at all, he must be fully and completely divine. On the other hand, if he were only partly human, he could not have taken our place and died for us on the cross. I can only be crucified with Christ, as Paul said, if Christ was crucified in the same way that I would otherwise have been.[30] If his death was something that I could not have experienced, then it has no bearing on me, and I am not saved by it.

The only solution that does justice to the biblical witness is to say that Jesus was *fully* God and *fully* man, not half one and half the other. But how could this be if he was a single individual? This question formed the substance of the great debates of the fourth and fifth centuries, in the course of which the biblical teaching was clarified and a terminology adequate to express it was developed. Its broad outlines were as follows:

A. Jesus of Nazareth was the eternal Son of God, the second person of the Trinity. This is clear from a number of New Testament passages that either state or strongly imply that he existed in eternity before becoming a man.[31] Those who met him in the flesh saw the Father, and, when he spoke, it was with the mind and voice of the eternal God.[32]

B. It was the Son's own decision to become a human being, and he must be regarded as the agent of his own incarnation.[33] This is important because his work of redemption was voluntary. It is true that he was sent by the Father to do his will, and that he submitted to the Father's will in humble obedience, but he was not forced to do this, and we who have been saved through union with him in his suffering and death can know that he died for us because he loved us, and not because the Father ordered him to do it.

C. The incarnate Son lost nothing of his divinity when he became a man. This is implied in John 1:14: "The Word became flesh and dwelt among us, and we have seen his glory . . ." In other words, the glory of the Word was seen *in* his flesh and not in spite of it. It is sometimes suggested that Philippians 2:7 states an opposite view because there Paul says that the Son of God "emptied himself," but this refers to his voluntary self-humiliation, not to a loss of divine power. As Jesus himself put it,

> I lay down my life that I may take it up again. No one takes it from me, but I lay it down of my own accord. I have authority to lay it down, and I have authority to take it up again.[34]

---

[30]See Gal. 2:20.
[31]John 1:1–14; 3:13; 17:5; Phil. 2:6–7; Col. 2:9.
[32]Mark 1:24; John 8:58; 14:9.
[33]Phil. 2:6–8.
[34]John 10:17b–18.

D. Jesus had everything he needed to be able to take our place on the cross and to die for us. As with every other human being, he had his own unique identity, but he lacked none of the attributes that make us all members of the same biological species. In the words of Paul,

> When the fullness of time had come, God sent forth his Son, born of a woman, born under the law, to redeem those who were under the law, so that we might receive adoption as sons.[35]

In other words, the Son of God identified himself with us so that we might be able to become identified with him in his relationship to the Father. He came down to earth so that we might be taken up into heaven, where we are seated with him in his glory forever.[36]

Put all this together and it soon becomes clear that the revelation of Jesus Christ changed not only the traditional perception of God but the way we think about human beings as well. The Christian revelation decreed that the three persons in God share the same nature and constitute a single substance or being, because there is only one God. Then it said that every human being shares a common humanity but is still an individual person. Our personhood unites us to God, giving us a relationship with him and the capacity to interact with him in a way that no other creature can. It is that personhood, not our common humanity, which gives us the right to be called "human."

Furthermore, it is the person who controls the nature and the substance, not the other way around. Whereas pre-Christian people thought that what we call the "person" was an expression of the underlying substance and its nature, Christians found that the New Testament revelation of Christ forced them to think the opposite. Jesus Christ was a divine person who showed that he was not bound by his divine nature by stepping out of it and assuming a second, human nature. He was one divine person manifested in two natures— one divine and the other human—both of which he controlled and united to himself by means of his person. The natures are mutually incompatible and have no relationship with each other on their own, but, as possessions of the divine second person of the Trinity, they come together to constitute the man Christ Jesus.

It took Christians a long time to work out the implications of this revolutionary doctrine, and they made many mistakes along the way. The old way of thinking did not die easily and even now it is not uncommon to find it lurking beneath the surface of many of the "difficulties" that people have with

---

[35]Gal. 4:4.
[36]Eph. 2:6.

the doctrine of the Trinity or of the divinity of Christ. But the fulfillment of God's self-revelation calls us to turn our minds around. As Paul put it,

> Even though we once regarded Christ according to the flesh, we regard him thus no longer. Therefore, if anyone is in Christ, he is a new creation. The old has passed away; behold, the new has come.[37]

The context of Paul's remarks is different from this one, but the principle is the same. A new way of thinking is required for a new revelation that cannot be understood purely within the boundaries of the old creation. The coming of Christ into the world not only changed how we perceive and experience God; it also defined humanity in a new way.

Jesus is a divine person with a human nature, and in that sense he is different from us, but human persons can relate to the divine because personhood has a relational aspect that is common to us both. As a person, Jesus can take our place and represent us before the judgment seat of his Father. Being divine, he has access to the other persons of the Godhead in a way that we do not. That is why he can be our mediator and reconcile us to God in the way that the Father intended when he sent his Son into the world.[38] Perhaps most important of all, it helps us to understand what Jesus meant when he told Nicodemus that God sent his Son to us out of his deep love for "the world."[39] This is not an abstract statement about something nebulous called the "world," but a clear affirmation that God loves those whom he has created in his image and likeness, and that it was out of his love for them that he sent his Son.

This assertion forces us to reconsider what the image of God in man is—or rather, what it is not. Could Jesus have possessed it, if he was God? What would he have needed his own image for? The question is made more difficult because for many centuries it was believed that the image and likeness of God was the rational soul, which inevitably raised the question of whether Jesus had a rational soul. If the rational soul was divine, why would he have needed one? This view was put forward in ancient times by Apollinarius, and was condemned at the first council of Constantinople in 381. Since that time, the church has taught that Jesus had a human mind and a human soul because otherwise he could not have taken our place on the cross. Sin is manifested by acts of the mind and will, not by inert skin and bones, so if Jesus did not have a soul he could neither have sinned himself nor become sin for us. His

---

[37] 2 Cor. 5:16b–17.
[38] See 2 Cor. 5:18–19.
[39] John 3:16.

sinlessness was not due to an inability to sin but to the perfect obedience of his human will to the will of God. That the incarnate Christ possessed two wills, a human and a divine one, is borne out by the evidence of the garden of Gethsemane, where Jesus prayed that the Father's will, and not his, should be done.[40] From the divine point of view, the will of the Son was identical to the will of the Father because there is only one will in God. From the human standpoint, Jesus could not have had a death wish and been a psychologically normal human being, but as God he could not diverge from the will he shared with his Father. What we see in the garden therefore is the submission of his human will to his divine one, or in other words, the submission of his human nature to his divinity.

The implication of this is that the mind and the will are not the image and likeness of God in us. They do not inhere in our persons but in our human nature. They can be corrupted or destroyed without removing our personhood, a matter of great importance for medical ethics. Does a man cease to be fully human if his mental faculties are impaired? Can euthanasia be justified in such circumstances because the loss of a certain quality of life is tantamount to a loss of personhood? Christians cannot accept such ideas. The example of Jesus shows us that our natural faculties, important and necessary as they are for living a normal human life, are nevertheless distinct from our existence as persons. The ultimate proof of this is that, after death, we shall continue to be the same persons as we are now, but the rest of us will change beyond recognition because human nature ("flesh and blood") cannot inherit the kingdom of God.[41]

Once we make this distinction, the problems surrounding traditional interpretations of the two natures of Christ fall into place. In his incarnate nature, Jesus had a normal human mind, with all that that entails. There is no evidence to suggest that he was specially gifted intellectually or had any remarkable talents, still less that he knew the deep secrets of the universe. This causes a problem for theologians because we have to explain how it was possible for the eternal Son of God to be so limited in his incarnate state. The answer has to be that, although he was a divine person, he was functioning within the parameters of his human nature and could not exceed them without compromising the integrity of his humanity. An analogy might perhaps be found by comparing him to a child who is bilingual, speaking one language to his father and another to his mother, perhaps without fully realizing what he is doing. Other people perceive this and wonder how it is possible to switch

---

[40]Matt. 26:42.
[41]1 Cor. 15:50.

so easily from one way of thinking to another, but, to the child, this seems natural. He seldom confuses the one with the other. To some extent, Jesus must have been like this, talking to other human beings in one way and to his Father in heaven in another way, but without any confusion or contradiction in his mind between them. There are some things that can be said in one language but not in another (at least not in the same way), and so it was with Jesus. What he knew as the Son of God he could not communicate as the son of Mary.

Something else that we must bear in mind is that the Son of God became a man with a mission given to him by his Father, and it was on fulfilling that mission that his efforts and interests were concentrated. When his disciples asked him when he would restore the kingdom to Israel, he replied, "It is not for you to know times or seasons that the Father has fixed by his own authority."[42] He does not tell them whether *he* knows the answer because that is irrelevant. The disciples were not *meant* to know, and so the information was withheld from them. Before his crucifixion Jesus told his disciples that neither the Son nor the angels in heaven knew when the last judgment would take place, because that information belonged to the Father only.[43] Can there be anything that one person of the Trinity knows but not the others? It would seem that that is possible, but as we have no way of penetrating the mind of God we must be extremely cautious about this. What is certain is that the incarnate Son was unable to convey the information to his disciples because the Father had not authorized him to do so. Beyond that we are reduced to speculation and cannot say for sure whether the Father's knowledge remains unique to him within the Godhead.

Another phenomenon that sets Jesus apart from us is that he was able to perform miracles as a man, sometimes using his body to do so. For example, he healed a blind man by spitting on the ground and making mud to cover his eyes.[44] Was there some divine property in his saliva that made healing possible? Even more remarkably, the woman with an issue of blood was healed when she touched Jesus' clothing, apparently without his being fully aware of what was happening.[45] Did his clothing radiate some healing property? The question is important because it is tied to the phenomenon of relics. There are no known relics of Jesus, but there are fragments that purport to be from his cross and there are innumerable relics of various saints to which healing power has been attributed. Many of the relics are fraudulent, but at least some

[42]Acts 1:6–7.
[43]Matt. 24:36
[44]John 9:1–7.
[45]Mark 5:28–34.

are genuine, and the question arises as to whether holiness attaches to them because of the person with whom they are associated.

At first sight, the evidence of the earthly life of Jesus suggests that there is some plausibility in this. To answer the question, let us begin with the case of the woman with the issue of blood. Jesus sensed that a power had gone out of him when she touched his clothing, but attributed her healing not to that but to her faith.[46] For him, healing was always tied to the faith and spiritual state of the person seeking the miracle, even if the power to heal came from him and not from them. This is made clear in the story of the paralytic let down through the roof.[47] When Jesus saw him, he ignored the paralysis and addressed the man's spiritual state, telling him that his sins had been forgiven. Only when that provoked a reaction from some of the onlookers, who wondered what power he had to forgive sins, did Jesus go on and heal him. The miracle was designed to prove his authority as a forgiver, not his power as a healer. He was not a miracle worker as such but a preacher of the gospel, which he had come to fulfill. His ability to perform miracles was a rebuke to those who refused to believe his message, a means to an end rather than the end in itself.[48]

Once we understand that, we can see that there is no reason to venerate relics, because they do not (and cannot) possess healing powers in their own right.[49] Nor is there any reason to think that there are specially qualified people called "saints" whose extraordinary devotion to Christ gives them the ability to perform miracles. To claim that they do, and to encourage their veneration on the ground that because the incarnate Christ possessed this power they can possess it too, is to deny the gospel by leading people to put their trust in miracles and not in the forgiveness of God. Miracles can and do occur, but they do so because God has heard the cry of his faithful people and responded to their request, not because some relic has been touched or some "saint" invoked.

Another question that arises concerning the humanity of Jesus is the extent to which it enables him to be the representative of the whole human race. The Son of God became incarnate as a first-century Jewish male, something that was probably necessary in order for him to fulfill his mission within

---

[46]Mark 5:34.
[47]Mark 2:3–12.
[48]John 14:11.
[49]There is, however, an unusual case recorded in Acts 19:12, where handkerchiefs that had touched Paul's skin were used to heal the sick. There is no evidence that this was a regular occurrence, or that the apostle approved of it, but it shows that he possessed something of the healing power of Jesus, whose garments also healed people who touched them. In neither case, though, is there any suggestion that this phenomenon was meant to be permanent.

the limited range of options available. The Messiah had to be a descendant of both Abraham and David, and the patriarchal nature of Israelite society ensured that he also had to be male, though there were other reasons for his masculinity as well. As we have already seen, a male birth from a virgin could only be the result of divine intervention, whereas a female birth could have occurred naturally. In a male virgin birth, moreover, both sexes play a part, whereas in a female one the male element is excluded, and so such a birth would be less representative of the human race as a whole. Most important of all, the maleness of Jesus was determined by the nature of the original creation—Adam had been made first, and Eve had been taken out of him. As the second Adam, he could include the female in a way that would not have been possible the other way around.[50] His masculinity should therefore not be seen as a barrier to the salvation of women but as a reminder that both men and women are beneficiaries of God's plan of salvation.

Where Christ's humanity is circumscribed and unrepresentative is in his Jewishness—not in any ethnic sense of the term but in the covenantal meaning attached to it. Jesus came to save those who were his, and they were to be found within the nation of Israel. There is virtually no evidence that Jesus had any connection with people outside the narrow Palestinian world in which he lived. It is true that there were occasions when he spoke to non-Jews, but these were exceptional, and he never hesitated to tell them that his ministry was primarily to the people of Israel. For example, when he talked to the Samaritan woman at the well, he reminded her that "salvation is from the Jews," even as he pointed out that the time was coming when the ancient distinction between Jews and others would no longer matter.[51] Similarly, when he was approached by a Canaanite woman seeking help for her daughter, he told her that he had been sent only to the lost sheep of Israel, but relented when she compared herself to a dog![52] On another occasion, he healed a centurion's servant and used it to rebuke his fellow Israelites, telling them not only that they did not have the centurion's faith but also that in the kingdom of heaven, there would be many who would come from the four corners of the earth to sit at table with Abraham, Isaac, and Jacob, whereas the natural heirs of the kingdom, the Jewish people, would be thrown into the outer darkness.[53]

Social activists scour the evidence of the four Gospels to show that Jesus ministered to outcasts of one kind or another, but their attempts to prove from this that he had a special mission to the poor, the homeless, or the oppressed

[50]1 Cor. 15:22, 45.
[51]John 4:21–24.
[52]Matt. 15:21–28.
[53]Matt. 8:5–13.

are usually strained and have an air of special pleading about them. It is certainly true that Jesus decried riches and had harsh things to say about those who cheated and oppressed the poor, but this was because they were worshiping the false gods of wealth and power, not because he thought that everyone was entitled to an equal share of the world's goods. He himself was homeless, and he expected his followers to act as if they were too.[54] He admired those who are poor *in spirit* and those who hunger and thirst *after righteousness*, which is not the same as saying that he had a bias toward poverty and destitution for their own sake.[55] It is simply not possible to understand Jesus in terms of economic or social class, and his message of repentance and new life was meant for everyone, rich and poor alike.

To sum up, the incarnation of the Son of God as a Jew "born under the law" was not an accident but part of the eternal plan of the Father for the salvation of the human race.[56] The people of Israel had been called into being as a gift of God to the nations, a glimmer of light in a world of darkness. Jesus came to make that light brighter, not to establish a rival light that would have called the validity of Israel's witness into question.[57] Whatever he did backed up what the Old Testament said and validated it as the revelation of a plan that had been conceived at the beginning of time. That plan would be fulfilled by gathering men and women from the four corners of the earth and transforming them into the likeness of Christ by putting them to death (as far as this world is concerned) and giving them a new life in the power of the Spirit of God. Who these people were and are is known only to God, just as only God could determine who among the elect of Israel would constitute the remnant of those who were saved. We cannot define them in terms of earthly distinctions, which no longer count even if they continue to exist.[58] But we can say that Jesus is their representative, wherever they may have come from, because they are grafted into the covenant people of Israel to whom he was sent. His humanity is adequate to embrace theirs and to redeem it.

THE SINLESSNESS OF JESUS

The ability of Jesus to represent the whole of mankind in his own humanity brings us to the question of his sinlessness, which the Bible insists was necessary for him to be our Redeemer.[59] What does "sinlessness" mean? Presumably

---

[54]Matt. 8:19–22; Luke 14:26–33.
[55]Matt. 5:3, 6.
[56]Gal. 4:4–5.
[57]Matt. 5:17–20.
[58]Gal. 3:28.
[59]Heb. 4:14–5:10.

God is sinless by definition, but if Jesus was sinless because he was God, how could he have been a man like us? Does his sinlessness mean that he was not fully human? Just as the incarnation of Christ transformed our perception of God and man, so it also changed what most people had thought (and perhaps still think) about sin. In the past, sin was generally thought of as some form of impurity or corruption. It could have originated in any number of different ways, not all of which would be regarded as sinful nowadays. For example, one very common way of becoming "sinful" both in ancient Israel and in the pagan countries that surrounded it, was by ritual defilement. Failure to perform the correct ablutions or make the right sacrifices could easily produce a situation displeasing to God (or to the gods), and the only way out of that was by ritual cleansing, which again could take different forms. Today, we are inclined to think of such things as superficial, even if we agree that laws should be obeyed and customs respected as much as possible. For example, on entering a mosque, we would take off our shoes as a sign of respect, but would not feel that we had done something terribly wrong if we had neglected to do so. To call it a "sin" would be taking the matter too seriously.

It takes some effort for us to think back to a world which thought very differently about such external acts, but a glance at the career of Jesus will show that it was a major issue in his day. Jesus taught his disciples that it was not what they touched or ate that defiled them, but what came out of their wicked and disobedient hearts.[60] He was constantly being upbraided by Jewish leaders for breaking one or other of their laws, especially regarding the keeping of the Sabbath.[61] Worst of all, he made claims about himself that were regarded as blasphemous, and it was these that eventually led to his condemnation.[62] By the standards of his own time, Jesus was far from being sinless—on the contrary, he could easily have been regarded as the worst of sinners because of the claims he made for himself. And yet, his disciples rejected such accusations and claimed that he had never committed any sin at all. What did they mean by "sin"?

On one point at least, all parties to this argument could agree: breaking the law was a sin. Jesus was born under the law and was expected to keep it just as any other Jew would have done. But Paul tells us that it is impossible to keep the law, partly because it is so complicated but partly also because we do not have what it takes within us to begin with. Even if I want to keep the law, he says, there is a law in my body that says something different and I am

---

[60]Matt. 15:18–21.
[61]Mark 2:26–27.
[62]John 5:18; Matt. 26:65.

dragged down by that.[63] But what was true of Paul obviously was not true of Jesus, since if it were, he would have been a sinner too. Yet there is no reason to suppose that the humanity of Jesus was different from ours, and Paul even says that he came to earth "in the likeness of sinful flesh."[64] Jesus spent the first thirty years of his life in a small village where everyone knew him intimately, and they never thought he was odd, which they presumably would have done if his sinlessness had been apparent to them. Indeed, so ordinary did he appear that when he began preaching in the synagogue at Nazareth, they threw him out for being arrogant.[65]

Most importantly, when the writer to the Hebrews discusses the sinlessness of Jesus, he makes sure to point out that this was not because Jesus was a special kind of human being. As he says,

> We do not have a high priest who is unable to sympathize with our weaknesses, but one who in every respect has been tempted as we are, yet without sin.[66]

It would seem clear from this that whatever we have to suffer he also suffered, including temptation, as the Gospels point out. We are not given specific examples of how Jesus was tempted in the ways that we are, perhaps because the Gospel writers did not find that sort of thing very interesting. Whether Jesus was tempted by sex or money, for example, is unknown, though various modern writers have speculated that he was and have sought to portray him as having been tempted by Mary Magdalene, though there is no evidence for that. One or two have even suggested that he was homosexual, but again, there is no evidence for that to be found anywhere in the Gospels, and those who think otherwise have played fast and loose with the text in their own preconceived interest. The temptations that Jesus endured were real enough, but they were not the sort of temptations that would be inflicted on us.

This is so because temptation is always something that we have the ability to fall into, since otherwise we would not be tempted by it. Jesus was tempted to turn stones into bread, something that is impossible for us but which he could do because he was God.[67] People in high and exposed positions are often tempted more than ordinary mortals because they have more options than we do. When we say that Jesus was tempted just as we are, what we mean is that he was tempted to the limit of his capacities, which in his case included

---

[63]Rom. 7:7–25.
[64]Rom. 8:3.
[65]Luke 4:16–30.
[66]Heb. 4:15.
[67]Matt. 4:3.

things that only God could do. Of course, Jesus resisted the temptations and so did not fall into sin, but resistance is something that is possible for any one of us. No one is tempted beyond his ability to say no, and the same was true of Jesus, great as his temptations were. As Paul says,

> No temptation has overtaken you that is not common to man. God is faithful, and he will not let you be tempted beyond your ability, but with the temptation he will also provide the way of escape, that you may be able to endure it.[68]

Jesus' resistance was not supernatural but was something that any one of us could manage, if we had our minds clearly focused on the will of God. It is this, in the end, that provides the clue to the sinlessness of Jesus. As the writer to the Hebrews put it,

> In the days of his flesh, Jesus offered up prayers and supplications, with loud cries and tears, to him who was able to save him from death, and he was heard because of his reverence. Although he was a son, he learned obedience through what he suffered. And being made perfect, he became the source of eternal salvation to all who obey him.[69]

From this we learn that, although Jesus was sinless in his humanity, he was not exempt from the sorrows and sufferings associated with normal human life. What this tells us is that we cannot regard such sorrows and sufferings as the inevitable or exclusive result of sin. Sinfulness is not an essential ingredient of humanity but a distortion of what it means to be human. There are no sinless human beings today because we are all heirs of Adam, but that does not rule out the possibility of a sinless human being existing, nor does it imply that such an individual would come across as a freak in a world full of sinners. Jesus was not an heir of Adam in the way that we are because although he had a human nature just like ours and was descended from Adam through his mother, that did not count where inheritance was concerned. Had sin been a defect in the body, as the medieval theologians who invented the concept of the immaculate conception of Mary thought it was, matters would have been different. The sin of Adam, however, is not to be found in the weakness of the flesh that causes us to suffer, but in the broken relationship with God which cuts us off from him. As the Son of God, Jesus was not cut off from his Father, and so the legacy of Adam does not apply to him. In theological

---

[68]1 Cor. 10:12–13.
[69]Heb. 5:7–9.

terms, sin is an act of the person, not of the nature, and the person of Jesus was the divine Son of God.

Once again, we find that by becoming a man, the Son of God defined the nature of humanity as much as he revealed that of divinity. It is completely wrong to suggest that human suffering is the direct result of sin or that if we were sinless we would not suffer in any way. It may be true to say that those who sin are liable to incur suffering as a result, but it cannot be said that those who suffer are necessarily paying the price of their sin. Jesus made that point in his healing of the man born blind, and he demonstrated it with even greater clarity in his own life and death. Sinlessness did not make his human nature invulnerable, a point which needs to be made in the face of those who preach a so-called "prosperity gospel," which says that health and wealth are the natural fruits of a godly life.

Could Jesus, as a man, have disobeyed the will of God? This is a tricky question. At one level, the answer to this must be yes because Jesus was tempted just as we are, yet he did not sin. If it had been impossible for him to sin, such a statement would be meaningless, and he could not have been tempted. On the other hand, Jesus was also God, and so if he had sinned as a man he would have been sinning against himself. That really makes no sense, so we have to say that, although he could have sinned in his human nature, he did not do so because he was the Son of God. For some people that will sound as if his humanity was compromised by his divinity, but that is not right. What stopped Jesus from sinning was not his divine nature but the relationship with the Father which was his from all eternity. That relationship, far from being beyond our grasp, is what he came to earth to give us, so that we might also become sinless in the sight of God. Thus, although the sinlessness of Jesus makes him different from other human beings, it does not cut him off from us because it is the very thing that he came to give us, who are just as capable of receiving it as he was of living it out in his earthly life. The difference is that he is sinless by nature, whereas we are made sinless by being united with him and thus gaining access to that nature. In other words, his sinlessness belongs to him and our sinlessness belongs to him as well, because it is only in and through him that we can acquire it.

THE EARTHLY MINISTRY OF JESUS

The Bible tells us that Jesus began his earthly ministry when he was baptized by John, which probably occurred in A.D. 29. This would have made it possible for him to be in Jerusalem for Passover on April 7, A.D. 30.[70] After that, he went to Galilee and was probably still there for the next Passover, since it is recorded that his disciples were plucking grain in Galilee, which would have happened around Passover time.[71] Jesus would then have been back in Jerusalem for Passover in A.D. 32, the third year of his ministry but only the second one that he spent in the city,[72] and his crucifixion would have occurred a year later, on Friday, April 3, A.D. 33. This chronology allows for an initial visit to Jerusalem shortly after his baptism, followed by an extended period of ministry in the north and completed with a return to Judaea for the final phase. The many other events recorded in the Gospels cannot be precisely dated, though some guesses can be made. For example, we are told that Jesus returned to Galilee when word got out that he was baptizing more people than John, which must have been sometime in A.D. 30, when John was still active. It was on this return journey that he met the Samaritan woman, which allows us to date that event with reasonable precision.[73]

If that reconstruction is correct, it was probably during his first Passover visit to Jerusalem that he met Nicodemus.[74] At that time, Jesus was still a novelty, and there was no organized hostility toward him on the part of the Pharisees, which would have made it easier for Nicodemus to establish contact in the way that he did. Working back from there, the wedding feast at Cana must have taken place late in A.D. 29 or early in A.D. 30 because the text tells us that it was there that he performed his first miracle.[75] Beyond that, it is hard to be precise because the Gospel writers were not interested in biographical details or in chronological sequence for their own sake.[76] Nevertheless, we know enough to be reasonably confident of the timescale for Jesus' ministry and can discern the broad outline of the direction it took.

From the theological standpoint, the first reason why Jesus' earthly ministry was important was its prophetic nature. Jesus was recognized as a prophet and as a teacher who had come from God, which amounts to much the same thing.[77] The main duty of a prophet was to proclaim the Word of God to his people, and Jesus did that throughout his ministry. But his way of proclaiming that Word was different from what had gone before because, instead of teaching that God had spoken to him and given him a message of judgment

---

[70]An event which is probably recorded in John 2:13.
[71]Matt. 12:1; Mark 2:23; Luke 6:1.
[72]John 6:4.
[73]John 4:1–7.
[74]John 3:1–2.
[75]John 2:11.
[76]It is interesting to note that it is John's Gospel, often regarded as unhistorical, which gives us the best clues for dating Jesus' earthly ministry, as the examples quoted here illustrate.
[77]John 4:19; 3:2.

and/or blessing to convey to Israel, he told them that he himself was the Word and the key to understanding all the earlier prophecies.[78] He had not come to continue the ministry of the prophets but to fulfill it, by doing the things that they had foretold.[79] This led to a comprehensive reinterpretation of the Hebrew Bible. Jesus taught his disciples that the Scriptures spoke of him and explained what he had come to do. He accepted their authority without reservation, but insisted that they must be read in the light of his own mission because that was what they were really all about.[80]

Jesus began his public ministry by acknowledging the authority of John the Baptist and asking him for baptism.[81] The importance of that event can be measured from the fact that it is one of the few things Jesus did that is mentioned in all four Gospels. John did not want to baptize Jesus, because he felt he was unworthy to do so. He understood his own limitations as a prophet, and that Jesus was the Lamb of God who had no need to repent and be baptized. Later on, Jesus paid tribute to John by saying that there had never been a prophet greater than he was, not least because his role had been to prepare the way for someone even greater to come, namely himself.[82]

In submitting to a baptism that he did not need, Jesus told his followers that it was necessary in order to "fulfill all righteousness."[83] The meaning of this phrase is somewhat puzzling because baptism was not one of the requirements of the Mosaic law to which Jesus was subject. But it reminds us that he had come to save us from our sins by taking our place and becoming sin for us, even though he was sinless himself.[84] His baptism is the proclamation of his representative and substitutionary role as the Lamb of God who would atone for the sins of the world. As the acknowledged beginning of his earthly ministry, it was a sign to everyone that everything he said and did was geared toward that one aim.

Following his baptism, Jesus set out to choose his disciples. It appears that one of the first to follow him was Andrew, who had been a disciple of John but who tagged along after Jesus following the latter's baptism.[85] Andrew went to find his brother Simon, whom Jesus promptly renamed Cephas, or Peter ("rock") in Greek. The Synoptic Gospels tell us that this happened by the sea of Galilee, which means that Andrew must have taken Jesus there immediately

---

[78]John 5:39; Matt. 11:13; Luke 16:16.
[79]See Luke 4:21.
[80]Matt. 5:17–20.
[81]Matt. 3:13–17; Mark 1:9–11; Luke 3:21–22; John 1:29–34.
[82]Matt. 11:7–11; Luke 7:24–28.
[83]Matt. 3:15.
[84]2 Cor. 5:21.
[85]John 1:40.

after his baptism. At the same time, Jesus spotted James and John, the sons of Zebedee, and he called them to be his disciples also.[86] The sequence of events is significant because although Andrew decided to follow Jesus, Jesus chose the other three and even renamed Simon in the process. Afterwards, Andrew receded from the spotlight somewhat, but Peter, James, and John became and remained the inner circle of Jesus' disciples. They went everywhere with him, even when the others did not, and they remained the pillars of the Jerusalem church for some time after his death and resurrection.[87]

The choosing of the disciples is important for two reasons. First of all, it reminds us that those who follow Jesus have been selected by him, not the other way around. Andrew might be a partial exception to this, but although he was not rejected, neither was his decision to follow Jesus to become the norm. There would be many others who wanted to become Jesus' disciples, but he almost always rejected them or imposed conditions on them that were too hard for them to fulfill.[88] Toward the end of his ministry, Jesus could turn to his disciples and say, "You did not choose me, but I chose you and appointed you that you should go and bear fruit."[89] This is the key. The true followers of Jesus know that he has chosen them and appointed them for a purpose, and their only desire is to fulfill his will.

The second reason why the choosing of the disciples is important for us is that they were the ones who would become the foundation on which the church would be built.[90] The Peter who stood up in Jerusalem on the day of Pentecost and proclaimed the resurrection of Christ was the same man whom Jesus had found fishing in the Sea of Galilee and had called to follow him. The men who saw the risen Lord had spent up to three years with him, absorbing his teaching, watching his miracles, and experiencing the opposition he aroused. Their witness could not easily be set aside, and the Gospels remind us what Jesus' message was and how it was worked out in his death and resurrection. What went before is consistent with what came afterwards, as Jesus himself explained shortly before his ascension.[91]

The teaching Jesus gave his disciples during his earthly ministry can best be understood as an internalization of the Jewish law. This is clear from the way he handled the Ten Commandments. The disciples hardly needed to be reminded that it was wrong to kill or to steal, but they thought about such things as external acts that today we would call crimes. Jesus taught them to

---

[86]Matt. 4:21–22.
[87]Gal. 2:9.
[88]See Matt. 8:18–22; 19:16–22.
[89]John 15:16.
[90]Matt. 16:18–19.
[91]Luke 24:44–48.

examine their hearts and ask whether they had ever had bad thoughts about other people, or envied them. Looked at from that perspective, there was no one who had not offended, and laws which at first glance seemed relatively easy to keep suddenly became swords piercing the disciples' hearts.[92]

Once this is understood, the rest falls naturally into place. The ethics of Jesus was not based on a legal code of dos and don'ts but on a transformed life in which the Holy Spirit bears witness with our spirit that we are children of God.[93] To those who are pure in heart, everything is pure, but to those whose hearts are corrupt, everything is defiled.[94] At the same time, purity and freedom from the law are not meant to be taken as a license to do whatever we want. Our primary duty is to love God and to love our neighbors as ourselves, and that demand sets clear boundaries to what we can and cannot do.[95]

A central theme of Jesus' teaching was the "kingdom of God," whose imminent coming he prophesied.[96] It was easy for his hearers to misunderstand this, and so it is not surprising that there is such great emphasis on the spiritual nature of his kingdom. Much of what Jesus said was in the form of parables, a teaching method especially characteristic of him.[97] A great deal has been written about parables, seeking to explain what they are like and how they should be interpreted, but the main principles are clear enough. A parable is a story or example taken from everyday life that is used to illustrate a spiritual principle. A good example of the technique is the parable of the sower who went out to sow his seed.[98] The seed fell on different types of ground and the results were correspondingly varied, ranging from the complete disappearance of the seed at one end because the ground was too hard and it was eaten up by the birds, to a fruitful harvest at the other end.

As a story from everyday life the parable can be understood, although it does not make much sense, since no real sower would be so careless as to sow his seed on unsuitable ground. But to understand it like that is to miss the point. The seed is the Word of God, which must be preached everywhere and to all without discrimination. However, the people who hear it are of very different kinds. Some simply reject it and the Word is lost. Others receive it but only half-heartedly, and before long its effects are compromised and then nullified. Finally, there are people who hear it, take it on board, and experience

---

[92]Matt. 5:21–32.
[93]Rom. 8:16.
[94]Titus 1:15.
[95]See Rom. 14:20–23.
[96]It is sometimes also called the "kingdom of heaven," probably because Jews did not pronounce the name of God.
[97]Matt. 13:34.
[98]Matt. 13:1–9.

its life-giving power. It is not the sower's job to decide who those people will be and restrict his sowing to them. God will reveal those who are his in the results that emerge from the sower's efforts, and we must be ready to see him at work in that process, as he is in everything else.[99]

Parables are paradigmatic of the teaching of Christ, which makes little sense to those who are not called and which may easily be misinterpreted and misapplied by people whose good intentions are not backed up by spiritual knowledge. Those who have the Spirit of God in them know what his teaching means and can see it bear fruit in their lives, which is ultimately what the presence of the kingdom of God is all about.

Another notable aspect of Jesus' earthly ministry is his miracles, which naturally attracted considerable comment at the time and a sizeable following of people who wanted to be there when they happened. But, like the parables, the miracles served to pave the way for the coming of the kingdom, and they must be understood in that light. When John the Baptist was in prison, he seems to have had doubts about his mission as the forerunner, and it is recorded that he sent some of his disciples to ask Jesus whether he really was the promised Messiah. Jesus' reply is illuminating:

> Go and tell John what you hear and see: The blind receive their sight and the lame walk, lepers are cleansed and the deaf hear, and the dead are raised up, and the poor have good news preached to them.[100]

From a modern perspective, it is strange to see that preaching good news to the poor is mentioned alongside the miracles, but in the stratified society of the ancient world it must have seemed almost as remarkable as they were. The point, however, is that the miracles were signs pointing toward the greater revelation that the coming of the kingdom would bring. Even the miracle of raising Lazarus from the dead was prophetic in this sense.[101] Lazarus did not come back to a better life than the one he was living before but to the same one, and eventually he died again. When Jesus first heard that Lazarus was ill, he recognized that his sickness was not terminal, but he also knew that it had come upon Lazarus as a means of bringing glory to God. Lazarus actually died before Jesus arrived on the scene, but that too was foreordained as a means of testing and strengthening the faith of his disciples and of those dear to the dead man. And that is what happened. Despite her fatalistic acceptance of the finality of Lazarus's death, his sister Martha nevertheless confessed her

---

[99]Matt. 13:18–23.
[100]Matt. 11:4–5.
[101]John 11:1–44.

belief in Jesus as the Messiah and in the promised resurrection on the last day. It is that confession which forms the focal point of the story, allowing Jesus to proclaim,

> I am the resurrection and the life. Whoever believes in me, though he die, yet shall he live, and everyone who lives and believes in me shall never die.[102]

Once that was clear, the miracle could follow on in due course because its real purpose was understood.

Closely connected to the miracles was Jesus' mission to subdue and defeat the demonic forces present in the world. The spiritual dimension of his ministry was understood by many people who saw him at work, even if their interpretation of his activities was wrong. Nicodemus recognized that Jesus must have come from God if he was doing such things, but his fellow Pharisees were less charitable. To them, the supernatural works of Jesus had to be diabolical because Jesus broke the law of Moses (at least as they understood it) and they could find no other explanation for his obvious powers.[103] Jesus did not hesitate to unmask their hypocrisy, and he even turned their accusation against them by telling them that it was they, and not he, who were the children of the Devil and were doing his will.[104] But the demons knew who they were up against and why. A man with an unclean spirit in him declared, "What have you to do with us, Jesus of Nazareth? Have you come to destroy us? I know who you are—the Holy One of God."[105] On another occasion, Jesus cured a demon-possessed man by casting the evil spirits out of him and sending them into a herd of pigs (unclean animals to begin with), which promptly went down into the Sea of Galilee and drowned.[106]

The spiritual significance of Jesus' earthly ministry culminates in the astonishing story of the transfiguration.[107] So strange is this account that some commentators have assumed it must have been a post-resurrection story that got transposed to the pre-resurrection phase of Jesus' life, though it would make little sense if that were the case. Jesus went up a mountain with Peter, James, and John, and there he was transfigured in their presence, revealing to them what his true glory was like. In the light of that event, the disciples saw Moses and Elijah, representing the law and the prophets, stand-

---

[102]John 11:25–26.
[103]Matt. 12:22–32.
[104]John 8:39–47.
[105]Mark 1:24.
[106]Mark 5:1–13; Luke 8:26–33.
[107]Matt. 17:1–8; Mark 9:2–8; Luke 9:28–36. See also 2 Pet. 1:16–18.

ing on either side of Jesus and speaking to him. This should remind us that it is only in the light of Christ than we can understand who Moses and the prophets were and why they had been sent into the world. It is also noteworthy that Moses and Elijah did not communicate with the disciples nor did the disciples speak to them—because their relationship was (and could only be) in and through Christ. Only in him can we understand what the Old Testament is all about, and only by him is its true character revealed.

The transfiguration also teaches us that, wonderful as the earthly revelation of Jesus was, it was not the whole story. When the disciples wanted to erect shrines to commemorate the event, Jesus prevented them from doing so because something greater was still to come. Many people today think it might have been better for us to have lived in the time of Jesus and to have known him during his life on earth. Jesus' reaction to his disciples' proposal suggests that there would have been no advantage to such firsthand experience. By no means did everyone who saw Jesus in the flesh recognize who he was, and many were deeply hostile to his message. But even those few who had some idea of what was going on were told that there was more and better still to come. We are not disadvantaged by not having seen Jesus with our own eyes. On the contrary, as Jesus told his disciples, we can do even greater things than they could because he has gone to the Father, and in the glory of his heavenly kingdom he has sent his Holy Spirit into our hearts.[108]

THE ATONING DEATH OF JESUS

Jesus did not sin, but on the cross he became sin for us.[109] What does this mean? It cannot be that there was any change in either of his natures. His human nature was subject to all the pressures we have to endure, but he did not succumb to them, and his divine nature could not be diminished or compromised by an external influence. Jesus did not become a sinner; thus his relationship with the Father was not affected. On the contrary, it was the fact that that relationship remained intact that made his atoning work on our behalf effective. Had Jesus sinned, that relationship would have been broken, and he would not have been able to make atonement for us. Sometimes people quote his words on the cross, "My God, my God, why have you forsaken me?" as evidence that his relationship with the Father had been cut off, if not by his sin, then by the Father's abandoning of him, but this is not an adequate explanation of this verse.[110]

---

[108]John 14:12–17.
[109]2 Cor. 5:21; Gal. 3:13.
[110]Matt. 27:46; Mark 15:24. See Ps. 22:1.

The words Jesus used were the opening line of Psalm 22, and it was customary to use the first line of a psalm as shorthand for the whole thing, as we often do with hymns today. If we read all of Psalm 22, we see that although it starts off looking like a cry of despair, it is in fact a hymn of victory and praise to God. But even if we do not want to press our interpretation that far, we must notice that in the moment of supreme crisis, Jesus addressed his words to his Father. Even in the depths of his desolation, Jesus is still speaking to him and calling him "My God." Someone who thought he had been abandoned would never have prayed like that. In these words, Jesus is expressing a relationship with the Father much deeper than what we commonly find in most people. It is easy to praise God and to relate to him when things are going well, but when trouble comes, it is a different matter. Many Christians feel that God has deserted them when they are afflicted, and cry out to him for an explanation of something they cannot understand. They may use words similar to those of Jesus on the cross, but if they do, it is because they are looking for God to explain something they cannot understand. In speaking this way, Jesus is demonstrating that he too feels the depths of human pain and suffering, and by identifying himself with people in such situations, he is reminding us that doubt and despair are not to be confused with loss of faith. On the contrary, they may be a way to strengthen faith by opening up a deeper level of connection with God that will only reveal its true strength once the storm clouds have passed.

Sin is not an objective thing that can be seen and measured, so to say that Jesus became sin for us does not mean that he looked any different from what he had been before. We can understand what this means only by using the analogy that he applied to himself, which was that of the Passover lamb. The lamb that was sacrificed for the sins of the people became sin for them, but it was not covered in blotches representing sins. On the contrary, it had to be completely free of blemish in order to be able to bear the burden of the people's sins.[111] If the lamb were less than perfect, someone might say that it was being sacrificed because of its own defects, but that was not true. It was not the lamb that was the problem but those for whom the lamb was dying. Exactly the same principle applies in the case of Jesus. He was not put to death for anything he had done wrong, but for the sins of those for whom he died.[112] His sinlessness exempted him from death and therefore made him suitable to be a sacrifice for the sins of others.[113]

---

[111]Ex. 12:5.
[112]1 Pet. 3:18.
[113]Heb. 10:11–14.

Jesus bore the punishment for our sins, took our place on the cross, and paid the price for us by his suffering and death. If he had not died for us, we would have had to die for our own sins, and would have been destroyed by their unbearable weight. Instead, we have been forgiven and promised that, just as Jesus was raised from the dead, we shall be raised with him to share in his eternal glory.[114] Those who protest that it was wrong of God the Father to send Jesus to his death have a point, because he had done nothing to deserve it. But before criticizing God for punishing Jesus, they should also protest that we have been unjustly spared our punishment because Jesus bore it for us. The death of Christ reveals to us the true nature of God, who does not condemn those whom he loves without providing the means to rescue them from condemnation. God's justice is balanced by his mercy and forgiveness, and nowhere is this more true than on the cross of Jesus Christ.

Furthermore, by dying for us, Jesus paid the price for our sins in a way that no lamb or other animal could ever have done.[115] By becoming a man, Jesus took on every part of our nature and therefore everything in us that is prone to sin or affected by it. He did not bear our sinfulness in the abstract but in a way that corresponds to every aspect of our being. There is no part of us that his atoning work does not include, and so our sinfulness is fully paid for by his death.[116] At the same time, Jesus also paid the price for every sin we have committed or can commit, and no sin is too great for him to be able to forgive it. In this respect, his atonement was universal—he died for the sins of the whole world. No one can claim (or complain) that he cannot be saved because he has sinned so much that the sacrifice of Jesus is unable to cover it. At the same time, however, Jesus came to lay down his life for his sheep,[117] and not every human being belongs to his flock. In that sense, his atoning work is restricted to those whom he claims as his own because it is effective only within the context of being called, chosen, and united to him.

Here there is an apparent paradox that many people have found hard to accept and impossible to resolve. How can the atoning work of Christ be limited to those who have been chosen when he has come to be the Savior of the whole world? The answer to this depends on how we look at the question. If we think in terms of sins, then Christ's atonement is universal because there is no sin too great for his blood to be able to forgive. But if we think in terms of sinners, then it is limited because not everyone is saved. The problem is knowing whether this limitation is imposed by God's immutable decree or

---

[114]Rom. 6:4–11.
[115]Heb. 10:4.
[116]Heb. 10:12.
[117]John 10:15.

whether it results from the voluntary refusal of human beings to take advantage of the offer of salvation. A little thought about this will show us that no one can come to Christ unless the Father draws him,[118] and so if a person fails to respond, it must ultimately be because God has not led that person to himself. Why this should be so is beyond our comprehension, but God cannot be blamed if not everyone is saved. As human beings, we have sinned against him and deserve nothing but his wrath and condemnation; the miracle is that anyone is saved at all, and for that we should be eternally thankful.

Nor can we say that the sacrifice of Christ failed to accomplish its appointed task. All those for whom Christ died are saved by his sovereign grace whether they want to be or not. It is foolish to think that we can resist the power of the God who made us, and to question his will is to rebel against him.[119] Those who accept this principle are faced with one of two choices. Either they can say that Christ died for everyone and so everyone is saved, whether they profess faith in him or not, or they can say that, since not everyone is saved, Christ did not die for everyone. The former option is popular among liberal theologians, who often use it as the basis for proclaiming universal reconciliation to God. They back this up by referring to what Paul told the Corinthians:

> As by a man came death, by a man has come also the resurrection of the dead. For as in Adam all die, so also in Christ shall all be made alive.[120]

According to their logic, every human being has died in Adam, and so every human being must be brought back to life in Christ. In a sense this is true, because the Bible does tell us that every human being will be raised from the dead when Christ comes again.[121] What they leave out, though, is that after the general resurrection will come the final judgment, when the sheep will be separated from the goats and only the former will be saved.[122] The Good Shepherd lays down his life for the sheep, not for the goats, even if the latter tag along hoping to sneak into the sheepfold without being noticed.[123]

Jesus assured his disciples that he had other sheep who were unknown to them, and that they too would have to be gathered in if the flock was to be complete,[124] but that is not the same thing as turning goats into sheep. Why

---

[118]John 6:44.
[119]Rom. 9:19–23.
[120]1 Cor. 15:21–22.
[121]John 5:29.
[122]Matt. 25:31–46.
[123]John 10:11, 14–15.
[124]John 10:16.

some people are sheep and others goats is unknown to us, but it will become clear at the end of time when all things are revealed. God knows those for whom Jesus Christ died, because they belong to him. Jesus said, "I was sent only to the lost sheep of the house of Israel,"[125] but the context in which he said this makes it clear that we do not always know who those lost sheep are. Jesus spoke those words to a Canaanite woman who would not have been regarded as a child of God by any of his disciples, but she showed such a degree of faith in him that he granted her the healing that she craved for her demon-possessed daughter. On another occasion, he reminded the Jews that Elijah was sent to a Phoenician widow in Zarephath and was told to help her in a time of famine, even though the famine had struck Israel just as hard. Later on, Elisha healed Naaman the Syrian of his leprosy, although there were also many lepers among the Jews at that time.[126] The lost sheep may be hidden from our eyes, but Jesus will not rest until every one of them is brought safely back into the sheepfold of his kingdom.[127] Hard though it may be for some people to accept, the message of Jesus is that some will be saved and others will be condemned, not just for what they have done but for what they are. That is why we speak of "limited" or "definite" atonement and why we can say that all the sheep, whether or not they have been gathered into the flock, will be saved in the end.

One question that often arises in connection with the satisfaction for sin that Jesus made for us concerns the ransom he paid on our behalf.[128] To whom has this ransom been given? In the early church, it was often assumed that it had been paid to the Devil, on the ground that a ransom is normally given to an enemy in order to secure the release of a hostage. As sinners, this argument goes, we have been held hostage by Satan, and in offering up his Son to death, God the Father bought Satan off and set us free. But in accepting the Son as payment for the release of the hostages, Satan was tricked into admitting his greatest enemy into his citadel, where the victorious Son of God promptly overthrew him and defeated the powers of hell once and for all. To people brought up on stories of the Trojan horse, that must have seemed like a particularly appealing interpretation, but it was not difficult to see its flaws, and it was soon being severely criticized. To trick anyone, even the Devil, was rightly regarded as unworthy of God. To pay him a ransom was to accord him a dignity he did not deserve and even to abdicate divine sovereignty. After all, since Satan was not a rival power but a subordinate who could not act without

---

[125] Matt. 15:24.
[126] Luke 4:25–27. See also 1 Kings 17:1 and 2 Kings 5:1–14.
[127] Luke 15:4–7.
[128] Matt. 20:28; Mark 10:45; 1 Tim. 2:6.

God's permission in the first place, paying him a ransom made little sense. The only person worthy to receive the ransom was God the Father himself, because it was his justice that had been offended by sin, and it was his decision as to who would be set free and who would not. Eventually, therefore, it was agreed that the Son paid the ransom to the Father, who then released those captured by sin, so that they might become citizens of the Son's new kingdom.

That answer is obviously closer to the truth than the theory that the ransom was paid to the Devil, but it probably needs to be refined somewhat further by reconsidering what exactly is meant by the term "ransom." It is not so much the underlying idea as it is the language used to describe it that is the problem. We need to understand the ransom as a satisfaction given to God for the sins that have cut us off from him. Our deliverance is not the result of a confrontation between the Son and the Father, but of a deep cooperation between them. Before he became a man, the Son of God chose to become a servant, giving up his claim to equality with the Father (even though he retained it) and voluntarily accepting the role of sacrificial victim.[129] Everything that the Son did as Jesus of Nazareth, he did in direct relation to the Father and the Father's will. As he constantly reminded his disciples, he had come to do the will of the one who had sent him, and his life and death cannot be understood in any other way.[130] It is in that sense and in that context that his death can be called a ransom, because it provided the means by which the Father's wrath was appeased, making the liberation of the captives possible.

The notion of the Father's wrath has disturbed many people, though once again the problem seems to be one of vocabulary as much as anything else. Some have objected that God cannot get angry because he is without passions of any kind. As they understand it, anger is a loss of self-control, and that cannot apply to God. Others have argued that any wrath in God would contradict his love, and therefore it cannot be present in him. Neither of these objections holds up when weighed against the evidence of the biblical texts. There, the "wrath of God" is not an emotional reaction to human sin but a just punishment which that sin deserves and must receive if it is to be taken seriously.[131] For God to have overlooked sin or wiped it out as if it did not matter would have been an abdication of his responsibility and a denial of his love for us. God rejects our sin because he values us and sees it as a barrier that we have erected against him.

In order to put our relationship with him right, God has to break that bar-

---

[129]Phil. 2:6–11.
[130]John 4:34, 5:30. See also Matt. 26:42.
[131]Rom. 1:18; 9:22; Col. 3:6; Heb. 3:11; 4:3.

rier down, which can be done only by removing it. If a child is buried beneath a pile of rubble, the zeal of the rescuers in removing the pile may be described as an expression of wrath against the rubble, and the pain of removing it will be felt by those engaged in saving the child. This is how we should look at the wrath of God against sin. He cannot tolerate it, and his wrath against it is the proof of his great love for us and of his determination to deliver us from the burden weighing us down. But unlike rubble on top of a child, sin is not something external to us but is a separation from God that makes us spiritually dead. If Christ becomes sin for us, then it must be expected that he will attract the wrath of God against that sin and will suffer the pain of death in consequence. That is not the end of the story, however, because even as Jesus shields us from the Father's wrath by taking it on himself and removing it, he is simultaneously delivering us from sin and restoring us to the fellowship with God that sin had broken. Jesus is not a barrier between God and man but the mediator, the one who reaches out to both sides in the estranged relationship and reconciles them to each other.[132]

Reconciliation between God and sinners is more than simple expiation for the sins of the sinners. Expiation was both possible and provided for under the Old Testament dispensation, with an elaborate sacrificial system designed to take away any number of particular sins and offenses. However, these sins kept recurring and therefore expiation had continually to be made, which is why there was an entire order of priests whose main task was to do just that. The death of Jesus Christ put an end to the need for constant expiation, not because the sinners he redeemed ceased to sin but because his sacrifice was sufficient for all eternity. As John put it,

> If we walk in the light, as he is in the light, we have fellowship with one another, and the blood of Jesus his Son cleanses us from all sin. If we say we have no sin, we deceive ourselves, and the truth is not in us. If we confess our sins, he is faithful and just to forgive us our sins and to cleanse us from all unrighteousness.[133]

There is no need for any repetition of Christ's sacrifice and no addition to it is either required or possible. This expiating power is available to us once we have been reconciled to God and have fellowship with him. Ideally we should not sin at all, but we are still human, and if we do sin, "we have an advocate with the Father, Jesus Christ the righteous. He is the propitiation for our

---

[132]1 Tim. 2:5; 2 Cor. 5:18–19.
[133]1 John 1:7–9.

sins."[134] It is our new relationship with God in Christ that makes him our advocate and gives us access to the Father, who in turn assures us that our sins will no longer count against us but are covered by the blood of the lamb who was slain for us.

JESUS' DESCENT INTO HELL

After Jesus died on the cross, he went down to hell. This is a very obscure event, as befits the nature of its subject. Hell is not something that we are meant to dwell on or even know much about because it is the home of Satan and of all who have rebelled against God. But neither can it be ignored. If Jesus had paid the price for our sins but not dealt with their ultimate cause, they would only have come back again sooner or later and his sacrifice would have lost its power to save. The root of sin is not to be found in our own will but in the rebellion of Satan, who tempted Adam and Eve into following him. They listened to him, so Satan claimed them (and through them, us also) as his own. When Jesus died on the cross, he paid the price for our rebellion against God, and that included the sufferings inflicted on us by Satan. But what about the possibility that Satan might try to reclaim us?

This is what the descent into hell is really all about. Jesus took his sacrifice on the cross to the depths of our rebellion against God, in order to show heaven and earth that the price of our deliverance had been paid and that the dominion of Satan over God's chosen people was at an end. Whether, and how far, Christ's descent affected those who were already in hell is another matter. In 1 Peter 3:18–20 we read that Christ was

> . . . put to death in the flesh but made alive in the spirit, in which he went and proclaimed to the spirits in prison, because they formerly did not obey, when God's patience waited in the days of Noah . . .

Exactly what this means is hard to say. If we take it literally, then Jesus went down to hell to preach to the rebellious spirits who were imprisoned there in the days of Noah. This presumably refers to those who were drowned in the flood, but why they should be singled out for particular attention is unclear. What about everyone else? Should they not have had a chance to hear the gospel as well? Perhaps we should understand Noah as the man who received God's promise that the sinful world would be preserved in spite of its wrongdoing. If we take it that way, then it may be that all those who died before

---

[134]1 John 2:1b–2a.

the coming of Christ were granted the chance to hear the gospel, though we cannot say how they responded to it if they did hear it.

The Bible says very little about those who die without any knowledge of Christ. We are told that those who sin without the law of Moses will be judged according to their own lights and not according to a law they have never heard of, but that is not the same thing as hearing the gospel. There is no suggestion that such people will be saved by the efforts of their own consciences.[135] If possession of the law condemns Jews because they invariably disobey it, there is little reason to suppose that ignorance of it will save Gentiles who can only guess at what right and wrong must be.

Another text that is sometimes quoted in relation to Christ's descent into hell is Ephesians 4:9, where Paul writes, "In saying 'He ascended,' what does it mean but that he had also descended into the lower regions, the earth?" This is a commentary on the previous verse, a quotation from Psalm 68:18, which says that when he ascended up on high "he led a host of captives." Some have interpreted this to mean that, when he descended to the dead, Jesus broke their bonds and set them free, leading them all up to heaven. Suffice it to say that there is no evidence to support such an interpretation, which seems fanciful and contrary to what the rest of the Bible teaches. There is much about Christ's descent into hell that remains a mystery, but we can be fairly confident that, although it entailed the final defeat of Satan, it was not the prelude to the universal salvation of mankind.

THE RESURRECTION OF JESUS

The resurrection of Jesus took place on the third day after his crucifixion.[136] By Jewish law, Jesus had to be buried before the Sabbath began, and it should come as no surprise that he spent the day of rest in the tomb. His resurrection on the first day of the week symbolizes the fact that he is the author of a new creation.[137]

Did the resurrection actually happen? The Gospels insist that it was a historical event and all four of them attest it. Those who went to the tomb on that Sunday morning found it empty, a fact that even those who refused to believe that Jesus had risen from the dead were forced to acknowledge.[138] The Gospel accounts are sufficiently different from each other in what they say about the resurrection that they do not represent a single narrative, which critics might argue had been concocted for propaganda purposes, but on the central point

---

[135]Rom. 2:12–16.
[136]By the inclusive reckoning common at that time, this meant the following Sunday (probably April 5, A.D. 33).
[137]2 Cor. 5:17; Gal. 6:15; Eph. 4:24; Col. 3:10.
[138]Matt. 28:11–15.

that Jesus came back from the tomb, they are all agreed. Moreover, there can be no doubt that those who claimed to have seen the risen Christ with their own eyes were prepared to brave persecution and martyrdom for that belief, which would be strange if they knew it were not true. The only disciple of Jesus who had any doubts was Thomas, and he was persuaded by a direct appearance of Jesus to him and to the others as well.[139] At least some of those who were present on that occasion were still alive when the account of it was written, so it would have been very difficult for John to have included the incident in his Gospel if both he and they knew that it had never happened.

The fact is that there were enough people who claimed to be eyewitnesses of Jesus' resurrection, and who were prepared to stake their lives on the truth of the events recounted in the Gospels, that the claims they made must be taken with the utmost seriousness. They had nothing to gain by lying. Given the reaction of the Jewish authorities, some of them might have made a considerable sum of money if they had been able and prepared to expose the whole thing as a fraud. But as we would say today, no one "broke rank," and those who saw Jesus after his resurrection remained firmly convinced and united in their testimony to the very end.

In more recent times, doubts about the resurrection have surfaced in liberal theological circles, but they have not gone unchallenged. On no other subject has the debate between believers and nonbelievers been so intense. It is fair to say that a conviction that Jesus rose bodily from the grave remains an indispensable tenet of Christian faith, even for those who are not otherwise orthodox. On this, more than on anything else, the truth or falsehood of Christianity has been made to depend, and rightly so, for as Paul put it,

> How can some of you say that there is no resurrection of the dead? But if there is no resurrection of the dead, then not even Christ has been raised. And if Christ has not been raised, then our preaching is in vain and your faith is in vain. We are even found to be misrepresenting God. . . . If Christ has not been raised, your faith is futile and you are still in your sins.[140]

The bodily resurrection of Jesus is an essential part of Christian belief because of the direct impact that it has on us as believers. It set the seal on Jesus' atoning work on the cross, which would not have been effective otherwise. Many people have died terrible deaths, but those deaths have had no saving effect on others. Jesus' death was intentional, but so was his resurrection because he died in order to put an end to death. His body did not decay in the tomb

---

[139]John 20:24–29.
[140]1 Cor. 15:12b–15a, 17.

but came back to life, and the promise is that one day we shall come back to life as well. In that sense, Christ's resurrection was a unique event only in historical time; at the end of time, we shall all be raised with our bodies and those who have believed in Christ will enter into eternal glory.[141] If Christ had not risen from the dead, that would be impossible, and the hope held out for us in heaven would be a delusion.

What was the resurrection body of Jesus like? After he rose from the dead it was transformed into a semi-heavenly state. It could appear and disappear at will but at the same time it was still possible for people to touch him,[142] and he was also able to eat.[143] It was also possible for him to pass unrecognized, as he did when he met Mary Magdalene near the tomb and she mistook him for a gardener, and when he spoke to Cleopas and his companion on the road to Emmaus.[144] He was not a phantom, but he could disappear and reappear at will, which no one with an ordinary human body can do.[145] A very significant feature of Christ's resurrection body was that it continued to bear the marks of his suffering and death. Nothing is said about this in Matthew's or Mark's accounts, and it is only alluded to indirectly by Luke,[146] but John is very specific about it.[147] Not only were the marks confirmation that the man who appeared to the disciples really was Jesus (and not an angel, for example) but they are also a reassurance that the price paid for our sins has not simply disappeared. It remains etched on the body of the risen Lord as proof that we have indeed been ransomed and redeemed for all eternity.

The semi-heavenly state that characterized Jesus' body after his resurrection was not permanent, and it would be transformed again at his ascension into heaven after forty days. But although it lasted only for a short time, it was not without its significance, for it was while he was in this transitional phase that Jesus gathered together his disciples and revealed to them the true meaning of his earthly ministry.[148] They had been with him for three years but understood hardly anything of what he had come to do. On the night that he was betrayed, they ran away, so little did they appreciate why this terrible event mattered and how deeply it would affect their eternal destiny. But rather than abandon them as they had abandoned him, Jesus came back and told them the meaning of the events they had witnessed (and had run away

---

[141]1 Cor. 15:52; 1 Thess. 4:16.
[142]Matt. 28:9; Luke 24:39; John 20:27.
[143]Luke 24:30; see also John 21:12–13.
[144]Luke 24:42–43; John 20:14.
[145]Luke 24:31, 36–39.
[146]Luke 24:40.
[147]John 20:20, 25–27.
[148]Luke 24:44–48.

from). During these last forty days of his earthly ministry, Jesus' disciples saw enough of his resurrection glory to be able to understand what his mission had been all about, and they were not left to figure it out for themselves. To the very end, Jesus interpreted himself to them, and did so by telling them that he was fulfilling Old Testament prophecy. After his ascension into heaven, the disciples would be empowered to proclaim the gospel message to others, but they did not need to have it explained any further to themselves because Jesus had already done that.

The very last thing Jesus did on earth was to commission his disciples for their mission.[149] He told them that all authority in heaven and on earth had been given to him, and that on that basis, his disciples were to go and preach the gospel to every nation, baptizing people for the forgiveness of their sins and teaching them to keep the commandments as Jesus had taught them to do. We know that the disciples could not do this immediately because, until he had ascended into heaven, had taken up his kingdom, and had sent the Holy Spirit to them, they would not be empowered to fulfill the charge he gave them.[150] But the main outlines of their future mission were established, and when that had happened, Jesus was free to return to his Father and bring his earthly mission to a triumphant conclusion around the throne of his heavenly grace.

THE ASCENSION AND HEAVENLY REIGN OF JESUS

When he ascended to heaven, Jesus took his humanity with him, complete with the scars of the wounds he had suffered. The ascension was an event witnessed by the disciples, who saw him go up into heaven and disappear out of their sight.[151] What difference, if any, did the ascension make to Jesus' resurrection body? The short answer to that question is that his body passed into a different dimension of reality. After his resurrection, Jesus remained on earth, and his body continued to manifest physical characteristics that we can recognize and identify with, even if it was no longer entirely like ours. In his ascension, however, that lingering attachment to the limitations of this world was removed and he entered into his heavenly glory.

At the time of the Reformation, there was a long and involved debate about the precise nature of this heavenly body of Jesus, a question that, despite its obscurity, continues to divide Lutherans from Reformed (or "Calvinist") Protestants to this day. The Lutherans argued that, because the body of Jesus

---

[149]Matt. 28:18–20.
[150]See Luke 24:49; Acts 1:4–5.
[151]Acts 1:9.

had been taken up into God, it must have acquired the characteristics of the divine nature, so that it is now to be found everywhere, just as God is. In other words, the ascended and glorified body of Christ is "ubiquitous." In answer to this, Reformed theologians, taking their cue from John Calvin, countered that a human body is by nature finite, and if it ceased to be so, it would no longer be a human body. They could not say how the body's finitude could coexist with the divine infinity in heaven, but they were convinced that it must do so. If it did not, they reasoned, the humanity of Christ would be merged into his divinity, the distinctiveness of his two natures would be lost, and our salvation, which depends on the mediating role of the man Christ Jesus, would dissolve and disappear into the infinite being of God.

Both of these views are true in what they affirm but neither is adequate to capture the fullness of the reality of the ascended Christ. On the one hand, his humanity has been preserved intact, but it is not so localized as to be inaccessible to those who are not in the right place at the right time. Anyone can know the presence of the risen, ascended, and glorified Christ wherever he may be, so in that sense his body may be said to be "ubiquitous." On the other hand, it remains a real body with all the definition and limitations which that word implies. Jesus spoke to Saul of Tarsus on the road to Damascus in his ascended body, though it is not clear whether Saul actually saw him in bodily form.[152] John also had a vision of him on the island of Patmos in which he appeared "like a son of man."[153] The context is so laden with symbolism that it could be argued that this should not be taken too literally, but the weight of the available evidence suggests that the Son of God can still be seen as incarnate in his heavenly glory. How this can be is a mystery that our finite minds cannot imagine or explain. Our eyes can see only what is finite, which his body must somehow be, but as he can appear anywhere at any time, it cannot be tied down to a single location or separated from the ubiquitous nature of God.

What similarity is there between the ascended body of Christ and our resurrection body? Will his glorified humanity carry over to us in any way? Paul tells us that when Christ returns those who are living on earth will "rise to meet [him] in the air," an expression which suggests that they will experience a transformation of their bodies and a kind of ascension into heaven at the same time.[154] Paul also tells us that "Christ has been raised from the dead, the firstfruits of those who have fallen asleep."[155] Our resurrection depends on

---

[152]Acts 9:3–5; 1 Cor. 15:8; see also Gal. 1:16.
[153]Rev. 1:13.
[154]1 Thess. 4:17.
[155]1 Cor. 15:20.

his, not as it was on the day he rose from the dead but as it is now, glorified in heaven. Jesus returned from the grave in a recognizable form, although not everyone who saw him immediately realized who he was. Even so, it is clear that he came back from the grave more or less as he had gone into it, as a man in his mid-thirties who was still bearing the wounds he had suffered on the cross. Will we return in the form in which we go down to the grave, or will we look different from that? Will we bear the scars caused by the wounds of our sufferings for Christ, or will they have vanished? It can be argued that Christ's wounds are still visible because he is our sacrifice, pleading for us in heaven. They have an ongoing purpose that makes their continuing visibility not only desirable but essential, but that will not be true of us in the same way. There may be some reason for us to go on bearing our scars as reminders of what we have suffered, but that might also lead to pride in our achievements and take us away from relying fully on what Christ has done for us. The arguments for keeping our scars in heaven must be weighed against those for leaving them behind in our earthly bodies, and no clear answer to this can be given.

However we conceive of it, the ascension of Christ completed the transformation of his body from its earthly to its heavenly state, and it remains that way. When he returns to earth at his second coming, his body will still be heavenly and will not reenter time and space as we know it. On the contrary, it is the earth that will be rolled away and cease to exist, being transformed or replaced by a new and heavenly creation.[156] The Lord of the universe will change the world to suit his heavenly body, not the other way around, and the whole creation will participate in the transformation of which his bodily ascension is the foretaste and prototype.

JESUS AS THE MEDIATOR OF A NEW COVENANT

In his ascended body, Jesus sat down at the right hand of the Father, who has entrusted him with the government of the kingdom he has obtained by the shedding of his blood—the assembled company of all those for whom he died.[157] The right hand is the hand of power, and symbolizes the authority that has been committed to the Son. That authority allows him to perform his ongoing work of mediation, using his sacrifice as the plea for the Father to forgive the sins which we continue to commit.[158] It is this aspect of Christ's work that is central to our life as Christians now, though few of us understand it properly. Some people have interpreted his words on the cross, "It is finished,"

---

[156]Rev. 21:1–4.
[157]Heb. 1:3; 8:1; 1 Cor. 15:25–28.
[158]1 John 2:1–2.

to mean that his work is done and that he is now at rest.[159] Whether or not these words from the cross are meant to signify the end of Christ's atoning work, we can agree that it was fully and finally accomplished by his death. But that does not mean that his work is at an end. It has been taken up into heaven, where he now intercedes for us in the Father's presence on the basis of his finished work on the cross.[160] Because of that, Paul is bold enough to say that nothing can now separate us from the love of God because, whatever trials and tribulations we may be subjected to in this life, we know that we are more than conquerors because of who he is and what he is doing for us in heaven.[161]

Finally, the mediatorial role of Christ is directly linked not only to the cross but also to the humanity that he assumed at his incarnation. Paul wrote, "There is one God, and there is one mediator between God and men, the *man* Christ Jesus."[162] It was in his manhood that the Son of God reconciled us to the Father. By becoming one of us, the Son made it possible for us to relate directly to him, but in doing that, we are put in a relationship with the Father that is analogous to his. It is because we have been grafted into the Son that we too have become sons, and that God has put his Son's Spirit in our hearts, crying "Abba! Father!"[163] Of course, we have to admit that even without the incarnation of the Son, we could have known something about God. It would have been possible to pray to him, to receive messages from him, and to do his will. All of these things were well known in ancient Israel and would have caused no problem. But the incarnation of Christ has given us a deeper relationship with God, one in which we know him as our Father because we have a brother who is his Son.

In Jesus Christ we see the fullness of the Godhead dwelling in a human body.[164] We can visualize him, conceptualize him, and feel that he is one of us, even though he is also the second person of the divine Trinity. The being of God that is beyond our comprehension has been made known to us in a way that we can understand and relate to. Furthermore, once the incarnation took place, it became a permanent feature of the Son's eternal, divine identity. We know that when the Son became a man, the Godhead was in no way diminished, and that in some mysterious fashion the Son continued to reign as Almighty God in heaven even as he was walking the earth as Jesus of Nazareth. Occasionally, we get glimpses of this in the Gospels, as when Jesus

---

[159]John 19:30.
[160]Rom. 8:34.
[161]Rom. 8:34–39.
[162]1 Tim. 2:5.
[163]Rom. 8:15; Gal. 4:6.
[164]Col. 2:9.

stilled the waves of the sea and walked on water, defying the laws of gravity because those laws were his to use or transcend as he chose.[165] What is more, he showed that he had the power to invite us to transcend the laws of gravity as well because he invited Peter to step out of the boat and walk on the waves with him. Peter failed in this attempt, but this failure was attributed to his lack of faith, not to the limitations of his human nature.

The power of faith in us is the power to move mountains—to do things that are impossible with man but not with God.[166] The mediatorial role of Christ must therefore include the extension of certain divine powers and prerogatives to us in the measure that we are united to him in faith. This is a truly glorious concept and makes it possible for us to say that we have a victory over the forces that assail us that no power on earth can resist or overcome. The means by which this is achieved is the indwelling presence of the Holy Spirit in our hearts, and it is to the sending and work of that Spirit that we must now turn.

---

[165]Matt. 8:27; 14:22–33; Mark 4:41; 6:45–51; John 6:15–21.
[166]Matt. 14:31; 17:20; 19:26; 21:21; Mark 9:23; 10:27; 11:23.

PART SIX

THE CONSUMMATION OF GOD'S LOVE

27

THE SENDING
OF THE
HOLY SPIRIT

THE PREPARATION FOR HIS COMING

The benefits of Christ's atonement and his righteousness are communicated to us by the presence of the Holy Spirit in our lives. By sending his Holy Spirit into the world, God the Father has fulfilled his promises to us and applied the work of his Son in the lives of his chosen people. This took place at the feast of Pentecost, fifty days after the resurrection of Jesus and ten days after his ascension into heaven, when God poured out his Spirit on the disciples.[1] The timing is significant, because the Holy Spirit did not come until the Son was seated in his heavenly glory. It was the ascension of Jesus that marked the transition from his earthly and temporal work to his heavenly and eternal mediation at the Father's right hand. This is why it is the ascension, and not Pentecost, that is the last event recorded in the Gospels and the first in the Acts of the Apostles. The coming of the Spirit is set firmly in the context of the heavenly reign of Christ, whose ambassador he is. The Holy Spirit did not come into the world to draw people to himself, as Jesus did,[2] but to confirm the truth of Jesus' message by making it come alive in our hearts. He sustains it in us so that we may be increasingly conformed to the likeness of Christ.[3]

The Bible does not explain why Pentecost was chosen as the date for this event to take place, but as it marked the end of the harvest of the later grains and was the day of the firstfruits, when the loaves made from those grains

---

[1]Acts 2:1–4.
[2]See John 12:32.
[3]Rom. 8:29. See also 1 Cor. 2:14–16.

were offered on the altar, the timing seems appropriate.[4] Paul picked up the symbolism of the firstfruits as a description of the indwelling presence of the Holy Spirit in the lives of believers, who are waiting expectantly for the redemption of our bodies as part of the new creation, so it seems that this connection was accepted in the early church as the reason why the Spirit came when he did.[5]

Pentecost has sometimes been compared to the incarnation of the Son because it marked the coming of another person of the Trinity into the world, but the parallel is not exact. The Son came to fulfill the promises made to Israel and to bring an end to the sacrificial system laid down in the law of Moses, but the Holy Spirit came to confirm that work, not to modify or extend it. Pentecost is therefore not to be understood as the beginning of a new era in the life of God's people that would take them beyond the gospel of Christ, but as the application of what Jesus had already done. The pattern for this had been set by Jesus before his crucifixion, when he told his disciples that he would confirm their love for him with this special gift:

> I will ask the Father, and he will give you another Helper, to be with you forever, even the Spirit of truth, whom the world cannot receive because it neither sees him nor knows him. You know him, for he dwells with you and will be in you.[6]

From this statement we learn that the Holy Spirit will come from the Father, but at the Son's request. When the Holy Spirit comes, says Jesus, he and the Father will also come and all three will dwell in the hearts of his disciples forever.[7] The coming of the Spirit is therefore a coming of the Trinity, just as the incarnation of the Son was also a revelation of the Father.[8]

The Holy Spirit is the Spirit of truth. There can be no love without the truth, as we are frequently reminded in the New Testament,[9] which is why the Spirit comes to convict the world of sin, of righteousness, and of judgment.[10] There can be no compromise of this tough message because to dilute it is to lie. "If we say we have no sin, we deceive ourselves, and the truth is not in us."[11] The work of the Holy Spirit could hardly be stated more clearly than that. Finally, Jesus tells his disciples that the world will not receive the Spirit or

---

[4]Ex. 23:16; Lev. 23:17; Num. 28:26.
[5]Rom. 8:22–23.
[6]John 14:16–17.
[7]John 14:18, 23.
[8]John 14:9.
[9]Eph. 4:15; 2 Thess. 2:10; 1 Pet. 1:22; 1 John 3:18; 2 John 1, 3; 3 John 1.
[10]John 16:8.
[11]1 John 1:8.

understand him because it is blind to who he is and what he has come to do. This may be the ultimate proof that the Spirit has come to continue Christ's work, because exactly the same was true of Jesus when he came. In the words of Jesus to Nicodemus,

> This is the judgment: the light has come into the world and people loved the darkness rather than the light because their deeds were evil. For everyone who does wicked things hates the light and does not come to the light, lest his deeds should be exposed.[12]

When the Spirit of truth came, Jesus told his disciples, he would teach them everything they needed to know and remind them of the things that Jesus had said to them during his earthly ministry.[13] As he put it,

> I still have many things to say to you, but you cannot bear them now. When the Spirit of truth comes, he will guide you into all the truth, for he will not speak on his own authority, but whatever he hears he will speak, and he will declare to you the things that are to come. He will glorify me, for he will take what is mine and declare it to you. All that the Father has is mine; therefore I said that he will take what is mine and declare it to you.[14]

Here Jesus reinforces the teaching role of the Spirit and defines its nature. We have the result of that work in the New Testament, the collected deposit of Christ's teaching that was retained by subsequent generations as the pillar and foundation of our faith.[15] What the Spirit teaches belongs to the Son, and the Son belongs to the Father. Everything he says is of God and about God because it is the name and work of God that he comes to glorify.

This is an important test because it is possible to receive a spiritual message that does not come from the Holy Spirit. Today we are prone to make this mistake because we tend to assume that whatever is "spiritual" must be of God, but that is not so. As John warned his people,

> Beloved, do not believe every spirit, but test the spirits to see whether they are from God, for many false prophets have gone out into the world. By this you know the Spirit of God: every spirit that confesses that Jesus Christ has come in the flesh is from God, and every spirit that does not confess Jesus is not from God. This is the spirit of the Antichrist, which you heard was coming and now is in the world already.[16]

---

[12] John 3:19–20.
[13] John 14:26.
[14] John 16:12–15.
[15] 1 Tim. 3:15; 2 Tim. 1:13.
[16] 1 John 4:1–3.

We are warned not to be deceived, and the litmus test is belief in the incarnation of the Son of God. That is what the Holy Spirit will speak to us about, and if that is denied, then the voice we are hearing is not his. In the modern world, where there is great tolerance in spiritual matters and little discernment, this message is more needed than ever if we are to avoid being led astray by a spirit that has not come from God.

THE HOLY SPIRIT AND THE CONVERSION OF GOD'S PEOPLE

The sending of the Holy Spirit at Pentecost inaugurated a new era in the life of God's people. We cannot say that he was not working in the lives of believers before then, and the depth of spiritual experience found in the Old Testament strongly suggests that he was, but the outpouring at Pentecost made a difference that was understood as fulfilling the prophecies about what would happen at the end of time:

> In the last days it shall be, God declares, that I will pour out my Spirit on all flesh, and your sons and your daughters shall prophesy, and your young men shall see visions, and your old men shall dream dreams; . . . And it shall come to pass that everyone who calls upon the name of the Lord shall be saved.[17]

The first great work that the Holy Spirit began was the work of converting Christ's chosen people to a living faith. It is notoriously difficult to say when the disciples of Jesus became believers, and it seems that some still had their doubts even after his resurrection.[18] Presumably, they must have believed something in order to give up their previous lives and follow him, but it is far from clear what that was or how deep it went. Peter was given enough insight to be able to confess that Jesus was the Son of God, but he also denied Christ on the night of his betrayal, and it was not until after the resurrection that he was reconciled to him.[19] Can we speak of him or of the other disciples as being "Christians" before this time? It is not for us to judge what the spiritual state of the disciples was at any given moment, and we must remain silent on a matter not explained in the Gospels. But whatever may have been the case before Pentecost, there can be no doubt that the disciples of Jesus were Christians in the fullest sense of the word after that. From then on, there was no more doubting or falling away, and they were equipped to be the foundation of the Christian church.[20]

---

[17]Acts 2:17, 21, quoting Joel 2:28–29, 32.
[18]Matt. 28:17.
[19]Matt. 16:13–18; 26:69–75; John 21:15–19.
[20]Eph. 2:20.

The first thing that the Holy Spirit does in a person's life is to convict him of sin, the root of which is unbelief.[21] It is, however, possible to assent to the facts of the gospel and to have a high view of Jesus Christ and the Bible, even to admit to being a sinner, without being truly convicted of sin. Conviction is more than mere knowledge. It is a firm persuasion that something must be done about our sin because knowing the truth about ourselves makes continuing to live our former lives intolerable. To be convicted of sin does not mean that a person will know every sin that he has committed or even fully realize how serious sin is. These are aspects of the matter that grow and develop over time, as we come to understand the depths of our own sinfulness more clearly. What is essential at the beginning is the knowledge that the presence of sin in our lives is unbearable and that there is no escape from it other than in and through Jesus Christ. As long as a person thinks that he has his faults under control and that he can deal with them as required, there is no conviction of sin, and therefore no deep work of the Holy Spirit in him.

Conviction of sin brings with it an understanding of righteousness—both what it is and how it can be obtained. The standard for human behavior is the one set by Jesus Christ and modeled by him.[22] Without his teaching and example, we would not be able to understand what righteousness is in practical terms. The ancient Israelites understood what righteousness was because they had the law of God, but since they could not keep the law, they could not obtain that righteousness for themselves.[23] By his incarnation, the Son of God brought divine righteousness into the world and made it known. To know what righteousness is, however, is one thing; to acquire it for oneself is quite another. How can a believer obtain something that is essentially alien to his nature and beyond his ability to achieve?

The answer is that righteousness can be acquired only by God's free gift of himself to us. This free gift is a work of the Holy Spirit in our hearts and is called "grace."[24] Grace is the foundation of the Christian life. Without God's grace we could not exist, let alone do anything that would win his favor. But although everyone agrees about this, there have been great differences about the ways and means by which this grace is given to us, and about what it means to have or to become the "righteousness of God."[25]

The first thing we must decide is what grace actually is. Is it a thing that can be objectified, quantified, dissected, and analyzed into various kinds of

---

[21] John 16:8–9.
[22] 1 Cor. 11:1.
[23] Rom. 2:12–24; 7:7–24; Gal. 3:10–14.
[24] Eph. 2:8.
[25] 2 Cor. 5:21.

grace, with designations like prevenient, cooperating, sufficient, and efficient? Can it be poured or infused into a person like a liquid, conveyed or imparted like a legacy, or reckoned or imputed like an entitlement? These questions have been hotly debated in the past and they need to be answered if we are to understand how the Holy Spirit works in God's people.

First of all, it must be understood that God's grace is the fruit of his love. It is because he loves us that he has extended his favor to us and has done for us what is needed to bring us back into his presence as his children.[26] It is not a thing, any more than love is a thing. Rather, it is God's action toward us that flows from a relationship he has with us that is governed by his love. Like love, grace is an abstract term used to describe something that we experience in a relational context, apart from which it is meaningless. Our relationship with God must begin with his grace toward us because he is our Creator. Even if we had never done anything wrong, the initiative in establishing that relationship would still be his because of who he is and who we are in relation to him. If he has decided to raise us above the state of our nature or that of the sinfulness into which we have fallen, it is because of his goodness and free will, and it does not depend on us in any way.[27]

Because we are personal beings created in the image and likeness of God, we are naturally capable of receiving his love and of responding to it. But because we have broken our relationship with God as his creatures, we cannot respond to him now unless and until what is broken in us has been repaired. That is what the Holy Spirit comes to do in our lives. By convicting us of our sin, he shows us what is wrong with us, persuades us that something must be done about it, and then does what is necessary. The Bible describes this as replacing a heart of stone with a heart of flesh, as being born again into a new life.[28] But this new life has no autonomous existence of its own; it is made possible only by the indwelling presence of Jesus Christ in his Holy Spirit.[29] When we say that we have been made the righteousness of God, we are not talking about a transformation of our created nature into something resembling the substance of God, but about the subduing of that nature by the power of God at work in us. There is no righteousness apart from his, and we cannot claim to have any righteousness that is not the result of his presence in us. For that reason it is possible for a believer to be righteous only if he is united with Christ and living Christ's life instead of his own.[30]

---

[26] John 3:16.
[27] Rom. 9:14–29.
[28] Ezek. 11:19; 36:26; John 3:7; Rom. 6:4.
[29] Gal. 4:6.
[30] Gal. 2:20.

It follows from this that righteousness is deeply relational and subjective. As an objective reality, it can exist only in God, but even in him it is not so much a thing in itself as a description of God's character. We can never be or become righteous in the sense that God is, and it is here that so much of the theological argument has been concentrated. Those who talk about infused or imparted righteousness believe that a real transformation of the human being is not only possible but is actually achieved by the working of the Holy Spirit in us. Depending on a number of factors ranging from the will of God to the disposition of the human recipient of grace, this righteousness may increase or decrease over time in any one individual and will be present to varying degrees in the different members of the church. This is the way the matter has often been viewed, but there is no basis for this view in the New Testament. For a human being to be righteous is to be in the right relationship with God, who is our righteousness, whether or not we have done anything to deserve it.

Much the same is true of sanctification, which is often viewed as a process in which grace increases over time, bringing greater righteousness along with it. But this is not possible. The righteousness of God cannot be transferred to human beings. If it is imputed to us by the sacrifice Christ made for us, that sacrifice does not increase over time and neither does the imputation of it to us. Sanctification is something we are called to work out in our daily lives, but we can do that only with the help of the Holy Spirit at work in us; we do not become better or more skillful people in our handling of some quantity of righteousness or grace that has been given to us.

In the end, when we talk about an "increase" of these things in the life of the believer, what we are really talking about is a deepening of our love for God.[31] His love for us cannot increase because it is total already, but our love for him can and does mature as we go on in the Christian life. A couple who have been married for forty years are not "more married" than they were on their honeymoon, but the marriage has matured and deepened over time, through shared struggles and experiences. So it is in our relationship with God. We are not more "born again" forty years after our conversion than we were at the beginning, but from living it out we have learned something more of what it means. Far from improving as human beings, what we discover about ourselves is just how irredeemably sinful we are and how much we need the grace of God to be at work in our lives. When we get to heaven we shall be fully united with him, that dependence will be complete, and God will be "all in all" in our lives.[32]

---

[31] 1 Thess. 3:12.
[32] 1 Cor. 15:28.

THE HOLY SPIRIT AND THE MISSION OF GOD'S PEOPLE

The pouring out of the Holy Spirit on the disciples was not the only fruit of Pentecost. It was also the occasion when Peter stood up with the other disciples to preach their new faith and three thousand people were converted. From the beginning, the presence of the Holy Spirit in the lives of believers has brought with it an evangelistic imperative—he has come to empower those who have been called and chosen for salvation to preach the gospel of Christ to the ends of the earth.

This mission was symbolized by the fact that the disciples were given the ability to speak in other languages, so that the pilgrims who were in Jerusalem for the festival would understand what they had to say, no matter where they came from. The text does not say so explicitly, but it has generally been assumed that Pentecost marked a reversal of what had happened at the Tower of Babel, where the languages of the nations were confused and people could no longer understand one another.[33] The New Testament records that speaking in tongues also occurred on later occasions, but the contexts are somewhat exceptional. For instance, when Peter went to Caesarea Philippi to preach the gospel to the centurion Cornelius, it is recorded that the Holy Spirit fell on everyone who heard him and that they all began to speak in tongues.[34] However, we must remember that Peter was very reluctant to go to Cornelius because he was a Gentile, and the phenomenon may have been meant to reinforce the message that the gospel was for Gentiles as well as for Jews. On another occasion, the same thing happened at Ephesus when Paul discovered that the disciples there had never even heard of the Holy Spirit. Once again, speaking in tongues seems to have reinforced the reality and importance of the sending of the Spirit for mission, and it is possible that the same thing happened in Samaria, though nothing is said about tongues on that occasion.[35] It would appear that although the gift of tongues was significant, it was not essential to the Holy Spirit's mission, and there is no mention of it among any New Testament fellowship of believers other than those cited in Ephesus, Corinth, and possibly Samaria.

At the same time, there are clear statements that the mission strategy of the first Christians was guided by the Spirit on a day-to-day basis, since he regularly told the apostles what to do and occasionally altered the plans they had made.[36] In the nature of the case, it is impossible to apply what happened

---

[33]Gen. 11:7.
[34]Acts 10:46.
[35]Acts 19:6; 8:14–17.
[36]Acts 10:19–20; 16:6.

to the apostles in a straightforward way because their circumstances were very different from ours, although like them, we also must be open to the Spirit's leading and guidance. The Spirit is sovereign and does what he pleases; our duty is to hear and obey the voice of his prompting when it comes to us. But however this works out in specific instances, we know that it is always the Holy Spirit's purpose to spread the Word of God and the message of salvation that it contains.[37] The church exists to further that aim, whose ultimate goal is the consummation of God's love in the kingdom of heaven.

How can we tell whether a particular development in church life is a work of the Holy Spirit? This is a very touchy subject today because so many people claim that what they think, say, or do is directed by the Spirit, which makes it almost impossible to criticize. What principles are there to help us decide whether a particular voice or initiative is of the Lord? In the Roman Catholic Church, and to a lesser extent in Eastern Orthodoxy, it is always possible to appeal to the authority of the pope or church hierarchy, who are supposed to be able to answer that question. But even there, history has shown that there have been movements of the Spirit of God that have met with opposition from the institutional church itself. In some cases, like that of Francis of Assisi, that opposition was eventually overcome and the new wave of spirituality was integrated into the existing church structures, but in other cases, notably at the time of the Protestant Reformation, that did not happen. Would anyone today be bold enough to claim that the papacy was right to condemn Martin Luther? If that was a mistake, how are we to trust the pope's judgment on anything else?

Within the Protestant world there is often wide latitude given to individual initiative, and there are any number of missions and ministries that have been started by people who felt that God was leading them to do so. We are more likely to hear about the success stories than we are to hear about the failures, but there have been a great many false starts, and those who are cautious in the face of private enthusiasms often have good reason to be so. The New Testament does not address this issue directly, but from what it says about the common life of the church there are certain principles that can be laid down.

First of all, the content of the gospel must not be altered. If anyone comes preaching a different gospel from the one found in the New Testament, he is to be rejected, even if he appears to have the authority of an angel from heaven.[38] This is of particular relevance in the so-called "mainline" Protestant churches, where in recent years bishops, theologians, and synods have promoted ideas

---

[37] 1 Cor. 12:13.
[38] Gal. 1:8.

and policies that are clearly incompatible with the Word of God. Christians in those churches have no option but to reject such teaching; they cannot defer to any human authority that goes against revealed truth.

Secondly, the witness of the church must not be brought into disrepute by internal disruption and disorder.[39] If a new initiative is generating more heat than light, it is probably wrong, even if it can be theologically justified. In the early church, there were those who had no problem eating meat that had been sacrificed to idols, while others had conscientious objections to doing so. Paul sided with the former in principle but told them that it was more important to accommodate the "weaker brethren" than to press their own beliefs to the point where the church would be divided on a matter of secondary importance.[40]

Finally, the Holy Spirit does not guide us in ways that would cause us to interfere with the missionary work of others. Some people have felt led to plant new churches in places where there is already a flourishing gospel witness, with the result that unnecessary division and duplication is created. Paul understood this problem and declared to the Romans that he had no intention of building on someone else's foundation.[41] If God was calling him to mission, then it would be to the extension of the church into places that remained unreached. In our fallen world, there will always be difficulties and hard choices to make. Should Protestant missionaries work in Latin America, for example, where the people are historically Roman Catholic, even though that church has often barely penetrated below the surface in its evangelistic efforts? Can we work within the existing structures, or do they force us to start something new? What are the limits of cooperation that we should aim for when dealing with those who differ from us? Sincere believers will sometimes give different answers to such questions and try to resolve the difficulties posed by them in different ways, but if we keep the basic principles in view, there is at least a chance that we shall be able to overcome such potential sources of conflict and work together for the ongoing mission of the Holy Spirit to present the claims of Christ to a dying world.

---

[39]1 Cor. 14:40.
[40]Rom. 14:20–23.
[41]Rom. 15:20.

28

THE CHRISTIAN LIFE

CHOSEN FOR SALVATION

To be a Christian is to know that you have been chosen by God. We cannot fathom his mind to know why we have been singled out, and since there is no visible or earthly criterion that has determined his choice, we cannot guess either. Jesus told his disciples that when he returned in glory, two people would be working side by side, and one would be taken and the other left.[1] The same principle applies to faith now. Two people may hear the gospel, but one repents and believes while the other does not. The circumstances and the message are the same, but the will of God draws one to himself and leaves the other behind, for reasons that we cannot know. Some people think that this is unfair of God, but to them Paul replies,

> Who are you, O man, to answer back to God? Will what is molded say to its molder, "Why have you made me like this?" Has the potter no right over the clay, to make out of the same lump one vessel for honorable use and another for dishonorable use? What if God, desiring to show his wrath and to make known his power, has endured with much patience vessels of wrath prepared for destruction, in order to make known the riches of his glory for vessels of mercy, which he has prepared beforehand for glory?[2]

Those who have been chosen by God know that they are unworthy of their calling and may well feel that others deserve it more than they do. But God's choice does not work on the basis of what we deserve because, if it did, no one would be saved. God reaches out to us and saves us by an act of his will that depends on nothing but his love for us. We have no idea why he has chosen us,

[1]Matt. 24:40–41; Luke 17:34–36.
[2]Rom. 9:20–23.

and we cannot say that he has rejected others because he does not love them. As the above passage suggests, the way he loves them is different from the way he loves us because he created them for a different purpose. If those who have been condemned have no right to complain, how can those who have been saved question the will of God?

To be chosen for salvation is a privilege, not a right, and if we presume on it there is a real possibility that it will be taken away from us.[3] The ancient Israelites thought they were safe because they were God's covenant people, but he rejected them and chose Gentiles to take their place. We have the assurance that nothing can separate us from the love of God and that we cannot lose our salvation,[4] but we also know that we cannot presume on his love. There is a mystery here that defies logical analysis but makes sense in the context of a living relationship. To know God and to love him is to understand how undeserving we are of the grace that has been given to us. Being sinful creatures, we may try to rebel against God, but he soon shows us how disastrous the consequences of such rebellion would be if it were successful, and he draws us back to himself.

Those who have been chosen for salvation also know that they really had no choice but to respond to God's call when it came. God has commanded everyone to repent, but those who do not hear and obey that command cannot be saved.[5] When Jesus called his disciples, they dropped what they were doing and followed him immediately. People who made excuses were turned away because they were not fit for the kingdom of God, and the same will happen to us if we behave the way they did.[6] As with Saul of Tarsus on the road to Damascus, meeting with Christ is an overwhelming experience that makes nonsense of the notion of "choice," even as it sets us free. In that sense, it is like falling in love, which is not a "choice" either, but which uplifts our spirit and frees our will to honor and serve the one whom we love. If that is true in human terms, how much more will it be true of the love of God?

Those whom God has saved also know that they have been chosen for a purpose. Salvation is not a reward for services rendered, nor is it comparable to winning a lottery. It is something that we have been given, and that we are called to work out "with fear and trembling" because it is God who is at work in us in order to fulfill his will and purpose.[7] There is no such thing as early retirement in the Christian life!

---

[3] Rom. 11:17–24.
[4] Rom. 8:38–39.
[5] Acts 17:30.
[6] Luke 9:62.
[7] Phil. 2:12–13; 2 Pet. 1:10.

Knowing that you have been chosen by God is a humbling experience, and humility is the chief hallmark of the Christian. It is a humility that gives us spiritual authority to proclaim the Word of God without fear because we are not furthering our own interests but the glory of Jesus Christ our Savior. This is well illustrated by Paul, who did not hesitate to call himself "the least of all saints" and the "foremost" of sinners, despite his high calling from God to preach the gospel and the honor in which he was held by all those touched by his ministry.[8] After rebuking the Corinthians for their spiritual immaturity and laying down the law as an apostle, Paul wrote,

> I am the least of the apostles, unworthy to be called an apostle, because I persecuted the church of God. But by the grace of God I am what I am, and his grace toward me was not in vain. On the contrary, I worked harder than any of them, though it was not I, but the grace of God that is with me.[9]

In those words breathes the spirit of a man who knows what it means to be chosen by God. Our sins may be different from Paul's, but the grace of God toward us is the same, and it is by that grace, not by our own efforts, that we are called to serve and please him now.

To know the grace of God is to submit to his authority in our lives. Even Jesus had to learn obedience to his Father's will, and that took him to his death on a cross for our sake.[10] As servants we are not greater than our Master, and we may be sure that if he was forced to bear his cross, we shall have to bear ours, and we shall have to do it on a daily basis.[11] Obedience is the hardest thing any Christian has to learn. Perhaps we can say that we know we have learned obedience only when God calls us to do something we do not want to do and we submit to his will because we know it is the right thing to do. Jesus did that in the garden of Gethsemane. He prayed that the suffering he would have to endure on the cross might be taken away from him, but after a spiritual struggle so severe that he sweated blood,[12] he surrendered his human will to his Father. For Jesus' sake, we are called to surrender everything, and as his example shows us, the cost of that surrender may be high indeed.

The spiritual struggles we are called to wage may be fierce, and there will be times when we shall long to run away and seek a quiet life. But being chosen by God means that he will not let us go. Jonah tried to escape, but God intervened and ensured that Jonah would fulfill his prophetic vocation, even

---

[8]Eph. 3:8–9; 1 Tim. 1:15.
[9]1 Cor. 15:9–10.
[10]Heb. 5:8.
[11]Luke 9:23.
[12]Luke 22:44.

though he was never fully reconciled to it.[13] The child of God knows this only too well. Every time we run away from God, his loving hand reaches out and brings us back because none of his sheep will be lost, however hard they try to get away.[14] We cannot pretend that this is an enjoyable experience; very often it is not. We may be angry with God for thwarting our desires. We may feel frustrated because we cannot do what we want. We may think we have been unfairly treated because we have not been given what we believe we are entitled to. In purely human terms, there may be some justification for those feelings, and those around us may even encourage us to believe that we have been treated unfairly. But God knows those who are his, and they know it too. In our heart of hearts we understand that these afflictions are part of his Fatherly chastening—so that we may prove to be worthier and more fruitful servants.[15]

Finally, to be chosen by God for salvation is to be set apart from the world around us. This separation is not physical but spiritual, which makes it harder to achieve. If all we had to do as Christians was to go into a monastery and lock ourselves away, it would be relatively simple. But living the Christian life means being in the world but not of it, and that is hard.[16] We have to turn away from the world's way of thinking and put on the mind of Christ, which is easy to say but very difficult to do.[17] Our priorities and our value systems must change, our interests must be transformed, and our sense of purpose in life must be radically altered by the work of the Holy Spirit in our lives. When we love God we must put him first, and that is bound to set us at odds with a world that does not love God or even know him. Those whom God has chosen will soon learn the pain of that separation, but we will also know that we have no choice—the Master has called, and we must obey and be grateful to him for having shown us such great love and consideration.

CALLED IN HOPE

Those who are chosen by God are called to suffer with Christ, but this suffering is not without hope. Hope is a major biblical theme and fundamental to the covenant God has given us in his Word, although it tends to be emphasized in some contexts more than in others. In the Old Testament, the theological use of the word is largely confined to the Wisdom literature (Job, Psalms, Proverbs, Ecclesiastes) and Jeremiah (including Lamentations). In the New Testament

---

[13]Jonah 4:1–3.
[14]Rom. 8:38–39.
[15]Deut. 8:5; Prov. 13:24; Heb. 12:6–7.
[16]John 17:11–16; 1 John 2:15–16; 2 Pet. 1:4.
[17]Col. 2:20–23.

it is used almost exclusively by Paul, in Hebrews, and in 1 Peter. Somewhat surprisingly, perhaps, it is not found at all in the Gospels, and only once in the Johannine literature.[18] Even so, the texts where the word "hope" occurs give us a clear idea of its importance. Paul mentions Abraham, saying that he hoped against all hope, believing that he would become the father of many nations even though his wife was past childbearing age.[19] Hope was therefore at the very foundation of the covenant, which cannot be understood without it.

Most of the other biblical passages about hope speak either about the "hope of Israel" or about those who had no hope, either because they were Gentiles or because they were disobedient Israelites. Paul describes the Ephesians in terms that make this perfectly clear:

> Remember that you were . . . separated from Christ, alienated from the commonwealth of Israel and strangers to the covenant of promise, having no hope and without God in the world.[20]

It was in the Psalms that Israel expressed its hope in God most clearly and frequently—no fewer than twenty-six times, in fact—which is particularly appropriate, since the Psalter was the hymnbook of the Jewish people. It was in their worship of God that they expressed themselves freely, reminding each other that God was their only hope of salvation:

> O Israel, hope in the LORD!
>   For with the LORD there is steadfast love,
>   and with him is plentiful redemption.
> And he will redeem Israel from all his iniquities.[21]

The hope of Israel was ultimately a trust in God's steadfast love for his people, whom he would not abandon to the destruction that he was going to unleash on the surrounding nations. Israel would be uprooted and tested almost beyond endurance, but even in the depths of despair, the prophet Jeremiah was still able to cry,

> O LORD, the hope of Israel,
>   all who forsake you shall be put to shame;
> those who turn away from you shall be written in the earth,
>   for they have forsaken the LORD, the fountain of living water.[22]

---

[18] 1 John 3:3.
[19] Rom. 4:18.
[20] Eph. 2:12.
[21] Ps. 130:7–8.
[22] Jer. 17:13. See also Lam. 3:21–30, which expresses the same idea at greater length.

This was the "hope of Israel" that Paul proclaimed had been realized in the coming of Jesus Christ.[23] As Paul understood it, the essence of this hope was resurrection from the dead, something that Jesus had brought about in his own life and that he subsequently promised to his followers. Resurrection hope was not new to Israel, but what had previously been a vague and contested belief was focused and made real in and by Jesus.[24] Believing in Jesus made hope come alive. On the basis of that hope, we experience the love of God in our hearts, and it changes our lives.[25] Hope produces a concrete change of attitude and perspective, giving us an entirely new perspective on the future. Most world religions and civilizations have operated on the belief that the past was better than the present and the future will only be worse. Even today, it is by no means uncommon to hear such a pessimistic view expressed both by ordinary people and by many so-called "futurologists," who paint various scenarios of Doomsday and Armageddon. From a purely material standpoint, it is hard to see how they can do anything else, because even if life gets better in the short term, in the long run the universe will run out of energy and implode, an event that will make everything we do now seem trivial and meaningless by comparison.

It is not always understood that the belief in a better future that so pervades Western thinking nowadays is the product of centuries of Christian instruction. In recent times, its leading exponents have dispensed with God and claimed that they can bring about the desired improvements by their own efforts, but the likelihood of their succeeding is not great. The twentieth century was the classical age of idealistic utopianism, but whether it took the form of communism, fascism, or free-market capitalism, it failed. The first two produced intense regimentation, and unspeakable horrors were inflicted on those who did not (or could not) conform to the "ideal." The last has been more subtle and is still with us, but it has bequeathed to us the emptiness of the consumer society and the awareness that money cannot buy happiness. Yet in spite of these reverses, it is still common to hear prophecies of hope from the secular world. Some come from the political "left," which tends to write off the failure of communism as a tragic mistake, and some from the "right," which dismisses the excesses of capitalist exploitation as no more than growth pains that require a correction.

We no longer live in a world without hope as the first Christians did, but in a world of false hope. In many ways, this false hope is worse because

---

[23]Acts 26:7; 28:20.
[24]On the disagreement about it among the Jews, see Matt. 22:23–32.
[25]Rom. 5:5; 15:13.

it poses as a caricature of the real thing. The Christian hope is very different from what goes by that name in the world today. For a start, we recognize the finitude of created things[26] and do not believe that they hold the key to our future well-being, even if technology and science can make life more enjoyable and productive than it is right now. Christians do not put their hope in technological advances that might improve the lives of their children and grandchildren, even if these things are to be welcomed. In the end, we shall all die, and, in that respect, future generations will be no better off than we are, even if they manage to live a little longer on average than we now do.

The Christian hope is fixed not on the future but on eternity. Our hope is laid up for us in heaven, where the corruptions of this world are unknown.[27] We are called to focus our attention on a dimension of reality that we cannot perceive with our physical senses and that those who disagree with us are inclined to dismiss as mythical. The historical resurrection of Jesus Christ is the objective basis for this, but that can no longer be seen. Instead, what we have is a hope rooted in faith, not only that his resurrection has occurred but also that one day we shall rise again as he did. That faith gives us the stamina to endure the hardships of the present, knowing as we do that "the sufferings of this present time are not worth comparing with the glory that is to be revealed in us."[28]

Hope in the face of disappointment, suffering, and death is what Christians are called to manifest to the world. How we behave in such situations is the real evidence of our faith and commitment to Christ. It is that which speaks to others most effectively, and often gives us an opportunity that we might not otherwise have to share our faith with them.[29] As Paul said about the way in which we should mourn the dead,

> We do not want you to be uninformed, brothers, about those who are asleep, that you may not grieve as others do who have no hope. For since we believe that Jesus died and rose again, even so, through Jesus, God will bring with him those who have fallen asleep.[30]

Nor should we be too distressed about failure. It is perfectly possible for a Christian to live in obedience to the commands of God, only to find that his efforts to preach the gospel have borne little or no fruit. Some missionaries have spent their entire lives in countries where virtually no one has responded

---

[26]Rom. 8:20.
[27]Col. 1:5. See also Matt. 6:19–21.
[28]Rom. 8:18.
[29]1 Pet. 3:15.
[30]1 Thess. 4:13–14.

to their message. Others have built churches, only to see them disintegrate for one reason or another. Experiences like these are particularly hard to bear when there are others who have had what looks like enormous and almost effortless success. That is almost certainly not the whole truth, but things can be presented in a way that makes it seem that, if you preach faithfully and work hard, a successful ministry will be the inevitable result. Lack of outward success can be made to seem like God's judgment on unfaithfulness, which is by no means always true. Paul founded churches in many important Mediterranean cities, but there were other places where he seems to have failed, Athens being a notable example.[31] Was it wrong for him to have gone there? Of course not. The sower must sow his seed wherever he can, knowing that only some of it will bear lasting fruit, and even then that the results will be uneven.[32] God will not judge us by our results but by our faithfulness, and that is our hope. Even in apparent failure we know that he is the Sovereign Lord—and that we belong to him because we have been called and chosen to be his.

Our inheritance is stored up for us in heaven, and our eyes must be focused on that. Those who are called in hope must actively seek to purify themselves, knowing that Christ is pure and that we shall be made like him when he returns.[33] Separation from the world and a closer union with Christ is our calling, and the zeal with which we pursue it is the true measure of the reality of the hope we claim to possess.

UNITED TO CHRIST

To be grafted into Christ is to be united with him in his humanity and subjected to him as the Lord of our lives. The biblical picture of this is that he is the head and we are the different members of his body.[34] Individual members can be pruned or even chopped off, but the head remains central to the body's existence. It is the head that determines what the members do and provides the coordinating principle that keeps them working in harmony with each other. Without the head, the members can do nothing. Understanding this is the key to realizing what it means to be united to Christ. We are branches grafted into the tree, as Paul says, and no branch can survive without a tree.[35]

The first thing that happens to us when we are united to Christ is that we discover who we really are and where we belong in his scheme of things. To

---

[31] Acts 17:32–34.
[32] Matt. 13:23.
[33] 1 John 3:3.
[34] 1 Cor. 12:12–31.
[35] Rom. 11:17–25.

take the analogy of the body that Paul uses in 1 Corinthians 12, if we discover that we are an eye or a hand, we soon realize that although we have our own integrity, we cannot act autonomously. The eye and the hand do not need each other in order to function, since their activities are completely different and there is no overlap between them. But an eye that is removed from the body or a hand that is cut off from it cannot function at all. It is in the body that the eye and the hand discover what they are for and how they ought to be used. They also discover what their limitations are, and why the other is useful for the well-being of the body as a whole.

No Christian can exist independently, even if there is nothing lacking in him. A believer finds out who he really is and where he belongs in the wider scheme of things only by being united to Christ, who gives shape to the body and direction to its individual parts. Only in union with Christ do we come to understand where other believers fit into things and appreciate how we can be of service to Christ and to one another. Our relationship with each other is governed by our relationship with Jesus Christ, who is the Lord and Master of us all. What unites us is our common submission to his direction, which we find in the Scriptures and apply by the prompting of the Holy Spirit, who interprets the Scriptures for us.[36] It is this spirit of obedience to the Word of God that bears witness that we belong to him and that makes union with him a reality in our experience.

When we are submitted to the Word of God, we have the mind of Christ, which is expressed in it.[37] This is a matter of the greatest importance because it is the mind of Christ that makes us spiritual people who can discern what the Holy Spirit is teaching us. As there is only one Christ, and he has a single mind, those who have his mind are joined to him and to one another in mutual fellowship. Having his mind in us, we not only discover who he is and what his purposes are, but we are given the will and the power to accomplish those purposes. This sounds simple, and in principle it is quite straightforward, but there is one big problem we have to face. We cannot be united with Christ or have his mind in us unless we first die to ourselves, and that is not so easy. As long as we live in this world, we are children of Adam and therefore inheritors of his sinfulness and the fruits of the broken relationship with God which that produced. God puts the relationship right, but there is still a lot of cleaning up to do, and that takes time and patience. It can also be very painful because self-love is a powerful force that is not easily overcome. Not the least of our problems is that it is often convenient to confuse our own desires with the will

---

[36] 1 Thess. 2:13.
[37] 1 Cor. 2:16.

of God, and to pursue those desires with a clear conscience, convinced that there is nothing wrong with them. Paul, however, saw things very differently. As he put it,

> I have been crucified with Christ. It is no longer I who live, but Christ who lives in me. And the life I now live in the flesh I live by faith in the Son of God, who loved me and gave himself for me.[38]

Paul did not pretend that this was easy or painless—crucifixion is a very unpleasant experience, but that is the analogy that he chose to use in this context. What makes it bearable, and indeed compelling, is that Jesus is not asking us to do anything for him that he has not already done for us. He was crucified because he loved us. He willingly sacrificed himself for us so that we might live with him and for him in eternity.

Most wonderful of all, not only have we been called to share in Christ's sufferings, but it has been given to us to fulfill and complete his sufferings in our own lives, as we serve him in the world.[39] Paul learned to rejoice in his sufferings for the sake of the gospel, and to see in them God's purpose being worked out for the salvation of his people. Of course, neither Paul nor anyone else can add anything to the saving significance of Christ's suffering and death, but that is not what Paul was talking about when he told the Colossians that he was "filling up what is lacking in Christ's afflictions."[40] That striking phrase can be properly understood only by putting it into the context of union with Christ. Just as Paul's life was not his own but Christ's, so his sufferings did not belong to him either—they were the sufferings of Jesus, taken up into heaven to plead for our salvation but continuing in his body on earth. That body cannot now appear without its wounds, and if we are parts of Christ's body then we must expect to share his wounds also. Paul did not hesitate to write to Timothy and encourage him to "share in suffering for the gospel by the power of God," since that is the calling of all true believers.[41]

Having the mind of Christ helps us understand who we are and gives us strength to bear the sufferings that come with our calling to be transformed into the likeness of his death. It also assures us that the purpose of this suffering is not annihilation but a new life, which is the beginning and promise of the resurrection that we shall one day share fully with him.[42] In our present life, the experience of that promise comes in and through the presence of the

---

[38]Gal. 2:20.
[39]Phil. 3:10; 2 Cor. 1:5; Col. 1:24.
[40]Col. 1:24.
[41]2 Tim. 1:8.
[42]Rom. 8:17–18.

Holy Spirit in our hearts, which expresses itself above all in a life of prayer. As Paul said,

> Because you are sons, God has sent the Spirit of his Son into our hearts, crying, "Abba! Father!"[43]

By ourselves, we do not know how to pray or what to pray for, but the Spirit of God intercedes for us, and the Father, who sent the Spirit and who knows his mind, hears the prayers he offers in and through us.[44]

There is no aspect of the Christian life more neglected today than prayer. Modern people are activists, and tend (often quite rightly) to be suspicious of those who sit back and do nothing, particularly if they try to justify their idleness by appealing to the power of "prayer." But the fact that such misunderstanding and abuse is possible shows how much this vital subject has been neglected, and it is a major reason why so much of our activism bears so little real fruit. Prayer is the lifeline that connects us with Christ and gives meaning to our relationship with him. To be a Christian without praying is like being married but never speaking to your spouse. It may be theoretically possible, but what kind of a relationship would that be? It would certainly not be one that is growing and flourishing!

To put it succinctly, the closeness of our union with Christ can be measured by the quality of our prayer life. This is not a matter of outward observance or formal rituals, nor does it have anything to do with eloquence. It is not uncommon to hear people praying in public at great length and with considerable passion, but all too often they are preaching to those listening and not speaking to God at all. Jesus told his disciples that when they prayed they should not be like the Pharisees, who were fond of great show and liked to create a big impression.[45] Instead of that, he told them to go into a secluded place and pray quietly, not using many words but making each of them count. The prayer that Jesus taught his disciples, and which virtually every Christian knows by heart, is fundamentally a prayer for union with him.[46] First of all, we are told to pray to God using the word that Jesus himself used—"Father." This did not come naturally to the Jews, who regarded Jesus' use of such language as presumptuous if not actually blasphemous.[47] But not only did Jesus use the term himself, he taught his disciples to use it as well, thereby putting them in the same relationship to God that he himself had.

---

[43]Gal. 4:6.
[44]Rom. 8:26–27.
[45]Matt. 6:5.
[46]Matt. 6:9–13.
[47]John 5:18.

The first purpose of prayer is to glorify God, which is why Jesus told his disciples to ask that his name might be "hallowed." This cannot mean that they were to pray that God should become holier than he already is, but rather that his name, that is to say, his reputation and glory, should be honored for what it is and set apart in our minds as something on which we must focus above everything else. Once we have done that, we can go on to pray for things, which as Jesus outlines them come under four main headings:

A. The coming of the kingdom.
B. The giving of God's gifts.
C. The forgiveness of our sins.
D. Deliverance from temptation and evil.

Each of these takes us deeper into the mystery of what it means to be united with Christ. First, there is the coming of the kingdom and the doing of God's will that must accompany it. There is no kingdom without the king, so what we are praying for is his presence in our hearts. As for doing his will, we have already seen that this was the prayer of Jesus as he prepared himself to make the supreme sacrifice on the night before his crucifixion. So what we are really praying for is a deeper experience of the crucified Christ, who brings his kingdom into our lives by subduing our will to his and making us live in him by the power of his Holy Spirit.

Of the gifts that we pray for, the greatest is the food we need for survival. Jesus was undoubtedly alluding to the manna that fed the people of Israel in the desert on a daily basis, and that image recurs in the New Testament as a picture of the spiritual food that is ours only if we are united with him.[48] Jesus is the bread that came down from heaven, and in him all our wants and needs are satisfied.

Forgiveness is the next thing we are told to pray for, and of course that can be had only in and through Christ and his sacrifice for us. Apart from him there is no atonement, no forgiveness, and no power to forgive. Just as we cannot love others without the love of God at work in our hearts, so we cannot forgive them unless we know his forgiveness by being crucified with him. The secret of being able to forgive others and to receive forgiveness ourselves is to be united to Christ.

Finally, we are told to pray for deliverance from temptation and evil. Temptation is something we are led into, while evil is something we have to be delivered from. The two things are not identical, but they are related, since

---

[48] John 6:35, 41; 1 Cor. 10:3.

it is the evil one who tempts us, and if we are not to be led into temptation, it is from him that we must be delivered. This is possible only if we are united to Christ, who has defeated the forces of evil and set us free from them. If we have been delivered from death, it is because he has been delivered from it; our new life is the one he gives us when we are grafted into him. Here too, the spiritual battle we are called to wage is a battle that he has already won for us, and our victory can be found only in and through him.

The life of prayer is a life of growing into deeper union with Christ, of knowing him and the power of his death and resurrection more fully in our lives. Prayer is not, and cannot be, an afterthought or something we resort to only in an emergency. Just as physical food is beneficial only if consumed in regular portions, so spiritual food must be absorbed on a regular and orderly basis. As for those who use "prayer" as an excuse for inaction, let us remember that just as material food is useful only if it is burned up in energy, so spiritual food is intended to give us new life and the power that goes with it. To sit back and do nothing but eat is the sin of gluttony, which can be as destructive spiritually as it is physically. True prayer is a spur to action, not an excuse to avoid it. When God speaks to us, we must hear—and obey.

BAPTIZED FOR FORGIVENESS

The Nicene Creed states in its final paragraph that we believe in "one baptism for the forgiveness of sins." The phrase is taken from the Gospels, where we are told that John the Baptist preached "a baptism of repentance for the forgiveness of sins."[49] John's message brought people to repentance but it could not forgive their sins because only God can do that. This was the big difference between his ministry and that of Jesus, and explains why Jesus was so much greater than John.[50] Oddly enough, though, it was possible to know the message of Jesus, and even to proclaim it, without realizing that his baptism went beyond repentance to forgiveness. That was the case of Apollos, who "taught accurately the things concerning Jesus, though he knew only the baptism of John."[51] There were also people who baptized in the name of Jesus and not in the name of the Father, the Son, and the Holy Spirit, although Jesus had told his disciples to do that.[52] These anomalies are enough to remind us that baptism has always been a difficult subject, largely because so many questions about it go unanswered in the Scriptures.

Was John's baptism good enough for those who received it, or did they

---

[49] Mark 1:4; Luke 3:3.
[50] See Acts 19:3–4.
[51] Acts 18:25.
[52] Acts 8:16. See Matt. 28:19.

need to be baptized again according to the Trinitarian formula given by Jesus? When Paul met Christians at Ephesus who had received only John's baptism, he instructed them in the difference, and the result was that they were rebaptized.[53] There is no indication, however, that this happened earlier. Some of the disciples of Jesus would almost certainly have been baptized by John, as Jesus himself was, but there is nothing in the Bible to suggest that they were baptized again later on. Perhaps the difference was that they were baptized before the death and resurrection of Jesus, when John's baptism was sufficient. After Pentecost it was superseded by Christ's baptism, which meant that anyone baptized with John's baptism after that time had to be rebaptized. That is not explicitly stated in Scripture, but it fits with the evidence.

John told his followers that Jesus would baptize not just with water but with the Holy Spirit "and fire," though the meaning of that was not explained. In fact, it seems that Jesus baptized no one during his earthly ministry, except by proxy through his disciples.[54] Furthermore, there was no sign of either the Holy Spirit or fire, so we do not know whether this "baptism of Jesus" that he entrusted to his followers was what John was talking about. The likelihood must be that it was not, because Jesus alluded to another baptism that he associated with casting fire on the earth, and challenged the willingness of his disciples to share in it, which they clearly did not understand.[55] The context leads us to assume that this was the "baptism" of his death, which Jesus assured them they would undergo as well, though in what way is not stated. None of the disciples was put to death alongside Jesus, and although some were later martyred, not all were.[56] Was this the baptism of fire to which John alluded, or was he referring to the descent of the Holy Spirit at Pentecost, when tongues of fire rested on the disciples' heads?[57] Once again, this is not clear, and the evidence has been read in different ways. Given that the accounts we have were all written after Jesus' death and resurrection at a time when a fairly standardized baptismal practice was being established in the church, this loose-endedness is truly remarkable and reminds us of how difficult it is to come to a coherent understanding of the Bible's teaching on the subject.

In the early church, baptism was administered to those who professed faith in Christ, apparently with little or no catechetical instruction beforehand.[58] From the limited evidence we possess, it seems that anyone could baptize a new convert without referring him to the wider church or even demanding

---

[53] Acts 19:5.
[54] Matt. 3:11; John 4:1–2.
[55] Luke 12:49–50; Mark 10:38.
[56] John 21:20–23.
[57] Acts 2:3.
[58] Acts 16:33.

an explicit confession of faith. This is apparent in the story of Philip and the Ethiopian eunuch, whom he met on the road from Jerusalem to Gaza.[59] The eunuch was reading Isaiah 53, which puzzled him, and Philip explained how it referred to the sacrificial death of Jesus. The text does not say how the eunuch responded to that explanation, other than to point out that when they passed a body of water, he asked Philip whether there was anything that would prevent him from being baptized. Jewish readers of this story might instinctively have replied that there was, since a eunuch could not enter the house of God,[60] but that did not bother Philip, who promptly baptized him. At no point in the story is there any mention of the eunuch's faith—we have to assume that he believed what Philip told him and put his trust in Jesus because that is what normally had to happen before a person could be baptized. But that is our assumption, and not what the text actually says.

The story of the Ethiopian eunuch reminds us that our questions about baptism are not necessarily ones that troubled the first Christians, nor are the problems they had with it always immediately comprehensible to us. If we were in Philip's shoes, we almost certainly would have deferred the eunuch's baptism until he could be properly instructed. We might not even think of mentioning that he was a eunuch, but that was clearly of some significance to Luke, and we may assume that the way he wrote up the story tells us what the priorities of his contemporaries were. What impressed them was not that baptism was so easily available, but that the grace of God was being extended to people who under Jewish law might have been disqualified from receiving it, because eunuchs were not allowed to serve in the temple. Luke's priorities do not mean that our modern concerns are unimportant, but they remind us that we must be cautious in the way we use biblical evidence to determine what our current practice should be.

Most peculiar of all the New Testament references to baptism is the mention of baptism for the dead, to which Paul alludes when arguing for the reality of the resurrection:

> What do people mean by being baptized on behalf of the dead? If the dead are not raised at all, why are people baptized on their behalf?[61]

These are good questions, but most people today would ask them for rather different reasons and would probably come up with different answers. Paul apparently did not object to the practice, though there is no sign of it any-

---

[59] Acts 8:26–39.
[60] Deut. 23:1.
[61] 1 Cor. 15:29.

where else in the New Testament. We may surmise that the people concerned were Christians who were worried about their ancestors who had died before the coming of Christ, and wanted to make sure that they did not lose out on the promise of salvation. Although that sounds reasonable enough, there is no evidence to support it, the practice never caught on, and it was soon discontinued. No one (except the Latter-day Saints) has thought to revive it in modern times. In this case, we can safely say that a potential controversy has failed to materialize, apparently because there is no real interest in the subject, even though the question of what has happened to our pre-Christian ancestors is still a concern in many parts of the world, especially in places where Christianity has only recently been planted.

Rediscovering what the practice of Christian baptism actually was in New Testament times is difficult, but the truth is that few people are genuinely interested in reviving it, whatever they may claim to the contrary. Today, the evidence of the New Testament is cited not so much for its own sake as to support positions and practices found in the church now. People naturally want to think that what they believe is what the New Testament teaches, but the fact that they can disagree so deeply about things that should be obvious is a good indication of the problems we have to face where this subject is concerned.

For a start, the normal practice today is not to baptize people immediately upon their making a profession of faith. Most churches examine the candidate for baptism and some enroll them in a course designed to teach them the rudiments of Christianity in order to make sure that they understand what they are committing themselves to. This practice has very ancient origins and may go back to New Testament times, though there is no clear evidence for that. In those days people being prepared for baptism were known as catechumens, and what we call catechisms were originally produced as manuals for their instruction. Catechisms are little used nowadays, but this is because methods of teaching have changed, not because the principle itself has been abandoned. Now there is a great variety of courses and other materials specially prepared for those seeking baptism, which is seldom administered on demand. It is especially interesting to note that Christians who disagree about many other aspects of baptism are virtually unanimous about this, and very few churches now follow what was clearly the standard New Testament practice in this respect: immediate baptism, with no special preparation.

The baptism of infants is more controversial, and although it continues to be the norm in most churches, it would be wrong to pretend that there is not serious opposition to it, or even that there is a justification for it that has attracted universal assent among those who practice it. No one can say for sure whether baptism was administered to infants in New Testament times, though if it was, it was almost certainly in the context of the so-called "household" baptisms that we read about in the missionary career of Paul.[62] As long as Christians were a minority in the Roman empire and the church grew by conversion more than by reproduction, infant baptism could not have become the norm. That happened only in the fourth and fifth centuries, when the last remnants of paganism were stamped out and the vast majority of the population made at least a nominal profession of Christianity.

The curious thing is that, although there were plenty of people who objected to the rapid rise in church membership and who complained about what they saw as a corresponding decline in standards among the members, there was no controversy about the spread of infant baptism. Whatever process led to its general adoption, the result was accepted without demur by the whole church and continued without serious dissent until the Reformation. During most of that period, the main theological justification for infant baptism was belief in original sin. Because every child was born sinful and needed the saving grace of Christ, baptism was administered as soon as possible after birth in order to take that sin away. At a time when infant mortality was high, this argument carried a lot of weight and the Reformers found it almost impossible to dislodge the idea from their congregations. Even today the idea lingers at the level of folk religion, and many people seek baptism for their children for what are essentially superstitious reasons, while having little idea what it is about.

Closely tied with the notion of cleansing from original sin is a belief in baptismal regeneration, which is still characteristic of Roman Catholic and Eastern Orthodox theology. According to this view, a person is born again by baptism and is therefore a Christian whether or not he has made a profession of faith. At first sight, there appears to be considerable New Testament justification for this interpretation. Consider for instance what Paul says to the Romans:

> Do you not know that all of us who have been baptized into Christ Jesus were baptized into his death? We were buried therefore with him by baptism into death, in order that, just as Christ was raised from the dead by the glory of the Father, we too might walk in newness of life.[63]

How literally are we meant to take this statement? Baptism is clearly a physical act, performed by someone qualified to exercise the authority of the church, and the transformation that produces the "newness of life" is presumably

---

[62]Acts 16:15; 1 Cor. 1:16.
[63]Rom. 6:3–4. See also Col. 2:12.

meant to be real as well. At the same time, our relationship to Christ's death and resurrection is obviously figurative in the sense that it is speaking of a spiritual experience which has no physical counterpart. Can a physical act produce a spiritual result? It would be very strange if it could, and such a view contradicts everything Paul had to say about circumcision only a few chapters earlier in the same letter. It also goes against what Peter said more specifically about the rite of baptism itself:

> Baptism . . . now saves you, not as a removal of dirt from the body but as an appeal to God for a good conscience . . .[64]

The physical act of baptism is neither here nor there as far as Peter is concerned; what matters to him is that the person being baptized should repent and ask God to clear his conscience. Jesus told Nicodemus that he had to be born again, but although he may have associated this with the rite of baptism, he did not identify the two in the way that the Catholic tradition has done.[65] That it is possible to be born again without being baptized is made clear by the witness of the thief on the cross, who professed faith in Jesus and was told that he would be with him in paradise that very day.[66] Some ingenious exegetes have tried to argue that the thief was in fact baptized with the water that flowed from Jesus' side when he was pierced,[67] but the fact that they have to go to such extravagant lengths shows how weak their case is, and we can safely disregard it.

Unfortunately, one of the strongest pieces of evidence against the validity of a doctrine of baptismal regeneration is the generally acknowledged existence of vast numbers of baptized people who have no real faith and a considerable number who have formally or informally renounced it. Adolf Hitler was baptized, but would anyone say he was a Christian? So was Josef Stalin, but what difference did that make? A rite not supported by any kind of faith has no power to regenerate, and if a baptized infant later rejects the faith professed by his parents on his behalf there can be no ground for assuming that he was ever born again.[68] Such a claim makes nonsense of baptism, and we can hardly be surprised that it has pushed many true believ-

---

[64]1 Pet. 3:21.
[65]John 3:5–7. Jesus said that we must be born "of water and the Spirit," but the meaning of the word "water" is not made clear. Even if it does refer to baptism, it is noticeable that he puts all the emphasis on the work of the Holy Spirit and none at all on the supposed effect(s) of the water.
[66]Luke 23:43–44.
[67]John 19:34.
[68]The same, of course, applies to those who were baptized upon their profession of faith but who later turned away from it.

ers into rejecting it altogether because of the way in which it so obviously has been abused.

For many centuries, the main theological justification for infant baptism was found in the words of Psalm 51:5: "Behold, I was brought forth in iniquity, and in sin did my mother conceive me." The widespread belief that baptism took away sin was therefore urged as a reason for baptizing newly born children, especially as the infant mortality rate was so high. We tend to forget this now, but at a time when up to a third of babies did not survive their first year of life, the fear that they would be sent to hell because of their innate sinfulness was very great, and baptism was a means of reassuring parents that their offspring would not be condemned for what was essentially an ancestral fault and not their own. At the time of the Reformation, people who rejected infant baptism were sometimes accused of believing that children are born sinless, which would make it theoretically possible for them to avoid sinning altogether. Presumably those who died before the age of responsibility would have gone to heaven automatically, an important consideration in a world where about a third of all babies died at or soon after birth.

That view has never been the official teaching of any church, but the idea that unbaptized people (of any age) necessarily go to hell is not widely held either. Protestants, including those who practice infant baptism, have never placed so much weight on the performance of the rite as to make it an essential condition of salvation, and other Christians, while they may officially teach something like that, seldom insist on it in practice. It is true that Roman Catholics will baptize stillborn children and those who die shortly after birth, a practice rooted in the belief that the unbaptized are eternally damned, but in recent years there has been a tendency to rely on "intention" as a way out of the more difficult cases: if someone intended to be baptized (or to have a child baptized) but was prevented from doing it for some reason, the intention would be taken as the equivalent of the act. Here again, the thief on the cross may be cited as an example, the assumption being that he would have been baptized if he could have been but that he was prevented from doing so by unavoidable circumstances!

Probably the most commonly heard justification for infant baptism nowadays is the one that associates baptism with circumcision and claims that it is the New Testament equivalent of the Old Testament practice. Those who adopt this view accept that there are differences of practice between the two dispensations of the covenant, the most obvious ones being that baptism is administered equally to both sexes and that it does not leave an identifiable mark on the body. On the other hand, baptism resembles circumcision in that it represents entry into the covenant community of God's people. Both parents and infants receive the promise that salvation is extended to the children of believers, but the analogy with circumcision is a reminder that this cannot be taken for granted. To be an heir to the promises is not the same thing as actually benefitting from them, as Paul reminded the Jews:

> No one is a Jew who is merely one outwardly, nor is circumcision outward and physical. But a Jew is one inwardly, and circumcision is a matter of the heart, by the Spirit, not by the letter.[69]

Those who equate baptism with circumcision also insist that membership in the covenant people is not a guarantee of salvation and are concerned that those who have been baptized as infants should make a personal confession of faith when they are old enough to do so. In liturgical terms, this is represented by the rite of "confirmation," which is the moment when someone baptized in infancy confirms that he or she has accepted the promised inheritance and has become a believer. Of course, formal profession of this kind ought to be grounded in genuine spiritual experience, without which it has no validity. In practice, it must be admitted that many people are confirmed too young or without sufficient examination of their spiritual state, which is one reason why less pressure is put on teenagers nowadays to go through a ceremony that they may be old enough to understand but whose true meaning they have not experienced. Certainly, those Reformed Protestants who practice infant baptism and confirmation do not believe that the rites guarantee anything, and they continue to press as strongly as those who reject infant baptism for the conversion of those who are formally within the bounds of the covenant.

Infant baptism is a reminder that everyone, even a newborn baby, is a sinner in need of God's grace. This is a particularly important thing to emphasize nowadays, when modern sentimentality and good intentions downplay original sin and assume that a child who dies before reaching the age of reason goes to heaven automatically. There is no support in the Bible for such a view, and the notion that infants are somehow "innocent" is false, however popular it may be. Those who baptize children are reminding the church that even the smallest infant needs a Savior because, whether or not it has committed actual sins, it has inherited the sinfulness that results from a broken relationship with God just as much as anyone else. We do not fall when we reach the age of responsibility, but merely express our alienation from God that has been there all along, and that no human being can escape.

---

[69]Rom. 2:28–29.

Those who reject infant baptism do so for two main reasons beyond the fact that the practice is not clearly attested in Scripture. The first is that infant baptism has been so widely abused that it has become meaningless for most people. If baptism really signifies new life in Christ, they argue, then it should be administered only to those who give evidence of participating in that new life. It is not easy to know what sort of evidence ought to be required, but in practice most "baptists"[70] seem to think of baptism in terms not dissimilar to confirmation. Often they will dedicate a newborn infant (instead of baptizing it), but they will instruct the child in much the same way and prepare it for receiving baptism, usually in the teenage years. It may be noted in passing that baptists who do this face the same difficulty as others, in that many young people submit to the rite without having had the spiritual experience that would justify it. This then raises the dilemma about what to do if they are genuinely converted later on. Some would counsel (and practice) rebaptism, but others do not, and there is no clear theological understanding on this point. Another difficulty, which may be unusual but which nevertheless occurs, is that there are people who for some reason cannot make a personal profession of faith, or whose profession must be suspect because they are mentally impaired. No one wants to discriminate against them but it is hard to know what to do in such cases, and a pastoral practice that relies heavily on the need for a personal profession of faith finds itself in difficulty at this point.

The second reason that baptists object to the baptism of infants is that they believe that baptism is a testimony to the grace of salvation that has already been received. This appears to be the pattern in the New Testament, and they think that that pattern should determine the meaning and practice of the rite today. An infant may theoretically have received the grace of salvation, but there is no way that we can tell, and a personal testimony from the child is obviously impossible. Baptism is therefore to be avoided until reasonable certainty can be obtained about a person's spiritual state. A baptism administered to an infant should probably be viewed as invalid, rather like an underage marriage. There is, however, some disagreement among baptists about whether an adult who was baptized as an infant must be baptized again upon profession of faith. Most say that he should be, but some argue that, since the earlier baptism has obviously taken effect, in the sense that the person concerned has made a subsequent profession of faith, it is not necessary to repeat it. A complication with this occurs when a believer who was baptized as

---

[70]The term is used loosely here to mean all who practice believer's baptism only, not all of whom are members of a Baptist church.

an infant wants to join a baptistic church, perhaps for reasons that have little or nothing to do with its baptismal beliefs or practice. Should people like that be rebaptized if they have made an adult profession of faith and have been living it out for many years? On this there is occasionally room for flexibility in baptist circles, but rebaptism continues to be the official policy in many (and probably most) baptist congregations.

Another question that often surfaces in the debates between those who baptize infants and those who do not concerns what is called the mode of baptism. Should a person be totally immersed in water, or is sprinkling over the head good enough? This is not really a theological question, but the symbolism of dying and rising with Christ which total immersion is supposed to represent is powerful among many baptists.[71] Some scholars go to great lengths to "prove" that because the Greek word *baptisma* means "dipping" or "immersion," nothing less than that will do. Others point out that so literalistic an interpretation is not warranted by the biblical texts, and that there are cases of baptism where total immersion is unlikely to have been the way in which it was done. How, for example, would the Philippian jailer and his entire household have been completely immersed in water in the middle of the night?[72] No doubt various ingenious solutions to this problem can be found, but they strain credulity and must be regarded as improbable. For what it is worth, the evidence of ancient frescoes and mosaics that depict baptism usually show the candidate going knee- to waist-deep in water and then having a jug of water poured over his head. That may well have been common practice, and would not be inconsistent with the description of Philip and the Ethiopian eunuch, who "went down into the water," and after the eunuch's baptism "came up out of the water."[73] As so often, we do not know exactly what happened, and it is unwise to be dogmatic one way or the other.

The best solution to difficulties of this kind is probably to adopt the policy that Paul recommended to the Romans with respect to the observance of Jewish customs like the food laws:

> Let not the one who eats despise the one who abstains, and let not the one who abstains pass judgment on the one who eats, for God has welcomed him. Who are you to pass judgment on the servant of another? It is before his own master that he stands or falls. And he will be upheld, for the Lord is able to make him stand.[74]

---

[71]Rom. 6:4.
[72]Acts 16:33.
[73]Acts 8:38–39.
[74]Rom. 14:3–4. See also the rest of this chapter.

Centuries of conflict over the practice and mode of baptism have demonstrated that universal agreement on this matter is not possible, but they have also shown that the gospel is professed and proclaimed with equal fervor by people on both sides of the argument. Letting people decide for themselves has not weakened the church to any noticeable degree, and while there will continue to be differences of opinion, tolerating them would seem to be better than encouraging potentially damaging controversy. As Paul said, "Let us pursue what makes for peace and mutual understanding" and leave the judgment up to God.[75]

Can we therefore come to an agreement about what baptism signifies? Whatever practice we adopt and whatever view we may have about particular aspects of the question, we should all be able to agree that baptism is a physical act with a spiritual meaning. However it is administered, it proclaims salvation by the death and resurrection of Christ and holds out the promise of participation in that resurrection by those who profess faith in him and who are united to him by his Holy Spirit. The exact relationship between the reality that the rite signifies, and the experience of that reality, is disputed, but the two things are clearly distinct. Whether baptism is administered before the experience, in anticipation of it, or only when there is good reason to believe that the recipient has already had it, the fact remains that the two things are not so closely connected that one can be mistaken (or substituted) for the other. Ultimately the experience is more important than the rite, since without it there can be no salvation, but as the rite is the means appointed by God to proclaim the experience and to explain what it means, it cannot be ignored or dispensed with.

Baptism expresses the need for believers to die with Christ and to be born again into a new life, but although this is a real spiritual experience in this world, it is not complete until we go to be with Christ in eternity. However much baptism may bear witness to what has already happened, it always points to something more that has not yet been fully realized. It looks back to the sacrifice and death of Christ and forward to his coming again, when we shall be caught up into his eternal glory. Right now, its presence in our lives and in the wider life of the church serves to challenge us to think more deeply about our commitment to Christ and to ask ourselves how the cleansing power of his Holy Spirit actually works in us. However we understand baptism and from whatever angle we look at it, it is not an end in itself but points to a spiritual reality above and beyond the confines of this world but also present in it through the Spirit of Christ who dwells in our hearts by faith.

---

[75]Rom. 14:19.

If we can agree about that, we can look back to the first mention of baptism in the New Testament and appropriate the message of repentance and the forgiveness of sins in a new and deeper way. Baptism proclaims the need for repentance, but because that has to come from us, it cannot guarantee it. Even a formal profession of faith is not proof that genuine repentance has occurred, and in any case repentance is ongoing because sin is a permanent fixture of our earthly lives. The fact that we have repented before being baptized does not mean that we shall never have to repent again! Forgiveness, however, is another matter. That comes from God, and although it is applied to us only when we repent, it is always there. If baptism proclaims the need for repentance, then it also proclaims the availability of forgiveness, which depends not on us but on God.[76] In practical terms, what this means is that I can know that I have been forgiven even for sins that I have not yet committed. I know that I shall go on sinning as long as I live in this world, and there is no way of knowing whether I shall repent. Failure to repent may not always be due to obstinacy or rebellion, because there are many sins we commit of which we are unaware. The real problem is not the sins we are guilty of, but our innate sinfulness, which ensures that everything we do will be tainted with sin one way or another. The paradox of the Christian life is that the more we know about God and his will for us, the more we are conscious of our failure to live up to it and of the resistance to his will which is a fundamental part of our experience as fallen human beings.[77]

But if the number of my sins is unknown and the depth and sincerity of my repentance is hard to measure, the forgiveness of God is permanent and total. He accepts me even when I cannot accept myself. He knows me at depths of my being which are hidden from my conscious awareness. He even forgives my inability to repent as much as I should because he knows that if I were to try to put right what I have done wrong, I would destroy myself in the process. His forgiveness is my life, but it is my life because I have been buried with Christ and brought to new life in him—in baptism! It is not something I have done by my good deeds or earned by my profession of faith, but something that he has done for me by the shedding of his blood in love. When all is said and done, baptism is a monument to the love of God, who gave himself for us so that we might be cleansed from our sinfulness and born again to newness of life in him. That is what it proclaims, and that is why it matters. It is nothing less than an expression of the gospel of Jesus Christ, who has sought me out and united me to him so that I may

---

[76]See Acts 2:38.
[77]Rom. 7:21–25.

be washed clean and clothed in the pure garments of heavenly and eternal righteousness.

JUSTIFIED BY FAITH

The promise that we can be set free from our burden of sinfulness, that instead of its filthy rags we shall be clothed in God's righteousness and reign with the risen, ascended, and glorified Son in his eternal kingdom, is the great message of the gospel to which our calling and our baptism bear witness. What prevents these things from being abstract and theoretical is the way they are grounded in our lives by the restoration of our broken relationship with God. That restoration is accomplished by faith, which delivers us from the condemnation we so richly deserve and ushers us into the state of righteousness that only God can claim as his own—and that he gives to us in love.

"Faith" is one of those words that everyone thinks they understand but that few people bother to define. Many people equate it with "belief," and in secular usage it has come to mean little more than "religion," as in terms like "faith schools" or "faith-based charities." It would obviously be wrong to pretend that faith has nothing to do with belief, but the two things cannot simply be equated. We all believe any number of historical or scientific facts, but we would not think of this as an act of faith. Some people might even say that it is the opposite, because to them "seeing is believing," whereas faith is believing when there is no evidence to support it. Atheists who attack Christianity often do so for precisely this reason. To them, our faith is irrational because (so they claim) it is based on fantasy and wishful thinking rather than on objective facts. We reject that claim, not because we agree with them that only objectively demonstrable "facts" ought to be believed, but because their analysis of the Christian understanding of faith is superficial and deficient. To put it simply, there is more to faith than simply believing a set of facts, whether or not these can be proved in a scientifically acceptable way.

Other people think that faith is an act of the will, which explains how it can survive and grow whether or not there are facts to support it. Many people convince themselves of things that are not true and go on believing them because they want to, regardless of the facts. Sometimes this can be more amusing than anything else, as with Irishmen who swear that they have seen a leprechaun and Americans who are convinced that they have had an encounter with extraterrestrial creatures. But faith of this kind can also be tragic and harmful, as when parents refuse to accept that their children can do anything wrong even when they are convicted of murder or theft on a grand scale. Critics of Christianity are not slow to point out that, in their view, our faith is a blend of the amusing and the dangerous. To believe that Jesus walked on water may be regarded as a charming eccentricity, but to claim that millions of people are headed for eternal damnation for not believing in him is outrageous, especially if it appears to lead Christians to support wars against those who do not share their beliefs. Once again, the Christian response to this is that such analyses are superficial and miss the point.

Faith is not an act of the human will that creates its own reality and then proceeds to act on it, but is a gift from God. It is not belief in a set of abstract principles or facts, but a relationship with a person—Jesus Christ. More than once, Jesus complained that his disciples were lacking in faith because, in one respect, they were just like the hardheaded atheists of today. To them, seeing was believing, and anything else was a fantasy to be rejected.[78] Even after Christ's death and resurrection, some of his disciples continued to doubt, and by no means everyone who heard and saw Jesus was prepared to believe in him, although they knew perfectly well that he could do miracles.[79] When we read the story of Jesus in the Gospels, we find that the religious experts of the day, the scribes and Pharisees, were often the ones who had the biggest problem with him, whereas the most unlikely people turned out to possess the deepest faith. No one would have expected a Roman centurion to know or care anything about Jesus, yet one particular centurion had a faith in him that was greater than that of most Israelites.[80] He had no theological training and presumably was not looking for the Messiah, yet what he knew about Jesus convinced him that here was the man he needed.

What was true of the centurion is true, one way or another, of every Christian. Our faith is not based on logical deductions or a moral code. It is not a traditional belief handed down from our ancestors that we dare not question. Rather, it is a knowledge and experience of Jesus that can come only when he reveals himself to us. It has always been possible to know about Jesus without encountering him personally. It is even possible to believe everything in the Gospels and yet not understand what they are all about. Most Europeans in premodern times probably believed in the Bible, but it did not make them Christians in any real sense. True conversion comes only by meeting Jesus, and the time and place of that meeting are decided by him.

The faith that God puts into our hearts is our relationship with him in and through his Holy Spirit. Yet again, we discover that it is being united with

---

[78]Matt. 6:30; 8:26; 14:31; 16:8.
[79]Matt. 28:17.
[80]Luke 7:6–9.

Christ that makes the difference. It is this relationship that governs our lives as believers and empowers us to live in a world that does not (and cannot) understand us. But for us, the trials and temptations of this life are the occasions when we realize that we cannot get away from Jesus, that his love draws us to himself, and that if we fail, he lifts us up and puts us back on the right track in spite of ourselves.

The writer to the Hebrews defined faith as "the assurance of things hoped for, the conviction of things not seen."[81] He then went on to give several examples, drawn from the history of Israel, of people whose lives illustrated the way this definition worked out in practice. The great models of faith turn out to be those who knew God and who acted on that knowledge. It was what they did, rather than what they said, that counted. At every stage, their actions were determined by their knowledge of God's will, which stemmed from their relationship with him. For hundreds of years they remained loyal to the promises made to Abraham, knowing that one day those promises would be fulfilled in Christ. What this might mean in particular cases is well illustrated from the history of Moses, who chose to be mistreated with the people of God rather than enjoy the fleeting pleasures of Pharaoh's sinful court:

> He considered the reproach of Christ greater wealth than the treasures of Egypt, . . . By faith he left Egypt, not being afraid of the anger of the king, for he endured as seeing him who is invisible.[82]

Some of those faithful Israelites performed great miracles because of their faith; others suffered severe torments for exactly the same reason. A few, like Elijah, did both. But in the end it did not really matter because what they did sprang from a deep conviction that it was what God was calling them to do. In the early church, many Christians gave their lives for the sake of the gospel, and it was this, more than anything else, that left the deepest impression on those who met them. As Tertullian remarked around the year A.D. 200, "the blood of the martyrs is the seed of the church,"[83] and so it has often proved. This is what true faith is, as James testified when he wrote,

> Count it all joy, my brothers, when you meet trials of various kinds, for you know that the testing of your faith produces steadfastness. And let steadfastness have its full effect, that you may be perfect and complete, lacking in nothing.[84]

---

[81]Heb. 11:1.
[82]Heb. 11:25–27.
[83]*Apologeticum*, 50.
[84]James 1:2–4.

From this it will be clear that justifying faith is not to be equated with belief in the right things, important as that is. Right belief must result in right behavior, and very often that will mean standing up and being counted when the going gets tough. There has never been a time when believers have been comfortable; even in the so-called ages of faith, when the institutional church was a power in the land, those within its ranks who tried to put gospel principles into practice were often given a hard time. Today, supposedly, there is greater freedom, but the pressure that can be put on people to tone down the gospel message, to show tolerance of other religious beliefs, and to compromise in one way or another with the world is just as strong as it has ever been. To stand up for Christian beliefs and values in the academic world or in the media is just as difficult today as it would have been to face the lions in the Roman coliseum, and perhaps even more so. In these situations our faith is severely tested, and it is in that process that we discover what it really is. As God told the high priest Eli, "Those who honor me I will honor, and those who despise me shall be lightly esteemed."[85] Eli discovered the truth of that to his cost, but succeeding generations have found from experience just how true it is, and have known that even if they walk through the valley of the shadow of death, if they go in faith, God is with them there, guiding and leading them to his eternal rest.[86]

Once we understand what faith is, it becomes clearer why the Bible says that we are justified by it in God's sight. Our faith in Christ is a trust born of our union with him in his suffering, death, and resurrection. This union is not physical but spiritual, but it is no less real because of that. On the contrary, it is more real and effective, because if we were obliged to die and rise again with him in the physical sense, we could never be Christians in this life at all. The miracle of the gospel is that we can live the new life of the risen Christ here and now, not because we have changed in any objective sense but because he has integrated us into his body by sending his Holy Spirit to apply his work of atonement to our lives.

This means that, although we are sinners and have nothing to offer to God other than the sinful state into which we have fallen because of our Adamic inheritance, God has taken us into himself and wiped out both our sins and our innate sinfulness by the blood of his Son. Because we are united to the Son, his righteousness has become our righteousness, and we can stand in the presence of our Father, knowing that we have been forgiven all that is past and have been granted the power to live in the newness of Christ's resurrection life. It is important to understand that, while justification includes the

---

[85] 1 Sam. 2:30.
[86] Ps. 23:4–6.

forgiveness of sins and would be inconceivable without it, it is not limited to forgiveness alone. It would be possible for us to be forgiven on a piecemeal basis without being justified, and there are many people who think in that way. They believe that every time they sin, they must repent and seek God's forgiveness, which is true, but they have no assurance that their fundamental sinfulness and separation from God has been dealt with. In their minds, God remains a distant judge whom they must try to satisfy, and they are always afraid that there are secret sins that they may not have taken into account, which will be held against them on the day of judgment.

Such people may be perfectly sincere believers, but they have been trapped by their ignorance of the true meaning of justification by faith and so are not able to live in the freedom of Christ. The sixteenth-century Reformers were concerned that the church was keeping people in spiritual bondage, either because its leaders were suppressing the truth about justification, or because they simply did not understand it. It was for this reason that Martin Luther said that justification was the "article of a standing or falling church" and believed that it was the central plank of the gospel. Without an understanding of justification, the message of redemption remains something external to the experience of the believer, and the church becomes a place of spiritual bondage rather than of spiritual freedom.

What does it mean to be justified and to share in the righteousness of Christ? Is his righteousness something that he gives to believers so that they can claim it for themselves, or is it something that is credited (imputed) to them because of their union with Christ but not imparted or transferred to them in any objective sense? This is the question that lies at the heart of the Reformation debate about the nature of justification. By being grafted into Christ, we are covered by his righteousness and share in it because of our union with him. We do not possess any righteousness of our own, and in that sense we have to say that Christ's righteousness is imputed to us. Not only are we dead in our trespasses and sins and therefore incapable of doing anything to get rid of them, but Christ has taken our death on himself and canceled the debt that we owe to God.[87] The life that we now live in this world is therefore a life that we live by faith in the Son of God, who lives in us and brings his righteousness to bear on our lives.[88] In the words of Paul:

> God, being rich in mercy, because of the great love with which he loved us, even when we were dead in our trespasses, made us alive together with

---

[87]Eph. 2:1; Col. 2:13–14.
[88]Gal. 2:20.

Christ—by grace you have been saved—and raised us up with him. . . . For by grace you have been saved through faith. And this is not your own doing; it is the gift of God, not a result of works, so that no one may boast.[89]

To say, as some people have done, that justification is an act that requires human cooperation, whether by works or by a form of mental assent that we call "faith," is mistaken. Before we are justified we are spiritually dead, and it is impossible for a corpse to do anything, let alone bring itself back to life. It is for that reason that justification by faith can only be a gift of God, freely given to us in spite of ourselves. And why did he do this? Paul makes it clear that there are two reasons. First, God is "rich in mercy," which means that he is fully able to wipe away our sins and is not bound, as a human judge would be, by some higher law or principle that would force him to punish us in spite of his own desires. But second, God shows his mercy toward us because of his love for us. His capacity to forgive is made real in his behavior toward us, and it is in that act that we are made alive in Christ, which is what being justified by his righteousness is ultimately all about.

ADOPTED AS CHILDREN

To be justified by the blood of Christ is to be set free from the burden of sinfulness and given the freedom to live a new life in the power of his righteousness, but that is not all. Sometimes we explain sin by describing it as a spiritual sickness from which Christ, our great physician, has cured us. This is not wrong, but like all analogies it has its limitations and must be used with caution. In this case, the danger is that we shall press the comparison too far and assume that, once the patient is healed of his illness, he is free to go away, just as the many people whom Jesus healed during his earthly ministry did. Few if any of them became his disciples, nor did Jesus necessarily expect them to. In the case of the ten lepers who were healed, for example, only one returned to give thanks, but although Jesus commended him for that, he did not hesitate to tell him to go back to his normal life.[90] There may have been a reason for that, in that the man concerned was a Samaritan whom Jesus might not have made one of his disciples even if he had wanted to become one, since salvation was from the Jews.[91] But whether or not that is true, we can safely say that this is not the way Jesus deals now with sinners whose sins have been forgiven.[92]

A justified sinner is not free to go his own way or to return to his previous

---

[89]Eph. 2:4–6, 8–9.
[90]Luke 17:19.
[91]John 4:22.
[92]Luke 17:16–18; John 4:22.

life, because the act of justification brings with it a new relationship with God that the Bible describes as "adoption." To quote Paul again,

> All who are led by the Spirit of God are sons of God. For you did not receive the spirit of slavery to fall back into fear, but you have received the Spirit of adoption as sons, by whom we cry, "Abba! Father!" The Spirit himself bears witness with our spirit that we are children of God, and if children, then heirs—heirs of God and fellow heirs with Christ, provided we suffer with him in order that we may also be glorified with him.[93]

The image of adoption is a particularly well chosen one because it illustrates, in a way that nothing else can, the nature of our relationship with God in Christ. An adopted child is not the natural offspring of his adoptive parents, but neither is his presence in the household an accident. His parents have deliberately chosen him and made him a member of their family by an act of will that is sealed in love and self-sacrifice. There is nothing in the child that puts these parents under an obligation to accept him, and there may be any number of considerations that would advise against it. For example, the child might be handicapped, which would make caring for him more difficult. He might be of a different race, which would draw attention to the fact that he is adopted and could cause problems in later life. His birth parents might not be reconciled to losing their child, and might try to reclaim him at some future point. The child himself might rebel against his adoption when he finds out about it, and actively seek out his birth parents, with serious consequences for the families involved.

One way or another, all these factors play into our adoption as children by God. There is nothing in us that would oblige him to take us under his wing. Our sins have handicapped us and make us more difficult to deal with because their consequences are still with us and have to be overcome. We are quite different from God, and when other people hear that we are claiming to be his children, they may point this out and dismiss our claims as wishful thinking on our part. Finally, Satan, the ruler from whom we have been rescued, is not happy about this and does all he can to win us back.[94] We may even be tempted to seek him out in times of spiritual discouragement or depression, wondering whether our old life was really as bad as it is made out to be. In short, adoption does not come naturally, and it is only by the witness of the Holy Spirit in our hearts that it takes root and becomes a kind of second nature to us.

---

[93]Rom. 8:14–17.
[94]See 1 Pet. 5:8.

If adoption is not a natural entitlement, however, its rewards are nonetheless very great. Adopted children are heirs just as much as the natural children are, which in spiritual terms means that we who have been grafted into Christ share in all the privileges and blessings that have been bestowed on him in his glorified human nature. Yet, however much we share in the heavenly reign of Christ, because he is still our Lord and Savior, we must recognize our debt to him by obeying him in all things. We must never forget that he is a divine person who took on a human nature like ours in order to identify with us. We, in turn, identify with him in his humanity, but not in his divinity, which remains above and beyond anything we can imitate or even imagine. It is because he ascended to his Father with his human body that we shall ascend and dwell with him in eternity. We do not know what our spiritual bodies will look like, but we do know that we shall still be human in heaven, just as he is still human there.[95]

That we must see things in this perspective is made clear by Paul when he adds that our inheritance with Christ is dependent on sharing in his sufferings. As a divine person, the Son of God cannot suffer because suffering is alien to his nature. It was in his humanity that he suffered and died for us, and it is in our humanity that we suffer and die for him. But this suffering and death with Christ is not an end in itself because, if we are united with him in those things, we shall be united with him in his risen glory. It is here that we see the real blessings of our spiritual adoption.

First, adoption in Christ gives us access to God the Father.[96] This means that we are free to take our problems and desires to him without fear of being ignored or rejected. Jesus has told us that the Father will give good gifts to his children, and being adopted into his family gives us the assurance that we shall receive them.[97] But the freedom to communicate with our heavenly Father is not just about receiving gifts from him. It is also about thanking him for who he is and for what he has done. It is about relating to him beyond the merely formal, about resting in his presence and knowing that we are safe in his everlasting arms.[98] It is a total experience, embracing every aspect of our lives and filling us with the joy of knowing that we are loved by the one whose love is the greatest gift that anyone can ever receive.

Second, adoption in Christ gives us a purpose for living. If we are members of God's family, then the family business becomes our business as well, and we must do what we can to represent it and further it as much as possible. Paul makes this clear when he says,

---

[95] 1 Cor. 15:42–53.
[96] Eph. 2:18; 3:12.
[97] Matt. 7:7–9.
[98] Phil. 4:7.

In Christ God was reconciling the world to himself, not counting their trespasses against them, and entrusting to us the message of reconciliation. Therefore, we are ambassadors for Christ, God making his appeal through us.[99]

We cannot save ourselves (or anyone else) by what we do, but we have been given the inestimable privilege of being entrusted with the message that Christ has done it for us, and for all who put their trust in him. As witnesses to his grace and beneficiaries of his love, we are ideally placed to act as his messengers, to tell the world that what has happened to us can happen to them also. Bearing the family name is one of the great rewards of adoption, and we must never forget that those who see us are meant to see the Lord Jesus Christ at work in us. How we behave, what we say, and the things we do all advertise who we are.[100] We have to pay careful attention to this because, if we fail, we are not rejected or disregarded, as we might prefer to be, but mocked and condemned as hypocrites by those who see only too clearly that we are not practicing what we preach.[101]

Third, adoption in Christ gives us a share in his rule over the world.[102] We have no right to this, but because we have been adopted, we are seated "in the heavenly places in Christ Jesus."[103] In the ancient world, only the king was allowed to sit—everyone else had to stand in his presence. In Christ's kingdom, however, those who belong to him will be seated along with him, sharing in his power and authority and reigning with him until he has destroyed every authority and power that is hostile to his rule.[104] Where he is, there we shall be also, basking in the glory of the Lamb who was slain for us, whose names were written in his book of life even before the foundation of the world.[105]

Finally, adoption in Christ gives us the means to grow spiritually so that we may become more like him.[106] Jesus told Nicodemus that he had to be born again, and this theme is found throughout the New Testament.[107] The analogy is taken seriously, and it is not assumed that those who are born spiritually are immediately or automatically mature in their thinking or behavior. Paul says that new Christians must not be given responsibilities in the church that are too great for them to bear because, if they are, they run the risk of becoming proud

---

[99]2 Cor. 5:19–20.
[100]See 1 Cor. 4:1.
[101]1 Cor. 6:12–20.
[102]2 Tim. 2:12; 1 Cor. 6:3.
[103]Eph. 2:6.
[104]1 Cor. 15:24–27.
[105]Rev. 13:8.
[106]2 Pet. 3:18.
[107]John 3:3–7. See also Gal. 4:29; 1 Pet. 1:23; 1 John 2:29; 3:9; 4:7; 5:1, 4, 18.

and being ensnared by the Devil.[108] Believers have to grow in their faith, and that means starting with the most simple and straightforward instruction, much of which consists in learning to reject the ways of the world. As Peter wrote,

> Put away all malice and all deceit and hypocrisy and envy and all slander. Like newborn infants, long for the pure spiritual milk, that by it you may grow up into salvation—if indeed you have tasted that the Lord is good.[109]

Important and necessary as the spiritual milk is, however, it is only a beginning. One of the problems Paul faced in the Corinthian church was that its members had not weaned themselves off the basics. He complained that he could not talk to them the way he normally would to spiritual people, but had to address them as "people of the flesh, as infants in Christ," who were stuck on milk and unable to move on to solid food.[110] Later on in the same letter, he returned to this theme and told them not to be children in their thinking, but to grow up and act like spiritual adults.[111] The writer to the Hebrews was even more direct:

> . . . you have become dull of hearing. For though by this time you ought to be teachers, you need someone to teach you again the basic principles of the oracles of God. You need milk, not solid food, for everyone who lives on milk is unskilled in the word of righteousness, since he is a child. But solid food is for the mature. . . .[112]

It is hardly surprising that the same writer went on to quote Proverbs 3:11–12, which speaks about the Lord disciplining his children, and then added,

> God is treating you as sons. For what son is there whom his father does not discipline? If you are left without discipline, in which all have participated, then you are illegitimate children and not sons. . . . For the moment, all discipline seems painful rather than pleasant, but later it yields the peaceful fruit of righteousness to those who have been trained by it.[113]

Spiritual discipline sounds unattractive and can be painful at times, but it is necessary if we are to grow into the maturity that God wants to see in us. Indeed, says the passage, if we are not disciplined, we are illegitimate children! In human terms, an illegitimate child has a claim on his parents' attention

---

[108]1 Tim. 3:6.
[109]1 Pet. 2:1–3.
[110]1 Cor. 3:1–2.
[111]1 Cor. 14:20.
[112]Heb. 5:11b–14a.
[113]Heb. 12:7–8, 11.

because he is their natural son, but God cannot have children who are not legitimate. The only way into his family is by adoption, and if we have not been adopted by him, then we are not his children at all. On the other hand, once we are integrated into his family we must accept his Fatherly role, and that includes all the instruction and discipline we require to become the kind of spiritually mature adults he wants us to be.

SANCTIFIED IN THE SPIRIT

Growth in spiritual maturity is the logical consequence of our adoption into the family of God and is what we call "sanctification." This means that we must acquire something of the characteristics that distinguish God from his creation and make him the loving spiritual Father that he is. There are many things about God that are beyond our reach. No matter how hard we try, we shall never become invisible, immortal, impassible, omnipotent, or omniscient. The very strangeness of these words shows us how far we are from ever being able to grasp their meaning, let alone participate in them ourselves. But holiness is different. This is one characteristic of God that we can share, and that he wants us to participate in as much as we are able. As the apostle Paul put it, our sanctification is the will of God.[114]

What does it mean to be or to become holy? One of the most unfortunate developments in the history of the church is the way in which this word has become restricted to a certain category of people who have been held up as models of virtue for everyone else to imitate. These so-called saints have been canonized either by tradition or by ecclesiastical authority, and so highly have they been regarded that people have been taught to pray to them on the understanding that, because their holiness makes them so much closer to God than we are, they can intercede more effectively with him than we can. At the present time, canonical "sainthood" of this kind is restricted by the Roman Catholic Church to those who can be credited with having performed at least two miracles. One miracle merits what is called "beatification," allowing the person so honored to be addressed as "blessed," but a second miracle is required for the full status of sainthood to be conferred. The Eastern Orthodox churches also canonize "saints," but their criteria for doing so are more flexible. Most other churches honor prominent members who have died, especially if they have been martyred for their faith, but they do not put them in a special category of "saints."

Sainthood of this kind has no scriptural basis and is quite alien to the

---

[114]1 Thess. 4:3.

spirit of the Bible, where every believer is regarded as a "saint" in both the Old and New Testaments.[115] In the Old Testament, the saints were primarily those who had gone through the ritual acts of purification required for entering the temple, and it is in the context of worship that the term is most frequently used. In the New Testament the imagery of cleansing is taken up by Paul, who told the Corinthians that they had been washed and sanctified by the Holy Spirit.[116] His indwelling presence in the hearts of believers makes them his temples, so the principles of holiness that applied to the ancient Israelite temple also apply to us.[117] Our bodies are temples of the Holy Spirit because he is the Spirit of Christ, who was himself the living embodiment of the Old Testament temple.[118] In other words, it is union with Christ that leads to our sanctification, not anything we do or have done that might earn us the accolade of "saint." As with our adoption, sanctification is something given to us at the moment of our conversion that we must develop and apply as we grow into maturity as believers. Perhaps we might say that growth in adoption means understanding more deeply who we are in Christ, whereas growth in sanctification is directed more specifically at how we behave in a spiritually hostile world. But this distinction is more notional than real because in practice it is impossible to do one without the other. Christian growth necessarily affects our appreciation of who we are, and that in turn will determine what we do with our lives.

Clear as this is in Scripture, however, so great has been the influence of the Catholic tradition that no one today would call himself a saint because it would leave the impression that he was big-headed and deluded. The very suggestion that we should strive for holiness is often met either with a sense of despair at being asked to do the impossible, or with a certain amount of derisory laughter because any such "holiness" is almost bound to be a form of legalism that leads to hypocrisy rather than true sainthood.

In this respect, the holiness movements of the nineteenth and early twentieth centuries, which promoted a kind of spiritual perfectionism among their adherents, have not helped matters. They almost always defined "holiness" in terms of self-denial—no drinking, no smoking, no dancing, and so on. Unfortunately, as those who come from such backgrounds know only too well, it is much easier to give up something like drinking than it is to abandon feelings of pride or hatred, which those who refrain from the proscribed

---

[115]In the Old Testament, most of the references to "saints" are in the Psalms and in Daniel 7–8. See, for example, Ps. 30:4; 52:9; 85:8; 148:14; and Dan. 7:18–27. In the New Testament, the term is often used by Paul when writing to the churches. See for example Rom. 16:2; 1 Cor. 6:1; 2 Cor. 1:1; Eph. 1:1; Phil. 1:1; Col. 1:4.
[116]1 Cor. 6:11.
[117]1 Cor. 3:16–17.
[118]Mark 14:58.

activities may all too easily direct at those who fail to do so. Critics of this way of thinking can easily show that the Bible says nothing about smoking, does not disapprove of dancing, and while it is not exactly favorable toward strong drink, restricts its condemnation of it to drunkenness and does not ban its use altogether.[119] It is therefore hardly surprising that, in reaction to the excesses of the holiness movements, many Christians have developed an aversion to the very idea of holiness. Pursuing it actively is now very rare indeed, even among those who are sincerely trying to do God's will in their lives.

This is a tragedy because the pursuit of holiness is one of the most fundamental aspects of the Christian life. It does not mean becoming a slightly peculiar person who lives a life of ascetic self-discipline, as if those things were somehow signs of greater closeness to God. By those standards, Jesus cut a very poor figure when compared with John the Baptist:

> For John the Baptist has come eating no bread and drinking no wine, and you say, "He has a demon." The Son of Man has come eating and drinking, and you say, "Look at him! A glutton and a drunkard, a friend of tax collectors and sinners!"[120]

It is hard to imagine many churches being willing to hire Jesus as their pastor, with references like that! Of course, by defying the conventions of Jewish society, Jesus was teaching his disciples that true holiness is not a matter of keeping superficial and distorted versions of the law but of having a heart and mind attuned to the being and character of God.

To be attuned to God means being focused on what is transcendent and eternal, on what reflects the nature of the Creator rather than the limitations of his creatures. At the most basic level, this means avoiding any kind of idolatry and the immorality associated with it. In the modern world, it is easy to think that idolatry is a sin of the past, since apart from Hinduism and its derivatives, no major world religion today practices idolatry in the way that it was known in ancient times. But of course, idolatry has not disappeared; it has merely become more subtle. Instead of temples filled with stone statues, we have a leisure culture in which sports and films have created a new aristocracy whose careers are envied and whose lifestyles are imitated, regardless of their moral or spiritual failings. Some of their more outrageous excesses may be condemned (as was also the case with the excesses of ancient paganism), but is there really any difference between decking a statue in gold and paying an athlete millions of dollars a year when all he can do is kick a ball around

---

[119]Luke 21:34; Rom. 13:13; 1 Cor. 11:21; Gal. 5:21; Eph. 5:18; 1 Tim. 5:23.
[120]Luke 7:33–34; Matt. 11:19.

a field? Looked at in that light, it might even be argued that the pagans were better off, because their idols were a lot cheaper than ours!

Ancient idolatry was frequently associated with immorality, especially of a sexual kind, and so it is not surprising to find that sexual immorality features prominently among the things that we are told we must avoid. This was the context in which Paul wrote to the Thessalonians, telling them that sanctification was God's will for them. He explicitly said that each one of them must "know how to control his own body in holiness and honor, not in the passion of lust like the Gentiles who do not know God."[121] The same connection is also apparent in his letter to the Corinthians, where he explicitly excludes the sexually immoral, idolaters, adulterers, and those who practice homosexuality from the kingdom of God.[122]

Until recently, there would have been little quarrel with this, but the decline of Christian values in modern Western society has not left the church unscathed, and now we find people not only tolerating but even advocating things that only a generation ago would have been regarded with horror. The practice of homosexuality is one obvious example of this. It is forbidden in the Bible, but today there are people who argue that those whose "orientation" is homosexual should be allowed to fulfill their desires in the same way that heterosexuals can. Too few Christians are prepared to point out that, while the Bible does not condemn sexual desire, neither does it elevate it to the point where it becomes the decisive factor in a relationship. Heterosexual love must be structured and developed within a lifelong commitment to a single partner. It is clearly possible for a man to desire another woman, as David desired Bathsheba, but that is lust, and when David succumbed to it, he was punished.[123] Most churches today would still condemn someone in David's position, but they have become much more tolerant of remarriage after divorce, forgetting that it too is a form of adultery.[124] There is no question that this is hard to bear—the disciples of Jesus found it just as difficult as people today do. Jesus was uncompromising on this subject, however, and his followers have no choice but to embrace and adhere to his standards.

Sexual immorality plays an important part in New Testament teaching about sanctification, but it is by no means the only thing that Christians are called to avoid. In writing to the Corinthians, Paul does not hesitate to add that thieves, the greedy, drunkards, "revilers," and swindlers will not inherit

---

[121] 1 Thess. 4:3–4.
[122] 1 Cor. 6:9.
[123] 2 Sam. 12:13–14.
[124] Matt. 19:9.

the kingdom of God either.[125] It is not immediately clear what a reviler is in this context, but it is probably best understood as a person who is critical of other people or things to the point of bearing false witness about them. Accusing someone of theft, for example, would not entail reviling him if the accusation is sincerely believed, but if it has no basis in fact and is simply a means of discrediting the person concerned, then it is a sin equivalent to theft because it is robbing the unfortunate victim of his reputation.

In his letter to the Galatians, Paul broadens the scope of what he sees as "the works of the flesh" to include things like sorcery as well as matters more likely to upset personal relationships, like enmity, strife, jealousy, fits of anger, rivalries, dissensions, divisions, and envy.[126] All these things and others like them, such as malice,[127] must be exposed for what they are and excluded from our lives, both as individuals and in community. They are passions that belong to the corruption of our fallen nature, and although they cannot be completely uprooted until that nature is itself transformed by death and resurrection, they can be held in check and prevented from taking control of the church. This is the first step along the road that leads to maturity in sanctification.

The next step is a reordering of our priorities. Many people do this at different stages in their lives, but for a Christian, it only makes sense to do it in conformity with the revealed will of God. Above all else, this means focusing on things that are of lasting value and contribute to our spiritual growth. Sometimes this is relatively easy, particularly when it comes to avoiding morally dubious or reprehensible activities that can only do us harm. But making a choice is not always that simple or straightforward. In our sports-crazed world, for example, many Christians are tempted to put athletics before the service of God, either as participants (if they are young and fit) or as spectators (if they are not). No one doubts that physical exercise is a good thing, and it can be very beneficial to those who take part in it. But as Paul wrote to Timothy,

> Train yourself for godliness; for while bodily training is of some value, godliness is of value in every way, as it holds promise for the present life and also for the life to come.[128]

It is also tempting for Christian scholars to crave academic respectability, even when this can be had only at great cost to their faith. Faced with peer review from colleagues who may have no sympathy for Christian belief, we can all too

---

[125]1 Cor. 6:10.
[126]Gal. 5:19–20.
[127]Eph. 4:31; 1 Pet. 2:1.
[128]1 Tim. 4:7b–8.

easily forget that "the word of the cross is folly to those who are perishing."[129] The sin of pride haunts academia, and Christians must flee it if they want to grow closer to God, remembering that he has chosen what the world sees as foolish in order to shame the wise, the weak in order to shame the strong, and things that have no reputation in order to show the emptiness of those who are highly regarded in the secular sphere.[130] Paul was mocked by the intellectuals at Athens, who had no idea what he was saying, [131] and the situation of Christian believers in the modern academy is not so very different from his. It is a hard lesson to learn, but intellectual brilliance is no substitute for faithfulness as an entry ticket to the kingdom of God.

In all these things, the believer who is striving for greater sanctification must seek to emulate the character of God. Paul tells us what this means when he describes the "fruit of the Spirit," which includes love, joy, peace, patience, kindness, goodness, faithfulness, gentleness, and self-control.[132] All these qualities reflect the nature of God and are present in the way in which he deals with us. Of love it is hardly necessary to speak, since it is the foundation of everything God is and does.[133] The joy of the Lord is a characteristic that he shares with all those who are faithful to him, and it undergirds and sustains everything we do for him.[134] The peace of God is again well known, as are the other attributes mentioned in the list. Self-control perhaps does not apply to God in the way that it does to us because he is absolute and we are not, but it could be said to be the reason why he told Noah that he would not destroy the earth with another flood, despite the provocation of ongoing human sinfulness.[135]

To sum up, sanctification is life in the Spirit, which is the only kind of life a Christian can have. The Spirit's presence in us may be described as our contact point with God, the reality that allows us to cry, "Abba! Father!"[136] It is in his strength that we go forward and by his empowering that we gradually reach the goal to which God has predestined us.[137]

PREDESTINED TO ETERNAL GLORY

There is, perhaps, no subject more thoroughly debated, and at the same time more completely misunderstood, than the great question of predestination.

---

[129]1 Cor. 1:18.
[130]1 Cor. 1:27–28.
[131]Acts 17:32.
[132]Gal. 5:22–23.
[133]1 John 4:16.
[134]Neh. 8:10.
[135]Gen. 9:11.
[136]Rom. 8:15; Gal. 4:6.
[137]Eph. 1:13–14.

To the average person, it tends to suggest that everything has been decided by God in advance, which seems to make any activity on our part redundant. After all, this logic goes, if what we do is going to happen anyway, why do it? The issue has been especially contentious in the field of evangelism, where it has sometimes been thought that people who have a strong belief in predestination will find preaching the gospel unnecessary because, if God has already decided whom he will save, nothing we say or do will make any difference. We think that people who make a profession of faith ought to do so of their own free will, since otherwise it is hard to see how such a profession could be genuine. Free will seems to be an essential condition of our humanity because, if it is not, then neither Adam nor any of his descendants can be blamed for a sinfulness that they could not have avoided. In response to this, Christians have always affirmed that human beings must take responsibility for their sins, but they have also insisted that God is in sovereign control of the universe. How these things can be reconciled is a mystery, but many people think that to put the emphasis on predestination is to diminish the part people must play in their own salvation. There is also the danger that some people may convince themselves that they are not predestined, and may lose any hope of redemption as a result. That, too, hardly seems right, and so for all these reasons, many people believe that the doctrine of predestination ought to be avoided, even if it contains important elements of the truth.

This is somewhat ironic because most secular ideologies in the modern world are deterministic, which is to say that they have a predestinarian flavor to them. According to this way of thinking, the order of the universe is governed by fixed laws that are built into it. There may be various explanations for these laws, including ones that allow for a divine Creator, but wherever it may come from, the system functions according to its own inner logic. Human beings are products of their heredity and environment, and they cannot be any different from what they are. To believe otherwise is to introduce an anomaly or element of randomness into the system which is alien to its nature and would cause it to collapse if it were true. Since the system clearly does not collapse, such unpredictable interventions do not occur and everything that happens can be explained by studying the patterns that govern the way things work.

To a large extent, modern science has been built on this assumption. It is true that, as time goes on and new discoveries are made, the system is revealed as being much more complex and subtle than was previously thought. The physics of someone like Sir Isaac Newton, for example, have been considerably qualified by more recent developments, notably by the theory of relativity associated with Albert Einstein. That famous example can be replicated hundreds of times over in virtually every scientific discipline, and no scientific researcher would suggest that the way we view things now is the definitive explanation of the way things are. Every scientific theory is open to falsification, at least in principle, and one of the aims of researchers is to come up with better theories by falsifying the currently dominant theories. Nevertheless, a belief in determinism remains fundamental to the whole enterprise, which would not be possible without it.

It will be obvious that Christians cannot accept a deterministic view of the universe. For a start, we cannot believe that human beings are incapable of being changed, because that is precisely what happens when a person becomes a believer. Nor can we agree that the universe is a closed system that is unable to tolerate anomalies, because if that were so, miracles would be impossible.

People who do not accept that there is such a thing as a miracle in the true sense of the term will, of course, regard Christians as naive, obtuse, or intellectually lazy. Christians, by contrast, are frightened by what they see as a mechanistic, clockwork universe that reduces people to the level of robots and leaves no room for a sovereign God who is free to operate outside the system he created. To the atheist, science is a liberation from the superstitions of the past, but to a believer it is a prison in which human freedom is crushed by impersonal forces in a way that it never is by a doctrine of divine predestination.

Given this background and these arguments, what can we say? Can we rescue predestination from the clutches of determinism, or do we have to abandon the idea (as many Christians have done) because it is fundamentally incompatible with human freedom and therefore is dangerous to our sense of who we are? In seeking to resolve this issue, the first point we must grasp is that, as the word itself suggests, predestination is not about where we have come from but about where we are going. The two things are related, but the primary emphasis of predestination is on the future, not on the past.

The next thing we have to understand is that, in the New Testament, predestination is usually mentioned in connection with our salvation in Christ. It is not to be seen as an iron law built into the mind of God or the structure of the created universe, but as a word of assurance from God that our experience of his saving power is both real and purposeful. We have been saved for a reason and are heirs to a promised eternal glory, which we know we shall enter into when the time comes.[138]

---

[138]Rom. 8:38–39.

On what is that assurance based? The answer can only be that it is rooted and grounded in the sovereign will of God. There is much about that will of which we are ignorant, but we have been told that we are privileged to play a part in God's plan. Because of our human limitations, we cannot always see where that plan is heading, but when we look back over our past experience we can often make sense of it. Indeed, we often come to think that what has happened to us so far has an air of inevitability about it. We may occasionally wonder about what might have been if we had taken a different turning at some point or other, but such speculations quickly fade into the realm of fantasy because, once one past event is altered in our minds, there is no way of telling how many other events would have worked out differently as a consequence of that. If I had married a girl when I was twenty and gone to live with her in Argentina, my life would undoubtedly have been very different from what it has been, but what more can I say conclusively than that? Nothing, really! All I can do is look back on what has actually happened and make sense of it, a process that for a Christian will inevitably mean seeing the hand of God in the great events of his or her life.

But would I find God at work only in the big things that have happened to me? Hardly. Quite apart from anything else, how could I decide what is important and what is not? Going to university for four years might seem important in a way that receiving a letter from a stranger might not, but if I never use my degree for anything and the unknown letter is the offer of a job that I still have, would it not seem sensible for me to alter my sense of what matters? This is obvious from hindsight, but it might not appear that way at the time. Faced with a choice of taking up a university place or accepting employment by someone I have never heard of, deciding which of the two to take would not be at all clear. At times like that, Christians must be guided by the sense that "for those who love God, all things work together for good, for those who are called according to his purpose."[139] This is when our belief in predestination becomes not only valuable but essential for our lives, since it helps us to understand what God wants of us and to make the right decisions accordingly.

When looking back at the past, predestination has a healing power that is one of God's greatest gifts to us. Paul knew this from experience because he was haunted by the knowledge that as a young man he had persecuted the church. But listen to what he says:

> You have heard of my former life in Judaism, how I persecuted the church
> of God violently and tried to destroy it. . . . But when he who had set me

---

[139]Rom. 8:28.

apart before I was born, and who called me by his grace, was pleased to
reveal his Son to me, in order that I might preach him among the Gentiles,
I did not immediately consult with anyone . . .[140]

The man who had so misunderstood the mind of God that he attacked those
who had given their lives to Christ nevertheless knew that he had been set
apart before he was born and had been called for a particular purpose. Why
did God deal with Paul in this way? Why did he allow his people to be persecuted by someone who would later become their great defender and advocate? We cannot say, other than to reflect on the pattern we find throughout
Scripture, according to which God humbles the proud by confounding their
desires and exalts the humble in ways they could never have imagined. As
Mary sang when she was told that she would be the mother of the one who
would turn the world upside down and save us from our sins,

> He has brought down the mighty from their thrones and exalted those of
> humble estate; he has filled the hungry with good things, and the rich he
> has sent away empty.[141]

Predestination is an intensely practical belief, very closely tied to what
we often call "guidance." If I have a clear sense of my long-term destiny, then
that will affect the way I live and will influence how I evaluate the events of
my everyday life. If I have put God first and have laid up my treasure in heaven
as Jesus advised us to do, I shall be less bothered about getting rich here on
earth, not just because I know that I cannot take it with me, but because my
energies will be spent in more useful ways.[142] That would undoubtedly affect
the way I view my career and the things that I would be prepared to get
involved in. In particular, it would have a powerful influence on my choice of
a spouse. Christians are warned not to marry unbelievers because those who
do not share our outlook on life cannot walk along the pathway set out for us
by God.[143] In fact, Christians are advised not to marry at all if they can help it,
not because there is anything wrong with matrimony but because the service
of God comes first and matrimony is liable to interfere with it.[144] Marriage is
an important life decision, but it is a decision for this life only—there is no
marriage in heaven, and it is to heaven that we are headed.[145]

These principles are clearly stated in the New Testament, but there is

---

[140]Gal. 1:13, 15–16.
[141]Luke 1:52–53.
[142]Matt. 6:19–21.
[143]2 Cor. 6:14.
[144]1 Cor. 7:1–9.
[145]Matt. 22:30.

no teaching more strongly resisted among believers than this one. Far from encouraging people to see matrimony in the context of God's will for our lives, most pastors are only too eager to act as matchmakers, and may even put pressure on those who resist their services in this respect. The intentions of these pastors may be good, but we have to wonder whether they have any sense that God's purposes for us are not bound or governed by the limits of this life. In this sense, predestination is an uncomfortable doctrine because it forces us to consider the claims that eternity has on our lives and to accept that, if there is a clash between what God has prepared for us in heaven and what we want to enjoy on earth, it is both our duty and in our interest to choose what we know he wants for us and not what we want for ourselves.

Is there such a thing as choice or free will? It is clear that if there is, it can be exercised only within a very limited sphere. We cannot choose the time, place, or circumstances of our birth and upbringing. We cannot go back into the past or leap into the future if we are not happy with our present situation. Factors of many kinds will inevitably play a part in the decisions we make, and these will limit our freedom of choice, often to a very considerable extent. We seldom have the luxury of being able to "choose" something in the abstract; usually, we are confronted with particular possibilities of which we have to pick one. Ironically, the degree of "freedom" we exercise in making such a decision may well be in inverse proportion to the importance we attach to it. For example, if the "choice" is between different flavors of ice cream, we may decide just to take whatever comes first and not spend too much time on it. But if we have to make plans that will affect our long-term future, we shall probably sit down and think carefully about it, weighing every relevant consideration we can think of, before coming to a decision. The more we do that, of course, the more circumscribed our decision will be, and after we have eliminated any number of alternatives, it may be debated just how "free" our final choice will be.

Having said that, though, there is no doubt that we feel we are free to decide, and this feeling is more than just an illusion. Human beings are not machines controlled by a supernatural mind. We are created in the image and likeness of God, and decision-making powers are part of that. The sphere in which we operate may be limited by our finitude, but within it we are "gods," as Scripture says, because we have a freedom similar to God's.[146] There is something in us that is more like him than like the world around us, and it is that which gives us the ability to make choices that other creatures cannot make. Ultimately, of course, we are also creatures, and God knows

---

[146]Ps. 82:6; John 10:34.

what he has made. In the depths of his being, he understands us in ways that we shall never be able to fathom; he knows the secrets of our hearts even when we do not know them ourselves. Trying to probe the depths of that mystery is impossible because our minds are not able to grasp all the factors involved. Inevitably we shall reduce the plan and purpose of God to the limits of our own understanding, which means that we shall distort it. All we know is that we are presented with choices and are expected to make them in the fear and knowledge of God. Moses expressed it very well when he told the Israelites,

> I have set before you life and death, blessing and curse. Therefore choose life, that you and your offspring may live, loving the LORD your God, obeying his voice and holding fast to him . . .[147]

We are free to disregard these words, but if we do, we shall be choosing death, which is the loss not only of freedom but of existence itself. Outside the will of God, all choice is ultimately self-destruction because apart from his will, the exercise of our free will can be nothing other than rebellion against him.

---

[147]Deut. 30:19–20.

29

THE FELLOWSHIP
OF BELIEVERS

INDIVIDUALS IN COMMUNITY

The Holy Spirit makes living the Christian life possible. Everything he does for us after our conversion is geared to that end and designed for that purpose. There are a few people who never get the opportunity to lead a Christian life because they die almost immediately after their conversion, but this is rare and cannot be regarded as the norm. Most of us remain on earth for some time after we have become believers, and we are therefore obliged to work out our salvation in a way that honors God in our own lives and in our witness to other people.

As Christians, we are called to do this both as individuals and in fellowship with others who share our faith. These two things go together, and rather like the chicken and the egg, it is hard to say which of them comes first. Logically speaking, conversion to Christ comes before fellowship with others because we cannot enjoy such fellowship if we are not converted. On the other hand, most people come to faith because they have been in contact with such a fellowship and heard the gospel preached by someone who already belongs to the Christian community. Converted individuals form a community, but that community then attracts other individuals and leads them to faith. The key to understanding the Christian life is not to give priority to the one over the other but to see individuals and communities interacting in a mutual relationship from which each draws strength and to which each contributes.

The fellowship of believers into which we are called is known as the church, a word with many layers of meaning. When they hear the word "church," most ordinary people think first of a building, and then perhaps of the organization that owns it, but they may never realize that those things are only the outward and visible manifestations of a spiritual and invisible reality. Buildings have their importance and cannot be neglected or ignored, but they point to something beyond themselves that the eye of the beholder cannot immediately see. The invisible church expresses itself in visible forms, and the buildings and organizations we call "churches" are evidence of that. To belong to the invisible church without also belonging to the visible one is like trying to be a spirit without a body. That may be imaginable in theory, but it is not practically possible in this world. Whether we like it or not, we are both spirit and body, and so is the church.

But just as our bodies are temporary and wasting away in their present form, so too, the visible church is a temporal thing that is subject to the law of decay and death. There is no visible church that can claim to be a perfect or complete manifestation of the invisible one, and every human organization will suffer from the limitations imposed on all human beings. It is important to understand this because many people find it difficult to belong to a visible church which they know is imperfect. They see that it is full of hypocrites, riven by political divisions, and exposed to scandals of various kinds. For some, the existence of different denominations, which often seem to be in competition with one another, makes a mockery of the claim that we are all one in Christ.[1] Surely it is much simpler just to follow him and put his teaching into practice, without getting wrapped up in such complications.

To this, various answers can be given. At one end of the spectrum are those who say that, just as there is only one invisible church, so there is only one visible church that represents it, even if it does so imperfectly. According to this way of thinking, other groups may claim the status of churches, but they are defective in one way or another. They may teach false doctrine, or be incapable of exercising discipline among their members. They may be too localized, belonging essentially to one geographical area or ethnic group, and not embracing the whole of mankind on an equal footing. Whatever the reason, they are inadequate to represent the one true, universal church and so their claim to be churches in the true sense of the word must be rejected, even if genuine Christians can be found in their ranks.

This is the position taken by the Roman Catholic Church, by the various Eastern Orthodox churches, and also by some Protestant churches, particularly those who hold to a "restorationist" view of the church. Restorationists say that it is possible to ignore the corruptions of the past two millennia, go back to the New Testament, and form a church based exclusively on what it says. If that is done, they claim, the visible church will be as perfect as it can be

---

[1] 1 Cor. 12:12; Gal. 3:28.

because the accretions of later times, which have no divine authority, will be excluded. In practice, of course, pure restorationism is not possible, and even the strictest of these churches have to compromise with modernity to some extent—just as the Roman Catholics and Eastern Orthodox are usually more flexible in practice than their official doctrine would suggest.

Unlike the restorationists, however, the Roman Catholic and Eastern Orthodox churches do not reject post-biblical traditions. On the contrary, they justify them by saying that the Holy Spirit has continued to speak to the church and in the course of time has led it to adopt certain beliefs and practices which are consonant with the historical development of Christian teaching. Such beliefs and practices are not meant to contradict what the Bible says but to clarify and supplement it when necessary. The great creeds of the early church are a prime example of this because they proclaim the truth of the Scriptures in language adapted to the needs of later times. In the course of history, certain doctrines and devotional practices have taken shape to deal with the challenges posed by specific circumstances or to help Christians grow deeper in their faith. At any given time, there will be a number of such things that are less emphasized or less official than others, and these are optional extras as far as the ordinary believer is concerned. But if the church is led to define them more precisely and make them official, there can be no further opting out—the decision taken by the church must be accepted by everyone. A good example of this is the Roman Catholic doctrine of papal infallibility. Before it was proclaimed in 1870, there were many people who either did not believe it or who would have expressed it in much looser terms, but now that it has become an article of faith, it must be believed by everyone who wants to belong to the Roman Catholic Church.

One of the biggest problems with this view of the visible church is its inherent inflexibility. If what is seen reflects what is unseen, and if that necessarily produces a single, united set of beliefs and practices, it is hard to see how genuine diversity can be accommodated within the visible structures. There have been times in the past when the need felt for visible unity has been taken to extremes, as when the Roman Catholic Church required its services to be conducted exclusively in Latin, the supposedly universal language. The Eastern Orthodox churches have usually been more flexible on the matter of language, but the forms of their liturgy have not changed in centuries and are easily recognizable all over the world. So rigid has this become, that even a modest reform of the calendar (to bring it into line with the reform made by the papacy in 1582, which is now universally accepted in the secular sphere) has been hotly contested and has led to a breach of the church's unity in spite of the essentially trivial and nontheological nature of the reform. It has even been claimed by some extremists that those Orthodox who have accepted calendar reform are out of line with the saints in heaven, who presumably are using the old Roman calendar, which was adopted by Julius Caesar in 46 B.C. and was in use in the time of Jesus.[2]

Most Protestants take a view of the visible church different from the one just described. They agree that there is only one spiritual, invisible church, but they do not accept that this is manifested in only one visible form. Even in the New Testament, the different cities and provinces of the Roman empire had autonomous local churches which submitted to apostolic authority but not to each other. The churches of Achaia (in southern Greece) sent money to the church at Jerusalem in order to help with famine relief there, but there is no sign that either one sought to influence or discipline the other in any way.[3] This is particularly significant because it is well known that the Jerusalem church was stricter in its observance of Jewish customs than most of the Gentile churches were, a fact that had caused tensions in the not too distant past.[4] But as long as these differences did not touch on an essential point of faith, they were accommodated within the overall fellowship of the wider church and did not act as a barrier that was destructive to Christian unity.

It is this model that most Protestants adopt, though they disagree about what constitutes a "local" church. For some, this means the individual con-gregation, which claims the freedom to order itself and to associate with other like-minded believers as it sees fit. For others, "local" means national or regional. Their churches are structured along customary or secular territo-rial lines, within which a common order is adopted, usually by the vote of a representative council or synod. Individual congregations must then conform to this common order or be disciplined. This discipline can take many forms and is often fairly lax, with provision being made for dissenters if they consti-tute a significant minority. In recent times, this has happened when a church has revised its forms of worship only to discover that many of its members remain attached to what was already in use. In such situations it is usual to allow them to continue to use the older forms, at least for a period of time, until the transition to the new order is complete. Nevertheless, the decision to allow exceptions of this kind is a commonly agreed one and operates within the guidelines accepted by the church as a whole, so that its visible unity is preserved. The underlying principle here is the desirability of distinguishing

---

[2]This does not mean that Jesus himself used it, however. It is more likely that the Jewish communities in which he lived followed the Jewish and not the Roman calendar, at least most of the time.
[3]2 Cor. 9:2; Acts 19:21.
[4]Acts 15:1–21.

what is essential from what is not, and allowing tradition and personal preferences to have their place when nothing essential is at stake.

For Protestants, learning to distinguish between what is essential and what is not is vitally important if the unity of the church is to be preserved and the truth of the gospel maintained. If nonessentials are allowed to become matters of debate that divide the church, the likelihood is that people will focus on them rather than on the far more important matters directly connected to the gospel. When the Roman Catholic Church made it optional to eat fish on Fridays (a discipline that had been imposed until the 1960s), many ordinary church members thought their whole faith had been changed. Some resisted this overreaction, of course, but many others proceeded to reject such things as the doctrine of the Trinity, on the ground that it too was just an outdated church ordinance that could safely be discarded along with the previously compulsory fish. Protestant churches tend not to have disciplinary rules like that, but many Protestants can be just as attached to forms of worship or versions of the Bible that have no particular authority, and feel that if they are abandoned something essential to their faith has been lost.

The history of Protestant denominationalism shows how problematic this can be. A comparison of the different confessions of faith that Protestant churches have adopted tends to show that the first half is much the same in all of them. This is the part that deals with God, the Bible, and the way of salvation. It is in the second half, which usually deals with church government, ritual practices, ministry, church-state relations, and social issues such as Sunday observance and pacifism, that significant differences appear. A look at the way denominations identify themselves will confirm this. Episcopalians are people who have bishops, Presbyterians are those who have synodical government, Congregationalists champion local autonomy, Baptists practice only believer's baptism, and so on. None of these things is central to the message of the gospel, but feelings about them have been strong enough to divide the church when compromise has been unattainable.

Unfortunately, the tendency to downplay the more essential matters is such that today there are people in all these denominations who deny or compromise the basic doctrines of the faith without being disciplined, but woe betide anyone who transgresses one of the so-called "denominational distinctives." An Episcopalian who accepted the validity of Presbyterian ordination, for example, or a Baptist who baptized an infant would probably be thrown out of his church, but the same church might happily let them preach unitarianism and get away with it! When this happens, priorities have been inverted, and the church must be called back to the distinction between the fundamentals, on which there must be unity, and the nonessentials, where each person can be allowed to make up his own mind and act accordingly.

Reflection on this distinction between what is central and what is secondary or even peripheral will soon show that one of the reasons why the distinction is so hard to maintain is that the secondary things tend to be material whereas the primary ones are more likely to be spiritual and therefore, to many minds, purely intellectual and theoretical. This is why preaching heresy from the pulpit is likely to attract less attention than reordering the furniture, introducing a new hymnbook, or altering the worship style. Those are things that ordinary people can relate to, and so trouble is likely to result from that kind of change. Nothing demonstrates more clearly than this that we are earthly beings, attached to what our physical senses tell us. In this respect, traditionalists and innovators may be equally at fault because both tend to concentrate on what is superficial. They either ignore what really matters or assume that by changing appearances the spiritual message will come across more clearly. The many reforms of liturgy and worship that have been introduced in the mainline churches since about 1960 have two things in common. The first is that they were supposed to bring people back to church by making Christianity more "relevant" to the upcoming generation. The second is that they have all failed in their aim, and the churches that have adopted them are more divided and weaker now than they have ever been.

Given this situation, the need to stress the underlying spiritual unity of the church is more pressing today than ever before. The church of God is first and foremost a creation of the Holy Spirit, as we can see from the experience of Pentecost, when the preaching of Peter and the other apostles led to the formation of the first Christian community.[5] That community came into existence through the proclamation of the Word of God and in direct response to it. There was nothing else that bound its members together, since as the text tells us, they came from every part of the known world and did not even speak the same language. Until the apostles got them organized, there was no church for them to belong to. The First Christian Church of Jerusalem (or if you prefer, the Cathedral Church of St. Peter and the Apostles!) never existed as such. What did exist was a community gathered by the preaching of the gospel, and that gospel came straight out of the pages of Holy Scripture.

What happened on the day of Pentecost became the pattern in the early church, as the Acts of the Apostles tells us. There we find a developing ministry of preaching which took the erstwhile disciples of Jesus from Jerusalem to all Judea, then to Samaria, and ultimately to the ends of the earth, as Jesus

---

[5] Acts 2:41–47.

had told them it would.[6] For this to be done with the maximum degree of efficiency, it was desirable to set aside certain people, who clearly had the gift of preaching, and commission them to do it on a full-time basis. Nevertheless, the officially appointed preachers did not monopolize the ministry. The degree to which the apostles were prepared to accept anyone as a preacher, provided the message itself was sound, is well illustrated by Paul, who wrote,

> Some indeed preach Christ from envy and rivalry, but others from good will. The latter do it out of love, knowing that I am put here [in prison] for the defense of the gospel. The former proclaim Christ out of selfish ambition, not sincerely but thinking to afflict me in my imprisonment. What then? Only that in every way, whether in pretense or in truth, Christ is proclaimed, and in that I rejoice.[7]

It would be hard to find a better endorsement of the primacy of the message over the preacher. The spiritual state and motivation of the preacher was less important to Paul than the content of what he had to say, and on that there could be no doubt or compromise. The gospel message has always been public, and there is no room for reasonable doubt about what it is. But that has not stopped some people from trying to twist it to their own predilections, and when that happens, those who know the truth are forced to react. Paul had this happen to him in Galatia. After preaching to the churches there and winning many to Christ, he was followed by others who tried to tell the Galatian Christians that the message they had heard was defective. To be a real Christian, they claimed, a person must first of all become a Jew, because the message of Jesus did not abolish the law of Moses. When Paul discovered this, he was quick to react:

> There are some who trouble you and want to distort the gospel of Christ. But even if we or an angel from heaven should preach to you a gospel contrary to the one we preached to you, let him be accursed.[8]

Once again, we see that the credentials of the preacher are of secondary importance. It is the message that counts because that is what wins people to Christ and constitutes the church. It is for this reason that purity of doctrine has always been of fundamental concern. It is perfectly possible to be an eloquent orator and yet preach a false message, as many famous dictators have demonstrated. People like that are especially dangerous because they sound so

---

[6] Acts 1:8.
[7] Phil. 1:15–18.
[8] Gal. 1:7b–8.

convinced of what they are saying and come across so persuasively. Over the years the church has known many people of that kind, who have gained a following, thanks to the power of their voice and personality. They may be very successful for a time, but after they are exposed or fade from the scene, their followers melt away and the church is back to where it was before, perhaps with a few extra scars to show what it has been through.

The Galatian Christians were fortunate in that they had Paul to put them straight, but we are better off still because we have the entire New Testament. Anyone can buy a copy and read what it says. It is perfectly possible to test what preachers say against the Bible itself, and this is what we are called to do as believers.[9] The intelligent Christian is one who is learned in the Word of God and recognizes it when he hears it—and who also knows when he does not hear it. But some people may ask, if reading the Bible is enough to teach us the truth, do we really need the ministry of preachers, especially nowadays when there are so many other means of mass communication readily available to us?

To those who are spiritual and who understand what it is saying, the Bible is an essential guide to the Christian life and speaks very powerfully to rebuke us when we stray from the right pathway. But to those who have no such understanding, the Bible is a closed book. It is sometimes said that the Bible can be read as great literature, but hardly anyone actually does so. Outside the sphere of the church or the synagogue, its contents are little known. Those unbelievers who know it well have almost always had a Christian education, but with the secularization of Western culture, that can no longer be taken for granted. At the other end of the spectrum, there are some people who have devoted their lives to studying the Bible in an academic way but who have no sympathy with its teaching and no real understanding of what it is saying. In that respect, the Bible, like any other aspect of the visible church, can be read and studied without any appreciation of the spiritual dimension to which it bears witness.

This is where preachers come in. They are men sent by God to bring his Word alive in the world. Their purpose is not merely to teach what the Bible says, though that is important, but to challenge their hearers to receive that teaching in their hearts. A sermon is not a lecture but a plea to us to hear and submit to the authority of the Word of God. The problem with ancient Israel was not that it had not heard that Word but that it had not submitted to it in humble obedience.[10] Unfortunately, what was true of them is also true of

---

[9]See Acts 17:11.
[10]Rom. 10:18–21.

many people today because true preachers (as opposed to lecturers and pulpit entertainers) are few and their message is neglected. The true preacher is a man filled with the Spirit of God, who can bring his Word alive in that Spirit. As the fire in him spreads to those who hear him, the dry wood is set alight, and men and women come to know the power of the Lord Jesus Christ in their lives.

When that happens, the conversion of individuals leads to the creation of the new community that we call the church. Fire can exist on its own, but only for a time because eventually it will grow cold and be extinguished. Individual sparks need to find the full body of the blaze to which they can contribute and from which they will draw new life. That fire and that life can be found in the visible institutions we call "the church," but the two things are not identical. When we are alive in the Spirit, we live in the visible church but we see beyond it, knowing that our true home, and indeed the true church of God, is the spiritual body, which the Spirit's heavenly fire brings to life in the world.

Before we move on to consider the way in which the different branches of the visible church see themselves and each other, something needs to be said about the eternal dimension in which the invisible church can also be found. The visible community of God's people exists only in time and space, but there is a whole body of saints in heaven who are also members of the church, even though we no longer see them and often do not know who they are. They constitute what is known as the "church triumphant," as opposed to those of us who are still engaged in spiritual warfare here below, who constitute the "church militant." There is evidence in Scripture to suggest that the church triumphant prays for us in our struggles here below,[11] but this is too vague for us to be able to draw any conclusions from it about our relationship with its members. There is certainly no evidence that we can pray to the saints in heaven and ask them to intercede for us; we have direct access to God the Father and do not need to go through his servants in order to speak to him. Even if communication with those who have gone before is theoretically possible, there is no evidence that it occurred in New Testament times, and attempts to contact them should be avoided. The saints in heaven are at rest, and they should be allowed to remain that way.

THE OLD TESTAMENT PEOPLE OF GOD

The origins of the church reach back into the distant past, to the time when God called Abraham to leave his father and mother and to go to a distant

---

[11]See Rev. 6:10.

country, where he would settle and become the ancestor of a great nation. Abraham believed what God said, and in spite of many hurdles and setbacks, he did indeed become the founder of a new people, known to us as Israel, the name God gave to Abraham's grandson Jacob.[12] It is a fundamental Christian belief that God's love has been poured out on the world in and through Israel, and no one can come to know God or experience his love as long as he remains a stranger to that nation. Every child of God is a descendant of Abraham, sharing his faith and entering into the same relationship that Abraham had with his Creator. For many centuries, that relationship was essentially confined to Abraham's physical descendants. Not all of them wanted it, and many were cut off from their inheritance because of their rejection and disobedience. On the other hand, there were a few who came to share Abraham's faith even though they were not physically descended from him, and they were subsequently integrated into his people along with his blood descendants. The most famous of these was Ruth the Moabitess, who became an ancestor of King David and, through him, of Jesus.[13] There were also isolated cases of individuals such as Naaman, who professed belief in the God of Israel but did not join the nation. Naaman was even excused for having to participate in pagan worship because of his high position in the Syrian kingdom, though this was unusual.[14] Both the large numbers of Israelites who turned away from God and the small numbers of foreigners who submitted to him were exceptions in a world where tribal and national allegiances determined religious beliefs most of the time. Renegade Israelites rapidly disappeared into the surrounding pagan societies, while believing foreigners were too few in number to constitute a distinct group.

The Old Testament people of God were a nation among the nations, and what we know about them reflects that. Their laws and their history are faithfully recorded for us, sometimes in great detail. From those records we learn that Israel was expected to demonstrate its character as God's chosen people in every aspect of its social life, and the great principles of justice that the law enshrines remain valid for believers today. But a detailed application of the ancient law is seldom if ever possible now because circumstances have changed beyond recognition. A good example of this is the law of jubilee, according to which all debts were to be canceled every fifty years.[15] The purpose of this law was to ensure that indebtedness did not become an insoluble problem, weighing the nation down and leading to a situation in which the

---

[12]Gen. 32:28.
[13]Ruth 4:17.
[14]2 Kings 5:18.
[15]Lev. 25:10.

poor would find themselves in semi-permanent slavery. Whether the law of jubilee was ever applied is doubtful, but the principle is a good one and is maintained today by various kinds of debt-relief schemes that try to do much the same thing. In other words, the principle has survived, even if the precise details are no longer applicable.

Maintaining this distinction is important in guiding our interpretation of the Old Testament. The Christian church is not a state in the way that ancient Israel was, and we cannot simply adopt laws originally intended for civil government back then if they make little or no sense in modern conditions. We also have to remember that no modern state is the embodiment of God's people on earth, and, although there may be some benefit in following particular biblical precepts, governments today are not under any divine obligation to do so. This has to be said because in the past, Christians have sometimes tried to justify things like slavery on the basis of Old Testament texts. The argument they used was that the institution existed in ancient Israel and so it was permissible in a Christian society as well, even though slavery was not encouraged in Israel and the economic and social circumstances that had made it hard to eliminate in ancient times no longer applied.

THE NEW TESTAMENT PEOPLE OF GOD

When God fulfilled his promise to Abraham and came to earth himself in the person of the Son, Jesus Christ, Israel's relationship to him changed forever. True descent from Abraham was thenceforth to be defined as a spiritual inheritance which could be enjoyed by anyone who shared his faith. The physical descendants of Israel, who thought of themselves as a race apart, were told that they had no grounds for thinking they had a special relationship with God on the basis of their human ancestry.[16] When the Son of God came to earth, many of those who were identified as Jews in human terms refused to accept their promised Messiah, but at the same time many non-Jews—far more, in fact—who had previously been excluded or untouched by the grace of God came to enjoy a saving faith in him. The new community these people formed is what we call "the church." It includes those faithful believers who lived before the coming of Christ, whether or not they were Israelites, but it is not a "nation" in the way that Israel was.[17] The essential difference between Israel and the church is that what was external in the former has now been internalized. The temple that once stood in Jerusalem as the focus of wor-

---

[16]Rom. 2:12–3:18.
[17]It was once customary to refer to Israel as the "Old Testament church" but we seldom do this nowadays, perhaps because Israel did not use the word to describe itself.

ship and the sign of God's presence has disappeared and has been replaced by the body of Christ, which was once present on earth in material form but is now spiritually manifested in each and every believer.[18] Christians do not constitute an ethnic community, but they are a particular people, chosen from among the nations and separated out as a special society that transcends and relativizes human barriers of every kind.[19]

The Christian church as we know it began fifty days after the resurrection of Jesus and ten days after his ascension into heaven, when he filled his expectant disciples with the Holy Spirit that he had promised to send after his departure.[20] From then on, the people of God were distinguished by the indwelling presence of that Holy Spirit, who taught them the meaning of God's love as revealed in Christ.[21] The relationship with God that had been held out to Israel as the sign and seal of that love now became a reality in their lives. No longer was it necessary to struggle to attain to a standard acceptable to God in order to enjoy his favor. Instead, it was clearly recognized that no one could ever satisfy God's requirements by his own efforts—and that it was pointless to make the attempt, because Jesus Christ had already done what was necessary on our behalf. Not only had he kept the law of God in his own life, but he had also taken our sins and shortcomings on himself and died in order to atone for them. Furthermore, he had defeated the forces of evil ranged against us, and although we must continue to struggle against them, they can no longer control our lives.

The church is primarily the community of those who have come to know the love of God as their Savior and Lord, but it has always also included unbelievers, who have been attracted to it for some reason but have never truly entered into the relationship of faith that characterizes the true child of God.[22] Why this should be so is a mystery, but whatever the explanation, we can be sure that it is part of God's way of showing his love to his creation and of glorifying himself. Perhaps he wants to show how wonderful the blessing given to the church is by demonstrating the power it has to attract even unbelievers. Maybe he wants to keep us humble by reminding us that belonging to an outward body of people is no guarantee of our spiritual state before him. There may be other explanations for it that are unknown to us. Whatever the case, the visible church has never been "pure" because it never has consisted exclusively of believers. In the words of Jesus himself, "The wheat and tares

---

[18]Matt. 26:61; 2 Cor. 6:16.
[19]Gal. 3:28.
[20]Acts 2:1–4; John 16:7.
[21]Gal. 4:6.
[22]See Acts 5:1–11.

grow together until the harvest," and attempting to root out the latter runs the risk of damaging the former in the process.[23] In the end, it is not through the church that we come to God, but through God that we come to the church and through him that we recognize who our spiritual brothers and sisters are.

THE CHURCH AND THE CHURCHES

The relationship between the church and the churches is essentially that between the invisible and the visible people of God. All who are born of the Spirit are members of the church, grafted into the olive tree as members of the body of Christ. No external rite, official ceremony, or formal document can produce that effect, nor is it possible for any ecclesiastical authority to detract from it. If the Holy Spirit is dwelling in our hearts, then no power on earth can separate us from the love of God in Christ.[24] We can and do have fellowship with all who belong to that church, whatever branch of the visible institution they may belong to. Conversely, we do not (and cannot) have fellowship with those who are not born again by the Holy Spirit, even if we both belong to the same denomination. We do not know what the boundaries of the invisible church are, and it is not our business to define them. Spiritual fellowship comes naturally to those who live in the Spirit, as people from all over the world can testify from their personal experience. But when we encounter those who do not know the Lord, no amount of common tradition or culture can bridge the abyss between us.

It is when we talk about the visible church that we use the word in the plural, especially when we are talking about individual congregations or different denominations. The New Testament gives us plenty of evidence for the first of these because there were congregations of believers in all the major cities of the Roman world, but it knows nothing of denominations. In those days, and for at least four centuries afterwards, there was really only one visible church, even though there were always sectarian offshoots or heretical groups that competed with the mainline body.[25] It was only in the fifth century that this church began to break up into different groups which exist to this day and are generally recognized as being "churches" in the modern, denominational sense.

The event that sparked the first of these lasting divisions was the Council of Chalcedon in 451, where the incarnate Christ was defined as being one divine person in two natures. The Antiochene party, which followed the

---

[23]Matt. 13:29–30.
[24]Rom. 8:39.
[25]Famous examples of these were the Donatists of North Africa and the Montanists of Asia Minor.

teaching of Nestorius (381?–451?), rejected this formulation because it felt that it obscured the completeness of Christ's humanity. These so-called Nestorians were forced to leave the Roman empire in 484 and go to Persia, where they were welcomed and allowed to settle. For many centuries, they evangelized Central Asia and established a number of flourishing churches there, but persecution and isolation gradually weakened them. Today there is only a small handful of them left, living mostly in northern Iraq and as exiles in the United States. Among themselves, they claim to be the only true church, but they are too small and obscure for this claim to be taken seriously.

The other group that rejected Chalcedon did so for the exact opposite reason. These were the followers of Cyril of Alexandria (d. 444), who insisted that the incarnate Christ had only one nature after his incarnation, a nature in which his humanity had effectively been absorbed into his divinity. We call them Monophysites because of their "one nature" Christology, and they became the main church in Egypt, Syria, and Armenia. Later on, they went to Ethiopia and also to South India, where they remain an important presence. Like the Nestorians, the Monophysites also claim to be the one true church, but again, their historical circumstances are such that it is hard to accept this.

The next major division in the Christian world occurred between the churches of what had been the Western and Eastern Roman empire. That empire had been divided for the first time in 313, shortly before Christianity became a legal religion (in 380), but the division was made permanent in 395, and the two sides moved further apart. The Western empire collapsed in 476 and was replaced by a number of Germanic kingdoms, most of which were Arian or pagan. In those circumstances, the Christian population came to see itself as essentially Roman and universal, or "catholic," because the church covered the area that had previously been part of the empire. Rome was its natural capital, and that city gradually assumed greater importance as time went on. Latin was its official language, not least because the Germanic tribes had no written languages of their own. Latin thus quickly established itself as the universal standard for worship and theology. In the East, however, the empire survived until 1453 and never developed the same cultural homogeneity. Greek was its main language, but not the only one, and the church was quite happy to use Georgian, Armenian, Syriac, and Coptic as well. Later on, Slavonic was added to this list as missionaries moved north to convert the Slavs to the Eastern form of Christianity.

Like the Nestorians and the Monophysites, both the Roman Catholic and the Eastern Orthodox churches claim to be the one true church, but as they are much larger and more influential, their claims have to be taken more seriously. The Eastern Orthodox churches do not have a single head or the kind of unity that typifies Rome. They are loosely grouped around the patriarch of Constantinople (Istanbul) and are held together by a common doctrine and liturgy, which compensates for the vast differences of language and culture that otherwise distinguish them from one another. Outsiders sometimes find it hard to believe that Greeks and Russians belong to the same church, but they may be even more surprised to discover that many Greeks and Russians share the same feeling.

The main problems with the Eastern Orthodox claim to be the one true church are that they are so obviously the products of a fractured European history that this claim makes little sense. How can Romanians and Bulgarians be real Christians but not Portuguese or Swedes? Of course there are doctrinal differences between Eastern and Western Christians, but the degree to which these have been bound up with politics is such that it seems audacious (to put it mildly) to make such a claim nowadays. Apologists for Orthodoxy like to insist that their church has retained the purity of the ancient one and that their essentially apophatic theology is the right way to approach God. Unfortunately for them, this ignores the rather obvious fact that the modern Orthodox churches bear little resemblance to anything found in the New Testament, despite a certain historical and geographical continuity with it. It also ignores the fact that apophatic theology is by definition one-sided in its approach, that it did not dominate the ancient Greek world in the way that its devotees like to claim, and that from the sixteenth century onwards, Orthodoxy has frequently borrowed Western models and adapted them to suit its own purposes.

In recent times the Eastern Orthodox churches have had to come to terms with a wider world, but they have not done this very successfully and they continue to struggle with even the most basic elements of modern life. Those in the West who have embraced this form of Christianity have often done so precisely because they reject modernity and are attracted by a theology and devotional life that seems to be able to resist it. But as a claimant for the role of universal church, Eastern Orthodoxy remains too exotic for most people who are not part of it, and the chance that it will ever reconcile the rest of the Christian world to itself are no greater than the chance that the rest of the world will adopt the Greek or Russian alphabet instead of the Latin one that most of us use.

That leaves the Roman Catholic Church, which is by far the largest and most important of all those who claim the title of "universal church." When nominal or cultural Christianity is taken into account, about a third of the world's population is "Christian" and two-thirds of these Christians are Roman Catholics. Although it clearly has its roots in the western Mediterranean, the Roman church has now spread so far and wide that it cannot easily be equated with a single cultural area. It does have a single language, Latin, but that is now used only in formal documents and very occasionally in worship. In its place, every major tongue on earth can be heard in Rome, and the church is well represented almost everywhere that Christians live. Furthermore, Rome actively pursues its vocation to universality and continues to make overtures to other churches in the hope of eventually bringing them back into union with itself.

So large and multi-faceted a church cannot be fairly assessed in a few paragraphs, though it must be said that statistics are deceptive. On paper, there may be more than a billion Catholics around the world, but many of these are nominal. Some are agnostics or have become Protestants, a phenomenon particularly noticeable in Latin America. There is a massive shortage of priests in many parts of the world, and places that only a generation ago were solidly Catholic, such as Spain, Ireland, and Quebec, have seen numbers fall dramatically in recent years. The reality is less impressive than the facade, and the future of the Catholic church is by no means as assured as one might think.

From the theological perspective, it is possible to find fault with many Catholic doctrines that go beyond the teaching of Scripture and are often tied to outdated ways of thinking. This is especially noticeable when discussing something like transubstantiation, a central Catholic teaching which was developed in the context of a now discredited Aristotelian philosophy and which no longer makes sense. Theologians know this and try to reformulate it in a way that will be acceptable today, but most lay Catholics continue to believe that when the priest consecrates the bread and wine at Communion, they become the literal body and blood of Christ. It is this belief that has traditionally underlain the great deference shown by Catholics to their clergy, who are set apart from them by compulsory celibacy and a professional culture largely insulated from the modern world.

The biggest problem with the Roman church, however, lies not in these aberrations, which can be corrected over time, but with its fundamental claim to be the universal church. The logic behind this claim is that it was founded by Jesus Christ's direct commands to Peter, who supposedly became the first bishop of Rome and bequeathed his divine commission to his successors. Biblical support for this idea, such as it is, comes from the following passage:

[Jesus said to his disciples], "Who do you say that I am?" Simon Peter replied, "You are the Christ, the Son of the living God." And Jesus answered him, "Blessed are you, Simon Bar-Jonah! For flesh and blood have not revealed this to you, but my Father who is in heaven. And I tell you, you are Peter, and on this rock I will build my church, and the gates of hell shall not prevail against it. I will give you the keys of the kingdom of heaven, and whatever you bind on earth shall be bound in heaven, and whatever you loose on earth shall be loosed in heaven."[26]

Scholars continue to debate the true meaning of Peter's confession, and to dispute whether the authority given to him really set him apart from the other apostles. It is certainly true that Peter took the lead on the day of Pentecost, which may suggest that he was the head of the Jerusalem church, but when Paul went there after his conversion, which cannot have been that much later, he seems to have thought that the church was governed by a triumvirate of Peter, James, and John.[27] Paul certainly did not believe that Peter was infallible, because he stood up to him on a matter of doctrine where he believed that Peter was in serious error.[28] If the Acts of the Apostles are anything to go by, Peter seems to have faded out as time went on, though Luke never says what happened to him. Only two New Testament letters are directly linked to Peter, although there is an ancient tradition that he dictated his memoirs to Mark, who then wrote them up as the Gospel attributed to him. As for a link with Rome, there is no sign of this anywhere in the New Testament. Peter was presumably not there when Paul wrote his letter to the Romans, since otherwise he would surely have been mentioned in the greetings in the last chapter. Nor is he mentioned at the end of Acts, when Paul went to Rome as a prisoner, which would be odd if he was the city's bishop at that time.

The most solid piece of evidence connecting Peter with Rome is the tomb under the Vatican that is thought to be his. As this tomb was venerated at a very early date, it may very well be where he was buried, but that is all we can say. Nothing we know about the Roman church in the first centuries of its existence supports the idea that Peter was its founding bishop, and current research suggests that the church at Rome did not have a single leader until well into the second century. The names of Peter's immediate "successors" may even be fictitious, as there is no evidence for any of them until about A.D. 180. Finally, while the other churches of the ancient world were generally happy to give Rome pride of place, and even accepted its Petrine origins, they

---

[26]Matt. 16:15–19. See also John 21:15–19.
[27]Gal. 2:9.
[28]Gal. 2:11–15.

did not submit to its jurisdiction in church affairs. Not one of the ancient councils, which established fundamental Christian doctrine, was attended by a Roman bishop or convened on his authority. It would not be until 1123, in very different circumstances, that the pope would preside over a general council of the Western church, which was not recognized in the East, although it is considered to have been "ecumenical" by the Roman Catholic church.

This is a slender base on which to build such weighty claims. Today even many Roman Catholic scholars and theologians are prepared to admit that the Roman primacy cannot be securely grounded in Scripture but must rest on tradition—in this case, much later tradition! Given the way that that primacy has been exercised, not only with respect to Protestants but also in relation to the Eastern churches and within the Catholic church itself, it is hardly surprising that other Christians are highly skeptical of the papal claims and are unwilling to join a church that bases itself on them.

This leaves us with the Protestant churches, which are too numerous and varied to be numbered, even in a major encyclopedic work! Hardly any of them would claim to be the one true church, though some erect barriers to fellowship with those outside their ranks that suggest that that is what they think about themselves. Feelings between different Protestant denominations have run high in the past, especially in situations where one of them has been an established state church and the others have suffered as a result. Today, however, those problems have been largely overcome. Lay people move from one denomination to another with relative ease, and there are any number of nondenominational community churches and interdenominational parachurch organizations that often carry more weight than the denominations do. Given that almost all of them contain a wide range of doctrinal convictions (or lack thereof) and of worship styles, individuals often find their level and stick with that, regardless of what denominational label a particular church might wear. It is not too much to say that, nowadays, denominational divisions are more of a problem for the clergy, who have to pay attention to them, than for anyone else. Some people regret this, but it is probably true to say that, for most ordinary Protestants, it is the fellowship of the invisible church that now determines what congregation they will join. If they are one in the Spirit with those with whom they worship, other things can be left to one side and the unity of the body of Christ can once again be manifested as it was originally intended to be.

The historical divisions of the church are a reality with which we have to live in a spirit of humility, recognizing that the present situation came about for a variety of reasons, not all of which can be justified. Christians in every church and denomination must feel a sense of regret for past actions, which have sometimes led to persecution and the exclusion of other believers from a particular church. We all share responsibility for this and must do our utmost to break down barriers that have occurred for the wrong reasons. It is our duty to reach out to fellow believers wherever they may be found, and not to impose artificial conditions on them before being willing to welcome them into our fellowship. Having said that, we must also recognize that in some cases, divisions have persisted because of very real disagreements, and that these cannot be overcome merely by good will and wishful thinking. In practice, it is usually the case that individuals from different churches, and especially lay people, can share a high degree of fellowship with one another because of their common faith, but the churches they belong to cannot merge into one another because of different and sometimes mutually contradictory beliefs and practices that distinguish them.

Leaving aside divisions that have occurred mainly for political or cultural reasons, there are two main types of schism that exist within the Christian world. The first of these concerns matters of faith and the second concerns matters of order. Whether these two aspects of the church's life can be separated from one another is a matter of debate, but they can certainly be distinguished as distinct components of any given ecclesiastical community. Protestants are divided from Roman Catholics and the Eastern Orthodox on matters of faith, which are more direct and more obvious in the case of the former. The separation between the Western and the Eastern churches was already complete at the time of the Protestant Reformation, which means that Protestants differ from the Eastern Orthodox in much the same way as Roman Catholics do. This needs to be said because some Protestants have looked for a reunion with the Eastern churches, bypassing Rome. This is not a realistic option, however, because any resolution of the differences that separate us from the East would have to resolve most of the difficulties the Roman Catholic church has and would potentially lead to reunion across the board. In practice, reunion with the East is unimaginable without a reunion of Western Christendom—a distant and probably unattainable goal.

The main problems that divide Protestants from Roman Catholics can be summed up under the heading of the work of the Holy Spirit. Rome believes that it has been uniquely entrusted with the witness of the Spirit at work in the offices and sacraments which it administers. Its head, the bishop of Rome, is regarded as infallible when he speaks in his official capacity as "pope." Its priests are empowered to turn bread and wine into the body and blood of Christ, and thereby to administer the grace of God to his people—or to withhold it from them. These basic beliefs are shored up by a wide range of devotional practices and spiritual disciplines, which have become part of church tradition even though they rest on no other authority. These additional requirements may even go against the teaching of the Word of God, as compulsory priestly celibacy does, for example, but this is justified on the ground that the leaders of the church, and in particular the pope, have the authority to reinterpret that Word and add to it as they think necessary. Many subtle distinctions are drawn between what is merely a matter of discipline (like celibacy) and what is a matter of fundamental belief (like the infallibility of the pope) but it makes little difference in practice. Roman Catholics are expected to accept everything their church teaches, regardless of how it is justified. Those who fail to do so find themselves out of communion with it.

Protestants cannot accept this. We share many things with Roman Catholics, but we do not believe that any human being or ecclesiastical body is (or can be) invested with infallible authority. The Holy Spirit may choose to work in and through the clerical order of a visible institutional church, but no individual church leader or body can claim this as a matter of right. Whether a person receives the grace of God through the ministry of the church depends both on the faithfulness of that ministry to the teaching of the gospel and the faith of the recipient. Protestants believe that Rome has departed from the pure gospel of Christ in its teaching and has devalued the faith of its members by making its validity ultimately dependent on its priesthood. We are not in communion with Rome because we believe that such disagreements touch on matters that are fundamental to the life and witness of the church. If we accepted the claims of Rome in these areas, we would be denying those of Christ.

When it comes to relationships between Protestant bodies, most of the differences concern matters of church order, including the ministry and the sacraments. Unfortunately, order is more visible than faith, and therefore differences over it have often provoked strong feelings. Whether a church has bishops or is governed by a college of presbyters should not affect the content or preaching of the gospel, but it does alter the structure of the church's organization. When a group insists on one of these things to the exclusion of the other it produces division within the visible church. Differences over the proper administration of baptism have also provoked splits and hard feelings, especially when those who reject the validity of infant baptism rebaptize those who received it and then later made a profession of faith as adults. In a case like that, the principled consistency of one church leads to the rejection of the ministry of another and so calls into question the validity of the faith proclaimed by that other church.

No denomination is innocent of the tendency to insist on matters of church polity to the point of excluding other believers from its fellowship. We must repent of this, whatever church we belong to. It is one thing to adopt a particular form of church government and sacramental practice because we believe that it is the one most faithful to the teaching and intention of Christ, but quite another to refuse to have fellowship with those who disagree with us on matters that are not clearly defined in Scripture. On matters like these we must accept that different opinions are possible and that other ways of doing things have advantages from which we can (and should) learn without denying the validity of our own procedures, whose benefits we must be prepared to acknowledge and recommend to others. Happily, we can say that here the ecumenical movement of recent times has made genuine progress, and that differences of church order have sometimes been overcome when it is clear that the underlying faith of the churches concerned is identical.

DIFFERENT TYPES OF CHRISTIANS

Alongside the different denominations there are a number of spiritual tendencies and movements in the Christian world which stand out for their distinctive emphases. The first of these appeared in the third century, when some Christians decided to lead solitary lives in the desert, seeking to get closer to God by intense spiritual devotion and asceticism. Some of these desert-dwellers, whom we call "hermits" (from the Greek word for "desert"), later banded together as "monks" (from the Greek word for "alone"), and many of them became the greatest evangelists of the early church. Spreading beyond the confines of the Roman empire, monks preached the gospel all over northern Europe, establishing monastery churches ("minsters") as outposts for the conversion of the pagan Germanic and Slavic tribes.

Given that hermits and monks fled the cities of the Roman empire because they thought that the Christians who lived there were becoming too worldly, it is not surprising that they had difficult relations with the mainline church. When the monasteries in turn became rich and "worldly," reform movements broke away, either to found new monastic orders or to become begging brethren ("friars"), earning their living from pious donations. The Protestant Reformation was largely the work of men trained in this way. In its early years, it could be seen almost as an attempt to create a monasticism for the masses. Many devotional practices such as daily Bible reading and hymn singing, for example, were monastic in origin, and Protestant evangelicals continue these traditions today, in spite of the vast cultural differences between them and the medieval monks. It is among evangelicals that one is most likely to find a deep interest in Bible study, fervent hymn singing (and writing), and evangelistic zeal, giving them a spiritual link with the past that other more superficially traditionalist churches do not necessarily possess.

At the other end of the spectrum are people who are much more attached to the structures of the institutional church. They prefer hierarchy, order, and submission to authority, as opposed to what they often see as the undisciplined, anarchic spontaneity of the evangelicals. These are the high church people, who are liable to think that building a cathedral is more important than conducting an evangelistic crusade, because they are thinking more long-term. To their minds, the cathedral will still be there bearing witness to the faith of those who built it, long after today's crusade will have been forgotten. For similar reasons, they may be more inclined to write books than to preach sermons—books last longer and reach further than the spoken word, even if they lack the latter's sense of immediacy. Needless to say, evangelicals and high-church people often find it hard to relate to one another, though both types can be found in most of the mainline churches. High-church people are naturally more prominent in the Roman church, and evangelicals feel more at home in Protestant denominations (though they often create denominations or independent churches of their own), but neither can be exclusively identified with any one church. There are evangelically minded Catholics (and Orthodox), just as there are high-church Baptists, Presbyterians, and Methodists. The Anglican Communion gives semi-official recognition to both tendencies and tries to hold them together, though it has not always been very successful in doing so.

In addition to these groups, there is a middle way, which is often termed the "broad church" or "mainstream," which consists of people who do not identify with either the high churchmen or the evangelicals but who see themselves as "ordinary" believers. They are the people who are most likely to be enthusiastic about the denominations they belong to and supportive of them as they stand, whereas both evangelicals and high-church people are more likely to want to reform them in their particular direction. Otherwise, the broad church is hard to define, which is one reason why it is often regarded as a lukewarm form of Christianity. Nevertheless, the life and career of men like C. S. Lewis (1898–1963) remind us that broad-church Christians can be fully orthodox in their theology and reach out to both of the others. The fact that many evangelicals and high churchmen today claim Lewis as one of their own (when in fact he was neither) shows that there is a common thread of Christian faith that is capable of uniting what might otherwise seem to be incompatible extremes.

Beyond these groupings, there are groups that over time have split off from the main churches and formed communities of their own, which are often viewed by other Christians as extreme and sectarian. The Amish, for example, would have to be classified among these, as would the Shakers. Groups like the Salvation Army are now more mainstream than they once were, but they still retain characteristics that set them apart from others and make them hard to label. In more recent times, the charismatic movement has swept across the Christian world and attracted followers from almost every denomination, but although charismatics often retain their original church loyalties, they undoubtedly form a spiritual fellowship that cuts across such barriers. At the same time, new divisions have emerged between charismatics and others. Fortunately, these have generally managed to avoid open hostility, at least so far, but there is a definite sense of difference, and some noncharismatics can be quite vocal in their opposition to what they believe is a false spirituality.

How should we deal with these differences? It must be admitted that many Christians get more worked up about them than they should and can often be quite uncharitable in their dealings with people whose spiritual outlook differs from their own. It is difficult to find exact biblical parallels because the early church was too small and too new to have developed these different streams, but there were differences within it that might offer us some kind of analogy. The most important of these was the division between Jewish and Gentile Christians, which erupted near the beginning of Paul's missionary activity and which had to be resolved by mutual forbearance. This allowed each side to hold to its own convictions and practices without anathematizing the other.[29] Based on that, we can perhaps offer the following suggestions as to how we should proceed when dealing with Christians whose beliefs differ from ours:

1. Be persuaded in your own mind that what you do and recommend to others is justified by the teaching of Scripture. People who have doubts about their own beliefs are more likely to be insecure and therefore more defensive and uncharitable in their dealings with others.[30]

2. Never do anything that goes against your conscience, even if others think it is unobjectionable.[31]

---

[29]Rom. 14:1–15:7.
[30]Rom. 14:5.
[31]Rom. 14:23.

3. Do not pass judgment on others or make life difficult for them.[32]

4. Remember that we belong to Christ and that our duty is to please him and not ourselves.[33]

5. Keep things in perspective. If something does not touch on the fundamentals of the gospel, do not overemphasize it.[34]

6. Try to see the other person's point of view and to learn from him. None of us is perfect, and we can all benefit from being balanced by our contacts with those whose insights and experiences are different from ours.[35]

7. Remember that love is the fulfilling of the law; our approach to other Christians must be governed by that spirit.[36]

Another kind of difference that troubles the church is the division between conservatives or "traditionalists" and liberals. These labels are often used to describe clearly defined sets of people, but it is often much harder to pin them down than appearances would suggest. In broad terms, liberals are more likely to be dissatisfied with the status quo, aware of its weaknesses (or some of them), and determined to press for change, whereas conservatives and traditionalists will be more inclined to resist such moves. In practice, however, a great deal depends on the issues being debated, and such a neat distinction is not always possible. For example, evangelicals are likely to be conservative on doctrinal matters but not on liturgical ones, and some of them are in the vanguard of technological innovation, which they see as an important aid to evangelism. Liberals, on the other hand, often cling to existing church structures, especially if they think that change is likely to disadvantage them by giving their opponents a greater voice. On social matters, too, there is no neat divide. Conservative Christians were certainly more likely to support racism in the United States and in South Africa, which liberals fiercely opposed. On the other hand, liberals were often uncritical of communist regimes, which conservatives fought in every way they could, even going to prison on account of their beliefs. No side can claim to have been in the right all the time, and neither should accuse the other of having betrayed the gospel without searching its own soul first.

One of the results of the secularization of modern Western society is that the conflict between tradition and innovation which once characterized conservatives and liberals has to a large extent given way to a struggle between orthodox Christianity and various diluted forms of belief. The modern lib-

---

[32]Rom. 14:13.
[33]Rom. 14:7–9.
[34]Rom. 14:20–22.
[35]Rom. 14:6–7.
[36]Rom. 13:10.

eral is not someone pleading for a scholarly approach to biblical study, or for ecumenical cooperation on the ground that what unites Christians is more important than what separates them. Nowadays, the word "liberal" is more likely to be attached to people who deny fundamental Christian doctrines, like the bodily resurrection of Jesus, and who are prepared to say that Paul (for example) was wrong in parts of his teaching. To these people, there can be only one response—they are not Christians at all. Jesus had to deal with "liberals" of this type, the Sadducees, a Jewish sect who denied the resurrection. He made no bones about it when he told them, "You are wrong because you know neither the Scriptures nor the power of God."[37] Paul had no time for such people either:

> Even if we or an angel from heaven should preach to you a gospel contrary to the one we preached to you, let him be accursed. As we have said before, so now I say again: If anyone is preaching to you a gospel contrary to the one you received, let him be accursed.[38]

Tolerance and understanding must be extended to all who are brothers and sisters in the Lord, but not to those who claim to be Christians and deny the fundamental truths of our faith.

---

[37]Matt. 22:29.
[38]Gal. 1:8–9.

30

BELONGING TO THE FELLOWSHIP OF BELIEVERS

THE BELIEFS WE HOLD IN COMMON

How do we know whether a person belongs to the body of Christ? Most churches test this by some form of instruction that leads to certain questions being asked at baptism or at the time the person concerned is received into church membership, or both. Generally speaking, the questions tend to be fairly simple, such as, "Do you believe in God the Father, who made the world?" A trained theologian may find great depth in a proposition like that, but for most people the issue is straightforward. As far as they are concerned, all they have to do is affirm that they believe there is a God who created the world and whom we regard as our heavenly Father. The average Christian will have little trouble assenting to that, and in all likelihood it will seem obvious to him.

Things get more complicated the further up the scale we go. Theological students, and those about to be ordained for pastoral ministry, will (not unreasonably) be expected to give a fuller account of their beliefs, even if they are answering the same questions. For example, where the ordinary person might have little to say in answer to the above question, the trained pastor may reflect on the meaning of creation, whether it can be attributed to God the Father as opposed to all three persons of the Trinity (or to God as opposed to an evolutionary selection process), and even how "the world" is to be understood. Is it planet earth, the whole universe, or a spiritual concept that describes everything that stands in opposition to God? Ordinary believers might conceivably discuss such matters, but they would not normally be expected to do so. No one would insist that a person who is unable to discuss theological questions at that level should not be admitted to church membership for that reason, but some churches will deny ordination to candidates unable to give satisfactory answers to such questions, and rightly so.

This has to be said because there is a persistent strand in church life which maintains that any sort of structured belief, of the kind found in the classical creeds and confessions of faith, is an imposition on believers that should not be required of anyone, or even tolerated. "No creed but Christ" is their rallying cry, or "The Bible alone is the religion of Protestants," as if other statements of faith were somehow obscuring our understanding of both Christ and the Bible. Of course, at one level we must agree with such people that the Christian faith cannot be reduced to a set of beliefs contained in a creed or confession of faith. It is a new birth in Christ, an experience of the living God that, by definition, goes beyond what words can describe. Assenting to a creedal statement may satisfy the outward criteria of formal church membership, but it says nothing about the presence or absence of true faith in the heart of the person seeking membership. That is a matter between the believer and God, who gives us the mind of Christ and shapes our every thought and action in conformity with his will.

Having said that, however, it is also true that the experience of individual believers ought to resonate with the official creeds and confessions of the church, even if they do not know or understand them. If it does not, either those statements of faith are wrong or the people concerned are mistaken. It is not impossible for the perception of a single individual to be right and the rest of the church wrong, but in the nature of things, that will be exceedingly rare. What that individual says will require careful proof if it is to be accepted. The common witness of the Christian community through the ages cannot easily be overruled, and those who claim to do so, either by some private revelation or by some new theological discovery unknown to earlier ages, must be treated with the greatest caution. The creeds of the church are not perfect, nor are they comprehensive, but the substance of what they affirm must be believed by every faithful Christian.

There will always be some people who do not like creeds, even though they agree with what they say, and we must be tolerant of this. They bear witness to the greatness of God, who goes far beyond what any human words can say about him, and they challenge us to remember that this must be true of our faith as well as of theirs. Nevertheless, their purist approach to such matters cannot be followed by the whole church because the absence of creeds makes it that much easier for false teaching to creep in. It is rather like pacifism or unilateral disarmament. The idea is a good one and Christians must surely be sympathetic to it, but the world we live in is not prepared to deal with it. We have to maintain our defenses until such time as the final victory of the Prince of Peace makes them unnecessary.

There are also those who have trouble with particular aspects of the creeds because they have not fully understood them. Here we must draw a distinction between those who are genuinely puzzled or troubled by something that they acknowledge as part of the Christian tradition but find difficult to understand, and those who say that Christians were wrong to canonize such beliefs, which they think are erroneous and must be rejected. The former group are believers seeking further understanding of their faith; the latter group have failed to understand it and are unwilling to be enlightened any further on the subject.

What cannot be accepted is preaching or teaching in the church that openly contradicts or denies some aspect of the creedal statements that express our common faith. A preacher or theologian who denies the bodily resurrection of Christ and ridicules those who believe it as being primitive "fundamentalists" is not a Christian and ought to be excluded from the pulpits of the church. Here we have a responsibility before God to maintain the purity of the message we proclaim as far as we are able to do so, and no compromise with unbelief is possible. There will always be some who will seize the authority of pastoral office in the church and use it for spreading false teaching. This was the case in the first generation, when false apostles went about subverting the gospel, and it is still the case today. Vigilance is always necessary, and the denunciation of such behavior, unpleasant as it is, is a duty imposed on us as faithful servants of Christ.

One of the most important functions of creeds and confessions is that they help us understand "the whole counsel of God," or the teaching of the Bible in its entirety, which must form the framework for our interpretation of individual parts of Scripture. In the early church there were people who said that Jesus was not God, but was a man whom God adopted as his Son. They did not make this up, but believed that it was the right interpretation of Matthew 3:17, which says that when Jesus was baptized, a voice from heaven said, "This is my beloved Son, with whom I am well pleased."[1] They were trying to figure out why Jesus had to be baptized, and the answer they came up with was that this was the moment when the Father adopted him and sent his Spirit down on him in the form of a dove.

The idea that Jesus was less than fully God was very popular in ancient

---

[1] See also Mark 1:11; Luke 3:22.

times because it seemed to resolve a number of questions that plagued people's minds. They did not believe that the infinite God could become finite, or that he could suffer and die for any reason, least of all by "becoming sin" for us. God was perfect, eternal, and good, and he had to remain that way. If the world was to be saved by the death of a perfect man, that man had to be a creature and not God. To the question of whether they believed that God the Father had created the world, they would have replied with an enthusiastic "yes," but they would also have understood the name "Father" to mean that the Son and the Holy Spirit were inferior to him and were excluded from his creative act. They regarded the Son as the highest of the creatures, closer to God than any other and therefore better able to intercede with him, but they denied that he was God in his own right.

This heresy may seem distant and obscure to many people today, but if you want to see how important it can be, ask the members of an average congregation whether or not Jesus is God. Many of them will probably be puzzled for a minute and then reply that he is the Son of God, but not quite the same as God himself. Without ever intending it, these people will have fallen into the very error that the creeds were designed to avoid. They will not realize that those who spoke of Jesus as a man whom God adopted, or as the highest of the creatures, were trying to solve one set of difficulties posed by the biblical text without taking all the evidence into account, or by twisting it to suit their preconceived theory. For instance, they might interpret a phrase like "the Word became flesh" to mean that the Word was transformed into a human being and ceased to be divine.[2] Other passages which talk about the Son of Man coming down from heaven, or about his returning to his eternal glory, they would either ignore or misinterpret in a similar way.[3]

The overall effect of such thinking was to deprive people of their salvation by trying to explain it in the wrong way. It was for that reason that the church leaders of the time had to come together and formulate their beliefs in language that would be true to the teaching of Scripture and would avoid the kinds of errors into which these false (though perhaps well-intentioned) teachers had led them. Their efforts were successful, and the true faith was preserved for future generations, for which we must be deeply grateful. But as a quick survey of an average congregation will show, error is never far below the surface and can easily creep in if our teaching is inadequate. Many of the controversies that rock the church today have occurred because some aspect of Christian teaching has been ignored or underemphasized. For example,

---

[2]John 1:14.
[3]John 3:13; 17:5.

we cannot assume that, because Martin Luther thought that justification by faith alone was a fundamental Christian truth, all those who claim his legacy today will agree with him. The reality is that many of them will never have heard the phrase and only a few can explain what it really means. Yet without the reality of justification by faith alone, the preaching of the gospel would be impossible and our churches would not exist.

In conclusion, it also has to be said that those who compose statements of faith must take great care to ensure that what they are saying is truly of central importance to our faith. For example, when Archbishop Thomas Cranmer was composing a series of "articles" to explain the doctrine of the Church of England, he included a couple that dealt with the end of time and criticized the millenarian tendencies that had erupted in the wake of the Reformation. When his articles were revised a decade or so later, however, those particular ones were left out. It is extremely unlikely that the revisers had changed their minds about the issues concerned, but they must have realized that those issues were not so fundamental that church members should have to accept one particular view of them. We believe that Christ is coming again to judge the living and the dead, but precisely when and how this will happen is a mystery and there is no one answer that can be imposed on all believers. The leaders of the church may have disliked the millenarians and disagreed with them, but they were not prepared to exclude them from the fellowship of Christ, and so they remained silent about what was, after all, unknowable.

Such forbearance is unfortunately rare, and it has been excess of zeal as much as anything else that has brought confessional theology into disrepute. The divines who composed the famous Westminster Confession of Faith, for example, were great and learned men, but occasionally their prejudices got the better of them and they insisted on things that have caused embarrassment to later generations who wish they had been more restrained. The most notorious instance of this occurs in chapter 25, section 6, where, in denying that the pope is head of the church, the Confession goes on to describe him as "that Antichrist, that man of sin and son of perdition that exalteth himself in the church against Christ and all that is called God."[4] That was a common sentiment at the time, but it cannot really be claimed that the bishop of Rome is the Antichrist of whom John spoke. Today, even those who agree with the general thrust of the statement usually wish that it had been expressed in less offensive (and more accurate) language. We must take care not to saddle future generations with embarrassments of this kind.

In composing creeds and confessions, therefore, we must be careful not

---

[4]See 1 John 2:18, 22; 4:3; 2 John 7.

to include things that are matters of personal or local interpretation and not fundamental to the faith once delivered to the saints.[5] If we find such things in statements inherited from the past, we should have the humility to recognize the error and remove them so as not to bring the rest of their contents into disrepute. We must also remember that false teaching is alive and active in every generation, and we may be obliged to write our own confessions, pointing out modern errors that have crept in and corrupted the truth. Future generations will decide whether we have expressed ourselves in the best way, and they may revise what we have said in the light of developments that we cannot now foresee, but our task is to be faithful to what we understand to be true and to pass that understanding on to those who come after us.

THE FREEDOM WE HAVE IN CHRIST

One of the great themes of the New Testament that was stressed with particular vigor at the time of the Reformation is that of the freedom we have in Christ. This freedom is rooted in the deliverance from sin that we enjoy because he died for us on the cross and rose again from the dead. The consequences of that for our lives now are many. First of all, we have been delivered from any need to keep the ancient Jewish law because its provisions have been fulfilled by Jesus and therefore are now redundant. Second, we have been set free to live a new life without having to carry the burden of our past sins and failures.

Few of us today are particularly bothered about keeping the Jewish law, which is not a major issue in the church in the way that it was for the first generation of (mainly Jewish) Christians. But there are still many people for whom the burden of guilt for their past sins is very much a reality, and we must deal with this as best we can. In principle, all sinners are equal in the sight of God because all have fallen short of his glory, and it makes little difference to him whether some have fallen further than others.[6] In practice, however, those who have committed serious crimes like murder, or who in various ways have to live with the consequences of their past actions, are more likely than others to feel the reproach of sin. To some extent, this may be due to their own inner sense of guilt, but it may also be due to the feeling that other people are still holding it against them. There will always be someone who will not let such things be forgotten, and it is easy to fall victim to the idea that nothing can be done about it. It is to this feeling of spiritual bondage that Paul spoke when he said,

---

[5] Jude 3.
[6] Rom. 3:23.

There is therefore now no condemnation for those who are in Christ Jesus. For the law of the Spirit of life has set you free in Christ Jesus from the law of sin and death.[7]

Freedom in Christ is not license to do whatever we want, and the moral precepts of the law are still as valid for us as they were for the people of ancient Israel. Lying, cheating, and stealing are just as intolerable in a Christian context as they are anywhere else, and indeed more so because those in whom the Holy Spirit dwells have the responsibility and the power to live as children of God. Most people understand this readily enough, but there are always gray areas where it is not entirely clear what we should do. In the New Testament, we come across this phenomenon in the case of those who felt at liberty to eat meat that had been sacrificed to idols.[8] Christians do not believe that idols exist, and so it ought to make no difference whether meat has been sacrificed to them. In terms of strict logic, this is undoubtedly true, and the apostle Paul recognized that, in principle, there was nothing wrong in ignoring such pagan habits. Those who had been brought up as Jews, however, were sensitive to this because even if the argument used by the people who ate such meat was logically flawless, the impression they were giving was quite different. People who saw them doing such things might easily have thought that they were indulging in a pagan practice, if only by association, and therefore they believed that it was better to avoid "idol meat" altogether.[9]

What we see here is the phenomenon that "perception is part of the reality." It might be theoretically possible for me to visit brothels as part of my ministry to prostitutes, and there need not be any untoward activity associated with that. But would people observing me draw such a high-minded conclusion? What impression would I give to others if I claimed to have a ministry to the poor but wore expensive clothing and drove a car that most of those people could not afford? There may be nothing objectively wrong with such things, but we have to be aware of the impact our behavior is likely to have on our witness and act accordingly.

What applies to individuals also applies to churches. It is not unknown for churches to invest in companies that do business in unethical ways, and that should be avoided as much as possible. Church property should not be used for activities such as gambling, even if it appears to be small-scale and relatively innocent, as it often does. Nor should church buildings be sold to developers who will turn them into nightclubs, or to adherents of other

---

[7]Rom. 8:1–2.
[8]1 Cor. 8:1–13.
[9]1 Cor. 8:1–13; Rom. 14:13–23.

religions who will use them as a place of worship. It may be true that a build-ing is "just a building," but when it is clearly associated with the worship of God, to use it for some other purpose sends the wrong message and is harmful to the witness of the gospel. We must not forget that, in some parts of the world, churches have been forcibly turned into mosques in order to make the point that the God of Islam is greater than the God of Christianity, so to do this voluntarily is short-sighted and ignorant of the way our action is likely to be perceived.

The trouble with freedom is that there are no fixed rules that can be applied in every circumstance. If there were, our freedom would be lost. Each situation has to be decided on its merits, and in the nature of things, different people are almost bound to come up with different conclusions. The one thing that Paul counsels in such circumstances is that the law of love should prevail. If I am doing something that wounds the conscience of another Christian, how important is that thing to me? Would it really matter to me if I gave it up? If the answer is no, says Paul, then the right thing is to give way and not cause unnecessary offense. In time, the conscience of my "weaker brother" may be healed by my humility and spirit of self-sacrifice, but if I am obstinate and insist on my "rights," it is virtually certain that I shall lose him, and that is simply not worth it.

Freedom in Christ applies to the way we are called to live with a clear conscience, which includes things that we do not know for sure and about which Christians hold different and even contradictory opinions. No one can know exactly what is going to happen in the future, but that has not stopped some people from giving what are occasionally very detailed descriptions of the "end times," which they then assume have the authority of revelation. Others come up with very different conclusions, but likewise think that their views ought to be accepted as correct. Faced with such a situation, the proper response is to examine the Scriptures carefully, and if the evidence in them is insufficient to form a definite doctrine, to have the humility to admit it. To say that we do not understand exactly how or when Christ will come again is not to say that we do not believe that he will, but only that we have not been told what we do not need to know about it.[10] Being humble in the presence of the unknown is not the same thing as being indifferent to it. After all, the being of God is unknown and yet it is the focus of our attention and the goal of our striving. No Christian would claim that, because we cannot fathom the nature of God, it does not matter, and so we might as well ignore it and get on with life!

---

[10] Acts 1:7.

At the same time, there are things pertaining to the life of the visible church that are not fully revealed in God's Word, and here we do have freedom to decide for ourselves. Obvious cases relate to church order and worship. Some Christians believe that faith and order go together, and justify this by saying that what we do must correspond to what we believe. That is true, of course, but it ignores the fact that we have the freedom to implement what we believe in different ways, so that our church order and forms of worship may legitimately differ without imperiling the unity of our faith. Here we must recognize that there is a difference between cultures that are literate and cultures that are not. In modern Western society, where everyone can read and write, variations in practice are less important than they are in places where people put a great deal of weight on gestures and ceremony. It is irrelevant to me whether the bread used at Holy Communion is leavened or unleavened, or even whether it is "bread" at all, but people who learn from symbols may think differently. To them, there may be great significance attached to such apparently minor details, and where that is the case, our practice must be tailored accordingly.

It is the same principle as that of the weaker brother all over again and may be equally difficult to resolve. In many developing countries, the gospel was introduced by different missionary groups who brought their traditional practices with them, whether or not they were essential (or even appropriate). Christians in those countries came to associate these practices with the content of their faith, which may create problems when attempts are made to unite churches across denominational boundaries. Can a common form of worship be devised, or is it practically necessary to allow different forms to coexist side by side, in order not to upset those who are used to them? There is no simple answer to that question, but at least a start can be made if we accept that the form of church order we adopt is part of the freedom given to us by God, and not something prescribed by the Bible or by ancient but alien traditions.

THE GIFTS OF THE SPIRIT

The church is the body of Christ, formed and preserved in being by the indwelling presence and power of the Holy Spirit. In order to maintain this body in good working order, the Spirit gives certain people gifts meant to be used for its growth.[11] There are four lists of these gifts in the New Testament, which can be compared as shown in table 30.1, on page 694.

---

[11] 1 Cor. 12:7.

Romans 12:6–8	1 Corinthians 12:8–10	1 Corinthians 12:28	Ephesians 4:11
		1. Apostles	Apostles
Prophecy	Prophecy	2. Prophets	Prophets
			Evangelists
			Pastors
Teaching		3. Teachers	Teachers
	Wisdom		
	Knowledge		
	Miracles	4. Miracle workers	
	Healing	5. Healers	
Service		6. Helpers	
		7. Administrators	
	Interpretation of tongues		
	Speaking in tongues	8. Speakers in tongues	
Exhortation			
Giving			
Leading			
Acting in mercy			
	Faith		
	Discernment of spirits		

TABLE 30.1

In the first two lists, Paul expresses the gifts in terms of their function, whereas in the third and fourth he does so in terms of the people appointed to exercise those functions. The third list is also the only one to be graded in order of importance, though it is interesting to note that Paul omits interpreters of tongues, whom he certainly regarded as more highly gifted than those who merely spoke in them.[12] Curiously enough, the gift of prophecy is the only one to appear in all four lists, though a case can be made for saying that those who are given the utterance of wisdom and knowledge were probably teachers.[13] What is certain is that no one list is definitive, and we need to look at them all in order to get a comprehensive picture of what the Holy Spirit was doing in the early church.

By their nature, some of the gifts are unlikely to have been the preserve of officers specially appointed for the task. In many churches there are people who are unusually generous donors, for example, but they often prefer to remain anonymous. Likewise, people with extraordinary powers of faith may take a back seat in the congregation, praying and encouraging others in a quiet way, and the same may be said for those who perform particular acts of mercy. Exhortation, leading, and the discernment of spirits are harder to define. It would probably be impossible to "lead" a congregation without having some kind of recognized authority, though there are people who have an ability to get others moving even if they have no special position, and Paul

[12] 1 Cor. 14:5.
[13] 1 Cor. 12:8.

may be referring to them. The same might be true of exhorters, a term which could refer to those who are called to remind people of their duties and tasks in the church, something that is often best done quietly on a one-to-one basis. The discernment of spirits is also hard to pin down, but some people do have an unusual ability to see through things, and that may be what is meant here. Paul clearly believed that every congregation would contain people of these types, and he did not think it necessary to single them out for special ordination or commissioning.

It is somewhat different with the third list because there it is clear that at least the first few gifts mentioned applied to specific people who had been called by God to exercise a particular ministry. The most important of these was the apostleship, which Paul himself had received, though not in the same way as the others had.[14] It is therefore with the gift of apostles that we must begin.

In order to make sure that the gospel would be maintained in its purity in the church, the Holy Spirit appointed the apostles as the supreme guardians of the gospel in the first generation after Christ. Most of them had been Christ's disciples during his earthly ministry, but the overlap between disciples and apostles was not total. As everyone knows, there was one famous disciple, Judas, who betrayed Jesus and did not become an apostle, and there was one famous apostle, Saul or Paul of Tarsus, who had not been a disciple. But all the apostles had seen the risen Christ, a criterion which was essential to their office and ministry. It seems in fact that the word "apostle" was originally used to refer to those who were witnesses of the resurrection (more than five hundred people in all) and who formed the first generation of evangelists.[15] It is to this category that Andronicus and Junia must have belonged, if the reference to them as "well known to the apostles" is to be interpreted as including them within the apostolic company.[16]

Further evidence for the existence of many apostles may be found in Paul's condemnation of the so-called false apostles who seemed to have followed him around with the intention of destroying his ministry.[17] If the number of apostles had been confined to the original disciples of Jesus, it would have been easy to detect imposters, but the fact that these men were able to convince the Corinthians of their status suggests that apostleship was not as closely defined as that. It must also be said, however, that very soon the term "apostle" was restricted to the Twelve, who had existed as a distinct group from the beginning. Here again we find a good example of how the early

---

[14] 1 Cor. 15:8.
[15] 1 Cor. 15:4–7.
[16] Rom. 16:7. The words may also be translated as "renowned among the apostles," which is more ambiguous.
[17] 2 Cor. 11:13. See also Gal. 2:4.

church developed its theological terminology. The word "apostle," which originally meant a variety of things, was narrowed down and turned into a technical term with a specific meaning, which is the one Paul appears to be using in 1 Corinthians 12.

The historic apostles had no successors, and the claims made for the bishop of Rome in this respect are without foundation. The same must be said for other churches of much more recent origin which have claimed to have "apostles" in their midst. To the extent that the apostolic ministry exists today, it does so in and through the New Testament, which is the authorized record of their teaching. When Paul handed on his ministry to Timothy and Titus, he did not grant them the same authority as he possessed, but told them to guard the deposit of faith that had been entrusted to them, which is what we continue to do today.[18]

There were almost certainly some apostolic practices that have not come down to us in written form, most likely because they were not particularly controversial. As far as we can tell, most of them related to the worship of the early church and existed as oral traditions handed down in the Christian communities. The difficulty is that we cannot be entirely sure what they were, and because they are not found in the New Testament, they have no binding authority on us. For example, the signing with the cross at baptism is an ancient practice that may well go back to the apostles, but they never told their churches that they must practice it and so it cannot be insisted upon today as a necessary part of the apostolic faith.

Next to the apostles in Paul's list come the prophets, an ambiguous term that is open to different interpretations. There were prophets in the Old Testament, of course, but that form of prophecy died out about four hundred years before the coming of Christ, and was revived only by John the Baptist. Even so, we read that Anna, the old woman who waited for the coming of the Messiah in the temple, was a prophetess.[19] So was Agabus, the man who went down from Jerusalem to Antioch and foretold the coming of a famine, and who afterwards met Paul on his return to Palestine and predicted that he would be arrested when he got to the city.[20] Whether Anna uttered similar prophecies is unknown, but Agabus's actions are reminiscent of what we might expect from an Old Testament prophet, and by Luke's account, it seems that he was not the only one to exercise that kind of ministry.[21]

That there were prophets recognized as such in the early church is also

---

[18]2 Tim. 1:13.
[19]Luke 2:36.
[20]Acts 11:28; 21:10.
[21]Acts 11:27.

clear from the fact that Philip the evangelist had four daughters who prophesied, and when Paul laid hands on some Ephesian disciples, they too began to prophesy.[22] More than that, Paul openly encouraged prophecy in the Corinthian church, and he seems to have assumed that there were people there who were claiming that gift.[23] The question for us is, what sort of gift was it?

The Old Testament prophets had been used by God to convey his word to Israel, but this cannot have been the function of the prophets we find in the New Testament, since that ministry had passed to the apostles, who tolerated no rivals. Paul did not hesitate to warn anyone at Corinth who claimed the gift of prophecy that, if his claim was genuine, he would have to accept what the apostle was teaching as the word of God and fall into line with it.[24] Whatever a prophet said or did had to conform to the apostolic teaching, and if it did not, it was to be rejected. In the sixteenth century, and still today in some circles, it was assumed that "prophets" in the New Testament referred to preachers, and prophecy was a term regularly used for the ordinary preaching ministry. But although the prophets may well have preached, that does not seem to have been their main function in the early church, and we cannot equate them with preachers as if there were no difference between the two functions.

It is virtually impossible to analyze the phenomenon of New Testament prophecy now because, apart from the predictions of Agabus, we have no example of anything they actually said. The only clue we have is what Paul tells us when he writes that "the one who prophesies speaks to people for their upbuilding and encouragement and consolation."[25] These qualities are those of a good pastor, and that may be what the New Testament prophets essentially were. In later times, as preaching came to be the main source of pastoral guidance in most congregations, it is easy to see how the two things could have been conflated, but there is no evidence that that was the case at the beginning, and from what little we do know, it seems that it probably was not.

Alongside prophets Paul mentions evangelists, who are called to preach the gospel. That preaching was their main activity seems clear, both from what is said about Philip, who was a traveling evangelist in Palestine, and from what Paul says about the need to preach the gospel if anyone was to hear it and come to faith.[26] It is the special task of the evangelist to engage in primary apologetics, explaining the meaning of Christianity and defending

[22]Acts 21:10; 19:6.
[23]1 Cor. 14:4–5, 37.
[24]1 Cor. 14:37.
[25]1 Cor. 14:3.
[26]Rom. 10:14–15.

its worldview in the face of ignorance and possible opposition. That is what Philip did when he spoke to the Ethiopian eunuch, and it seems that he went on to preach the gospel all along the coast of Palestine, in towns where it had not previously been heard.[27]

Evangelism remains a vital ministry in today's church, which is often disadvantaged by an unwillingness or inability to engage outsiders with the gospel. An evangelist has to keep abreast of contemporary trends in intellectual life and in popular culture, and must know how to deal with the questions and problems that arise from them. At the same time, he must be faithful to the gospel message and know how to transpose it into the language of his hearers. In a world where the main emphasis seems to be on dialogue and mutual understanding between different religions and philosophies, and where it is considered to be in poor taste (to put it mildly) to try to persuade others of the rightness of your own point of view, evangelism is more needed than ever. The Christian gospel can never be reduced to the level of one religious or philosophical option among many. It commands attention by its uniqueness and demands a response from those who hear it. It is the special gift of the evangelist to remind us of those things and to present the message of Christ in a clear and challenging way to all who are in need of the salvation it brings.

Pastors are named specifically in only one of the lists, but a number of things mentioned elsewhere (such as exhortation and even the discernment of spirits) could probably be put in this category, since that is a vital part of pastoral ministry. The specific duty of a pastor is to shepherd those who have responded to the preaching of the gospel and to guide them along the pathway to spiritual maturity. It is almost always the case that there are things a new Christian has not heard or has failed to grasp, and part of the pastor's job is to fill in those gaps, so that spiritual weakness may be avoided. Another thing that he must do is prepare the young Christian for the spiritual warfare in which he will soon be engaged. It often happens that people who have responded to the gospel are soon afterwards put through a time of testing, in order to see how strong their commitment really is. At times like that, the pastor is especially needed to provide support and give direction to the person undergoing trial. Even at a later stage, spiritual guidance remains an important part of every Christian's life, and no congregation can thrive without pastors to help it along the way.

Next to pastors come the teachers, who seem to have been appointed for the instruction of new converts, but who were probably preachers as well, since there is no sign that New Testament teachers merely lectured in the way

[27] Acts 8:40.

that a modern instructor might. The whole point of teaching was to persuade the hearers to accept the message, although there is no doubt that catechetical instruction was also necessary for that to be effective. We can see this from the Acts of the Apostles. Paul had great success in the synagogues, where his audiences had been prepared by years of teaching from the Old Testament, but he had very little success when he went to Athens, where the locals had received no such teaching and did not understand even the basics of what he was saying.[28] To put it another way, preaching about Abraham and his faith is of little value if people have no idea who Abraham was and why he matters to us today. The more people know about the Bible, the more effective preaching based on it will be. This is especially true in our modern world, where the presuppositions of the Christian faith concerning the nature of mankind and the need for salvation are often little understood, or are even totally rejected by the secularism rampant in once-Christian lands and among the non-Christian religions and ideologies dominant elsewhere.

Failure to understand even the basic principles of Christianity impedes the spread of the gospel and runs the risk of causing serious misunderstandings. This can be seen in many mission contexts, where syncretistic forms of Christianity, mixed with local religious traditions, have occasionally sprung up and been very influential. The early church had its gnostic heretics who did this, and today there are the Kimbanguists in Congo and the followers of Sun Myung Moon in Korea, among others, who follow in their footsteps. It is sometimes said that Christianity in Africa today is a mile wide but only an inch deep. If this is true, it must be the result of preaching based on inadequate or nonexistent teaching. People have been converted in huge numbers, but they have not studied their faith in depth and are therefore unable to apply it in everyday life. What is true of Africa is increasingly true elsewhere as well, as basic Christian instruction is no longer given in the way that it once was, and there are more and more people who are as ignorant of what Christians believe as were the Athenians whom Paul addressed.

Next in the list come miracle workers and healers. Though not identical, there would appear to be a real overlap between these two, not least because most of the miracles done by Jesus and his disciples involved some form of healing. There is no question that the early church knew miracles and had a (non-miraculous) healing ministry as well, but it is not clear that there were particular people who were identified as having the gift of healing.[29] Paul seems to assume that they existed. We have to take his word for it, but it is impos-

---

[28] Acts 17:22–34.
[29] James 5:13–16.

sible to say who they were or how they operated. Probably they were discreet in exercising their ministry, which explains why we know so little about it. In the modern church there are "faith healers" who appear from time to time, but their reputation is not usually very good, and the church is extremely cautious about recognizing miracles. We do not deny that they occur, but they are rare. Professional healing ministries are more common and generally well respected, but confidentiality is obviously important. We seldom hear much about them, and if miracles occur we are unlikely to find out. Nevertheless, their continued existence shows that this form of ministry still operates today and brings its particular gift to the wider witness of the church.

After healers come helpers and administrators, two categories that can probably be linked together and were most likely related to the diaconal ministry established by the apostles to relieve them of such duties.[30] Support staff remains crucial to the working of any church, and it is important to remember that their ministry is a spiritual gift as much as any other.

Finally, we come to speaking in tongues and their interpretation. In recent years, more attention has been paid to this than to all the other spiritual gifts combined. Yet Paul was quite clear that it was, and presumably still is, the least important of them all because, by itself, it is of no benefit to the church as a whole.[31] Paul had no problem with this gift as a form of personal devotion, and he himself possessed it to an unusual degree, but he was very clear that it should not be overused in public worship, and that is the main thrust of his remarks about it.[32]

Speaking in tongues began on the day of Pentecost, when it had a functional purpose, enabling people from all corners of the Roman empire to hear the gospel message in their own language.[33] Later manifestations of the phenomenon did not have that purpose, but were a sign that the Holy Spirit had truly descended on believers.[34] In the Corinthian church, tongues were a regular part of worship and Paul did not forbid them, though he strongly encouraged those who had the gift to use it responsibly and to seek interpretation, so that others might also be edified.[35]

In later times speaking in tongues seems to have died out, and for centuries the phenomenon was regarded as defunct. Occasional outbreaks of it were treated as hysteria and were discounted, so much so that by the beginning of the twentieth century it was generally assumed that any such manifestation

---

[30]Acts 6:1–7.
[31]1 Cor. 14:5–12.
[32]1 Cor. 14:18–19.
[33]Acts 2:8–11.
[34]Acts 19:6.
[35]1 Cor. 14:13–17.

must be false. That, however, began to change as speaking in tongues returned to a considerable section of the church and new Pentecostal denominations were formed. These churches came out of the holiness movement of the nineteenth century, which stressed the need for a "second blessing" that would be the seal of the Spirit in the life of the believer, protecting him from sin and guaranteeing his future salvation. In the 1960s, Pentecostal phenomena spread to the mainline denominations, including the Roman Catholic Church, sometimes to the discomfiture of old-time Pentecostals, whose theology was generally more conservative and identifiably Protestant. In this form, it is generally known today as the charismatic movement and is distinguished from classical Pentecostalism because it has no connection to the holiness movement, nor is it necessarily tied to a conservative theology. In general terms, the charismatic movement appears to offer a release of inner spiritual energy to those who participate in it rather than a "second blessing" in the traditional sense.

What can we say about this phenomenon? On the one hand, we have to admit that speaking in tongues can no longer be regarded as defunct or dormant in the life of the church. It may be true that glossolalia, to use the official term for it, can be psychologically induced, but this is unlikely to account for every manifestation of it. If that were the case, the charismatic movement would probably have faded away by now. On the other hand, however, charismatic churches seldom follow Paul's advice to keep the phenomenon strictly under control and in its place. On the contrary, they often tend to make it central to their self-identity and sometimes try to insist that people must demonstrate a charismatic gift if they are truly filled with the Spirit. Furthermore, the range of these gifts has expanded considerably and without any biblical warrant, to include seeing "pictures" and even barking like a dog. Alleged "prophecies" can be given great weight in these circles, and the emphasis sometimes seems to be on what is strange and even bizarre. It is hard to know what all this has to do with the real work of the Holy Spirit in the life of a believer, except that we are saved by the shed blood of Christ and not by extraordinary manifestations claiming to come from the Holy Spirit. If that emphasis is lost or obscured, the phenomenon cannot be of God because it takes people away from the centrality of the cross and the atoning sacrifice of Christ.

THE MINISTRY OF THE CHURCH

Alongside these charismatic gifts are two orders of ministry that were established by the apostles for the maintenance of the local church as a functioning community. As far as we can tell from the evidence, the first to be established was the order of deacons, followed by that of elders, or "presbyters."[36]

The diaconal ministry originated when it became clear that the apostles could not minister to the daily needs of the congregation because that left them with no time to pray and preach the Word. They therefore appointed seven men "of good repute, full of the Spirit and of wisdom," to take over their pastoral duties and leave them free to evangelize.[37] It would be a mistake, however, to assume that this division of labor was rigid. Very soon after they were appointed, we find deacons like Stephen and Philip preaching the Word. Stephen was the first person to lose his life for his Christian faith because of his bold witness to the gospel,[38] and Philip could claim to have been the first Christian who took the gospel to the ends of the earth, as he preached to the Ethiopian eunuch.[39] Later on, Paul instructed Timothy to appoint as deacons men who were sober, honest, and well-grounded in their faith. He also insisted that their wives should be respectable women and that their children and households should be properly supervised. He was well aware that the reputation of the church was at stake in the appointment of its deacons, and he wanted Timothy to make sure that whoever assumed that office would be a credit to the faith of Christ.[40]

Deacons played an important part in the life of the early church, but since New Testament times their role has often been undervalued and obscured. In the Middle Ages, and still today in those churches that have retained the medieval orders of ministry, a deacon is little more than an apprentice priest, seldom serving for more than a year in that office and sometimes for a much shorter period.[41] In other churches, the office of deacon is usually given to lay people who do the work on a part-time, unpaid basis. Inevitably, such an arrangement limits the scope for developing the office and contributes to the widespread feeling that pastoral administration is somehow inferior to preaching and teaching. Few areas of church life are in greater need of reform than this one, but the experience of centuries is not encouraging. A full-time diaconate would be the ideal, but despite occasional attempts to create one, there is little sign that it will become the norm anytime soon.

We do not know precisely when eldership came into being, but it was not long after the emergence of deacons. The New Testament evidence seems to

---

[36]"Presbyter" is a word adapted from Greek which originally meant "elder."
[37]Acts 6:3–4.
[38]Acts 7:60.
[39]Acts 8:26–39.
[40]1 Tim. 3:9–13.
[41]The Roman Catholic Church today has a number of permanent deacons, most of whom substitute for priests because of the acute shortage of the latter.

suggest that, at the very beginning, the apostles themselves were the "elders" of the church at Jerusalem,[42] but if so, that situation did not last long. By the time a council met there to deal with the question of Gentile converts, probably around A.D. 48 or 49, there were elders in the Jerusalem church in addition to the apostles, and the practice of appointing them to head local churches had apparently become the norm elsewhere by that time.[43] There seems to be no doubt that this practice was taken over from Judaism, where there were elders in every synagogue as well as in Jerusalem, where they formed a recognized group that operated alongside the chief priests and the scribes.[44] The elders seem to have acted mainly as guardians of tradition with acknowledged expertise in the law. It is possible that, if any of the elders in the synagogues where Paul preached followed him and became Christians, they also became elders in the newly founded churches, though we cannot say whether that was an established pattern. Certainly those churches had elders appointed by Paul before he moved on elsewhere, and it is hard to see where they would have acquired the necessary spiritual maturity if it were not from the synagogue. On the other hand, if Gentiles were appointed elders in the churches, as they apparently were, they could not have been Jewish elders beforehand, although they would probably have been "God-fearers," the name given to Gentile adherents of the synagogue who worshiped the God of Israel without becoming Jews.[45]

Elders were held in high esteem, and it seems that the apostles were happy to apply the term to themselves when writing to different churches, and to regard the elders in those churches as their equals.[46] This would have meant that elders were engaged in the same preaching and teaching ministry as the apostles, but while the apostles had a roving commission to all the churches, as did their personal assistants like Timothy and Titus, there is no indication that an elder in a local church could or did exercise this ministry elsewhere.

It seems probable that the elders were regarded as overseers of their churches and that the two terms could be used interchangeably of them. Thus, we find that Paul gives instructions to Titus, telling him to appoint "elders in every town" on Crete, and then goes on to describe what their qualifications as overseers ought to be.[47] These qualifications are virtually identical to those required of deacons, the one possible difference being that overseers were also expected to "be able to give instruction in sound doctrine and also to rebuke

---

[42] Gal. 2:9.
[43] Acts 15:2. See also Acts 11:30; 14:23.
[44] Matt. 26:3, 57–59; Mark 8:31; 11:27; Luke 9:22; 22:66.
[45] Acts 13: 50; 16:14; 17:4, 17; 18:7.
[46] 1 Pet. 5:1; 2 John 1; 3 John 1.
[47] Titus 1:5, 7.

those who contradict it."[48] Otherwise, elders had to show the same level of spiritual maturity demanded of deacons and to be a good advertisement for the faith in their local communities.[49]

One question not directly addressed in the New Testament is how many elders there were in any given church, and whether one of them took precedence over the others. The word is normally used in the singular only when it refers to an apostle,[50] and the general impression is that each local congregation had a number of people who exercised this responsibility. It stands to reason that one of them must have presided over their meetings, if only to keep order, but there is no indication that there was a particular individual appointed for that purpose or that one elder exercised authority over the others. Leadership at the local level seems to have been collegial, though we cannot say how that operated in practice. Did everyone have to agree on everything, or was a majority vote enough to carry a particular motion? No doubt consensus would have been sought as much as possible, as the proceedings of the Jerusalem council indicate, but whether that was achieved everywhere, and what happened if it was not, is impossible for us to say.[51] Paul and Barnabas were sent to Antioch at the council's request, but no sooner had they got there than they fell out with each other and parted company, which is perhaps indicative of what transpired when there was serious disagreement.[52]

As long as the apostles were alive, this form of church government seems to have continued unaltered, but after they died a change took place. In every congregation, it seems that one of the elders rose to prominence as the chief overseer, who took special responsibility for preserving and proclaiming the apostolic message. Timothy and Titus may perhaps be regarded as their prototypes, not least because they exercised a ministry of oversight in churches other than their own. As the church grew and established new congregations, this overseer extended his ministry to them as well, even if there were also local elders appointed to govern them. In this way, the classical system of bishops and dioceses gradually took shape.[53] Every major city had its bishop, who would be responsible for all the congregations in it and in the immediate neighborhood. Not surprisingly, special importance was soon being attached to the bishops of the biggest cities, a pattern that was

---

[48]Titus 1:9.

[49]1 Tim. 3:1–7.

[50]1 Tim. 5:19 is an exception, but the reason for the exception is easy to understand, as it speaks about accusations made against one of the elders.

[51]Acts 15:1–29.

[52]Acts 15:36–41.

[53]"Bishop" is the Anglicized form of the Greek word *episkopos*, which means "overseer." A diocese was originally an administrative unit of the Roman empire, and the term was taken over by the church for practical reasons.

formally established after the legalization of Christianity in the fourth century. At the top of the hierarchy were the three bishops of Rome, Alexandria, and Antioch (in that order), who were given the honorary title of "patriarch." Later on, Constantinople was added to this list (in second place, immediately after Rome), and Jerusalem was tacked on at the end because it had been the first church, though by that time it was of no special importance. Individual dioceses were also grouped into provinces headed by an archbishop, a system that is still found today in most of the historic churches.

Compulsory celibacy for bishops (and archbishops) was imposed in 692, and has remained the norm in both the Roman and the Eastern churches. At the time of the Reformation, the Protestants who broke away from Rome approached this inheritance in different ways. Where they could, they often kept the medieval system of bishops and archbishops, as the modern Anglican and Lutheran churches demonstrate. Where that was not possible, largely for political reasons, the Reformed churches reorganized themselves along what seemed to them to be biblical lines. Generally speaking, they revived a presbyterian system of collective leadership, usually with one of their number appointed as president (or "moderator"), who served for a fixed term. Disputes arose about how far, and in what way, the presbyters of one congregation would be accountable to those elsewhere, and further division resulted between those who opted for greater centralization and those who preferred more local independence. But these differences apart, the basic structure was similar in most non-Episcopal Protestant churches, and that remains the case today.

Is there a biblical case to be made for having bishops or their equivalents in the church? We cannot decide this question simply by examining the meaning of the words "elder" and "overseer" in the New Testament, nor by the fact that the apostles, the only people known to have exercised authority beyond the bounds of a single congregation, occasionally identified themselves as "elders." The people most like a modern bishop are Timothy and Titus, Paul's assistants who had a supra-congregational commission like his but without enjoying full apostolic authority.[54] The practical advantages of having someone with general oversight over a group of churches become apparent when trouble erupts in one of them that only a neutral but authoritative observer can resolve. This is what the apostles often did, and there is no reason to suppose that the need for an umpire is any less today than it was then.

It is also good to have someone with recognized authority who can speak for the church as a whole and coordinate its activities by calling the elders

---

[54]Titus 1:5.

together and presiding over their deliberations, and it can be useful for the elders to have someone to turn to for pastoral advice and support, as the New Testament elders turned to the apostles. Having said that, the historical reality is that bishops have often failed to live up to their responsibilities, and some of them have become tyrants when they have been allowed to rule unchecked. The ministry of oversight can work only if it is organically tied to the body of the church and answerable to it. Granting anyone unfettered power and life tenure is a recipe for disaster, and it certainly cannot be justified on the biblical principle of the need for congregational oversight.

One problem that the Reformers had to confront was that, during the Middle Ages, the ancient eldership had given way to an order of ordained men who were no longer answerable to the local congregation, but who could exercise their functions wherever the bishop sent them. At the same time, the way these functions were understood had also changed. In theory, the elders remained responsible for teaching the faith and rebuking error, but many of them were barely educated and hardly suited to such a task. Instead, they focused on baptizing babies and celebrating Holy Communion, which became the central act of Christian worship. As time went on, that came to be understood as a re-presentation of Christ's sacrifice on the cross, with the result that the elder assumed a role analogous to that of an Old Testament priest. The collegiate aspect of this priesthood was maintained at the diocesan level, but in local churches there was usually only one man appointed to the task. After 1123, the Western church required priests to be celibate as well as bishops, which greatly increased the distance between them and their flocks.

At the time of the Reformation, all Protestants abandoned compulsory celibacy, and the teaching role of the eldership was once more brought to the fore. The more conservative Anglican and Lutheran churches continued to use the word "priest," but the others preferred less tendentious terms such as minister or pastor. But there is one feature of the medieval system that has continued almost unchanged in virtually every Protestant church. This is that the pastor retains a unique place in his congregation, even when there is a body of elders which is theoretically supposed to share his authority. These elders, like deacons, are mostly part-time and unpaid, whereas the pastor is generally a full-time professional, which gives him a built-in advantage. Attempts to resurrect the New Testament form of eldership have been pursued more seriously than attempts to revive the diaconate, but they have not succeeded very well, and the residual legacy of the medieval priesthood is still very much with us in the church today. Members of the church are told to be submissive to their leaders,[55] but given the diverse pattern of leadership in many congregations and the relative ease with which those who are unhappy can go elsewhere, this biblical precept is hard to apply in practice.

One question that has surfaced in modern times is whether women can be admitted to these forms of ministry. As a general rule, the more emphasis a church places on the status of its ordained clergy, the less likely it is to approve of women's ordination. Because of this, many Protestants see restrictions placed on women as a legacy of the rejected Catholic past and believe that the time has come to grant women full ministerial equality with men. The difficulty is that this is not the teaching of the Bible, which maintains a distinction between the roles given to men and women in the life of the church that effectively excludes women from the eldership, though not from the diaconate.[56]

Those who argue in favor of women's ordination have employed all kinds of ingenious arguments in order to get around the witness of the Bible. At one end of the spectrum are somewhat eccentric claims that Junia was an apostle,[57] that Mary Magdalene was the first person to see the risen Christ and therefore was also an apostle,[58] and that the Greek word for "head" means "source,"[59] with no implication that there is any underlying authority involved. Rather more serious is the argument that there is "no male and female" in Christ, and so no distinctions should be made between them in the church.[60] Appeal is made to cultural conditioning (that of the ancients, of course, not ours!) and to something called the "trajectory" of biblical thought, which maintains that freedom in Christ was gradually breaking down ancient barriers, and so we are entitled to go further than the New Testament does in trying to achieve this aim. Despite such ingenuity, however, the Scriptures are perfectly clear and straightforward on this matter. Paul did not mince his words when he wrote to Timothy,

> I do not permit a woman to teach or to exercise authority over a man; rather, she is to remain quiet. For Adam was formed first, then Eve; and Adam was not deceived, but the woman was deceived and became a transgressor.[61]

Two things must be observed about this. First, Paul is talking about the eldership (teaching and exercising authority) not about participation in worship. He was certainly prepared to let women pray and prophesy in the

---

[55]Heb. 13:17.
[56]For evidence of deaconesses in the New Testament, see Rom. 16:1.
[57]Rom. 16:7.
[58]John 20:14–18.
[59]1 Cor. 11:3.
[60]Gal. 3:28.
[61]1 Tim. 2:12–14.

church, insisting only that they should cover their heads as a sign of their submission to the authority of men.[62] It might be argued today that there are more culturally appropriate ways of signifying that in modern Western society, where the significance of covering the head has been lost, but the principle remains valid even if it requires new forms of expression in our particular circumstances.

Second, the Bible gives two reasons why women must submit to the authority of men. The first has to do with the order of creation and the second with the way in which the human race fell away from God's plan. Some people try to argue that the death and resurrection of Christ has reversed the effects of the fall, but this instruction was given after that, so clearly Paul did not think that the sin of Adam could be ignored. Even if that were the case, though, the creation ordinance would remain in place, and it is the more fundamental of the two. Men and women relate to one another the way they do because of how they were made. Women are not inferior to men, but they are different, and that difference must be respected. When it is not, the result is liable to be chaos, as happened when Eve was deceived and Adam allowed himself to be persuaded by her. It is to fulfill the creation mandate and to avoid the pitfalls of disobedience that this command has been given, and it is for that reason that women cannot exercise an eldership role in the church.

Lest anyone think that this gives special privileges to the man, let us consider what Paul had to say in a different context. Talking about marriage, he said that wives should submit to their husbands as their heads, just as the church submits to Christ as its head.[63] When he speaks to the men, however, he tells them to love their wives and to sacrifice themselves for them, just as Christ gave himself up to death so that the church might live.[64] It is a tall order, but those who are called to a particular honor are also called to greater self-denial, and no one more so than the shepherd (pastor) who is expected to lay down his life for his sheep.[65]

THE WORSHIP OF GOD

Among the main tasks assigned to ministers of the church today is the conduct of public worship, though whether this was the established pattern in New Testament times is not clear. We know that the early church worshiped together, but who presided at their services and how they were organized is

---

[62] 1 Cor. 11:4–11.
[63] Eph. 5:22–24.
[64] Eph. 5:25–28.
[65] John 10:11.

not known. To some people this is problematic because they do not want to do anything that is not specifically authorized in Scripture, but when it comes to the public worship of God, there is simply not enough in the Bible to dictate what our order of service should be. As a result, every church is obliged to supplement what is found in the New Testament with provisions of its own that it regards as being compatible with biblical principles.

In the modern world, worship falls into two main types—liturgical and nonliturgical. Broadly speaking, the more a church has retained its medieval heritage, the more likely it is to be liturgical, since that was the norm before the Reformation. Liturgical worship grew up over many centuries and was eventually codified in a number of different forms. During the Reformation, the churches that retained those forms reduced their number and standardized them still further, with the aim of protecting the uniformity of the church's doctrine by making sure that everyone worshiped according to the same pattern. The key to understanding liturgy is to recognize that it is designed to provide both breadth and depth in our devotional life. A good liturgy will cover all the main biblical and doctrinal themes in a way that allows the worshiper to memorize them and reflect on them more deeply over time. Usually it will include a regular cycle of readings from Scripture based on the Christian year, which begins at Advent and continues through Christmas and Easter, culminating with the sending of the Holy Spirit at Pentecost. The time from then until the next Advent, which is nearly half the year, is not specifically organized and may be devoted to other doctrinal themes.

By its nature, liturgical worship cannot be sampled on a casual basis. It demands commitment and yields its benefits over time as its principles and emphases are absorbed by the worshiper. For this reason, it is often unappealing to the young and to those who want instant spiritual gratification, whereas older people can become very attached to it and resent changes that interrupt the flow of their prayers and distract them from concentrating on God. Liturgical worship can also nourish congregations who lack a good preaching and teaching ministry as it helps to make up for that defect. This is not ideal, of course, and liturgies were not composed for that reason, but Christians who are deprived of spiritual nourishment in other forms have good reason to be grateful for the liturgies which they have learned and that sustain them in such times of dryness.

Supporters of nonliturgical worship often argue that it is superior to any liturgy because it is "free." To their minds, this means that it is more in tune with a community that lives in the Spirit, but this is not so obvious if we compare the two styles objectively. Nonliturgical worship tends to be much more predictable and monochromatic than liturgical worship is because the spontaneity needed to keep it fresh is hard to maintain over time. Liturgical churches may have a bewildering variety of prayers to choose from, and its ministers can easily get caught up in minute details of order, but nonliturgical ones usually end up with a "hymn-sandwich" pattern (hymn, prayer, hymn, reading, hymn, etc.) which is often meaningless. Even in charismatic churches, it is astonishing how repetitive the "voice of the Spirit" can sometimes be in practice! Practicalities to do with the use of time and the need to ensure a standard of doctrinal orthodoxy may work in favor of adopting a common liturgy, as was done in ancient times and still continues in many churches today. Useful and practical as liturgies can be, however, they should not stifle the practice of private prayer, or of prayer by individual members of the congregation. Even the best of forms can be abused, and if prayer becomes mere repetition it ceases to fulfill its proper role in the life of the church.

Our modern worship must reflect the teaching of the apostles, but it is not bound to follow their practices in every detail. Even if that were possible, it would impose a rigidity on the church that would hamper its mission in the world because so many of those practices were geared to the needs of their time, and our needs are often quite different. Equally dangerous is the habit of reviving "traditions" gleaned from an ancient source and grafted onto the modern church in the name of authenticity. There may be some substance to this, but such artificial revivals can easily distort the meaning and intention of the original (possibly without realizing it) and hamper the mission of the church. A good example is the growing tendency in some Protestant churches for the clergy to wear vestments that reflect the fashions of the late Roman empire but which have no connection to modern life. There may be some advantage in having church officers dressed in a kind of uniform so that other people will know who they are, but to choose one that is totally out of step with the modern world, to invest it with theological meaning, and then to insist that everyone must wear it is absurd and damaging to the church's credibility as the bearer of an eternal message, as relevant to our times as it was to those of the fourth century.

Whatever pattern of worship we adopt, we must ensure that all things are done "decently and in order," so as not to bring shame and disgrace on the church.[66] In principle, any church member is free to exercise his spiritual gifts in the congregation, and opportunity should be given for that. In the New Testament, open prayer was something that everyone was entitled to take part in, and the singing of psalms, hymns, and spiritual songs was encouraged

---

[66] 1 Cor. 14:40.

as a communal activity.[67] Circumstances will inevitably dictate how this is done, and what is possible in a small gathering may be unworkable in larger churches. Here we have to rely on sanctified common sense, and we may be grateful that the Bible gives us the freedom to adapt our practices to the needs of each community and congregation.

At the heart of Christian worship are the ordinances that we normally refer to as "sacraments." The word "sacrament" derives from the Latin word for "oath" and was originally applied to baptism, which was seen as analogous to the oath a Roman soldier took on entering the army. The church was the army of the Lord, and by submitting to baptism, a believer was swearing allegiance to him. The word "sacrament" does not occur in the New Testament, unless we take the Greek equivalent (*mystērion*) in this sacramental sense, which does not fit the contexts where it occurs, and which most scholars believe is an incorrect translation of the word.[68] By the fourth century, however, *mystērion* was coming to be used of what we would now call the sacraments, and a whole theology has subsequently grown up around it.

The Western understanding of the sacraments was codified by Peter Lombard (d. 1160) in his *Sentences*, which became the theological textbook of the Middle Ages. Peter categorized the sacraments as means of grace and declared that there were seven of them, apparently because he thought that seven was a sacred number. Neither this definition nor this categorization was ever officially approved by the church, but the influence of the *Sentences* was such that it was taken for granted and used as the basis of debate by all sides in the Reformation era.

Peter Lombard subdivided the seven sacraments into five and two, depending on whether they were intended for every Christian or only for some. The five universal sacraments were baptism, confirmation, penance, Holy Communion, and extreme unction. The other two were ordination and matrimony, neither of which was necessary for any one individual to have, and both of which could not be held by the same person.[69] Because Peter believed that the sacraments were the means by which the church dispensed the grace of God to its members, he saw their administration as the main function of the ministry of bishops and priests. One of the oddities of Peter's categorization is that of all the seven "sacraments," only one—Holy Communion—is a regular act of public worship, though in the Middle Ages even it tended to

---

[67]Eph. 5:19; Col. 3:16.
[68]See, for example, Eph. 3:9; 5:32; 6:19.
[69]That was decided during Peter Lombard's lifetime, when the first Lateran council (1123) made celibacy compulsory for all bishops and priests.

be privatized, with priests performing the ritual by themselves or with only the tiniest of flocks.

The Protestant Reformers restructured this sacramental system on a different principle. In their minds, a sacrament was an extension of the preaching of the gospel, and if an ordinance did not do that, it had no right to be called by that name. Given that the word "sacrament" does not appear in the New Testament, it is possible to argue that their restructuring was no more biblical than Peter Lombard's had been. We must certainly be careful about lumping together ordinances that are not connected in the Scriptures, but at least everyone agrees that baptism and Holy Communion proclaim the gospel of Christ and are found in the New Testament. The other five have either been abandoned on the ground that they developed out of a misunderstanding of biblical teaching, or have been relegated to a different category. Confirmation, for example, continues to be used in churches that practice infant baptism, but it is now usually regarded as a completion of that baptism and not as a distinct sacrament in its own right. Penance and extreme unction are no longer practiced on a regular basis, although there is clearly nothing wrong with repenting of one's sins or with prayers for the sick and dying. The difference is that these things are no longer ritualized or integrated into a system of confession to a priest, followed by specific acts of contrition determined according to the gravity of the fault being atoned for.

Ordination and matrimony are both ordinances of the modern church, but Protestants do not regard them as mutually exclusive.[70] Ordination is a public recognition by the church of a particular ministry, but it does not confer a special status based on the reception of some additional grace, and cannot be interpreted in sacramental terms. Matrimony is also practiced by the church (which was not the case in New Testament times), though in most countries there has been growing interference from the state that has led to a number of complications. Generally speaking, the church recognizes the validity of a marriage performed by the state and does not repeat the ceremony, which means that in countries where civil marriage is compulsory, the church can only bless a union so contracted.

The church is also obliged to accept civil divorce, but it does not dissolve marriages, so that a divorced person who remarries during the lifetime of a previous spouse is committing adultery in the eyes of the church.[71] Unfortunately, it is often difficult to enforce this in practice, and some divorced people are remarried in a religious ceremony, in defiance of the Bible's teach-

---

[70]Not all Protestant denominations recognize ordination, but matrimony is universally practiced.
[71]Matt. 19:9.

ing on the matter. In some churches marital discipline is so lax that remarried divorcees may even be admitted to preaching and teaching offices, a scandal which threatens the moral integrity of the Christian community and compromises its witness to the wider world. Same-sex unions, which are recognized by some civil jurisdictions as marriages, are forbidden by the Bible and cannot be legitimately performed or blessed by any Christian body, though again, lax enforcement of this means that these things do occasionally happen, and there is a vocal body of liberal protesters who want the church to abandon the truth of the gospel and recognize such immorality as legitimate.[72]

THE LORD'S SUPPER

The most important sacrament, and the one that ordinary Christians are most likely to take part in on a regular basis, is Holy Communion, also known as the Lord's Supper, the Eucharist, or the Mass. The different names reflect different theological traditions, and it is difficult to find one that is genuinely neutral. Evangelical Protestants tend to prefer "the Lord's Supper," which was also the term preferred in ancient times. Scholarly ecumenists go for "Eucharist," and those of high church inclinations say "Mass," even though this word is nothing but a corruption of the Latin word *missa*, which occurs at the end of the service in the dismissal of the congregation (*ecclesia missa est*). It has no theological meaning in itself, but it signals to participants that the celebrant holds to the Roman Catholic doctrine of eucharistic sacrifice, and Catholics continue to use it for that reason. In whatever guise, the Lord's Supper has always been the central act of Christian worship, though the forms it takes and the frequency with which it has been celebrated have varied widely over time and have been the subject of much controversy.

Its origin goes back to the Last Supper of Jesus and his disciples, when he broke bread and gave it to them, telling them that it was his body which was to be broken for them. He also passed around a cup of wine, telling them that it was his blood, which would be poured out for them.[73] Whether this Supper was a Passover meal has been disputed, but that there is a connection with Passover is clear from the fact that Christ was called the Passover Lamb.[74] After his resurrection, Jesus accepted the hospitality of two men whom he had met on the road to Emmaus and to whom he explained the events of his crucifixion, which had taken place just a few days before. He was not recognized by them until they sat down to eat and he broke bread, a clear reminder of what

---

[72]1 Cor. 6:9; 1 Tim. 1:10.
[73]Luke 22:19–20.
[74]1 Cor. 5:7. Christ was also called the "Lamb of God, who takes away the sin of the world," though that was at his baptism, and not at the Supper (see John 1:29).

had taken place at the Last Supper. The text does not say that this was a celebration of Holy Communion, and given that as soon as the men recognized him, Jesus vanished out of their sight, it almost certainly was not, but the breaking of bread was enough to trigger their memories, and the symbolism of this has passed into eucharistic worship.[75]

Later on, we find Paul giving the Corinthians details of how the Communion service should be conducted. It is virtually the only time that he refers directly to words that Jesus uttered before his resurrection, which indicates how significant that occasion was.[76] We are given the impression that the memorial of Christ's death was celebrated frequently at Corinth, probably weekly and perhaps even daily, and that it may have been part of a wider fellowship meal, known today as the agape feast. Whether that was true (or typical of the early church in general) is hard to say, but the focus was always on the remembrance of his death and the promise of his future coming. Before long, that was the only purpose of the Communion meal, which then became stylized in the life of the church as part of its worship. As far as we know, only baptized believers were admitted to the Lord's Table because Holy Communion was understood as representing the gift of the Holy Spirit to live the Christian life in conformity to the death and resurrection of Jesus Christ. Having died and been raised to new life with Christ in baptism, the believer was expected to go on growing in that new life by constantly being brought back to the foot of the cross and challenged again to take it up and follow him. Anyone who did not understand this and who ate and drank without "discerning" the Lord's body was bringing down damnation on himself and even risking sickness and death.[77]

Oddly enough, the earliest Christian witnesses outside the New Testament tell us far more about baptism than they do about Holy Communion, perhaps because conversion was seen as more fundamental to the Christian life. Whatever the reason, it is not until the fourth century that we start to find extended theological reflection on the Lord's Supper, which by then had become the centerpiece of an increasingly elaborate liturgy. It was universally acknowledged that Christ was present in the celebration, feeding his people. That this was done by the mediation of the Holy Spirit was also agreed, though it was not explained precisely how that happened. Only much later, during the Middle Ages, did theologians venture to describe what went on in the Supper, and when they did so they concentrated on what supposedly

---

[75]Luke 24:13–35.
[76]1 Cor. 11:23–26.
[77]1 Cor. 11:27–30.

happened to the elements of bread and wine. A minor controversy erupted in 692 when the Council in Trullo[78] legislated that only leavened bread should be used in the ceremony, since (according to the council) unleavened bread was too Jewish. Unfortunately, the Western churches mostly used unleavened bread in the form of wafers[79] and continued to do so, sparking a controversy that lasted until the Council of Florence in 1439 and continues in some circles to this day. Silly and unnecessary as it was, this dispute is a reminder to us of the deep sensitivities that have always attached to the rituals surrounding this sacrament, where even the smallest differences in practice can provoke a reaction from those unused to the new practice, and where theological significance can be accorded to almost anything, whether or not this is justified. Sorting out the core doctrine from the pious practices that surround it has never been easy, and in different ways this problem continues to affect the church today.

It was not until the ninth century that the first suggestion of transubstantiation arose. Transubstantiation is the belief that, when the bread and wine are consecrated, their substance changes into the body and blood of Christ, even though their outward appearance (the so-called "accidents") remains the same. This theory was based on the physics of Aristotle, and became untenable when his view of matter was discarded, but that has not prevented the Roman Catholic Church from insisting on it and building an array of devotional practices around it. By itself, transubstantiation might have been less important had it not been connected with another development, which was the progressive integration of the Old Testament into the life of the church. By the sixth century, church buildings were being erected following the blueprint of the Jerusalem temple as described in 1 Kings 6–7. The dignity that attached to the priesthood of the Old Testament was applied to the Christian clergy, even to the point of assigning them tithes on the Old Testament model. It is therefore hardly surprising that the functions of the Old Testament priesthood were transferred to the clergy of the Christian church, who came to be seen as men who offered sacrifices to God in the same way as those who served the ancient Jerusalem temple had done.

There was, however, one big difference between ancient Jewish priests and their Christian counterparts. The Old Testament priesthood was hereditary, in line with the nature of the Jewish dispensation through the generations of Abraham, Isaac, and Jacob. The New Testament church was not a nation in the physical sense but a new kind of human community. The Mosaic law had specified that the priests should not have a portion of the Promised Land to

---

[78]The Trullum was a wing of the imperial palace at Constantinople.
[79]Known as *azymes*, from the Greek word for "unleavened."

call their own, because they were to be scattered among all the tribes of Israel and were meant to live off their tithes. This was reinterpreted in the medieval church to mean that the Christian priesthood was to remain celibate (and therefore to have no inheritance).[80] The introduction of a doctrine of transubstantiation greatly increased the mystique of the Christian priesthood, underscoring not only the difference between the Old and New Testaments but (more importantly) the superiority of the priests of the New over the Old. After all, anyone could sacrifice a lamb for the sins of the people, since no special power from God was required for that. But only someone endowed with the power of the Holy Spirit could turn bread and wine into Christ's body and blood, an act that quickly became known as "the miracle of the altar."

As that belief grew stronger, supplementary devotional practices grew up around it. Consecrated bread and wine was reserved in the church and venerated as if it were really the body and blood of Christ. Sometimes they would be placed in a "tabernacle" (another throwback to Old Testament imagery) and taken around the streets to encourage popular devotion to them as if they were Christ. Thieves would steal the consecrated bread, known as the "host,"[81] and use it for the occult practice known as the black mass, on the assumption that it contained some spiritual power that they could manipulate. So sacred did the bread become that lay people were forbidden to touch it; it could only be put directly on the recipient's tongue by the priest. The cup was gradually withdrawn from the people, possibly originally as a hygienic measure in time of plague, but eventually as a theological principle. When this was objected to as a nonbiblical practice, theologians cleverly concluded that the blood was contained in the body, so that whoever received the bread was receiving Christ's blood as well. Meanwhile, the priest continued to drink from the consecrated cup, thereby enhancing his status as a mediator between God and the people. All this was a far cry from the New Testament picture of the Last Supper, and it was inevitable that when the Reformation came, it would focus on the Mass and the practices surrounding it as one of the chief abuses that had to be put right.

Unfortunately, even before the Reformation got off the ground, there was a disagreement between Martin Luther and the Swiss reformer Huldrych Zwingli that continues to reverberate to this day. Both men agreed that transubstantiation was a false and untenable doctrine, but they differed about what ought to be put in its place. Luther continued to focus on the real presence of Christ in the sacrament, and to locate that presence in the elements of bread

---

[80]Num. 18:20.
[81]From the Latin word *hostis*, which means "victim" or "sacrifice."

and wine. He differed from the Roman view, however, in believing that Christ was present in, with, and "under" the elements of bread and wine, not by a process of transubstantiation but in a way that we now call "consubstantiation." In Luther's view, the body and blood of Christ were spiritually present in the Supper and linked to the elements by association. The bread and wine remained what they were, but they conveyed the body and blood of Christ as a spiritual reality, which was attached to their natural substance in such a way that the person who consumed the physical elements partook of the body and blood of Christ, whether or not he believed in him. Those who ate and drank worthily were blessed by this, but those who did not were condemned and exposed to numerous perils, including disease and death, as Paul had said.[82]

Zwingli, on the other hand, said that bread and wine remain what they are and cannot become anything else. In the Lord's Supper, they serve as a remembrance of Christ's body and blood without being or becoming those things in any way. The benefit of the Supper was to be found in its value as a memorial, a reenactment of the death of Christ that was supposed to stir the hearts of believers to seek him spiritually in their lives. Those who were convicted of the meaning of his death would benefit from the sacrament, whereas those who failed to discern this would get nothing out of it.

These differences were taken very seriously and led to such bitterness that they almost killed the Reformation before it started. A mediating position was developed by Martin Bucer and transmitted through his disciple, John Calvin, to the wider Protestant world. Bucer and Calvin rejected the consubstantiation theory because it focused on the elements rather than on the recipients, but they did not like the memorialist ideas of Zwingli either. What they wanted was a *via media*, something that would retain the spiritual value of the rite without falling into medieval superstition or some approximation thereof. The solution they came up with was to tie the celebration of the Lord's Supper to the preaching of the Word of God. The message of salvation in Christ was never a purely intellectual thing. Included in it was the doctrine of the resurrection of the body, and so it was necessary to include the body in the message of the gospel. This was done by means of the Lord's Supper, when believers took the death and resurrection of Christ into their bodies by means of the sacrament. But since the bread and wine contained no supernatural powers that could do anything to transform the body of the recipient, this benefit had to be understood in a spiritual way, as the promise of the resurrection of the body that would occur when the Lord returns. This is why Paul stressed the eschatological dimension of the sacrament—it looked

---

[82]1 Cor. 11:29–30.

forward to the consummation of all things, as well as backward to the once-for-all sacrifice of Christ on the cross.[83]

In the meantime, the function of the Supper is to reinforce the message that the new life in Christ reaches into every part of our being. There is no division between the religious and the secular, the spiritual and the material. Everything comes under the lordship of Christ and everything must be subjected to and transformed by him. The Supper is indeed a memorial, in the sense that it recalls the historical sacrifice of Jesus on the cross and his resurrection on the third day. But what took place on a single occasion in time and space has now been taken up into the heavens, where the risen, ascended, and glorified Christ pleads for our forgiveness by presenting his broken body and poured out blood to the Father as the propitiation for our sins. This heavenly reality is brought home to us by the Holy Spirit, who uses the elements of bread and wine in the Supper as a means of making us aware of what Christ is doing for us and of challenging us to accept it for ourselves. It has an eschatological dimension that is easily ignored, but which Paul was careful to emphasize in his instructions to the Corinthian church. The Lord's Supper faces both ways—it looks back to the sacrifice of Jesus in time and space and forward to the consummation of that sacrifice in eternity. What Jesus did once for all on the cross he is now doing eternally in heaven. We cannot go back in time to ancient Palestine, but that does not matter because we are seated in the heavenly places in Christ Jesus, and it is in that context that we partake of the Supper of the Lamb who was slain.[84]

The believer who partakes of the Supper on earth is demonstrating his commitment to the mediatorial work of Christ for him in heaven, and he benefits from it accordingly. The person who takes the bread and wine but does not acknowledge its significance eats and drinks damnation to himself because he does not discern the Lord's body. To attempt to bring that body back to earth by some kind of transubstantiation is to try to bypass the work of the Holy Spirit. Those who do this may not be diminishing the mediatorial role of Christ as such, but by attempting to gain access to it by material means they are subverting the work of the Spirit and denying people access to the very thing that they are claiming to provide. This was the true scandal of the Mass and the reason why Bucer and Calvin condemned it as idolatrous—it tried to replace a heavenly and spiritual reality with an earthly caricature that promised access to it but actually denied it, just as Satan had promised access to God for Adam and Eve but actually cut them off from him. Only when

---

[83]1 Cor. 11:26.
[84]Matt. 26:29; Mark 14:25; Rev. 19:6–9.

this is understood can the vehemence with which the Reformers attacked the medieval church be properly appreciated, and only then can we understand why it is so important not to lose sight of their vision in our own worship and practice. If the Lord's Supper is central to our worshiping life as Christians, this is because it is one of the chief means by which God draws us closer to himself in the power of his Holy Spirit, whom he has sent to proclaim the truth of the gospel of Christ which the Supper so eloquently reveals to us. Distort that and we are lost; remember it and we shall find that the Lord's Supper is a blessing given to us by God so that we can ponder and experience his love more deeply than mere words could ever allow.

THE BOUNDARIES OF BELONGING

Who has the right to participate in the Lord's Supper? In principle this would seem to be an easy question to answer, in that all baptized members of the church should be welcome as communicants at the Lord's Table. In practice, however, things are not that simple. For a start, infants who have been baptized have generally been refused permission to receive Communion until they have made a personal profession of faith and been confirmed as church members. This is a sensible precaution in churches that practice infant baptism, and can be defended on the ground that a communicant must be able to "discern" the Lord's body,[85] which presumably means that he must be able to understand what he is doing. However, there have always been those who believe that there should be sacramental consistency—anyone who has been baptized should be admitted to the table as well. In the Eastern Orthodox churches infants are given Communion after their baptism but then they usually do not receive it again until they are older and able to take it for themselves. This precedent is sometimes cited by liturgical reformers in the West, but it is of limited value because regular Communion is much less common in the Eastern churches and refraining from taking the sacrament is not as odd as it would be in most Protestant or Roman Catholic congregations today.

One of the effects of modern liturgical reform has been to make Holy Communion the chief form of worship in many churches on a Sunday morning, but although this can be justified in liturgical and theological terms, the effects have been far from uniformly positive. The biggest problem is that when Communion becomes the norm, it is difficult, if not impossible, to exercise any spiritual discipline. The New Testament tells us that we should prepare ourselves to receive the sacrament by sorting out our affairs before we

---

[85]1 Cor. 11:29.

come,[86] but if we are expected to receive it as a matter of course every week, that is very difficult to do. The structure of most modern services also makes it virtually impossible not to receive the Communion when it is offered, which can create embarrassment when there are visitors present who, for one reason or another, do not wish to participate. Opting out of Communion has become more difficult, and preparation, with the discipline which that implies, is virtually unknown. Contrary to the intentions of the liturgical reformers, the sacrament has been trivialized and devalued by overuse, and so its significance in the life of the believer and the congregation has been obscured.

Difficulties can also occur with members of other churches. Most Protestant denominations are happy to admit anyone from another church to their Communion table, but this is not true of Roman Catholics or Eastern Orthodox, whose authorities not only refuse to admit others to their tables but forbid their members from receiving Communion in other churches.[87] The logic behind this is that these churches believe that they and they alone are the true church, and it is only within the communion of that church that the sacrament has any meaning. Protestants rarely claim that their denomination is the true church to the exclusion of all others, and so are usually prepared to admit nonmembers, especially if they are visitors from elsewhere. The consequence of this is that, if the decision to partake is generally left up to the recipient, no discipline can be exercised. This tendency has even been stretched to the point where some Protestants hold Communion services outside the church context altogether, where no oversight or discipline is possible.

This is clearly an unsatisfactory situation that has to be addressed at the level of principle and then put into practice. The authorities of the church have a responsibility to ensure that, as far as they are able, Holy Communion should be confined to those who are ready and prepared to receive it. It should always be accompanied by the preaching of the Word and by a sufficiently clear and strong exhortation to repent and turn to Christ, because forgiveness and reconciliation is basically what it is all about. When these things are lost sight of the sacrament is profaned, the Holy Spirit withdraws his blessing, and the church loses a precious opportunity to help its members grow in the love of God for them.

In years gone by, exclusion from the church was marked by excommunication, which meant that the sacrament was withdrawn and the person so affected was excluded from the fellowship of others. A few small congrega-

---

[86]Matt. 5:24.
[87]This practice can also be found among some Anglicans and Lutherans, as well as in smaller Protestant bodies such as the Exclusive Brethren.

tions still practice this, but on the whole it has disappeared from the modern church, which tends to accept whoever is prepared to come. The advantage of this approach is that it does not discriminate unfairly against those who might come into conflict with church authorities. In England, for example, it was once customary to excommunicate people who failed to pay their tithes or who were held to be in contempt of an ecclesiastical court, and there was considerable abuse of the practice in contexts that were essentially secular.

Today we have gone to the other extreme and seem to be prepared to admit people who have no discernible belief at all or who are living openly immoral lives. The effect of this is that the credibility of the church is compromised to the point where it is impossible to maintain any kind of standards at all. Yet it is clear from the New Testament that those who did not believe the doctrine of the church or who lived immoral lives in defiance of its teaching were excommunicated and not allowed to pretend that their behavior was compatible with Christian discipleship.[88] Unless and until the modern church recovers that sense of discipline it will be weak and ineffective, unable to feed its members with the food of the Holy Spirit's teaching and unable to preach the gospel of Christ to an unbelieving world.

---

[88] 1 Cor. 5:9–13.

31

FROM TIME
TO ETERNITY

LIVING IN THE LAST DAYS

One of the most pervasive themes of the New Testament is that we are living in the "last days" and that time will come to an end suddenly and without warning. Many scholars have thought that this was merely a part of Jesus' message that held a particular attraction for his disciples, who supposedly believed that the end would come in their lifetimes, when Christ would return to earth in his heavenly glory. This event was known as the *parousia* ("presence") of Christ, and the phrase "parousia hope" is often found in descriptions of New Testament theology. As time went on and that did not happen, the early Christians are supposed to have gradually abandoned this hope and settled down to construct a church that would last for the indefinite future. To put it a different way, Jesus was portrayed as an apocalyptic figure who preached catastrophe and judgment, but his disciples toned his message down for popular consumption and the church has followed their lead ever since.

It will perhaps come as no surprise to discover that this theory was developed by liberal German scholars of the nineteenth century who were unhappy with the constraints imposed on them by the institutional church of their day and sought to counter it by proposing a vision of early Christianity quite different from the commonly accepted view. There was just enough truth in their presentation of Jesus and his disciples to make it seem that they were right, and although their views have been considerably modified and supplemented since their time, the basic picture they painted is still widely accepted today.

History, however, does not support the thesis that the "parousia hope" declined after the first generation of disciples passed away. In the second century there was the prophet Montanus, who believed that Christ would come back to earth in Asia Minor, and whose followers gathered at a place called Pepuza in expectation of that event. Later on, after Christianity became the official religion of the Roman empire (in 380) and Rome was sacked by the barbarian King Alaric (in 410), it was widely assumed that the end was nigh, and the great Augustine of Hippo (354–430) was forced to write his magisterial *City of God* to show that this interpretation of history was mistaken. After that, we hear of similar outbreaks of apocalyptic fervor at times of great social and political crisis. The Islamic conquests in the seventh century, the arrival of the year 1000, the black death in the fourteenth century, the sixteenth-century Reformation, the French Revolution, and the massive upheavals of the twentieth century all produced crops of doomsday prophets who attracted a following.

Some of these prophetic movements petered out fairly quickly, but others had a much longer life. It is not often appreciated that modern millennialism, with its pre-, post-, and a-millenarian variants, emerged in the wake of the French Revolution, whose rationalist and atheistic tendencies were widely believed to portend the reign of the Antichrist, a feeling that has only intensified now that Darwinism, Marxism, Freudianism, and other secular ideologies have arisen in its wake. The "culture wars" that mark our generation's struggle against such forces and fuel so much of the current interest in apocalyptic scenarios have actually been going on for more than two hundred years and were of major importance in the early years of the United States. How many people now remember that Thomas Jefferson rewrote the New Testament in order to remove the unacceptably miraculous bits, and that in the 1800 presidential election his opponents accused him of atheism, a force which (thanks to the excesses of the French Revolution) was then thought to be on the verge of destroying the world?

This historical perspective is necessary, not because it shows that much of the talk about the end times is a fantasy, but because it helps us to see the teaching of Jesus for what it is and to focus on the true meaning of what has been revealed to us in the New Testament. To do this properly, we must begin with the great theological statement that opens the letter to the Hebrews:

> Long ago, at many times and in many ways, God spoke to our fathers by the prophets, but in these last days he has spoken to us by his Son, whom he appointed the heir of all things, through whom also he created the world.[1]

The message of the letter to the Hebrews is that Jesus Christ is the culmination of Jewish history, the end point to which the prophets of old had pointed

---

[1]Heb. 1:1–2.

and the perfect fulfillment of what had up to then been revealed only partially and sporadically. There can be no further revelation from God because in Christ we have seen the Son, who is both the Creator and the heir of all things. There is no opening left for anyone else to come, and whatever happens now must be understood in the light of the revelation we have received from him.

The first practical consequence of this is that we must reject any message that claims to add to or replace what Jesus said. Jesus warned his disciples that there would be many who would come and lead people astray by telling them that they were the promised Messiah.[2] Later on, the early Christians were warned about false prophets, who were also trying to take them away from the truth.[3] Deception can take many forms and is inevitably going to be subtle, since otherwise it would be easy to detect, but we are promised that if we hold fast to the faith we have received, we shall be protected and preserved from all such deception.[4]

The second consequence is that when we look at the development of world history, we must remember that whatever happens, Christ is seated on the throne of glory and remains in control of events. This is the basic message of the book of Revelation, which describes the many horrors that will come in the future but at the same time begins with the vision of Christ the King, "who is and who was and who is to come, the Almighty," and culminates in the great judgment that destroys the power of evil and remakes the created order.[5] There have been many attempts to connect the visions of Revelation with specific historical events, but such attempts constitute a half-truth that is bound by our limited human perspective. It is certainly true that the march of human history does exemplify the disasters foretold in Revelation, and Jesus told his disciples to expect wars and rumors of wars.[6] Nothing could have been more foolish than the optimistic hope, expressed during the First World War, that it would be the "war to end all wars." Many of those who said that lived to see the rise of Hitler and Stalin, and to be eyewitnesses of atrocities that the men of 1914–1918 could not have imagined. Even in times of "peace," there are always wars going on somewhere or other. We may live in plenty, but others suffer from hunger, and there are still appalling famines in various parts of the world. We may enjoy the benefits of modern medicine, but strange and lethal epidemics are still common.

The scenarios portrayed in New Testament apocalyptic literature are

---

[2]Matt. 24:5; Mark 13:6; Luke 21:8.
[3]2 Pet. 2:1; 1 John 4:1; Jude 4–18.
[4]Jude 20.
[5]Rev. 1:8; 19:1–22:5.
[6]Matt. 24:6; Mark 13:7; Luke 21:9.

familiar, and will remain so until Christ returns. They cannot be tied down to particular events, as if they had no wider application. An exception to this general rule is what Jesus told his disciples when he said,

> When you see the abomination of desolation spoken of by the prophet Daniel, standing in the holy place (let the reader understand), then let those who are in Judea flee to the mountains.[7]

As Luke's version confirms, this refers to the destruction of Jerusalem, which took place in A.D. 70, and which the Christians in the city managed to escape by fleeing as Jesus had told them to. From the Jewish point of view, the events of A.D. 70 were indeed apocalyptic in their significance because the ancient polity of Israel was destroyed and has never been resurrected. But even here, the Gospel accounts, which most scholars think were written after these events, are curiously open-ended. If the destruction of Jerusalem had been the fulfillment of Jesus' prophecy, then surely the Gospels would have said so. But the warnings given to the disciples remain applicable because at bottom they are spiritual in nature. Jerusalem is a historical city, but one that has eternal significance, as the New Testament reminds us.[8] The destruction of what is earthly must take place in order for what is heavenly to appear, and in warning his followers to be ready for what was about to happen to them, Jesus is also reminding us that in this world we have no permanent home. If we are truly following him, then we must be prepared to go "outside the camp" as he did, and bear the reproach that he endured, in expectation of the glory that is to come when he returns.[9]

THE TRIALS OF THE SAVED

There are many who will tell us that we are deluding ourselves if we think that good will come out of what we suffer in this life. It is all very well, they may say, for comfortable, middle-class people to think this way, because nothing very bad ever seems to happen to them. But those who suffer nightmarish pain or who are condemned to a marginal existence of poverty cannot afford such detachment. Christians who appear to excuse suffering by saying that our reward is not here on earth but in the kingdom of heaven will readily be accused of preaching "pie in the sky when you die" as a way to condone injustice and avoid taking responsibility for alleviating the sufferings of our fellow human beings. There is no easy answer to such charges, although it is

---

[7]Matt. 24:15–16; Mark 13:14; Luke 21:20. The reference is to Dan. 9:27; 11:31; 12:11.
[8]Gal. 4:25; Heb. 12:22; Rev. 3:12; 21:2.
[9]Heb. 13:12–14.

remarkable how often they are made by people who are merely observing the pain of others and not experiencing it themselves. No human being is excused from suffering, and every one of us must play our part in helping its victims, whether or not they are believers. Whether we are called to share the pain of others or expected to endure tragedies of our own, we must stand with people everywhere in their hour of need.

There is no exemption from suffering in this life, but for Christians that can never be an end in itself. As Paul told the Christians of Thessalonica, "We do not want you to be uninformed, brothers, about those who are asleep, that you may not grieve as others do who have no hope. For since we believe that Jesus died and rose again, even so, through Jesus, God will bring with him those who have fallen asleep."[10] Bereavement is something that comes to us all, but death is not the end. The Son of God came into the world, not to ignore our suffering but to take it on himself and to transform it into new life. However severe our trials may be, Christians resonate with the words of the patriarch Job:

> For I know that my Redeemer lives,
>   and at the last he will stand upon the earth.
> And after my skin has been thus destroyed,
>   yet in my flesh I shall see God,
> whom I shall see for myself,
>   and my eyes shall behold, and not another.[11]

This is our experience—the true knowledge of God and the essence of what we call "theology." It is not something given to everyone, nor is it automatically revealed, even to those who look for it. There have been people in the history of mankind who have sought the truth but have not found it, who have looked for salvation and peace with God, but have been denied it. The Bible tells us that those who wholeheartedly seek the Lord will find him,[12] but this promise is addressed to the covenant community of Israel and seems to imply that the seekers will know who it is they are looking for. Why God reveals himself to some and not to others is a mystery, but the testimony of great men and women who have left us their memoirs bears witness to this reality. On the other hand, there are those like Saul of Tarsus, who never wanted to meet with God or have their lives turned around, yet who were given no choice. God came to them when they least expected it, and there was nothing they could do except fall on their faces and surrender their lives to him.

---

[10]1 Thess. 4:13–14.
[11]Job 19:25–27a.
[12]Deut. 4:29; Jer. 29:13.

The Bible tells us that God accepted Abel but rejected Cain,[13] that he loved Jacob but hated Esau.[14] We are not told why he did so, and from what we know about the men concerned, it is quite possible that we would have made a different choice had we been given the chance. Cain and Esau were great hunters and "men's men," as we would say today, but God chose the foolish things of this world in order to shame the wise, the insignificant in order to humble the self-important, the poor in order to embarrass the rich.[15] Why? Self-made men may be admired in this life, but no one can pull himself up by the bootstraps and earn his way into the kingdom of heaven. Getting there is not the result of human achievement but an act of God's grace. He is the one who opens the door and lets us in, and if we are not humble enough to see that, then the door will not be opened for us. Nor would we be happy if it were, because our pride would prevent us from accepting the free gift of God.

There is something seemingly noble about people who do not want to be a burden to others, who insist on paying their own way, and who cannot stand being in debt. In human terms these are good qualities and we are right to encourage them. But in relation to God they are not only useless, they are harmful. God cannot accept anyone who thinks that he has done something to deserve eternal life, because eternal life is not something that can be earned or deserved. It is a gift that is freely given and that must be humbly received. If this sounds demeaning to our sense of self-worth, we should remember that it is an act of God's supreme love, for if he had imposed a standard of achievement on us, what chance would we have of being saved? Even Cain and Esau could not have reached the required level, as their reactions to the way they were treated shows. As we have already noted, the truth is that "all have sinned and fall short of the glory of God";[16] not one of us is righteous in his sight.[17] We have no claim on his love, but the miracle of salvation is that in his love he has come to claim us in spite of ourselves.

BELIEF IN THE FUTURE

It is easy to focus so much on the apocalyptic elements in the New Testament that we can forget that one of the most distinctive features of Christianity is its belief in the future. Most ancient religions taught that the distant past had been an age of bliss which had been progressively eroded with the passing of time, and that the future would be even worse. What would happen in the end

[13]Gen. 4:1–16.
[14]Mal. 1:3.
[15]See 1 Cor. 1:18–31.
[16]Rom. 3:23.
[17]Rom. 3:10b, quoting Ps. 14:3.

was explained in different ways, but there was nothing much to look forward to. Judaism was different from those religions because, although it believed that mankind had fallen from its original paradise, it also believed that there would be a future intervention by God, when his anointed one (the Messiah) would come and rescue them (that is, the Jewish people who belonged to God) from all their troubles. Christianity emerged as a faith that proclaimed that the Messiah had come in the person of Jesus Christ, and that his chosen people had been redeemed by his death and resurrection. But the Christian gospel went beyond this by adding that the risen Christ, who had ascended into heaven, would come again at the end of time. At that point, the world would be judged and transformed into a kingdom fit for God.[18]

Believers in Christ are therefore encouraged to watch and to pray for that day to arrive. No one can say when Christ will return, but everyone is expected to be prepared for an event that could occur at any moment and catch us unawares.[19] Those who are not ready for Christ's return will suffer the consequences, but those who are ready will inherit the kingdom that has been prepared for them from the foundation of the world.[20] The importance of this for us is that it gives us hope. The material world will decay and disappear, but our life is neither hopeless nor meaningless. What we do matters to God, and in the end it will be rewarded.[21] As Paul put it, "The sufferings of this present time are not worth comparing with the glory that is to be revealed in us."[22] None of us can say for certain what that will be like, and we are warned by Jesus not to presume on God, who has a place prepared for each one of us irrespective of what we want or think we are entitled to.[23] The future hope is a great comfort to us and a great blessing, but it is also cause for humility in the presence of the awesome judgment of the Lord.

DEATH AND ETERNAL LIFE

The implications of this teaching are far-reaching. Pessimism and despair at the turn of events in the world is replaced by a deep sense of optimism that all things work together for good for those who love God. However hard it might be to understand or accept particular occurrences, the end result will reveal the triumph of good over evil, of the kingdom of God over the rebellious powers of Satan and his hosts.[24] This conviction is seen most clearly at

---

[18] 1 Cor. 15:20–28.
[19] Matt. 25:1–13.
[20] Matt. 25:34.
[21] 1 Cor. 3:12–14.
[22] Rom. 8:18.
[23] Matt. 20:23; Mark 10:40.
[24] Rom. 8:28–39.

the point of death. Christians are told to mourn, not as pagans did, but as those who have in them the hope of resurrection to eternal life and glory.[25] Far from being the end of it all, death is the transition from this life to a better one.[26] Christians should not be afraid of death but should welcome it as the gateway to a better life and embrace it as the fulfillment of everything we have been waiting for and working toward.

The way we approach death is the most telling index of the quality of our Christian belief. The secular mind cannot see beyond death, and tries to put it off as long as possible. In extreme cases, people do everything they can to prolong their youth, and some have even thought of having their bodies frozen until the ailments they are suffering from can be cured and they can live indefinitely. In modern society, death is the great unmentionable subject, and, when it occurs prematurely, it is almost impossible for some people to come to terms with it. There are many who say that they cannot believe in God because death has robbed them of a loved one, and there are famous people, such as Charles Darwin, who lost their faith because of this.[27]

To the Christian mind, however, death appears in a very different light. Christians do not despise life on earth or seek to end it before its natural term. Like anyone else, we believe that earthly life should be preserved and enhanced as far as possible. It is a gift from God, who has given us the created order to develop and enjoy, and we struggle against disease and disasters for that reason. Yet, at the same time, we know that life on earth is temporary and should be treated as a preparation for a greater life to come. However wonderful earthly things may be, they pale in comparison with what lies beyond. For a believer, to die young is sad in the sense that an earthly life has not come to its full term or developed its full potential, but it is also the transition to the better life that we so much desire. It therefore cannot be regarded as an unmitigated tragedy. From the perspective of eternity, a day is as a thousand years, and whether or not we live out our allotted threescore years and ten, once we are in the courts of heaven, we shall never look back.[28] Our life in Christ is eternal, and when we grasp that, how much of our spiritual life we spend here on earth hardly matters one way or another.

When we die, time ceases to exist for us, and we go immediately into the presence of God.[29] Some people have maintained that there is a period of "soul-sleep" before the return of Christ, but that is only the way it

---

[25]1 Thess. 4:13.
[26]Phil. 1:21.
[27]Darwin apparently lost his faith in God when his young daughter died.
[28]See 2 Sam. 12:23.
[29]Phil. 1:23; Luke 23:43.

appears from the earthly point of view. Those who are still alive on earth at the return of Christ will see the dead rise from the grave, but for the dead themselves, that experience will be instantaneous, because they have already made the transition from the temporal to the eternal realm.[30] It is true that the Bible says the saints of the Old Testament were not permitted to receive the blessings promised to them until we who believe in Christ could be added to their number,[31] but it is not clear how that should be understood. Moses and Elijah were certainly in heaven when they appeared on the Mount of Transfiguration,[32] yet Moses was apparently among those who were held back. Most likely, when the Old Testament believers died they entered the same eternal realm as we Christians do when we die. On earth they looked forward in faith to the coming of Christ, but as time does not exist in heaven, it cannot be said that they enjoyed the blessings of salvation before we did.

How time and eternity coexist is a mystery we cannot solve in our present state. If we are alive in eternity, does this mean that our eternal selves can look down on the world of time and space and see our earthly life flashing before us? How will it be possible to experience time and space reality once we have left it behind? What is our relationship to the eternal world here and now? Can we communicate with it in any way, and if so, how? We are told that we already enjoy the firstfruits of eternal life, but what does that mean? All these questions and more surface as soon as we start to consider this subject, and there are vast areas in which we can only confess our ignorance. One day we shall know just as we are known by God, but until we get there, we see "in a mirror dimly" and must rely on the promises held out to us.[33] We trust those promises because we have seen some of them already fulfilled in our lives. We experience the presence and the power of the eternal God at work in us now, and that gives us the confidence to believe that what we have experienced so far will grow and deepen as we move on to eternity. We walk in faith, but the God of the past and the present is also the God of the future and we believe that, as he has not failed us in the past, so he will guide and protect us until we arrive at the destination he has prepared for us in eternity.

The relationship between this life and the next is portrayed to us in Scripture by the image of the seed and the plant.[34] The seed is sown as it is, a bare kernel of wheat or something like that. When it comes back, however, it

---

[30] 1 Thess. 4:13–17.
[31] Heb. 11:39–40.
[32] Matt. 17:1–8; Mark 9:2–8; Luke 9:28–36.
[33] 1 Cor. 13:12.
[34] 1 Cor. 15:35–58.

will come with a body chosen for it by God, which will be quite different from the body it now has. As Paul put it,

> What is sown is perishable; what is raised is imperishable. It is sown in dishonor; it is raised in glory. It is sown in weakness; it is raised in power. It is sown a natural body; it is raised a spiritual body.[35]

What is certain is that, in whatever form we shall return, it will be geared toward a life of eternal fellowship with the ascended Christ. Whatever we need in order to enjoy that fellowship will be given to us, and there will be no need for anything else. The details are hidden from us now, but they will be revealed to us when the transformation takes place, and we shall go to live forever with the Lord.[36]

THE FINAL JUDGMENT

Hard as it is to see how time and eternity can coexist in different dimensions of reality, we know that time's end will be marked by the experience of judgment. On the last day, everyone who has ever lived on earth will be raised from the dead and will stand before the judgment seat of Christ. Those who have done what is right will go to eternal bliss, and those who have not will go to eternal punishment.[37]

When Christ comes again, it will not be as the child in a manger at Bethlehem but as the king of glory, riding on the clouds of heaven.[38] The clouds are a symbol of his divine majesty, which remains cloaked in unfathomable mystery even when it is clearly revealed to us. The judgment will be a judgment of our works, and from what we are told in Scripture, there will be three different kinds of results. Those who have done evil will be refused entry into the kingdom of heaven and consigned to everlasting punishment.[39] Those who have done good will be rewarded with the blessings of paradise.[40] But among this latter group there will be some whose works will be destroyed because they are not acceptable to God, yet they will nevertheless be admitted into the kingdom of heaven as if they were naked.[41]

At first sight, this appears to contradict the belief that we have been justified by faith and not by works, but it is the category of people who are saved

---

[35] 1 Cor. 15:42–44. Note that the Greek word for "natural" is *psychikon*, not *physikon*, as we might expect. We have no exact word for this and would have to say "unspiritual" or perhaps "unregenerate."
[36] 1 Thess. 4:17.
[37] Matt. 25:31–46; Rev. 20:11–15.
[38] Acts 1:11; 1 Thess. 4:16; Rev. 1:7.
[39] Matt. 25:41–46.
[40] Matt. 25:34–40.
[41] 1 Cor. 3:15.

even though their works are destroyed that makes us see what the judgment is really all about. God will not judge people merely on the basis of their works because, if he did, those who escape by the skin of their teeth would also be condemned.[42] They are saved because they have been chosen in spite of their works, and this provides the clue for understanding who the other two groups are. Those whose works are evil and who are punished for them were never chosen in the first place. If they had been, either their works would have been good or they would have been saved in spite of them. Likewise, those who do good and are admitted to heaven do good because they have been chosen for salvation. These are the people who have lived lives consistent with their calling, and they will be rewarded for that when they come to the judgment.

What kind of punishment is meted out to those who are rejected? This is one of the most debated questions in Christian theology and has caused a good deal of negative reaction in modern times. The standard answer is that they are sent to hell, where they are punished for eternity. Is such a view justified? Hell as a concept is vague in the Old Testament, where it is usually referred to as Sheol, or the place of the dead. What went on there is unclear, although it seems that its inhabitants were cut off from God in some way or other. Whether they were punished by being burned or otherwise tormented is not stated, nor is anything said about Satan being in control of them.[43]

A clearer picture of hell emerges in the teaching of Jesus during his earthly life. It is sometimes forgotten that he is the one who speaks about hell more clearly and more insistently than anyone else in the Bible—and given who he is, he speaks with greater authority as well. In the words of Jesus, hell is a place of fiery torment, and those who go there are cut off forever from the bliss of heaven.[44] Can such a concept be reconciled with the love of God? This question has intrigued theologians for many centuries, and different solutions have been proposed. Perhaps the most enlightening is the one apparently put forward by an eighth-century monk known as Isaac the Syrian, which has occasionally been echoed in later Orthodox tradition.

According to Isaac, those who go to hell are people whose greatest desire is to get as far away from God, the source of all life, as they possibly can. But God made these rebellious souls, and because he hates nothing that he has made,[45] he will not let them achieve their desire. This frustrated desire is felt by the rebellious souls as torture, but in God's eyes it is preservation from destruction and therefore a sign of his love. We cannot say whether Isaac was

---

[42]See Job 19:20.
[43]See, for example, Num. 16:30–33; Deut. 32:22; Ps. 9:17; 16:10; 30:3; Isa. 5:14; 38:18; Hos. 13:14; Jonah 2:2.
[44]Matt. 5:22, 29–30; 10:28; 11:23; 18:9; 23:33; Mark 9:43–47; Luke 12:5; 16:23.
[45]Gen. 1:31.

right, but at least he showed how the notion of eternal punishment can be reconciled with the love of God. In his interpretation, an act of divine love is experienced by the recipients as torture because they have turned away from God and cannot appreciate his love for what it is.

An alternative view put forward in recent years says that the souls consigned to hell are eventually annihilated. Proponents of this view argue that there is no point in God's consigning anyone to eternal punishment because it has no redemptive purpose, and, they assume, God would not do such a thing to any of his creatures. But since the people sent to hell have not merited eternal salvation, there is no reason why they should be pardoned and admitted to heaven. The answer offered to resolve this problem is to say that God annihilates the souls consigned to hell, in order to preserve them from a pointless eternal punishment! It sounds like a good and even humane theory, until we realize that what is being proposed is euthanasia beyond the grave. The basic idea is that people are put out of their misery by being annihilated, but if this is what is happening, it can be argued that the cure is worse than the disease. While there is life, there is hope, but hope is extinguished if the people concerned are put to death. Proponents of annihilationism would probably argue that it is not euthanasia because, in the case of living people, there is always a chance that a cure may be found to end their suffering, while in hell there is no chance of a reprieve, so it is better to end their agony rather than see it perpetuated. The intentions of this argument are good, but the idea that compassion should lead to extinction is abhorrent and must be resisted.

A third solution, one generally adopted in liberal circles today, is to say that all talk of hell is mythological. The claim here is that when people die they are redeemed in Christ, whether or not they are conscious of this. They contend that Jesus died for the sins of the whole world, and therefore everyone is saved in the end. The chief objections to this view are that it is not just and that it is not what Jesus himself taught. Sin is a reality that deserves to be punished. In dying for us on the cross, Jesus paid that price and set us free to live with him in eternity. In principle, he may have paid the price for the sins of every human being, but not everyone accepts it. Some have never heard of it, but others have consciously and consistently rejected the offer of salvation. Why should such people not get the punishment they deserve? To say that God saves them anyway is to impose his will on theirs in a way that does not respect their individual freedom or integrity. It also diminishes the significance of Christ's work on the cross. Why did he come to earth to die for us if universal salvation was guaranteed in advance?

Another view that has had considerable currency in the past, and which is still the official doctrine of the Roman Catholic Church, is that there is a place called purgatory, where those not yet ready for the kingdom of heaven go after they die. In purgatory they are given a second chance. There they can work off the penalty of sin in the hope that when the price is finally paid, they will go to heaven. Purgatory was very popular in the Middle Ages, and it was even possible for people on earth to earn merits on behalf of their dead friends and relatives, thereby enabling them to go to heaven eventually. Over time, certificates granting the dead time off in purgatory, which were called "indulgences," were not only granted to people but were actually sold—a scandal that sparked the Reformation. The idea has no biblical basis, and it is easy to see how it subverts the gospel of salvation by grace because it presupposes the idea that, after death, sinners must work off their sins by remedial action. Purgatory and the sale of indulgences have played a large part in the history of the church, but there is no support for them in Scripture. They are a prime example of how misguided the teaching of the church can become when it gets away from the teaching of the Bible.

LIFE IN HEAVEN

In contrast to the fate the New Testament describes for the wicked stands its picture of the eternal bliss of God's children in heaven. As with hell, this teaching has often been caricatured, in this case by an exaggerated sentimentality. Pictures of fat little cherubs playing harps on fluffy white clouds are all too familiar, but that is not what the Bible says heaven will be like. It is true that we shall have fellowship with the angels there, but we should not picture that as some sort of kindergarten after death. The life of heaven will be the fulfillment of life on earth, a deeper fellowship with God than anything we enjoy here and a greater opportunity for praising and glorifying him with everything that gives us our being. Far from being a retreat into childish immaturity, it will be a progression into the full responsibility given to the children of God, who are called to reign with Christ forever.[46] In our heavenly state we shall be everything that Adam and Eve were meant to be and more. Perhaps the most important thing is that, not only shall we be delivered from our sinfulness but we shall also be protected from the possibility of falling away. Once we have been fully integrated into the life of Christ, it will be impossible for us to rebel against him again because then we shall be an integral part of his body.

It is important to understand this because many people picture heaven as a place of healing, when the sins of earth will be wiped away and we shall

---

[46]2 Tim. 2:12; Rev. 5:10; 20:4; 22:5.

be the free and autonomous beings that God intended Adam and Eve to be. But although pain, suffering, and death will cease to exist in the new creation, heaven will not be a return to the garden of Eden, even on a lofty and eternal scale.[47] When Jesus ascended into heaven he took his sacrifice with him, and there, at the right hand of God the Father, his wounds continue to plead for our salvation.[48] When we get there, we will be grafted into his body and will draw on the benefits of the sacrifice that he made for us. To use an earthly image, his body will be our life-support machine. Cut off from it, we would die, but attached to it we shall live forever, and no one will have the power or the authority to pull the plug on us.

THE ETERNAL REIGN OF CHRIST

To live with Christ in eternity is to be seated with him on the throne of his heavenly kingdom. What does this mean? Few subjects are more controversial than the nature of the kingdom of Christ. Everyone agrees that Jesus came preaching the kingdom, but what he meant by that has been hotly disputed, especially in the last hundred years or so. Some have interpreted it as a social transformation meant to occur on this earth. In past years people may have seen this as a reestablishment of the ancient Israelite monarchy,[49] but nowadays it is more likely seen as a constructing of societies in which social justice is the main characteristic of community life. Others have interpreted the kingdom of Christ in a more spiritual sense, but this has gone in two main directions. Some have understood it as the establishment of the church as a kind of super-society that reconfigures natural human relationships according to principles derived from the kingdom of heaven. This was what happened in the Middle Ages, when monastic life and compulsory clerical celibacy were justified by claiming that the church was the presence of the heavenly kingdom on earth. The argument was that because angels do not marry and neither do the resurrected saints, those who want to be like them ought to imitate them in this respect! Others have reacted against this interpretation, and have preferred to think of the kingdom as something that will be realized only at the end of time.

Which of these options we choose will depend on how we understand the future, and this has often been connected to different interpretations of the millennium spoken of in the book of Revelation.[50] Speaking of those who had stood fast and had been martyred for their faith, John says,

---

[47]Rev. 21:1–4.
[48]Heb. 10:12–14, 19.
[49]Acts 1:6.
[50]Rev. 20:1–6.

They came to life and reigned with Christ for a thousand years. The rest of the dead did not come to life until the thousand years were ended. This is the first resurrection. Blessed and holy is the one who shares in the first resurrection! Over such the second death has no power, but they will be priests of God and of Christ, and they will reign with him for a thousand years.[51]

In the early church, most people read the book of Revelation as predictive prophecy and concluded that it described the age of persecution in which they were living. After that was over there would come a time of peace when the gospel would be preached to all the nations, following which there would be another round of persecution and then Christ would come again. This interpretation is generally known as chiliasm, the Greek word for millennialism. Chiliasm was attacked by Augustine, who insisted that the book of Revelation was essentially allegorical and should not be interpreted as history. His view prevailed, particularly after A.D. 1000, when it became clear that Christ was not going to return at the end of a thousand years. In the later Middle Ages, a popular form of chiliasm reappeared but it was never accepted by the church and generally spread underground until the Reformation, when it erupted in a number of extreme forms. They were eventually discredited and disappeared, but millennialism came back in the wake of the French revolution and has remained popular in some Protestant circles to the present time. In periods of economic or political crisis, it has seemed to have special relevance as an interpretation of the difficulties being faced by Christians, and a tradition has grown up of interpreting the text with reference to current events. These interpretations change as time moves on, but the fundamental belief that the book of Revelation is prophetic history remains.

Most of the people who read the text in that way are premillenarian, believing that Christ will return before the millennium and reign on earth for a thousand years. There are any number of subtle variations on this theme, ranging from a dispensational premillennialism, which stresses the conversion of the Jews at the end of time, to beliefs that focus on the rapture and the tribulation.[52] Will believers be raptured before the tribulation, during it, or afterwards? What will happen to those who are left behind at the rapture? Can we tell in advance when these things are likely to happen? A great deal of popular literature has appeared on these subjects, most of it pure fiction. How many people really believe premillenarian theories is impossible to say, but there are still seminaries (mainly in the United States) that require such beliefs as part of their confession of faith and evidently take them seriously.

---

[51]Rev. 20:4b–6.
[52]The rapture is based mainly on 1 Thess. 4:14–17 and the tribulation on Rev. 7:14.

At the opposite end of the spectrum is postmillennialism, which is the name given to the belief that the Christian church is now living through the millennium. The spread of the gospel across the world and the progress of Christianity and Christian values is taken to be the sign of the extension of God's kingdom here on earth. This will continue indefinitely until the whole world acknowledges the reign of Christ. This view is based on a curiously literal exegesis of a number of biblical passages outside the book of Revelation, to which it is only loosely connected.[53] Postmillennialism is an optimistic and even triumphalist belief which was common at the beginning of the twentieth century but has waned since then and is seldom heard of nowadays. The terrible persecutions of the twentieth century and the decline of religious faith in traditionally Christian countries has made postmillennialism much less plausible, and the circles that were once attracted to it have largely disappeared. Predictions are dangerous, but it would seem that the market for postmillennialism has largely dried up, at least for the time being.

This leaves the Augustinian viewpoint, which in its modern form is known as amillennialism and is the standard belief of most of the major churches. This view holds that the return of Christ will be the definitive event that signals the end of time, and that the book of Revelation is a symbolic representation of the spiritual warfare that Christians are currently waging. When the end comes, that warfare will be wrapped up in the victory of Christ over the forces of Satan, who will then be permanently disabled. Whether being "thrown into the lake of fire" means that they will be annihilated or simply consigned to eternal punishment is disputed, but as the text says that they will be tormented there forever and ever, it is safer to say that it refers to eternal punishment and not to absolute destruction.[54] We must never forget that God hates nothing that he has made and that even Satan was created good. As with fallen human beings, God is more likely to punish him in eternity than to wipe him out of existence altogether.

The amillenarian approach has received a substantial boost, not to say a confirmation of its validity, by the modern rediscovery of apocalyptic as a literary genre in its own right. Apocalyptic has affinities with prophecy but it cannot be regarded as the same thing. Still less can it be understood as history, though it definitely emerged out of particular historical circumstances, which today we might call times of transition and crisis. What is clear is that John was tapping into an existing tradition of writing and adapting it to serve as a vehicle for the Word of God. It is no exaggeration to say that his Apocalypse

---

[53]Among the passages used to support it are John 12:32; Rom. 11:25–26; Heb. 10:13; Isa. 2:4; 9:7; Matt. 5:18.
[54]Rev. 20:10.

is in many ways the most profoundly theological book of the New Testament, but a sophisticated hermeneutical key is required to interpret it correctly. For example, John's Apocalypse never quotes the Old Testament directly, but almost nothing in it can be understood without a deep knowledge of the Hebrew Bible. Its symbolism is complex but internally coherent, and once it is grasped it can be decoded and used to explain the nature of spiritual warfare and its outcome.

The result does not discredit the various millenarian views so much as transcend them, taking the discussion to a new level. The reign of Christ is not something to look forward to in some unknown future but a reality right now. He is seated on the throne in heaven, ruling the world by the Word of his power. The activities of Satan are being allowed to continue for a time, but he has been cast out of heaven and confined to a limited sphere on earth. Here we do battle with him, but the victory has already been won. Even in our sufferings we can sing a song of triumph, knowing that the Lamb who was slain from before the foundation of the world is in control of our lives and of human events in general. The final act in the drama may not yet be fully played out, but we live in the end times and the consummation is at hand.

What will life in eternity be like? We know that we shall enter it as ourselves—who we are on earth is who we shall be in heaven. It must be so, because otherwise salvation would have no meaning. To come back as someone else would be a form of reincarnation and a denial of our identity, which goes against the witness of the New Testament. Our earthly bodies will be transformed, but they will still be bodies, which implies that we shall still be finite beings but also spiritual ones—rather like the angels. There will be no reproduction of the species in heaven, and so marriage will no longer exist.[55] We shall presumably be ageless and timeless, hard as that is to imagine now. Will babies who die come back as adults? Will we look the way we do when we die, or when we were converted? We do not know, and from the perspective of eternity such questions are probably irrelevant. More to the point is that the created order in which we now live will be transformed into a new kind of reality, designed for our eternal life. There will be a new heaven and a new earth. The sea will disappear, and there will be no sun or moon to give light because the Lord himself will be the light of the city that will come down from heaven as the New Jerusalem in which we shall live.[56]

Here we are dealing with high symbolism, and it would be foolish to try to interpret it in terms of a new physical reality. What we know is that in the

[55]Matt. 22:30.
[56]Rev. 21:23–24.

new creation we shall live in eternal fellowship with God, and that all our sufferings here on earth will be wiped away. In the heavenly city there will be no
sorrow, only endless joy and praise for the Lamb who sits on the throne. There
his wounds will continue to plead for our salvation[57] and unite us forever with
the Father in the Holy Spirit.

Beyond that we are not told, and it would be unwise to speculate. We
know that we shall have fellowship with the redeemed of every tribe and
nation and of every time and circumstance. Does this mean that we shall con-
verse with them directly? Probably not—as the examples of Moses and Elijah
on the Mount of Transfiguration remind us. Will we look down on those in
hell and rejoice in their confinement? Some theologians have thought so, and
have even gone to the point of saying that contemplating the punishment of
the wicked will be one of the joys of heaven for the redeemed! This sounds
implausible, and there is nothing in Scripture to encourage us to think like
that. Our focus will be on Christ, not on the reprobate, and what they are
doing may never cross our minds once we are completely taken up with him.

Heaven is also a place where all our latent potential will be fulfilled. The
things we are meant to be on earth but cannot be because of our sinfulness
will be given to us in heaven, and we shall reign in glory with the Lamb who
is our Savior. We shall even judge angels alongside him as part of our being
integrated into his heavenly life.[58] It is hardly possible that this judgment will
depend on us, since all judgment belongs to him, but it is a sign of how closely
we shall be associated with him in his heavenly kingdom. Ultimately, that
kingdom is focused not on the external world but on the inner life of God. We
are told that when the judgment is complete, the Son will deliver his kingdom
up to the Father so that God may be all in all.[59] When that happens, our life
will be caught up completely in God. By the power of his Holy Spirit, we shall
be fully adopted into the life of the Father and the Son, a life that is lived out
in love. Love is our eternal destiny, the heart and foundation of what we were
made for and what we are being prepared for as we make our way through life
here on earth. The wedding feast is ready, the Spirit and the bride say, "Come."
The prayer of the Christian can only be, "Amen. Come, Lord Jesus!"[60]

---

[57]Heb. 9:11–10:18.
[58]1 Cor. 6:3.
[59]1 Cor. 15:28.
[60]Rev. 22:17, 20.

GENERAL INDEX

SCRIPTURE INDEX

Acts